Fundamentals of Criminal Law

Caught in the Act

Daniel E. Hall

Miami University

SAGE

Los Angeles | London | New Delhi
Singapore | Washington DC | Melbourne

FOR INFORMATION:

SAGE Publications, Inc.
2455 Teller Road
Thousand Oaks, California 91320
E-mail: order@sagepub.com

SAGE Publications Ltd.
1 Oliver's Yard
55 City Road
London, EC1Y 1SP
United Kingdom

SAGE Publications India Pvt. Ltd.
B 1/I 1 Mohan Cooperative
Industrial Area
Mathura Road, New Delhi 110 044
India

SAGE Publications Asia-Pacific
Pte. Ltd.
18 Cross Street #10-10/11/12
China Square Central
Singapore 048423

Printed in Canada

Library of Congress Control Number: 2022902213

ISBN (pbk) 978-1-0718-1173-3

ISBN (loose-leaf) 978-1-0718-6289-6

Acquisitions Editor: Josh Perigo

Content Development Editor:
Laura Kearns and Emma Newsom

Production Editor: Rebecca Lee

Copy Editor: Amy Hanquist Harris

Typesetter: diacriTech

Cover Designer: Candice Harman

Marketing Manager:
Victoria Velasquez

This book is printed on acid-free paper.

22 23 24 25 26 10 9 8 7 6 5 4 3 2 1

BRIEF CONTENTS

CONTENTS

PREFACE

The goal of this textbook is to offer students a comprehensive survey of criminal law in an accessible format with examples that are relatable to college students in the 2020s. After 30 years of textbook writing, I have learned that student readings do not have to be dense and impenetrable to be effective. On the other hand, students need to be challenged to dig into concepts, to learn terminology and doctrine, and to apply the law. To accomplish these apparently conflicting goals, several writing and pedagogical techniques have been employed.

WRITING STYLE AND PEDAGOGY

In what I believe to be a unique feature, nontraditional headings are used to ease the reader into the subject and to provoke student curiosity. The section on battery, for example, is titled "Sticks and Stones May Hurt Me," followed by the section on true threats, which is titled "Words May Hurt Me."

The study of criminal law involves a considerable amount of element learning, and it is common to embed the elements in the author's narrative discussions. Often, these discussions leave students unsure about a crime's specific elements, particularly when jurisdictional variances are acute. For clarity and to frame my narratives, I have included a specific listing of the elements, often at the start of a discussion. This approach not only frames the discussion but acts as an easy reference for the student who later returns to the material for a quick refresher.

Most significantly, the book is written specifically to the undergraduate student who may be taking their first law course. Legal terms are defined as they are encountered for the first time, and the writing style is purposely accessible. The writing level and style is intended to speak to, but not down to, students. These objectives aren't accomplished at the expense of learning. Students are eased into more challenging material.

PEDAGOGY

An introductory text naturally includes lower-level cognitive learning. But it doesn't have to be limited to it. To push students up the Bloom's taxonomy, examples that illustrate how the law applies to specific factual scenarios appear throughout the book. Students themselves are asked to apply what is learned through questions and problems that appear in every topical section, as opposed to the traditional method of having students do this after an entire chapter has been read.

I believe that reading judicial opinions is good for learning, for many reasons. They reinforce the narrative discussion, develop analytical and reasoning skills, and often humanize the subject. Students are interested in real people engaged in real conflict. Cases speak to them. Of course, there isn't room in a textbook for 20-page judicial opinions, nor is it important that every student read every case in full. So highly edited cases appear in every chapter in a feature titled Digging Deeper. The case excerpts are not used exclusively to teach the law, as is often done in law school. Rather, they supplement the narrative discussion. Accordingly, the cases can be skipped without any loss of content if you don't have the time or interest in the case method.

There are many factors that influence my case selection and editing decisions. Obviously, relevance and how well a case illustrates the subject are the most important. How amenable a case is to reduction, its age, and the quality of the court's writing also are considered. To make the cases more reader-friendly, editorial liberties have been taken. Sting citations and other references have been removed without indication. Other redactions are signaled with ellipses.

Graphics can be good learning tools. Many graphics and charts that compare, summarize, and illustrate concepts appear throughout the text. Photos have also been included to break up the text and to connect the subject to contemporary or historic events.

To appeal to students "where they are," many examples are drawn from contemporary events. Chapters open with crime stories, often from the headlines, and similar references to contemporary events and problems are found throughout the chapter discussions. There has been a lot of change to criminal law in recent decades, and more is to come during the 2020s. Although the objective of this book is to teach what the law "is," contemporary questions about what it "ought" to be are acknowledged and, on occasion, given brief exploration.

CONTENTS

The first chapter begins with a brief history of the Common Law and how it has shaped American criminal law. The centrality of the due process model, the distinction between civil and criminal law and between criminal law and procedure, the purposes of punishing offenders, the sources of criminal law, and how crimes are classified are all examined.

An introduction to the United States Constitution, with an emphasis on the amendments that limit the authority of the state to criminalize conduct, is the subject of the second chapter. The exclusionary rule and the role of state constitutions in the protection of liberty are highlighted.

The third chapter details the architecture of crimes and their essential elements. Mens rea, actus reus, attendant circumstances, concurrence, and causation are examined closely. This is followed in Chapter 4 with a discussion of the parties to crimes and incomplete crimes. Many authors cover this material later in their books. But I believe that earlier is better; it prepares the students to apply causation and relative liability to the crimes and defenses that follow.

Defenses to crimes are split into two chapters. Justifications and factual defenses are found in Chapter 5 and excuses in Chapter 6. Many good recommendations were made by the reviewers. One was to address crimes against the person before homicide, so Chapter 7 is devoted to crimes less than murder and Chapter 8, to homicide. Special attention is given to civil rights crimes, including the laws that apply to police misconduct.

Chapter 9 turns from crimes against people to crimes that involve property, including trespass, arson, burglary, and theft. Chapter 10 expands on Chapter 9 by taking a deeper dive into two growing areas of crime—commercial offenses and cybercrime. Problems that students will recognize from the lives of their contemporaries, such as sexting and cyberbullying, are included.

Chapters 11 and 12 cover crimes against the public and state. Specifically, Chapter 11 covers morality-based and other public welfare offenses. Chapter 12 offers broad coverage of crimes against the state as a political entity. In a post–9/11, post–U.S. Capitol insurrection world, this chapter contains timely and important material. It uses select prosecutions of the breach of the Capitol on January 6, 2021, as a platform to discuss many of the crimes featured in the chapter. Both Chapters 11 and 12 build on earlier discussions of the First Amendment by applying the Miller and O'Brien tests to the offenses discussed.

SUMMARY OF PEDAGOGICAL FEATURES

- Accessible, student-friendly writing style

- Comprehensive coverage, but not so long to be overwhelming or so dense to be dull

- Fun, thought-provoking headings

- Excerpted cases in the Digging Deeper feature that illustrate content and enable analytical development (if preferred, may be omitted without any loss of content)

- Contemporary problems, examples, and content

- Questions and problems at the end of every section

- Examples and factual hypotheticals throughout

- Graphics, data tables, summary tables, illustrations, and photos throughout

- Running glossary

ANCILLARY MATERIALS

- **Chapter test banks** provide a diverse range of pre-written options as well as the opportunity to edit any question and/or insert personalized questions to effectively assess students' progress and understanding

- **Lecture notes** summarize key concepts by chapter to ease preparation for lectures and class discussions

- Editable, chapter-specific **PowerPoint®slides** offer complete flexibility for creating a multimedia presentation for the course

- **Sample course syllabi** for semester and quarter courses provide suggested models for structuring one's course

- **Class activities** for individual or group projects provide lively and stimulating ideas for use in and out of class reinforce active learning.

- A **course cartridge** provides easy LMS integration

SUGGESTIONS FOR THE USE OF THIS BOOK

For lower-division courses that emphasize content learning, the book and its ancillary resources can be used exclusively. If an awareness of local law is part of the curriculum, the book is easily supplemented by asking students to read the counterpart state statute (or local ordinance). This offers the opportunity for students to compare the Common Law—or the dominant approach—that is described in the book with your state's specific laws. This type of comparative analysis enriches students' learning.

If the learning objectives of a course are to develop higher-order cognitive skills, as well as to learn the content, case analysis is a good supplement to the readings. In my classes, I have all students in my classes read all of the case excerpts in the book. In addition, I assign each student two or more cases, depending on the size of the class, to find, read fully, brief, and present to the class. Typically, I add more recent cases (or state-specific cases) to the cases that appear in the book. Students enjoy being the master of their cases, and I have discovered that the case method, as old as it is, is a very good pedagogical tool for developing analytical and communication skills.

Criminal law is exciting beyond legal doctrine. Police accountability, juvenile culpability, the legitimacy of holding one person responsible for the actions of others, the insanity defense, the balance of free speech and regulating harmful expression, whether plea bargaining is unfairly coercive, police and prosecutorial discretion, decriminalization of drug and petty social welfare offenses, and the nation's evolving values about sexual assault are issues of continual discussion in social media; they command the headlines in the mainstream media, and quite likely, they are important to students. Tapping into these topics through supplemental readings, debate, research, and presentations allows students to explore the complexities of crime, criminal law, and punishment.

Daniel E. Hall

ACKNOWLEDGMENTS

Thanks to Antje for her help in identifying appealing headings and, most of all, for listening to me when I need to mentally process my writing.

The suggestions of the reviewers greatly improved this text in organization and content. Thanks to each of the following people:

Troy Cochran, Director of Criminal Justice, Northern Oklahoma College

Catherine D. Sanders, JD, Triton College, Criminal Justice Administration

Traqina Q. Emeka, PhD, Lone Star College—North Harris

Stacey L. Callaway, JD, MBA, Rowan College of South Jersey

Mary Hiser, Professional Educator of Criminal Justice, Western New England University

Russ Pomrenke, Program Chair, MA, Gwinnett Technical College

Dr. Michael R. Salter, Cedar Crest College

Brandon L. Bang, West Texas A&M University

Alex O. Lewis, III, JD, Adjunct Professor, Department of Forensic Science, Southern University at New Orleans

The encouragement of Jessica Miller, Laura Kearns, Brian Craig, and the other behind-the-scenes folks at SAGE has been invaluable. I love your commitment to producing a scholarly, visually attractive, and student-friendly text!

ABOUT THE AUTHOR

Daniel E. Hall earned his bachelor's degree at Indiana University, Juris Doctor at Washburn University, and Doctor of Education in higher-education curriculum and instruction at the University of Central Florida. After law school, Daniel clerked for both the Honorable Gene E. Brooks, Chief Judge, U.S. District Court for the Southern District of Indiana, and the Supreme Court of the Federated States of Micronesia.

He has practiced law in the United States and in Micronesia, where he served as assistant attorney general following his judicial clerkship. In this capacity, he litigated some of the young nation's first cases that addressed important criminal, constitutional, and traditional law issues. He has been a member of the faculties of the University of Central Florida, the University of Toledo, and Miami University, where he is currently professor of Justice and Community Studies and Political Science, and Affiliate Professor of Global and Intercultural Studies. He is also a visiting professor of law at Sun Yat-sen University in Guangzhou, China. Daniel is the author or coauthor of 28 textbooks, including revisions, and a dozen journal articles on public law subjects. He is father of Grace and Eva, stepfather to Thea, and partner to Aryana. Your comments and suggestions for the next edition of this book are invited. Email them to hallslawbooks@gmail.com.

1 OVERVIEW OF CRIMINAL LAW

Criminal law is an exciting subject. Criminal conduct is interesting because it represents the worst of humanity—scandalous, selfish, and sometimes cruel and inhumane acts. Some crimes get attention because they are clever, occasionally genius. If you are like most people, most of what you know about criminal law has been learned from media in the form of news reports, movies, television, and streaming crime dramas. Unfortunately, *Law and Order* doesn't always get it right. That is where this book, and your criminal law course, step in. By the time you have completed reading this book, you will be able to impress, or possibly annoy, your friends and family by explaining what is right and wrong in their favorite crime shows.

A LONG HISTORY

Learning Objective: Explain the development of the Common Law, as applied to criminal law, from its origin to today.

When threatened, humans have two natural responses: fight or flight. And for most of human history, one or the other happened when a person was threatened or harmed. The response was personal, reflexive, and driven by the instinct to survive. Several thousand years ago, however, these in-the-moment responses were supplemented. Vendetta, or seeking revenge after the fact, is an example. Vendetta transcended the fight-or-flight instinct. It is cognitive, reflecting either a desire for retribution or to incapacitate offenders so they are no longer a threat. In time, personal responses evolved into collective action. The community, not the victim or the victim's family, began to hold offenders accountable. Unbounded vengeance was replaced with norms of justice and proportionality. These ideas were often expressed in written codes or court decisions.

The earliest known code of law in human history, Ur-Nammu, dates back to 2000 B.C.E. in Mesopotamia. It includes several crimes and punishments, including death for committing murder and robbery as well as fines for poking out the eye, cutting off the nose with a copper knife, or severing the foot of another person. Other ancient laws, such as the Code of Hammurabi (mid-1700s), also contain what the modern world would consider criminal laws.

Criminal law: A branch of law, and legal study, that defines criminal offenses and defenses to criminal accusations.

By the 11th century, two families of law emerged in Europe: **Civil Law** and **Common Law**. Civil Law was first seen in Italy in the 7th century, faded away, and was revived in the 11th century. It then spread from Italy to nations throughout Europe, and those nations spread it around the world as they expanded their colonial empires. It is found in the majority of the nations of the world today. Civil Law relies on written codes made by legal experts—and later legislatures—as the primary source of law.

The Civil Law's **inquisitorial system** of adjudicating cases empowers judges over prosecutors and defendants to oversee investigations, develop the factual theories of cases, and run trials. Inquisitorial systems are run as continuous, somewhat cooperative investigations.

The Common Law traces its roots to the Norman Conquest of England in 1066. The Norman kings brought a very different form of law to England. Before the Norman invasion, the law was feudal. Wealthy landowners made and enforced the laws and, therefore, law varied from place to place. These geographic spaces were known as shires and hundreds. In the early years of Norman rule, judges, not a legislature, made the laws. Eventually, through a system of hierarchy, lower courts were expected to follow the precedent of higher courts (stare decisis). This resulted in England's first national laws—or laws that were "common" to all people. Unlike the Civil Law, where law was changed abruptly through legislation, the Common Law evolved incrementally, as judges interpreted and applied the law to new cases.

Common Law nations use the **adversarial system** of adjudication. Differing considerably from the inquisitorial system, the adversarial system empowers the parties to advance their own theories of the case and to put on their own evidence. Judges are passive, acting as referees in a competition to find the truth.

Although the judges in old England were less active in developing the facts of cases, they were, and continue today, to be responsible for deciding the law and procedure of individual cases. The effect of hundreds of years of decisions, creating law that was applied in future cases through stare decisis, is a large body of judicially created substantive and procedural law.

Outside of the courts, many historical events also shaped Common Law. One of the most significant events was the **Magna Carta**, or "Great Charter of Liberty," of 1215. The Magna Carta was a political–legal document forced upon King John by rebelling nobles. Through the

---

Civil law: A branch of law concerned with the private rights of individuals. It is intended to provide individuals with a legal mechanism to be compensated for their injuries by the people who harm them.

Common Law: A comprehensive approach to law that relied, in its early development, on courts—not legislatures—to create law. They did this by deciding the law of individual cases. That law then became precedent for future like cases. Founded in 11th-century England, it spread to England's colonies and territories and was brought to the United States by colonists. The Common Law is a lower form of law than constitutional and statutory law.

Inquisitorial system: A method of investigation and adjudication found in Civil Law nations, such as France and Italy. Characterized as a continuous investigation, courts play an active role in the entire process, including the evidence gathering and theory development of a case.

Adversarial system: A method of investigation and adjudication found in Common Law nations. Characterized as a competition, the parties are active, and the judge is in the role of referee, only becoming involved periodically to resolve disputes or ensure justice.

Magna Carta: Also known as the Great Charter of Liberty. Forced upon King John in 1215, it represents the first appearance of rule of law.

Magna Carta, the King recognized that he was subject to the law, promised not to interfere with churches, and recognized several individual rights, including a right to inherit property, to be free from oppressive taxation, to be tried by a jury of peers, to receive due process, and to be free from arbitrary imprisonment. Just as the Magna Carta was compelled under threat of sword, it failed shortly after the sword was sheathed. Lasting only 3 months, King John, with the support of the Catholic Pope, suspended the Magna Carta. John died months later, leaving a 9-year-old heir to the throne, Henry III. Too young to rule, a regent was appointed to rule until Henry III reached adulthood. The regent reinstated a modified version of the Magna Carta in 1216 and another version in 1217. Henry III issued the final version of the Magna Carta in 1225, 2 years after he assumed control.

While previous rulers in world history had granted rights to the people, the Magna Carta is regarded as the first demonstration of **Rule of Law**, the idea that laws should apply to everyone, because King John acknowledged that he didn't give the rights to the people—they existed with, or without, his consent. Of course, it was a different time and not all people enjoyed these rights. Only the powerful were protected by them. Regardless, the Magna Carta set the stage for the development of the rights that are protected by the federal and state constitutions today.

Subsequently, other important laws about crime and criminal procedure were issued by Parliament, with the consent of the monarch, including the Petition of Right of 1628, which reinforced the Common Law right to have imprisonment reviewed for lawfulness (habeas corpus), prohibited martial law (the suspension of law and rights) during peacetime, limited the authority of the monarch to tax, and forbade the quartering of troops in citizens' homes. Sixty-one years later, another important law protecting the rights of people was issued. Through the English Bill of Rights of 1689, the Crown recognized the supremacy of Parliament over the monarchy, as well as the rights to free speech in Parliament, to petition the King with grievances, to be free from the quartering of troops in one's home, to receive a jury trial in certain cases, to be free of cruel punishments, and to be free from excessive fines.

The English courts also created important legal principles, many that are found in England, the United States, and other liberal democracies today. The requirements that a defendant be convicted by a high standard of proof, beyond a reasonable doubt, and the presumption of innocence are examples. Add to these developments the philosophical influence of the Enlightenment, with its ideas of proportional punishment, due process, freedom of speech, and empiricism, the adversarial system was molded to not only find factual guilt but to protect the rights of defendants. This combination of **factual guilt** (did the defendant actually commit the crime?) and a requirement of a fair process is known as **legal guilt**.

As happened with Civil Law, the English Common Law followed England to the peoples it colonized. This included peoples from all over the world. India, Australia, New Zealand, Belize, Barbados, most of Canada, Fiji, Ghana, Hong Kong, and of course, the United States

---

Rule of law: The idea that all people, including government leaders, are subject to the law.

Factual guilt: To commit the elements of a crime.

Legal guilt: The idea of investigating and adjudicating criminal suspects using a just process. Factually guilty people may be punished less harshly or not at all when treated unfairly in the process.

are among the many Common Law jurisdictions. The rights found in the U.S. Constitution and its first 10 amendments, the Bill of Rights, often mimic and sometimes extend what first developed in England.

An authoritative expression of the early Common Law that is still relied upon today is Sir William Blackstone's *Commentaries on the Laws of England* published in 1765. These books were so important that early American lawyers and judges would keep a set in their saddlebags as they traveled from town to town to practice law or to hear cases.

The influence of the Common Law didn't stop at the ratification of the Constitution. You will find references to old British Common Law in court decisions issued today. The presumption of innocence and proof beyond a reasonable doubt, for example, are not found in the U.S. Constitution, but the Supreme Court of the United States (SCOTUS) has found them to be implicit in the guarantee of due process because they have been a part of the Common Law for centuries. British roots can also be seen in U.S. courts every day, where defendants and prosecutors compete to persuade juries of their respective truths while judges stay on the sidelines, except to referee disputes and ensure fairness. See Figure 1.1 for a timeline of important dates in the history of the Common Law.

FIGURE 1.1 ■ Timeline of Common Law

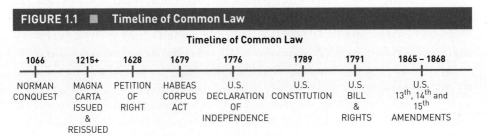

Timeline of Common Law

1066	1215+	1628	1679	1776	1789	1791	1865 – 1868
NORMAN CONQUEST	MAGNA CARTA ISSUED & REISSUED	PETITION OF RIGHT	HABEAS CORPUS ACT	U.S. DECLARATION OF INDEPENDENCE	U.S. CONSTITUTION	U.S. BILL & RIGHTS	U.S. 13th, 14th and 15th AMENDMENTS

QUESTIONS AND PROBLEMS

1. What was the Magna Carta, and why is it significant to U.S. law today?
2. Distinguish factual guilt from legal guilt.

WHAT CRIMINAL LAW IS

Learning Objective: Define criminal law.

A crime is an act that society finds so harmful, threatening, or offensive that it is forbidden and punished. Not all social wrongs are crimes. Has someone with a cold ever shook your hand or not covered a cough when standing near you? These are socially unacceptable acts, but they don't lead to arrest and punishment. However, if the person has a disease that is more dangerous and infectious than a cold, such as COVID-19, the same act may be a crime.

SCOTUS: Supreme Court of the United States.

Every society has informal ways of life. Social expectations about behavior are known as norms. There are several types of norms. A folkway is an expectation that makes life more orderly and predictable. But it is not grounded in morality. For example, it is customary in the United States to permit people on an elevator to get off before entering. There are good reasons for this practice. It speeds up the process of stopping between floors and makes it easier for passengers to get on and off the elevator. But to step on before others have had time to get off doesn't violate a moral code; it is just inconsiderate. A norm that is grounded in morality is known as a more. An extramarital affair is an example of a violation of a more because most people believe this conduct to be immoral.

Laws are a third type of norm. The key distinction between law and other norms is the use of a community's authority to enforce laws. In criminal law, that means to create formal laws and to adjudicate and punish people who violate them. In most cases, crimes are also violations of folkways or **mores**. Rape, for example, is both immoral and criminal. On the other hand, fewer mores are crimes. Recall the earlier example: extramarital affairs. At one time illegal, today they are not, but regardless of the law, most people find sexual cheating to be morally wrong.

Criminal law, as a branch of law and as an academic field of study, defines crimes and the defenses to criminal accusations. As you will learn later in this chapter, many legal authorities can declare an act to be a crime. These same authorities can also declare that people charged with certain crimes are entitled to use a defense. In some cases, the Constitution of the United States, as well as each state's constitution, may offer a defense. Said another way, constitutions sometimes protect the rights of people to act. The First Amendment, for example, protects many rights, including the freedom to believe and practice any religion. If the United States were to make it a crime to attend a Catholic mass and Nadia were arrested for violating this law, she would hold up the First Amendment as her defense, and unless the judge knows nothing about the law, the case would be dismissed.

QUESTIONS AND APPLICATIONS

1. Define criminal law.
2. Caroline is enjoying lunch at BigBurrito. The restaurant is very crowded. Near the end of her meal, Caroline belches very loudly. It is heard by nearly everyone in the restaurant. Some people are disgusted; others think it is funny. Has Caroline violated a norm? If so, was it a folkway, more, or crime?
3. Identify a crime in your state that is also a violation of a more. Identify another crime that is not a violation of a more. Explain both of your answers.

Norms: Expected behaviors.

Folkways: Expected rules of behavior that have evolved to give order to life.

Mores: Expected rules of behavior that are grounded in morality. The word is pronounced "more-ray."

Crime: An act that society finds so harmful, threatening, or offensive that it is forbidden and punished.

Defense: Law or fact that is used to reduce or fully eliminate criminal liability.

WHAT CRIMINAL LAW ISN'T

Learning Objective: Compare and contrast criminal law, criminal procedure, and civil law.

Criminal law is substantive; it defines crimes and defenses to crimes. What is required to prove murder? What if a defendant murdered, but in self-defense? These are substantive criminal law questions. And they will be answered in this book!

Criminal Procedure

Substantive criminal law must be brought to life; processes are needed to put it into action. Criminal procedure is the field that defines these steps and processes; it makes criminal law "real." The process that a court case goes through is known as adjudication.

- How are criminal cases filed with courts?

- How does a defendant challenge an illegal search by police?

- At trial, does the defendant or the state address the jury first?

These are criminal procedure questions. Criminal procedure also includes the constitutional aspects of criminal adjudications. As examples, the following constitutional questions also fall into the academic study of criminal procedure:

- When is probable cause required?

- May a police officer search a person's home without a warrant?

- May border agents turn on a traveler's phone and look at its contents?

- May a confession that has been beaten out of a defendant be used at trial?

- When is a defendant entitled to an attorney?

Although constitutional criminal procedure is not a criminal law topic, it is too important and too fun to skip entirely. You will take a quick tour of important constitutional requirements in a later chapter, and there will be references to the Constitution throughout this book.

Substantive criminal law: The law that identifies and defines crimes and the defenses to criminal accusations.

Criminal procedure law: (1) The steps and processes that are used to adjudicate a criminal case. (2) The constitutional limitations on the state's criminal law authority.

Adjudication: The process of a case in court, from start to finish. It is also used to refer to the final outcome, or judgment, of a case. In criminal law, this refers to a finding of guilty or not guilty.

Civil Law

When learning new subjects, structuring the subject can be helpful. Indeed, there is an organization of law that is commonly used by lawyers, courts, legislators, and professors. That organization divides law into different categories, also known as branches or fields. There is a lot of overlap between the various branches. But there are also important differences. One distinction is drawn between **public law** and **private law**. Most law that deals with the relationship between a person and their government falls into the public law category. Criminal law, administrative law, and constitutional law are examples of public law.

Most of the time, public law applies when there is **state action**—that is, a government acting in some manner against a person. By the way, don't let the term "state" confuse you. It refers to government at all levels, not just the 50 states. For the remainder of this book, "state" and "government" will both be used to refer to the United States, a specific state (e.g., California, Wyoming, etc.), or a local government (e.g., Boston, Cincinnati). In criminal law, a legislature's decision to forbid an act, a police officer's decision to arrest a violator, and a prosecutor's decision to file charges and to try an individual for a crime are all state actions.

As you learned earlier, not all violations of norms are legal wrongs. Similarly, not all legal wrongs are crimes. A common distinction in law is between criminal law and civil law. Law that concerns the relationship of one person to another person falls into the private law category also known as civil law.

The biggest difference between criminal law and civil law is their differing objectives. Criminal law has several objectives, including punishment and deterrence. We will explore the objectives of criminal law in greater detail in a moment. Civil law is different. Its objective isn't to punish; it is intended to compensate people for harms caused by other persons.

During your study of law, you will discover that exceptions exist for every rule. In some cases, the rule is smaller than its exceptions. So here is your first exception: **punitive damages**. In some cases, a plaintiff in a civil lawsuit can receive a damages award that exceeds the actual proven harm. Instead of compensating the plaintiff, punitive damages are intended to punish and deter future misconduct by the defendant. One high-profile punitive damages case was *Liebeck v. McDonald's Restaurants*. In 1992, Stella Liebeck put a cup of McDonald's coffee between her legs while sitting in a parked car. As she removed the lid to the coffee to add sugar and cream, coffee spilled out onto her legs and groin. The coffee was so hot that it caused third-degree burns, requiring skin grafts. Attempts to settle with McDonald's for her medical bills were unsuccessful, so she sued. The jury found for Ms. Liebeck; however, it concluded that she was 20% responsible for the accident. Both the high temperature of the coffee and a history of injuries and complaints about the heat of the coffee factored into the jury's

---

Public law: Any law that concerns the relationship of an individual and government.

Private law: Also known as civil law; any law that concerns the relationship of one person to another.

State action: A command, decision, or act that can be attributed to a government.

Punitive damages: Money damages in a civil suit that exceed compensation and are intended to punish and deter future misconduct.

deliberations. Actual damages were found to be $200,000, so the jury awarded $160,000, or 80%. Additionally, it recommended $2.7 million in punitive damages. That amount equaled 2 days of McDonald's revenues from coffee sales. Finding it excessive, the trial judge reduced the punitive damages award to $480,000, and ultimately, the parties settled for about $500,000.[1] The case garnered international attention and has been used by people of different legal and political perspectives to advance their causes. Tort reform advocates continue to use the case as evidence that civil juries are out of control. On the other side, advocates for using the law to control corporate greed and to increase corporate responsibility see the case as a success. Regardless, it is an illustration of the use of civil law to accomplish what are traditional criminal law objectives. The opposite is also true. There is a feature of criminal law that looks more like civil law. In some cases, the state may request that an offender compensate a victim for actual damages caused by a crime. This is known as restitution. Contrast this with a fine, which an offender pays to the state itself.

There are many types of civil law. **Contract law** is one. Contracts are about promises. Most people expect others to live up to their promises. Quite often, this is a social expectation, such as when Grandma promises to cook Thanksgiving dinner. Let's say Grandma chooses to go to a casino instead of cooking dinner. While she may disappoint her family, who were looking forward to her deep-fried turkey and green bean casserole, she hasn't committed a breach of contract. But business and professional affairs depend on promises. Imagine the harm that would befall Apple if one of the suppliers of materials needed for the production of its newest iPhone were to decide, at the last minute, to sell the materials to another company. This would likely cause a delay in the release of the new iPhone, reduce sales, cause Apple's stock to decline in value, and possibly lead to employee layoffs and terminations. To prevent this from happening, Apple can enter into a legally enforceable contract with the supplier. The contract would bind the supplier to provide the materials and for Apple to pay for them. A violation of contract, known as a breach, can be taken to court, and the breaching party can be ordered to pay for any harm (damages) it causes.

Another type of civil law is **tort** law. A tort occurs when one person hurts another person or another person's property. There are three forms of torts. You are likely familiar with the first: *negligence*. Have you ever seen an advertisement that urges you to contact an attorney if you have been injured in a slip and fall, car accident, or because you became sick at work? Those are examples of negligence—the tort of being harmed by another person who has behaved unreasonably, but not necessarily intentionally. The McDonalds coffee case discussed earlier is another example of a **negligent tort**. Let's consider another example that is common today: the person who causes an accident because they are texting while driving. The driver is responsible for compensating the victims of their negligence for their injuries and property losses.

Contract law: A form of civil law where two or more persons create an agreement that may be enforced in court.

Tort: A civil wrong not arising out of a contract. There are three forms of tort: negligence, intentional, and strict liability.

Negligent tort: Injury to a person or property damage resulting from another person's failure to act reasonably.

A change in our car crash facts illustrates the second type of tort. If the driver sees their enemy driving on the same street, swerves to hit the enemy, and indeed makes impact, they are committing an **intentional tort**. As may be obvious to you, the difference between negligence and intentional torts is what is in the driver's head: Do they want to hit the other car, or are they simply careless? Assault, battery, trespass, and false imprisonment are intentional torts; they are also crimes. Our driver's intentional collision with her enemy may result in both a civil lawsuit and criminal charges.

There is a third type of tort that isn't concerned with a defendant's fault at all: **strict liability**. In cases of strict liability, a defendant is liable for damages resulting from their conduct—*period*. It doesn't matter if the injuries were unintended, and it doesn't matter if the defendant acted reasonably. Strict liability is rare. It is imposed when an act is highly dangerous or the likelihood of harm is very great. The use of explosives, serving alcohol to intoxicated persons who subsequently injure others in car accidents, and the defective manufacturing of some consumer products are examples. Of course, plaintiffs like strict liability because it is easier to win when intentionality or negligence don't have to be proved.

There are other forms of civil law, including the law that determines what happens to a person's property after death (probate); the law of marriage, divorce, and children (family); and the law governing disputes over ownership and rights to property (property).

Recall that the objective of civil law is to restore a plaintiff to the position they weres in before the injury happened. The law uses money to "remedy" injuries most of the time. These monies are referred to as damages. Returning to the texter who causes a crash, the defendant could be ordered to pay for the plaintiff's medical bills and loss of income if work was missed. Sometimes, money isn't enough. Instead, a plaintiff wants a court to order the defendant to do something or to not do something. If a precious family heirloom is stolen, the victim of the theft will likely want the ring back more than they want its value in cash. So the plaintiff may ask the court to issue an order, known as a **writ**, for a return of the property.

In addition to objectives, civil law cases are similar in other ways that are different from criminal cases. First, the standard of proof in civil cases is lower than in criminal cases. Known as **preponderance of the evidence**, a party in a civil case wins if the **fact finder** (jury or judge) believes a party's version of the facts and damages are more likely true than not. This is a quantified standard: Greater than 50% wins. But it's not about quantity; it is about quality. Having

---

Intentional tort: Injury to person or property damage that was intended by the defendant.

Strict liability tort: A form of liability that is not concerned with state of mind, or fault. If a person is responsible for the act that results in injury or damages, even though unintentional and the person was acting reasonably, liability exists.

Writ: A court order.

Preponderance of the evidence: Standard of proof used to decide who wins in a civil case. It is also used in criminal law for specific questions, but never in the determination of guilt. A plaintiff must persuade the fact finder that its claim is more likely true (greater than 50%) than not to satisfy the preponderance standard.

Fact finder: The person or body responsible for weighing the evidence and deciding what evidence is true. Both judges and juries are fact finders. In criminal law, a defendant has a right to have a jury of peers find the facts in the ultimate determination of guilt. Judges find facts when issues arise before, during, and after trial. Judges only find the facts in regard to the ultimate question of guilt when a defendant has waived the right to a jury trial.

more evidence doesn't win a case. Persuading the fact finder that one's version of the case is more likely to be true than the other party's version is what is required.

The standard in criminal cases is different. Because the punishment in criminal cases can be so severe, the state has the burden of proving guilt by a very high standard: **beyond a reasonable doubt**. Unlike preponderance of the evidence, beyond a reasonable doubt is not quantified. Although the standard is not mentioned in the Constitution of the United States, SCOTUS has held that it is constitutionally required by due process.[2] But SCOTUS has not defined "beyond a reasonable doubt," so state definitions vary. Although the standard is higher than preponderance, proof beyond *all doubt* is not required anywhere. Some state definitions refer to moral certainty of guilt. To use everyday language, beyond a reasonable doubt means that a person is "damn sure of guilt." In the more precise words of one federal court,

> Proof beyond a reasonable doubt does not mean proof beyond all possible doubt or to a mathematical certainty. Possible doubts or doubts based on conjecture, speculation, or hunch are not reasonable doubts. Reasonable doubt is a fair doubt based on reason, logic, common sense, or experience. It is a doubt that an ordinary reasonable person has after carefully weighing all of the evidence, and is a doubt of the sort that would cause him or her to hesitate to act in matters of importance in his or her own life. It may arise from the evidence, or from the lack of evidence, or from the nature of the evidence.[3]

At trial, the state must prove every element of the crime beyond a reasonable doubt for the defendant to be convicted. Elements are the parts of a crime. You will learn much more about elements later.

The different standards of proof between criminal and civil law sometimes lead to conflicting outcomes. Consider the famous O.J. Simpson case. The former professional football player and actor was criminally charged with the murder of his ex-wife, Nicole Brown Simpson, and her friend, Ron Goldman. His 1995 televised criminal trial was commonly referred to as the "trial of the century." Although this is an exaggeration, the trial was a sensational event that gripped the nation. Represented by 11 prominent lawyers known as the "Dream Team," Mr. Simpson was acquitted of both murders. Later, however, the father of Ron Goldman sued Mr. Simpson for the wrongful death—a tort—of his son. The jury returned a verdict of $33.5 million in favor of Mr. Goldman. The outcome confused many people, who didn't understand how Mr. Simpson could be acquitted in one trial and found responsible in another. The answer is found in the difference between civil and criminal law. Because the beyond a reasonable doubt standard is so much greater than the 50% plus a feather preponderance standard, it is possible for a defendant to be acquitted in a criminal case but found liable in a civil case. In the *Simpson* case, the criminal jury didn't find proof of O.J.'s guilt beyond a reasonable doubt, but the civil jury found proof of his guilt by preponderance of the evidence.

Beyond a reasonable doubt: Standard of proof required to convict a defendant in a criminal case. While the standard has not been precisely quantified, it is less than beyond all doubt and considerably more than preponderance of evidence.

PHOTO 1.1 O.J. Simpson shows the jury a new pair of Aris extra-large gloves, similar to the gloves found at the Bundy and Rockingham crime scene on 21 June 1995, during his double-murder trial in Los Angeles, CA.

VINCE BUCCI/AFP via Getty Images

Guilt isn't the only decision that is made in criminal cases. Judges make many decisions before trial, during trial, and after trial. Each decision requires one of the parties, either the defendant or the state, to prove its position by a certain level of confidence. Rarely does the beyond a reasonable doubt standard apply in these decisions. Rather, lesser standards of confidence are required. Preponderance of the evidence, which you already learned applies in civil law cases, is common. Another standard, **clear and convincing evidence**, is used in a few, specific cases. As an example, the Eighth Amendment to the Constitution of the United States entitles a defendant to be released from jail pending trial, subject to posting money (bail) to ensure the defendant's appearance in court. But the right to bail isn't absolute. Defendants who are a threat to others or who are flight risks may be held without bail. Many jurisdictions require the government to establish dangerousness or flight risk by clear and convincing evidence. Clear and convincing evidence is more than preponderance and less than beyond a reasonable doubt; it exists when the truth of the party's allegation is substantially more likely to be true than not.

Clear and convincing evidence: Standard of proof that is applied in civil and administrative cases in which substantial personal interests are at stake (e.g., deportation and retraining orders). It is also applied to specific criminal law matters, such as the determination of whether a defendant's right to bail should be limited. The standard is defined as evidence that is substantially more likely to be true than not.

There are two other important standards in criminal law. One is so common that it is part of every American's vocabulary. **Probable cause** is required by the Fourth Amendment to the Constitution of the United States before law enforcement officers may conduct searches or seize persons or property. Like the beyond a reasonable doubt standard, probable cause is not precisely quantified. But its relationship to the other standards is known, and that helps to understand how much is required to satisfy the probable cause standard. Probable cause is less than preponderance of the evidence and more than a scintilla of evidence. SCOTUS has held that probable cause exists when the facts available to an officer warrant a person of reasonable caution in the belief that contraband or evidence of a crime is present.[4]

Another frequently used evidentiary standard of proof is reasonable suspicion. This standard, which is less than probable cause but more than a mere scintilla of evidence, is applied to specific searches and seizures where the probable cause standard isn't used. A well-known reasonable suspicion case was the 1968 SCOTUS decision *Terry v. Ohio*.[5] In *Terry*, SCOTUS held that police may conduct a short investigatory stop of a suspect, but not an arrest, if the officer has a **reasonable suspicion** of criminality that is supported by specific and articulable facts. A police officer's hunch is not adequate, although the officer's experience may be factored into the reasonable suspicion determination. SCOTUS permitted the stop with less than probable cause because it involved a brief, less intrusive encounter than a full arrest.

You just learned a lot of standards of proof; let's use Figure 1.2 to put it all together.

FIGURE 1.2 ■ Standards of Proof

Standards of Proof

LEVEL OF PROOF	WHEN APPLIED
Beyond All Doubt	Never Expected
Beyond a reasonable doubt	Required for criminal convictions
Clear and convincing evidence	Used in civil and administrative cases when liberties are at issue; occasionally in criminal cases for specific questions—never guilt
Preponderance of the evidence	Standard to win a civil case. Also used in criminal cases for specific questions—never guilt
Probable cause	Required for many searches and seizures
Reasonable suspicion	Required for specific, limited searches and seizures
Scintilla	Never used
No evidence	Never used

Probable cause: The standard of proof required by the Fourth Amendment to the Constitution of the United States for a search or seizure to be conducted. An officer has probable cause when the facts available to the officer warrant a person of reasonable caution in the belief that contraband or evidence of a crime is present.

Reasonable suspicion: Less than probable cause, and therefore an exception to the Fourth Amendment's probable cause requirement; police officers are sometimes permitted to conduct brief detentions and limited searches when a reasonable suspicion of criminality, supported by specific and articulable facts, is present. Reasonable suspicion is but more than a mere scintilla or a hunch, although an officer's experience may inform the decision.

In addition to differences in objectives and standard of proof, criminal and civil law vary in how they proceed. First, the parties, or litigants, are different. In all criminal cases, the individual charged with the crime is the defendant. In criminal cases, the plaintiff is always the government. This is true even if a specific individual was harmed by the defendant. Known as the victim-in-fact, the harmed individual doesn't have the authority to file a criminal prosecution. Instead, the state, as the victim-in-law, must file and prosecute the criminal charge. Governments identify themselves differently in the official court filings. The state may be expressed in the formal name of the government (e.g., *State of Texas v. Pagel, United States of America v. Wang*) or on behalf of the people (e.g., *People of the State of Illinois v. Smith*). There is no difference between the two.

Civil cases, on the other hand, are between private parties. So both parties are persons or corporate entities (e.g., *Reginald Teel v. Grace Kathryn* or *Amazon, Inc. v. Nikole Casey*). The government can be a private party when it is acting as a legal person, not as a public prosecutor. The state of Alabama, for example, may sue a contractor who has negligently constructed a public building that is falling apart (e.g., *State of Alabama v. Buildo, Inc.*). This is an example of a civil case, even though a government is the plaintiff. If the building were to fall, killing several occupants, the government could file a criminal case against Buildo, Inc., and its employees who were responsible for the deaths. In this instance, the government is both a civil plaintiff in the civil case and a prosecutor in the criminal case.

An important difference between criminal and civil cases is the application of the Constitution of the United States. Because criminal cases are filed and pursued by the state and the consequences can include serious punishments, including imprisonment and death, the Constitution is always present. Criminal defendants enjoy the protection of many constitutional rights that civil defendants do not. Here are a few examples:

- Speedy, public trial

- Privilege against self-incrimination, including the right to not be called as a witness by the prosecution at trial

- Representation by an attorney, paid for by the state in cases where defendants can't afford to hire their own

- Proof beyond a reasonable doubt

- No double jeopardy (to not be tried or punished twice for the same act)

- Questions of law that are unclear are to be decided in the favor of the criminal defendant over the state

---

Parties: The persons involved in a dispute. If the dispute is in court, the parties are also known as litigants.

Defendant: A litigant who is sued is referred to as the defendant.

Plaintiff: A litigant who files a civil suit is referred to as a plaintiff.

Victim-in-fact: A person or legal entity that is harmed by another. In civil cases, the victim-in-fact may sue to be compensated for injuries. In criminal law, a victim-in-fact does not have the legal authority to prosecute the offender.

Victim-in-law: The government when acting as a public prosecutor.

The Constitution's protections make a difference; in some cases, they can change the outcome of a case. Returning to the O.J. Simpson case, Mr. Simpson was made to testify in his civil case while he chose to invoke his privilege against self-incrimination in his criminal trial. This difference, along with the differing standards of proof, may explain why he was acquitted by the criminal jury and found liable by the civil jury.

TABLE 1.1 ■ Criminal, Civil, and Juvenile Law Compared			
	Criminal	*Civil*	*Juvenile*
Parties	State files an indictment or information against an individual or corporation	Individual, corporation or government files the case against another individual, corporation, or government	State files petition against juvenile
Objectives	Deterrence, retribution, rehabilitation, incapacitation	Compensation	Rehabilitation
Burden of proof	Beyond a reasonable doubt	Preponderance of evidence	Beyond a reasonable doubt
Outcomes	Death, imprisonment, fine, restitution, supervision, and more	Money damages, court orders	Education, counseling, treatment, detention
Constitution's role	Limits what acts can be made criminal; substantial protections of defendants (e.g., right to an attorney, right not to testify)	Limits what acts can lead to liability; smaller role in the process than in criminal law	Similar, but more limited, than in criminal law

Juvenile Delinquency

The law of juvenile delinquency is closely related to criminal law. In many respects, the two appear to be the same. Both deal with bad behavior, the state initiates both criminal and juvenile delinquency actions, and often the police are involved in both. But the two also differ in a couple of important ways. First, the objectives of the two are more different than alike. Criminals are punished; juveniles are rehabilitated. As you will learn, rehabilitation is one of many dimensions of criminal punishment. Juveniles determined to be delinquent, on the other hand, are provided with psychological, emotional, and drug and alcohol treatment; education; and life skills development with the intention of preparing them for a productive and law-abiding life.

Juvenile law is not uniform. The definition of who is considered a juvenile varies, for example. The minimum age in the United States is 6, although older is more common. Most states set the age of adulthood at 18. There is sometimes overlap between the jurisdiction of the juvenile justice and criminal justice system. In these cases, authorities decide whether to charge the offender as an adult in criminal court or as a juvenile. In most states, a minor can be declared delinquent for offenses that fall into one of two categories: status offenses and acts that are crimes for adults. Status offenses are acts that are not crimes if committed by adults, such as school truancy.

Because the juvenile justice system isn't focused on punishment, the constitutional rights that defendants enjoy in criminal court only partially apply. Like a criminal defendant, a juvenile is entitled to have an attorney, to remain silent, to cross-examine witnesses, and to have the state prove delinquency beyond a reasonable doubt. But other rights, such as to a jury trial, do not apply. For a summary of the differences between criminal, civil, and juvenile law, see Table 1.1.

QUESTIONS AND APPLICATIONS

Eva Small is upset with her city government. She posts the following on Snapchat on June 1: "The city council and mayor's support of the new shopping mall is nonsense. A beautiful park will be lost, an ugly mall will be built, and all of it so a rich developer can get richer."

The month before Eva's posting, the city council enacted an *ordinance* (local law) that made it a misdemeanor crime, punishable with a fine of $100 to $1,000 and a jail sentence of 7 to 60 days, to "utter, in person or through social media, opinions about the city council or the mayor of the city that are disparaging or offensive."

On June 3, two city police officers stopped Eva on the street, took her phone over her objection, turned it on, and searched for her Snapchat app. While searching her phone, the officers discovered a picture of her breaking into the city's administration building. She was arrested and charged with violating the new ordinance *and* with breaking and entering into a public facility.

Eva has responded with the following defenses. Label each as either an issue of criminal law or criminal procedure.

1. The statement she posted on Snapchat doesn't fall within the scope of the conduct prohibited by the ordinance.
2. The statement she posted on Snapchat is protected speech under the First Amendment to the Constitution of the United States.
3. Her stop by the police officers violates the Fourth Amendment to the Constitution of the United States.
4. The seizure and search of her phone by the police officers violates the Fourth Amendment to the Constitution of the United States.

Label the facts in Questions 5–7 as presenting a civil case or a criminal case. If a civil case, identify it as negligence, intentional, or strict liability tort.

5. Kym is with her friend Zoe, in Zoe's home. Kym entered the home through the back door and proceeded directly up the home's back stairs to Zoe's bedroom. The two chatted while awaiting a third friend, Zack. The three planned to go to see a movie together. Zack arrived later than planned, honked the horn of his car, and Kym jumped up and said to Zoe, "Let's go, we can still make the movie before it starts." She ran out of the room and down the home's master stairway. Kym followed closely behind Zoe. In her rush, Kym didn't see a banana peel on the stairs. She slipped on the peel and fell down the stairs, breaking an arm and a leg. She wants Zoe to pay for her medical bills.[6]
6. Kym is studying criminal law with her friend Zoe in Zoe's home. Zoe excuses herself to the bathroom during their studies. While in the bathroom, Kym looks for a highlighter marker on Zoe's desk. She inadvertently discovers a picture of Zoe and Kym's girlfriend, Sandi, kissing. Enraged, Kym begins shouting at Zoe. Confused about

what is happening, Zoe exits the bathroom to find Kym waiting outside the door. Kym immediately strikes Zoe in the face. Zoe falls to the floor and hits her head on a table. She suffers cuts and bruises to her head, requiring medical care. She wants Kym to pay for her medical bills.

7. Kym is studying criminal law with her friend Zoe in Zoe's home. Zoe excuses herself to the bathroom during their studies. While in the bathroom, Kym looks for a highlighter marker on Zoe's desk. She inadvertently discovers a picture of Zoe and Kym's girlfriend, Sandi, kissing. Enraged, Kym begins shouting at Zoe. Confused about what is happening, Zoe exits the bathroom to find Kym waiting outside the door. Kym immediately strikes Zoe in the face. Zoe falls to the floor and hits her head on a table. She suffers cuts and bruises to her head, requiring medical care. Kym offers to pay Zoe's medical expenses. Zoe refuses the money, calls the police, and Kym is arrested and charged by the prosecutor.

8. Do you believe punitive damages should be available in civil cases? If so, should a defendant be protected by the same rights found in criminal law? Explain your answers.

WHY PUNISH?

Learning Objective: Identify and describe the five primary objectives of criminal law punishment.

As you have learned, the differing objectives of criminal and civil law are important. The differing objectives are so important that the nation's most fundamental law, the Constitution, applies differently to them. Why do we punish wrongdoers? The Christian theologian St. Augustine wrote, "Punishment is justice for the unjust."

There are two dominant philosophies of punishment: retribution and utilitarianism. To a retributivist, punishment is deserved; offenders should suffer to pay for their crimes. To the utilitarian, punishment is needed to maximize the greatest good for the greatest number of people. There are six commonly recognized objectives that spring from these two rationales. Two objectives, retribution and restitution, are retributive. The other four—deterrence, rehabilitation, incapacitation, and restoration—are intended to protect, or benefit, society. Let's take a look at each.

Deterrence

Stopping crime before it occurs is a significant objective of criminal law. Using fear, the law deters people from criminality. There are two forms of deterrence. The first is *general deterrence*. Under this theory, the public at large is deterred from committing crimes when they see offenders punished. *Specific deterrence*, on the other hand, focuses on the individual. Punishing a person for today's offense is intended to deter that individual from future offenses.

Classical (older) theory suggested that there are three elements to deterrence: certainty, celerity, and severity. The first is the certainty of getting caught. The more likely a person believes they will be caught, the greater the deterrent effect of the law. The second element of deterrence is celerity, or the speed of justice. Punishing an offender months after a crime has been committed is more effective than years later when few people will connect the crime to its punishment. The third element is the severity of the punishment. The assumption of this element is that people engage in rational choice; they balance the benefits of offending against the costs. These theories assume people make rational choices about being involved in crime. This assumption is questionable and the efficacy of deterrence is unclear.

Retribution

The second objective of criminal law punishment is *retribution*, or giving an offender their *just desserts*. The idea is also expressed as paying one's debt to society. Under this theory, the offender owes a debt to the community, rather than (or in addition to) the individual victim. Vengeance is a very old practice, quite possibly a natural instinct. The idea of public vengeance is also very old. One of the most ancient laws known to us was Hammurabi's Code. Dated to about 1750 B.C.E., Hammurabi's Code contained the principle of an "eye for an eye" and a "tooth for a tooth" long before it appeared in the Jewish Torah and Christian Old Testament.

In addition to satisfying the public's need for vengeance, retribution may also deter the victim from seeking personal retribution, thereby reducing further violence and preventing the victim from becoming an offender. To many people, vengeance is an archaic, cruel act that governments should not commit. Regardless, SCOTUS has upheld retribution as a legitimate criminal law objective,[7] and it often underpins state and federal criminal law.

Rehabilitation

The third objective of criminal law is the *rehabilitation* of the offender. Rehabilitation is focused on helping an offender to mature, to become self-sufficient, and to reintegrate into society. Rehabilitation programs typically involve formal education, occupational training, mental health counseling, and other programs that are designed to separate the offender, both psychologically and physically, from the causes of their criminal behavior. Like deterrence, rehabilitation has been heavily researched, and its efficacy is unclear.

Incapacitation

Incapacitation, the fourth objective, is the use of physical restraint to protect the general public. Imprisonment, house arrest, the use of technology to track and limit where offenders may travel and visit, and the death penalty are the most common forms of incapacitation. By limiting an offender's geography, the public is protected from the drug dealer, the violent from visiting a victim's home, the child sex predator from being near schools, and the burglar from breaking into another home. One criticism of the use of imprisonment is that it doesn't stop the offender from reoffending; it only reduces the pool of possible victims to fellow inmates.

Restitution

The final objective is *restitution*. Different from retributive justice, restitutive justice seeks to make the actual victim, not the public at large, whole again. The most common way to do this is to order an offender to compensate their victim for the harm they have caused. The accountant who steals $10,000 from a client is ordered to repay the loss, for example. In some cases, courts may also order restitution of wages or other indirect losses. Like civil law, monetary restitution seeks to compensate the victim. But restitution can involve more than money. A defendant who damages property, for example, may be ordered to repair it.

Restorative Justice

Restorative justice emphasizes healing those who are harmed by an offense, making the offender whole again, and returning him to full status in the community. The individuals harmed include the victim, victim's family, offender, offender's family, and the larger community. Restoration is premised on the idea that through inclusive open dialogue, mutual respect and understanding will result in healing and community harmony. Outcomes may include restitution, an apology by the offender and forgiveness by the victim, community service, and possibly agreed-upon incarceration. Restorative justice is found in traditional communities and takes many forms, including healing circles and formal apology ceremonies. Although there is little history of restorative methods in the United States, they are receiving increased attention as an alternative to imprisonment. Restorative justice doesn't fit squarely in the retributive or utilitarian models. But of the two, it is more utilitarian because its benefits everyone: offender, victim, and community.

Retributivism and utilitarianism are not mutually exclusive. Both approaches to justice can be found in the ancient and modern world. Today, both are seen in the punishments found in state and federal criminal laws. So which is best? As is so often true in law and justice, the answer is *it depends*. It depends on the objective sought; do you want to reduce how many times the crime occurs (deterrence), do you want to get a pound of flesh (retribution), do you want to prepare the individual to be a better neighbor (rehabilitation), do you want to protect the community (incapacitation), do you want to make the victim whole (restitution), or do you want some combination of these results? The last option is appealing. Why not accomplish more than one if possible? In many cases, multiple objectives are achieved automatically. For example, incarcerating a violent felon serves both retributive and utilitarian (incapacitation) objectives.

The punishment decision isn't just about society's intentions. Efficacy and efficiency are also factors. After all, there is no point in imposing a punishment to deter misconduct if it doesn't deter misconduct. Considerable research has been conducted on the relative successes and costs of various forms of punishment. What has been learned is that punishment is complex—there is no magic pill. Individuals respond differently, and individual responses are not static; they are contextual. As one scholar wrote about deterrence theory, it is "confusing... [and] very difficult to state with any precision how strong a deterrent effect the criminal justice system provides."[8] See Table 1.2 for a chart of the philosophies, objectives, and methods of punishment.

TABLE 1.2 ■ Philosophies, Objectives, and Methods of Punishment		
Philosophy	*Objectives*	*Examples of Methods*
Retributive	Retribution	Death, incarceration, hard labor, community service, shaming, forfeiture
Utilitarian	Deterrence, incapacitation, rehabilitation, restitution, restoration	Incarceration, education and training, psychological treatment, drug and alcohol treatment, repaying victim for losses, apologizing for harm and asking for (or giving) forgiveness, sex offender registration, chemical castration of sex offenders, forfeiture

QUESTIONS AND APPLICATIONS

The practice of passing through an intersection after a stoplight turns red is on the rise in the United States. The result has been a steady increase in accidents, injuries, and fatalities. The city of Colishun, Ohio, has experienced a 60% increase in accidents caused by red-light running in the past 5 years. Three of these accidents have resulted in deaths. The members of the city council have been urged by their police chief, director of traffic and roads services, and director of public health to act.

Which punishment objective is most emphasized in each of the scenarios in Questions 1 through 4? Explain your answer.

1. The city council enacted an ordinance requiring red-light cameras to be installed at all busy intersections and enacted a progressive system of fines for violations. The first violation is fined $200, the second $500, and subsequent violations are fined $1,000 and bring 1 week to 3 months in jail. The ordinance further required that tickets be issued to all violators. They directed the police chief and the two directors to develop a social media and television information campaign to educate the public about the dangers of red-light running, the law, the penalties, the zero-tolerance policy, and the 100% effective rate of catching violators using the cameras. The campaign is to include the names and punishments of every violator. When enacted, the mayor stated on behalf of the entire council, "We want everyone to know that red-light running is serious business. We are killing one another. If you run a red light, you will be caught and punished. Please think when you are driving and don't do it!"

2. After 6 months of the public information campaign and enforcement measures described in Question 1, there was no decline in red-light running. The police chief presented data that showed red-light runners are often repeat offenders. In another attempt to address the problem, the city council enacted an ordinance requiring every person convicted of red-light running to enroll in a traffic safety program. The curriculum of the program includes a module on the dangers of red-light running, discussions with individuals who have been injured by red-light runners, and in-car driving instruction.

3. After 6 months of the public information campaign and enforcement measures described in Question 1, there was no decline in red-light running. The police chief presented data that showed red-light runners are often repeat offenders. Frustrated, one member of council stated, "I have had it. These people are killing others because they are so selfish and uncaring. We tried education and light punishment to prevent this, and it didn't work. They owe it to everyone to pay for their crimes." The other members shook their heads in agreement, and one commented, "Commit the crime, do the time." They then enacted an ordinance changing the penalties for red-light running to a $1,000 fine and 5 to 30 days in jail for the first conviction, $1,500 and 30 to 60 days in jail for the second conviction, and $1,500 to $3,000 and 60 to 120 days in jail for three or more convictions.

4. The city council learns that insurance coverage often doesn't pay all of the expenses of accidents resulting from red-light running. Further, because it is expensive and time-consuming for victims to sue in civil court, they often don't recover the expenses not covered by insurance. The city council enacts an ordinance requiring the criminal court to order red-light violators who caused accidents to pay all of their victims' expenses not otherwise covered by insurance.

5. Marshan is 16 years old. He is an only child. He has never known his father. His mother is an alcoholic who has physically abused him most of his life. His mother's abuse put him into the hospital twice. He was once removed from the home by state child protective services officers, but he was returned to his mother after 2 weeks. During the time he was removed from his family home, he received a psychological assessment. The psychologist concluded that he is emotionally immature and suffers from an anger management problem. However, he is intelligent and academically motivated. In spite of his hardships at home, he has maintained a B average and expressed an interest in attending college. He met another 16-year-old boy, Samuel, on social media. The two share an interest in guns. Samuel invited Marshan over to see his guns. During the visit, the two began to argue about politics. Samuel told Marshan to leave, but Marshan refused, so Samuel grabbed Marshan and pushed him. Instinctively, Marshan pointed the gun at Samuel and pulled the trigger. To his surprise, the gun fired. Samuel died from the gunshot. Apply the five punishment objectives to Marshan and discuss whether each is satisfied. Decide what punishment fits the crime, if any. Explain your decision.

WHERE DOES CRIMINAL LAW COME FROM?

Learning Objective: Identify and describe the various forms of law that are important to criminal law.

Recall that law is a norm that a collective group of people enforces; they punish individuals who violate the norm. The United States is a constitutional republic. Laws are created by elected government officials, by appointed government officials, and, on occasion, by the people directly. There are several forms of law. In criminal law, the following forms of law declare crimes and defenses to crimes, protect civil liberties, and detail the process that courts use when hearing criminal cases.

Constitutional Law

Constitutional law is the first form of law. The United States (federal government) and each of the states have a constitution. The highest form of law in the United States is the Constitution of the United States. In this book, references to the "Constitution" are to the federal Constitution. As the highest form of law, all laws, federal and state, must fall in line with it. Laws that violate the Constitution are void.

The Constitution outlines the structure of government (i.e., federal and state governments' three branches), defines the authority of those governments, and also lists individual rights. A few rights are found in the original Constitution, but most are found in the amendments. The freedom from unreasonable searches and seizures, the right to a jury trial, and the right to

---

Constitutional law: The most fundamental law of the United States. As the highest form of law, all other forms of law are invalid if contrary to the U.S. Constitution.

be free from cruel and unusual punishment are examples. You will explore the rights that are important in criminal law in greater detail later.

Statutory Law

Statutory law is the second form of law. As you already read, the United States and each of the states have statutory law. Statutes are laws created by legislative bodies. At the federal level, the U.S. Congress is the lawmaker. Each state also has a legislature. They are known by different names, such as Arkansas General Assembly, California State Legislature, and Massachusetts General Court. Yes, you read that correctly—the Massachusetts General Court is a lawmaking body, not a court of law.

It is statutory law that declares acts to be crimes and establishes punishments. Occasionally, legislatures also protect liberties. As you will learn later, legislatures may extend individual rights beyond what constitutions protect, but they may not reduce them. When legislatures publish their laws, they group them together by subject matter to make it easier to find specific laws. These groups of statutes are known as codes, so you can find most criminal statutes organized into criminal codes. At the federal level, you can find both criminal law and criminal procedure in Title 18 of the United States Code, "Crimes and Criminal Procedure."

Model Penal Code

Because each state and the federal government have the authority to prohibit, punish, and process cases differently, criminal laws vary. With the objective of bringing some standardization and modernization to criminal law, a group of legal scholars began writing a unified criminal code in the 1950s. They completed their work in 1962. The product, known as the Model Penal Code, is not law. Rather, it was created as a model for the states to consider. Today, a majority of the states have adopted portions of the Model Penal Code (MPC). Because it represents the closest thing the United States has to uniform criminal law, it will be discussed throughout this book.

Referendum

Statutory law is a *republican* method of making law; the people elect representatives to make law. About half of the states also permit the people to directly make law through popular referendum, also known as a ballot initiative or ballot question. This is a form of *democracy*, or direct lawmaking by the people. There is no referendum at the federal level; all statutory law is made by Congress. Referenda processes vary between the states. Some states enable referenda to

---

Statutory law: Law made by the U.S. Congress and state legislatures. Statutory law is the primary form of law that defines crimes, defenses to crimes, and the processes used in criminal cases. A lower form of law than constitutional law.

Model Penal Code (MPC): A recommended criminal code created by a group of scholars and practicing attorneys. Most states have enacted portions of the MPC.

Referendum: Law created directly by the people through a process of gathering a minimum number of voter signatures to place a constitutional amendment or a statutory equivalent on an election ballot for consideration by the general voting public.

create statutory law, others permit it to be used to amend their constitutions, and many provide for both. In many states, a referendum may be started by the people after a minimum number of signatures have been obtained. In some states, the legislature may place questions on the ballot for popular vote. The referenda process can be powerful. Several states in recent years have decriminalized the use of marijuana through referenda, and in 2018, the people of Florida voted to restore the voting rights of ex-felons who were not convicted of murder or felony sex offenses.[9]

Ordinances

Ordinances are the local government counterpart of state statutes. They are created by local government lawmaking bodies, such as city and county councils, and occasionally directly by the voters. If properly enacted, ordinances have the authority of a statute. But as a lower form of law, they must not conflict with statutory and constitutional law.

Administrative Law

Administrative law is a somewhat odd feature of U.S. law. Although administrative agencies fall into the executive branch of government, which doesn't normally make law, they are empowered to "promulgate" (a fancy word for making and announcing to the public) law, commonly known as either rules or regulations. Most agency rules are civil or administrative, but sometimes agencies create criminal rules. All of the constitutional limitations that are imposed on statutory law apply administrative rules. Today, there are far more administrative rules than statutes. Administrative rules are organized into codes, in the same manner as statutory law.

Common Law

The *Common Law* was brought to the United States by our early English colonists. Common Law is judge-made law. In the early years of England, before Parliament existed, judges made most of the law. Eventually, the English Parliament became the primary creator of new law. But the role of courts in interpreting, and occasionally announcing, new law continues today. It is the courts, for example, that are the final word on what law means. Very important to criminal law and procedure, SCOTUS is the final word on the meaning of the Constitution. All of the states have adopted the Common Law to some degree. Louisiana, which was founded by French colonists, more closely follows the French (Civil) law, although it has adopted many features of the Common Law, particularly in the realm of criminal law. Because legal history informs our understanding of modern law, there are references to the old Common Law throughout this book.

Interpretation is the process that gives meaning to a law. For example, imagine a state statute that forbids "sexual cyber harassment." The statute makes it a crime to (1) post a picture of

---

Ordinance: Law made by local legislative bodies, such as city councils. A lower form of law to constitutional and statutory law.

Regulation: Law that is created by administrative agencies. A lower form of law to constitutional and statutory law.

another person who is nude or engaged in a sex act (2) on a social media platform (3) with the legal name or address of that person (4) without that person's permission. As an example of how the Common Law is made, consider Karli Makalini, a social media sensation. She has hundreds of thousands of subscribers to her YouTube channel, where she posts cooking videos. Her online persona is Cooking Karli—she has never posted her legal name on social media. Her former lover posted a nude picture of Karli on Facebook with the caption "Cooking Karli, cooking it up hot." If the lover were to be charged under the sexual cyber harassment statute, a question of interpretation that the trial court would have to answer is whether Karli's online persona is a "legal name." After it is decided, the case would be *precedent*. Under the doctrine of **stare decisis**, the decision in the case would apply to cases in the future that involve the same question: Is an online alias a legal name under the sexual cyber harassment statute?

Executive Orders

The final form of law has been in the news a lot in recent years: **executive orders**. The president of the United States, governors of the states, and other officials issue orders. Most executive orders concern the functioning of government or the execution of the executive's responsibilities. That is the duty of an executive. Ordering government offices to close during a crisis or to lower flags to half-mast to honor someone who has died are examples of orders that aren't lawmaking and therefore are valid. Sometimes, these orders are inherent, or they simply come with the executive officer's job. In other instances, the legislature empowers the executive officer. The recent COVID-19 directives to stay home, close businesses, and socially distance are examples. The states had legislation in place to address emergencies long before COVID-19 was known to the world. Most state statutes specifically empowered governors and health officials to act during public health emergencies. For example, Minnesota's peacetime emergencies law delegates to the governor the duty to "protect the public peace, health, and safety, and preserve the lives and property of the people of the state." It further provides that the governor may direct and control "the conduct of persons in the state," "the entrance or exit from any stricken or threatened public place, occupancy of facilities, and the movement and cessation of movement of pedestrians, vehicular traffic," and "the evacuation, reception, and sheltering of persons." It was under this law that the governor declared a peacetime emergency and issued stay-at-home, social distancing, and other executive orders.[10] In Photo 1.2, you can read a poster summarizing a similar order by the governor of Idaho.

A criminal law executive order that finds itself in the news on occasion is a pardon, commutation, or reprieve. A pardon absolves a person of criminal liability, a commutation reduces a sentence, and a reprieve is an order to suspend or delay a punishment. In the federal system, the president has absolute authority over pardons and commutations. In the states, this authority is held by governors, boards, or sometimes both.

Stare decisis: Latin for "stand by a thing decided." The doctrine holds that prior legal decisions shall be binding on future cases when the facts of the prior and current case are similar.

Executive orders: Law and declarations created by the president of the United States and the governors of states that are issued to implement their responsibilities. The status of an executive order, relative to other forms of law, varies.

Idaho COVID-19

coronavirus.idaho.gov

GUIDANCE FOR GOVERNOR BRAD LITTLE'S STATEWIDE STAY-HOME ORDER

Updated March 25, 2020

Self-isolate

ALL residents of Idaho must self-isolate and stay and work from home as much as possible, unless you work in healthcare, public safety or an identified "essential business" as defined in order.

Residents can leave homes to obtain or provide essential services.

People at higher risk (over 65 and/or health-compromised) should avoid leaving their homes.

Employers that do not provide essential services as defined in order must take all steps necessary for employees to work remotely from home.

"Essential" facilities & services open

Grocery stores, healthcare facilities, gas stations, pharmacies, essential state and local government functions, laundromats/laundry services, financial institutions, residential and home-based care, veterinary services, hardware stores, limited child care for essential workers, infrastructure, and other businesses essential to the safety and well-being of the residents as defined in the order remain open. Restaurants open but only for drive-thru, carry-out, or delivery.

"Non-essential" facilities & services closed

Includes indoor gyms, recreational facilities, nightclubs, bars, entertainment venues, convention centers, hair and nail salons, public events and gatherings, dine-in restaurants (drive-thru, carry-out, delivery to continue), and other facilities and services not included in "essential" businesses as defined in order.

Limit public transit

Only to provide or obtain essential services.

Limit travel

All non-essential travel must cease.

No gatherings

Limit all non-essential gatherings of any number of individuals outside the household.

Outdoor activity OK

Outdoor activity *near your home* is not prohibited but residents are encouraged to keep distance of 6-feet from others not in their household.

Practice good hygiene

Wash hands, clean high touch surfaces, cover coughs and sneezes, and do not shake hands.

Order in effect Wednesday, March 25, 2020, and will remain in effect for at least 21 days
Governor Little and public health officials will reassess before end of 21-day period
Final Stay-Home Order will be available at coronavirus.idaho.gov

PHOTO 1.2 In March 2020, Idaho Governor Brad Little issued an order requiring his state's residents to stay home whenever possible.

Idaho governor's office

Sometimes, executives issue orders that involve policy, particularly when frustrated with a legislature that won't act to address a problem; these orders are new law. For example, President Barack Obama issued an executive order known as Deferred Action for Childhood Arrivals, which permitted individuals who were in the nation illegally but who were brought to the country as children, to defer their deportation, and President Donald Trump issued an executive order banning immigrants from specific nations from entering the United States. An executive order that goes too far into the business of the legislature or the courts is unconstitutional. Ultimately, it is the courts that decide if executive orders are constitutional, just as they do with statutes.

QUESTIONS AND APPLICATIONS

1. The New York Association of Public School Administrators is concerned about bullying in the public schools. Police are often reluctant to respond to calls by parents and school officials in cases of bullying because officers believe bullying is a school or parent concern, not a criminal justice matter. They agree to advocate for a law requiring police to respond to bullying complaints by school officials. Should the group ask a court, the New York State Legislature, or the governor to make the new law?

2. The state of Delaware enacts a statute that mandates whipping as a form of punishment for theft if the value of the item stolen exceeds $500. Dora has been charged with the theft of an item valued at $1,000. Dora believes that whipping violates the Eighth Amendment of the U.S. Constitution, which forbids cruel and unusual punishment. She offered to plead guilty if the prosecutor would recommend a jail sentence. The prosecutor refused. She wrote to the governor for help. The governor replied that she agrees that the law is unconstitutional but that she can't help because she has no authority over locally elected prosecutors. Who has the authority to hear and decide Dora's cruel and unusual punishment claim?

WHAT ARE THE TYPES OF CRIMES?

Learning Objective: When presented with a crime, you will be able to identify it is a felony, misdemeanor, infraction, malum in se, or malum prohibitum.

Two categorizations of crimes are very common in criminal law. Because these categories will be referred to throughout this text, you are introduced to them now. One divides crimes by the seriousness of punishment and the other by the nature of prohibition (see Table 1.3).

Felony, Misdemeanor, and Infraction

Crimes are often categorized by their seriousness. For our purposes now, seriousness refers to the possible punishment that a court can impose for a crime. Although imprisonment isn't the only form of punishment, it is used to distinguish felonies, misdemeanors, and infractions. Serious offenses are felonies. Crimes that can result in serious personal injury, significant loss to the value of property, and where a defendant had an evil intent are commonly treated as felonies. A crime that can result in imprisonment for a year or longer is a felony. Murder, sexual assault, arson, treason, intentionally causing serious injury, terroristic threat, and theft of property exceeding a minimum value are examples of felonies. Not all felonies are the same. They are "graded" by seriousness. Florida's grading scheme, for example, recognizes capital (death possible), life, third-degree, second-degree, and first-degree felonies.

A crime that can lead to less than 1 year of imprisonment is a misdemeanor. Touching another person without their consent but not causing serious injury, stealing a small amount of money, and multiple violations of traffic laws are misdemeanors. Just like felonies, misdemeanors are graded.

There is an even less serious offense than a misdemeanor: an infraction. Parking offenses, jaywalking, and littering are examples. Depending on the state and the specific offense, an infraction may be considered a minor crime or not. If not, imprisonment may not be possible, and an administrative agency or a civil court may process the case. Although infractions may be punished with short imprisonment, most result in fines or administrative action, such as the disciplining of a driving, business, boating, or fishing license.

Malum In Se and Malum Prohibitum

The distinction between felonies and misdemeanors dates back to the old Common Law in England. The Common Law also distinguished between crimes malum in se and malum prohibitum. The former is a Latin phrase that means an act is inherently wrong. The act is punished because it is commonly understood by people to be harmful or immoral. Murder and rape, for example, are each malum in se. Crimes that are not so obviously wrong but have been declared to be crimes by a legislature, such as tax evasion, illegal drug use, and trespassing on property, are each malum prohibitum.

Several chapters of this book are devoted to explaining crimes that are found in the statutes of the states and the federal government. Those chapters use yet another common form of classification: the victim. Crimes may be committed against persons, property, the public, and the state. These are useful for teaching and organizing the law. But they are artificial. For example, the burning of a home, known as arson to the law, is a crime against property. But in reality, property doesn't feel pain, and it doesn't suffer financial loss. Crimes against property hurt people. So don't give this categorization too much attention. It is just a convenient way to organize crimes.

Felonies: Serious crimes that may be punished with imprisonment of 1 year or longer.

Misdemeanors: Crimes that are punished with imprisonment of less than 1 year.

Infractions: Minor offenses that may be treated as civil or administrative offenses or as minor crimes. These are typically punished with administrative sanctions, fines, and rarely with very short terms of imprisonment.

Grading: A system of classifying crimes by seriousness and corresponding punishment.

Malum in se: An act that is prohibited because it is inherently wrong.

Malum prohibitum: An act that is prohibited by law but isn't inherently wrong.

TABLE 1.3 ■ Types of Crimes	
Type	**Description**
Felony	A crime that is punished with imprisonment of 1 year or longer
Misdemeanor	A crime that is punished with imprisonment of less than 1 year
Infraction	A minor offense, often punished with a fine, community service, or a short jail sentence
Malum in se	A serious offense; inherently wrong
Malum prohibitum	An offense that is not inherently wrong, but prohibited by statute or ordinance

QUESTIONS AND APPLICATIONS

Identify each of the following as malum in se or malum prohibitum:

1. Erecting a business sign that is higher than allowed by a statute
2. Underpayment of a property tax
3. Sexual assault of a minor
4. Shooting a parking meter enforcement officer for issuing a parking ticket
5. Urinating in public

HOW DOES THE U.S. CRIMINAL JUSTICE SYSTEM WORK?

Learning Objective: Explain federal and state jurisdiction over criminal law and describe the roles of the legislative, executive, and judicial branches of government in criminal law.

This is a criminal law book, not a book about criminal procedure. But the basics of how criminal cases are processed will help you learn criminal law by framing how the criminal law is put into action. What follows is an overview of the U.S. criminal justice system.

The United States: A Common Law Nation

Over a long span of time, European nations colonized most of the world. In most cases, where a nation went, so went its legal system. Some European counties, such as France and Italy, follow the "Civil Law." England, on the other hand, has a different history; it was the birthplace of a legal tradition known as the Common Law. Because the United States was once a collection of British colonies (as well as a few colonies from other European nations), it falls into the English, or Common Law, tradition.

Don't confuse the Civil Law tradition with the civil law of the United States. The Civil Law tradition refers to a family of nations that share a legal history and continue to have similar justice systems. The civil law of the United States, on the other hand, refers to noncriminal cases, such as when two people disagree over who owns a cell phone.

There are many differences between Civil Law and Common Law. One big difference is in how and who made law in the early years. In Civil Law nations, small groups of experts made the law. These groups evolved into legislatures.

In the early Common Law in England, judges played an important role in not only hearing cases but in making law. This has changed over time. Today, Parliament in the United Kingdom and state legislatures and the Congress in the United States are responsible for making their country's new laws. Regardless of the rise of legislatures in Common Law nations, courts continue to be important players in the criminal justice systems of all Common Law nations. Judges interpret law, hear cases (adjudicate), and are guardians of freedom. Also, old Common Law principles and processes continue to be followed in the United States, though one exception is Louisiana. As a former French colony, Louisiana employs a hybrid Civil/Common Law system.

An important feature of Common Law courts is the doctrine of *stare decisis*. Translated from its original Latin, stare decisis means *to stand by things decided*. The way it works is simple. If the facts of an earlier case are similar to a present case, the law of the prior case is applied in the present case. The prior case is known as **precedent**. What makes stare decisis so powerful is that the precedential decision binds not only the court that made the decision, but all lower courts as well. In its 2019 decision for *Gamble v. United States*, SCOTUS decided that thedouble jeopardy clause doesn't forbid a state and the federal government from both punishing an individual for the same acts. So as the last word on the U.S. Constitution, SCOTUS's decision in *Gamble* binds all courts in the United States, should they be asked to determine whether an individual can be punished by two sovereigns for the same crime.

Absolute Power Corrupts Absolutely

The idea of absolute power corrupting absolutely, which is attributed to Lord John Dalberg-Acton of England in the late 1800s, was fully embraced by the Framers of the United States Constitution. To prevent absolute corruption, the Framers divided the powers of government. They also protected the rights of people, but we will explore that subject in the next chapter. Governmental power was divided in two ways: horizontal and vertical. You are likely familiar with the **separation of powers**, or the horizontal division of power into the legislative, executive, and judicial branches. The legislative branch has the authority to make laws. Only Congress, the state legislatures, and municipal bodies (e.g., city councils) may declare acts to be crimes. The enforcement of these laws falls to the executive branch. Police at all levels of government are executive branch officials. Finally, the third branch is the courts. Courts have several duties, including adjudicating legal cases and protecting individuals from oppressive governmental action.

To understand how courts protect liberty, a quick trip back in time to the presidential election of 1800 is illustrative. A rematch from 4 years earlier, it was a contest between two titans: Thomas Jefferson, a Democratic-Republican, and the incumbent, John Adams, a Federalist. The suggestion that politics is nastier today than in the past is proved wrong by the election of 1800. The supporters of Adams and Jefferson, and sometimes the men themselves, were fierce and ugly to one another. The sexual behaviors, religious beliefs, and integrity of the candidates were front and center. After a highly contentious election, Jefferson won. In an effort to extend the influence

---

Precedent: A prior case that is similar in facts.

Separation of powers: The division of governmental authority between the legislative, executive, and judicial branches.

of the Federalist agenda into the future, President Adams and the Federalist-controlled Congress changed laws and created new judgeships. The final hours of the Adams presidency were chaotic. Secretary of State John Marshall was busy into the wee hours of the final night of Adams's term, delivering the new appointments created under the new laws. But he ran out of time before they were all put into the hands of the new judges. Subsequently, President Jefferson's secretary of state, James Madison, refused to deliver them. William Marbury, who had been nominated by Adams and confirmed by the Senate to be a justice of the peace, sued.

In what may be one of its most famous decisions, *Marbury v. Madison*,[11] SCOTUS announced that courts have the authority to declare the acts of the legislative and executive branches unconstitutional and void. Today, this authority, known as judicial review, is a given. But it wasn't before *Marbury*. This decision is very important to criminal law. Through it, every trial judge in the country can declare bad laws void and exclude evidence that has been illegally obtained by police from trial. Take, for example, the controversy over the impact cell phones are having on family life, education, bullying, and the emotional health of youth. If a state legislature were to outlaw the use of cell phones by teenagers and prosecute a teen for making a call with one, the trial court (if the judge is doing their job) would declare the law to be a violation of the defendant's free speech and association rights under the First Amendment and Fourteenth Amendment, strike down the law, and dismiss the criminal case. At the top of the legal pyramid is SCOTUS. As such, it has the final word on the meaning of all federal laws, including the U.S. Constitution. It is said of the court, "It is not final because it is right; it is right because it is final."

PHOTO 1.3 The United States Supreme Court Building, also referred to as "the Marble Palace," houses the Supreme Court of the United States.

fstockfoto via iStock

Judicial review: The authority of courts to review the acts of the legislative and executive branches for constitutionality.

Oh, by the way, Marbury lost his case. Although SCOTUS decided that he was entitled to his appointment, it also decided that the statute that gave the court the authority to hear Marbury's case was unconstitutional. So the court pulled a fast one. It announced that it has the authority to tell the president what to do, but it avoided a conflict with President Jefferson, which it most likely would have lost because the republic was young, the court hadn't established its authority, President Jefferson may have refused to comply with its order, and the court has no way to enforce its orders against an obstinate president. But by invalidating the statute and leaving the president's decision to withhold Marbury's appointment alone, the court planted the seed that it is final interpreter of federal law.

Judicial review is an example of another feature of the U.S. system of **checks and balances**. Few powers held by any branch of government are absolute; most involve two branches. Congress's authority to make laws is checked by the president's role in approving or vetoing those laws. A president's veto is further checked, as Congress can override it with a supermajority (two-thirds) vote. The Senate must approve treaties and presidential appointments to important positions. SCOTUS itself is checked through the appointment process, which requires presidential nomination and Senate approval, and through the authority of Congress to define most of the jurisdiction of the federal courts. Judicial review, in turn, is a big check on the president and Congress.

OK, that was the horizontal division. The vertical division is known as **federalism**—the existence of both the federal government and the government of the states.

Making a Federal Case of It

"Don't make a federal case out of it" is a phrase that is sometimes used to express the idea that someone is making a problem bigger than it really is. But the phrase is legally inaccurate. Federal criminal cases are not more serious, or higher forms of crime, than state cases. The authors, or Framers, of the U.S. Constitution created a federal system of government. A federal system is one where there are two levels of government, and each is semi-independent of the other. For the Framers, state governments were to be responsible for the general welfare of the people. The responsibility for the general welfare is also known as *police power*. Police power refers to the authority of a state to regulate in the interest of the general welfare, security, and health of the people. This includes many of the authorities that are commonly associated with government: controlling and prosecuting crimes, providing courts for people to sue one another, enforcing health codes, ensuring that tradespeople and professionals are adequately trained and ethical, and much more.

In the criminal law context, the Framers intended for the states to be the epicenter of activity, where crimes are declared and courts adjudicate cases. So the least significant of crimes to the most serious (e.g., murder and rape) fall into the jurisdiction of the states. The federal government was to be different—it was to have limited authority. Most of the powers of the

---

Checks and balances: A structural feature of government that keeps the three branches of government accountable through the sharing of powers with one another.

Federalism: The division of governmental power between the federal and state governments.

federal government are listed in Article I, Section 8 of the Constitution. Some examples of what the federal government has the power to do are to create a national military, to declare war and to defend the United States from foreign nations, to make rules about business between the states and with foreign governments and Native Americans (Indians, in the words of the Constitution), to coin and make money, to regulate immigration, and to create a post office.

There is another provision, the necessary and proper clause, that empowers Congress to make whatever laws are needed to do these things. Consequently, there are federal criminal laws. To counterfeit money, for example, is a federal crime because only Congress has the authority to create a national money. Under the necessary and proper clause, it can also make it a crime to counterfeit money or to use the U.S. postal system to steal from others. The United States also has the authority to protect itself, so an assassin of the president of the United States has committed a federal crime. Although the number of federal crimes has grown over the years, the states continue to be the heart of criminal law. About 95% of all criminal cases are adjudicated in state courts. By the way, the use of the word "adjudicated," as opposed to "tried," was intentional because most criminal cases don't make it to trial—95% of state cases and 98% of federal cases are resolved through guilty pleas.[12] The most common method of reaching a plea is through a plea agreement, where a prosecutor agrees to recommend a specific sentence, to reduce the charge, to dismiss one or more charges, or to some combination of these acts in exchange for the defendant's guilty plea. The second form of plea is "straight up," or when defendants throw themselves at the mercy of the court without negotiating with the prosecutor.

Sometimes, federal and state jurisdictions overlap. Consider, for example, the assassination of the president mentioned earlier. Of course, the federal government has laws to protect the president and to punish an assassin, but assassination is also murder. So both the state where the president is killed and the United States have jurisdiction over the murderer. Which government gets to prosecute the murderer? Both. But the **supremacy clause** of the Constitution makes clear that when concurrent jurisdiction exists between a state and the federal government, the federal government win. That doesn't mean that the state can't prosecute. It only means that the United States has the option of trying the assassin first. And, yes, the president's assassin can be tried twice without violating the double jeopardy clause of the Fifth Amendment. SCOTUS has held, as recently as 2019,[13] that while the same jurisdiction can't try a person twice for the same offense, two different jurisdictions (two states or a state and the federal government) can punish a person for the same crime. Crazy, huh? This is known as **dual sovereignty**. The Constitution only recognizes the states and federal government as sovereign; local governments are subunits of states. Accordingly, a city and its state or two cities in the same state can't prosecute a person for the same crime. The decision in *Gamble v. United States,* discussed earlier, is an example. SCOTUS's decision that multiple sovereigns can prosecute a person for the same offense is precedent, binding every court in the United States.

In many instances, the federal government works closely with the state governments to address a problem. The COVID-19 pandemic of the 2020s is an example. As you now know, the federal

---

Supremacy clause: Article IV, Clause 2 of the Constitution of the United States makes clear that when the federal government and states have concurrent jurisdiction, federal law is superior when the two are in conflict.

Dual sovereignty: A doctrine that empowers multiple sovereigns to prosecute and punish an individual for the same crime without violating the prohibition of double jeopardy.

government has little authority over health emergencies. Historically, they have been assumed to be part of the state police power. But that doesn't mean that a national response isn't possible. The president, Congress, and other national officials can provide leadership and vision. More concretely, the federal government's authority over immigration empowered President Trump, as authorized by Congress, to restrict travel and close borders in 2020. Congress's authority to oversee interstate commerce, to support science and research, and to provide financial assistance to individuals and businesses was significant in the fight against the spread of the virus. But there is no national martial law provision in the Constitution; there is only a provision for the suspension of habeas corpus when the nation is under attack or is involved in civil war. Health emergencies are not mentioned. The authority to issue and enforce stay-at-home orders, social distancing, and masking appear to be mostly local. Hence, it was governors, state legislatures, and local officials who managed, in consultation with the federal government, these dimensions of the COVID-19 crisis.

Prove It!

All adjudication systems are designed to find the truth: Did the accused (defendant) commit the alleged crime? This question concerns factual guilt. As you learned earlier, Common Law criminal justice systems also emphasize the fairness of the process itself: Did the government play by the rules, and are the rules fair? Did the state prove guilt beyond a reasonable doubt? These questions transcend factual guilt; they are about legal guilt.

The impact of including fairness and a high confidence of guilt in the process is that some guilty people will go unpunished. As Blackstone once wrote, "It is better that ten guilty persons escape than that one innocent suffer." It is possible for a criminal jury to decide that a defendant most likely committed the crime, but for the defendant to be acquitted because more than likelihood (preponderance of the evidence) is expected; the prosecutor must prove the defendant's guilt beyond a reasonable doubt. However, the same case and the same finding in civil court will result in the defendant being found liable. Another example of the impact of requiring a fair process is the inadmissibility of illegally seized evidence at a defendant's trial. In the rare case when illegally seized evidence is essential to a prosecutor's case, its omission from trial can result in a guilty person going free.

The adversarial process is often likened to a sporting competition. The state and defendant are independent players, conducting their own investigations, developing their own theories of the case, and presenting their own cases at trial. Judges in the adversarial system act as referees. They oversee the process, ensure fairness, and become involved only as needed. This is different from inquisitorial systems, where courts are more involved, sometimes directing evidence collection, developing the theories of the case, and deciding what witnesses will be heard.

Adversarial systems are **accusatorial**; the state bears the burden of proving its case under the **presumption of innocence doctrine**. That means a defendant can sit back, remain silent, and say to the prosecutor, "Prove it," without offering any defense. The prosecutor has the obligation

---

Accusatorial: An element of the adversarial system that places the burden of proof on the state and otherwise gives the benefit of doubt to the defendant.

Presumption of innocence doctrine: In the United States and many other nations, the state has the obligation to prove a defendant's guilt. In the United States, the state must prove every element of the crime beyond a reasonable doubt. A defendant begins the process innocent and is not obliged to put on a defense.

to overcome the presumption of innocence. The prosecutor's burden of proof is twofold. First, the prosecutor must introduce evidence that the crime occurred and that the defendant committed it. This is known as the burden of production. Second, the prosecutor must persuade the jury that the defendant committed every element of the crime beyond a reasonable doubt. Unsuprisingly, this is referred to as the burden of persuasion. Although defendants don't have to prove their innocence, many find it necessary to call their own witnesses and to present their own physical and documentary evidence in order to avoid conviction.

The **rule of lenity** is an additional safeguard. It holds that a defendant is to get the benefit of the doubt in most instances. For example, if two or more reasonable interpretations of a law exist, the interpretation that is best for the defendant is to be adopted by the court. Imagine, for example, a statute reads that "any person convicted of the crime of theft of identity shall be subject to 180 days in prison." Does the statute require 180 days imprisonment, or does it establish a maximum penalty of 180 days? Applying the rule of lenity, a person convicted under the law may be sentenced up to, but no more than, 180 days in prison.

QUESTIONS AND APPLICATION

For each of the following, identify whether the facts present a situation of legitimate dual sovereignty or double jeopardy.

1. Chanda robs a federally funded bank in the state of Alabama. Both Alabama and the United States charge her with robbery.
2. The City of Wobble, Tennessee, has an ordinance that makes burglary a misdemeanor crime. The state of Tennessee has a statute that declares burglary to be a felony. Both the city of Wobble and the state of Tennessee charge Burt Ler with the burglary of a home.
3. Kid Napper and his ex-wife have a shared parenting order that splits the time of their children between them. They live in California. The parenting order also requires the parents to notify one another if they take their child out of state. On a day when the child was in the care of her mother, Kid showed at the child's school, took her out early, and left the state. After several days, the police determined that he didn't intend to return. He was caught several months later in Oregon, the child was returned to her mother, and Kid was charged with kidnapping by the state of Oregon, the state of California, and, because he crossed state lines, the United States.

For each of the following, identify whether factual guilt, legal guilt, both, or neither exists.

1. A jury in a criminal case agrees the defendant likely committed the charged crime, but the state didn't prove the case beyond a reasonable doubt. The jury renders a not-guilty verdict.
2. A jury in a criminal case finds a defendant guilty. On appeal, the defendant alleges that the prosecutor failed to disclose evidence of his innocence and that there was

Rule of lenity: If there are two or more reasonable interpretations of a statute, the interpretation that most favors the defendant is to be adopted.

> insufficient evidence to support the jury's verdict, even without the challenged evidence. The appellate court disagrees with both claims and upholds the verdict.
>
> 3. A jury in a criminal case finds a defendant guilty. On appeal, it is determined that the bloody knife, a vital piece of evidence, was unlawfully seized by police. The appellate court decides that the trial court should not have allowed it to be presented to the jury. It also decides that without it the state can't prove guilt beyond a reasonable doubt. It orders the case to be dismissed.

IN A NUTSHELL

Humans naturally guard against, and respond to, threats and harm. For thousands of years, norms have been formally enforced through law. Today, criminal law is an important part of social control and the management of serious social problems.

There are two overarching philosophies of punishment: retributivism and utilitarianism. The weight each of these is given and the ways they are operationalized evolves. Each philosophy gives birth to different operational objectives. For retributivism, classical punishment is employed; utilitarianism relies on incapacitation, rehabilitation, restitution, and restoration. Although it is retribution- and incapacitation-focused, modern criminal law also embraces the objectives of deterrence, rehabilitation, restitution, and restoration. These objectives are operationalized through incarceration, death, fines, restitution, community service, restoration, and the occasional public shaming.

The political and legal history of the United States frames a criminal justice system that emphasizes individual liberty, including the rights of criminal defendants to a fair process and to proof beyond a reasonable doubt. The emphasis on liberty isn't without its costs. As Blackstone pointed out, the occasional offender goes unpunished.

In addition to the direct protections of the individual found in the Constitution (e.g., habeas corpus) and the Bill of Rights, the Framers of the Constitution constructed a government of divided powers. Through federalism and separation of powers between the branches, absolute power was avoided, and a "government of laws, not of men" was established. In this system, the states were delegated the authority to regulate for the general welfare of the people, known as the police power. This includes the criminal law, except when the federal government has a direct interest or when a crime crosses state or international borders. So we look to our state legislatures to make criminal laws, state and local police to enforce criminal laws, and state courts to adjudicate criminal cases. As you will see in a future chapter, this doesn't mean that federal law isn't present in state criminal justice. Just the opposite is true: The U.S. Constitution is omnipresent.

LEGAL TERMS

accusatorial (p. 32)

adjudication (p. 6)

adversarial system (p. 2)

beyond a reasonable doubt (p. 10)

checks and balances (p. 30)

Civil Law (p. 2)

clear and convincing evidence (p. 11)

Common Law (p. 2)

Constitutional law (p. 20)

Contract law (p. 8)

crime (p. 5)

Criminal law (p. 1)

Criminal procedure (p. 6)

defendant (p. 13)

defense (p. 5)

dual sovereignty (p. 31)

executive orders (p. 23)

fact finder (p. 9)

factual guilt (p. 3)

federalism (p. 30)

felonies (p. 26)

folkway (p. 5)

grading (p. 26)

infractions (p. 26)

inquisitorial system (p. 2)

intentional tort (p. 9)

judicial review (p. 29)

legal guilt (p. 3)

Magna Carta (p. 2)

malum in se (p. 26)

malum prohibitum (p. 26)

misdemeanors (p. 26)

Model Penal Code (p. 21)

more (p. 5)

negligent tort (p. 8)

norms (p. 5)

Ordinance (p. 22)

parties (p. 13)

plaintiff (p. 13)

precedent (p. 28)

preponderance of the evidence (p. 9)

presumption of innocence doctrine (p. 32)

private law (p. 7)

Probable cause (p. 12)

public law (p. 7)

punitive damages (p. 7)

reasonable suspicion (p. 12)

referendum (p. 21)

regulations (p. 22)

Rule of Law (p. 3)

rule of lenity (p. 33)

SCOTUS (p. 4)

separation of powers (p. 28)

stare decisis (p. 23)

state action (p. 7)

Statutory law (p. 21)

strict liability (p. 9)

substantive criminal law (p. 6)

supremacy clause (p. 31)

tort (p. 8)

victim-in-fact (p. 13)

victim-in-law (p. 13)

writ (p. 9)

NOTES

1. B. Bertram, "Storm Still Brews Over Scalding Coffee," *New York Times*, October 25, 2013, http://nytimes.com.

2. *In Re Winship*, 397 U.S. 358 (1970).

3. "Model Final Jury Instructions. United States Court of Appeals for Third Circuit," January 1, 2020, https://www.ca3.uscourts.gov/model-criminal-jury-table-contents-and-instructions.

4. *Florida v. Harris*, 568 U.S. 237 (2013).

5. 392 U.S. 1.

6. The classic banana peel slip and fall has been fodder for comic relief for decades. But the risk is real. You can see the death certificate of a man who died as a result of slipping on a banana peel at McClurg's Legal Humor, as well as several tort cases that have been filed by customers against grocers to recover damages resulting from banana peel falls at https://lawhaha.com/tortland/interesting-tort-cases/.

7. *Gregg v. Georgia*, 428 U.S. 153 (1976).

8. K. Tomlinson, "An Examination of Deterrence Theory: Where Do We Stand?," *Federal Probation* 80, no. 3 (2016): 33–38.

9. "Initiative Information," Florida Division of Elections, January 19, 2020.

10. Minnesota Statutes 2019, Section 12; Executive Order 20–20 (March 25, 2020).

11. *Marbury v. Madison*, 5 U.S. 137 (1803).

12. John Gramlich, *Only 2% of Federal Criminal Defendants Go to Trial, and Most Who Do Are Found Guilty* (Pew Research Center, June 11, 2019). Pewresearch.org on October 9, 2020.

13. *Gamble v. United States*, 587 U.S. __ (2019).

2 THE CONSTITUTION AND CRIMINAL LAW

THE FEDERAL SAFETY NET

Learning Objective: Identify and explain the three reasons the U.S. Constitution plays a much larger role in criminal law today than in the past.

On May 23, 1957, three Cleveland, Ohio, police officers received an anonymous tip that a bombing suspect could be found in the home of Dollree Mapp. But this wasn't an ordinary case, and Ms. Mapp wasn't an ordinary citizen. The bombing victim was a well-known gambling racketeer, Don King. Mr. King would later promote some of the best boxers of the world, including Muhammad Ali, Larry Holmes, and Mike Tyson. Mr. King is a larger-than-life character who has had many encounters with the law. In the future, Ali, Holmes, and Tyson, and many other people would sue him. Several years before the bombing of his home, Mr. King killed a man for attempting to rob one of his gambling houses, and in 1967, he was convicted of second-degree murder. Ms. Mapp was also known to police. She was independent, feisty, and outspoken.

The officers appeared at Ms. Mapp's door, demanding entry. She refused to allow them to enter and called her lawyer, who told her to demand that the officers produce a warrant. She made the demand, and the officers left, only to return 3 hours later with 7 to 12 additional officers. When Ms. Mapp again demanded to see a search warrant, one of the officers waved a piece of paper in front of her, claiming it to be a warrant. Ms. Mapp grabbed the paper, and a scuffle began, during which Ms. Mapp shoved the paper down her blouse. In response, one of the officers reached down into Ms. Mapp's blouse and retrieved the paper. The officers then entered her home. They found the suspected bomber, who was later cleared of the crime, but they didn't stop there. They searched her home from top to bottom, during which they found obscene materials (by 1950s standards), arrested Ms. Mapp, and subsequently charged her with felony possession of obscenity.

As Ms. Mapp suspected, the police didn't have a warrant. But it was true that she had violated Ohio's obscenity law, and the state could prove it. At the time, Ohio permitted evidence that police obtained illegally to be used at trial. But this wasn't true everywhere; the states were split on the use of illegal evidence. This was true of many rights. Each state decided what rights criminal defendants enjoyed in their courts. And recall, most criminal prosecutions happen in state courts. The effect of these facts was that the United States Constitution's protections didn't mean much. But this would change in a big way, due, in part, to Ms. Mapp and many other people who have fought the system.[1]

Why the U.S. Constitution Is Important

That the U.S. Constitution plays a much larger role in criminal law today than in the past is being referred to as constitutionalism in this book. As you will learn in this chapter, there are three reasons the U.S. Constitution is more important in criminal law, state and federal, today than in the past:

1. Incorporation doctrine

2. Expansion of rights

3. Exclusionary rule

America's current constitution is not its first; it's the second. The nation's first constitution was the Articles of Confederation and Perpetual Union of 1781. Under the Articles of Confederation, the states were superior to the national government. Believing that the weak national government was inhibiting the economic growth and military security of the young nation, the states sent delegates to Philadelphia in the summer of 1787 to "revise" the Articles of Confederation. These men, commonly known as the Framers, chose to scrap the Articles of Confederation and to write an entirely new constitution. They didn't have their states' permission to do this. In fact, they voted to keep their work secret until it was completed. Can you imagine a group of representatives to a Constitutional Convention meeting in secret today? Not likely. Either masses of people would descend on the gathering, insisting on openness, or the delegates would use texting and social media to continuously leak what was happening inside.

While the Framers intended to strengthen the federal government, they also wanted to leave the states as the primary governors. To accomplish these two objectives, they created a federal government that had specific, limited powers (that it didn't have under the Articles of Confederation) but left most governmental authority in the hands of the states. As you learned earlier, the states retained the general police power.

One of the issues that was debated at the Constitutional Convention was whether a list of individual rights should be included. The delegates advocating for a strong federal government, known as Federalists, opposed including a bill of rights. Among those men were James Madison and Alexander Hamilton. They had four reasons for their pushback against a bill of rights. First, they believed that the government's architecture, most notably federalism and the separation of powers, would protect the people from the centralization of power. Second, they didn't find a listing of rights necessary because the new Constitution didn't empower the federal government to violate liberty. In a third related argument, they believed that the protection of liberties was best handled by the states. And fourth, they believed it wasn't possible to identify and list all the freedoms of people, and to create a list would have the effect of limiting individual rights to what appears in the list. Ultimately, the Federalists won unanimous support to exclude a bill of rights. Consequently, the proposed Constitution identified only a few specific rights. These

---

Constitutionalism: Having fundamental law that limits the authority of government. In this text, it is a reference to the increasingly important role of the U.S. Constitution to criminal law.

include **habeas corpus**, which provides courts with the authority to review detentions; prohibiting **ex post facto laws**, or the declaration that an act is criminal after it occurs; prohibiting legislatures from acting as judge and jury, known as **bills of attainder**; and finally, a guarantee of a jury trial in federal criminal cases.

But the absence of a full set of rights proved to be a problem when the proposed Constitution was sent to the states for ratification. Many people screamed foul, and several states preconditioned their ratifications on the addition of a bill of rights. To ensure that the required nine states, of 13, would ratify, the Framers agreed. Consequently, the Constitution was ratified in 1788 and became effective in 1789. That same year, the first Congress under the new Constitution proposed, as promised, 12 amendments. Ten of those amendments were ratified and went into force in 1791. Today, we know them as the Bill of Rights. As a side note, one of the two amendments that wasn't approved was finally ratified in 1992, 202 years later! The amendment isn't dramatic; it simply states that any raise Congress gives itself isn't effective until the next session of Congress. Congressional sessions are 2 years long. The other unratified amendment changed the calculation for the number of members in the House of Representatives. If it were to be ratified, the House of Representatives would grow from its current number of 435 to as many as 6,000. Congress can't seem to get its work done with 435 members of the House of Representatives and 100 senators. Imagine a House of Representatives with over 6,000 members!

Historical records make clear that the Bill of Rights was intended to apply to the federal government but not to the states. That meant that the federal government had to respect freedom of speech, couldn't force defendants to confess, and so on. But the states were free to respect these rights, or not. Consequently, rights varied from state to state. And remember, more than 90% of prosecutions take place in state courts. The differences in individual rights between the states were real.

The Civil War would result in a second phase of constitutional liberty and equality. Three new constitutional amendments were ratified during Reconstruction: the Thirteenth, Fourteenth, and Fifteenth. The Thirteenth Amendment abolished slavery and involuntary servitude, and the Fifteenth Amendment recognized the right of all men, including those formerly enslaved, to vote. Sorry, ladies—you didn't acquire the right to vote until the adoption of the Nineteenth Amendment in 1920. The Fourteenth Amendment, ratified in 1868, is the most important amendment to criminal law, and it is broken into five sections. Section 1 protects the following rights:

- Citizenship: All people born or naturalized in the United States, and subject to the jurisdiction of the United States, are citizens of the United States and of the state where they reside.

Habeas corpus: A Latin phrase that translates to "you have the body." In law, it is a command to bring a detained person to a court to determine if the detention is lawful.

Ex post facto law: A law that declares an act to be criminal after it has occurred. The Constitution forbids ex post facto laws.

Bills of attainder: A legislative decision to punish a person or legal entity (e.g., companies) without a judicial trial. The Constitution forbids bills of attainder.

- **Privileges or immunities:** SCOTUS has defined this clause narrowly. It includes a few specific rights, including the right to travel between the states and the right to be protected from violence while in custody.

- **Equal protection:** This provision demands that the states not discriminate between people for racial, ethnic, and other reasons.

- **Due process:** Under this provision, a state may take a person's life, liberty, or property only after providing due process (fair process). SCOTUS has also held that this clause protects substantive rights, such as the right to privacy.

The Fifth Amendment also has a due process clause that is identical in language to the Fourteenth Amendment's due process clause. Remember that, at the time of its adoption, the Bill of Rights only limited the power of the federal government. This changed with the Fourteenth Amendment, which was intended to create a national minimum—a safety net—of fairness. And that is precisely what due process means: to have a fair process. The states are free to raise the safety net higher (e.g., to add or enlarge rights), but they must respect the safety net's minimum protections.

Fairness in the States: Incorporation

Determining the height and width of the national safety net hasn't been easy. After all, the phrase "due process" is very vague. What is due, or fair? Does fairness include the rights found in the Bill of Rights, for example? Interestingly, courts were not pressed to answer this question for many decades. But eventually, they did, and that leads us to the first reason the United States Constitution means more to criminal law today than in the past: the incorporation doctrine. When SCOTUS first began considering the meaning of the Fourteenth Amendment's due process clause, the justices wrestled with different theories. These included the following:

Theory 1. Independent meaning doctrine: The Fourteenth Amendment's due process clause is not connected to the Bill of Rights. Some of the rights overlap, but the rights found in the Bill of Rights are not the basis of "due process," and therefore, they do not automatically apply in state courts.

Privilege and immunities: Found in both Article IV and the Fourteenth Amendment, these clauses guarantee a limited number of rights against the federal government and fair treatment of states between their citizens and citizens of other states.

Equal protection: Found expressly in the Fourteenth Amendment and implicitly in the Fifth Amendment, a guarantee that government won't, without a compelling reason, treat people differently because of race, national origin, religion, or alienage.

Due process: Found in the Fifth and Fourteenth Amendments, a requirement that government provide a fair process when taking life, liberty, or property. In addition to procedural requirements, due process also includes substantive rights, such as the right to privacy.

Theory 2. Fundamental fairness doctrine: A right found in the Bill of Rights applies against a state when justice demands it. This decision is made on a case-by-case basis.

Theory 3. Total incorporation doctrine: The Bill of Rights *is* due process; all of the rights found in the first 10 amendments apply in state courts—automatically.

Theory 4. Total incorporation plus doctrine: As is true of total incorporation, all of the rights found in the Bill of Rights apply against the states. However, rights deemed fundamental that are not found in the Bill of Rights also apply.

Theory 5. Selective incorporation doctrine: Only the most important (fundamental) rights in the Bill of Rights apply against the states. Unlike fundamental fairness, this isn't a case-by-case determination. Once a right is found to be fundamental, it applies against the states, in all cases.

After years of disagreement between the justices, SCOTUS settled on the **selective incorporation doctrine**. Incorporation refers to extending a right found in the U.S. Constitution from the federal government to the states, using the due process clause. A right is "selected" to be applied to the states if it is (1) fundamental and (2) necessary to an ordered liberty. Said another way, a right is incorporated if it is really, really important. Today, nearly all of the rights found in the Bill of Rights have been incorporated. The first to be incorporated was the First Amendment's protection of free speech. That happened in 1925. Since then, SCOTUS has added, one by one, nearly all of the criminal law rights. The last "textual" right to be incorporated was the freedom from excessive fines in 2019. See Figure 2.1 for a listing of the status of each right found in the Bill of Rights.

In the last sentence, the word "textual" was enclosed in quotation marks to draw your attention to a detail about incorporation. A textual, or enumerated, right is one that you can find written in the Constitution, such as the Eighth Amendment's right to be free from excessive fines. But there are rights that are not written (unenumerated), but implicit. These too can be incorporated. This happened in 2020 in *Ramos v. Louisiana*.

The question in *Ramos* was whether the right to a jury trial includes the right to have all of the jurors agree to convict. The Constitution is silent on the number of jurors needed to convict. In fact, it has nothing to say about the number of jurors at all. However, SCOTUS decided in 1898 that in federal courts, juries of 12 are required, as is jury unanimity for conviction. Many years later, SCOTUS chose not to incorporate the unanimity requirement, and two states, Louisiana and Oregon, permitted convictions with as few as 10 of 12 jurors. In *Ramos*, SCOTUS reversed its earlier decisions and incorporated the right to jury unanimity, making *it* the most recently incorporated right, not the excessive fines clause.

Selective incorporation doctrine: The determination that a right found in the Bill of Rights is fundamental and necessary to an ordered liberty, and therefore, applies to the states.

FIGURE 2.1 ■ Is a Defendant Protected in State Court?	
What Right?	**Has it Been Incorporated by SCOTUS?**
First Amendment - speech	Yes, in *Gitlow v. New York*, 268 *U.S. 652* (1925)
First Amendment – religion	Yes, in *Everson v. Board of Education*, 330 *U.S. 1*(1947) and *Cantwell v. Connecticut*, 310 *U.S. 296* (1940)
First Amendment - press	Yes, in *Near v. Minnesota*, 283 *U.S. 697* (1931)
First Amendment - assembly	Yes, in *DeJonge v. Oregon*, 299 *U.S. 353* (1937)
First Amendment -grievances	Yes, in *Edwards v. South Carolina*, 372 U.S. 229 (1963)
Second Amendment – arms	Yes, in *McDonald v. Chicago*, 561 *U.S. 742* (2010)
Third Amendment – quartering of troops	No, but lower courts have said yes
Fourth Amendment	Yes, through several cases including *Mapp v. Ohio*, 367 *U.S. 643* (1961)
Fifth Amendment – grand jury	No
Fifth Amendment – self incrimination	Yes, in *Malloy v. Hogan*, 378 *U.S. 1* (1964)
Fifth Amendment – double jeopardy	Yes, in *Benton v. Maryland*, 395 *U.S. 784* (1969)
Fifth Amendment - takings	Yes, in *Chicago, Burlington & Quincy Railroad Co. v. City of Chicago*, 166 U.S. 226 (1897)
Fifth Amendment – due process	Fourteenth Amendment has its own Due Process Clause
Sixth Amendment – counsel	Yes, in *Gideon v. Wainwright*, 372 *U.S. 335* (1963)
Sixth Amendment – public trial	Yes, in *In re Oliver, 333 U.S. 257* (1948)
Sixth Amendment – jury trial	Yes, in several cases upholding right to impartial jury, number of jurors, etc.
Sixth Amendment – speedy trial	Yes, in *Klopfer v. North Carolina*, 386 *U.S. 213* (1967)
Sixth Amendment – confront accusers	Yes, in *Pointer v. Texas*, 380 *U.S. 400* (1965)
Sixth Amendment – compulsory process	Yes, in *Washington v. Texas*, 388 U.S. 400 (1965)
Sixth Amendment – notice of charge	Yes, in *In re Oliver* 333, U.S. 257 (1948)
Seventh Amendment – jury trial in civil cases	No
Eighth Amendment – cruel punishments	Yes, in *Robinson v. California*, 370 *U.S. 660* (1962)
Eighth Amendment – excessive bail	No, but it is likely
Eighth Amendment – excessive fines	Yes, in *Timbs v. Indiana*, 586 U.S. ___ (2019)
Ninth Amendment	Although no right has been found exclusively through the 9th, it has been used as secondary support for rights found under the 14th
Tenth Amendment	Although it refers to powers of the people, no rights have ever been declared under the 10th

DIGGING DEEPER 2.1

Does a jury have to be unanimous to convict a defendant?

Case: *Ramos v. Louisiana*
Court: Supreme Court of the United States.   Citation: 590 U.S. ___.
Year: 2020
Justice Gorsuch delivered the opinion of the Supreme Court.

[Facts]

Accused of a serious crime, Evangelisto Ramos insisted on his innocence and invoked his right to a jury trial. Eventually, 10 jurors found the evidence against him persuasive. But a pair of jurors believed that the State of Louisiana had failed to prove Mr. Ramos's guilt beyond a reasonable doubt; they voted to acquit.

In 48 states and in federal court, a single juror's vote to acquit is enough to prevent a conviction. But not in Louisiana. Along with Oregon, Louisiana has long punished people based on 10-to-2 verdicts like the one here. So instead of the mistrial he would have received almost anywhere else, Mr. Ramos was sentenced to life in prison without the possibility of parole.

Why do Louisiana and Oregon allow non-unanimous convictions? Though it's hard to say why these laws persist, their origins are clear. Louisiana first endorsed non-unanimous verdicts for serious crimes at a constitutional convention in 1898. According to one committee chairman, the avowed purpose of that convention was to "establish the supremacy of the white race," and the resulting document included many of the trappings of the Jim Crow era: a poll tax, a combined literacy and property ownership test, and a grandfather clause that in practice exempted white residents from the most onerous of these requirements.... Seeking to avoid unwanted national attention, and aware that this Court would strike down any policy of overt discrimination against African American jurors as a violation of the Fourteenth Amendment, the delegates sought to undermine African American participation on juries in another way. With a careful eye on racial demographics, the convention delegates sculpted a "facially race-neutral" rule permitting 10-to-2 verdicts in order "to ensure that African American juror service would be meaningless."...

The Sixth Amendment promises that "[i]n all criminal prosecutions, the accused shall enjoy the right to a speedy and public trial, by an impartial jury of the State and district wherein the crime shall have been committed, which district shall have been previously ascertained by law." The Amendment goes on to preserve other rights for criminal defendants but says nothing else about what a "trial by an impartial jury" entails.

Still, the promise of a jury trial surely meant *something*—otherwise, there would have been no reason to write it down....

One of these requirements was unanimity. Wherever we might look to determine what the term "trial by an impartial jury trial" meant at the time of the Sixth Amendment's adoption—whether it's the common law, state practices in the founding era, or opinions and treatises written soon afterward—the answer is unmistakable. A jury must reach a unanimous verdict in order to convict.

The requirement of juror unanimity emerged in 14th-century England and was soon accepted as a vital right protected by the common law....

This same rule applied in the young American States. Six State Constitutions explicitly required unanimity. Another four preserved the right to a jury trial in more general terms.

But the variations did not matter much; consistent with the common law, state courts appeared to regard unanimity as an essential feature of the jury trial.

It was against this backdrop that James Madison drafted and the States ratified the Sixth Amendment in 1791. By that time, unanimous verdicts had been required for about 400 years. If the term "trial by an impartial jury" carried any meaning at all, it surely included a requirement as long and widely accepted as unanimity....

Nor is this a case where the original public meaning was lost to time and only recently recovered. This Court has, repeatedly and over many years, recognized that the Sixth Amendment requires unanimity. As early as 1898, the Court said that a defendant enjoys a "constitutional right to demand that his liberty should not be taken from him except by the joint action of the court and the unanimous verdict of a jury of 12 persons."...

There can be no question either that the Sixth Amendment's unanimity requirement applies to state and federal criminal trials equally. This Court has long explained that the Sixth Amendment right to a jury trial is "fundamental to the American scheme of justice" and incorporated against the States under the Fourteenth Amendment. This Court has long explained, too, that incorporated provisions of the Bill of Rights bear the same content when asserted against States as they do when asserted against the federal government. So if the Sixth Amendment's right to a jury trial requires a unanimous verdict to support a conviction in federal court, it requires no less in state court.

The effect of the selective incorporation doctrine is that every judge in every courtroom in the United States has an obligation to enforce incorporated rights. And they do. Judges often tell local, state, and federal police that they are wrong. This is an awesome power that most judges around the world don't possess. Said another way, people around the world aren't as protected as Americans against governmental abuse. We will now turn to what rights are guaranteed, and later in this chapter, you will learn what happens when the police violate a person's rights.

QUESTIONS AND APPLICATIONS

1. Let's role-play. You are a SCOTUS associate justice in the early 1900s. How would you have defined due process? Would it have included the rights found in the Bill of Rights? Or would you have defined due process differently? Explain your answer.
2. Are the following rights incorporated? Answer yes or no.
   a. Freedom from self-incrimination
   b. Grand jury indictment
   c. Jury trial
   d. Freedom from unreasonable searches and seizures

TREAT ME FAIRLY

Learning Objective: Describe the most significant constitutional rights that apply to criminal law.

Recall that there are three reasons the U.S. Constitution means more in criminal law today than in the past. Incorporation was the first; the horizontal expansion of the Bill of Rights. The second is the vertical expansion of those rights. Each right simply protects more than in 1791. Let's begin with the general idea of a fair process and then examine specific rights.

The due process clauses demand that the federal and state governments play by fair rules. They don't forbid the government from punishing people or making laws that burden individual rights. The clauses simply require that the government be reasonable when doing these things. Specifically, both clauses state that "*no person...shall be deprived of life, liberty, or property without due process of law.*" When applying due process to a given situation, two questions must be asked: First, does due process apply to a case? And if it doesn't, what process is required?

Starting with the first question, the reach of the clauses is quite broad. If the government intends to take life or liberty or property, it must use a fair process. Defining these three interests, particularly liberty, is sometimes tricky outside of criminal law. But the most common forms of criminal punishment (e.g., death penalty, imprisonment, and fines) clearly fall within the zone of the three interests protected by due process. Therefore, question number one is easily answered in criminal law.

Let's now return to the thorny issue of what process is "due." You already know (I hope) that most of the rights in the Bill of Rights are part of due process. And we will soon examine these in greater detail. Before we do, let's think about rights that aren't found in the Bill of Rights. A few of these are explicitly found in the Constitution itself; others are "implicit" in due process.

Ex Post Facto and Bills of Attainder

An example of a right found outside the Bill of Rights is the requirement that the government tell a person that an act is a crime and that it will be punished *before it occurs*. This principle is so obvious, so natural, that it doesn't need to be explained. Every time a parent tells a child "I am only going to tell you once," the idea that it isn't fair to punish without a warning is expressed. In law, the prohibition of retroactive lawmaking, or ex post facto (after the fact), is hundreds of years old. There is a Latin phrase that expresses this principle: *nullum crimen sine lege, nulla poena sine lege*, which roughly translates to "no crime or punishment without law." Before the Constitution, this rule was known as the *principle of legality*. Today, the Constitution demands a warning before punishment. First, the Constitution has two ex post facto clauses—Article I, Section 9 applies to Congress, and Article I, Section 10 applies to the states.

There is more than one type of ex post facto law. All of the following are forbidden because they are ex post facto:

1. A law that declares an act, which is lawful when taken, to be a crime after it occurs.

2. A law that increases the punishment for a criminal act, after it occurs.

3. A law that changes the evidence or procedural rules to a defendant's disadvantage after the criminal act occurs.[2]

The prohibition of ex post facto laws guarantees that the government can't change the rules in the middle of a game or after the game is over to increase its chances of winning. A legislature may, however, change the rules in ways that favor a defendant. This is known as *legislative amelioration.* A real-life example of this is the First Step Act, a federal law that shortened the prison sentences of many offenders. In addition to early release, the offenders were provided with training and programming intended to reduce the likelihood that they would become involved in crime again, known as recidivism. The First Step Act was intended to address a couple of problems. One was the expense and unfairness of having the largest per capita prison population in the world. The second was the discovery of a racial disparity in punishment. Crack cocaine, more common among African Americans, resulted in much longer prison sentences than powder cocaine, which was more common among European Americans. Several thousand inmates were granted early release under the law.[3]

In addition to the Constitution's prohibition of ex post facto laws, due process guarantees a person a warning, known as "notice," of new crimes. The due process requirement of notice doubles down on the prohibition of ex post facto laws. In a specific case, it also requires that the defendant be fully apprised of the law that has been allegedly violated, the basic facts of the offense, and time to prepare a defense before trial. There are other procedural rights, both explicit and implicit in the Constitution.

Another right that is found directly in the Constitution is the freedom from bills of attainder. Like ex post facto laws, the federal government is prohibited from bills of attainder in Article I, Section 9 and the states in Article I, Section 10. A bill of attainder is a legislative act that punishes without trial. In the United States, only a court may try a person for a crime. Any legislative act that "punishes" is a bill of attainder, even if not strictly for a crime. For example, it was a bill of attainder for Congress to order that three federal employees not be paid for their work because Congress found them to be subversive communists.[4]

Void for Vagueness

Remember the rule of lenity, which states that if multiple reasonable interpretations of a criminal statute are possible, the interpretation that most benefits the defendant is to be applied? Let's take that situation one step further. Imagine a law is so broad, so hard to pin down, that it's not possible for a person to know if their act violates the law—for example, if there was a law that forbids "causing trouble" to other people, what is "trouble"? Would playing loud music in a public park be a violation of the law if it annoys others? How about running up behind people and screaming, with the intention of startling them? Or what about an employer who fires an employee for stealing company funds, but it results in the employee's bankruptcy—hasn't the employer caused the employee trouble? Because this law isn't specific about what conduct is illegal, it violates due process. Specifically, it is void for vagueness.

In addition to not providing a person with notice of what acts will be punished, vague laws also overempower police and prosecutors by giving them the authority to decide what conduct should lead to arrest and prosecution. This violates the separation of powers because

---

Recidivism: To commit a new crime after being punished for a different crime.

Void for vagueness: A criminal prohibition that is so imprecise that a person doesn't know if a specific act is prohibited. Vague statutes violate due process and are invalid.

the authority to declare criminal laws belongs to the legislative branch. Also, too much discretion can lead to racial and other forms of discrimination, in violation of the Fourteenth Amendment's guarantee of equal protection. SCOTUS has invalidated many laws for being too vague. A city ordinance that criminalized "persons wandering or strolling around from place to place without any lawful purpose or object, habitual loafers" was held to be too vague,[5] and the court has invalidated several federal laws in recent years for being vague.[6]

Overbreadth

The first cousin of void for vagueness is the overbreadth doctrine. A law that criminalizes acts that may be criminalized but also includes acts that are constitutionally protected is overbroad. Consider a free speech problem. The First Amendment protects speech, but with exceptions. Laws regulating speech must be written with precision to avoid including protected speech. For example, consider the following statute:

> Criminal Code, Chapter 45. Child Sex Abuse: Images
> Purpose: The intent of this law is to protect children under the age of 12 from sexual abuse.
> Section 1: A child is any person under the age of 12 years old.
> Section 2: A person who produces, distributes, sells, displays, or communicates any image
>   of a child's genitals is guilty of a Class B felony.

The conduct the statute prohibits is clear, so the law is not vague. However, it is overbroad. Consider, for example, a medical school text that has images of nude children that is used to teach pediatric medicine. And what about a mom's photo of her baby playing in the bathtub? Both of these acts fall within the grasp of the law, yet they are protected expression under the First Amendment.

Often, vagueness and overbreadth are seen together. Let's consider the criminalization of cyberbullying. Ubiquitous smartphone use by children, widespread social media, and the meanness that sometimes comes with youth have combined to make cyberbullying a common and harmful phenomenon. Lawmakers across the United States have scrambled to address it. But it is one of many crimes that is hard to define, at least in a way that is constitutional. For example, consider this law:

> Criminal Code, Chapter 120: Cyberbullying and Cyberthreat Prevention Act
> Section 1: Any person who shall use a computer network, social media, or other internet
>   service to post a statement about another person that is insulting, harassing, annoying,
>   or offensive shall be guilty of cyberbullying, a Class B misdemeanor.
> Section 2: Any person who shall use a computer network, social media, or other internet
>   service to post, on three or more occasions, statements directed at a specific person with
>   the intent to cause the person to fear imminent serious bodily injury or death, and that a

---

Overbreadth doctrine: A criminal prohibition that includes acts that may be criminalized and constitutionally protected acts. Overbroad statutes are invalid.

reasonable person would interpret the postings as a threat of imminent bodily injury or death and would also believe the person who made the posting has the ability to cause such harm, is guilty of cyberthreat, a Class A misdemeanor.

Section 1 of this law is vague. Reasonable people can, and will, disagree over what constitutes an insult, harassment, an annoyance, or what is offensive. Section 1 is also overbroad. Likely, you have not studied free speech, so you may not be aware that the First Amendment protects a wide range of expression, including "hate speech." Although there are limits to the First Amendment's protection of speech, including what is known as a "true threat," Section 1 criminalizes much more than true threats, and therefore, it is unconstitutionally overbroad. Section 2, on the other hand, is specific in its criminalization of true threat, so it is constitutional.

When confronted with an overbroad or vague criminal statute, a court has two options. First, it can treat the case as a **facial challenge** and strike down the entire law, or it can invalidate the specific prosecution under the theory the law is only invalid **as-applied**. This leaves the law standing to be used in the future.

In some instances, a court can "fix" the law by interpreting it narrowly or by removing the bad language, a process known as **severability**. In our cyberbullying and cyberthreat example, a reviewing court could invalidate the entire law, or it could leave Section 2 intact while invalidating Section 1.

Either way, the legislature has the authority to pass a new law or to amend the severed law, using language that doesn't offend the Constitution. In our child sex abuse images hypothetical example, the statute could be amended to specifically exempt images that serve medical and scientific purposes, and it could also require that children appear in sexually suggestive ways. These changes would narrow the law to better achieve its purpose—to prevent child sex abuse—and it would preclude the law from being used to unfairly prosecute parents, pediatricians, and medical school professors.

Innocence, Reasonable Doubt, and Damnation

Even though it's not spelled out in the Constitution, the presumption of innocence has been recognized as a fundamental right since at least 1895.[7] This right places the burden of proving guilt squarely on the state.

You have already learned that the state must prove guilt beyond a reasonable doubt. As is true of the presumption of innocence, you won't find the beyond a reasonable doubt requirement anywhere in the Constitution. But SCOTUS has held that due process demands it. This is also true in juvenile delinquency cases.[8] As you read in Chapter 1, Blackstone posited that a high standard of proof, and other due process protections, will result in guilty persons going free. That is a tradeoff we make in a free society.

Facial challenge: An assertion that a statute is invalid on its face and, therefore, should be stricken in its entirety.

As-applied challenge: An assertion that a statute is invalid as it is applied in a specific case, even though it is valid generally.

Severability: A doctrine that enables a court to remove unconstitutional provisions of a law, leaving the remainder of the law intact.

The beyond the reasonable doubt standard is an important feature of the U.S. criminal justice system. In theory, it reduces the number of wrongful convictions and keeps police and prosecutors in check. While it is a highly regarded right of defendants today, an interesting fact is that the original purpose of the standard wasn't to protect defendants. Rather, it was created to protect jurors and judges from eternal damnation. According to scholar James Q. Whitman, it was a mortal sin in old Christian law for a judge or juror to render a conviction while harboring a doubt about a defendant's guilt. The beyond a reasonable doubt standard was intended to protect the souls of those decision-makers.[10]

First Amendment

Only 45 words in length, the First Amendment packs a punch:

> Congress shall make no law respecting an establishment of religion, or prohibiting the free exercise thereof; or abridging the freedom of speech, or of the press; or the right of the people peaceably to assemble, and to petition the Government for a redress of grievances.

Often referred to as the "first among equals," the First Amendment protects six very important rights:

- Freedom of speech

- Freedom of press

- Freedom to exercise religion

- Freedom from the establishment of religion

- Freedom to assemble peaceably

- Freedom to petition the government to redress grievances

Laws that violate these rights can be stricken by the courts. Remember judicial review from the last chapter? In a criminal case, this means that the charges against a defendant are dismissed and the defendant is released. Of the six rights, controversies around free speech and religious freedom are most common. There is a lot of case law defining these rights and their limits. For example, you have already learned that the First Amendment's protections have been incorporated. Even though the First Amendment only tells Congress to respect its rights, case law makes clear that the president of the United State, the states, and local forms of government must also respect them.

Another question that has been heavily litigated is what is meant by the word "speech." Does the First Amendment limit its protection to oral communication? The courts have answered this clearly: no. All forms of expression—written, digital, nonverbal, and creative (art, sculpture, etc.)—are considered "speech." And, on occasion, speech and conduct are combined. An example of this is what happened during the 1984 Republican National Convention held in Dallas, Texas. As part of a larger protest of the nomination of Ronald Reagan to be president,

Gregory Johnson burned the flag of the United States in the streets near the convention. At the time, Texas made it a crime to desecrate venerated objects, including the flag. Johnson was criminally charged under the desecration statute. In this defense, Johnson asserted that what he did was protected under the First Amendment.

PHOTO 2.1 Flag-burner Gregory Johnson won his case for burning the U.S. flag on free speech grounds.

Allan Tannenbaum/Getty Images

DIGGING DEEPER 2.2

Is burning the U.S. flag protected speech?

Case: *Texas v. Johnson*
Court: Supreme Court of the United States.   Citation: 491 U.S. 397
Year: 1989
Justice Brennan delivered the opinion of the Court.

After publicly burning an American flag as a means of political protest, Gregory Lee Johnson was convicted of desecrating a flag in violation of Texas law. This case presents the question of whether his conviction is consistent with the First Amendment. We hold that it is not....

We must first determine whether Johnson's burning of the flag constituted expressive conduct, permitting him to invoke the First Amendment in challenging his conviction....

The First Amendment forbids the abridgment only of "speech," but we have long recognized that its protection does not end at the spoken or written word. While we have rejected "the view that an apparently limitless variety of conduct can be labeled 'speech' whenever the person engaging in the conduct intends thereby to express an idea," we have acknowledged that conduct may be "sufficiently imbued with elements of communication to fall within the scope of the First and Fourteenth Amendments."...

In deciding whether particular conduct possesses sufficient communicative elements to bring the First Amendment into play, we have asked whether "[a]n intent to convey a particularized message was present, and [whether] the likelihood was great that the message would be understood by those who viewed it."

Hence, we have recognized the expressive nature of students' wearing of black armbands to protest American military involvement in Vietnam, *Tinker v. Des Moines Independent Community School Dist.*, of a sit-in by blacks in a "whites only" area to protest segregation, *Brown v. Louisiana*, of the wearing of American military uniforms in a dramatic presentation criticizing American involvement in Vietnam, and of picketing about a wide variety of causes....

Especially pertinent to this case are our decisions recognizing the communicative nature of conduct relating to flags. Attaching a peace sign to the flag, refusing to salute the flag, and displaying a red flag, we have held, all may find shelter under the First Amendment.

That we have had little difficulty identifying an expressive element in conduct relating to flags should not be surprising. The very purpose of a national flag is to serve as a symbol of our country; it is, one might say, "the one visible manifestation of two hundred years of nationhood."...

"[T]he flag salute is a form of utterance. Symbolism is a primitive but effective way of communicating ideas. The use of an emblem or flag to symbolize some system, idea, institution, or personality, is a shortcut from mind to mind. Causes and nations, political parties, lodges, and ecclesiastical groups seek to knit the loyalty of their followings to a flag or banner, a color or design."

Pregnant with expressive content, the flag as readily signifies this Nation as does the combination of letters found in "America." Johnson burned an American flag as part—indeed, as the culmination—of a political demonstration that coincided with the convening of the Republican Party and its renomination of Ronald Reagan for President. The expressive, overtly political nature of this conduct was both intentional and overwhelmingly apparent. At his trial, Johnson explained his reasons for burning the flag as follows:

"The American Flag was burned as Ronald Reagan was being renominated as President. And a more powerful statement of symbolic speech, whether you agree with it or not, couldn't have been made at that time. It's quite a just position [juxtaposition]. We had new patriotism and no patriotism."

In these circumstances, Johnson's burning of the flag was conduct "sufficiently imbued with elements of communication," to implicate the First Amendment.

The government generally has a freer hand in restricting expressive conduct than it has in restricting the written or spoken word. It may not, however, proscribe particular conduct *because* it has expressive elements.

Texas claims that its interest in preventing breaches of the peace justifies Johnson's conviction for flag desecration. However, no disturbance of the peace actually occurred or was threatened to occur because of Johnson's burning of the flag....

The State's position, therefore, amounts to a claim that an audience that takes serious offense at particular expression is necessarily likely to disturb the peace and that the expression may be prohibited on this basis. Our precedents do not countenance such a presumption. On the contrary, they recognize that a principal "function of free speech under our system of government is to invite dispute. It may indeed best serve its high purpose when it induces a condition of unrest, creates dissatisfaction with conditions as they are, or even stirs people to anger."

Nor does Johnson's expressive conduct fall within that small class of "fighting words" that are "likely to provoke the average person to retaliation, and thereby cause a breach of the peace." We thus conclude that the State's interest in maintaining order is not implicated on these facts....

The State also asserts an interest in preserving the flag as a symbol of nationhood and national unity. In *Spence*, we acknowledged that the government's interest in preserving the flag's special symbolic value "is directly related to expression in the context of activity" such as affixing a peace symbol to a flag....

If there is a bedrock principle underlying the First Amendment, it is that the government may not prohibit the expression of an idea simply because society finds the idea itself offensive or disagreeable....

We have not recognized an exception to this principle even where our flag has been involved. In *Street v. New York*, we held that a State may not criminally punish a person for uttering words critical of the flag. Rejecting the argument that the conviction could be sustained on the ground that Street had "failed to show the respect for our national symbol which may properly be demanded of every citizen," we concluded that "the constitutionally guaranteed 'freedom to be intellectually. . . diverse or even contrary,' and the 'right to differ as to things that touch the heart of the existing order,' encompass the freedom to express publicly one's opinions about our flag, including those opinions which are defiant or contemptuous."

Nor may the government, we have held, compel conduct that would evince respect for the flag. "To sustain the compulsory flag salute, we are required to say that a Bill of Rights which guards the individual's right to speak his own mind left it open to public authorities to compel him to utter what is not in his mind."

"If there is any fixed star in our constitutional constellation, it is that no official, high or petty, can prescribe what shall be orthodox in politics, nationalism, religion, or other matters of opinion or force citizens to confess by word or act their faith therein."...

Johnson was convicted for engaging in expressive conduct. The State's interest in preventing breaches of the peace does not support his conviction, because Johnson's conduct did not threaten to disturb the peace. Nor does the State's interest in preserving the flag as a symbol of nationhood and national unity justify his criminal conviction for engaging in political expression. The judgment of the Texas Court of Criminal Appeals (which held for Johnson) is therefore Affirmed.

The United States protects expression to a greater extent than any other country. The protection of speech includes ideas that are offensive. After all, there is no reason to protect speech that everyone agrees with. Even more, who would decide what speech is too offensive? Do you trust whoever is in power at any moment to decide what speech is acceptable or not? The prospect of the law becoming a political or personal moralistic tool of those in authority is why SCOTUS has chosen to leave it to individuals, through a "free market of ideas," to decide. As Justice Robert Jackson wrote, "If there is any fixed star in our constitutional constellation, it is that no official, high or petty, can prescribe what shall be orthodox in politics, nationalism, religion, or other matters of opinion or force citizens to confess by word or act their faith therein."[11] For this reason, racist, sexist, ageist, and other forms of "hate speech" are protected.

As is true of all rights, however, there are limits. SCOTUS has been careful in narrowly defining these limits and is cautious in creating new ones. Here is a short list of exceptions, though there are others:

- *Obscenity.* Seriously objectionable material, beyond common pornography.

- *Child pornography.* Because children are more likely to be harmed by involvement in pornography than are adults, child pornography may be punished. This includes both involving a child in a sex act and exhibiting nude children in sexually suggestive ways. The objective of this free speech exception is to protect children from harm, not to prevent others from viewing the material. So digitally created, or virtual, images of child pornography are protected, unless they rise to the level of being obscene.

- *Defamation.* Written statements (libel) or oral statements (slander) that are untrue and harmful are not protected. The state may allow defamed people to sue and win money awards, but defamation may not be criminally punished.

- *True threats.* An expression that is intended to cause fear of imminent bodily harm or death, and if the speaker has the apparent ability to do what is threatened, may be criminalized. A true threat must be directed at a specific individual or group of people.

- *Incitement to imminent lawlessness.* Words that are likely to cause imminent lawlessness may be punished.

You will learn more about these exceptions when we explore the specific crimes that criminalize speech—for example, threat—later in the book.

Second Amendment

The Second Amendment reads "A well regulated Militia, being necessary to the security of a free State, the right of the people to keep and bear Arms, shall not be infringed." The relationship between the militia clause and the bear arms clause is unclear. Scholars and others continue to debate whether they are connected or independent of one another. If connected, then the right to bear arms only exists for members of the militia. If not, then all people possess a right to bear arms.

Regardless of the ongoing academic debate, SCOTUS found the two clauses to be independent in a case where it held that an individual has a right to possess a handgun in the home.[12] Two years later, the court incorporated the Second Amendment.[13] But the right to bear arms, as presently understood, is limited to a handgun in the home. Many states and the federal government regulate firearms in many other ways, including owning or possessing only certain types of guns, mandatory licensing or registration, safety training, prohibiting sales to people with criminal or psychological histories, restricting public possession, and limiting sales and distribution. These laws are being aggressively challenged, and it is likely that SCOTUS will soon better define the Second Amendment.

Fourth Amendment

One of the most important protections of rights in criminal justice is the privilege against unreasonable searches and seizures. This right is found in the Fourth Amendment. It is short and to the point:

> The right of the people to be secure in their persons, houses, papers, and effects, against unreasonable searches and seizures, shall not be violated, and no warrants shall issue, but upon probable cause, supported by oath or affirmation, and particularly describing the place to be searched, and the persons or things to be seized.

The amendment is fully incorporated, so all searches and seizures by any government officer must follow the amendment's commands. The words "searches and seizures" have special Fourth Amendment meaning. A seizure of the person, for example, is more than just an "arrest." Whenever a government officer makes a person feel unfree to leave the situation, a seizure has occurred, subject to a couple of conditions. First, the person's conclusion that they were not free must be reasonable, and second, the government officer must be acting under official authority, not as a private person. The Framers listed the spaces protected by the amendment—persons, houses, and papers and effects. These three interests include almost everything—the human body, homes, apartments, cell phones, cloud accounts, automobiles, water bottles, and purses and wallets are all protected.

No right is absolute; the Fourth Amendment doesn't ban all searches. Of course, police officers conduct searches and seizures of people and things thousands of times every day. The Fourth Amendment establishes the rules police must follow when doing these things.

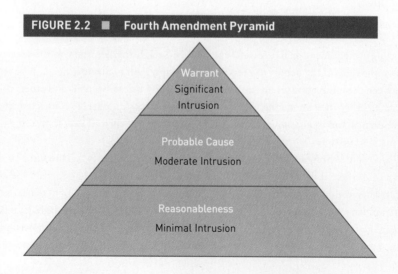

FIGURE 2.2 ■ Fourth Amendment Pyramid

To understand those rules, review Figure 2.2. The baseline, or minimum, requirement of the Fourth Amendment is that the government act reasonably. Searches and seizures must *always* be reasonable; and sometimes, police only have to be reasonable. That is the bottom of the pyramid. In other cases, being reasonable isn't enough. The state must also have probable cause. It takes credible evidence, not just a suspicion or a hunch, to prove probable cause. Many searches and seizures are permitted when the government has probable cause and has acted reasonably. Finally, you see the warrant requirement at the top of the pyramid. A warrant is a court order to conduct a search, make an arrest, or seize property. Whenever a warrant is required, everything below it on the pyramid is also required (reasonable behavior and probable cause). The point of a warrant is to protect society's most private spaces by interposing a judge between the individual and the state. Only a neutral judge may issue a warrant, the officer who has asked for the warrant must swear that the facts presented to establish probable cause are true, and the warrant must satisfy the particularity requirement. "Particularity" simply means details—what precisely is to be searched or seized. A warrant can't authorize police to go on fishing expeditions.

To make sense of the pyramid, think of it in terms of the level of privacy that the government has intruded upon. Less is required of the government at the bottom of the pyramid because the individual's privacy interests are minimal. The government's privacy intrusion is the greatest at the top of the pyramid, so the full warrant, probable cause, and reasonableness requirements are required. There are many exceptions to the warrant requirement. In Table 2.1, you will find a list of some of the most common searches and seizures and where they fall on the pyramid. A more thorough discussion of the Fourth Amendment can be found in a criminal procedure textbook.

TABLE 2.1 ■ Requirements of Specific Searches and Seizures		
Action	*Description*	*Pyramid Location*
Home search	With rare exceptions, police must have a warrant to search a home.	Top/Warrant
Plain view seizure	An officer may seize evidence that is in plain view, and probable cause exists to believe it is contraband or evidence of a crime.	Center/Probable cause
Automobile search	A car may be searched with probable cause to believe contraband or evidence of a crime will be found. A warrant isn't required.	Center/Probable cause
Terry frisk	Officer may "pat down" the outer clothing of a person subject to a Terry stop, provided a reasonable belief that the suspect is dangerous exists. Also named for the *Terry* case.	Bottom/Reasonableness

(Continued)

Probable cause: The standard of proof required by the Fourth Amendment to the Constitution of the United States for a search or seizure to be conducted. An officer has probable cause when the facts available to the officer warrant a person of reasonable caution in the belief that contraband or evidence of a crime is present.

Warrant: A judicially issued authorization for police to conduct a search or seizure.

TABLE 2.1 ■ Requirements of Specific Searches and Seizures *(Continued)*		
Action	*Description*	*Pyramid Location*
Terry stop	Officer may temporarily detain a suspect when there is a reasonable suspicion of criminality supported by specific and articulable facts. Named for *Terry v. Ohio*, 392 U.S. 1 (1968).	Bottom/Reasonableness
Search of an arrested person	For the safety of the officer and others, and for administrative reasons (to make a list of the arrestee's possessions), an arrested person may be searched without evidence that contraband will be found. The "search incident to arrest" is automatically authorized.	Bottom/Reasonableness

Fifth Amendment

Another important set of criminal justice rights is found in the Fifth Amendment, which reads as follows:

> No person shall be held to answer for a capital, or otherwise infamous crime, unless on a presentment or indictment of a Grand Jury, except in cases arising in the land or naval forces, or in the Militia, when in actual service in time of War or public danger; nor shall any person be subject for the same offense to be twice put in jeopardy of life or limb; nor shall be compelled in any criminal case to be a witness against himself, nor be deprived of life, liberty, or property, without due process of law; nor shall private property be taken for public use, without just compensation.

Under this Amendment, a defendant can't be made to testify (at all); can't be tried twice; is entitled to due process; and is entitled to have a group of citizens, known as a **grand jury**, decide whether charges, known as an **indictment** or true bill, should be filed in the first place. All of the rights in the Fifth Amendment, except indictment by grand jury, have been incorporated. Regardless, many states require grand jury indictment for serious crimes. When grand jury indictment isn't required, a prosecutor can file the charge, known as an *information*, directly.

Sixth Amendment

Like the Fifth Amendment, the Sixth is short but packed full of rights:

> In all criminal prosecutions, the accused shall enjoy the right to a speedy and public trial, by an impartial jury of the State and district wherein the crime shall have been committed, which district shall have been previously ascertained by law, and to be informed of the nature and cause of the accusation; to be confronted with the witnesses

---

Grand jury: A group of citizens who decide if probable cause to believe a suspect has committed a crime exists.

Indictment: Also known as a true bill, a formal criminal charge issued by a grand jury.

against him; to have compulsory process for obtaining witnesses in his favor, and to have the Assistance of Counsel for his defense.

The reach of the amendment is clear: It only applies in criminal cases. Of the rights found in the Sixth Amendment, a speedy trial has been one of the most difficult and most contentious. SCOTUS has refused to set hard dates and has recognized that there are legitimate reasons for delays. Most states provide for a right to trial within 90 days if the defendant is in custody and 180 days if the defendant is free.

The speedy trial determination is case-specific. The impact COVID-19 will have on speedy trial and public trial rights is yet to be seen. There is precedent for delays due to natural causes. As a consequence of Hurricane Katrina in Louisiana, many trials were postponed well beyond the normal limits of speedy trial. Also, many courts chose to use virtual hearings and trials.

The rights to confrontation and cross-examination are inherent to the "orality" of the adversarial system. The adversarial system assumed that direct, real-time testimony that is subject to interrogation is the best way to find the truth. The state can't introduce written statements or other evidence without producing the witness to testify at trial.

The Sixth Amendment's right to counsel is a good example of the expansion of a right. First, it wasn't incorporated until 1963, although SCOTUS had previously decided that it was incorporated in a very minimal way.[14] Beyond expanding it to the states, the right now applies to many cases it didn't before. In the early years, only defendants charged with crimes that could be punished with death were entitled to counsel. Over time, the right expanded to felonies, then misdemeanors, and today, every defendant charged with a crime that may be punished with a single day in jail is entitled to have an attorney. This includes the right to have an attorney appointed at the government's expense if a defendant can't afford an attorney.

Privacy

Privacy is not specifically protected by the Constitution. The Fourth Amendment has the effect of protecting privacy, but it isn't a source of any specific right to privacy. SCOTUS has found, however, a number of privacy rights to be implicit in other rights. The most significant source is due process. Of course, due process is about procedure. But it also protects substantive rights. In some instances, the court has primarily relied on due process to protect privacy, but it has also thrown other rights into the mix. An example is the Ninth Amendment, which was the Framers' way to express that there are more rights than appear in the Constitution. In spite of the obvious intent of the Framers, the Ninth Amendment has never been used by itself to secure a right. But it has been cited as a supporting cast member to the star of the show: substantive due process.

Several areas of private life have been deemed "fundamental" and protected under the due process clauses. These include reproductive, sexual, and marriage rights. The landmark case where the right to privacy was announced was *Griswold v. Connecticut*, 381 U.S. 479 (1965). In *Griswold*, a Connecticut statute that criminalized prescribing contraceptives for married couples was invalidated. Justice Douglas wrote, "Would we allow the police to search the sacred precincts of marital bedrooms for telltale signs of the use of contraceptives? The very idea is repulsive to the notions of privacy surrounding the marriage relationship." Subsequently, this decision was extended to unmarried couples in *Eisenstadt v. Baird*, 405 U.S. 438. Additionally, the right to interracial marriage was found in *Loving v. Virginia*, 388 U.S. 1 (1967), the right of a woman to elect abortion in *Roe v. Wade*, 410 U.S. 113 (1973), the right to sex with a person of the same sex in *Lawrence v. Texas*, 539 U.S. 558 (2003), and the right to same-sex marriage in *Obergefell v. Hodges*, 576 U.S. 644 (2015).

PHOTO 2.2 Supporters of gay marriage rally in front of the Supreme Court in Washington.

Allan Tannenbaum/Getty Images

QUESTIONS AND APPLICATIONS

In Questions 1 and 2, identify the laws as either ex post facto or a bill of attainder.

1. Ty is convicted of theft and sentenced to 18 months in prison. During his second month in prison, the state legislature changed the theft statute to include orders of restitution in addition to jail time. The statute applied to all convictions that occur after the law is enacted and to all convictions that occurred within 2 years before the law was enacted. Ty received a notice from the court where he was convicted that he has been ordered to pay the victim of his theft $2,500 in restitution.

2. Terri Trustworthy, a licensed financial investment consultant, was sued by a large group of investors who claimed they lost millions of dollars in savings due to her embezzlement and carelessness. The lawsuit is dismissed, and in response to pleas from the investors, Congress enacts a statute that finds Terri liable and orders her to repay the investors' losses.

3. Is the following law vague, overbroad, both, or neither? Explain your answer.

COVID-19 Health Emergency Protection Act

Any person who meets with a large number of people in any space, real or virtual, for any reason other than to provide important and essential services is guilty of a Class B misdemeanor.

In Questions 4 through 6, explain which right is implicated by each scenario and then list in which amendment that right is found.

4. State enacts a statute that declares it a misdemeanor to "utter, publish, or write any statement concerning the governor's COVID-19 orders to wear masks, socially distance, or to close businesses that are not approved by the governor's office."

5. HappyTown City Police Officer James Smiley stops a man on the street for appearing to be grumpy. Officer Smiley asks him what is bothering him. The man replies, "I don't have to talk to you," and begins to walk away. Officer Smiley grabs the man and searches his body.

6. Darian is on trial for involuntary manslaughter. The prosecutor calls him to testify. He refuses, and the judge tells him that he will be found in contempt of court if he doesn't take the stand.

TREAT ME EQUALLY

Learning Objective: Describe the three levels of review under the equal protection clause and identify the classifications that fall under each.

In addition to protecting due process, the Fourteenth Amendment forbids the states from denying "to any person within its jurisdiction the equal protection of the laws." Even though there isn't an express counterpart that applies to the federal government, SCOTUS has held that the Fifth Amendment's protection of due process includes the equal protection of the laws.[15] So today, both the federal government and the states must provide equal protection of the laws *and* due process.

A straightforward reading of the equal protection clause appears to demand that the states and federal government treat every person identically all the time. But this rarely happens—nor should it. Discriminating between people is both necessary and common. For example, few people would disagree that there should be a minimum age to drive a car or that a medical school education should be required to obtain a license to practice medicine. Thankfully, the equal protection clause hasn't been interpreted to require the states to issue driver's or medical licenses to 7-year-old applicants. But some forms of discrimination are more troubling than these examples. Indeed, the equal protection clause was specifically created to address racial discrimination, so there is, therefore, legitimate and illegitimate discrimination in the eyes of the equal protection clause. Stated another way, the law discriminates between different forms of discrimination. (I admit, that was fun to write.)

SCOTUS has developed a method of analysis for equal protection claims. The first step in the analysis is to determine whether the court should apply strict scrutiny, intermediate scrutiny, or rational basis review of the government's action. Most laws and government actions are constitutional if there is a rational basis for them. Under the *rational basis test*, the government must have a legitimate purpose for making the law, and the law must be rationally related to that purpose. Let's use our medical license example from earlier. The state has a legitimate interest in protecting people from poor medical care, and it is reasonable to assume that a person who graduates from medical school will be better prepared to provide quality medical care than a person who hasn't attended medical school, so the medical school requirement easily passes the rational basis test. The rational basis test is the default test that is used by courts to determine if the equal protection clause has been violated.

There are a few classifications, however, that are "suspect" under the equal protection clause. Over the years, SCOTUS has considered several factors when deciding if a classification is suspect. Included are whether people are grouped by immutable conditions, or biological traits, over which a person has no control; whether there is a history of discrimination against a group; and whether the group has a history of being disadvantaged in the political system. Applying these factors, race, alienage, national origin, and religion has been found to be **suspect classification**.

Suspect classifications are not tested under the rational basis test. Instead, the **strict scrutiny test** is applied. This is a hard test for a law to pass because it requires more than simple rationality. It demands these items:

1. The government must have a compelling interest in the regulation.

2. The law is narrowly tailored to accomplish that compelling interest.

3. The law uses the least restrictive means possible, or to put it another way, can the government accomplish its purpose in a way that doesn't classify people? If so, it must follow that path.

The first element concerns the government's interests, and the last two elements concern the means, or manner, it uses to accomplish its goal. To be compelling, an interest must be necessary, vital to the public good. For shorthand, think of this as the "damn good reason test." The second and third elements are focused on the means used to accomplish the damn good reason—did the government narrowly tailor the law to avoid the classification?

In addition to requiring a compelling purpose and a narrowly drafted law, another big difference between the strict scrutiny standard and the rational relationship standard is the burden of proof. If the rational basis test applies, the law is presumed constitutional and the person challenging the law must prove it to be illegitimate or not designed to achieve its objective. In strict scrutiny review, however, the government must prove that its compelling interest is real; it must put on evidence that there is a problem, that the law will help solve that problem, and that the law is narrowly tailored.

Suspect classification: Laws that discriminate between people by race, alienage, national origin, and religion are suspect.

Strict scrutiny test: Laws that discriminate using a suspect classification or that encroach upon a fundamental right are reviewed by courts under the strict scrutiny test. To satisfy equal protection or due process, such laws must be supported by a legitimate compelling governmental interest, be narrowly tailored, and use the least restrictive means possible to accomplish the government's purpose.

Most, but not all, laws that are put under the strict scrutiny microscope are found to be unconstitutional. Although you will explore fundamental rights later in the chapter, it is worth noting now that the strict scrutiny test applies in a second situation: when laws burden fundamental rights. A law that makes it a crime to express dissatisfaction with the government encroaches on the First Amendment. It would, therefore, be subject to strict scrutiny when reviewed by a court for constitutionality. And by the way, the law would unquestionably fail.

A third test has developed that falls in between strict scrutiny and rational basis; it represents an intermediate level of judicial review. Known as the substantial relationship test, a law is constitutional if it furthers a legitimate and important governmental interest and is substantially related to the government's purpose. Sex classifications are an example.

Examples of common forms of discrimination that are not recognized as protected classes are age and wealth. Without a doubt, both exist. There are statutory laws that forbid age discrimination in employment and in certain other circumstances, but the Fourteenth Amendment does not provide any special protection. Income or wealth, on the other hand, is not protected by statute or the Constitution. Laws that distinguish by wealth only need to be rational. This is why people of greater income can be taxed at a higher rate than people of lower income and why it was legal for the government to send COVID-19 support checks to some people but not others. See Figure 2.3 for a flowchart of how to step through an equal protection problem.

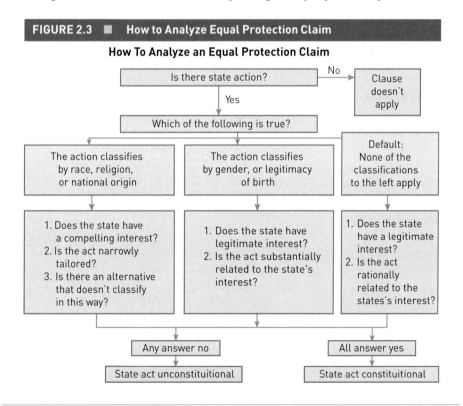

FIGURE 2.3 ■ How to Analyze Equal Protection Claim

How To Analyze an Equal Protection Claim

Substantial relationship test: Laws that discriminate between people by sex are reviewed by courts under the substantial relationship test. To satisfy equal protection, such laws must be supported by an important and legitimate governmental interest, and the law is substantially related to that interest.

Now, let's apply what you have learned about equal protection to criminal law. By its very nature, criminal law treats people differently. Criminals are punished; the general population isn't. Being a "criminal" doesn't put a person into a protected class, so criminal classifications have to pass the rational relationship test. The government's interest in protecting people from crime is a legitimate governmental purpose, and a law prohibiting and punishing an offender for constitutionally unprotected conduct is rationally related to that purpose. Consequently, criminal laws don't wrongly discriminate between offenders and others.

Although a law stands a good chance to be found constitutional when tested under the rational relationship standard, that doesn't always happen. The conviction of a police officer in Ohio is an example. The officer, aged 35, met a girl on a dating app. In their conversations, she claimed to be 18. They met and began to have sex, only to be discovered by her mother. The girl, as it turns out, was 14. The officer was charged with two crimes: statutory rape and sexual battery under a statute that prohibits sexual conduct when one person is a minor and "the offender is a peace officer, and the offender is more than two years older than the other person." The statutory rape charge was dismissed after the jury couldn't reach a verdict, but the judge found the defendant guilty on the count of sexual battery by a police officer.

The defendant challenged the law as violating equal protection, asserting that police officers shouldn't be treated differently from other people. The Ohio Supreme Court agreed. The battery law in question protected minors, and adults in some circumstances, from abuses by school officials, physicians, clerics, police, corrections officials, and other authority figures. However, all of the other listed professionals could only be convicted if they used their position of authority to take advantage of a victim. For example, the law made it a crime for a mental health professional to "induce the other person to submit [to sex] by falsely representing to the other person that the sexual conduct is necessary for mental health treatment purposes." But no such connection between the authority of a police officer and the resulting crime existed under the statute. In the defendant's case, there was no evidence that the victim knew, or that he used, his status as a police officer to coerce or lure her into sex. The law simply punished the defendant differently because he was a cop. The Ohio Supreme Court found the classification to be a violation of both the U.S. Constitution's and Ohio Constitution's guarantees of equal protection; it found the law to be irrational.[16]

Criminal laws that group people into protected classes are less likely to survive equal protection testing. Today, it is rare for a law to violate equal protection on its face. Most equal protection violations occur when race, ethnicity, and religion influence the decisions of police and prosecutors. A decision to pursue an investigation or prosecution may violate equal protection, even though the law itself doesn't mention one of the protected statuses. This is known as *selective prosecution*.

Rational basis test: The default test under the equal protection clause and due process clauses. It is applied whenever a law doesn't involve a suspect classification or a fundamental right. The least demanding test under the Fourteenth Amendment, a law will survive review if it is supported by a legitimate governmental interest and the law is rationally related to that interest.

What happened to Yick Wo is an example. In 1880, during a period of anti-Chinese sentiment in the United States, San Francisco enacted an ordinance that forbade laundries from operating in wooden buildings unless a permit was obtained. At the time, nearly all of the laundries in the city operated out of wooden buildings, which were susceptible to catching fire. At the time, there were over 300 laundries, most owned by people of Chinese descent. Yick Wo had operated his laundry for over 2 decades when the law went into effect. As required, he applied for a permit, but it was denied. As it turned out, there were over 200 applications from Chinese launderers. All but one was denied, while nearly every permit application was granted to white applicants. In violation of the law, Yick Wo continued to operate his business, was charged, convicted, and fined—and when he failed to pay the fine, jailed. He appealed his conviction, eventually reaching SCOTUS. The court held that while the law was neutral and its intent, to prevent fires in the city, legitimate, the manner in which it was enforced was racially discriminatory. The court dismissed Yick Wo's charges and ordered his release, as well as the release of other launderers of Chinese descent who were jailed under the law.[17]

Today, concerns about the unequal treatment of racial minority groups by police are much in the news. In an effort to combat crime in high-crime areas, New York City employed a large "stop and frisk" program for a decade. The program was intended to be proactive attempt to prevent crime. Several million people were stopped and frisked for contraband and weapons during the life of the program—over 600,000 in 1 year alone. Most of the detainees were people in racial minority groups, which caused concern that race was playing a significant role in the decision-making of police officers. City officials, however, credited the stop-and-frisk program as a major factor in a decline in crime during the period of the program and claimed that data didn't support the assertion that racist decisions were being made. Eventually, a federal district judge ruled that the program violated equal protection. That judge was later removed from the case by the New York Court of Appeals for having suggested that the plaintiffs bring a lawsuit to challenge the program. Since she had shown a bias in favor of the lawsuit, the appellate court said she should have recused herself from the lawsuit that the plaintiffs eventually filed.[18]

In addition to race, ethnicity, and religion, laws sometimes classify by gender. This is illustrated by one case involving statutory rape laws. Statutory rape law presumes that young people are emotionally and psychologically incapable of consenting to sex. To protect minors from potentially harmful sexual liaisons, statutory rape laws make it a crime for an older person to have sex with a younger person under the age of consent within the state, regardless of whether the minor consents or even initiates and encourages the liaison. Laws vary considerably in the minimum and maximum ages for victims and offenders. For a long time, statutory rape laws were gendered; only males could commit the offense and only females were protected. When a 17-year-old male was convicted of the statutory rape of a 16-year-old girl, he challenged the law's sexual classification under the equal protection clause. The case made its way up to SCOTUS, which applied the substantial relationship test because the law classified the victims and offenders by gender. In a controversial decision, SCOTUS found the classification to be legitimate and substantially related to the purpose of the law: to protect girls from sexual intercourse and pregnancy at an age when the physical, emotional, and psychological consequences are particularly severe.[19]

QUESTIONS AND APPLICATIONS

Identify whether the following classifications will be tested under the strict scrutiny, substantial relationship, or rational basis test. Explain your answer.

1. State law declares it a misdemeanor for a person to perform genital circumcision of a male younger than 1 year in age as part of a Brit milah or other Jewish practice.
2. State law declares that any person convicted of a felony shall lose the right to vote until that person's punishment has been completed.
3. A state legislature investigates the problem of binge drinking by youth. The legislators hear testimony that young men are more likely than girls to binge drink. Further, when the effects of alcohol on young men and women are compared, they discover that boys are more likely than girls to commit violent crime or to become involved in automobile accidents. Consequently, the state legislature, with the governor's signature, enacts a statute that permits men to begin drinking at 21 and women at 19.

DON'T BE CRUEL

Learning Objective: Identify the three rights found in the Eighth Amendment.

Up to this point, you have learned about rights that limit the government's authority to declare acts to be crimes and other rights that empower defendants to demand a fair process. The Eighth Amendment is concerned with the other end of the criminal justice process: punishment. It is shorter than the amendments discussed already:

> Excessive bail shall not be required, nor excessive fines imposed, nor cruel and unusual punishments inflicted.

There are three distinct rights in the Eighth Amendment—no excessive bail, no excessive fines, and no cruel and unusual punishment. The excessive fines and cruel and unusual punishments clauses have been incorporated, but the excessive bails clause has not. But it is expected to be, eventually, and all the states and the federal government have rules limiting bail and making pretrial release possible in many cases.

Defining cruelty isn't easy. Whatever it is, however, isn't what it used to be. Instead, cruelty is defined using society's "evolving standards of decency." Although familiar to early Americans, lopping off an ear and drawing-and-quartering (when a horse was used to split a person into four pieces) are no longer allowed. In two separate opinions, SCOTUS held that it is cruel and unusual punishment to execute the rapists of an adult and a child.[20] There are many cases that address the methods that may be used to execute offenders and the conditions of prison confinement. Prisoners are entitled to sanitary conditions, clothing, minimal nutrition, personal space, and medical care. It is unknown whether there is a limit to the length of imprisonment that may be imposed for minor crimes.

QUESTIONS AND PROBLEMS

1. What are the three protections found in the Eighth Amendment?
2. When the Constitution was ratified, branding was still a lawful form of punishment in some of the states. If it could be proved that most people at that time believed branding to be acceptable, could we employ it today? What evidence would you need to answer this question? Explain your answer.

DON'T USE ILLEGAL EVIDENCE

Learning Objective: Define the exclusionary rule and identify its constitutional source and the case where it was incorporated.

Remember Dollree Mapp from the opening of this chapter? Her Fourth Amendment right was violated by the officers who entered and searched her home without a warrant. The evidence they seized was used at trial to obtain her conviction. That may not be fair, but what is to be done is unclear. The Constitution declares rights, but it doesn't spell out what is to happen when those rights are violated.

Ms. Mapp appealed her case all the way to SCOTUS. Her appeal resulted in the third reason the Constitution means so much in criminal law today: the exclusionary rule. Read about this rule in your next Digging Deeper..

DIGGING DEEPER 2.3

Can illegally seized evidence be used to convict a defendant?

Case: *Mapp v. Ohio*, 367 U.S. 643
Court: SCOTUS
Year: 1961
MR. JUSTICE CLARK delivered the opinion of the court.

Appellant stands convicted of knowingly having had in her possession and under her control certain lewd and lascivious books, pictures, and photographs in violation of § 2905.34 of Ohio's Revised Code. As officially stated in the syllabus to its opinion, the Supreme Court of Ohio found that her conviction was valid though "based primarily upon the introduction in evidence of lewd and lascivious books and pictures unlawfully seized during an unlawful search of defendant's home."....

Exclusionary rule: A judicially created rule that requires evidence that is illegally obtained by the state to be excluded from the trial of the defendant.

The State says that, even if the search were made without authority, or otherwise unreasonably, it is not prevented from using the unconstitutionally seized evidence at trial... [even though the court had previously decided that illegally seized evidence may not be used in federal courts].

Since the Fourth Amendment's right of privacy has been declared enforceable against the States through the Due Process Clause of the Fourteenth, it is enforceable against them by the same sanction of exclusion as is used against the Federal Government. Were it otherwise... the assurance against unreasonable federal searches and seizures would be "a form of words," valueless and undeserving of mention in a perpetual charter of inestimable human liberties; so too, without that rule, the freedom from state invasions of privacy would be so ephemeral and so neatly severed from its conceptual nexus with the freedom from all brutish means of coercing evidence as not to merit this Court's high regard as a freedom "implicit in the concept of ordered liberty."...

Moreover, our holding that the exclusionary rule is an essential part of both the Fourth and Fourteenth Amendments is not only the logical dictate of prior cases, but it also makes very good sense. There is no war between the Constitution and common sense. Presently, a federal prosecutor may make no use of evidence illegally seized, but a State's attorney across the street may, although he supposedly is operating under the enforceable prohibitions of the same Amendment. Thus, the State, by admitting evidence unlawfully seized, serves to encourage disobedience to the Federal Constitution which it is bound to uphold. Moreover... "[t]he very essence of a healthy federalism depends upon the avoidance of needless conflict between state and federal courts."

Nothing can destroy a government more quickly than its failure to observe its own laws, or worse, its disregard of the charter of its own existence.

In the abstract, the exercise of a right should be free. But in reality, there are costs. Litigation, civil and criminal, can be protracted, time-consuming, financially expensive, and invasive of one's privacy. In some cases, there are social expenses. Through the exclusionary rule, evidence that police seize illegally is excluded from trial. That can jeopardize the possibility of bringing an offender to justice. That was true of Ms. Mapp. Her case was dismissed, and she was set free. She was later convicted of possession of a controlled substance, served time in prison, was released, and died in 2014 at the age of 91. But freedom doesn't occur automatically when the exclusionary rule is applied. If the state has other evidence, the case will proceed without the excluded evidence.

QUESTIONS AND APPLICATIONS

1. Like judicial review, the exclusionary rule isn't in the Constitution. Should SCOTUS have the authority to create such rules? Construct arguments in favor of and in opposition to the court's creation of the exclusionary rule.
2. What are the costs and benefits of the exclusionary rule? Consider the individual, the community, and the legal system.

DON'T FORGET STATE CONSTITUTIONS

Learning Objective: Define new judicial federalism and provide one example of it in action.

You are now familiar with the importance of the U.S. Constitution in criminal law. Much of the expansion of criminal procedure rights you learned about occurred during the 1960s, when Earl Warren was Chief Justice of SCOTUS. The period is often referred to as the Warren Court Era. Warren was appointed by President Dwight D. Eisenhower, but as a conservative who opposed what the Warren Court did, President Eisenhower referred to Warren's appointment as his "biggest damn fooled mistake." Warren retired in 1969 and was replaced by Warren E. Burger. Chief Justice Burger moved the court in a more conservative direction, often limiting the impact of the criminal justice decisions of the Warren Court.

Dismayed by the direction of the court, Justice William Brennan published an article in 1977, calling on the states to strengthen their constitutional protections.[21] For Brennan, if the U.S. Constitution wasn't going to expand its protection of the people, state constitutions should. This became known as **new judicial federalism**. In response, many state courts began turning to their own constitutions more than they had in the past. For example, in 2019 the Colorado Supreme Court held that under its constitution a police dog sniff of a vehicle for marijuana is a search requiring probable cause. The same sniff is not a search under the Fourth Amendment.[22] A few other state high courts have been somewhat aggressive in expanding rights beyond what the U.S. Constitution protects. For example, you learned earlier that gender-based discrimination under the federal equal protection clause is tested using the intermediate substantial relationship test. But the California Supreme Court reviews sex discrimination by the state by the strict scrutiny standard.[23] In regard to an exception to the exclusionary rule that the U.S. Supreme Court adopted, and thereby permitting illegally seized evidence to be used against a defendant, the Pennsylvania Supreme Court wrote, "We flatly reject the notion."[24] The lesson of these cases is clear: do not forget state constitutional law. While it may not reduce U.S. constitutional rights, it sometimes bolsters them.

QUESTIONS AND PROBLEMS

1. New judicial federalism results in greater protection of rights in some states than in others. Is this fair to the people in the states with less protection? What can they do to change their rights?

New judicial federalism: The interpretation of state constitutions independent from the U.S. Constitution. State constitutions may enlarge, but not reduce, the rights found in the U.S. Constitution.

IN A NUTSHELL

The political DNA of the United States includes a suspicion of governmental authority and a respect for the rights of the individual. The Constitution's Framers chose to divide the government, both horizontally and vertically, to protect liberty. The federal system can be complex, clunky, and inefficient. But to the Framers, that was a reasonable price to pay to guard against tyranny.

The Framers believed that people have a greater voice, and laws are better tailored to the needs of the people when created at the state and local levels. It is easy to understand their reasoning, given the size of the country at the time. There were fewer than 4 million people spread across 13 states at the time of the adoption of the Constitution. The largest state, Virginia, had a population of about 750,000 inhabitants, and the smallest state, Delaware, had only around 60,000. Consequently, they placed most governmental authority, including the police powers, with the states. Even today, 90% of all criminal cases are adjudicated in state courts. Most crimes, their punishment, and, to some extent, the defenses that may be asserted to criminal charges are made and enforced by the states.

But state authority is not without its limits. Although the individual rights found in the Constitution were originally intended to restrict the federal government and not the states, this changed after the Fourteenth Amendment was ratified. Through selection incorporation, most of what is found in the Bill of Rights, as well as the few rights found in the original Constitution, acts to restrict state authority. The practical impact of this on criminal law can't be overstated. Every defendant in every courtroom in the United States can assert the Fourth Amendment's protection against unreasonable searches and seizures, can demand a public jury trial of peers, is free from self-incrimination, and so on. When added to the more expansive interpretation of those rights, particularly after the 1960s, the United States Constitution is a powerful force of liberty.

LEGAL TERMS

as-applied (p. 48)

bills of attainder (p. 39)

constitutionalism (p. 38)

Due process (p. 40)

Equal protection (p. 40)

exclusionary rule (p. 65)

ex post facto laws (p. 39)

facial challenge (p. 48)

grand jury (p. 56)

habeas corpus (p. 39)

indictment (p. 56)

new judicial federalism (p. 67)

overbreadth doctrine (p. 47)

Privileges or immunities (p. 40)

probable cause (p. 55)

rational relationship test (p. 62)

recidivism (p. 46)

selective incorporation doctrine (p. 41)

severability (p. 48)

strict scrutiny test (p. 60)

substantial relationship test (p. 61)

suspect classification (p. 60)

void for vagueness (p. 46)

warrant (p. 55)

NOTES

1. *Mapp v. Ohio*, 367 U.S. 643 (1961); Ken Armstrong, "Dollree Mapp, 1923–2014: The Rosa Parks of the Fourth Amendment," *The Marshall Project*, April 15, 2020, https://www.themarshallproj ect.org/2014/12/08/dollree-mapp-1923-2014-the-rosa-parks-of-the-fourth-amendment.

2. *Calder v. Bull*, 3 U.S. 386 (1798).

3. Matt Zapotosy, "3,100 Inmates to Be Released as Trump Administration Implements Criminal Justice Reform," *Washington Post*, July 19, 2019, accessed April 16, 2020, TheWashingtonPost.com.

4. *United States v. Lovett*, 328 U.S. 303 (1946).

5. *Papachristou v. Jacksonville*, 405 U.S. 156 (1972).

6. See, for example, *United States v. Davis*, 588 U.S. __ (2019).

7. *Coffin v. United States*, 156 U.S. 432 (1895).

8. *In Re Winship*, 397 U.S. 358 (1970).

9. William Blackstone, *Commentaries on the Laws of England in Four Books* (Philadelphia: J.B. Lippincott Co., 1893).

10. James Q. Whitman, *The Origins of Reasonable Doubt* (New Haven, CT: Yale University Press, 2008).

11. *West Virginia Board of Education v. Barnett*, 319 U.S. 624 (1943).

12. *District of Columbia v. Heller*, 554 U.S. 570 (2008).

13. *McDonald v. Chicago*, 561 U.S. 742 (2010).

14. Incorporated in *Gideon v. Wainwright*, 372 U.S. 335 (1963); partially incorporated in *Powell v. Alabama*, 287 U.S. 45 (1932).

15. *Bolling v. Sharpe*, 347 U.S. 497 (1954).

16. *State v. Mole*, 149 Ohio St.3d 215 (2016).

17. *Yick Wo v. Hopkins*, 118 U.S. 356 (1886).

18. See *Floyd v. New York*, 959 F. Supp. 2d 540 (S.D.N.Y. 2013) for the district court's decision.

19. *Michael M v. Superior Court of Sonoma County*, 450 U.S. 464 (1981).

20. *Coker v. Georgia*, 433 U.S. 584 (1977); *Kennedy v. Louisiana*, 554 U.S. 407 (2008).

21. William J. Brennan, *State Constitutions and the Protection of Individual Rights*, 90 Harv. L. Rev. 489 (1977).

22. *Colorado v. McNight*, Case No. 17SC584 (May 20, 2019).

23. *In Re Marriage Cases*, 43 Cal.4th 757, 76 Cal.Rptr.3d 683, 183 P.3d 384 (2008).

24. *Commonwealth v. Edmunds*, 526 Pa. 374 (1991).

3 THE ELEMENTS OF A CRIME

Pat Cogdon, 19, was awakened one night by her mother, who was touching her face. When Pat asked her mother why she woke her, Ms. Cogdon replied that she was tucking her into bed. At bedtime the next night, Ms. Cogdon prepared a hot water bottle and warm milk for her daughter, and the two had a short talk, during which Ms. Cogdon expressed fear of the Korean War. Pat replied to her mother's concerns, "Mum, don't be so silly worrying about the war, it's not on our front doorstep yet." The two then went to sleep. Later in the night, Ms. Cogdon returned to Pat's room. But she didn't have warm milk; she had an axe. And with that axe, Ms. Cogdon struck Pat twice in the head, killing her. As it turns out, Ms. Cogdon had previously seen ghosts in her own bedroom and said to them, "Well, you have come to take Pattie." And the night before she killed Pat, she wasn't tucking her into bed—she was brushing away spiders that she saw on Pat's face. On the night of the homicide, Ms. Cogdon dreamed that the Korean War was waging around them and that a soldier was on Pat's bed, attacking her. Ms. Cogdon's axe swings were taken in defense of her daughter. Ms. Cogdon's first memory after waking was of herself running to her sister's home, next door. When her sister opened the door, Ms. Cogdon fell into her sister's arms and exclaimed, "I think I've hurt Pattie." Ms. Cogdon was charged with murder. The testimony at trial revealed no disagreement between mother and daughter. On the contrary, Mr. Cogdon testified that his wife adored Pat. Ultimately, the jury acquitted Ms. Cogdon of the crime because she didn't act voluntarily; she was sleepwalking. In criminal law terms, there was no **actus reus**.[1]

ACTING LIKE A CRIMINAL: ACTUS REUS

Learning Objectives: Describe the two fundamental elements of a crime and the voluntariness requirement of actus reus. Identify two examples of involuntary acts under the Model Penal Code (MPC).

For hundreds of years, the law has held that there are two fundamental elements of a crime. The first is a criminal act, the *actus reus*, and the second is a guilty mind, or **mens rea**. In what you can

---

Actus reus: A voluntary physical movement—a muscle contraction—that is part of a crime. Some crimes do not require a physical act; the voluntary decision to not act satisfies the actus reus of a crime.

Mens rea: The mental aspect of criminality. The intention or knowledge part of a crime.

think of as a third element, the act and the guilty mind must happen together. This is referred to as **concurrence**. Sir William Blackstone, whom you learned about in Chapter 1, penned that

> an unwarrantable act without a vicious will is no crime at all. So that to constitute a crime against human laws, there must be, first, a vicious will; and, secondly, an unlawful act consequent upon such vicious will.[2]

The requirement of a guilty mind and voluntary act has a due process dimension; they reduce the likelihood of wrongful convictions. At the same time, they have a liberty dimension. They limit the authority of government to punish. Ultimately, the objective of criminal law is to prevent and punish harm. But harm isn't the only factor in the equation. The driver who accidentally hits and kills a small child who unpredictably darts into the road has caused great harm. But peoples around the world have excused this type of harm from punishment for thousands of years.

As you will hear many times in this book, there is an old Latin language legal phrase that expresses these elements: *Actus Non Facit Reum Nisi Mens Sit Rea.* This roughly translates to *an act isn't guilty unless the mind is guilty.* Many crimes have a fourth element that isn't exactly an act or state of mind; these are known as attendant circumstances. You will now explore these historic, basic elements. The first up in the queue is actus reus.

Acting Like A Criminal

Let's test your memory. What is the Model Penal Code (MPC)? If you don't recall, return to Chapter 1 to refresh. The MPC will be referred to many times in the upcoming chapters. As your first reference to it, the MPC has this to say about actus reus:

2.01 Requirement of Voluntary Act; Omission as Basis of Liability; Possession as an Act

1. A person is not guilty of an offense unless his liability is based on conduct which includes a voluntary act or the omission to perform an act of which he is physically capable.
2. The following are not voluntary acts within the meaning of this Section:
   a. a reflex or convulsion;
   b. a bodily movement during unconsciousness or sleep;
   c. conduct during hypnosis or resulting from hypnotic suggestion;
   d. a bodily movement that otherwise is not a product of the effort or determination of the actor, either conscious or habitual.
3. Liability for the commission of an offense may not be based on an omission unaccompanied by action unless:
   a. the omission is expressly made sufficient by the law defining the offense; or
   b. a duty to perform the omitted act is otherwise imposed by law.
4. Possession is an act, within the meaning of this Section, if the possessor knowingly procured or received the thing possessed or was aware of his control thereof for a sufficient period to have been able to terminate his possession.

Concurrence: The requirement that an act be the product of mens rea.

Before we dig into the specifics of the law, notice the style of writing. This is how "statutory" law is written. It is formal and highly structured. Don't be intimidated by it. Anytime the MPC, or other statutory language, is presented, it will be explained. Now, let's look at Section 2.01 of the MPC in greater detail.

The MPC uses the word "conduct," not "act." The two are synonyms in criminal law, and you will see both used in this text and in the case law. An act is something more than a thought; it is a muscle contraction. It is not a crime to spend hours a day imagining ways to hurt a former lover, to blow up a building, or to steal a neighbor's high-tech gaming computer. Thought doesn't satisfy the actus reus element.

Turning thought into speech is a more complicated matter. Speech, verbal or nonverbal, commonly involves muscle contractions of the mouth or hands. And a person can express themselves with other parts of the body as well. The belly dancer's abdominal muscles, a happy person's jump for joy, and even a frustrated person's middle finger extended upward when the other fingers are clenched are examples. Therefore, expression can be the actus reus of a crime. But there is a big limitation on the power of the state to punish speech—the First Amendment.

Recall from Chapter 2 that the free speech clause has been interpreted by SCOTUS to protect all forms of expression, not just the spoken word. And the First Amendment prohibits the state from punishing a person for the "content" or "viewpoint" of their expression. The state can't, for example, punish a person for suggesting that climate change is a hoax, advocating for a more socialist form of government, or for organizing people to protest in favor of greater accountability in policing. However, there are very narrowly drawn limits to free speech. As you learned in Chapter 2, expression that is likely to cause imminent lawlessness, defamation, and obscenity are not protected. You will learn later that speech uttered during the planning of a crime may be used to prove a crime. But the speech of conspirators is not enough for conviction; action to further the criminal objective beyond speech must be taken for there to be criminal liability.

So a thought is not an act, and expression is often protected from prosecution, even when it constitutes an act. Sometimes, even pure acts that hurt people don't create guilt. As you saw in the opening story, whether Ms. Cogdon took the swings of the axe wasn't in question. She did. But she wasn't guilty because her swings were involuntary. MPC 2.01(1) specifically requires the act (or omission, but we will discuss that shortly) to be voluntary. To be voluntary, an act must be the result of a conscious, free choice. The MPC provides examples of involuntary acts. Let's examine a few.

A convulsion is an involuntary and uncontrolled muscle contraction. An example is an epileptic seizure. Epilepsy is a disease that causes brain seizures and sometimes body convulsions. Consider a hypothetical case. Emil is unaware that he has epilepsy. He has his first seizure while driving a car. He convulses, loses control of his car, and hits several schoolchildren walking home from school. Four children are killed. As awful as the loss of four lives is, Emil is not criminally culpable because his act was involuntary. Let's change the facts. The same accident occurs, but Emil had been diagnosed with epilepsy several years earlier and experienced as many as 20 seizures a year. Does this change the outcome? This isn't a hypothetical; it happened. In the real case, Emil was found guilty of negligent homicide. He appealed his conviction on the grounds that his seizure was involuntary. But the court that heard his appeal decided that the act that formed the basis of the charge of negligent homicide wasn't Emil's loss of control of the car; it was his decision to drive the car in the first place.[3] This, the court found, was voluntary and negligent.

Reflexive conduct is also listed as involuntary under the MPC. Reflex is an involuntary, automatic muscle contraction. You know reflex—it happens when a doctor hits a patient's knee with that little hammer. The patient who reflexively kicks the doctor after being hit in the knee with the hammer has not committed the crime of battery.

Other examples of involuntary conduct under the MPA are unconsciousness and sleep. Although rare, Ms. Cogdon isn't the only person who has injured or killed another or caused property damage while sleepwalking. In the film *Sleepwalk With Me,* comedian Mike Birbiglia tells his true story of being a sleepwalker. On several occasions, Birbiglia injured himself while acting out his dreams. The most dramatic episode occurred when he was on tour. In the middle of the night, he dreamed that a guided missile was heading for his hotel room. He consulted the military personnel around him, and they told him that the missile was specifically targeting him. With that information, he decided to end his life by jumping out of his window. Unfortunately, the window was closed, and his room was on the second floor. In his pajamas, Birbiglia jumped through the glass, fell two stories while screaming, hit the ground, got up, and began running.

PHOTO 3.1 Comedian Mike Birbiglia has caused property damage while sleepwalking.

Photo by Bryan Smith/ZUMA Press/Alamy Stock Photo

Eventually, he woke, returned to the hotel, and sought medical attention. To minimize the possibility that he will hurt himself in the future, he goes to bed in a sleeping bag that closes to his face, wears mittens, and takes sedatives. One author, citing other research, found that sleepwalking has been an accepted defense for at least 700 years.[4]

A person is also not criminally liable for acts taken while under hypnosis. So the audience member who is hypnotized and instructed by the hypnotist to punch holes in the wall of the theater is not responsible for the punching or its consequences. However, as with the epilepsy case discussed a moment ago, the facts can be changed to reach a different conclusion. If, before hypnotized, the audience member watched as two earlier audience members were hypnotized and instructed to damage property, then the third audience member's consent to be hypnotized forms the actus reus of the crime of destruction of property.

TABLE 3.1 ■ Summary of Actus Reus		
What Is in Question?	*Common Law*	*MPC/Modern Statutes*
Reflexes, convulsions	Not an act	Not an act
Thoughts, beliefs	Not an act	Not an act
Speech, expression	An act	An act, but often protected by First Amendment
Physical status	Not an act	Not an act
Failing to act (omission)	Not an act	Not an act unless explicitly required (e.g., duty by relationship, contract, statute, assumption, creating danger)

Not Acting Like a Criminal

You have learned that the general rule is that there must be an act for there to be a crime. With the old Common Law, this rule was absolute. It even applied to situations where it is possible to rescue people from danger. As was remarked over a hundred years ago, "Thou shalt not kill but needst not strive, officiously, to keep another alive."[5] Yes, you read that right. The default rule is that people have no legal obligation to help one another. You can ignore your drowning neighbor's pleas for help and close your door on a woman who is fleeing an attacker—immoral, yes; criminal, no.

But there are exceptions to this rule. By the way, get used to hearing about exceptions; there are always exceptions in law, and often, there are exceptions to the exceptions! Returning to actus reus, a crime that doesn't require an act is known as a **crime of omission**. A crime of omission is the opposite of the general rule: Failure to act is a crime. Because omission is an exception, the law must affirmatively impose a duty to act. A duty to act can be established by special relationship, creating danger, contract, and statute. See Table 3.1 for a summary of actus reus.

Duty by Special Relationship

Many crimes of omission fall into the category of special relationship. Familial and professional relationships often create a duty of care or to rescue another person. While you may ignore your drowning neighbor's pleas for help, the law demands that you attempt to save your drowning child. Some states extend the duty to protect children further than to parents and guardians; California explains it like this:

a. Any person who, under circumstances or conditions likely to produce great bodily harm or death, willfully causes or permits any child to suffer, or inflicts thereon

---

Crime of omission: A crime that involves a failure to act. The actus reus is omitted from the standard requirement of actus reus, mens rea, and concurrence for there to be a crime.

unjustifiable physical pain or mental suffering, or having the care or custody of any child, willfully causes or permits the person or health of that child to be injured, or willfully causes or permits that child to be placed in a situation where his or her person or health is endangered, shall be punished by imprisonment in a county jail not exceeding one year, or in the state prison for two, four, or six years.

b. Any person who, under circumstances or conditions other than those likely to produce great bodily harm or death, willfully causes or permits any child to suffer, or inflicts thereon unjustifiable physical pain or mental suffering, or having the care or custody of any child, willfully causes or permits the person or health of that child to be injured, or willfully causes or permits that child to be placed in a situation where his or her person or health may be endangered, is guilty of a misdemeanor.[6]

As you can see, California's law applies to everyone, and it contains both a felony violation, which applies to situations where a child is at risk of great bodily harm or death, and a misdemeanor violation, which applies when there is less risk. Most states have other laws that impose duties to protect children, such as from sexual assault.

Physicians, psychologists, and other medical care professionals have a duty to protect their patients from the harms related to the service they provide. Notice the reference to "the service they provide." A surgeon must attempt to save the life of a patient who is in distress during surgery. However, the same surgeon doesn't have to jump into a pool to save a patient who is drowning during recreational swimming.

Creating Duty by Creating Danger

The first example of a duty to act arises when a person puts someone at risk. For example, assume John stops his car in the middle of the road, near a curve, to look at the ocean. At that moment, Janice drives around the bend, swerves to avoid hitting John's car, and strikes a tree. A branch of the tree breaks through her window and impales her in the chest, leaving her bleeding, too weak to get out of the car, and unable to reach her cell phone. Normally, John wouldn't have a responsibility to rescue Janice. But because he created Janice's predicament, he has a *duty* to attempt to rescue her. How much he must do to help her varies between the states. In many, a 911 call is enough. In others, he may be expected to do more. However, no law demands that a person risk their own life to rescue another.

A tragic crime of omission that involved modern technology and bullying is found in *Commonwealth v. Carter.* Conrad Roy and Michelle Carter met in 2012, became romantically involved, and because they lived over 30 miles from one another, maintained what was largely a distance relationship. They frequently communicated by text and phone. Physically abused at home, Roy suffered from depression. He attempted suicide in 2012 at the age of 17. Between 2012 and 2014, Carter repeatedly encouraged Roy to get psychological help. He did as she recommended and was prescribed an antidepressant that was known to cause suicidal thoughts in some people. On July 13, 2014, Roy parked his truck in a Kmart parking lot and killed himself by carbon monoxide poisoning. Text and phone records showed that in spite of her efforts to help Roy for nearly 2 years, Carter had encouraged him to commit suicide in the weeks before and on the day of his suicide. She went so far as to encourage him to return to the truck, which was filled with carbon monoxide, after he began to have second thoughts. Subsequent to his death, Carter told a friend that she "helped ease him into it... his death is my fault." At the age of 17, Carter was charged, waived a jury trial, and was convicted by the trial judge of involuntary manslaughter.

Although the trial judge didn't issue a written decision, he emphasized the special relationship that the two shared and Roy's fragile emotional state in explaining the conviction. But he didn't find that she had a duty to protect him because of their special relationship. Instead, he found that she created the risk to his life when she encouraged him to return to the truck.[7] The case received considerable attention because it was the first manslaughter conviction for bullying and because it represented a significant departure in law. Whether this decision will expand the law on crimes of omission remains to be seen.

Duty by Contract

A third manner in which duty is created is by contract. A contract, you may recall, is an agreement between two parties. Employment is a form of contract. The employer agrees to pay a salary in exchange for the labor of the employee. In some circumstances, this relationship can create a duty that can be enforced by criminal law. Duty by contract can overlap with duty by special relationship. To illustrate, consider a lifeguard who makes no effort to save a drowning swimmer or a caretaker who causes the death of a ward by failing to administer needed medicine. Both are contractually obligated to act, and both are special relationships. For this reason, both the lifeguard and caretaker are accountable in criminal (and civil) law.

Assumption of Duty

Mitchel and Omar, work colleagues, are with their children at a secluded area of beach in Florida. Mitchel's child is 4 years old, and Omar's child is 5 years old. They position their chairs next to each other. The two have discussed how both of their children need to learn to swim. After an hour, Omar expresses a need to use the restroom and reaches for his daughter's hand. Mitchel says, "It is OK, I will keep an eye on her. You go ahead." While Omar is in the restroom, his daughter wanders close the water's edge, is caught up in a wave, and drowns. Mitchel had fallen fast asleep. Did Mitchel have a legal duty to save the child? There is no legally binding contract between the two men, and one of the traditionally recognized special relationships doesn't exist. A different doctrine, assumption of duty, fills in the gap in this case. A person who voluntarily assumes the legal duty of another is held to the same standard as the person who originally held the duty.

Duty by Statute

State legislatures and Congress often impose duties to act. Again, like the other forms of duty, this is often done to protect the innocent and vulnerable. Today, statutes impose duties on many people whose only relationship to the victim is knowledge of a crime. Mandatory reporting of child abuse and child neglect is common in the states. These statutes don't demand intervention; they criminalize not contacting the authorities. Typically, professionals who come into contact with children, such as physicians, nurses, police officers, emergency medical technicians, teachers, and school administrators, are required to report suspected child abuse or neglect.

Generally, there is no duty to report crime. But some states require witnesses of felonies to report them to police. And Ohio has the broadest mandatory reporting of crime statute in the United States:

29 Ohio Revised Code sec. 2921.22(A)(1)

[N]o person, knowing that a felony has been or is being committed, shall knowingly fail to report such information to law enforcement authorities.

Other situations where reporting is required include registering related to punishment (e.g., as a sex offender); the discovery of human remains; tax returns; spills of hazardous waste; and knowledge of exotic wild animals running freely.

Possessing Like a Criminal

The laws of all of the states and the federal government prohibit the possession of certain items. The possession of illegal drugs, or as they are referred to in the law, controlled substances, is a well known possession crime. Possession is discussed in this section of the book because possession, as opposed to receiving, is passive; it is a physical state, not an act.

The Model Penal Code, Section 201(4) states that "possession is an act, within the meaning of this Section, if the possessor knowingly procured or received the thing possessed or was aware of his control thereof for a sufficient period to have been able to terminate his possession." This definition includes both actual and constructive possession. The law often uses constructs. A **construct** is a legal fiction that is used to connect a gap between reality and legal doctrine. As defined by the MPC, a person has constructive possession when she is aware of the presence of an item within her control, even though she wasn't responsible for placing the item in the space and she doesn't exercise physical control over it. These principles can be seen in the following scenarios:

- Jamal borrows Nell's car. Two days after he returns it, she discovers a transparent bag full of what she believes may be cocaine in the trunk. If Nell doesn't remove it immediately, she will be guilty of possession of a controlled substance, even though she didn't take physical possession of it or place it in the trunk. Let's say, however, that she calls her attorney, who advises her to take it to the police. Nell immediately drives to the nearest police station with the bag in her passenger seat. In her haste to rid herself of the contraband, Nell speeds while en route to the police station. Deputy Dooright pulls her over for speeding, approaches her car, and sees the bag. He immediately identifies it as cocaine and arrests Nell for possession. In this case, Nell didn't possess the contraband long enough to terminate possession, so she is not guilty of possession.

- Continuing with this hypothetical, assume Nell opens her trunk and sees a tennis bag. It is zipped closed but the handle of a tennis racquet can be seen extending out from the racquet pocket. She knows Jamal plays on a club team and assumed he forgot to remove

---

Legal construct: A fiction that is used to connect reality with legal doctrine; an adjustment to the law through a logical presumption, inference, or imputation.

the bag. She closes the trunk, forgets about the bag, and is pulled over the next day for speeding. The officers who pulled her over have a K-9 in their car. Deputy Dooright instructs his partner to walk the dog around Nell's car while he writes her ticket. The dog alerts to contraband, and believing there is nothing to find, Nell consents to a search of the trunk and bag. The cocaine is found, and she is charged with possession. In this case, time could be an issue again. But she has a better defense; she lacked the mens rea required for possession. She didn't know that she was in control of the drugs. You will learn more about the mens rea later in this chapter.

In addition to controlled substances, statutory law commonly forbids possession of burglary tools, specified hazardous substances, firearms and other weapons (subject to Second Amendment limitations), stolen property, open containers of liquor in vehicles, and obscenity and child pornography.

It's OK to Be Me

Most aspects of a person's identity, state of being, and status are not acts. Imagine a person standing perfectly still. No muscle contraction is necessary for that person to be Asian, Black, white, or brown; or to be tall or short; or to have blonde, brown, black, or red hair. Status is similar to an involuntary reflex, for purposes of actus reus.

Regardless, states have enacted laws that appear to regulate status. As you saw earlier, states can omit the actus reus element from a crime. This is OK in the elements of a crime world—except there is another issue: the Constitution. The First Amendment's protection of religion prohibits laws that make it illegal to be of a religion or to be of no religion. The equal protection clause adds race, national origin, and sex to protected statuses. This is also true of physical and mental illness and disease.

The Eighth Amendment's ban on cruel and unusual punishments has also been relied upon to strike down status offenses. The landmark case in this area of law is *Robinson v. California*, where SCOTUS invalidated a California law that criminalized the condition of being a drug addict.

DIGGING DEEPER 3.1

Can a state punish a person for being addicted to drugs?

Case: *Robinson v. California*
Court: Supreme Court of the United States.   Citation: 370 U.S. 660
Year: 1962
Justice Stewart delivered the opinion of the Court.

A California statute makes it a criminal offense for a person to "be addicted to the use of narcotics.". . .

The appellant was convicted after a jury trial in the Municipal Court of Los Angeles. The evidence against him was given by two Los Angeles police officers. Officer Brown testified that he had had occasion to examine the appellant's arms one evening on a street in Los Angeles some four months before the trial. The officer testified that at that time he had observed "scar tissue and discoloration on the inside" of the appellant's right arm, and "what appeared to be numerous needle marks and a scab which was approximately three inches below the crook of the elbow" on the appellant's left arm. The officer also testified that the appellant, under questioning, had admitted to the occasional use of narcotics.

Officer Lindquist testified that he had examined the appellant the following morning in the Central Jail in Los Angeles. The officer stated that at that time, he had observed discolorations and scabs on the appellant's arms, and he identified photographs which had been taken of the appellant's arms shortly after his arrest the night before. Based upon more than ten years of experience as a member of the Narcotic Division of the Los Angeles Police Department, the witness gave his opinion that "these marks and the discoloration were the result of the injection of hypodermic needles into the tissue into the vein that was not sterile." He stated that the scabs were several days old at the time of his examination, and that the appellant was neither under the influence of narcotics nor suffering withdrawal symptoms at the time he saw him. This witness also testified that the appellant had admitted using narcotics in the past.

The appellant testified on his own behalf, denying the alleged conversations with the police officers and denying that he had ever used narcotics or been addicted to their use. He explained the marks on his arms as resulting from an allergic condition contracted during his military service. His testimony was corroborated by two witnesses.

The trial judge instructed the jury that the statute made it a misdemeanor for a person

> either to use narcotics or to be addicted to the use of narcotics. . . .That portion of the statute referring to the "use" of narcotics is based upon the "act" of using. That portion of the statute referring to "addicted to the use" of narcotics is based upon a condition or status. They are not identical. . . . To be addicted to the use of narcotics is said to be a status or condition, and not an act. It is a continuing offense, and differs from most other offenses in the fact that [it] is chronic, rather than acute; that it continues after it is complete, and subjects the offender to arrest at any time before he reforms. The existence of such a chronic condition may be ascertained from a single examination if the characteristic reactions of that condition be found present.

The judge further instructed the jury that the appellant could be convicted under a general verdict if the jury agreed either that he was of the "status" or had committed the "act" denounced by the statute. . . .

The broad power of a State to regulate the narcotic drugs traffic within its borders is not here in issue. . . .

Such regulation, it can be assumed, could take a variety of valid forms. A State might impose criminal sanctions, for example, against the unauthorized manufacture, prescription, sale, purchase, or possession of narcotics within its borders. In the interest of discouraging the violation of such laws, or in the interest of the general health or welfare of its inhabitants, a State might establish a program of compulsory treatment for those addicted to narcotics. Such a program of treatment might require periods of involuntary confinement. And penal sanctions might be imposed for failure to comply with established compulsory treatment procedures. *Cf. Jacobson v. Massachusetts.* Or a State might choose to attack the evils of narcotics traffic on broader fronts also—through public health education, for example, or by efforts to ameliorate the economic and social conditions under which those evils might be thought to flourish. In short, the range of valid choices which a State might make in this area is undoubtedly a wide one, and the wisdom of any particular choice within the allowable spectrum is not for us to decide. . . .

This statute, therefore, is not one which punishes a person for the use of narcotics, their purchase, sale, possession, or for antisocial or disorderly behavior resulting from their administration. It is not a law which even purports to provide or require medical treatment. Rather, we deal with a statute which makes the "status" of narcotic addiction a criminal offense. . . .

It is unlikely that any State at this moment in history would attempt to make it a criminal offense for a person to be mentally ill, or a leper, or to be afflicted with a venereal disease. A State might determine that the general health and welfare require that the victims of these and other human afflictions be dealt with by compulsory treatment, involving quarantine, confinement, or sequestration. But, in the light of contemporary human knowledge, a law which made a criminal offense of such a disease would doubtless be universally thought to be an infliction of cruel and unusual punishment in violation of the Eighth and Fourteenth Amendments. *See Francis v. Resweber.*

We cannot but consider the statute before us as of the same category. In this Court, counsel for the State recognized that narcotic addiction is an illness. Indeed, it is apparently an illness which may be contracted innocently or involuntarily. We hold that a state law which imprisons a person thus afflicted as a criminal, even though he has never touched any narcotic drug within the State or been guilty of any irregular behavior there, inflicts a cruel and unusual punishment in violation of the Fourteenth Amendment.

You may recall from an earlier discussion that juveniles may be adjudicated for both crimes and so-called status offenses. Being a truant from school or a runaway are juvenile status offenses. Because juvenile proceedings are intended to rehabilitate, not punish, these statuses may be the basis for a juvenile offender finding.

QUESTIONS AND APPLICATIONS

1. Grace sneaks up on Raygen while she is sleeping and screams, "Surprise!" Raygen simultaneously opens her eyes, screams in fear, and punches Grace in the nose. Has Raygen committed a battery? Explain your answer.

Are the following acts crimes of omission? Explain your answers.

1. Reginald is sleeping. He hears a woman scream for help from the alley beneath his bedroom window. He goes to the window and hears what sounds like a muffled voice and people struggling. He returns to bed and goes to sleep. He learns in the morning that a woman was sexually assaulted and murdered. Was Reginald's choice to not call the police or to help in some other way a crime of omission?
2. Perry Police Officer arrests Robert for robbery. Robert is known to Perry as a member of a street gang, the Puffs. He handcuffs Robert and places him in the back seat of his police cruiser. As he is taking a witness statement, he notices that a man with the insignia and tattoos of a rival gang of the Puffs approaches his police cruiser. He watches as the man yells at, spits on, and strikes Robert in the face several times and then runs away. Perry makes no effort to stop the man from assaulting Robert or to arrest him. Has Perry committed a crime of omission?

THINKING LIKE A CRIMINAL: *MENS REA*

Learning Objectives: Define and compare types of intent and the four states of mind recognized by the MPC, strict liability, and vicarious liability.

Now that you are an expert in the physical element of the crime, it is time to explore the mental element. One of your author's favorite legal quotes is from the preeminent SCOTUS justice, Oliver Wendell Holmes. He served on the court from 1902 to 1932. He wrote that

> [e]ven a dog distinguishes between being stumbled over and being kicked.[8]

In 11 words, Justice Holmes expressed a complex and fundamental principle—and in a very relatable way, particularly for dog lovers. The distinction between intentional and unintentional harm is so basic, so natural, that it transcends humanity. It is often said there are two natural responses to threat: fight or flight. The dog doesn't flee or bite when stumbled over because it is not threatened.

The law has distinguished between the kick and stumble for thousands of years. The oldest laws known to humanity, including the famous Code of Hammurabi which dates back to about 1750 B.C.E., punished unintentional harm less harshly than intentional harm. Often referred to as the "guilty mind," mens rea refers to the state of mind that is required to prove a crime. As you will learn shortly, a guilty mind is not always required in modern criminal law.

Old School

Judges in the old Common Law required both an act and mens rea for criminality. These elements were used to ensure guilt and to limit the power of the government. This was very important in the early years of the Common Law because there was only one punishment for crime: death. A person either committed murder and was executed or not.

Over time, however, judges began to "grade" crimes, or distinguish them by the defendant's state of mind and the severity of the harm. This resulted in crimes of specific intent, general intent, constructed intent, and transferred intent. If a defendant *intends to cause the result* (the harm the law is addressing) of an act, there is specific intent. If a defendant *intended to act, but not to cause the result*, there is general intent. Typically, general intent crimes are punished less than their specific intent counterparts. These scenarios illustrate the difference:

- Francine is involved in a protest. She is carrying a pistol in a holster. A counterprotestor approaches her and says, "You know you are wrong about this; you are exaggerating the problem. In fact, you *are* the problem. Because of people like you, our community

---

Specific intent: Purposely acting with the intention of causing a specific outcome (harm).

General intent: Purposefully causing an act, but not the outcome (harm) of the act.

Constructive intent: A legal fiction; an inference. Proof of intent from the act itself, context, or other facts.

Transferred intent: A legal fiction. If the harm that a defendant specifically intends to inflict on a person or object falls to another, the defendant's specific intent applies to the unintended victim.

is at war with itself." Francine becomes angry, removes the gun from its holster, takes aim at the counterprotestor's chest, and screams, "One more word, dirtbag, and you are d-e-a-d, dead!" The counterprotestor replies, "Really, you are going to—" and before he could finish the sentence, Francine pulls the trigger, killing the individual. It is reasonable to conclude from her statement and conduct that Francine had specific intent to cause the outcome (the death of the counterprotestor). Therefore, she is guilty of a specific intent crime.

- Assume the same facts, until the point when Francine replies to the counterprotestor. In this scenario, Francine becomes angry, removes the gun from its holster, holds it in the palm of her hand, no finger on the trigger, and screams, "One more word, dirtbag, and I am going to kick your b-u-t-t, butt!" The counterprotestor replies, "Really, you are going to—" and before he could finish the sentence, Francine swings and strikes the counterprotestor's head with the gun. When the gun hits his head, it discharges, killing the counterprotestor. It is reasonable to conclude from her statement and conduct that Francine intended the act that caused the harm (striking the victim with the gun). But is equally reasonable to conclude that she didn't intend the outcome (for the gun to discharge and kill the victim), so Francine is guilty of a general intent homicide, but not a specific intent homicide.

Don't fret about justice for our dead counterprotestor. Francine can be punished in both cases. But she would likely be punished less for the general intent crime. There is more to come about the mens rea of homicide in a future chapter.

The likelihood of success of a defendant's method to cause harm is immaterial to mens rea. Imagine that Randy is hiking in a mountainous park. While standing on a cliff, he sees his former lover, Craig. The relationship ended on bad terms a month before, and Randy, who is angry about Craig's infidelity, decided to take advantage of the opportunity to kill him. He had prayed for Craig's death every day since their breakup. Although he didn't think it would work, he pushed a large bolder off the cliff in the direction of Craig. As it rolled, he whispered to himself, "Please, please, rid the earth of that cruel man." Much to his surprise, the boulder hit a rock, propelling it into the air, ultimately falling on Craig. He is immediately killed. Although the probability of the boulder striking Craig was very small, Randy possessed the intent to cause Craig's death using the boulder. Therefore, he committed a specific intent homicide.

Scienter exists when a person is in possession of specific knowledge at the time of the act. For example, to prove that a defendant has committed "the purposeful battery against a legally authorized law enforcement officer who is performing the duties of office," two mens rea must be proved. The first is the mens rea of battery—the intent to harmfully touch another person. The second is a scienter requirement—specific knowledge that the touched individual is a "legally authorized law enforcement officer who is performing the duties of the office." To be guilty of passing counterfeit money requires knowledge that the money is fake, and the crime of possessing stolen property requires knowledge of the property's stolen character.

Scienter: A form of specific intent; having specific knowledge.

Proving specific intent can be difficult. In the occasional case, the state may have direct evidence (e.g., a defendant's confession). Because this rarely occurs, specific intent can also be proved constructively. Remember, constructs are fictions. In this case, intent is constructed through a factual inference rather than direct evidence. In fact, prosecutors rarely have direct evidence of intent. Instead, they prove intext through the actus reus itself, context, and other facts. Inferences must be reasonable and supported by the facts. Some courts have said that an inference must reflect a *natural and probable consequence* of the actus reus.

- Example of direct evidence of intent: In a text, Kaili tells Linda that she has two cell phones that were given to her by a friend who stole them from work. She also wrote, "I don't need 2. Will sell 1 for $100." Linda reports the crime to police, provides them with the texts, and Kaili is charged with possession of stolen property, a specific intent crime. Kaili's text is direct evidence of her knowledge of the stolen character of the phones.

- Example of inference of specific intent: In a text, Kaili tells Linda that she has a box of cell phones to sell at $100 each. She also writes, "They are worth $500. Great deal. Want to get rid of them fast." Linda agrees, meets Kaili for the purchase, and is handed a cell phone that is in its original packaging with a Best Buy price sticker on it. Feeling uncomfortable, Linda doesn't open the box and turns the phone over to the police. Kaili is charged with possession of stolen property, a specific intent crime. Although the state has no direct evidence of Kaili's knowledge of the cell phone's stolen character, it can be reasonably inferred by her act of attempting to sell them quickly, far below market value, and by the packaging and price sticker.

Finally, specific intent can be transferred. Well, it isn't like a bus pass, but it can move from one person or object to another. This is another legal fiction. Transferred intent occurs when a defendant intends to harm one person, or property, but injures another person, or property, instead. Let's return to our example of battery on a police officer:

- Officer Dooright responds to a report of violence on Fremont Street in Las Vegas, Nevada. Officer Dooright arrives at a chaotic scene of fighting and screaming. At the center of the melee are two women, Candy and Carmine. Carmine is wielding a knife. The officer instructs them to back away from one another. As instructed, Candy moves away, but Carmine pursues and thrusts the knife at her. Carmine missed her aim and pushes the knife into Officer Dooright's abdomen. Carmine's intent to cause serious common bodily harm, an element of aggravated battery, transfers from Candy to Officer Dooright. So Carmine is guilty of aggravated battery, even though she intended to hurt Candy, not the officer.

There are limitations to transferring intent. First, the harm that befalls the victim must be similar to the defendant's original intended harm. For example, Bob shoots his gun at the propane tank on Patrick's grill, hoping to cause it to explode. He has the specific intent of causing the destruction of property. Unknown to him, Patrick is standing nearby. Bob shoots and hits the tank, but instead of piercing it, the bullet ricochets and kills Patrick. Although Bob had specific intent to cause harm, it is too different from the resulting harm for the intent to transfer. However, as you will learn later, Bob is still guilty of a crime. But he is guilty of a lesser form of homicide than intentional murder.

Another limitation on criminal liability through transfer of mens rea is that a defendant gets to transfer defenses as well. So if Bob shoots at Patrick in self-defense, but misses and kills an innocent bystander, Bob is entitled to use self-defense against a prosecution for killing the bystander.

New School

The law of mens rea has changed considerably since the early Common Law. The Industrial Revolution of the 1800s brought new risks to workers, who were crowded into factories with few safeguards and few workplace safety laws. It was common for employees to be seriously injured and killed on the job. Outside of the factory, employees crowded into cities with poor sanitation and few fire, construction, or legal protections. The criminal law of the period, specifically the law of mens rea, made prosecution of factory owners, landlords, and others who didn't possess the intent to injure people (but who showed little regard for their safety) very difficult. So the criminal law changed. Today, some crimes require less than specific or general intent. You will read about these states of mind later in this chapter.

Model Penal Code and Mens Rea

State and federal criminal laws were wildly different in their treatment of mens rea for most of U.S. history. Literally, hundreds of words were used to describe various states of mind. Malice, intentional, willful, evil, deliberate, knowing, and vicious are but a few examples. As you read before, one of the objectives of the MPC was to bring consistency and coherence to American criminal law. One aspect of the MPC that has been more widely adopted has been the MPC's approach to mens rea. Section 2.02 identifies four states of mind: purpose, knowing, reckless, and negligent. These are listed in the order of mental culpability. Purpose reflects the guiltiest mind; negligence, the least guilty.

Being *purposeful* is the MPC's closest mental state to the Common Law's specific intent. To act with purpose, a defendant must desire to cause the result. To act *knowingly*, a defendant

---

Purpose: The Model Penal Code's highest level of mens rea; similar to the Common Law's strict liability. A defendant acts with purpose when there is a desire to cause the result.

Knowing: The second-highest form of mens rea under the Model Penal Code. A defendant knowingly acts when the result of an act is "practically certain."

Reckless: A defendant acts with indifference to consequences and indifference to the safety and rights of others. Recklessness involves less care than ordinary negligence.

Negligence: A defendant acts negligently when the resulting harm or material element of a crime occurs because the defendant has taken a substantial and unjustifiable risk, even if the risk is not perceived, so long as the risk involves a gross deviation from the standard of conduct that a law-abiding person would observe.

must be "practically certain" that his act will cause the result. But unlike acting with purpose, the defendant who acts knowingly doesn't desire to cause the result. Practical certainty has been defined to mean very likely, a high probability.

- Ken and Abbie are sitting in a car in a crowded public park. Ken has a rifle. He points it and remarks that he could shoot and kill the person who was standing the furthest away from them. Abbie challenges him to do it. Ken takes aim and pulls the trigger, striking and killing his intended victim. Ken acted with purpose.

- Ken and Abbie are sitting in a car in a crowded public park. Ken has a rifle. He points it and remarks that he could shoot through the crowd without hitting anyone, striking a bottle that is sitting on a picnic table. Abbie challenges him to do it. Ken takes aim, pulls the trigger, striking and killing a person who is throwing a Frisbee with his son. Ken has acted knowingly. He didn't intend to shoot or kill his victim. In fact, his goal was to not shoot and kill his victim. Regardless of his objective, killing the victim was practically certain.

In late 2018, Dr. Dan Gladish, a Miami University botany professor and director of a university greenhouse known as The Conservatory, and that facility's manager received a surprise visit by university police officers and special agents of the federal Drug Enforcement Administration (DEA). The officers were there to investigate a report that among the nearly 1,000 species of plants in The Conservatory was the obscure *Tabernanthe iboga*; iboga, as it is commonly known, is native to western Africa. Because of its hallucinogenic effects, the bark of iboga is used in religious and cultural practices.

The seeds to the plant were donated to The Conservatory by Dr. John Cinnamon, an MU anthropologist who studied religion in West Africa, over a decade before the DEA and police came calling. Unknown to the men, ibogaine, the compound that can be extracted from the plant's bark, is illegal under the federal Controlled Substances Act (CSA) and its counterpart Ohio statute. Consequently, the university immediately suspended the two professors and began disciplinary proceedings against them, as well as the manager of the facility. The three had never been disciplined before, had no history of drug offenses, and it was never alleged that they intended to process the root into ibogaine or to sell the plants. The plant was included in the collection because it was interesting, both culturally and botanically.[9] To further complicate the case, the plant isn't mentioned in the CSA, but it is included in the regulation implementing the statute, as a trade name for ibogaine. Whether this means the plant is a controlled substance, like ibogaine, is unclear.

Neither the police nor the DEA chose to pursue criminal charges against anyone involved. Had a prosecution been pursued, one of many legal challenges the prosecutors would have faced was proving mens rea. In a similar case involving an exotic plant, *United States v. Caseer*, the Sixth Circuit Court of Appeals reversed a conviction because prosecutors failed to prove that Caseer knowingly possessed a controlled substance. The important fact in this case was that the substance was exotic. Presumably, you know cocaine is illegal, regardless of whether you have ever seen, used, or handled it. But do you know about khat?

DIGGING DEEPER 3.2

Can a person be expected to know the chemical composition of plants he imports?

Case: *United States v. Caseer*
Court: Sixth Circuit Court of Appeals.   Citation: 399 F.3d 828
Year: 2005
Karen Nelson Moore, Judge, delivered the opinion of the court.

For centuries, persons in East African and Arabian Peninsular countries such as Somalia, Kenya, and Yemen have chewed or made tea from the stems of the native khat shrub (*Catha edulis*), which is known to have stimulant properties. Khat is often consumed in social settings, and many men in the East African/Arabian Peninsular region use khat. Khat is legal in many parts of East Africa, the Middle East, and Europe; however, khat is illegal in the United States because it contains cathinone, a Schedule I controlled substance, and cathine, a Schedule IV controlled substance. . . .

At the time of his trial in 2001, Daahir Caseer had lived in the United States for approximately three years, having spent the first sixteen years of his life in Somalia and seven years in Kenya. The events in question began in the spring of 2000, when Caseer approached John Eldridge, a bookkeeper at the Nashville, Tennessee, taxicab company where Caseer worked, about the possibility of Eldridge traveling to Amsterdam, the Netherlands, to transport about fifty pieces of khat to the United States. Caseer explained to Eldridge that he could not make the trip himself because of visa issues. Caseer assured Eldridge that khat was an agricultural product, and, at worst, customs might confiscate the khat and assess a fine. At trial, Eldridge testified that taxicab drivers in Nashville (80% to 90% of whom he believed to be of Somali or East African descent) frequently chewed khat and that, from his observations, khat was no stronger than caffeine.

Eldridge agreed to go to Amsterdam along with his girlfriend, Shannon Adams. . . .

Eldridge and Adams returned to the United States on June 5, 2000, landing at the airport in Detroit, Michigan. A drug-detection dog at the Detroit airport alerted on one of the bags filled with khat, and a DEA agent approached Eldridge and Adams. The pair agreed to cooperate with the investigation, and Eldridge placed a recorded telephone call to Caseer informing him that he had arrived and had cleared customs. At trial, Eldridge testified that during the telephone call, he complained about the amount of khat being greater than Caseer had indicated and reiterated his understanding that Caseer would pay his travel and related expenses. Caseer told Eldridge to trust him and that Eldridge did not need to discuss the matter with anyone else. Eldridge also testified that he met with Caseer after returning to Nashville and that Caseer told him they had not done anything illegal and would not be prosecuted, that he would take care of it, and that Eldridge should just stay quiet and not say anything about Caseer's involvement.

Agent Panning then traveled to Nashville and arrested Caseer. During questioning, Caseer admitted knowing Eldridge, Adams, and Awale. Caseer initially stated that Eldridge had purchased the airplane tickets; however, Caseer later said that a Hussein Abugar had made the purchase. At trial, Caseer stated that he may have lied to Agent Panning, but that he only did so because he was shaky and scared. . . .

Eldridge, Adams, and Caseer were indicted on two counts: (1) conspiracy to import cathinone; and (2) importation of cathinone, and aiding and abetting the importation of cathinone. Eldridge agreed to testify against Caseer and pleaded guilty to misdemeanor possession of cathinone pursuant to a plea agreement recommending six months' probation. Caseer waived his right to trial by jury and was tried before a district judge for the Eastern District of Michigan.

Cathinone was not listed in the original Controlled Substances Act schedules but was added by agency rule as a Schedule I controlled substance in 1993:

Stimulants. Unless specifically excepted or unless listed in another schedule, any material, compound, mixture, or preparation which contains any quantity of the following substances having a stimulant effect on the central nervous system, including its salts, isomers, and salts of isomers:

* * *

(3) Cathinone. . . 1235 Some trade or other names: 2-amino-1-phenyl-1-propanone, alphaaminopropiophenone, 2-aminopropiophenone, and norephedrone

Although [the applicable federal regulation] makes clear that cathinone is a controlled substance, neither the U.S. Code nor the Code of Federal Regulations controlled substances schedules refers to the plant from which cathinone is derived, *Catha edulis*, commonly known as "khat." [The Court then detailed examples where other chemicals are listed, along with the names of the plants from which the chemicals are extracted.] . . .

However, the Supplementary Information published in the Federal Register along with the text of the rule adding cathinone as a Schedule I substance does explain the connection between khat and cathinone. "Cathinone is the major psychoactive component of the plant Catha edulis (khat). The young leaves of khat are chewed for a stimulant effect. Enactment of this rule results in the placement of any material which contains cathinone into Schedule I. When khat contains cathinone, khat is a Schedule I substance. During either the maturation or the decomposition of the plant material, cathinone is converted to cathine, a Schedule IV substance."

[The court then addressed Caseer's assertion that the listing was unconstitutionally vague and, therefore, violative of due process. The court rejected the vagueness argument because the Controlled Substances Act included a mens rea requirement, *knowing*, that when applied, had the effect of narrowing the scope of the Act. The court then turned its attention to Caseer's mens rea claim.]

Here, the term "cathinone" is sufficiently obscure that persons of ordinary intelligence reading the controlled substances schedules probably would not discern that possession of khat containing cathinone and/or cathine constitutes possession of a controlled substance. Persons seeking clarification of [the regulation] would be unaided by many mainstream dictionaries, as they contain no definitions for "cathinone" and make no reference to the chemical in their definitions of "khat." . . .

[T]he district court found that Caseer was "aware of the stimulant effect of khat" based on Caseer's trial testimony that "khat is a stimulant and gives energy like tea or coffee." Although actual knowledge that a substance is controlled might in some cases be inferred from the physical effects caused by the substance, in this case, the stimulant effect of khat is too mild to permit a reasonable inference that Caseer knew that khat contained a controlled substance. The district court's opinion indicates that Caseer knew only that khat had a mild stimulant effect and indeed seems to suggest that chewing khat is the Somali equivalent of drinking coffee or tea in the United States. The seeming ubiquity of coffee houses in the United States attests to the fact that consuming products with stimulating effects is common custom in the United States, and the average American coffee drinker most likely does not pause to consider while drinking his or her morning "cup of Joe" whether he or she may be subject to criminal sanction for possession of a controlled substance. . . .

Thus, Caseer's awareness of the mild stimulant effect of khat provides little support for the conclusion that Caseer actually knew that the khat he was importing was a controlled substance. . . .

In sum, the evidence cited by the district court in its determination of whether Caseer had the requisite scienter for conviction lends, at best, only tenuous support for the conclusion that Caseer knew that he was participating in the importation of a controlled substance. Even drawing all inferences in the light most favorable to the government, a rational trier of fact would have reasonable doubt that Caseer knew that khat was a controlled substance. Thus, Caseer's conviction cannot stand.

The third mental state under the MPC is *recklessness*. A defendant acts recklessly when there is a conscious disregard for a substantial and unjustifiable risk of a specific outcome. The difference between a knowing act and a reckless act is in the degree of risk—practical certainty versus substantial risk. The MPC defines a substantial risk as a "gross deviation from the standard of conduct that a law-abiding person would observe in the actor's situation." Although the defendant is conscious of the risk, and it is substantial, it is not practically certain to happen.

The fourth and final state of mind under the MPC is *negligence*. The definition of negligence is similar to recklessness—that is, there must be a "substantial and unjustifiable risk." But unlike a reckless act, the actor has no conscious awareness of the risk. A negligent defendant hasn't perceived an existing risk, and that failure amounts to a gross deviation from a law-abiding person's standard.

- John and Katrina have a 7-year-old child, Jamie. In March 2020 in the midst of the coronavirus pandemic, Jamie begins to show symptoms of the virus. John and Katrina belong to a religion that believes medical care should not be sought to fight viruses and infections. They believe that God's intervention, sought through prayer, heals. Also, they were of the understanding, from news reports, that young people are highly unlikely to die from COVID-19. Jamie's condition slowly worsened, the family continued its regimen of prayer, and 11 days later, she died. John and Katrina were negligent in their care of Jamie.

- Assume the same facts in the previous paragraph, except add that Jamie suffers from severe asthma. This condition was diagnosed years before when Jamie was rushed to the hospital by school officials because she was unable to breathe. John and Katrina have been treating her condition with prayer. Being asthmatic puts Jamie at high risk for developing COVID-19. Jamie's condition worsened quickly, the family increased its regimen of prayer, and 4 days later, she died. John and Katrina were reckless in their care of Jamie.

See Table 3.2 for a comparison of mens rea under the Common Law to the MPC.

TABLE 3.2 ■ Mens Rea Under the MPC and Common Law		
Model Penal Code	*Common Law*	*Modern Development*
Purposeful	Specific intent	
Knowledge	General intent	
Recklessness	Didn't exist	
Negligence	Didn't exist	
Strict liability permitted only for offenses not punished with imprisonment	Didn't exist	Strict liability crimes punished with imprisonment found throughout the United States

Strict Liability

In 1996, famed racing car driver Bobby Unser and a friend went snowmobiling near Unser's ranch in New Mexico. A sudden snowstorm swept through the area. The men became lost, abandoned one of the snowmobiles after it became stuck, and spent 2 nights in the freezing weather. Both Unser and his friend were suffering from hypothermia, Unser was vomiting blood, and Unser's friend had given up on life when they were found by a search party. After their rescue, the men received a surprise. They were charged and convicted of violating the National Forest Wildnerness Act. Their crime: snowmobiling on federal land. One of Unser's defenses was that he didn't intend to be on federal land, that the snowstorm caused them to wander from unprotected land into the wilderness area. But the law forbidding snowmobiling in the area didn't have a mens rea requirement, so the government only had to prove they were present on the land. Ultimately, an appellate court upheld his conviction, finding that the law didn't have an intent element—of any kind![10] This is known as a **strict liability crime**, or a crime with no mental state. A prosecutor only needs to prove the actus reus in a strict liability crime. In Unser's case, simply being on the land was enough.

If Unser's conviction appears inconsistent with what you have learned in this chapter, you are right. Strict liability crimes are deviations from the Common Law. They are also inconsistent with the MPC, which requires mens rea for all crimes, except minor violations that are punished only with fines.[11] Regardless, Congress and the states have created many "public welfare" or regulatory crimes that don't require mens rea. Many of these regulatory offenses have been created by administrative agencies, not legislatures, and they are malum prohibitum, not malum in se. Speeding and other traffic offenses, selling alcohol to and otherwise contributing to the delinquency of minors, environmental, and public health violations are commonly strict liability offenses.

Even though most strict liability crimes are malum prohibitum, there are malum in se crimes that don't require a showing of intent. An example is statutory rape, or sex with a minor.

Strict liability crime: A crime that has no mens rea element; proof of actus reus is all that is required for guilt.

In some jurisdictions, proof that a defendant knew, or should have known, that a victim was under the age of consent is not required.

Strict liability offenses that are punished more harshly have been criticized as inconsistent with principles of liberty, particularly substantive due process, and a few state courts have stricken strict liability crimes on due process grounds. SCOTUS has endorsed congressional authority to create strict liability offenses, although it has also emphasized that they should not be punished severely. Courts have struggled with criminal statutes that don't mention mens rea at all. The MPC instructs courts to add one of the three highest forms of mens rea—purpose, knowing, or recklessness—to statutes that don't have an explicit mens rea requirement.

In recent years, there has been a growing concern by scholars, judges, and legislators about overcriminalization and racial inequality in punishment. There are many contributing factors to overcriminalization, including too many criminal laws, the growing number of strict liability crimes, excessive penalties, overzealous prosecution, and the largely unbounded discretion of police and prosecutors. This has led to a number of reforms, or calls for reform, to the criminal justice system. One possible reform is to strengthen mens rea. State and federal courts have moved in this direction in small measure, and Congress has on a couple of occasions considered bills that would explicitly require the courts to add mens rea when it is missing from a statute.

Vicarious and Corporate Liability

Generally, people are not criminally liable for the acts of others, yet there are a few instances when one person may exhibit vicarious liability for something someone else has done. For there to be vicarious liability, the actor must in some way be under the control of the person to be held vicariously liable. A parent, for example, may be held responsible for the acts of a child.

- R. E. Onna is teaching her 13-year-old daughter, Maria, to drive. Under state law, a person isn't eligible for a driver's permit or to drive on public roads until the age of 15. But R. E. wants Maria to be "street ready" when she turns 15, so she started the lessons early. The first lesson was in a parking lot. For the second lesson, they hit the city streets. During the lesson, R. E. averts her eyes from the road to text a friend. During R. E.'s texting, Maria, observing that the light at the next intersection is yellow, punches the gas. Consequently, she enters the intersection 10 miles over the speed limit when the light is red. They hit a car in the intersection, killing the driver. The state's vehicular homicide law makes it a Class D felony to "kill a human being with a motor vehicle while driving that motor vehicle in a negligent manner." R. E. is vicariously liable for vehicular homicide.

Like a parent, a corporation may also be vicariously liable. But this wasn't always the case. Throughout most of history, a corporation was not liable for crimes because it had no "soul"

Vicarious liability: Criminal culpability for the acts of another person.

and was "destitute of the natural organs of man."[12] In Common Law, the rationale for this policy was that corporations didn't possess a mind to form mens rea nor a body to commit actus reus.

But corporations are treated differently by the criminal law today; they are legal persons. SCOTUS recognized corporations as persons that could be criminally prosecuted as early as 1908.[13] The MPC incorporates the idea that "[a]corporation may be convicted of the commission of an offense if . . . the conduct is performed by an agent of the corporation acting in behalf of the corporation within the scope of his office or employment."[14] So corporate entities, including corporations, partnerships, and other business organizations, may be guilty of crimes so long as the criminal acts of their agents were (1) within the scope of employment and (2) taken on behalf of the corporation. The MPC doesn't require that senior corporate leadership order, consent, or be aware of the specific acts.

Because a corporation can't be imprisoned, fines are the most common punishment. Regulatory action is also possible, such as revoking a corporation's charter to conduct business. Of course, the employee of a corporation who commits the criminal act for which the corporation is vicariously liable may be also be prosecuted.

Two companies that have been convicted of homicide are Pacific Gas and Electric (PG&E) and Film Recovery Systems. PG&E is a large electrical company in California. The company pled guilty to 84 counts of involuntary manslaughter in 2020 for death resulting from wildfires caused by poor maintenance of its electrical grid. The company was charged again in 2021 for deaths resulting from another fire that prosecutors allege was caused by PG&E's negligence.[15]

People v. Film Recovery Systems, Inc. (FRS) was in the business of extracting silver from used photographic film. In the early 1980s, the company was growing quickly. It had recently hired new employees and expanded its processing. Almost all FRS employees were foreign, undocumented, and had limited English language skills. During this time of expansion, FRS didn't adequately expand its facilities or worker safety measures. The business heavily used cyanide, a dangerous gas. The drums of cyanide had warning labels, but because they were in English, most of the employees could not read them. Safety inspectors had cited FRS for this and many other unsafe conditions, including inadequate ventilation and personal protective equipment. In 1982, Stefan Golab, an employee who was responsible for stirring vats of cyanide, reported that he was being made ill by the cyanide. He asked to be moved to another job within the company. Four days later, he was in the same job. When he reported to work, fellow workers noticed that his skin was pale, and he was having difficulty breathing. While working, he began to foam at the mouth. Golab's peers carried him outside to the company parking lot, where he died from acute cyanide toxicity.[16] At trial, the coroner who examined his body testified that the smell of bitter almonds, commonly associated with cyanide, filled the examination room after he made the first incision into Golab's body.[17]

At trial, three officers of the company were found guilty of murder and reckless conduct, and FRS was convicted of involuntary manslaughter and reckless conduct. In regard to the corporation's defense that it was not a natural person capable of committing crime, the trial judge wrote

PHOTO 3.2 One of the most fundamental principles of criminal law is that a person should have both a guilty mind and a guilty act to be culpable.

rudall30/Shutterstock

The mind and mental state of a corporation is the mind and mental state of the directors, officers and high managerial personnel because they act on behalf of the corporation for both the benefit of the corporation and for themselves; and if the corporation's officers, directors and high managerial personnel act within the scope of their corporate responsibilities and employment for their benefit and for the benefit of the profits of the corporation, the corporation must be held liable for what occurred in the work place.

The trial judge sentenced each of the three corporate officers to 25 years of imprisonment for murder, with concurrent 1-year sentences for each of the recklessness convictions. FRS and another involved company were fined $48,000. Although corporate criminal liability is possible, it happens rarely in cases involving crimes against the person (e.g., murder and battery). It is more common in white-collar criminal cases, including fraud and antitrust violations. The most common methods of holding corporations accountable are regulatory actions and civil cases.

Don't Question My Motives

Criminal law scholar Jermone Hall (no relation to your author!) wrote that "hardly any part of penal law is more definitely settled than that **motive** is irrelevant."[18] Motive is not mens rea.

Motive: A person's reason for acting or for desiring the outcome of an act. Motive leads to mens rea and actus reus. Prosecutors are not required to prove motive but often do.

Motive is the underlying reason for desiring an outcome. Jack may want Jill dead. When he pushes her down and over a cliff, his specific intent is to cause her death. Why Jack wants Jill dead is his motive. Criminal law doesn't require proof of motive. So the prosecutor doesn't have to offer a reason for Jack's conduct—only that he intended to cause her death to prove murder or carelessly caused her death to prove manslaughter. In terms of their relationship to one another, motive precedes mens rea, which precedes the actus reus. See Figure 3.1 for a graphic of the sequence of motive to harm.

FIGURE 3.1 ■ From Motive to Harm

From Motive to Harm

	MOTIVE	MENS REA	ACTUS REUS
FACTS	Norman discovers that his wife is having an affair. He is so deeply hurt, embarrassed, and angry that he wants vengeance. He wants her "to pay."	Norman decides to kill his wife using his shotgun.	Norman shoots and kills his wife with his shotgun.
STATE'S BURDEN OF PROOF	None	That Norman desired to cause his wife's death by shooting her must be proven beyond a reasonable doubt	That Norman shot his wife after forming the mens rea (only a second before is adequate) must be proven beyond a reasonable doubt.

The *why* of a bank robbery is easily inferred—it's about the money. On the other hand, motive for murder isn't always so obvious. Because jurors often want to understand the "why," prosecutors will try to explain it. Motive is also considered at other stages of the process. Prosecutors and police often consider motive in making investigation and prosecution decisions, and judges consider motive at sentencing to mitigate (reduce) or aggravate (increase) punishment. And, deviating from the general rule, a few crimes have motive as an element. This is true of some civil rights crimes. You will learn more about this later in this book.

QUESTIONS AND APPLICATIONS

Identify each of the following statutes as general intent or specific intent crimes under the Common Law or as strict liability. Explain your answer.

1. It shall be the offense of Promoting Unhealthy Lifestyle Through Sugary Drinks for any business to sell or serve to any person a nonalcoholic carbonated or noncarbonated

beverage that is sweetened by the manufacturer or selling establishment with sugar or another caloric sweetener that has greater than 25 calories per 8 fluid ounces of beverage.

2. It shall be the offense of simple battery for a person to willfully touch another person without the person's consent.

3. It shall be the offense of aggravated battery for a person to intentionally cause serious bodily harm during a battery.

MIND AND BODY: CONCURRENCE

Learning Objectives: Define concurrence and identify its two aspects.

The idiom "mind, body, and soul" is intended to express the totality of being human. Two of these—mind and body—are the default elements of crimes. The law excludes a person's soul from the equation.

There is another dimension, a third element if you wish, of mind and body: *concurrence.* The act must be the product of a mens rea. For a crime that has both a mens rea and actus reus element, concurrence requires that the two be joined with intent (1) preceding and (2) causing the act (see Figure 3.2). These two aspects of concurrence are known as temporal concurrence and motivational concurrence. The temporal, or time between an actor's formation of intent and acting on that intent, can be short or long. Theoretically, the time between the formation of intent and the act can be less than a second.

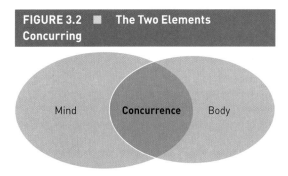

FIGURE 3.2 ■ The Two Elements Concurring

The following three scenarios illustrate, respectively, when concurrence exists, where there is no temporal concurrence, and where no motivational concurrence appears.

- Angry over disagreements about work, Cheryl decides to kill her coworker, Naomi. They work as ironworkers for HiRize, a construction company. As ironworkers, they assemble and repair the structures of tall buildings. Although they are normally harnessed, they must occasionally be unharnessed. Cheryl decides to push Naomi off their current jobsite, 80 stories high, on Friday. She chose Friday because the two women are alone in the same area of the building. Friday arrives, they both start working, and Naomi unharnesses to move from one beam to another. Cheryl pushes her, and she falls to her death. There is concurrence of mens rea and actus reus.

- Cheryl hates her coworker, Naomi. They work as ironworkers for HiRize, a construction company. As ironworkers, they assemble and repair the structures of tall buildings. One day when the two are not harnessed, Cheryl loses her footing and accidentally stumbles into Naomi, who is pushed off the building to her death. Cheryl and her coworkers gasp. Then Cheryl smiles and says, "Damn, it's OK. She has always been a pain. I probably would have pushed her off someday anyway." There is no temporal concurrence in this case because Cheryl didn't form the mens rea to cause Naomi's death before the act.

- Angry over disagreements about work, Cheryl decides to kill her coworker, Naomi. They work as ironworkers for HiRize, a construction company. As ironworkers, they assemble and repair the structures of tall buildings. Although they are normally harnessed, they must occasionally be unharnessed. Cheryl decides to push Naomi off their current jobsite, 80 stories high, on Friday. She chose Friday because the two women are alone in the same area of the building. On Thursday, Cheryl, Naomi, and another employee are unharnessed, eating their lunches on a high beam. As she stands, Cheryl loses her footing and stumbles against Naomi, who is pushed off the building to her death. There is no motivational concurrence in this case because Cheryl didn't intend to push Naomi off the building .

QUESTIONS AND APPLICATIONS

1. Define concurrence and explain its two aspects.
2. Explain why there is or is not concurrence in this scenario:

Chelsea is a computer hacker. She enjoys breaking into secure computer systems. She has been successful in breaking into college, banking, and social media systems. She has never stolen anything or harmed a system. She simply enjoys the challenge of breaching firewalls. Confident after so many successes, she decides to try her hand at the U.S. Department of Defense (DOD) system, a notoriously secure asset. After weeks of effort, she finally gets into the system. While poking around, Chelsea discovers troubling information. She found a folder full of documents labeled "confidential," detailing assassinations and assassination plans carried out by the military and Central Intelligence Agency. Some of the names didn't bother her much—foreign intelligence officers, foreign dictators, and terrorist leaders. But there were citizens of the United States on the list, including journalists. What troubled her the most was Elmo from Sesame Street. She thought, If they will kill Elmo, they will kill anyone. So she downloaded the folder onto a flash drive with the intention of sharing it with her fellow Americans. But the DOD was on to her. She was arrested and charged with violating an espionage law. Specifically, the law makes it a felony punishable by 10 to 25 years in

> prison to "knowingly and without authorization enter a secure computer system of the Department of Defense for the purpose of reading, downloading, copying, distributing, or photographing confidential records."
> **3.** Return to the scenario in Question 1. Rewrite the espionage law in such a way that Chelsea's conduct would be more clearly prohibited.

ATTENDANT CIRCUMSTANCES AND ELEMENT ANALYSIS

Learning Objectives: Define attendant circumstance and element analysis.

As you learned earlier, the prosecution must prove guilt beyond a reasonable doubt. More precisely, every element of an offense must be proved beyond a reasonable doubt. Elements are the parts of a crime. You have learned that *most* crimes have two types of elements: actus reus and mens rea.

However, all crimes have elements, or facts, that are not mens rea or actus reus. These elements "accompany" one of the two essential elements and are essential to proving that a crime occurred. These are known as attendant circumstances. A murder, for example, involves an intent to cause death and an act that causes death. Those are easily identified as the mens rea and actus reus. But the victim's death must also be proved. To die isn't an act. It is a condition, and in our example, it is an outcome. Establishing that the victim is dead in a murder case is as important as proving that the defendant intended the death and committed the act that caused the death. The victim's death, therefore, is an attending circumstance that must be proved beyond a reasonable doubt.

The MPC recognizes that they are elements of crimes that don't fall squarely into the mens rea or actus reus boxes. It requires prosecutors to prove attending circumstances and, in some instances, that a specific result or outcome occurred (e.g., death in a murder case).

In the very early years of the Common Law, the only mens rea that had to be shown was general moral culpability—that the defendant acted with malice or an evil mind. As you have learned, the idea of culpability was refined over the years, and eventually, courts distinguished between two forms of intent, general and specific. Every crime was committed with one of these states of mind. The difference was real. Specific intent crimes were typically punished with death and general intent crimes with life imprisonment. This single mens rea approach is known as offense analysis.

The MPC and many contemporary criminal codes offer an alternative to offense analysis. They recognize the possibility that a crime may have *mentes raea*, or multiple mens rea, that attach to the varying elements of the crime. Under the MPC, each act (conduct), attendant

---

Element: A part of a crime. For conviction, each element must be proved beyond a reasonable doubt.

Attendant circumstances: Facts or conditions that must be proved, along with the mens rea and actus reus, for a defendant to be convicted.

Offense analysis: The assignment of a single mens rea to an offense.

circumstance, and result may have its own mens rea requirement. This approach is known as **element analysis**. Consider the crime of burglary, which may be defined as the unlawful breaking and entering of a home of another person with the purpose to commit a felony. The act, attendant circumstances, result, and the mens that attaches to each of these are as follows:

Unlawful [*mens rea/scienter—knowledge of the absence of a right to break and enter*]

breaking [*actus reus*] and

entering [*actus reus*]

the home [attendant circumstance]

of another [*mens rea—knowledge that the home belongs to another person*]

with purpose [*mens rea for committing the felony when inside*]

to commit a felony [*attendant circumstance/result*]

In this example, there are two acts—breaking and entering. There are three states of mind—knowledge of the lack of legal authority to break, knowledge that the home belonged to someone else, and the high mens rea of purpose for the element of committing a felony when inside. And finally, there are two attendant circumstances that must be proved—that the building broken into was a home and that the crime intended was a felony.

Let's look at another example, the federal crime of falsely representing oneself as a federal employee:

18 U.S.C. §912.

Whoever falsely assumes or pretends to be an officer or employee acting under the authority of the United States or any department, agency or officer thereof, and acts as such, or in such pretended character demands or obtains any money, paper, document, or thing of value, shall be fined under this title or imprisoned not more than three years, or both.

Let's break the statute down into its elements:

Whoever falsely [*mens rea/scienter; requires proving knowledge of falsehood*]

assumes or pretends to be an officer or employee [*actus reus*]

under the authority of the United States . . . [*attendant circumstance*]

and acts as such, or in such pretended character [*actus reus*]

demands or obtains [*actus reus*]

any money, paper, document, or thing of value [*attendant circumstance*]

Element analysis: The assignment of a separate mens rea to each element of an offense.

Pretending to be an officer is an act. But the "under the authority of the United States" is neither an act nor a state of mind. It is an attending circumstance. This is also true of the status of the items received, which must be "money, paper, document, or thing of value." All elements—mens rea, actus reus, and attending circumstances—must be proved, individually, beyond a reasonable doubt.

Jurisdictions vary in their approach to mens rea. Both offense and elements analysis continue to be applied. Indeed, the MPC provides that offense analysis is to be the default method, so element analysis is applied only when there is clear legislative intent for it.

Proving mens rea can be troublesome to prosecutors, especially when the prosecution has to prove specific intent. Specific intent, you may recall, refers to a desire to cause a specific outcome. This requires getting into a defendant's head. But humanity has yet to create a mind reader, so in cases where there isn't a confession, prosecutors have to use indirect evidence to prove intent. You learned how this is done earlier in the chapter; prosecutors rely on inferences and presumptions.

QUESTIONS AND PROBLEMS

1. Define attendant circumstance.
2. Compare and contrast element and offense analysis.
3. Identify the acts, attendant circumstances, results, and mens rea in the following crime:

    It is a felony for any person who is a candidate for elective federal office to receive a contribution of money or something of value from a person knowing that the person is not a citizen or permanent resident of the United States with the purpose of supporting the candidate's election campaign.

I'M NOT THE CAUSE

Learning Objectives: Define and compare the two forms of causation and how an intervening superseding cause impacts an individual's culpability.

To be guilty of a specific intent crime, a defendant's act must be the "cause" of the resulting harm. To commit murder, for example, an act of a defendant must be the cause of the victim's death. There are two forms of causation, factual and legal.

To prove that an act is the **factual cause** of the prohibited harm, courts apply the *sine qua non* or "but-for" test to determine if the act and result are sufficiently connected to hold the actor accountable. In the words of the MPC, "Conduct is the cause of a result when ... it is an

---

Factual cause: For an act to be a substantial factor in an outcome. Most jurisdictions use the "but-for" test to determine if an act is the factual cause of a harm.

antecedent but for which the result in question would not have occurred." Typically, factual cause is easy to prove. All that has to be shown is that a defendant's actions created a sequence of events that led to the result. If a defendant is responsible for knocking over the first domino, then she is responsible for all of the fallen dominos, regardless of the number of dominos or the distance they stretch before the final crime occurs.

However, factual cause isn't the end of the causation question. **Legal cause** must also be proved, and it is more defined than factual causation. Legal causation is concerned with the similarity between the intended result and the actual result, and the similarity between the intended manner used to bring about a result and the actual manner that caused the result. The more similar these two, the more likely an act is the legal cause.

A harm may be the result of several causes. To be just, a person should only be held accountable for harm that flows, at least in part, from their actions. Borrowing from tort law, most jurisdictions define legal cause as **proximate cause**. Proximate means "near" or "close." Proximate doesn't mean the only cause, or the only factor, in the outcome. The result must be a consequence of the act, not a coincidence. A result is proximately caused if it is **foreseeable** to a reasonable person.

- Curtis is president of MegaOil, Inc., an international company that extracts, processes, and sells oil and natural gas. Ted is a self-proclaimed environmental ecoterrorist. Ted drives to Curtis's house, scales a fence, and when he is about 15 feet from the house, throws a brick with a message that reads "Stop killing Mother Earth" through a window. It turns out to be the bedroom of Curtis's 8-year-old daughter, who is hit in the head. The blow lacerates her skull, requiring four stitches. She also suffers a concussion. Ted is guilty of destruction of property and trespass. In addition, he is guilty of battery because the possibility of a brick that is thrown through the window of a home striking a person is foreseeable.

- Curtis is president of MegaOil, Inc., an international company that extracts, processes, and sells oil and natural gas. Ted is a self-proclaimed environmental ecoterrorist. Ted drives to Curtis's house, scales a fence, and when he is about 15 feet from the house, throws a brick with a message that reads "Stop killing Mother Earth" through a window. It turns out to be the bedroom of Curtis's 8-year-old daughter, who is hit in the head. The blow lacerates her skull, requiring four stitches. She also suffers a concussion. Scared to return in her room, the daughter asks to be moved to a different room. She is moved to a room on the backside of the house. Unknown to the family, their heating system was leaking carbon monoxide into the daughter's new bedroom. Consequently, the daughter died during her sleep. Ted is guilty of destruction of property, trespass, and battery. He is not guilty of murder because the cause of the girl's death was not a foreseeable consequence of Ted's act.

Legal cause: Similarity between the intended and actual result of an act, and the similarity between the intended manner used to bring about a result and the actual manner that caused the result.

Proximate cause: A test used to determine if an act is the legal cause of a result. A result must be foreseeable to be the proximate cause of an act.

Foreseeable: An outcome of an act that a reasonable person anticipates as possible.

In some cases, the chain of events between an act and a result may be broken by an **intervening superseding cause**. To negate a defendant's culpability, an intervening cause must be an independent act (or external force) that is unforeseeable and breaks the causal chain between the defendant's act and the result. The intervening superseding cause doctrine is closely related to foreseeability. The previous hypothetical involving the girl dying from carbon monoxide illustrates the relationship. Her death by carbon monoxide was unforeseeable *and* the carbon monoxide acted as an intervening superseding cause of her death. The Washington State Supreme Court addressed a question of causation in *State v. Leech*.

DIGGING DEEPER 3.3

Is an arsonist responsible for the death of a negligent firefighter?

Case: *State v. Leech*
Court: Supreme Court of Washington.   Citation: 114 Wn.2d 700
Year: 1990
Opinion by Anderson

At issue, in this case, is whether a fire fighter's death occurred in the furtherance of an arson, thus rendering the arsonist liable for the crime of first-degree felony murder.

On July 12, 1987, a fire broke out at the largely abandoned Crest apartment building in Seattle. Robert Earhart was one of nearly 70 City of Seattle firefighters who responded to the alarm. Fire investigators suspected arson, and Clyde Dale Leech, the defendant herein, was arrested at the scene. The substantial evidence against the defendant included his having been seen leaving the Crest just minutes before smoke emerged from the vacant area he had been in.

Robert Earhart died of carbon monoxide poisoning while fighting the fire inside the Crest. When his body was found, his breathing apparatus was on the floor beside him and the air bottle read at or near zero. Subsequent tests showed that the breathing apparatus was not defective but was simply empty.

The defendant was charged with first-degree felony murder. His main defense was that the negligence of Earhart and the Seattle Fire Department, rather than the arson, was the proximate cause of Earhart's death. A safety inspector for the Washington State Department of Labor and Industries testified that if Earhart had obeyed state safety regulations and gotten a new air bottle when the alarm in his breathing apparatus sounded, his death could have been avoided. (The apparatus was designed to sound an alarm when less than 5 minutes of oxygen remained in the air bottle.) The inspector also testified that Earhart was allowed to freelance, or fight the fire without proper supervision. The safety inspector opined that if Earhart had been properly supervised, his death might have been avoided. . . .

The defendant claimed before the Court of Appeals that the felony murder statute was inapplicable to his case because (1) Earhart's negligence was not a "specifically foreseeable" result of the arson; (2) the arson fire was not the proximate cause of Earhart's death; and (3) Earhart's death was not caused in the course of and in furtherance of the arson.

Intervening and superseding cause: An independent act (or external force) that is unforeseeable and breaks the causal chain between the defendant's act and the result.

We agree with the Court of Appeals disposition of the defendant's first two contentions. With regard to the claim that Earhart's alleged negligence was not foreseeable, the court noted that RCW 9A.48.020 defines first-degree arson as including fires that are knowingly and maliciously set which are "manifestly dangerous to any human life, including firemen." In addition, the court cited its holding in *State v. Levage*:

> experience teaches that one of the certainties attendant upon a hostile fire is that firemen will be called and will come. Danger inheres in fire fighting. In setting a hostile fire, the arsonist can anticipate that firemen will be endangered.

While the arson statute and *Levage* establish that Earhart's *death* was foreseeable, they do not squarely address the issue of whether his *negligence* was foreseeable. According to one respected authority, however, foreseeability is not required in a felony murder case when death occurs as a consequence of an intervening response to the defendant's conduct.

[C]ourts have drawn the perimeters of legal cause more closely when the intervening cause was a mere *coincidence*... than when it was a *response* to the defendant's prior actions (i.e., a reaction to conditions created by the defendant). Foreseeability is required as to the former, but in the latter instance, the question is whether the intervening act was abnormal—that is, whether, looking at the matter with hindsight, it seems extraordinary.

It does not seem to us that human error in fighting a fire is an extraordinary occurrence. The implication of the defendant's argument is that an arsonist is entitled to have his fire fought in a perfect, risk-free manner by a fire department; this is not the law. Thus, the Court of Appeals properly rejected the contention that the defendant was not guilty of felony murder because Earhart's alleged negligence was not specifically foreseeable.

We also agree with the Court of Appeals conclusion that the arson fire proximately caused Earhart's death. We find it sufficient to simply note here that the fire fighter's alleged negligence in using his breathing apparatus was not the sole cause of his death. Since his failure to use the apparatus would not have killed him had the defendant not set the arson fire, the defendant's conduct in setting the fire was a proximate cause of Earhart's death. . . .

The . . . defendant's conviction of the crime of first-degree felony murder is affirmed.

Time can sometimes confound causation. Edgar Allen Poe wrote that "[t]he boundaries between life and death are at best shadowy and vague. Who shall say where one ends and where the other begins?"[19]

If the victim of a blow to the head by a blunt object dies immediately, causation is clear. But it is less clear if the victim becomes comatose and lives a month, a year, or many years before dying. At the old Common Law, when medical science was less developed, it was assumed that if an act and the victim's death were too far apart in time, that the act wasn't the cause of death. The law set that time limit as a year and a day. Today, few jurisdictions follow the rule. Most have abolished it altogether; others have extended the time. That is true in California, which has a 3-years-and-a-day rule:

> Cal. Pen. Code §194. To make the killing either murder or manslaughter, it is not requisite that the party die within three years and a day after the stroke received or the cause of death administered. If death occurs beyond the time of three years and a day, there shall be a rebuttable presumption that the killing was not criminal. The prosecution

shall bear the burden of overcoming this presumption. In the computation of time, the whole of the day on which the act was done shall be reckoned the first.

Unlike the old year-and-a-day rule, however, California's rule isn't absolute. It imposes a rebuttable presumption that an act isn't the cause of a death that occurs 3 years and 2 days or more later. The rebuttable presumption simply means that a prosecutor can prove murder after 3 years and a day with solid medical evidence that the defendant's act was the legal cause of death. See Figure 3.3 for an illustratiion of the causation chain.

FIGURE 3.3 ■   Causation Chain in Illustration 3D

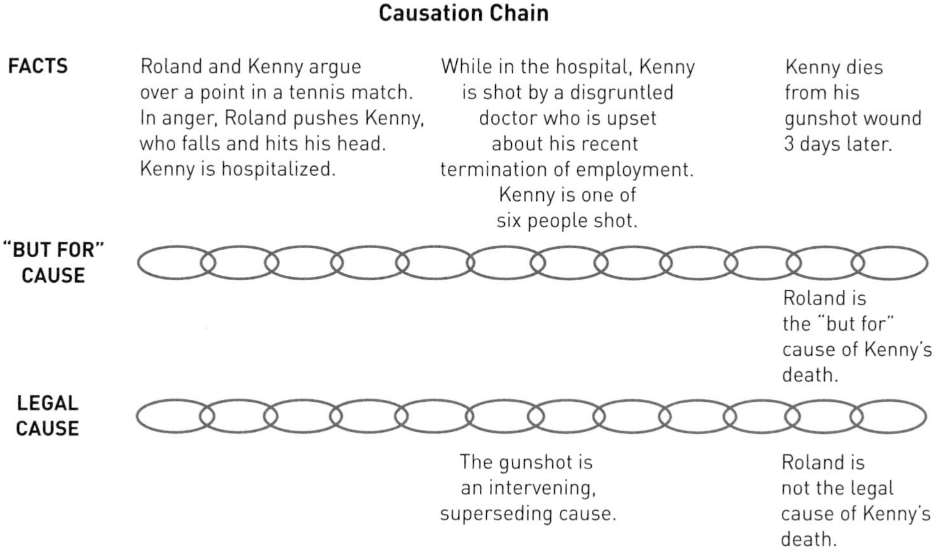

Causation Chain

FACTS	Roland and Kenny argue over a point in a tennis match. In anger, Roland pushes Kenny, who falls and hits his head. Kenny is hospitalized.	While in the hospital, Kenny is shot by a disgruntled doctor who is upset about his recent termination of employment. Kenny is one of six people shot.	Kenny dies from his gunshot wound 3 days later.

"BUT FOR" CAUSE

Roland is the "but for" cause of Kenny's death.

LEGAL CAUSE

The gunshot is an intervening, superseding cause.

Roland is not the legal cause of Kenny's death.

QUESTIONS AND APPLICATIONS

Steff stalks Melissa for months. In response, Melissa changed her telephone number twice, installed cameras on her property, and obtained a protective order. Steff was jailed twice for violating the orders; regardless, he continues to stalk her. Fearing for her life, Melissa decides to move. She finds a job in another town, sells her home, packs her belongings, and climbs into her car to make the drive to her new home over an hour away. During the drive, a truck that is driving in the opposite direction crosses the center line and hits Melissa's car head-on. Melissa is killed.

1. Is Steff the factual cause of Melissa's death in this scenario? Explain.
2. Is Steff the legal cause of Melissa's death? Explain.
3. Is it just to hold a person accountable for a death that occurs years after the person caused the original injury to the victim? Explain your answer.

Year-and-a-day rule: An old Common Law rule that relieves a defendant of murder if the victim lives longer than a year and day. Many jurisdictions have abolished the rule, extended it to 3 years and a day, or modified it in other ways.

IN A NUTSHELL

One of the most fundamental principles of criminal law is that a person should have both a guilty mind and a guilty act to be culpable. To limit punishment to those who understand and intend the harm they cause appears to derive from the state of nature and from a shared humanity.

At the Common Law, the primary mens rea distinction was between specific and general intent, the former requiring a defendant to intend the outcome of an act, and the latter, only the intent to act. Over time, many terms were used to describe these two states of mind, such as malicious, wanton, evil, willful, deliberate, and intentional. To add to the confusion, the definitions of each varied between jurisdictions. The MPC and modern statutes have attempted to bring order to this area of law. The MPC recognizes four states of mind: purposeful, knowing, reckless, and negligent. The industrial and digital eras brought with them new challenges and a change in criminal law—the emergence of crimes that don't require proof of a guilty mind. So-called strict liability crimes can be found in all of the states and the federal government. They are mostly, but not entirely, confined to regulatory offenses.

A voluntary act is also required for criminal liability. Involuntary acts, thoughts, and a person's physical status are not considered acts and, therefore, may not be criminalized. With rare exceptions, there was no duty to help others at the old Common Law. Modern law deviates from this principle in several situations, such as when a person has a special relationship with another person that creates a duty of care.

Finally, the actus reus must be the consequence of the mens rea, not a coincidence. The intent, if required, to commit the act or to attempt to cause the outcome must occur before the act. Temporally, this can occur in a moment. This joining of the two essential elements is known as concurrence.

LEGAL TERMS

actus reus (p. 71)

attendant circumstances (p. 97)

concurrence (p. 72)

construct (p. 78)

constructed intent (p. 82)

crime of omission (p. 75)

element (p. 97)

element analysis (p. 98)

factual cause (p. 99)

foreseeable (p. 100)

general intent (p. 82)

intervening superseding cause (p. 101)

knowing (p. 85)

Legal cause (p. 100)

mens rea (p. 71)

motive (p. 93)

negligent (p. 85)

offense analysis (p. 97)

proximate cause (p. 100)

purpose (p. 85)

reckless (p. 85)

Scienter (p. 83)

specific intent (p. 82)

strict liability crime (p. 90)

transferred intent (p. 82)

vicarious liability (p. 91)

year-and-a-day rule (p. 103)

NOTES

1. *King v. Cogdon* (S.Ct. Victoria, 1950) (Australian court).

2. William Blackstone, *Commentaries on the Laws of England* (1769).

3. *People v. Decina*, 138 N.E.2d 799 (N.Y.1956).

4. See B. E. Teacher, "Sleepwalking Used as a Defense in Criminal Cases and the Evolution of the Ambien Defense," *Duquesne Criminal Law Journal* 2, no. 2 (2016): fn 27.

5. Commonly attributed to Arthur Hugh Clough (1819–1861).

6. Cal. Penal Code § 273a.

7. *Commonwealth v. Carter:* Trial Court Convicts Defendant of Involuntary Manslaughter Based on Encouragement of Suicide. 131 Harv. L. Rev 918 (2018).

8. Oliver Wendell Holmes, *The Common Law* (1881).

9. See Karen Raterman, *Conservatory Controversy: Iboga Confiscation and Professor Suspensions at Ohio's Miami University.* 125 HerbalGram 38, 2020, CMS.HerbalGram.org; Daniel E. Hall, "Miami University Must Reverse Unjust Decision to Terminate Professors," *Cincinnati Enquirer*, July 5, 2019, accessed June 21, 2020, www.cincinnati.com/story/opinion/2019/07/05/opinion-miami-university-must-reverse-unjust-decision-terminate-professors/1557192001/.

10. *United States v. Unser,* (10th Cir. 1999).

11. MPC §2.02(1) and 2.05.

12. W. Robert Thomas, How And Why Corporations Became (And Remain) Persons Under The Criminal Law, 45 Fla. St. U.L. Rev. 479, 487 (2018).

13. *Berea College v. Kentucky*, 211 U.S. 45 (1908) and *N.Y. Cent. & Hudson River R.R. Co. v. United States*, 212 U.S. 481, 494–95 (1909).

14. MPC §2.07 (1)(a).

15. Lozana, A. (Sept. 24, 2021). PG&E Charged with Manslaughter in Claiforria Wilfire Last Year That Killed 4. NBC News. Retrieved at https://www.nbcnews.com/news/us-news/pg-e-charged-manslaughter-california-wildfire-last-year-killed-4-n1280045.

16. Most of the facts of this case were taken from Jeffrey P. Grogin, *Corporations Can Kill Too: After Film Recovery, Are Individuals Accountable for Corporate Crimes*, 19 Loyola of Los Angeles L. Rev. 1411 (1986).

17. Ray Gibson, "3 Guilty in Cyanide Death," *Chicago Tribune*, June 14, 1985.

18. Michael T. Rosenberg, *The Continued Relevance of the Irrelevance-of-Motive Maxim*, 57 Duke L. J. 1143 (2008), citing Jerome Hall, *General Principles of Criminal Law*, 2nd ed. (1960), 88.

19. Edgar Allen Poe, *The Premature Burial* (1950).

4 PARTIES TO CRIME AND INCHOATE CRIMES

On March 12, 2019, 50 people were charged with federal crimes in a high-profile case that would become known as the Varsity Blues scandal. Additional defendants would be named over the next year. At the heart of the scandal was William Rick Singer. Working through two firms he controlled, Mr. Singer received tens of millions of dollars to help parents fraudulently obtain college admission for their children. Many prominent people were involved in the affair, including actress Lori Laughlin and her husband, Mossimo Giannulli, who paid $500,000 in bribes to get their two daughters admitted to the University of Southern California; actress Felicity Huffman; Georgetown University's tennis coach, who also coached Michelle Obama and her daughter; coaches from a variety of sports at several other colleges; and investment bankers and attorneys. Tao Zhao, the chairman and cofounder of a multibillion-dollar international pharmaceutical company, allegedly paid Singer $6.5 million to get his son into Stanford University.

PHOTO 4.1 William "Rick" Singer leaves the federal courthouse after facing charges in a nationwide college admissions cheating scheme.

Singer used a variety of methods to get kids into colleges. He paid third parties to pose as children of clients to take entrance exams, photoshopped a picture of an applicant to look more athletic, and bribed test officials to change entrance exam scores. In some cases, he falsified athletic records and bribed coaches to support the admission of applicants under the ruse that the student would participate in college athletics. One couple paid $1.2 million to have an elaborate athletic record created that resulted in their child's admission to Yale University.

Singer pled guilty, cooperated with authorities, and was awaiting sentencing when this book went to press. Huffman, Laughlin, and several other defendants pled guilty and were sentenced to fines and short jail terms.[1]

The charges against the defendants varied, but included mail fraud, money laundering, and bribery. And there was another: conspiracy. In addition to actually committing fraud or one of the other crimes, many of the accused were also charged with plotting with others to do those things. Every time Singer worked with a parent to create a false record or hired a brainiac to take an exam for someone else, the parties were conspiring to commit a crime. That intended crime in a conspiracy is known as the target crime, or the substantive offense.

In practice, prosecutors commonly include a conspiracy charge when there are two or more defendants involved in the same crime. This practice is controversial for several reasons. First, it can be reasonably argued that charging both the target crime and the conspiracy amounts to double charging the same bad act. Second, conspiracy laws often carry hefty penalties. When combined with the target crime (e.g., bribery and conspiracy to commit bribery), prosecutors have considerable coercive power over defendants. This can result in unfair plea deals. Third, the heart of many conspiracies is communication between the parties. That raises First Amendment free speech concerns. Regardless, conspiracy is an often used and powerful prosecutorial tool.

This chapter presents the various parties to crimes, including conspirators; crimes that involve multiple people; and so-called inchoate, or unfinished or preparatory, crimes. The discussion begins with the parties to crimes.

THICK AS THIEVES

Learning Objectives: Compare and contrast the Common Law and MPC approaches to parties.

Crimes can be committed by individuals or groups of people. When an individual is accused of committing a crime alone, it is obvious that the state must prove that the defendant committed every element of the crime. However, it is more complicated when multiple people work together to commit a crime. Must all of the members of the conspiracy be involved in every element? If not, how "involved" does an individual have to be before criminal liability attaches? We begin by labeling the different parties in crime.

Target crime: The crime that conspirators plan to commit. Also referred to as the substantive offense.

I Wasn't Alone

Principals and Accessories

The Common Law recognized four possible parties to a crime: principal in the first degree, principal in the second degree, accessory before the fact, and accessory after the fact. A **principal in the first degree** is the person who commits the prohibited act, and a **principal in the second degree** is physically present during the commission of a crime and assists the principal in the first degree but doesn't commit the prohibited act.

At one time, the difference between a first-degree and second-degree principal was clearer. Today, technology can blur the lines between the two. Consider, for example, the terrorist attacks in Mumbai, India, in 2008. Many people regard the attacks as India's 9/11; 174 people were killed, including nine terrorists in attacks on several targets, which included the famous Taj Mahal Hotel. During the attack on the hotel, 10 gunmen were under the control of handlers in Pakistan, who used the internet to identify guests for assassination and to monitor police operations. The command center personnel were virtually present with the gunmen during the siege, transmitting data and issuing tactical and assassination orders.[2] Although not physically present in the hotel, their virtual presence walked the line between first-degree and second-degree status. Regardless of their status, had it been in the United States, their punishment would not differ from the gunmen, or at least not significantly.

An **accessory before the fact**, as the name implies, is involved before the crime occurs but isn't present as it happens. Accessories before the fact are commonly referred to as accomplices. An accomplice is liable for the acts of their principal. An **accessory after the fact** provides a principal or the principal's accomplice with assistance in avoiding arrest or prosecution after a crime is committed. As may be obvious, an accessory after the fact is a specific intent crime. More specifically, there are both scienter and specific intent requirements—knowledge of the fugitive status of the person helped and an intent to hinder the arrest or prosecution of that person.

Wayne, Thobias, and Robyn hatch a plan to burglarize the home of a wealthy jeweler, Allison. She lives in her home with her husband, Tim. They had heard rumors that Allison keeps a cache of jewelry in the home. They meet on several occasions, develop a plan, divide the labor, and agree to equally share the proceeds of their ill-gotten gains. Wayne surveys the property over a week. Over a 3-week period, he records the patterns of the couple and makes an inventory of cameras, lights, and other security. He discovers that they have a routine of going out on Saturday night until the early hours of Sunday morning. He recommends a Saturday burglary and maps out the security devices he found. He gives this information to Thobias and Robyn. The following

---

Principal in the first degree: A person who commits a prohibited act.

Principal in the second degree: A person who is present and provides assistance in the commission of a crime but who doesn't commit the prohibited act.

Accessory before the fact: A person who is involved in the planning or preparation of a crime but isn't present during its commission.

Accessory after the fact: A person who assists a principal or accessory in avoiding arrest or prosecution after a crime is committed.

Saturday at 10 p.m., Robyn picks up Thobias in her car and drives them to Allison's home. As planned, Robyn stays in the car as a "lookout," while Thobias uses Wayne's map to navigate the security system. Alas, Wayne didn't see a camera near the street. Allison received an alert on her phone, called the police, and Thobias was caught in the house with a bag full of Allison's jewels in his hands. The police didn't see Robyn in the car, and she successfully left the area. During the night, Thobias chose to turn "state's evidence," or to be an informant, in exchange for leniency. He told them the whole story. The police immediately arrested Wayne. But Robyn chose not to go home when she left Allison's. Instead, she drove to her friend Rocky, who agreed to let her spend the night. She told Rocky the whole story. He told her to not worry and that she "could stay with him until the police stopped looking for her."

Thobias is a principal in the first degree.

Robyn is a principal in the second degree.

Wayne is an accessory before the fact.

Rocky is an accessory after the fact.

State laws vary, but principals and accessories before the fact are punished more severely than accessories after the fact. A defendant's specific contribution to the crime and potential or resulting harm are factors in the punishment decision. In this example, Thobias, Wayne, and Robyn would likely be sentenced to greater prison time than Rocky.

Let's play with the facts. The group decides that no acts of violence were acceptable and agreed, as they did, to make every effort to enter the home when no one was present. They also decide that Thobias is to be unarmed and he is to take no chances of harming anyone or being harmed. If Thobias enters the home unarmed, he, Wayne, and Robyn will likely be punished similarly, or he may receive a marginally longer prison sentence. But what if Thobias disobeys the group's decision and enters the home with a handgun? Likely, he would pay for the decision with a longer prison sentence. Let's take this out another step. Thobias is surprised to find Allison alone in the home. He sexually assaults her before stealing the jewels. Whether his accomplices are responsible for the sexual assault differs by jurisdiction. In some states, principals in the first degree and accessories before the fact are responsible for all of the acts of the principal in the first degree that occur during the planned crime. In a state following this rule, Robyn and Wayne could be convicted of rape. However, some jurisdictions require an accessory to share the same intent with the principal in the first degree to be liable, or they adhere to the natural and probable consequences doctrine, which holds that Robyn and Wayne would be criminally liable for the rape if it was foreseeable and likely to occur. Given their commitment to nonviolence and because the crime of rape is so different in its nature and the resulting harm from theft, they are not responsible for the assault on Allison. The outcome would be different if Thobias decided to steal an antique statue while in the house, even though they had only planned to steal jewelry.

Natural and probable consequences doctrine: A rule that holds that accomplices are criminally liable for the unplanned but foreseeable crimes of the principal in the first degree that are committed during the planned crime.

Jurisdictions vary considerably in their statutory language and how they structure the law around the parties to a crime. The term accomplice, for example, is sometimes used to refer to principals in the second degree and accessories—and in some cases, only to accessories. The terms "aiders" and "abettors" are also used to refer to accessories before and after the fact. And in a few states, the distinctions have been abolished, at least formally. Texas is an example:

Texas Penal Code § 7.01. PARTIES TO OFFENSES

a. A person is criminally responsible as a party to an offense if the offense is committed by his own conduct, by the conduct of another for which he is criminally responsible, or by both.

b. Each party to an offense may be charged with commission of the offense.

c. All traditional distinctions between accomplices and principals are abolished by this section, and each party to an offense may be charged and convicted without alleging that he acted as a principal or accomplice.

A Utah court reviewed a conviction of a principal in the second degree in *State v. Grunwald*, featured in the next Digging Deeper.

DIGGING DEEPER 4.1

Does a jury care about *who* and *to* in a murder?

Case: *State v. Grunwald*
Court: Supreme Court of Utah.   Citation: 2020 UT 9
Year: 2020

[The following account of the facts was presented by the Utah Court of Appeals in its decision that was reversed by this decision. That court's description of the events has been substituted for the Supreme Court's because they are more detailed.]

In June 2013, when Grunwald was 16 years old, she was introduced to Garcia by a mutual friend. Garcia had been previously convicted of manslaughter and was on parole. Although Garcia was almost 10 years older than Grunwald, they became romantically involved. By September, Garcia had moved into the Grunwald family home in Draper, Utah. Garcia's presence in the home and his intimate relationship with Grunwald resulted in friction between Grunwald's parents.

In January 2014, Grunwald's parents decided to separate, and Grunwald planned to move with her mother to St. George, Utah. Garcia told his parole officer that he wanted to transfer his supervision to St. George so that he could stay with Grunwald. His parole officer directed Garcia to stay with his brother in Provo, Utah, and to report in on January 27. When Garcia failed to report, the parole officer applied for an arrest warrant.

On January 30, Grunwald and her mother were packing their belongings when Garcia asked Grunwald to "go on a ride" with him so they could talk. Grunwald agreed, and she and Garcia drove away in her truck, with Grunwald behind the wheel.

Accomplice: Depending on the jurisdiction, a synonym for a person involved in a crime that is not a principal in the first degree.

At some point during the drive, Garcia told Grunwald that there was a warrant out for his arrest. The circumstances surrounding this announcement were disputed at trial, but Grunwald became sufficiently upset to pull off to the side of Highway 73 and turn on her hazard lights.

Sergeant Cory Wride, with the Utah County Sheriff's Office, noticed the truck on the side of the road and notified dispatch that he was conducting a "motorist assist." He approached the driver's window and asked Grunwald if she was OK. Although she was crying and her face was red, Grunwald told him she was fine. He asked for her identification and car registration and then went back to his vehicle to confirm her information with a police dispatcher. When Sergeant Wride returned to the truck, he gave the documents back to Grunwald and asked her again if she was sure she was OK. When she assured him that she was, he turned his attention to Garcia. Garcia provided a false name and birthdate, and Sergeant Wride again returned to his vehicle to verify the information.

According to Grunwald, Garcia told her to put her foot on the brake while he shifted the truck into drive. With a gun in hand, Garcia announced to Grunwald that he was "going to buck [the officer] in the fucking head." Grunwald held her foot on the brake with the car in drive for more than 3-and-a-half minutes. During this time, a passing motorist noticed that Grunwald was checking her driver's-side mirror. When there was a significant lull in traffic, Garcia slid open the truck's back window and fired seven shots at Sergeant Wride as he sat in his patrol vehicle. Immediately after Garcia fired the shots, Grunwald accelerated back onto the road and drove away.

Two bullets struck Sergeant Wride, one piercing his forehead and the other puncturing his neck. When Sergeant Wride did not answer his radio or calls to his mobile phone, another officer drove to his last known location. The officer found Sergeant Wride dead. He notified the dispatch center, and other officers began searching for Grunwald's truck.

About an hour and a half after the shooting, police first spotted the truck traveling southbound on I-15 between the two Santaquin exits. When police gave chase, Grunwald pulled into an emergency turnaround and made a U-turn to head northbound on I-15.

Another officer, Utah County Sheriff's Deputy Greg Sherwood, spotted Grunwald's truck as she exited the interstate at the Santaquin Main Street exit and began to follow. When Deputy Sherwood activated his siren and overhead lights, Grunwald suddenly reduced her speed, which closed the gap between the two vehicles. In that instant, Garcia fired at Deputy Sherwood through the truck's back window. One bullet struck Deputy Sherwood in the head, causing serious injury. Fortunately, Deputy Sherwood survived the shooting.

Immediately after Garcia fired at Deputy Sherwood, Grunwald made another abrupt U-turn and headed back to the I-15 on-ramp. Utah Highway Patrol Trooper Jeff Blankenagel spotted Grunwald's truck once it was back on the interstate. As Trooper Blankenagel followed the truck, Garcia fired two shots in his direction from the truck's back window. Trooper Blankenagel reduced his speed to create a safe following distance between his vehicle and Grunwald's truck. Ahead on I-15, other officers had deployed a spike strip to stop the truck. Grunwald maneuvered around it, but the spike strip disabled Trooper Blankenagel's vehicle. As Grunwald continued driving, she crashed into another vehicle, resulting in damage to the front end of the truck that impaired her ability to steer and brake.

Undeterred, Grunwald continued driving and passed a semi-trailer truck traveling southbound on I-15. As they went by, the truck driver saw Garcia lean out of the truck's passenger window and fire shots at his semi-trailer. The truck driver pulled over to examine his vehicle and found that the gunshots had damaged parts of the truck.

Shortly after passing the semi-trailer truck, Grunwald took the Nephi Main Street exit off I-15, and she and Garcia abandoned the disabled truck. Garcia ran down the middle of the road away from the truck, and Grunwald followed. Officers yelled at them to "stop" and "[g]et down." Ignoring these commands, Garcia fired at an officer while Grunwald ran directly toward a moving car, waving her arms. The driver saw Grunwald flagging her down and stopped her vehicle. While Grunwald opened the passenger side door and climbed in, Garcia opened the driver's door, waved his gun at the driver, and ordered her to get out. The driver asked if she could get her daughter out of the back seat, to which Garcia replied, "[Y]ou better hurry." As soon as the driver retrieved her daughter, Garcia drove away, with Grunwald in the passenger seat.

Garcia returned to I-15, but police successfully deployed tire spikes, slowing the vehicle and eventually causing a tire to become dislodged. When the disabled vehicle came to a stop, Garcia abandoned it, running toward another vehicle, with Grunwald following him. Officers yelled at them to stop and get down. As Garcia neared the other vehicle, gunfire erupted. Grunwald stopped and dropped to her knees.

Garcia continued to flee and aimed his gun at an approaching officer. The officer yelled, "Show me your hands." When Garcia failed to do so, the officer fired two shots. Grunwald saw one bullet strike Garcia in the head, and she began to scream. The officer who fired heard her yell, "You shot him in the fucking head." A bystander saw Grunwald pacing frantically, acting distraught and hysterical. She appeared angry at the police and screamed, "You fucking ass holes, you didn't have to shoot him. You fucking shot him. Oh, my God, you fucking shot him."

Garcia, on the ground but still conscious, continued to struggle as officers wrestled away his gun and placed him in handcuffs. Once he was subdued, officers attempted to administer first aid. Garcia asked them for water then said, "Why don't you let me kiss my girlfriend with my last dying breath?" Garcia died later that day.

After Grunwald was arrested and placed in a patrol vehicle, she claimed that Garcia had threatened to shoot her and her family if she refused to go with him and that she "tried to get him to stop."

The state charged Grunwald with 12 counts associated with these events. On Counts 1–7 and Count 11, the state charged Grunwald as an accomplice. She pled not guilty to all charges and the case proceeded to trial.

[W]e turn to the accomplice liability instructions in this case. Instructions 33, 38, 40, 44, 45, 46, and 50 each contain identical language, replacing only the name and elements of the principal crime. In relevant part, these instructions required the jury to find:

1. That the defendant, Meagan Dakota Grunwald,
2. "Intentionally," "knowingly," or "recklessly" solicited, requested, commanded, encouraged, *or* "intentionally" aided [Garcia] *who*: [elements of principal crime]
3. And that the defendant, Meagan Dakota Grunwald,
   a. Intended that [Garcia] commit the [principal crime], or
   b. Was aware that [Garcia's] conduct was reasonably certain to result in [Garcia] committing the [principal crime], or
   c. Recognized that her conduct could result in [Garcia] committing the [principal crime] but chose to act anyway. . . .

This instruction appears to be based on the Utah Model Jury Instruction on accomplice liability, which reverses the order in which the elements appear in the statute. The first statutory element—"acting with the mental state required for the principal offense"—is addressed in paragraph 3 of the instruction. The second element—"solicits, requests, commands, encourages, or intentionally aids another person to engage" in the principal offense—is addressed in paragraph 2.

Chief Justice Durrant, opinion of the [Supreme] Court:

* * *

I. There is a Reasonable Probability the Jury Found That Ms. Grunwald Was Reckless as to the Results of Her Conduct, While Also Finding That She Did Not Intend for Sergeant Wride to Be Killed or Know That His Death Was Reasonably Certain to Result

The first error in the jury instruction is that it permitted the jury to convict Ms. Grunwald based on a finding that she acted recklessly, rather than intentionally or knowingly. This constitutes a serious error.

In *State v. Briggs*, we held that "[t]o show that a defendant is guilty under accomplice liability, the State must show that an individual acted with both the [requisite mental state] that the underlying offense be committed and the [requisite mental state] to aid the principal actor in the offense." Accordingly, "the first step in applying accomplice liability is to determine whether the individual charged as an accomplice had the [requisite mental state] that an underlying offense be committed."

The requisite mental state for an aggravated murder conviction is "knowing" or "intentional.". . .

Although the jury instruction included an instruction regarding intentional and knowing mental states, it also permitted the jury to convict Ms. Grunwald based on a reckless mental state. It stated that the jury could convict if it found that Ms. Grunwald "recognized that her conduct could result in [Mr. Garcia] committing the crime of Aggravated Murder but chose to act anyway." The inclusion of the reckless mental state instruction permitted the jury to convict Ms. Grunwald if it found that she was aware that her interactions with Mr. Garcia could possibly assist Mr. Garcia in murdering Sergeant Wride. So even if the jury had found that Ms. Grunwald did not intend for Mr. Garcia to kill Sergeant Wride or know that her interactions with Mr. Garcia would most likely lead to Sergeant Wride's death, the jury was nevertheless permitted to convict her. This was an error.

II. There is a Reasonable Probability the Jury Convicted Ms. Grunwald for Aiding Mr. Garcia in Some Way Unconnected to the Commission of the Murder at Issue

In this case, the jury instruction permitted the jury to convict Ms. Grunwald if she intentionally aided Mr. Garcia, *who* committed the crime. The instruction should have read that Ms. Grunwald was guilty if she intentionally aided Mr. Garcia *to* commit the crime. As the court of appeals pointed out, by "substituting the word 'who' [for the word 'to'], the instruction permitted the jury to find [Ms.] Grunwald guilty if she . . . aided [Mr.] Garcia in any way, so long as [Mr.] Garcia committed [aggravated murder]." Thus, this instruction permitted the jury to convict Ms. Grunwald based on conduct that was not directly connected to the murder. This was also error.

Although the court of appeals recognized that this error in the jury instruction permitted the jury to convict Ms. Grunwald based on a finding that she helped Mr. Garcia in some way unrelated to the commission of the crime at issue, it ultimately concluded there was "no reasonable probability that the jury convicted [Ms.] Grunwald because she aided [Mr.] Garcia in some way other than to commit the crime of aggravated murder." In support of this conclusion, the court of appeals explained that the "undisputed evidence showed that, after [Mr.] Garcia announced his intention, [Ms.] Grunwald applied the brake, enabling the truck to shift into drive" and that she "held her foot on the brake for 3-and-a-half minutes while [Mr.]

Garcia shifted in his seat to get into position to fire." But as we explained earlier, the timing of events in this case is far from undisputed. And the court's reliance on a disputed timeline is even more problematic in regard to this issue.

Whether Mr. Garcia stated that he wanted to "buck" Sergeant Wride before or after Ms. Grunwald placed her foot on the brake is crucial to determining whether Ms. Grunwald intentionally aided Mr. Garcia to commit the murder. As the court of appeals noted, the State focused primarily on Ms. Grunwald's act of putting her foot on the brake while Mr. Garcia prepared to fire. So if the jury believed that Mr. Garcia made his "buck" comment immediately before he began shooting, all of her conduct, which allegedly constituted intentional aid, would have occurred before Ms. Grunwald heard the comment. In other words, there would be no evidence that Ms. Grunwald's conduct was done with the purpose of helping Mr. Garcia prepare to commit the crime. We therefore cannot be certain that the jury found that Ms. Grunwald's act of putting her foot on the brake was intentionally done *to* aid Mr. Garcia in committing the murder.

Instead, the jury could have determined that Ms. Grunwald had placed her foot on the brake at Mr. Garcia's insistence, or for some other reason, even though she did not know that by so doing she was assisting him in committing a murder. Under this factual scenario, Ms. Grunwald would be assisting someone *who* committed murder, but she would not be assisting someone *to* commit murder. So because it is unclear from the record whether Ms. Grunwald put her foot on the brake before Mr. Garcia stated his intention to "buck" Sergeant Wride, there is a reasonable probability the jury would not have concluded that Ms. Grunwald's act of putting her foot on the brake was done to intentionally aid Mr. Garcia to commit the murder.

[The Supreme Court remanded the case with an order to retry the defendant.]

Historically, accomplices could only be convicted if a principal was first convicted. This rule has been universally abandoned. Today, an accomplice can be convicted and punished, even when the principal has not been charged, or even if the principal was charged and acquitted. This is the Model Penal Code's (MPC's) approach:

> "[A]n accomplice may be convicted on proof of the commission of the offense and of his complicity therein, though the person claimed to have committed the offense has not been prosecuted or convicted or has been convicted of a different offense or degree of offense . . . or has been acquitted."[3]

Although a conviction of the principal in the first degree is no longer required, most jurisdictions continue to condition the liability of accomplices on the liability of the principal in the first degree—which means, no principal in the first-degree liability, no accomplice liability. In some states, the reason an actor who has committed a crime is not liable determines whether an accomplice may be liable. You will learn later, for example, the difference between excuses and justifications. Both of these refer to situations where a principal has committed all the elements of an offense, but the crime goes unpunished. Self-defense is an example of a justification, and insanity is an example of an excuse. In states that distinguish between the two forms of defense, accomplices continue to derive liability from defendants who have been excused, but not from defendants who were justified.

- Angry about a work disagreement, Laura chases Jessica around the office with a knife. Preston hands Jessica a handgun to defend herself. Jessica's warnings to Laura are ignored, and Laura is shot and killed as she attempts to stab Jessica. Jessica has committed a justified homicide. Therefore, Preston, her accomplice, is also not liable for Laura's death.

- Angel Jake is a member of a cult, Aqon, that believes Lizard people inhabit the earth in the form of elected officials, intent on eliminating the human race. He enlists the assistance of his brother, Randal, to kidnap and kill their city mayor, who he believes is a Lizard. Randal doesn't share Angel's beliefs, but he agrees to help out of love for his brother. Randal's contribution is to track the mayor's daily routine so that Angel can identify the best time to attack. The plan is successful; Angel kidnaps and kills the mayor. Angel is tried first and determined to be legally insane. Even though Angel's acts are excused, Randal continues to be liable as an accomplice for the kidnapping and murder.

As mentioned earlier, however, each party's contribution to, and threatened or realized harm, is a factor at sentencing. So the consequence (i.e., punishment) isn't as different between the Common Law and modern law as may be inferred from the differing legal terminology.

FIGURE 4.1 ■ Liability of the Parties to Crimes		
Party	Description	Liability
Principal in the first degree	Commits the intended crime	Liable for their acts
Principal in the second degree	Complicit and present during the intended crime, but doesn't commit it	Liable for the foreseeable acts of the principal
Accessory before the fact/ accomplice	Involved in the planning and preparation but not the commission of a crime	Liable for the foreseeable acts of the principal
Accessory after the fact	Assists a principal or accomplice in avoiding justice	Liable only for their acts of assistance
Vicarious liability	Not directly involved in the crime, before, during, or after; responsible due to supervisory, control, or oversight authority	Liable for the foreseeable acts of the principal, who is under the control or authority of the defendant

Vicarious Liability

To impute one person's criminal liability to another person was discussed in the last chapter. Vicarious liability is not the same as accomplice liability. Accomplices are personally involved in a crime before, during, or after its commission. This is different from vicarious liability, where a defendant's culpability is imputed (assigned) by virtue of position or relationship. See Figure 4.1 for a listing of the parties and their relative liabilities.

QUESTIONS AND APPLICATIONS

Ashley is an electrician. While installing new outlets and light fixtures in Kevin's home, she notices a collection of rare, valuable baseball cards. Later that night, she discusses what she witnessed with her husband, Walter. The two have fallen on difficult financial times. Four months ago, their apartment rent was increased by 20%, they have had over $50,000 in medical bills in the past year, and they recently lost all of their savings in bad investments. Out of desperation, the two decide to steal and sell Kevin's cards. Ashley is scheduled to return to Kevin's home the following day to finish the electrical work. Kevin, who lives alone, is to give Ashley entry using a remotely controlled smart lock. Walter suggests that they make it appear as though someone burglarized the home before Ashley arrives. They decide that Walter should go to work the next day, lest they will invite suspicion. The next morning, Walter loads Ashley's car with boxes to hold the cards and with burglary tools, which she is to place in the house to direct attention away from them. The theft goes as planned, but they are immediately suspected by the police. In the week after the crime, both are questioned by detectives twice, and they learn that the detectives have made inquiries about them with neighbors, Walter's employer, and others. During the last visit to their home, detectives ask if they can look around, and they deny the request. They conclude that the police will soon appear with a search warrant for their home. They call a friend, Karen, to explain the situation and ask her to hide the cards in her home. Karen, a deacon in her church and a law-abiding person, reluctantly agrees. They hide the cards in her garage. The next day, Karen becomes overwhelmed with a fear of getting caught, but she doesn't have the heart to tell Ashley and Walter that she changed her mind. So she asks a friend, Amy, if she will keep the cards for her. She explains that she purchased the cards as an investment and didn't realize that they need to be stored in a dry, cool environment and her home is not air-conditioned. Amy agreed. The cards are now in Amy's basement. Identify each of the following people as a principal in the first degree, principal in the second degree, accessory before the fact, accessory after the fact, or not criminally liable for the theft of the cards. Explain your answers.

1. Ashley
2. Walter
3. Karen
4. Amy
5. What purpose is served in punishing attempted crimes? What risks or disadvantages are presented by punishing attempted crimes?

EMPOWERING THE VICTIM

Learning Objectives: Discuss how the rights of crime victims are different today than during most of U.S. history, including the use of victim impact evidence in sentencing.

The academic study of criminal law typically limits the discussion of the people involved in crimes to criminals. The secondary role of victims is mirrored in the law itself. For most of U.S. history, victims played a small role and enjoyed very limited rights in the criminal justice system. For example, most prosecutors relied on victims to testify and to provide other support, but often, that cooperation wasn't reciprocated. Victims were often not consulted, not offered assistance, not apprised about the progress of a case or of hearing dates, and at times, were not permitted to participate in sentencing. This began to change in the 1980s, when a victims' rights movement gained momentum. Since that time, all 50 states and the federal government have, through statute or state constitutional amendment, recognized victims' rights. The federal government's victims' rights statute is a good illustration of what is commonly expected of prosecutors and judges:

> 18 U.S.C. § 3771. Crime Victims' Rights
> **a.**   RIGHTS OF CRIME VICTIMS. A crime victim has the following rights:
> 1.   The right to be reasonably protected from the accused.
> 2.   The right to reasonable, accurate, and timely notice of any public court proceeding, or any parole proceeding, involving the crime or of any release or escape of the accused.
> 3.   The right not to be excluded from any such public court proceeding, unless the court, after receiving clear and convincing evidence, determines that testimony by the victim would be materially altered if the victim heard other testimony at that proceeding.
> 4.   The right to be reasonably heard at any public proceeding in the district court involving release, plea, sentencing, or any parole proceeding.
> 5.   The reasonable right to confer with the attorney for the Government in the case.
> 6.   The right to full and timely restitution as provided in law.
> 7.   The right to proceedings free from unreasonable delay.
> 8.   The right to be treated with fairness and with respect for the victim's dignity and privacy.
> 9.   The right to be informed in a timely manner of any plea bargain or deferred prosecution agreement.
> 10.   The right to be informed of the rights under this section and the services described in section 503© of the Victims' Rights and Restitution Act of 1990 (42 U.S.C. 10607©) and provided contact information for the Office of the Victims' Rights Ombudsman of the Department of Justice.

There are constitutional limitations to victims' rights. The Sixth Amendment's right to confront an accuser and to cross-examine witnesses is an example. For example, a law that allows adult accusers in sexual assault cases to testify virtually in an effort to protect them from emotional distress violates the confrontation clause. However, in a reasonable exception to the rule, a young child is permitted to testify remotely, and a defendant's cross-examination of an alleged child victim can be limited in manner to protect the child from emotional harm.[4]

One issue in victims' rights that has been controversial has been the use of victim impact evidence in sentencing, parole, pardon, and clemency decisions. Victim impact evidence refers

---

Victim impact evidence: Oral or written testimony by a victim of the physical, psychological, financial, and other harm caused by a crime. This evidence may not be considered in the guilt determination but may be considered at sentencing or in parole, probation, clemency, and pardon decisions.

to a victim's testimony about the physical, emotional, and financial harm caused by a crime. This evidence may not be heard at trial because it is not material to the guilt decision. But it is used for other purposes, including sentencing, parole, pardon, and clemency. Its influence in parole, pardon, and clemency is less contentious than its use at sentencing. Even SCOTUS has waffled on this question. In *Booth v. Maryland,* 482 U.S. 496 (1987), SCOTUS held that consideration of victim impact evidence in a capital case violates the Eighth Amendment's prohibition of cruel and unusual punishments because it may be wholly unrelated to the blameworthiness of a particular defendant, and may cause the sentencing decision to turn on irrelevant factors such as the degree to which the victim's family is willing and able to articulate its grief, or the relative worth of the victim's character. Thus, the evidence in question could improperly divert the jury's attention away from the defendant. Moreover, it would be difficult, if not impossible, to provide a fair opportunity to rebut such evidence without shifting the focus of the sentencing hearing away from the defendant.

Just 2 years later, the court expanded *Booth* in *South Carolina v. Gathers,* 490 U.S. 805 (1989), to include victim impact statements by prosecutors to juries. And then again, only 2 years later, the court handed down another decision on victim impact evidence. But the court had changed in this 2-year period: Two of the justices who voted in the 5–4 majority in *Booth*, William J. Brennan and Lewis F. Powell, had retired and were replaced with justices who saw things differently. Consequently, in a 6–3 vote, the court overruled Booth's conclusion that the use of victim impact evidence is per se unconstitutional in *Payne v. Tennessee,* 501 U.S. 808 (1991). And that decision stands. So victims are heard by judges and juries at the sentencing stage in most jurisdictions. But *Booth* wasn't overruled entirely. A few of the limitations announced in *Booth* continue today, such as limiting the testimony of victims to the harm they personally experience. They may not comment on the punishment they deem appropriate or speak to the crime itself, except as witnesses in the guilt phase of the trial. Also, the due process clauses of the Fifth and Fourteenth Amendments empower trial judges to limit or exclude evidence that is unduly prejudicial or duplicative.[5]

Victims are also more likely to be compensated for their financial losses than in the past. Trial courts can order convictees to pay restitution to their victims, and many states and the federal government have publicly funded victim compensation funds. Ohio, for example, allows victims of violent crime to apply for compensation up to $50,000 for medical, psychological, crime scene cleanup, funeral, and other expenses. Between 1976 and 2019, Ohio paid more than $380,000,000 to crime victims. The fund also reimburses medical facilities for sexual assault testing and offers grants to victim support services, domestic violence shelters, child advocates, and similar programs.[6]

Restorative justice has received a lot of attention in recent decades. The guiding purpose of a restorative justice approach is to restore the victim, offender, and community to

---

Victim compensation fund: Public monies that reimburse crime victims for their medical, psychological, property, and other expenses.

Restorative justice: A philosophy of justice that focuses on repairing the harm caused by a crime and restoring the victim, offender, and community to their pre-offense state. The restorative justice model is less formal and more focused on the needs of the parties and community than the adversarial model.

their preharm places. Retribution and incapacitation are deemphasized. Restorative justice is holistic; it equally considers the interests of all of the parties involved. Its method is less formal than the traditional adversarial approach. The victim, offender, and possibly others are brought together in an effort to repair the harm to the victim and to find a way to restore the offender's standing in the community through a process aimed at reaching consensus. Admission of guilt, apology, forgiveness, service, compensation of the victim, and rehabilitation are common objectives. This doesn't preclude incarceration, fines, or other traditional punishments, but they are deemphasized. The process is believed by some to facilitate the psychological healing of the parties, in addition to satisfying retributive, rehabilitative, and deterrence objectives. Communities around the United States are experimenting with restorative justice in different ways. Regardless of the model, victims have a greater role in restorative justice than in the traditional adversarial system.

Finally, as you learned earlier, victims may sue their offenders in civil court for intentionally and negligently caused harm. Damages in civil law are broader than court-ordered restitution. Restitution is limited to "out-of-pocket" expenses, including medical and psychological services, loss of income, and property damages. Civil damages, on the other hand, include out-of-pocket expenses as well as pain and suffering and loss of marital consortium (sex and companionship). Both criminal and civil courts may also order the return of property.

Recall from an earlier chapter that the burden of proving liability is lower in civil cases, typically preponderance of the evidence, so it is easier to prove that a defendant committed the alleged offense in tort law. Regardless of the differing standards for proving commission of the offense, the standard for proving the harm is the same for criminal restitution and civil damages: preponderance of the evidence. In criminal law, after a defendant is found guilty beyond a reasonable doubt a separate sentencing hearing occurs, at which the prosecutor is only expected to prove a victim's harm by the lower preponderance standard.

There is another important difference between civil and criminal law: Most of the constitutional protections of criminal law are not applicable in civil court. As examples, a defendant may be called to testify and the exclusionary rule doesn't apply. One limitation on restitution that doesn't exist for civil damages is a defendant's ability to pay. Although SCOTUS has not decided it, many courts assume the Eighth Amendment's prohibition of excessive fines limits restitution. Beyond the Eighth Amendment, many states have imposed this limitation statutorily. Civil courts are not limited in this manner. Indeed, the largest barrier to victims receiving financial compensation is the inability of perpetrators to pay.

From the victim's perspective, restitution is often preferable to civil action because the prosecutor, not a hired attorney, is responsible for proving the case, it often occurs more quickly, and it can be enforced through contempt citations, while civil judgments rely on less effective enforcement methods. This isn't true, however, if a victim wants to recover loss of consortium or pain and suffering damages.

You may also recall from Chapter 1 the principle that criminal charges are not a precondition to a victim bringing a civil suit. Also, acquittal in a criminal court does not preclude a civil judgment, as happened in the O.J. Simpson case.

QUESTIONS AND APPLICATIONS

Through a referendum, a state enacts the following state constitutional amendment:

Prevention of Revictimization Act

Any woman (1) who is the subject of felony crime of sexual violence and (2) can establish by a preponderance of evidence that she will be emotionally traumatized by testifying at the trial of the person accused of committing the felony crime of sexual violence against her may elect to testify remotely. The defendant shall be entitled to cross-examine the woman, regardless of location.

1. Is the remote testimony provision constitutional? Explain your answer.
2. Drawing on what you have learned in an earlier chapter, can you identify another constitutional problem with this statute?

UNFINISHED BUSINESS

Learning Objectives: Identify the elements of attempt, solicitation, and conspiracy, fully explaining the mens rea and actus reus of each crime.

Not all intended crimes are finished. Perry Pickpocket reaches into Penni's purse, only to discover it is empty. Mary Murderer adds poison to her husband's dinner, only to discover that she put chili powder in it, not poison. Neither Perry nor Mary hurt anyone. Should they be punished?

An uncompleted crime is known in criminal law as an inchoate crime. In some instances, inchoate crimes are punished—and sometimes, punished severely. The idea of punishing acts that have not reached the point of being otherwise criminal is controversial. There are at least two concerns: First, if defined too broadly, many acts not seriously intended to reach the point of causing harm would be criminalized; and second, it is possible, even when there is an intent to harm, for the actor to have a change of mind. In both instances, some people believe it is unjust to punish the acts. On the other hand, many argue that attempts should be punished to deter both the actor and others and to incentivize law enforcement to intervene before harm occurs. Our discussion of inchoate crimes begins with attempt.

Tried and Failed

Attempt refers to a failed crime. There are many reasons people fail to complete a crime. Police intervention, natural occurrences, a defendant's fear of getting caught, a change of facts, and

---

Inchoate crime: A started but unfinished crime.

Attempt: When a person intends to cause prohibited harm, takes steps in furtherance of the intent, but the harm doesn't occur.

poor execution can all lead to failure. Attempt was not a crime until the late 1700s. Today, every state and the federal government have many attempt crimes in their criminal codes.

There are two forms of attempt: complete and incomplete. A **complete attempt** occurs when a person commits all of the acts required for the crime, but the intended harm doesn't occur. When a sniper plans an assassination, drives to the location at the time and date planned, loads the rifle, takes aim, fires, and misses, that is a complete attempt—in this case, attempted murder. An **incomplete attempt** occurs when a person commits some, but not all, of the required acts. A sniper who plans an assassination, drives to the location at the time and date planned, loads the rifle, and is then forced to abandon the plan because of a stumble and fall that breaks the shooter's arm is an example of an incomplete attempted murder. Complete attempts are nearly always crimes. Incomplete attempts may, or may not, be crimes. It depends on how close the actor came to completing the crime.

Generally, the elements of attempt are (1) an intent to commit a target crime; (2) some conduct to accomplish the target crime has occurred; and (3) the target crime wasn't completed. As for the mens rea, the target offense must be a specific intent crime. Otherwise, it isn't possible to form the state of mind required to commit attempt. It is possible to attempt to murder, for example. But it is not possible to attempt to negligently kill or harm someone. The MPC follows this approach, requiring that a person act with purpose, the highest level of mens rea.

MPC §5.01. Criminal Attempt

1. *Definition of Attempt:* A person is guilty of an attempt to commit a crime if, acting with the kind of culpability otherwise required for commission of the crime, he:
   a. purposely engages in conduct which would constitute the crime if the attendant circumstances were as he believes them to be; or
   b. when causing a particular result is an element of the crime, does or omits to do anything with the purpose of causing or with the belief that it will cause such result without further conduct on his part; or
   c. purposely does or omits to do anything which, under the circumstances as he believes them to be, is an act or omission constituting a substantial step in a course of conduct planned to culminate in his commission of the crime.

The actus reus of attempt can be confounding. Recall from the actus reus discussion in Chapter 3 that thinking about committing a crime isn't actus reus. Beyond thinking about committing a crime, when does a terrorist cross the line from evil idea to attempted terrorism?

Early attempt law held that an actor committed an attempt only if the last act before the crime was fully completed occurred. This was known as the **last act test**. No United States

---

Complete attempt: When a person completes all the acts required to commit a specific intent crime, but the prohibited harm doesn't occur.

Incomplete attempt: When a person starts but doesn't complete all of the acts required to commit a specific intent crime.

Last act test: A test to determine if an actor crossed the line from preparation to attempt. An actor commits an attempt if the final step toward completion of a crime occurs.

jurisdiction uses this test today. Over time, four different tests developed across the nation. They are the (1) dangerous proximity; (2) res ispsa loquitor; (3) substantial steps; and (4) probable desistence tests.:

A person is dangerously proximate to the completion of a crime when it is possible to complete it immediately—when the final step has been started. This requires close proximity of both time and location. **Res ipsa loquitur**, which translates to "the thing speaks for itself," works like an inference. Under this test, an attempt has taken place if, at the moment the actor stopped moving toward the completion of the crime, it was clear that the actor's purpose was to commit the crime. Evidence of the actor's purpose must "manifest," or be self-evident, from the acts themselves. Unlike substantial steps and dangerous proximity, an early act that has many steps to go before completion can be deemed a criminal attempt.

The Model Penal Code and a large number of states use the substantial steps test. Under this approach, a person must take a "substantial step" toward completing the target crime to be guilty of attempt. The MPC offers several examples of acts that may constitute a substantial step:

Conduct shall not be held to constitute a substantial step under Subsection (1)(c) of this Section unless it is strongly corroborative of the actor's criminal purpose. Without negating the sufficiency of other conduct, the following, if strongly corroborative of the actor's criminal purpose, shall not be held insufficient as a matter of law:

a. lying in wait, searching for or following the contemplated victim of the crime;
b. enticing or seeking to entice the contemplated victim of the crime to go to the place contemplated for its commission;
c. reconnoitering [to scout/check out] the place contemplated for the commission of the crime;
d. unlawful entry of a structure, vehicle, or enclosure in which it is contemplated that the crime will be committed;
e. possession of materials to be employed in the commission of the crime, which are specially designed for such unlawful use or which can serve no lawful purpose of the actor under the circumstances;
f. possession, collection or fabrication of materials to be employed in the commission of the crime, at or near the place contemplated for its commission, where such possession, collection or fabrication serves no lawful purpose of the actor under the circumstances;
g. soliciting an innocent agent to engage in conduct constituting an element of the crime.

Res ipsa loquitor test: A test to determine if an actor crossed the line from preparation to attempt; translates to "the thing speaks for itself." An attempt has taken place if at the moment the actor stopped moving toward the completion of the crime, it was clear that the actor's purpose was to commit the crime. Evidence of the actor's purpose must "manifest," or be self-evident, from the acts themselves.

Substantial steps test: A test to determine if an actor crossed the line from preparation to attempt. An act(s) that strongly corroborates an actor's purpose to commit a specific harm is a substantial step. It is the MPC approach, followed by many states.

For an act to constitute a substantial step, it must be *strongly corroborative of the actor's criminal purpose.* The examples listed here are not per se substantial, but they are presumed to be.

The MPC's substantial steps test has been adopted by more jurisdictions in the United States than the others. It is much broader in its scope than the other tests. For example, simply lying in wait or surveying a site wouldn't be adequate under the other tests, but both are listed as examples of substantial steps by the MPC. Accordingly, it is easier for prosecutors to prove attempt under the substantial steps test than under the others, particularly the last steps test.

The probable desistence test asks whether in the ordinary and natural course of events, without interruption from an outside source, the actor would have completed the crime. The three earlier tests look backward at what happened. This test looks forward; but for the interruption, would the crime have been completed? The test is objective. It is not a matter of what the actor would have done; it is what a reasonable person would have done if not interrupted. A classic example is the bank burglar who is caught outside of a bank in the middle of the night, wearing black clothing and carrying electronic equipment capable of disabling the bank's security system, explosives, and empty bags. (OK, just for fun, add the classic black burglar mask.) A reasonable conclusion would be that the burglar would have gone through with the robbery but for being caught by the police. Accordingly, the probable desistence test is satisfied, enabling a conviction for attempted burglary.

See Table 4.1 for a summary and comparison of the tests.

TABLE 4.1 ■ Comparison of Attempt Act Tests		
Test	*Defined*	*Comparative Difficultly to Prove Attempt*
Last act	Did the defendant commit the last act of the crime?	Most difficult
Dangerous proximity	Was the defendant dangerously close to completing the crime?	Difficult
Res ipsa loquitur	Looking forward, was it clear that the defendant's purpose was to commit the crime?	Medium
Probable desistence	Considering what the defendant had done up to the point of stopping, would the defendant have completed the crime if the intervention hadn't occurred?	Medium
Substantial steps	Did the defendant commit a substantial act toward completing the crime?	Easiest

Let's apply these tests to answer the question asked earlier: When does a terrorist cross the line? This is not science, so feel free to make your own arguments! We need to know more about the terrorist's activities. Here is a hypothetical sequence of events leading up to the planned bombing:

- For years, a person reflects on their hatred of the United States and ways they can harm the greatest number of people.

- June 1: Ideas about bombing various targets are sketched out on paper.

- June 15: A Google search is conducted to find bombmaking supplies. They are ordered.

- June 17: The supplies arrive.

- June 20: The time and location to detonate a bomb are decided—July 4 at the community fireworks display and Independence Day celebration.

- July 1: The bomb is built.

- July 3, 10 p.m.: Terrorist drives 30 minutes to the target location.

- July 3, 10:30 p.m.: Terrorist surveys the area for over an hour, looking for a good hiding place for the bomb.

- July 3, 12 a.m.: Terrorist hides the bomb in the viewing stands.

Beginning with the easiest test—the last step test—the terrorist commits an attempt when the bomb is planted in the stands of the sporting event. This is the last step before the crime is completed.

The dangerous proximity test likely pushes the moment back one step, to when the terrorist surveys the location. This puts the person dangerously close to completion. The immediately preceding step, driving to the location, is not "dangerously close" because of the physical distance between the offender and the intended target and the time remaining between the drive and the target crime.

For the res ipsa loquitur and probable desistence tests, the jury is out. Reasonable people can disagree on whether the determinative act was purchasing the supplies, deciding on a location and time, or constructing the bomb. Neither test would require that the crime proceed to the driving-to-the-location stage.

At the other end of the spectrum, a substantial step was taken when the terrorist purchased the bombmaking supplies. The MPC specifies "possession of materials to be employed in the commission of the crime which are specially designed for such unlawful use or which can serve

---

Dangerous proximity test: A test to determine if an actor crossed the line from preparation to attempt. A person is dangerously proximate to the completion of a crime when it is possible to complete it immediately, or when the final step has been started.

Probable desistence test: A test to determine if an actor crossed the line from preparation to attempt. It asks whether in the ordinary and natural course of events, without interruption from an outside source, would the defendant have completed the crime?

no lawful purpose of the actor under the circumstances" as a substantial step. Considered in tandem with the sketch, the terrorist's purpose is strongly corroborated.

Finally, to avoid the unfairness of punishing a person twice for one act, the **merger doctrine** applies to attempt when the target offense is proved. The merger doctrine holds that if one act proves two crimes, the lower crime drops out. Since attempt is a lesser included of a target offense, it merges into the target offense. For example, Ainsley is charged with attempted fraud and fraud. If Ainsley is convicted of fraud, the attempted fraud charge merges into her conviction, and she is only punished for fraud. Of course, if Ainsley is acquitted of fraud, she may be convicted of the attempt charge. Merger is a Common Law rule. Today, the Fifth Amendment's prohibition of double jeopardy also requires merger in many cases.

Quitter

In some cases, defendants are excused from attempts. Abandonment of a started but unfinished crime is one of those cases. Abandonment falls into a special class of defenses, known as *affirmative defenses*. An affirmative defense is different from the standard factual defenses (e.g., "It wasn't me!," or "The government didn't prove it was me"). An affirmative defense is a justification or excuse for having committed a crime. You will learn more about affirmative defenses in the next chapter. What being an affirmative defense means for abandonment is that a defendant must acknowledge that they began the crime, but that they had a change of heart and decided to not complete it. The MPC's abandonment defense reflects the law of most jurisdictions. It reads:

Section 5.01(4) Renunciation of Criminal Purpose

When the actor's conduct would otherwise constitute an attempt . . . it is an affirmative defense that he abandoned his effort to commit the crime or otherwise prevented its commission, under circumstances manifesting a complete and voluntary renunciation of his criminal purpose. The establishment of such defense does not, however, affect the liability of an accomplice who did not join in such abandonment or prevention. Within the meaning of this Article, renunciation of criminal purpose is not voluntary if it is motivated, in whole or in part, by circumstances, not present or apparent at the inception of the actor's course of conduct, that increase the probability of detection or apprehension or that make more difficult the accomplishment of the criminal purpose. Renunciation is not complete if it is motivated by a decision to postpone the criminal conduct until a more advantageous time or to transfer the criminal effort to another but similar objective or victim.

For abandonment to be legitimate, a defendant's decision to stop must be voluntary—an actual change of heart. If the defendant chooses to abandon a plan because of a change of circumstance that (1) increases the likelihood of getting caught or (2) that makes completion of the crime more difficult, abandonment isn't a defense. Let's apply these principles:

- Aryana the Arsonist has targeted a building for destruction. But she blows out the match intended to start the blaze when she discovers that the building has a fire suppression (sprinkler) system and concludes that the fire will not spread. Aryana has not voluntarily renounced the crime because her decision to stop was driven by discovering the suppression system, which made "more difficult the accomplishment of the criminal purpose."

- Aryana the Arsonist has targeted a building for destruction. But she blows out the match intended to start the blaze when she discovers that the building has a video surveillance system. Aryana has not voluntarily renounced the crime because her decision to stop was driven by discovering the video surveillance system, which increased "the probability of detection or apprehension."

- Aryana the Arsonist has targeted a building for destruction. As she is about to light the match, she begins to think about her parents, Oma and Opa. She thinks about how they taught her to be law-abiding and to do no harm. She worries about how disappointed and hurt they would be by her actions. Overwhelmed with guilt, she leaves without lighting the fire. Aryana has voluntarily renounced the crime.

One Is the Loneliest Number

Under the Model Penal Code and the laws of all states, it is a crime to get others involved in crime. The MPC provides that "a person is guilty of solicitation to commit a crime if with the purpose of promoting or facilitating its commission he commands, encourages or requests another person to engage in specific conduct which would constitute such crime."

There is no requirement that money exchange hands or that the defendant coerce the other person to be involved. A request or encouragement is adequate. The MPC allows for abandonment if the defendant "after soliciting another person to commit a crime, persuaded him not to do so or otherwise prevented the commission of the crime, under circumstances manifesting a complete and voluntary renunciation of his criminal purpose."[7]

Solicitation is a specific intent crime and an affirmative defense. It is possible to solicit others to commit misdemeanors and felonies. Solicitation of prostitution is common, but soliciting another person to commit any crime falls within the scope of solicitation laws. Uniformly, solicitation is punished less severely than the target crime. North Carolina's law exemplifies the grading of solicitation.

N.C. Gen. Statutes §14-2.6. Punishment for Solicitation to Commit a Felony or Misdemeanor

a. Unless a different classification is expressly stated, a person who solicits another person to commit a felony is guilty of a felony that is two classes lower than the felony the person solicited the other person to commit, except that a solicitation to commit a Class A or Class B1 felony is a Class C felony, a solicitation to commit a Class B2 felony is a Class D felony, a solicitation to commit a Class H felony is a Class 1 misdemeanor, and a solicitation to commit a Class I felony is a Class 2 misdemeanor.

b. Unless a different classification is expressly stated, a person who solicits another person to commit a misdemeanor is guilty of a Class 3 misdemeanor.

Like attempt, solicitation merges into the target offense, so only the target offense is punished.

Teamwork Makes the Dream Work

One of the most famous conspiracies in United States history occurred on April 14, 1865, when President Abraham Lincoln was shot in the head by John Wilkes Booth. Lincoln, who was attending a play at Ford's Theater in Washington, DC, when he was attacked, died the next day. Booth acted alone the moment he shot the president, but he wasn't alone in the crime. He was a member of a larger conspiracy, and President Lincoln wasn't the only intended victim; the conspirators also planned to assassinate Vice President Andrew Johnson and Secretary of State William H. Seward. The conspirator who was appointed by the group to kill Johnson backed out of the plot. The attack on Seward was carried out but failed, leaving Seward and others injured.

A large national hunt for the conspirators ensued. Booth was found and killed, and scores of people were detained. Ultimately, eight conspirators were captured, tried, and convicted. Their charges varied, but all were charged with conspiracy to commit murder. Four were hanged; the others received prison sentences. Mary Surratt was one of the conspirators hanged, making her the first woman executed by the United States.[8]

Today, conspiracies are often in the news. Terrorists, drug dealers, murderers, and white-collar criminals are often accused of conspiracy. Prosecutors and courts alike have suggested that conspiracies are uniquely dangerous because they increase the likelihood of success of a crime and reduce the possibility that an individual will abandon a plot.

A conspiracy occurs when (1) two or more people (2) agree to jointly commit a crime or to commit a lawful act (3) in an unlawful manner and (4) an overt act in furtherance of the conspiracy has been taken. Conspiracy is classified as an inchoate offense because the target crime doesn't have to be completed for the crime to occur. Imagine that Eva, Grace, and Thea, high school students unhappy with their grades in chemistry class, decide to kill their chemistry teacher. They hatch a plot for Grace and Eva to create a distraction during class, during which Thea add a dangerous chemical to the teacher's coffee. They are successful in adding the chemical to the coffee without getting caught, and the teacher becomes very sick, but she recovers fully. Even though Eva, Grace, and Thea are not guilty of murder, they are liable for conspiracy to commit murder.

Conspiracy is controversial. Many scholars and jurists have raised concerns that conspiracy laws are so broad that they ensnare innocent people, and because conspiracy doesn't merge with the target offense, guilty people are being punished twice. Learned Hand, a well-known legal scholar, penned that "so many prosecutors seek to sweep within the drag-net of conspiracy all those who have been associated in any degree whatever with the main offenders. That there are opportunities of great oppression in such a doctrine is very plain, and it is only by circumscribing the scope of such all comprehensive indictments that they can be avoided."[9]

There are dozens of federal conspiracy statutes, and to ensure that there aren't any gaps, Congress enacted the following "catch-all" statute:

18 U.S.C. §371 Conspiracy to Commit Offense or Defraud United States

If two or more persons conspire either to commit any offense against the United States, or to defraud the United States, or any agency thereof in any manner or for any purpose, and one or more of such persons do any act to effect the object of the conspiracy, each shall be fined under this title or imprisoned not more than five years, or both.

If, however, the offense, the commission of which is the object of the conspiracy, is a misdemeanor only, the punishment for such conspiracy shall not exceed the maximum punishment provided for such misdemeanor.

The breadth of modern conspiracy law can be seen in the MPC:

SECTION 5.03. CRIMINAL CONSPIRACY

1. *Definition of Conspiracy.* A person is guilty of conspiracy with another person or persons to commit a crime if with the purpose of promoting or facilitating its commission he:
   a. agrees with such other person or persons that they or one or more of them will engage in conduct that constitutes such crime or an attempt or solicitation to commit such crime; or
   b. agrees to aid such other person or persons in the planning or commission of such crime or of an attempt or solicitation to commit such crime.

The provision makes clear that conspirators are like the Three Musketeers—it's *all for one and one for all.* Said another way, they are equally responsible for conspiracy regardless of their individual contributions. Involvement as a principal in the target crime is immaterial. A co-conspirator may be an accessory who plans and participates in advance of the target crime. As you learned earlier, a co-conspirator is liable for the *foreseeable* acts of co-conspirators, even if they were not agreed upon. This is known as the Pinkerton rule.[10]

Conspiracy has a double mens rea requirement. First, there must be specific intent to enter into an agreement, and second, conspirators must specifically intend the target crime. As for the act, the agreement is itself actus reus. If possible, a prosecutor will prove this through the conspirators' communications. These can be written, digital, nonverbal, and verbal. In the absence of communicative evidence, it can also be inferred from the conduct of the conspirators.

In many places, an overt act must be proved in conspiracy cases. This is true under the MPC, except for the two highest grades of felonies. An overt act is conduct taken in furtherance of the target offense of a conspiracy. The overt act doesn't have to be illegal. It simply has to further the conspiracy. Purchasing the chemicals required to build an explosive and the creation of software to breach a bank's digital security are examples of overt acts for the crimes of terrorism and computer theft. As an aside, the Constitution, which has little to say about crime, requires an overt act to prove treason.[11] The next Digging Deeper case examines whether fantasy postings and chats in cyberspace are real enough to be overt acts. The defendant in the case, who was a New York City police officer, was dubbed "Cannibal Cop" by the media.

Pinkerton rule: A conspirator is liable for the foreseeable acts of co-conspirators that occurred during the planning and commission of the target crime.

Overt act: An act taken in furtherance of a crime. Proof of an overt act in furtherance of the target crime is required to prove conspiracy in some jurisdictions.

DIGGING DEEPER 4.2

When does a group's cyber fantasy cross the line to criminal conspiracy?

Case: *United States v. Valle*
Court: United States District Court for the
Southern District of New York.   Citation: 301 F.R.D. 53
Year: 2014

Paul G. Gardephe, U.S.D.J.:
On March 12, 2013, a jury convicted Defendant Gilberto Valle of conspiracy to commit kidnapping (Count One), in violation of 18 U.S.C. § 1201(c), and of conducting a computer search of a federal database that exceeded his authorized access (Count Two), in violation of 18 U.S.C. § 1030(a)(2)(B). Valle has moved for a judgment of acquittal pursuant to Fed. R. Crim. P. 29 or, in the alternative, for a new trial under Fed. R. Crim. P. 33. For the reasons set forth below, Valle's motion for a judgment of acquittal will be granted as to Count One but denied as to Count Two. Valle's motion for a new trial as to Count One will be conditionally granted pursuant to Fed. R. Crim. P. 29(d)(1). To the extent that Valle seeks a new trial on Count Two, that motion will be denied.

The highly unusual facts of this case reflect the Internet age in which we live. To prove the kidnapping conspiracy alleged in Count One, the Government relied on numerous Internet "chats" in which Valle and three alleged co-conspirators discuss in graphic detail kidnapping, torturing, raping, murdering, and cannibalizing women. Valle and his three alleged co-conspirators "met" on Dark Fetish Network or darkfetishnet.com ("DFN"), which bills itself as a fantasy sexual fetish website. Valle's DFN profile page stated: "I like to press the envelope but no matter what I say, it is all fantasy." Many of Valle's Internet communications involved him transmitting Facebook photographs of women he knew—whether his wife, her colleagues from work, or his college friends—and then "chatting" with other DFN users about committing acts of sexual violence against these women. . . .

[This section was written by the court, but appears later in the decision. It was moved here for continuity of the statement of the facts]: Gilberto Valle was raised in Forest Hills, Queens. He graduated from Archbishop Malloy High School and the University of Maryland. After college, Valle returned to New York, and in 2006 he became a police officer in the NYPD. At the time of his arrest six years later in October 2012, Valle worked as a patrol officer in the 26th Precinct on the Upper West Side. There was no evidence at trial that Valle had ever acted violently toward a woman, had ever threatened a woman, had ever been the subject of any misconduct complaint as a police officer, or had ever been involved in criminal activity prior to this case. Kathleen Mangan, Valle's estranged wife, testified that he had never been violent toward her or their child, and that he had no drug or alcohol problems. Valle and Mangan met on a dating website in 2009. Their relationship quickly became serious and they soon moved in together. Mangan described these early months as "fun." "We laughed together. It was nice. He opened doors, pulled out chairs." The relationship declined, however, after Mangan—a New York City schoolteacher—became pregnant in the fall of 2011. As an NYPD officer, Valle worked a 3:00 p.m. to midnight shift. After arriving home from work, Valle would typically spend a few hours "play[ing] video games, watch[ing] TV, [or] go[ing] on the Internet." In the months after Mangan became pregnant, Valle "started staying up really late or not coming to bed at all." The couple's relationship did not improve after their June 2012 wedding. According to Mangan, "[t]he wedding was nice. The marriage was not." Valle continued to spend the early morning hours online. Unbeknownst to his wife, Valle spent much of this time "chatting" over the Internet with others about kidnapping, raping, torturing, murdering, and cannibalizing various women he knew, including Mangan. Mangan became increasingly concerned about Valle's nighttime behavior. In August 2012, she discovered two image files on a MacBook laptop computer that the couple shared, after Valle had neglected to log out of his account. Although the images did not load, Mangan was able to discern the URL for the website from which the images had been downloaded. After entering the URL into the computer's web browser, a website Mangan recalled as "Fetish Net" appeared on the screen. Mangan recalls that a "girl [shown] on the [website's] front page was dead." Mangan confronted Valle about what she had discovered, but his late-night online activities continued, and their relationship steadily deteriorated.

On September 9, 2012, Mangan installed spyware on the couple's MacBook computer. The spyware recorded every keystroke and website entered by the computer's users and took "pictures every five minutes or so of whatever [was] happening on the computer screen." The next morning, Mangan found several disturbing images captured by the spyware, including "pictures of feet that were not attached to bodies." Mangan was also alarmed by several screen names that Valle had been using to communicate with others, including "girldealer" and "girlmeathunter," as well as websites he had visited, including "[d]arkfetishnet," "sexyamazons," "darkfet," "motherless," and "fetlife."

After confronting Valle a second time about his Internet activities, Mangan left the couple's Queens apartment with their infant daughter and flew to her parents' home in Nevada. Once in Nevada, Mangan further inspected the contents of the MacBook. Using the couple's shared password, she was able to log-in to an email account whose address—"Mhal52@yahoo.com"—she did not recognize. Mangan's review of this email account uncovered Facebook images of herself and several other women she knew. Mangan's search regarding her own name revealed a lurid Internet chat in which Valle discussed butchering her: "I was going to be tied up by my feet and my throat slit and they would have fun watching the blood gush out of me because I was young[.]" Mangan testified that one participant wrote, "[']if she cries, don't listen to her, don't give her mercy.['] And Gil just said, [']It's okay, we will just gag her.[']" In other chats Mangan read, Valle discussed raping and torturing women Mangan knew, including Alisa Friscia, Kimberly Sauer, and Andria Noble. In connection with "the pictures of the girls [Mangan] knew," she also recalled reading, "this is a fantasy[.]"

Shortly after discovering these communications, Mangan contacted the FBI and authorized agents to make a copy of the MacBook's hard drive. She also provided agents with keys to the couple's apartment and authorized them to seize an HP laptop computer that had been used by both Mangan and Valle.]

With respect to the kidnapping conspiracy charge, the primary issue raised in Valle's motion for a judgment of acquittal is whether the evidence and the reasonable inferences that may be drawn from that evidence are such that a rational jury could find that "criminal intent ha[d] crystallized," that is, that Valle and his alleged co-conspirators entered into a genuine agreement to kidnap certain women and had the specific intent to actually kidnap these woman.

Valle contends that his Internet chats are fantasy role-play and that the Government did not prove beyond a reasonable doubt that he and his alleged co-conspirators entered into a "real" agreement to kidnap one or more women. The Government argues that the evidence shows that Valle entered into an illegal agreement to kidnap women with (1) a New Jersey man named Michael Van Hise; (2) an individual located in India or Pakistan who uses the screen name "Aly Khan"; and (3) a man using the screen name "Moody Blues," who lives in England. The alleged kidnapping conspiracy thus spanned three continents.

Although the alleged conspiracy lasted nearly a year, all communications between Valle and his alleged co-conspirators in New Jersey, India or Pakistan, and England took place over the Internet. None of the conspirators ever met or took steps to meet, nor did they ever speak by telephone. This is a conspiracy that existed solely in cyberspace. There is no evidence that the alleged conspirators ever exchanged telephone contact information or accurate information about the area in which they lived, or that they ever knew or sought to learn each other's true identities. Communication between the alleged conspirators was episodic and generally infrequent; months often passed between chats, with the alleged conspirators forgetting what had previously been discussed.

After reviewing thousands of Valle's Internet communications, the Government determined that Valle had discussed kidnapping, torturing, raping, murdering, and/or cannibalizing women with twenty-four individuals. At trial, the Government conceded that—as to twenty-one of these individuals—Valle's communications about kidnapping, torturing, raping, murdering, and cannibalizing women are nothing more than fantasy role-play. The Government nonetheless contends that Valle's communications with the remaining three—Van Hise, Aly Khan, and Moody Blues—reflect a "real" kidnapping conspiracy.

As is discussed in detail below, however, Valle's "chats" with a number of the individuals who the Government concedes are fantasy role-play correspondents are substantively indistinguishable from his chats with Van Hise, Aly Khan, and Moody Blues. Both sets of chats involve discussions about Facebook photographs of women Valle knows; dates for planned kidnappings; prices Valle will charge for kidnapping these women; surveillance Valle has allegedly conducted of these women; the use of chloroform to incapacitate victims; acts of sexual violence that will be perpetrated on these women; and fantastical elements such as human-size ovens and rotisseries, and the construction of soundproofed basements and pulley apparatuses that will be used for purposes of torture.

Moreover, the nearly year-long kidnapping conspiracy alleged by the Government is one in which no one was ever kidnapped, no attempted kidnapping ever took place, and no real-world, non-Internet-based steps were ever taken to kidnap anyone. While the alleged conspirators discussed dates for kidnappings, no reasonable juror could have found that Valle actually intended to kidnap a woman on those dates. For example, under the Government's theory, Valle separately "agreed" with two co-conspirators to kidnap three different women on or about the same day, February 20, 2012. Valle was to kidnap one woman in Manhattan; lure another to India or Pakistan; and kidnap a third in Columbus, Ohio.

No one was kidnapped on February 20, 2012, however, and no one was kidnapped on any other date "agreed to" or discussed by Valle and his alleged co-conspirators. Moreover, neither Valle nor any of his alleged co-conspirators ever even raised the issue of whether a "planned" kidnapping had taken place, and if not, why not. Dates for "planned" kidnappings pass without comment, without discussion, without explanation, and with no follow-up.

The kidnapping conspiracy alleged by the Government also featured a steady stream of lies from Valle to his alleged co-conspirators about himself and numerous critical aspects of the alleged conspiracy. Valle lied about his age, about his marital status, about the city and area in which he lived, about whom he lived with, and about his job and the hours he worked. He also lied about whether he owned a house "in the middle of nowhere . . . in Pennsylvania;" about whether he owned a van that could be used to transport victims; about whether he had a "pulley-apparatus" in his basement; about whether he was soundproofing his basement; about whether he had a human-size oven and rotisserie; about whether he possessed address and contact information for the purported targets of the kidnapping conspiracy; about whether he was conducting surveillance of targeted women; about how often he was in contact with these women; and about whether he had obtained, or would obtain, rope, duct tape, and a stun gun for purposes of committing a kidnapping.

Similarly, the details Valle provided to his alleged co-conspirators concerning the targets of the kidnapping conspiracy were—as to identification information—all false. Valle lied about where the purported kidnapping targets lived, their last names, their occupations, their dates and places of birth, where they had attended or were attending college, and the degrees they had obtained. Despite repeated requests, Valle never provided his alleged co-conspirators with the last names and addresses that would have permitted them to locate and identify these women.

The Government, of course, is not required to prove that conspirators planning a kidnapping met in person, spoke over the telephone, or shared accurate information about their names and where they live, the names and addresses of kidnapping targets, or the resources each conspirator will contribute to the enterprise. Those engaged in criminal activity frequently lie to each other about all manner of things, including, for example, the amount and purity of drugs they possess, the value of items to be stolen, and the likelihood of getting caught. There is likewise no legal requirement that a kidnapping actually take place in order for a kidnapping conspiracy conviction to be sustained. Moreover, the fact that Valle had fantasy chats with twenty-one individuals about kidnapping, raping, and murdering women does not establish that his conversations with Van Hise, Aly Khan, and Moody Blues are likewise fantasy.

But the kidnapping conspiracy here was formed and is alleged to have taken place almost exclusively in cyberspace, and in a context in which—according to the Government—the Defendant engaged in countless fantasy role-play conversations with at least twenty-one other individuals about the same topics: kidnapping, torturing, raping, murdering, and cannibalizing women. Under these unique circumstances, in determining whether the Government proved beyond a reasonable doubt Valle's criminal intent—his specific intent to actually kidnap a woman—the fact that no kidnappings took place and that no real-world, concrete steps toward committing a kidnapping were ever undertaken, is significant. And in determining whether Valle and his alleged co-conspirators ever intended to actually commit a kidnapping, the fact that dates for kidnappings are repeatedly set and then pass without incident, inquiry, or comment is powerful evidence that Valle and the three individuals engaged in these allegedly "real" chats understood that no actual kidnapping was going to take place.

Likewise indicative of Valle's lack of criminal intent is the fact that he provided his alleged co-conspirators with a veritable avalanche of false, fictitious, and fantastical information concerning himself and the steps he had allegedly taken to facilitate a kidnapping, including representations about a non-existent van that would be used to transport victims to a non-existent cabin in rural Pennsylvania, where they would be held in a non-existent soundproofed basement with a non-existent pulley mechanism, and cooked in a non-existent human-size oven or using a non-existent human-size rotisserie. The presence and quantity of concededly fictitious and fantastical elements in the chats and emails that the Government claims are "real" preclude any reasonable inference that Valle actually intended to kidnap a woman, particularly given the Government's concession that nearly all of the kidnapping-related chats and emails that Valle engaged in are, in fact, fantasy.

Once the lies and the fantastical elements are stripped away, what is left are deeply disturbing misogynistic chats and emails written by an individual obsessed with imagining women he knows suffering horrific sex-related pain, terror, and degradation. Despite the highly disturbing nature of Valle's deviant and depraved sexual interests, his chats and emails about these interests are not sufficient—standing alone—to make out the elements of conspiracy to commit kidnapping. There must be evidence that Valle actually intended to act on these interests with an alleged co-conspirator.

Under the unique circumstances of this extraordinary case, and for the reasons discussed in detail below, the Court concludes that the evidence offered by the Government at trial is not sufficient to demonstrate beyond a reasonable doubt that Valle entered into a genuine agreement to kidnap a woman, or that he specifically intended to commit a kidnapping. Accordingly, the jury's verdict on Count One, conspiracy to commit kidnapping, cannot stand, and Count One will be dismissed.

Requirements to Sustain a Conspiracy Conviction

Conspiracy statutes reflect a societal choice to detect and punish criminal wrongdoing at its inception, before the object of the illegal agreement has been realized or achieved. "The essence of a conspiracy is 'an agreement to commit an unlawful act.'". . .

Conspiracy law is premised on the long-standing belief that criminal agreements themselves warrant punishment separate and apart from the substantive crimes that are their objects. . . .

The elements of conspiracy are generally more easily proved than the elements of either a substantive offense or an attempt, the latter of which typically requires proof that a defendant took a "substantial step" toward completing a crime. Conspiracy merely requires proof of "(1) an agreement among the conspirators to commit an offense; (2) specific intent to achieve the objective of the conspiracy; and (3) [here] an overt act to effect the object of the conspiracy.". . .

"As an added protection to defendants against punishment for mere talk, in some instances, an overt act must take place in furtherance of the conspiracy." Whereas here— the applicable conspiracy statute contains an overt act requirement, the purpose of that element is to require the Government to demonstrate that the conspiracy was actually "at work.". . .

"[B]ecause conspiracy is a specific intent crime," the Government was required to prove, beyond a reasonable doubt, both that Valle entered into a genuine agreement to commit a kidnapping, and that he had the specific intent to actually kidnap one or more women. . . .

Given the Government's concession that nearly all of Valle's thousands of online communications about kidnapping, rape, murder, and cannibalism are fantasy role-play, the foundation of the Government's case at trial was its argument that Valle's forty chats and emails with Van Hise, Aly Khan, and Moody Blues are meaningfully different, in that they evince true criminal intent. . . .

While Agent Walsh testified that he concluded that the Van Hise/Aly Khan/Moody Blues chats as "real" because "they describe[d] dates, names, and activities that you would use to conduct a real crime," the fantasy chats also contain agreed-upon dates for kidnappings, the names of the same real women, and discussion of the same activities—kidnapping, rape, torture, murder, and cannibalization of women. . . .

[The Court then analyzed the specific facts of each allegation in detail, concluding that none rise to the level of an overt act.] Given that the weight of the evidence supports Valle's contention that he was engaged in fantasy role-play rather than in planning a series of real kidnappings [he is entitled to a new trial].

[Note: *The court denied Valle's motion for a new trial on the unauthorized use of the computer database, which he used to gather information about the women in his stories. On appeal, the trial court's dismissal of the conspiracy to kidnap charges was affirmed, and its decision on the unauthorized use of the computer conviction was reversed. Valle was freed after spending a year in prison.*]

As was true of attempt, it is possible in most jurisdictions to abandon a conspiracy. The MPC provides that "it is an affirmative defense that the actor, after soliciting another person to commit a crime, persuaded him not to do so or otherwise prevented the commission of the crime, under circumstances manifesting a complete and voluntary renunciation of his criminal purpose." In some jurisdictions that require an overt act, abandonment must occur before the overt act.

There are several special rules in conspiracy cases. Unlike attempt, for example, the crime of conspiracy is independent from its target crime. So neither merger nor the Fifth Amendment's double jeopardy clause prevent a person from being punished for both. And in many jurisdictions, the punishment for conspiracy is identical or similar to that of the target crime. Consequently, anytime people join together to commit a crime, they may double their time.

Given the nature of conspiracy crimes, there is a strong preference that the conspirators be tried together in federal and most state courts. At one time, courts imposed a rule of consistency between co-conspirators. Under the rule, one conspirator couldn't be convicted if all of the other conspirators had been acquitted. This rule is no longer applied universally, and it is less likely to be applied when defendants are tried separately. Moreover, it is possible for only one conspirator to be charged. But the prosecutor must prove the involvement of a co-conspirator to the jury, lest it wasn't a conspiracy.

Under Wharton's Rule, also known as the concert of action rule, conspiracy may not be punished when the target offense itself requires multiple people. For example, dueling, gambling, and prostitution are offenses that can only be committed by two or more people. Since the target offense inherently involves a conspiracy, the courts have held that a person should not be punished for both the target offense and conspiracy to commit the target offense. However, this is not a constitutional demand, so a legislature may allow for both.[12]

The co-conspirator hearsay rule is another special rule for conspiracy cases. Hearsay is a statement that is made out of court. It limits trial testimony to what a witness personally knows. The statement "I heard from Peggy that Amy said the defendant broke into the home" is hearsay. The general rule of evidence is that hearsay evidence is inadmissible at trial. But the

---

Rule of consistency: A person may not be convicted of conspiracy if all of the alleged co-conspirators have been acquitted.

Wharton's Rule: A prohibition of punishment for conspiracy when the target offense requires two or more people.

Co-conspiratory hearsay rule: An exception to the hearsay rule for statements by conspirators made during the planning and commission of a target crime.

Hearsay: A statement about what someone else said (or wrote or otherwise communicated). Generally, hearsay evidence is inadmissible at trial to prove the hearsay's truth. There are many exceptions to the hearsay rule.

co-conspirator hearsay rule is an exception that allows the statements of the conspirators that are made out of court to be admitted. The rule applies only to statements made during the planning and commission of the conspiracy. Statements made after a conspiracy has ended are subject to the regular evidentiary rules for hearsay.

Because conspiracies are often ongoing, stretching over long periods of time, applicable statutes of limitations don't usually begin until the final act of the conspiracy occurs. If a statute of limitations is 10 years and the last act doesn't occur until 5 years after the conspiracy is hatched, prosecutors have 15 years to file charges.

Finally, a shout-out to a specific conspiracy law, the Racketeer Influenced and Corrupt Organizations Act.[13] This federal statute, commonly referred to as **RICO**, has made a big splash in criminal and civil law since it was enacted in 1970. Originally intended to be a tool to fight habitual organized crime, prosecutors quickly learned that RICO's broad language and severe penalties could be used effectively well beyond mafia and international drug dealer prosecutions. Long before he was an advisor to President Donald J. Trump or mayor of New York City, Rudy Guiliani was a federal prosecutor. Often referred to as a modern Eliott Ness, the famous federal agent who was responsible for bringing Al Capone to justice, Guiliani used RICO to pursue the top mob bosses in New York, who collectively were known as the Commission. In a national cause célèbre, Guiliani successfully won convictions against many leaders of the most powerful crime families in the United States, leaving them hampered to this day. Guiliani also used RICO to prosecute Wall Street and government corruption. His many prosecutions included Ivan Boesky, who was sentenced to nearly 2 years in prison and a fine of $100 million, and Michael Milken, who was convicted of racketeering, insider trading, and securities fraud. With the help of RICO, Miliken went to prison for almost 2 years and paid $900 million in fines.[14]

RICO provides for both criminal and civil prosecutions. The elements of RICO are

1. conduct
2. of an enterprise
3. through a pattern
4. of racketeering activity.

For purposes of RICO, an enterprise is any group of people. Formal association status is not required. Managed health care facilities, mafia families, biker gangs, business corporations, the Catholic Church for alleged sexual abuses by priests, and the defendants in the Varsity Blues scandal have all been prosecuted under RICO.

A pattern of activity is defined as two or more "predicate acts" within a 10-year period. RICO lists the 35 federal and 10 state crimes that constitute racketeering activities. These include murder, dealing drugs, kidnapping, mail and wire fraud, and extortion. The objective of the law is to address dangerous racketeering schemes, not to punish two unrelated predicate acts. SCOTUS has held that the predicate acts must not only be related, but there must be a threat of continuing activity. Along those lines, SCOTUS decided that "two isolated acts of racketeering activity do not constitute a pattern."[15] The acts must arise of a common scheme.

RICO: An acronym for Racketeer Influenced and Corrupt Organizations Act, a federal conspiracy statute.

That doesn't mean they are the same scheme, but they must be related by purpose, method, participants, or intended victims. Also, two is the minimum number of acts. It is possible that it may take more to prove a pattern.

RICO is serious business. Convictees can be sentenced up to 20 years in prison, have assets seized, and be ordered to pay large fines for each racketeering violation. Don't forget, conspiracy doesn't merge with its target offense. RICO's harsh penalties are added to any sentences for underlying predicate offenses.

A number of different combinations of crimes can arise from a conspiracy. It is possible in a conspiracy of three for two to commit conspiracy, attempt, and the target crime; for three to commit conspiracy and the third to commit attempt and the target crime; for three to commit conspiracy and two to commit attempt; and so on. To further complicate the matter, the parties to the commission of the target crime can be divided into principals and accessories, and there is also the crime of solicitation, which often attends a conspiracy. But remember, attempt merges into its target crime; conspiracy doesn't. See Figure 4.2 for an illustration of the parties and inchoate crimes.

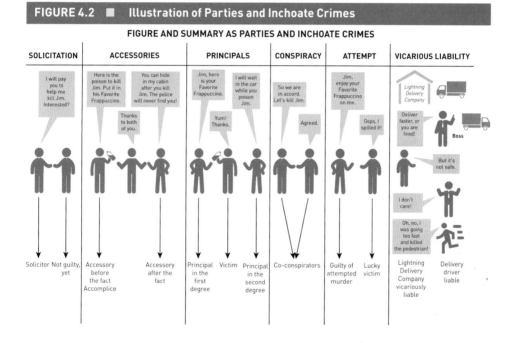

FIGURE 4.2 ■ Illustration of Parties and Inchoate Crimes

FIGURE AND SUMMARY AS PARTIES AND INCHOATE CRIMES

QUESTIONS AND APPLICATIONS

1. What are the elements of attempt?
2. Describe and compare the four tests used today, in addition to the Common Law test that is no longer used, to determine if an act crosses the line to attempt.
3. Define abandonment.

4. Define merger. Does it apply to attempt, solicitation, and conspiracy?
5. What are the elements of solicitation?
6. What are the elements of conspiracy?
7. What is RICO? Why has it proved to be significant in criminal law?

Applying the MPC, analyze each of the following scenarios and explain if the crime of attempt has been committed.

1. Johnny is texting while driving. Because he is distracted, he swerves his car and comes close to hitting a child. He is charged with attempted negligent homicide.
2. Johnny decides to kill Robert, who has been having an affair with Johnny's wife. Johnny purchases a gun, practices shooting the gun at a gun range, and watches Robert's house for 2 days to identify a good time to commit the murder. Robert sees Johnny outside of his home and calls the police. The police report to the scene and investigate. Johnny is charged with attempted murder.

IN A NUTSHELL

There are four parties to crimes: principals in the first degree and second degree and the accessories before and after the fact. Historically, a principal after the fact—typically an individual who helps an accessory before the fact or helps a principal to evade arrest—is punished less severely than the other three.

There are two breeds of inchoate crimes. The first is attempted, but uncompleted, crimes. A complete attempt refers to the situation where a person completes all of the acts required to commit the crime, but the crime doesn't occur. An incomplete attempt refers to a crime that is begun, but all of the acts required for the crime have not been completed. There are two competing goals in this situation. On the one hand, there is a policy argument in favor of giving the wrongdoer the opportunity to withdraw from the plan. That is more likely to happen if the individual can walk away without fear of prosecution and punishment. There is a contrary policy argument in favor of deterring malicious conduct. The law balances those two objectives by drawing a line between the earlier stages, which are not criminalized, and the later stages, which are criminalized. Four tests are used in the United States to draw this line: dangerous proximity, probable desistance, res ipsa loquitur, and the MPC's substantial steps.

The second breed of inchoate crime goes back earlier in time than attempt, all the way to the planning stages. The crime of solicitation is an example. The act of encouraging or rewarding another to commit a crime is a crime itself, even if the targeted crime is never committed. Working with others to commit a crime is also a crime in itself. Two mens rea must be proved for conspiracy: the intent to enter into an agreement and the intent to commit the target offense. In nearly all jurisdictions, an overt act in furtherance of the conspiracy must be taken. If the law were otherwise, the criminal ramblings of any group of people, regardless of seriousness or ability, could be punished. For an act to constitute a substantial step, it must be *strongly corroborative of the actor's criminal purpose.* The examples listed here are not per se substantial, but they are presumed to be.

LEGAL TERMS

accessory after the fact (p. 109)

accessory before the fact (p. 109)

accomplice (p. 111)

Attempt (p. 121)

co-conspirator hearsay rule (p. 135)

complete attempt (p. 122)

dangerous proximity test (p. 125)

Hearsay (p. 135)

inchoate crime (p. 121)

incomplete attempt (p. 122)

last act test (p. 122)

natural and probable consequences doctrine
(p. 110)

overt act (p. 129)

Pinkerton rule (p. 129)

principal in the first degree (p. 109)

principal in the second degree (p. 109)

probable desistence tests (p. 125)

Res ipsa loquitur (p. 123)

Restorative justice (p. 119)

RICO (p. 136)

rule of consistency (p. 135)

substantial steps test (p. 123)

target crime (p. 108)

victim compensation funds (p. 119)

victim impact evidence (p. 118)

Wharton's Rule (p. 135)

NOTES

1. See Moriah Balingit, Susan Svrluga, and Emily Yahr, *The People Charged in College Admissions Scandal Operation Varsity Blues; They Include Parents, Coaches and an Allegedly Corrupt College Admissions Counselor. Washington Post* Blogs. March 13, 2019; and Tom Huddleston, Jr., *How an Ex Basketball Coach Tried to Pull Off the Biggest College Admissions Scam Ever, Allegedly Roping in CEOs and Celebs,* cnbc.com on June 19, 2020.

2. Marc Goodman, "A Vision of Crimes in the Future," TED video, July 12, 2012, https://www.bing.com/videos/search?q=Marc+Goodman%2c+"A+Vision+of+Crimes+in+the+Future%2c".+TED+video%2ced+Talk.+July%2c+2012&docid=608034732087729525&mid=A8A99326105013C593E4A8A99326105013C593E4&view=detail&FORM=VIRE.

3. Model Penal Code § 2.06(7).

4. *Maryland v. Craig*, 497 U.S. 836 (1990).

5. *Bosse v. Oklahoma*, 580 U.S. 137 (2016).

6. *2019 Crime Victim Service Report.* Office of the Attorney General of Ohio. Available at ohioattorneygeneral.gov.

7. MPC §5.02.

8. Douglas O. Linder, Famous Trials (website), accessed June 27, 2020, https://famous-trials.com.

9. *United States v. Falcone*, 109 F.2d 579, 581 (2d Cir. 1940).

10. *Pinkerton v. United States*, 328 U.S. 640 (1946).

11. U.S. Const. Art III, sec. 3.

12. *Iannelli v. United States*, 420 U.S. 770 (1975).

13. 18 U.S.C. §1962.

14. "Rudolph Giuliani," The Mob Museum, accessed June 28, 2020, https://themobmuseum.org/notable_names/rudolph-giuliani/.

15. *Sedima, S.P.R.L. v. Imrex Co., Inc.*, 473 U.S. 479, 496 n.14 (1985).

5 DEFENSES: FACTUAL AND JUSTIFICATIONS

In 2009, three brothers were accused of drug trafficking in Malaysia. One died prior to trial. Regardless, the prosecutor knew that only one of the defendants committed the crime, and it wasn't the brother who died. With eyewitnesses, the case would appear to have been a slam dunk. But there was a twist. The two remaining brothers were identical twins, and the court was unable to distinguish between them, so they were both acquitted. For one of the brothers, the confusion made the difference between freedom and hanging, the punishment in Malaysia for the crime.[1]

In a case from Japan, "pinup" model Serena Kozakura was charged with trespass. Allegedly angry over her boyfriend's suspected infidelity, prosecutors claimed that she kicked a hole in the front door of her boyfriend's apartment and crawled through it. Ms. Kozakura countered that she couldn't have committed the crime because her 44-in. bust made it impossible for her to pass through the hole. She was acquitted by the judge. Ms. Kozakura later remarked, "I used to hate my body so much, but it was my breasts that won in court."[2] Although these stories are from abroad, they are fun, outlandish examples of factual defenses that are recognized in the United States.

This chapter and the next are about defenses—the various ways people declare that they are not criminally liable. There are two broad categories of defenses: factual and legal. Legal defenses are further divided into justifications and excuses. In this chapter, you will explore factual defenses and justifications. Excuses are covered in Chapter 6.

Defenses are characterized as *perfect* and *imperfect*. The discussion begins there.

IN PURSUIT OF PERFECTION

Learning Objective: Define and distinguish perfect and imperfect defenses.

A defense that wholly absolves a defendant of criminal liability is known as a perfect defense. A defense that is accepted but only reduces a defendant's culpability is an imperfect defense. Imperfect defenses sometimes result in convictions for lesser crimes; they always result in lesser punishment. It is a perfect defense, for example, when a defendant can prove that the actus reus was protected by the Constitution. The state may not, for example, criminalize speech that is hateful or offensive. If a state were to prosecute a person for uttering offensive words, the case

---

Perfect defense: A defense that completely relieves a defendant of criminal liability.

Imperfect defense: A defense that partially relieves a defendant of criminal liability or mitigates punishment.

would be dismissed on First Amendment grounds. And, by the way, the law would likely be stricken as unconstitutional. As you will learn shortly, if a person kills another in self-defense, but the jury determines that only nonlethal force was necessary, the defendant is guilty of some form of homicide, but not intentional murder.

QUESTIONS AND PROBLEMS

1. Define and distinguish perfect from imperfect defenses.

MAY I BE EXCUSED?

Learning Objective: Define affirmative defense and describe how an affirmative defense is different from a standard factual defense.

As you learned in the last chapter, affirmative defenses are special defenses, procedurally. They turn the standard rules of burden of proof upside down. Instead of the state bearing the burden of proof, the defendant must raise and prove the defense. Either statutory law or a court rule establishes a deadline for raising an affirmative defense. A defendant who doesn't have good cause to miss the deadline loses the right to argue the defense to the jury. Typically, the defendant is also expected to produce a small amount of evidence to support the affirmative defense claim. At the pretrial stage of the case, this is presented to the judge, who decides whether the defendant may offer the defense to the jury. Little evidence is required to get beyond this point, but again, if the evidence isn't produced, the defendant will not be allowed to present the defense to the jury.

If the defendant satisfies this requirement, then the question to be answered is who bears the burden of persuading the fact finder (jury or judge) that the defense is legitimate. Depending on the defense and the jurisdiction, a defendant may be expected to prove the truth of an affirmative defense by either the preponderance of evidence or a clear and convincing standard. In other jurisdictions, or for other defenses, the burden of persuasion may "shift" back to the state to disprove the claim. See Figure 5.1, which maps the process of raising and proving affirmative defenses. If the jury finds the defense to be legitimate, they either return a verdict of not guilty or guilty to a lesser crime if the defense is imperfect. If they don't believe the defense, they must still decide the ultimate question: whether the state proved the elements of the crime beyond a reasonable doubt.

There are many affirmative defenses, including alibi (a claim that the defendant was not present at the crime), duress, necessity, self-defense, insanity, entrapment, and mistake. Our discussion of defenses begins with two factual defenses: the claim of factual innocence, which is not an affirmative defense, and alibi, an affirmative defense in many jurisdictions.

Affirmative defenses: Special defenses that must be raised and proved by a defendant. Affirmative defenses involve facts that reduce or fully extinguish a defendant's culpability, even if the forbidden acts are committed.

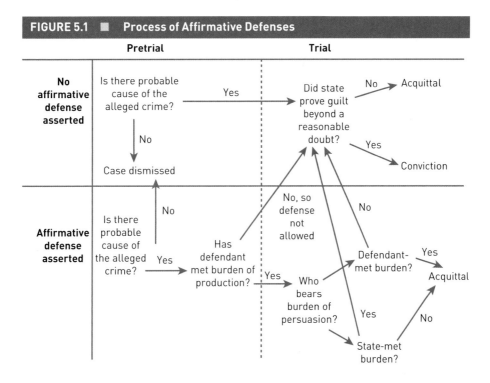

FIGURE 5.1 ■ Process of Affirmative Defenses

QUESTIONS AND PROBLEMS

Derrick is charged with murder. He is confident that the state can't prove his guilt beyond a reasonable doubt. He instructs his attorney, "Be cool. Make 'em prove it. They ain't got nothing on me." His attorney disagrees and urges a more proactive defense. Derrick tells the attorney to stand down. At trial, Derrick becomes worried. He can see an impending conviction in the faces of the jurors. He tells his attorney that he was somewhere else at the time of the murder and that he has a witness to prove it. He wants his attorney to move for a continuance of the trial to find the witness. The attorney complies with Derrick's demand and moves for a continuance. What is the most likely outcome of the motion?

I DIDN'T DO IT

Learning Objective: Define factual defense and alibi. Identify several causes of wrongful convictions.

A common defense is the claim of factual innocence. Because of the presumption of innocence and the right to be free from self-incrimination, a defendant can choose to be passive throughout the proceeding. There is no requirement that a defendant present a defense, and the Fifth Amendment's self-incrimination clause forbids the state from calling a defendant to testify at trial. Regardless, many defendants choose to present evidence of innocence or to suggest an alternative theory of the case to the police during the investigative stage or at trial.

Alibi, or evidence that a defendant was in a different location when a crime was committed, and evidence that someone else committed the crime are examples of perfect factual defenses. Alibi is an affirmative defense. To enable the state to conduct its own investigation of an alibi and certain other defenses, a defendant must plead them—make the court and prosecutor aware of them—by a certain date, and often, the defendant must prove them.

In recent years, wrongful convictions have been in the spotlight. The advent of DNA technology has revealed that eyewitness identification and confessions, often critical evidence in convictions, are not as reliable as once believed. Normal human error, prosecutorial misconduct and overzealousness, laws providing for excessive punishment, an increasing criminalization of behavior in the United States, and (some believe) an inherently coercive plea bargaining system also contribute to the number of wrongful convictions.

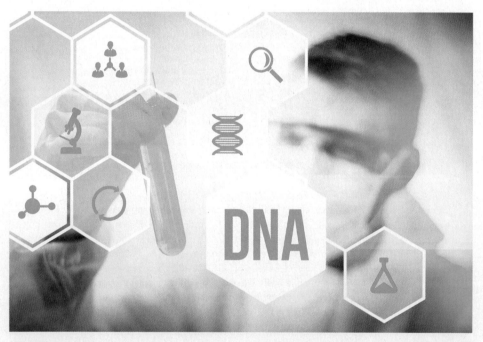

PHOTO 5.1 Instead of relying on eyewitness identification, forensic scientists can use DNA profiles to identify criminals.

Mikko Lemola/iStock

The National Registry of Exonerations at the University of Michigan reports that there were over 2,600 exonerations between 1989 and 2020, with over 23,000 years of free life lost.[3] One organization, the Innocence Project, has assisted in the exoneration of nearly 400 people. Most of these people were serving very long sentences, and more than 20 were sentenced to die.[4]

Alibi: A affirmative, factual defense where the defendant alleges that they were in another location at the time of a crime.

The number of wrongful convictions is not easy to determine; consequently, estimates vary considerably. Most researchers cast the number between 1% and 6%, with most researchers tending toward the lower end.[5] Regardless of whether the truth is at the high or low end, the raw number is large when understood in the context of 1 million felony convictions annually in the United States.

QUESTIONS AND PROBLEMS

1. Define factual defense and alibi.
2. Identify four factors that contribute to wrongful convictions in the United States.
3. What is an acceptable level of false guilt findings in criminal cases, as a percentage of the whole? Explain your answer.

I HAD TO DO IT

Learning Objective: Define and distinguish the defenses of necessity and duress.

Imagine that you are kidnapped and told that you would be killed if you refuse to sell a bag of illegal drugs to a dealer. If you comply, you have committed the crime of drug trafficking. Regardless, you are not guilty. This is an example of an excused crime. Excuse refers to conduct that is illegal but forgiven, or at least the punishment is reduced because of the circumstances faced by the defendant. A closely related defense, justification, refers to conduct that is not considered illegal to begin with, even though it causes harm. Justified conduct is thought to be universal. It is focused on society's interests, while excuses are personal to the actor. All people are entitled to defend themselves from harm, so self-defense is justified. Relieving a specific person of responsibility for a murder because of that individual's insanity is an excuse; it is personal to the actor. The distinction between the two is vague. Legal philosophers enjoy debating where the line between the two is found, if a distinction exists at all.

Today, excuses and justifications operate similarly, except that excused conduct can be either perfect or imperfect, and justified conduct is always a perfect defense. Often, justifications and excuses contain both questions of law and questions of fact. What that means in practice is that a judge must agree, as a matter of law, that a defendant can present the defense to the jury, or to the judge if a bench trial. If the answer is yes, then the defendant bears the burden of proving the defense. We begin our examination of excuses and justifications with the defenses of necessity and duress.

Excuse: Conduct that is illegal but forgiven, or at least, the punishment is reduced because of the circumstances faced by the defendant.

Justification: Conduct that is legal, even though it causes harm.

BREAKING NEWS   THE DEATH OF GEORGE FLOYD MURDER TRIAL   LIVE

Judge Instructs Jury Before Opening Statements   COURT

'O INVESTIGATORS, COMMON PRACTICE IN COLORADO.   TWO WEEKS LATER, THEY WERE STI   10:30 AM ET

PHOTO 5.2 A judge instructs the jury on the first day of the trial of former Minneapolis police officer Derek Chauvin, who was charged with second-degree murder and manslaughter in the death of George Floyd.

ZUMA Press, Inc. / Alamy Stock Photo

Necessity

In rare circumstances, compliance with the law can lead to greater harm than violating the law. In such cases, the excuse of **necessity**, also known as choice of evils, may shield the actor from liability. The prisoner who runs out of a prison when it is engulfed in flames has chosen the lesser of two evils—life over compliance with court-ordered incarceration. Of course, the prisoner is expected to remain at the scene and to immediately surrender to authorities. This hypothetical offers an opportunity to point out the interrelationship of the various legal principles you have learned. Let's consider our prisoner's escape and the two essential elements. Did the prisoner act voluntarily? Likely, but it is also reasonable to conclude that fleeing imminent death is reflexive. Did the prisoner possess the mens rea of escape? The answer to that question depends on the specific language of the escape statute. Yes, if the statute imposes strict liability—for example, "It shall be a crime for a person to leave the custody of the state while lawfully confined." However, if the statute were to read, "It shall be a crime for a person to leave the lawful custody of the state with the *purpose of escaping confinement*," the outcome would be different. In the latter instance, a prisoner who flees custody to avoid burning to death could defend against an escape charge through both the defenses of necessity and the absence of mens rea.

The elements of necessity under the MPC §3.02(1)(a) are as follows:

1. Conduct which the actor believes to be necessary to avoid an evil to himself or another is justifiable, provided that:
   a. the evil sought to be avoided by such conduct is greater than that sought to be prevented by the law defining the offense charged; and

---

Necessity: A doctrine that excuses illegal conduct because it was necessary in order to avoid greater harm. Also known as "choice of evils" defense.

b. neither the Code nor other law defining the offense provides exceptions or defenses dealing with the specific situation involved; and

c. a legislative purpose to exclude the justification claimed does not otherwise plainly appear.

2. When the actor was reckless or negligent in bringing about the situation requiring a choice of evils or in appraising the necessity for his conduct, the justification afforded by this section is unavailable in a prosecution for any offense for which recklessness or negligence, as the case may be, suffices to establish culpability.

Therefore, under (1), the evil that is avoided by breaking the law must be greater than the evil that is chosen. A boat captain who chooses to moor to a private dock during a violent storm to save a boat full of passengers has chosen the lesser of two evils: trespass over loss of life. In a case from New York, an intoxicated driver caused a minor traffic accident. He stopped to exchange insurance and driver's license information with the driver of the other vehicle. During their exchange, the other driver became belligerent and reached into the backseat of his car. Believing the driver was reaching for a gun, the defendant jumped into his car and fled. A few miles into his escape, he struck and killed a pedestrian. On appeal of his conviction of negligent homicide and other charges, the appellate court decided that the trial court was wrong in not allowing him to assert necessity—that he was speeding to avoid a threat to his life.[6]

Subsection (1) acknowledges that statutory law may make necessity unavailable as a defense, even if a person has chosen a lesser harm. For example, the intentional taking of life is not a permitted choice in most jurisdictions, even if it is the lesser evil. There is a well-known scenario that illustrates this rule. In this story, a trolley is running at a high speed when its brakes fail. Ahead, the trolley operator can see five people on the track—the train will undoubtedly kill them. The track splits, with a spur running to the right, just before the train reaches the people. The trolley operator can divert the train to the right, away from the five people. However, there is an employee on the spur who will be killed. The scenario presents interesting moral, philosophical, and legal problems. But the law of necessity is clear. If the switch operator chooses to divert the train to the right, the homicide of the employee isn't excused, even though a total of four lives were saved. Why wouldn't the law incentivize the decision to take one life to save four? Likely, it is not the trolley case that is driving the policy; it is more subtle cases. The law doesn't want people to engage in evaluating the value of life or in comparing the value of multiple lives. Blackstone wrote in his commentaries that a person "ought rather to die himself than escape by the murder of an innocent."[7] Reasonable people disagree about this point. Again, this is a place where the moral choice may diverge from legal choice. In reality, however, morality may still be a factor; many prosecutors wouldn't file charges, and many juries wouldn't convict in situations like the trolley case. Or at least, the trolley operator's reasonable fear of the death of the people on the tracks may have the effect of reducing a murder charge to something lower (e.g., manslaughter).

Another limitation of the necessity defense is that a defendant who is responsible for creating the threat is not entitled to the defense's protection. Take our boat captain, for example. If the captain had been warned that the violent storm was approaching and chose to take the passengers out on the water anyway, necessity won't protect the captain from a trespass prosecution. Section (2) of the MPC, quoted earlier, incorporates this principle, at least insofar as a defendant has negligently or recklessly caused the situation.

Necessity has arisen frequently in civil disobedience cases in recent years. Civil disobedience refers to an intentional, nonviolent violation of law intended to achieve a larger social purpose. Civil disobedience is to be distinguished from nonviolent, lawful demonstrations, which are protected by the First Amendment as well as state free speech and assembly laws. Antiabortion, environmental, animal, and civil rights activists have all asserted necessity in defense of their conduct.

The legal theory of protestors who assert the right to claim necessity is that the harm they are protesting about outweighs the harm caused by their crimes. The idea isn't entirely new. In 1974, Samuel Lovejoy, a farmer and writer in Massachusetts, had environmental objections to a nuclear power plant that was to be constructed near his home. Early one morning, he attached a chain from his truck to a meteorological tower that had been constructed as part of the nuclear power project, detached the anchors that secured the tower to the ground, and put the "pedal to the metal," pulling the tower down. He then hitchhiked to a police station and surrendered himself. (In a funny twist, it was a police car that offered Lovejoy a ride to the station.) He was criminally charged with destruction of personal property. There was a groundswell of local support for Lovejoy, in part because of a growing skepticism of the safety of nuclear power. Much to everyone's surprise, the trial judge dismissed the complaint, even though the defendant didn't make a dismissal request (this is known as sua sponte) on the theory that the tower was real property (like home or land) because it was secured to the ground. Apparently influenced by public opinion, and maybe Lovejoy's purpose, the prosecutor didn't appeal or file new charges.[8]

But Lovejoy's success is atypical. Other activists have had little success in convincing courts to permit necessity to be presented to juries. The fear of the impact of an unfiltered use of the defense was expressed by a California court this way:

> To accept the defense of necessity under the facts at bench would mean that markets may be pillaged because there are hungry people; hospitals may be plundered for drugs because there are those in pain; homes may be broken into because there are unfortunately some without shelter; department stores may be burglarized for guns because there is fear of crime; banks may be robbed because of unemployment.[9]

Further, to permit the widespread application of the necessity defense would be to convert juries from fact finders in individual cases into legislators and policymakers. To permit this would be a violation of the separation of powers. Courts may not engage in lawmaking, and naturally, they may not empower juries to do so. And there are other concerns about empowering juries in this way, including whether they are competent to make these decisions, and the suitability of the adjudicative process, as opposed to the legislative investigatory process, to policymaking.

In one federal appellate case, defendants who trespassed and threw faux blood on furniture and walls of an Internal Revenue Service office in protest of U.S. involvement in El Salvador were not permitted to argue the necessity defense because the harm they were protesting wasn't immediate, they were not protesting a legal wrong (the United States was lawfully involved in

El Salvador), and because their protest was indirect.[10] Their actions were indirect because the law they violated wasn't the object of their protest. Direct civil obedience, on the other hand, involves a violation of a law that is itself the object of the protest. For example, during the civil rights movement of the 1960s, Blacks would violate segregation laws in "sit-ins," where they would seat themselves in areas reserved for whites. In these cases, accepting the consequences of nonviolent civil disobedience may satisfy ethical and social principles, as well as uphold the rule of law. Civil rights leader Dr. Martin Luther King, Jr. penned that

> [o]ne who breaks an unjust law must do so . . . with a willingness to accept the penalty. I submit that an individual who breaks a law that conscience tells him is unjust, and who willingly accepts the penalty of imprisonment in order to arouse the conscience of the community over its injustice, is in reality expressing the highest respect for law.[11]

Duress

Another excuse is **duress**. The MPC says this about duress at §2.09:

1. It is an affirmative defense that the actor engaged in the conduct charged to constitute an offense because he was coerced to do so by the use of, or a threat to use, unlawful force against his person or the person of another, which a person of reasonable firmness in his situation would have been unable to resist.
2. The defense provided by this Section is unavailable if the actor recklessly placed himself in a situation in which it was probable that he would be subjected to duress. The defense is also unavailable if he was negligent in placing himself in such a situation, whenever negligence suffices to establish culpability for the offense charged.
3. It is not a defense that a woman acted on the command of her husband, unless she acted under such coercion as would establish a defense under this Section. [The presumption that a woman acting in the presence of her husband is coerced is abolished.]
4. When the conduct of the actor would otherwise be justifiable under Section 3.02, this Section does not preclude such defense.

The elements of duress are as follows:

1. The defendant was threatened and
2. the threat caused a reasonable belief
3. that the only way of avoiding serious personal injury or death to oneself or others
4. was to commit the crime.

Duress requires a reasonable belief of death or serious bodily injury by the defendant. Recall that reasonableness means objectively acceptable—in the range of what a person with ordinary reason, foresight, and intelligence might do. It is reasonable for a bank manager to help her

Duress: A doctrine that excuses illegal conduct because it was caused by a threat of serious bodily harm or death.

child's kidnappers steal from the bank when her assistance is demanded under threat of killing the child. But it isn't reasonable for the bank manager to help a stranger steal from the bank under a threat that the stranger will use a paper straw to kill one of the tellers. As to the third requirement, avoiding serious bodily harm or death, duress would not be available to the bank manager if she helped the thief under threat of being punched in the arm. It may hurt, but she has to suffer the punch. As is true of necessity, duress doesn't excuse intentional homicide, but if reasonable, it may reduce a murder charge to something lower (e.g., manslaughter).

Duress is sometimes an issue in prostitution and human trafficking cases. By definition, trafficked persons are controlled by another person through financial debt, withholding of passports and visas, and threats of violence. Most trafficking victims are exploited for labor, but others are used for sex and drug business. It is common for trafficking victims to be ordered to commit a variety of crimes, including prostitution, theft, and drug dealing. Today, there are "safe harbor" laws in many states that codify the duress defense specifically for trafficked and enslaved persons. You will learn more about this later in the book. See Table 5.1 for a comparison of necessity and duress.

TABLE 5.1 ■ Necessity and Duress Compared		
Defense	*Elements*	*Example*
Necessity	A criminal act that is taken to avoid a greater harm to oneself or others is excused, provided the defendant didn't create the harm that is avoided.	Defendant with an expired driver's license drives his son to the emergency room during a life-threatening allergic reaction.
Duress	A criminal act that is taken under threat of harm; the defendant reasonably believed the act was necessary to avoid the harm.	Defendant breaks the window and steals a car under a threat by a fellow gang member that if he doesn't do it, he will be shot.

Duress has also been successfully used by people who have been forced to commit crimes by their spouses. *People v. G. M.* is an example.

DIGGING DEEPER 5.1

Is a person liable for the crimes ordered by an abusive spouse?

Case: *People v. G. M.*
Court: City of New York, Criminal Court.   Citation: 922 N.Y.S.2d 761
Year: 2011
Opinion by: Judge Toko Serita

Introduction

During a five-month span, from September 1997 through January 1998, defendant G. M. was arrested on six separate occasions, twice each for prostitution, criminal trespass and drug possession. As a result of the guilty pleas taken in each of these cases, she was ultimately convicted of two violations and four class B misdemeanors. The defendant now moves to vacate these convictions pursuant to Criminal Procedure Law § 440.10 on the grounds that, among other things, she was a trafficking victim at the time these offenses occurred. On April 1, 2011, this court issued an oral ruling granting the defendant's motion to vacate the convictions and dismissing the accusatory instruments, indicating that a written decision would follow.

Factual Background

In 1989, the defendant, a native of the Dominican Republic, met D. S. while on a tourist visa to the United States. The defendant decided to stay in the United States with D. S., in part, to earn money for her two children who were still living in the Dominican Republic. In 1994, the couple married. Soon thereafter, the relationship took a turn for the worse as D. S. began to physically abuse the defendant, something which had never happened before the marriage. As a result of this abuse, the defendant returned to the Dominican Republic later that year.

In early 1996, D. S. went to the Dominican Republic and begged the defendant to move back with him to New York, promising to find her a good job and to help her with her immigration status. She decided to do so "in the hope that it would improve my life and the lives of my children" (affidavit of G. M. at 2). Upon her return to New York, the defendant discovered that her husband was addicted to crack cocaine. The abuse resumed, and was often more severe when he was under the influence of drugs.

The continued violence at times resulted in visits to the hospital and left the defendant scarred and disfigured. D. S. also raped her when he was high on crack cocaine and imprisoned her against her will, sometimes for an entire weekend. He succeeded in completely isolating her from others and exerted control over almost every aspect of her life, taking all the income she earned working at various jobs. He exercised complete control over her, physically and psychologically, such that her "every move was tracked by [D. S.]" and she was not "allowed" to leave the room or apartment without him. He would often drop her off and pick her up from her jobs, waiting in a car parked outside to make sure she did not go somewhere else.

It was during this period of abuse that the defendant was arrested on six separate occasions. From September 1997 through January 1998, defendant was arrested twice for prostitution (Penal Law § 230.00), twice for criminal trespass in the third degree (Penal Law § 140.10), and twice for criminal possession of a controlled substance in the seventh degree (Penal Law § 220.03), all misdemeanor offenses. The defendant pleaded guilty on each of these cases, often at arraignments, resulting in two noncriminal convictions for disorderly conduct, a violation, and four Class B misdemeanor convictions.

According to the defendant's affidavit, D. S. forced her to engage in these illegal activities, including prostitution, upon threat of physical harm or actual violence if she did not comply. She was also forced to purchase crack cocaine for her husband because D. S. feared getting arrested himself. If she refused to comply with any of his demands, he would threaten to kill her or harm her children in the Dominican Republic. D. S. would drive the defendant to brothels and wait inside his car while he made her do his bidding. If she did not earn enough money for him, he would become angry and violent. The defendant was never allowed to keep any of the money she earned. "[D. S.] would pay for my food, clothes, and everything else. He would not give me money for my own necessities."

In 2003, the defendant tried unsuccessfully to leave her abusive husband. That year, she escaped from him and returned to the Dominican Republic to be with her children, whom she had not seen in over eight years. He ultimately tracked her down and forced her to return by issuing threats to harm a close family friend. When she returned to New York City, she found that "nothing had changed. I just went back to the nightmare I was living. The beatings were even worse because [D. S.] was angry that I went to the Dominican Republic" (*id.*). The defendant's ordeal ended in January 2005, when D. S. left one day and never returned. To date, the defendant does not know where he is and he has not attempted to contact her. The defendant eventually sought assistance from outside organizations to help her put her life back together, and in 2009, she received a "T Visa" (T-1 Nonimmigrant Classification Status), after proving to the federal government that she was a victim of human trafficking.

Yet despite the defendant's status as a trafficking victim, her criminal record has created a severe hardship for her. For example, her job as a home health care attendant, which she held for approximately five years, was jeopardized when the Department of Health (DOH) did a background check on her and discovered her criminal convictions. As a result of this discovery, the defendant was first put on suspension by DOH in 2007 and then terminated. With the assistance of the Sex Workers Project of the Urban Justice Center, she was approved to work again after successfully contesting DOH's decision. This process, however, took almost three years. The defendant now makes this application to clear her criminal record in part, because she will be otherwise vulnerable to having her background exposed to future employers, creating further embarrassment, humiliation and financial hardship.

The original basis for the defendant's CPL article 440 motion, filed on June 3, 2010, was that the defendant, a non-English-speaking Dominican woman, took these pleas without the effective assistance of counsel, and that these pleas were neither knowing nor voluntary. During the pendency of this litigation, however, the New York State Legislature amended Criminal Procedure Law § 440.10, allowing the New York courts, for the first time, to vacate the convictions of those arrested for prostitution-related offenses if they were sex trafficking victims at the time of the arrest. After the passage of that amendment, in a supplemental motion dated August 24, 2010, the defendant moved this court to consider these new provisions as additional grounds for granting the article 440 motion.

On December 17, 2010, the Queens County District Attorney's Office, represented by Assistant District Attorney Kimberly Affronti, the Deputy Bureau Chief of the Criminal Court, issued an oral response to the defendant's application in which it stated:

"Your Honor, you know the People have spent a great deal of time reviewing all of the facts of this case. While every 440.10 motion is viewed on its own merit, this case was an exceptional case and the merits of the case were based totally on the People's reliance on the defendant's truthfulness of what she disclosed in the affidavit on May 13th as well as her interview on November 22nd. . . . The People are exercising discretion in this particular case, the People are not looking to expand the statute. This defendant was convicted of four crimes and two violations, only two of the crimes are covered by [this statute]. It is the People's position that based on our reliance on the defendant's truthfulness, the right thing to do is to consent to the defendant's motion. Again, the People are stressing that we are not looking to expand the statute, this is not a case to refer to in future 440 motions. This case in no way sets a precedent for how the People will view other cases, nor do the People expect this decision to effect the defendant's cases in any other county. Having said all of that your Honor, the People do consent to defense's 440.10 motion."

In a ruling from the bench on April 1, 2011, this court granted the defendant's article 440 motion by vacating the judgment of conviction in each of the defendant's six cases and dismissed all of the accusatory instruments.

In August 2010, the New York State Legislature amended Criminal Procedure Law § 440.10 to allow sex trafficking victims to vacate their convictions for prostitution-related offenses. Specifically, this new legislation allows for the vacatur of convictions where the underlying charge was for prostitution (Penal Law § 230.00) or loitering for the purpose of engaging in a prostitution offense (Penal Law § 240.37) and the defendant's arrest on that charge "was a result of having been a victim of sex trafficking victim... "

[T]he defendant has provided a very compelling narrative of the circumstances surrounding all of her arrests, demonstrating that they were the product of years of brutal physical, psychological and sexual violence by her husband, which resulted in having been trafficked by him. While the defendant has moved to vacate all six convictions based on the provisions of the new amendment, and even though only two are prostitution offenses technically covered by the scope of CPL 440.10 (1) (i), this issue need not be addressed in the instant case because the People have consented to the defendant's motion in its entirety. Based upon the unique circumstances presented here, this court concurs with the People's position that all of the defendant's convictions are entitled to the relief requested. Thus, under the provisions of the new amendment, this court "must vacate the judgment and dismiss the accusatory instrument."

For the foregoing reasons, the defendant's application to vacate the judgments of conviction on all six cases is granted and the accusatory instruments in these matters are dismissed.

QUESTIONS AND PROBLEMS

1. Define and distinguish an excused crime from a justified crime.
2. Define and identify the elements of necessity.
3. Define and identify the elements of duress.

Identify whether necessity or duress is the better defense for each of the following scenarios and analyze the likelihood of the success of the defense.

1. Mabel and Steve are shopping. Steve drove to the mall because Mabel's driver's license was suspended for failure to renew it. While walking from a clothing store to UniqueBrewry to have lunch, Steve is shot by a drive-by shooter. With the assistance of other shoppers, Mabel is able to get Steve into their car and rushes him to the hospital. They arrive at the hospital safely, and Steve recovers after surgery. Mabel is charged with operating a motor vehicle on a public road without a driver's license.
2. Lewei takes control of Guo's bank account. Lewei tells Guo that if he doesn't kill Irina, he will transfer all of the money in Guo's account to an account Lewei has in the Cayman Islands. Having worked hard to save his money and because he is relying on the money in the account to retire, Guo acquiesces and kills Irina. Guo is charged with murder.
3. Kendra and Brian, a married couple, are on a walk. Three miles away from home, Kendra begins to have a diabetic insulin reaction. Brian concludes that Kendra needs sugar, immediately. There is a gas station with a small grocery nearby. He runs to the store, grabs a bottle of orange juice, and dashes to the checkout. At that moment, he realizes that he has no way to pay for the juice. He tells the employee what is happening and promises to pay for the item later. The employee refuses to let Brian have the juice, so he runs out of the store without paying for it. Brian is charged with theft.

I PREFER TO BE TRIED BY 12 THAN CARRIED BY SIX

Learning Objective: Identify the elements of defense. Define and describe the relationship between the castle doctrine, retreat doctrine, and stand-your-ground laws.

Darrell Roberson was with friends playing cards when he became concerned about his wife, Tracy Denise Roberson, who wasn't answering their home phone or her cell phone. He reached their daughter by phone, who told Darrell that she couldn't find her mom in the house. Darrell instructed the daughter to be sure the door to the home was locked, and he returned home. When he arrived, he discovered Tracy, partially nude, in a truck with another man, Devin LaSalle. Tracy saw Darrell arrive and yelled, "Darrell, Darrell, Darrell, he's trying to rape me, he's trying to rape me, he's trying to rape me." At some point, Darrell retrieved a gun from his car and ran toward the car. In response to seeing Darrell with the gun, Devin punched the accelerator of the car so hard that rubber from his tires was found on Darrell's clothes. His wife still in the truck, Darrell fired at Devin, killing him. Subsequently, it was discovered that Tracy wasn't being raped; she and Devin were lovers. Did Darrell commit a crime? The prosecutor decided that he had not because he was protecting his wife. Tracy, on the other hand, was found guilty of involuntary manslaughter and sentenced to 5 years in prison.[12] In an interview after Tracy's conviction, Darrell said that he took their marriage vows seriously and intended to wait for her release from prison so they could be together again.[13]

Self-defense is one of the most commonly asserted justification defenses, and there is a large body of statutory and case law about it. Self-defense can relieve a person of responsibility for several crimes against a person, including assault, battery, false imprisonment, and homicide. Self-defense exists in both imperfect and perfect forms. The title of this section reflects a commonly held value—don't be so fearful of being prosecuted for murder that you leave yourself vulnerable. It is better to be tried for murder by 12 jurors than to be killed and have your coffin carried by six pallbearers. There are several "use of force" defenses, including self-defense, defense of habitation, defense of others, defense of property, authority to use force, and resisting unlawful arrest.

Self-Defense

The MPC § 3.04(1) holds that force against another person is "justifiable when the actor believes that such force is immediately necessary for the purpose of protecting himself against the use of unlawful force by such other person on the present occasion." It also recognizes several limitations on the use of force.

This discussion will begin with the elements of self-defense, followed by several limiting doctrines. There are five elements of the defense:

1. An unprovoked

2. imminent threat

3. of bodily harm

4. requiring force to avoid the harm, and

5. the amount of force used was reasonable.

Let's begin the discussion with the MPC's fifth element, the demand that the amount of force used in self-defense be reasonable. Generally, proportional force is reasonable. The defensive force doesn't have to be precisely in proportion to the attack to be reasonable. For example, if Ramon slaps Gary and Gary's immediate response is to punch Ramon in the face, knocking him to the floor, Gary has acted reasonably even though his force, and the resulting injury, were greater than he suffered. If he continued to hit Ramon after he was down, that would be different.

Deadly force is only permitted in response to an attack that threatens death or serious bodily harm. Conversely, it is unreasonable to use deadly force to resist an attack that only threatens a minor injury, such as a slap to the face. As you will learn later, deadly force isn't permitted to defend property, although the presence of an owner or occupier during an assault on property may entitle the use of deadly force.

To determine whether the force used is reasonable, the fact finder will consider the facts known to the defendant at the time the defensive act was taken. It would be unfair to judge the defendant from the clear advantage of hindsight or from the perspective of the victim or others. Although it is the defendant's facts that frame the inquiry, the defendant's belief about the amount of force that was needed to repel the attack is not dispositive; the amount of force must be objectively reasonable—that is, reasonable to the fact finder. So the jury goes back in time and views the facts through the eyes of the defendant, but it makes its own conclusion about whether the amount of force was reasonable.

Returning to the MPC's first element, a defendant isn't entitled to self-defense if he provokes the confrontation. But there are exceptions to this rule. First, if the person attacked responds with excessive force, the defendant can claim self-defense. For example, Janie and Freddie disagree on who is next in line to be served at SuperQwik, a convenience store. Janie grabs Freddie by the arm and attempts to pull him behind her. Freddie responds by striking Janie in the face, knocking her to the ground. While she is down and fazed, he draws back to hit her again. She is able to swing her leg into his, causing him to fall and hit his head. Although Janie provoked Freddie's battery, she was privileged to knock him down because his response to her provocation was unreasonably excessive. He would have been privileged to push her away or possibly to strike her to force her to release his arm, but his attempt to strike her while she was already down was unnecessary to abate the threat. It is no surprise to you that under this **excessive force exception**, lethal force is never reasonable in response to nonlethal force.

A change of facts will illustrate the second exception, **withdrawal exception**. Assume the same facts, except that after Freddie hits Janie, she gets up and runs out of the store, and Freddie

---

Excessive force exception: An exception to the rule that a person who provokes an attack is not entitled to the protection of self-defense. It applies when the person attacked responds with unreasonable force.

Withdrawal exception: An exception to the rule that a person who provokes an attack is not entitled to the protection of self-defense. It applies when the person who provoked the attack retreats from the encounter but is pursued by the person initially attacked.

pursues her, screaming, "You are not getting away from me, bitch. I am going to teach you a lesson!" Although she initially provoked Freddie, she is entitled to defend herself anew because of her attempt to withdraw.

The second element is self-explanatory. A threat of future violence doesn't justify a violent response. The law demands that threats of future violence be addressed by nonviolent means, such as a call to police or other authorities. An exception to the imminence doctrine is made in many jurisdictions for the so-called **battered person syndrome defense**. BPSD, originally known as battered women syndrome defense, is a special form of self-defense that applies to circumstances where an intimate partner is subject to psychological and physical abuse so intense that they fear for their life and, sometimes, the lives of children or other family members. On March 9, 1977, Francine Hughes poured gasoline around her live-in ex-husband's bed and lit it on fire. He died from smoke inhalation, and the house was destroyed. She committed the act in response to years of physical and psychological abuse, but she had been beaten and raped by her husband shortly before she struck the match. She was charged with murder, chose to go to trial, and the jury acquitted her, finding that she was temporarily insane at the time she committed the crime. The case was memorialized in a book and movie of the same title, *The Burning Bed*. But this section isn't amount insanity. *The Burning Bed* is mentioned because some legal scholars have argued that self-defense is more appropriate in cases of abuse. But to make self-defense work, imminence has to be reimagined to include the likelihood of future harm, supported by a history of abuse. Most defendants have been unsuccessful in persuading trial courts that their violence was justified.

The third element of self-defense is bodily harm. Any physical harm qualified, but as you will learn in a moment, the amount of force used to repel an attack must be proportionate to the threat. Defending property will also be discussed later.

The fourth element is more complex than the others, particularly in cases of deadly force. With the old Common Law, many jurisdictions imposed a duty to retreat, when safe, before using deadly force to repel an attack. Known as the retreat doctrine or **retreat to the wall doctrine**, a person under attack was expected to flee before defending with **deadly force**. For purposes of self-defense, and defense of others and property, there doesn't have to be death for there to be deadly force. Deadly force is defined as any force that a reasonable person believes is likely to result in death or serious bodily injury.

Returning to the retreat doctrine, retreat wasn't required under the Common Law when retreating was dangerous, nor was it expected of police officers and other officials who enforced the law. The Model Penal Code says of retreat that "the use of deadly force is not justifiable . . . [if] the actor knows that he can avoid the necessity of using such force without

---

Battered person syndrome defense: Where a person who inflicts lethal or nonlethal force on an intimate partner asserts either self-defense or insanity due to psychological and physical abuse so intense that they fear for their life and, sometimes, the lives of children or other family members.

Retreat to the wall doctrine: A rule that a person must avail themselves of all safe opportunities to retreat from an attack before using deadly force to repel the attack.

Deadly force: An amount of force that a reasonable person believes is likely to result in death or serious bodily injury.

complete safety by retreating or by surrendering possession of a thing to a person asserting a claim of right thereto or by complying with a demand that he abstain from any action which he has no duty to take, except that (1) the actor is not obliged to retreat from his dwelling or place of work, unless he was the initial aggressor."[14]

Also, notice that the MPC requires not only retreat, but that "thing[s]" be surrendered and one comply with another's demands before deadly force is used. Of course, one can later use civil law to recover unlawfully taken items or to recover for complying with a demand that caused damage. The aggressor will be liable both civilly and criminally for such unlawful demands.

Defense of Habitation

The MPC and most states do not require one to retreat from his home. This is known as the castle doctrine. The castle doctrine developed in the old Common Law and continues to be recognized today. The castle doctrine is premised on the idea that the home is a space where a person should feel both safe and private: "A man's home is his castle." A home, usually referred to as a dwelling in statutes, can be a permanent or temporary structure and often includes the "curtilage," the area immediately around a home and attachments to the home (e.g., porch, garage).

The elements of the castle doctrine vary by jurisdiction. They commonly include one or more of the following:

1. A rejection of the Common Law retreat doctrine for residents of a home.

2. A rebuttable presumption that intruders are a threat to life or limb.

3. Immunity from criminal and civil liability for residents of homes who use deadly force on intruders.

As to the second element, some states create a rebuttable presumption in all instances for intruders, subject to a few narrow exceptions mentioned later. Other states limit the use of deadly force to intruders who are entering to commit a felony or who enter in a violent or tumultuous manner. The MPC has an even more limited rule. It permits deadly force only if the intruder "is attempting to commit or consummate arson, burglary, robbery or other felonious theft or property destruction" *and* poses a threat of serious bodily harm to a resident either in the commission of the act or would if less than deadly force was used in an attempt to stop the intruder.[15]

As you were warned, all rules have exceptions. The castle doctrine is no exception to the rule about exceptions. For example, deadly force may not be used against people who have a lawful right to be on the premises. Police officers and firefighters who enter a home without permission during the execution of their duties are examples. Under the Common Law, firefighters were implicitly invited by the homeowner into the home because of the benefit received. A police

---

Castle doctrine: A rule that a person is not required to retreat from an attack in a home. Today, statutory law in some states includes automobiles and other spaces in the zone where retreat is unnecessary.

officer is permitted to enter as a matter of law, presuming that the Fourth Amendment's rules on searches and seizures has been respected.

Another change to the castle doctrine in recent years has been the definition in the area protected. For example, Ohio is one of several states that has extended the castle doctrine to automobiles. Per the relevant statute, "Every person accused of an offense is presumed innocent until proven guilty beyond a reasonable doubt, and the burden of proof for all elements of the offense is upon the prosecution. The burden of going forward with the evidence of an affirmative defense, and the burden of proof, by a preponderance of the evidence, for an affirmative defense, is upon the accused."[16] Of course, general self-defense rules apply in the home. Regardless of the specific castle doctrine rules, a resident is always privileged to use deadly force when objectively necessary to protect life and limb.

Thirty-four states have enacted so-called **stand-your-ground** laws.[17] Stand-your-ground laws extend the castle doctrine from homes and cars to public spaces. The subject of an attack that threatens life or limb in any space is under no legal obligation to retreat, even if a safe retreat is available. Florida is a stand-your-ground state:

> A person is justified in using or threatening to use deadly force if he or she reasonably believes that using or threatening to use such force is necessary to prevent imminent death or great bodily harm to himself or herself or another or to prevent the imminent commission of a forcible felony. A person who uses or threatens to use deadly force in accordance with this subsection does not have a duty to retreat and has the right to stand his or her ground if the person using or threatening to use the deadly force is not engaged in a criminal activity and is in a place where he or she has a right to be.[18]

So in Florida and other states, a person who is attacked outside of the home can stand their ground and repel the attack, subject to a few exceptions that were discussed earlier, such as when a person provokes another and when a person attempts to withdraw.

In most jurisdictions, a defendant bears the burden of proving a stand-your-ground claim. But in Florida, the defendant is only required to make a "prima facie" showing. *Prima facie* is a procedural requirement that imposes a duty on a defendant to raise and support a claim with minimal evidence. Thereafter, the prosecution must overcome the claim with clear and convincing evidence. This represents the most extreme form of self-defense in the United States.

Stand-your-ground laws have led to many controversial cases, including the shooting of Treyvon Martin by George Zimmerman in 2012. Critics of stand-your-ground laws claim that they create a shoot-first, get-the-facts-later approach. It is contended that stand-your-ground laws tip the balance between respect for life and self-defense too far away from the former. In support of this contention, opponents of stand-your-ground laws point out that researchers have discovered that these laws increase homicides.[19] See Figure 5.2 for a comparison of deadly force doctrines.

Stand-your-ground doctrine: A rule that a person is not required to retreat from an attack, in any space, before defending with lethal force.

FIGURE 5.2 ■ Deadly Force Doctrines Compared

Deadly Force Doctrines Compared

Least Protection		Self-Defense		Greatest Protection
Retreat to Wall	Castle Doctrine	Castle Doctrine Plus	Castle Doctrine Enhanced	Stand-Your-Ground
Person has duty to retreat in the home before using deadly force.	Deadly force may be used by residents of homes against intruders without first retreating. Person using deadly force may have to prove it was reasonable.	The use of deadly force by the resident of a home is presumed reasonable, unless the victim had fight to enter premises.	Castle doctrine is extended to cars or other venues.	Deadly force may by used to repel an attacker in any location without first retreating, so long as reasonable that attacker threatens life or limb.

Defense of Others

The use of force to defend life and limb is not limited to protecting oneself. A person may protect another to the same extent that an individual may protect themselves. If Jana is entitled to use deadly force against an attacker, so is any person who defends Jana. An interesting problem arises when a Good Samaritan is reasonable for using force to protect a person who is not privileged to use force to protect themselves. For example, there is an active arrest warrant for Norm. Norm is 4'11" and 115 lbs. He is standing in a teller line at his local bank. An undercover police officer, Kris, is also in line at the bank. Kris is 5'10" and weighs 165 lbs. Kris recognizes Norm, confirms that there is a warrant for his arrest, and grabs him while is standing in line at a bank. As she takes hold of him, Kris identifies herself as a police officer and says, "You are under arrest for an outstanding warrant." The two begin to struggle. The bank security guard didn't overhear Kris's statement but witnessed her assault. He punches Kris in the face in defense of Norm. Norm isn't privileged to use force against a police officer who is performing the duties of office, so normally a third party wouldn't be privileged to use force to protect him. But it was objectively reasonable for the security guard to defend Norm. The jurisdictions are split on this problem. Some permit the security guard to present the defense of Kris to the jury; others don't. Of those that do, there is a further split between requiring the defender to have a reasonably objective belief that the victim will suffer serious bodily harm or death and those that ask if the defender subjectively believed the force was necessary.

Defense of Property

Both the Common Law and modern statutory law privilege people to use force to protect property. This includes both real property (land, home, and other structures) and personal property (everything else). Because property isn't valued as highly as life, the use of force to defend property is more limited than in the defense of the person. Deadly force may never be used to protect property. As is true when defending one's life, reasonable force must be used in the defense of property.

The Model Penal Code allows force to be used to defend property when it is immediately necessary to (1) prevent or end a trespass or (2) to stop another from walking away with, or to recover, stolen property. The act must be immediate, or in the case of an attempt to recover taken property, the owner's pursuit must be "fresh."

When defending property, an owner is to request that the property be returned or the trespass end before using force unless such a request would be useless, it would be dangerous to the owner or another person to ask first, or the property will suffer substantial harm as a result.[20] The classic example would be the ejection of a ship's stowaway into the ocean. The risk to the stowaway is too great to justify the use of force. The captain will have to wait until they reach land to eject the stowaway.

In some states, if there is time to call the police to remove a trespasser or to retrieve one's property, that must happen before using force. Finally, if there is a genuine dispute over ownership or possession, then the owner shall refrain from using force and rely on legal remedies.

Trespassing is an intentional crime in most states. Accidental trespassing, such as a hunter who mistakenly wanders onto another's land, is not a crime. That is one reason the law imposes a duty to ask a trespasser to leave before using force to eject them. The rule reduces the likelihood of an unnecessary and potentially harmful encounter by giving innocent parties the opportunity to correct their mistakes.

There is a body of law defining trespass and its exceptions. For example, the law recognizes both explicit and implicit invitees to property. In most states, if a no-trespass notice isn't posted and the property has a sidewalk, the law assumes the property owner is inviting people to the home. This includes salespeople, candidates for political office, and others. Of course, a FedEx driver who is delivering an ordered package is an express invitee.

Van D. Bilt discovers Lars Oney, a stranger, on his property. Lars has Bilt's expensive bike in his hands. Van yells, "Get away from that bike and get off my property." Lars throws Van the bird and jumps on the bike. Van strikes Lars in the face, knocking him off the bike. Van has acted appropriately in defense of his property because he used reasonable force to recover personal property that was about to be stolen.

Or consider this: The same basic facts, except Van hits Lars in the head with a shovel. Van suffers a concussion. Van is not entitled to the protection of defense of property because he used deadly force.

Finally, Van D. Bilt discovers Lars Oney, a stranger, sitting on a chair in Van's garden gazebo. Van walks up to Lars, hits him in the face, and then guides him off the property while tightly holding his arm. Van is not entitled to the protection of defense of property because he didn't demand that Lars leave, nor did he call the police before he used force.

Cameras, geofences, dogs, alarms, and locks are a few of the many ways people protect their property. Some property owners, frustrated and fearful, have turned to dangerous devices to protect their property. This is the subject of your next Digging Deeper (*Katko v. Briney*). Although *Katko* is a civil case, the announced legal principle applies to both tort and criminal law.

DIGGING DEEPER 5.2

Can a deadly device be used to protect property?

Case: *Katko v. Briney*
Court: Supreme Court of Iowa.   Citation: 183 N.W.2d 657 (Iowa 1971)
Year: 1971
Chief Justice Moore

The primary issue presented here is whether an owner may protect personal property in an unoccupied boarded-up farm house against trespassers and thieves by a spring gun capable of inflicting death or serious injury. We are not here concerned with a man's right to protect his home and members of his family. Defendants' home was several miles from the scene of the incident to which we refer infra.

Plaintiff's action is for damages resulting from serious injury caused by a shot from a 20-gauge spring shotgun set by defendants in a bedroom of an old farm house which had been uninhabited for several years. Plaintiff and his companion, Marvin McDonough, had broken and entered the house to find and steal old bottles and dated fruit jars which they considered antiques.

At defendants' request plaintiff's action was tried to a jury consisting of residents of the community where defendants' property was located. The jury returned a verdict for plaintiff and against defendants for $20,000 actual and $10,000 punitive damages....

Most of the facts are not disputed. In 1957 defendant Bertha L. Briney inherited her parents' farm land in Mahaska and Monroe Counties. Included was an 80-acre tract in southwest Mahaska County where her grandparents and parents had lived. No one occupied the house thereafter. Her husband, Edward, attempted to care for the land. He kept no farm machinery thereon. The outbuildings became dilapidated. For about 10 years, 1957 to 1967, there occurred a series of trespassing and house-breaking events with loss of some household items, the breaking of windows and "messing up of the property in general." The latest occurred June 8, 1967, prior to the event on July 16, 1967, herein involved.

Defendants through the years boarded up the windows and doors in an attempt to stop the intrusions. They had posted "no trespass" signs on the land several years before 1967. The nearest one was 35 feet from the house. On June 11, 1967, defendants set "a shotgun trap" in the north bedroom. After Mr. Briney cleaned and oiled his 20-gauge shotgun, the power of which he was well aware, defendants took it to the old house where they secured it to an iron bed with the barrel pointed at the bedroom door. It was rigged with wire from the doorknob to the gun's trigger so it would fire when the door was opened. Briney first pointed the gun so an intruder would be hit in the stomach but at Mrs. Briney's suggestion it was lowered to hit the legs. He admitted he did so "because I was mad and tired of being tormented" but "he did not intend to injure anyone." He gave no explanation of why he used a loaded shell and set it to hit a person already in the house. Tin was nailed over the bedroom window. The spring gun could not be seen from the outside. No warning of its presence was posted.

Plaintiff lived with his wife and worked regularly as a gasoline station attendant in Eddyville, seven miles from the old house. He had observed it for several years while hunting in the area and considered it as being abandoned. He knew it had long been uninhabited.

In 1967 the area around the house was covered with high weeds. Prior to July 16, 1967, plaintiff and McDonough had been to the premises and found several old bottles and fruit jars which they took and added to their collection of antiques. On the latter date about 9:30 p.m. they made a second trip to the Briney property. They entered the old house by removing a board from a porch window which was without glass. While McDonough was looking around the kitchen area plaintiff went to another part of the house. As he started to open the north bedroom door the shotgun went off striking him in the right leg above the ankle bone. Much of his leg, including part of the tibia, was blown away. Only by McDonough's assistance was plaintiff able to get out of the house and after crawling some distance was put in his vehicle and rushed to a doctor and then to a hospital. He remained in the hospital 40 days. Plaintiff's doctor testified he seriously considered amputation but eventually the healing process was successful. Some weeks after his release from the hospital plaintiff returned to work on crutches. He was required to keep the injured leg in a cast for approximately a year and wear a special brace for another year. He continued to suffer pain during this period. There was undenied medical testimony plaintiff had a permanent deformity, a loss of tissue, and a shortening of the leg....

Plaintiff testified he knew he had no right to break and enter the house with intent to steal bottles and fruit jars therefrom. He further testified he had entered a plea of guilty to larceny in the nighttime of property of less than $20 value from a private building. He stated he had been fined $50 and costs and paroled during good behavior from a 60-day jail sentence....

The main thrust of defendants' defense in the trial court and on this appeal is that "the law permits use of a spring gun in a dwelling or warehouse for the purpose of preventing the unlawful entry of a burglar or thief"....

"[T]the law has always placed a higher value upon human safety than upon mere rights in property, it is the accepted rule that there is no privilege to use any force calculated to cause death or serious bodily injury to repel the threat to land or chattels, unless there is also such a threat to the defendant's personal safety as to justify a self-defense . . . . Spring guns and other man-killing devices are not justifiable against a mere trespasser, or even a petty thief. They are privileged only against those upon whom the landowner, if he were present in person would be free to inflict injury of the same kind."

In *Hooker v. Miller*... we held defendant vineyard owner liable for damages resulting from a spring gun shot although plaintiff was a trespasser and there to steal grapes. At pages 614, 615, this statement is made: "This court has held that a mere trespass against property other than a dwelling is not a sufficient justification to authorize the use of a deadly weapon by the owner in its defense; and that if death results in such a case it will be murder, though the killing be actually necessary to prevent the trespass. At page 617 this court said: "[T]respassers and other inconsiderable violators of the law are not to be visited by barbarous punishments or prevented by inhuman inflictions of bodily injuries."...

In addition to civil liability many jurisdictions hold a land owner criminally liable for serious injuries or homicide caused by spring guns or other set devices....

[To learn what happened to Katko and Briney after the case was decided and to see the wire used in the spring gun, go to https://lawhaha.com/new-artifact-from-katko-v-briney-the-infamous-spring-gun-case/.]

The MPC follows *Katko's* reasoning. It allows a device to be used to protect property, provided

a. the device is not designed to cause or known to create a substantial risk of causing death or serious bodily harm; and

b. the use of the particular device to protect the property from entry or trespass is reasonable under the circumstances, as the actor believes them to be; and

c. the device is one customarily used for such a purpose or reasonable care is taken to make known to probable intruders the fact that it is used.

Hands Behind Your Back: Authority to Use Force

To enforce the law and to protect the public, police must sometimes use force. Police use of force is a contentious political issue in the United States. This discussion is exclusively about the law of use of force; it is not an exploration of use-of-force research, policies, or practices.

The rules were simple with the early Common Law; police could use deadly force to arrest felons who resisted, and they could use all but deadly force to arrest misdemeanants. While this is harsh by contemporary standards, consider the historical context. All felonies were punished with death in the early Common Law, all misdemeanors with either life or very long prison sentences, various forms of corporal punishment were common, and prison conditions were awful.

Advancing to the law today, the use of force and the arrest (seizure, imprisonment) of a person by a police officer give rise to several questions:

1. Is the officer criminally liable for the act?

2. Is the officer civilly liable for the act?

3. Is any resulting prosecution of the arrestee impacted by officer's act?

The first two questions are a matter of statutory and common law. The third question is addressed by the Fourth Amendment's search and seizure clause and the Fourteenth Amendment of the United States Constitution and state constitutional and statutory counterparts.

Whether an officer has the authority to seize, or arrest, a person is largely defined by the Fourth Amendment. As you learned in Chapter 2, a law enforcement officer must have probable cause, and sometimes a warrant, to conduct a search or make an arrest. In some circumstances, less than probable cause—reasonable suspicion—justifies lesser intrusions. Under the Fourth Amendment, a person may be arrested for any violation of law, no matter how small. Some states limit the arrest authority more than the Fourth Amendment. Concerning traffic offenses, Texas law permits a "motorist receiving a traffic citation in his home jurisdiction... except for certain violations, to accept the citation from the officer at the scene of the violation and to immediately continue on his way after promising or being instructed to comply with the terms of the citation."[21]

The MPC recognizes a *public duty defense* when an officer is acting pursuant to (1) a law defining the duties of a government officer; (2) a law pertaining to the execution of legal process; (3) an order of a court; or (4) any other law imposing a public duty on the actor. Additionally, an officer is immune when she believes that her conduct has been authorized or ordered by a court. This defense applies to trespass, assault, battery, false imprisonment, and other acts that are taken in the performance an officer's duties.

Nonofficials are also immune from prosecution for arrests, but to a more limited degree than officials. Dating back at least a thousand years, English people were encouraged to arrest when they personally witnessed a felony or a misdemeanor that amounted to a breach of the peace. This practice was encouraged because there were no standing police at the time. This became known as a citizen's arrest, although the defense isn't limited to citizens.

Citizen's arrest continues to be recognized throughout the United States, but in different forms. Most laws permit arrests for felonies and breaches of the peace committed in the presence of the person making the arrest. Some states widen the offenses to include misdemeanors that are not breaches of the peace, and others broaden the knowledge of the crime requirement from actually observation to probable cause or another standard of proof. Arkansas, for example, has a rule that favors arrestors, requiring only that they have "reasonable grounds" that a felony was committed.[22] In those jurisdictions that require the crime to be committed in the presence of the arrestor, the immunity from criminal and civil prosecution only applies if the arrestor was correct that a crime was being committed. For those jurisdictions requiring probable cause or reasonable grounds, the arrestor is protected if the evidence standard is met, regardless of whether the person arrested actually committed the crime.

We have examined whether a person has the authority to make a seizure. A related but separate issue is the amount of force that may be used in seizing a lawbreaker. Arrests can be peaceful and violent. With the authority to arrest comes the authority to use force to make the arrest. But that authority has limits. Arrests by police officers are bounded by the Common Law, statutory law, and constitutional law. The Constitution doesn't apply to private action, so only the Common Law and statutory law address a citizen's arrest. Because the authority to use force is more limited than the authority to arrest, there are cases where the arrestor will have to permit the lawbreaker to go free, to be caught another day.

In most states, police officers are authorized to use whatever force is necessary to effect an arrest, subject to two large constraints. First, whatever force is used must be objectively reasonable. Using a baton or pepper spray on an arrestee who has complied with all of the instructions of an arresting officer is unreasonable. Using pepper spray on an arrestee who refuses to comply with orders and strikes at an officer is reasonable. Reasonability is gauged from the perspective of the officer conducting the arrest. SCOTUS held that reasonability is required by the Fourteenth Amendment's due process clause in *Graham v. Conner.*[23]

The second constraint is in the use of deadly force. Unsurprisingly, the law doesn't permit officers to kill fleeing jaywalkers. Deadly force may only be used to protect life or limb. Specifically, an officer must have probable cause to believe the subject poses a threat of serious physical harm or death to the officer or others. SCOTUS announced this rule in the 1985 case *Tennessee v. Garner*,[24] where a police officer shot and killed an 15-year-old unarmed flee-ing thief who wasn't an apparent threat to others. This was a change in policy for some police departments, which had previously permitted deadly force to stop all fleeing felons. Obviously, an officer can use deadly force anytime an arrestee threatens the officer's life, regardless of the seriousness of the crime the arrestee committed.

Garner is a Fourth Amendment case that applies to suspects. Typically, the law treats con-victees differently, and the rules of use of force are no different. When a person is convicted, the Fourth Amendment drops out of the equation and the Eighth Amendment's prohibition of cruel and unusual punishment rules. By its very nature, the Eighth Amendment presumes pun-ishment is legitimate; it simply prohibits cruel and unusual punishments. Similarly, the Eighth Amendment permits corrections officers to act to ensure security in ways that would violate the Fourth Amendment. For example, deadly force may be used to prevent the escape of offenders who aren't a danger to life or limb, even though a police officer couldn't use the same force to stop the offender from fleeing before conviction.

An unanswered question is how deep this rule reaches. While it is likely that the use of deadly force to stop the escape of a convicted dangerous felon is permissible, regardless of future dangerousness, it is less likely that deadly force can be used against a prisoner who was convicted of a nonviolent felony or misdemeanor. The MPC doesn't limit the use of deadly force to dangerous offenders. In a very broad grant of force authority, it allows the "use of force to prevent the escape of an arrested person from custody is justifiable when the force could justifiably have been employed to effect the arrest under which the person is in custody, except that a guard or other person authorized to act as a peace officer is justified in using any force, including deadly force, which he believes to be immediately necessary to prevent the escape of a person from a jail, prison, or other institution for the detention of persons charged with or convicted of a crime."[25]

Not Without a Fight: Resisting Unlawful Arrests

The amount of force that may be used by citizens varies by state. In some states, citizens have less authority; they are not permitted to ever use deadly force for the sole purpose of making an arrest or preventing an arrestee from escaping. If an arrestee turns violent, then the normal rules of self-defense come into play. Contrary to this, some jurisdictions permit citizens to use deadly force, when needed, to effect an arrest or to prevent the escape of felons. But the citizen must be right in their conclusion. Typically, a citizen's reasonable but mistaken belief that deadly force is needed doesn't excuse the homicide. Finally, the law distinguishes between a "citizen's arrest" and a person who assists a law enforcement officer in making an arrest. If the latter, the citizen is entitled to the same protections from prosecution as the officer that was assisted.

Citizen's arrest has its critics. They point out that the law is complex, citizen's arrest rules are vague, that police are widely available today unlike when citizen's arrest developed in old England, and citizens are not trained in law or the techniques of arrest and use of force.

These concerns, critics contend, combine to create a perfect storm of unnecessary violence and liberty. One author points to several cases where unjustified shootings and batteries have occurred, illustrating how the law of citizen's arrests has gone wrong.[26] Other examples of how the citizen's arrest law has gone wrong include a group in New Mexico that attempted to arrest a police chief for "harboring" fugitives who worked for him, a group in Illinois who arrested all of the members of the Clark County (Illinois) Park Board for allegedly not following "government in the sunshine" rules, and several citizen patrol organizations, including a self-proclaimed Xtreme Justice League where the members dressed as superheroes. Still others claim that race plays a role in the use of force, and therefore, there should be greater limitations on it. This is particularly true when citizen's arrest, stand-your-ground, and race intersect. They point to the shootings of unarmed Black men and women, including the 2020 killing of Ahmaud Arbery by two white men who believed he was committing larceny as evidence of this proposition.

Obviously, resisting a lawful arrest is a crime, and as you learned earlier, police officers and citizens are privileged, within a few limitations, to arrest and to use force to arrest lawbreakers. In earlier England and until the 19th century in the United States, an arrest had much more serious consequences than today. Detainees were often held for months, sometimes years, before trial; few people were released before trial; there were no civil remedies for false imprisonment; and prison conditions were so harsh that prisoners often died from malnutrition or disease. For these reasons, people were privileged to resist unlawful arrests. But the situation is different today. There are civil remedies, jail conditions have improved, arrestees are immediately seen by a judge, bail is common, and a speedy trial is the norm. Consequently, the drafters of the MPC recommend against permitting resistance of unlawful arrests,[27] leaving such violations to be addressed by courts at a later date. Most states have followed the MPC recommendation and abolished the Common Law right to resist unlawful arrest. But not all. Following an Indiana Supreme Court decision[28] abolishing the Common Law right to resist unlawful arrest, the Indiana General Assembly reestablished the right. Specifically, the statute provides that

> [A] person is justified in using reasonable force against a public servant if the person reasonably believes the force is necessary to
>
> 1. protect the person or a third person from what the person reasonably believes to be the imminent use of unlawful force;
> 2. prevent or terminate the public servant's unlawful entry of or attack on the person's dwelling, curtilage, or occupied motor vehicle; or
> 3. prevent or terminate the public servant's unlawful trespass on or criminal interference with property lawfully in the person's possession, lawfully in possession of a member of the person's immediate family, or belonging to a person whose property the person has authority to protect.

A person isn't justified to resist in obvious situations, such as when they provoked the officer and when the person is committing a crime. Deadly force may be used only when the officer threatens serious bodily injury and the person reasonably believes the officer is acting unlawfully.[29]

QUESTIONS AND APPLICATIONS

1. What are the elements of self-defense?
2. Define and describe the relationship between the castle doctrine, retreat doctrine, and stand-your-ground laws.

Discuss the following scenarios in the context of defense of persons and property. Specifically, identify and fully discuss the most applicable defense doctrine (self-defense, castle doctrine, etc.).

3. Monty owns an electronics warehouse. He has had eight break-ins at the warehouse in a single year. Over $25,000 in merchandise has been stolen. Monty installed cameras, but they have not been effective because the thieves have been able to avoid them and to cover their faces when in front of them. He has been in continuous contact with the police, but they said there is little they can do. He installed new, highly secure locks. Consequently, the burglars entered through the roof in each of the three most recent burglaries. Frustrated, he created a trap where the burglars would fall through the roof into a pit of snakes. One morning he arrived to work to find two burglars dead, each in the grip of a python.
4. Brittany, who lives alone, is sleeping in her bed at home. There is only one door into her bedroom, and she doesn't have a master bathroom. The only bathroom in the home is in the hallway outside of her bedroom. A noise awakens her in the middle of the night. Frightened, she reaches into her nightstand, takes hold of her revolver, and sits quietly in her bed. After 15 seconds, she hears the wood floor outside of her bedroom squeak, and the figure of a person appears in her bedroom doorway. She shoots and kills the person.
5. Tammy drives to the mall to shop at WhiteLinens, a company founded by James White that sells bed linens, towels, and other bedroom and kitchen items. Unknown to her, a civil rights protest was planned in the neighborhood during her shopping spree. One of the marchers sees the WhiteLinens sign and yells, "Racist, racist. That place sells white sheets!" The protestors, 25 in number, move in front of the store and begin chanting, "No. More. White. Sheets." Tammy, who is about to enter the store, states, "Get out of my way. I am going in there to shop." The leader of the protest replies, "Oh, no, you aren't. Only racists shop here. Turn around and go away." Tammy replies, "You don't know what you are talking about. Get out of my way, moron." The protestors move closer to Tammy, their front line only a foot away from her, many waving their arms and screaming more loudly than before, and their leader lifts her wooden sign over Tammy's head in a threatening manner. Tammy pulls a handgun from her purse and delivers a fatal shot into the leader. Discuss these facts in the context of a traditional self-defense jurisdiction and a stand-your-ground jurisdiction.

I DID IT WITH THE VICTIM'S CONSENT

Learning Objective: Identify the elements of consent and describe two crimes or circumstances to which a person may not consent to being a victim.

In most crimes against the person and against property, the victim's consent to the act negates culpability. Consent is often alleged in sexual assault cases. But it is also commonly pled in property cases, such as "The owner said I could use his car." Consent in rape and sexual assault cases is discussed in the chapter on crimes against the person. This discussion applies to consent in other cases.

Consent must be (1) voluntary, (2) knowing, and (3) not specifically prohibited by law to be valid. Under the MPC, consent is not valid if given by a person who is any of the following:

- Legally incompetent to authorize the conduct

- A juvenile

- Suffering from a mental disease or defect or intoxication and is manifestly unable to make a reasonable judgment

- Induced by force, duress, or deception[30]

Even when knowing and voluntary, there are limits to consent. The Thirteenth Amendment to the U.S. Constitution forbids enslavement and involuntary servitude, so a person may not consent to be enslaved. And no state recognizes the right of a person to consent to serious bodily harm. Consent to acts that result in minor injury or are the consequence of the "reasonably foreseeable hazards of joint participation in a lawful athletic contest or competitive sport," in the words of the MPC, are legitimate, so a football player is not guilty of battery for tackling an opponent. A similar doctrine, mutual combat, is recognized in many states. If two people consent to fight, neither is responsible for minor injuries. In sports or mutual combat, all force must be reasonable, given the norms and expected physical contact of the particular sport or situation. Generally, deadly force is never privileged, except in response to deadly force.

A controversial issue in consent law is physician-assisted suicide. Although most states do not recognize the consent of patients who want to die as a defense to accessory to suicide or murder, a few do. Oregon is one. Its law allows physicians to prescribe life-terminating drugs to terminally ill patients, with the express purpose of assisting the patient to die. No person, including the physician, is permitted, however, to administer drugs that take life; the patient must perform that act. In states without this type of legislation (often referred to as death with dignity laws), the acts of prescribing the drugs and counseling the patient could result in a criminal charge of accessory to suicide.[31]

QUESTIONS AND PROBLEMS

1. What are the elements of consent?
2. Explain why physicians should, and shouldn't, be permitted to assist another in suicide. Discuss both the moral and legal aspects of this question.

Mutual combat: A rule that participants who agree to fight are not liable for minor injuries resulting from the fight.

IN A NUTSHELL

A defendant has the right to sit quietly and demand that the state prove its case. In addition to this nondefense strategy, there are many other defenses that can be raised. All of these can be put into one of three boxes: factual, excused, or justified.

A factual defense consists of evidence that the defendant didn't do it, including that the defendant was elsewhere when the crime was committed (alibi) or evidence that another person did it. The exoneration of hundreds of factually innocent people in recent decades, thanks to scientific developments and the hard work of attorneys and activists, is a reminder that wrongful convictions are a real thing. Many of these convictions were a product of eyewitness misidentification and false confessions. In the years to come, courts are likely to give both more attention than in the past.

Legal defenses, which manifest as excuses or justifications, are many. A defendant who is charged with committing an act that is legally protected may admit the act and rely on the law to stop the prosecution. The consent of the victim to the act is a legitimate excuse, except when public policy demands otherwise. Because of the nation's value of life, one person can't consent to being killed by another, but it isn't battery for one boxer to hit another during a match. As a matter of policy, preventing or minimizing harm to others is encouraged. The defense of necessity enables a person to choose the lesser of evils, and duress respects an individual's interest in minimizing harm to themselves, provided the harm caused to others isn't greater than the harm avoided.

Defending oneself, others, and property are excuses that periodically find themselves in the headlines. Recent police shootings of Black men and women, stand-your-ground killings, and batteries in defense of property during protests are examples. The law always recognizes the rights of people to use reasonable, proportional force to defend against an attacker. Deadly force is only proportional against an attack that threatens death or serious bodily harm. Deadly force is never excused for defense of property or against minor injuries. Although the facts used to determine the reasonability of a defendant's use of force are seen through the eyes of the defendant at the time the act occurred—and not through the lens of hindsight or of the victim—the use of force must be objectively reasonable. What the defendant believed at the moment is not dispositive, although what the defendant saw and experienced frame what is reasonable.

LEGAL TERMS

affirmative defenses (p. 142)

Alibi (p. 144)

battered person syndrome defense (p. 156)

castle doctrine (p. 157)

deadly force (p. 156)

duress (p. 149)

excessive force exception (p. 155)

Excuse (p. 145)

imperfect defense (p. 141)

justification (p. 145)

mutual combat (p. 168)

necessity (p. 146)

perfect defense (p. 141)

retreat to the wall doctrine (p. 156)

stand-your-ground (p. 158)

withdrawal exception (p. 155)

NOTES

1. *Indo-Malaysian Twins Escape the Noose Over Identity Confusion*, accessed July 1, 2020, https://mumbaimirror.indiatimes.com.

2. *A Good Offense Is the Breast Defense*, accessed July 1, 2020, JonathanTurley.org.

3. See National Registry of Exonerations at law.umich.edu.

4. See Innocenceproject.org, National Registry of Exonerations.

5. See Charles E. Loeffler et al., "Measuring Self-Reported Wrongful Convictions Among Prisoners," *Journal of Quantitative Criminology* 35 (2019): 259; and Paul Cassell, "Overstating America's Wrongful Conviction Rate? Reassessing the Conventional Wisdom About the Prevalence of Wrongful Convictions," *Arizona Law Review* 60 (2018): 815.

6. *People v. Maher*, 79 N.Y.2d 978 (1992).

7. William Blackstone, *Blackstone Commentaries* (Philadelphia: J. B. Lippincott, 1893).

8. Harvey Silvergate, "Crime for a Cause: Massachusetts and the 'Necessity Defense,'" October 4, 2014, accessed July 6, 2020, Forbes.com.

9. *People v. Weber*, 162 Cal. App. 3d Supp. 1 (Cal. App. Dep't Super. Ct. 1984).

10. *United States v. Schoon*, 939 F.2d 826 (9th Cir. 1991).

11. Martin L. King, Jr., letter from Birmingham Jail, discussed in *The Autobiograhy of Martin Luther King, Jr.*, 187, 194 (Clayborne Carson ed., 1998).

12. *Tracy Denise Roberson v. Texas*, (Tex.App.—Ft. Worth[2nd Dist] 2010).

13. Melody McDonald and Nathaniel Jones, "Tx. Man Who Killed Wife's Lover Says He Won't Divorce Her," *Ft. Worth Star-Telegraph*, May 7, 2008, accessed July 8, 2020, https://www.mcclatchydc.com.

14. Model Penal Code § 3.04(2)(b)(ii).

15. MPC §3.06.

16. O.R.C. §2901.05.

17. There are 25 states with stand-your-ground laws, according to the National Conference of State Legislatures [*Self-Defense and Stand Your Ground*, May 26, 2020, accessed July 8, 2020, ncsl.org]. According to RAND, an additional nine states have expanded the castle doctrine beyond the home [RAND, *The Effects of Stand-Your-Ground Laws*, accessed July 9, 2020, Rand.org].

18. §776.012, Fla. Sta.

19. RAND study, supra, note xvii.

20. MPC §3.06.

21. Texas Transportation Code § 703.002.

22. Ark. Code § 16-81-106.

23. *Graham v. Conner*, 490 U.S. 386 (1989).

24. *Tennessee v. Garner*, 471 U.S. 1 (1985).

25. MPC §3.07(3).

26. Ira P. Robbins, "Vilifying the Vigilante: A Narrowed Scope of Citizen's Arrests," *Cornell Journal of Law and Public Policy* 25 (2016): 557.

27. MPC §3.04(2)(i).

28. *Barnes v. State*, 946 N.E.2d 572, 576 (Ind. 2011).

29. Burns Ind. Code Ann. § 35-41-3-2.

30. MPC §2.11(3).

31. ORS §127.800 s.1.01.

6 DEFENSES: EXCUSES

On June 23, 1993, Lorena Bobbitt committed one of the most celebrated crimes in United States history when she "pulled back the covers on her sleeping husband [and] sliced his penis clean off with a kitchen knife." She would subsequently toss the severed organ outside of a 7-Eleven convenience store. It was found by police, put into a hot dog container, covered with ice, and transported to hospital, where it was reattached to her husband, John Wayne Bobbitt. Lorena later explained that she did it because her husband sexually assaulted herearlier that evening—his last act of violence against her after years of abuse. Ms. Bobbitt defended against a charge of malicious wounding by asserting that she suffered from an irresistible impulse, a form of insanity. The jury agreed, finding her not guilty by reason of insanity. She was committed to a psychiatric facility for 45 days and released.[1]

The last chapter covered factual defenses and justified crimes. This chapter continues the discussion by examining excused crimes, such as Ms. Bobbitt's.

I LOST MY MIND

Learning Objectives: Define and distinguish the McNaghten, irresistible impulse, Model Penal Code (MPC), Durham, and GBMI (guilty but mentally ill) tests. Explain the intoxication defense, including insanity, diminished capacity, and intoxication.

Insanity

This chapter opened with the story of the Lorena Bobbit. She did what few defendants have successfully done. Sure, slicing off a penis is rare. But that isn't what makes her case unusual, from a legal perspective. That she was successful in persuading a jury that she was legally insane, specifically "temporarily insane," is unusual. Less than 1% of criminal defendants assert that defense, and only about a quarter of those who make the claim are successful.[2] Often, insanity defense cases are high-profile news. The defense is perennially discussed in scholarly circles, and it is periodically debated in Congress and state legislatures. It is understandably controversial. Insanity results in acquittal, even for the most heinous crimes.

The rationale for the defense is twofold. First, it is argued that it is an extension of the most fundamental of ideas: There must be a mens rea for a crime. But as you will see soon, the way the insanity defense is framed overlaps with, but is sometimes different from, mens rea. The second reason goes to the heart of the criminal justice system: its purpose. Aruguably, no generally recognized penological purpose is served by punishing a person who was insane at the time of a crime. Remember the many purposes of criminalizing conduct—deterrence, rehabilitation, incapacitation, and retribution. Assuming the offender's insanity "caused" the person to commit the crime, punishment won't deter similar future misbehavior. Similarly, no rehabilitative purpose is possible because there wasn't purposeful conduct or judgment to rehabilitate. Incapacitation may be appropriate, if the offender's insanity continues to be a threat. But the nation has a long history of using civil commitment to deal with people who are a danger to themselves or others. Civil commitment's focus on the mental health and welfare of the individual and society at large is regarded by many experts as preferable to the punishment objectives of the criminal justice system. Finally, the moral grounds for retribution are questionable. Does society benefit from, or even want, an ounce of flesh from a mentally ill offender?

The law has its own definition of insanity. While the expertise of psychiatrists and psychologists is important to the determination of whether a person is legally insane, the standards of their fields are not used to decide criminal culpability. There are four active tests used to determine legal insanity today: M'Naghten, irresistible impulse, Model Penal Code (MPC), and Durham.

M'Naghten

In 1843, Daniel M'Naghten, who was suffering from a paranoid delusion that the British prime minister was plotting to kill him, decided to strike first. But he mistakenly killed the prime minister's secretary, believing him to be the prime minster. McNaughten was found not guilty of murder by reason of insanity by a jury.[3] The decision created controversy, and the House of Lords asked the justices of the Queen's Bench to explain the decision.[4] The justice's response included a set of standards that were used to determine whether M'Naghten was morally culpable for his act. These have become known as the **M'Naghten test**.

The elements of M'Naughten test were identified as follows:

1. At the time that the act was committed,

2. the defendant was suffering from a defect of reason, from a disease of the mind, which caused

3. the defendant to not know
   a. the nature and quality of the act taken or
   b. that the act was wrong.

Historically, insanity was recognized as a defense, but it focused on the inability of a person to control their actions. M'Naghten was different because it incorporated a moral, or normative, element. For this reason, the M'Naghten test is also known as the right–wrong test. M'Naghten is the most commonly used test in the United States.

M'Naghten test: A test to determine legal insanity. It is also known as the right–wrong test.

Let's discuss each of M'Naghten's elements. First, the defendant must have been suffering from a disease of the mind at the time the act occurred. Disease isn't a reference to those formally recognized by the mental health professions; in fact, a defendant doesn't have to prove, for example, that his mental condition appears in the *Diagnostic and Statistical Manual of Mental Discorders* (*DSM*) to be found insane. Instead, any mental condition that can cause the other elements to be satisfied is a mental disease. In at least one case, extremely low intelligence was found adequate.[5] Of course, diseases that are recognized by psychiatry, such as schizophrenia, delusional disorder, and paranoia, may satisfy this element.

As to those other elements, the requirement that "the defendant must not know the nature and quality of the act" simply means that the defendant did not understand the consequences of his or her physical act. The MPC offers the following illustration: A man who squeezes his wife's neck, believing it to be a lemon, does not know the nature and quality of his actions.[6]

What is meant by "wrong," as used in the M'Naghten test? Courts have defined it two ways. One asks whether the defendant knew that the act was legally wrong, and the other asks whether the defendant knew that the act was morally wrong. A defendant who attempts to hide their crime or who experiences guilt likely knows right from wrong and, therefore, won't be successful in establishing insanity under M'Naghten.

Let's say Betty kills two neighbor children because she found them out after dark. When the police arrive 10 minutes after the murders, they find Betty sitting on her porch, drinking iced tea. She appears relaxed. When asked why she killed the children, she replied, "Kids shouldn't be out after dark. It isn't safe for them. Their parents don't have to worry now." Betty is insane under the M'Naghten test because she doesn't appreciate that what she did was wrong.

In a similar scenario, Betty kills two neighbor children for being out after dark. After the murder, she runs home, changes clothes, and puts her bloodied clothes into the laundry. When the police arrive 10 minutes after the murders, she appears distraught. Betty is not insane under M'Naghten because changing and laundering her clothes along with her emotional reaction evince an awareness of the wrongness of her act.

Irresistible Impulse

One criticism of M'Naghten is that a defendant who knows that an act is wrong, but who could not control his or her behavior because of mental disease, would be found sane. To cure this defect, a few states supplemented M'Naghten to include the inability to control one's behavior as a reason for acquittal, even if the defendant understood the nature and quality of the act or knew that the behavior was wrong. This is known as **irresistible impulse.** The elements of this defense are the same as M'Naghten, except that the inability to control one's conduct is added as an alternative to being able to distinguish right from wrong.

Irresistible impulse tests can be found in American cases as far back as 1863.[7] The largest challenge with implementing the irresistible impulse test is distinguishing acts that can be resisted from those that cannot. Colorado and Texas are two states where this test is used.

Irresistible impulse test: A test to determine legal insanity; the loss of control due to mental disease that is so great that a person cannot stop from committing a crime.

Consider this example: Ed watches as a car, driving quickly in a parking lot, hits his 10-year-old daughter, Ava, throwing her into the air to fall to the pavement 15 feet away. In rage, Ed attacks the driver as he exits the vehicle, knocks him to the ground, and repeatedly pounds his head into the pavement. After he inflicts several blows, he hears Ava's voice: "Daddy, I am OK. Stop, please stop." Ed pauses, looks at the driver, head broken and bloodied, and utters, "Oh my God, I am so sorry. Oh my God, what have I done." Under the M'Naghten test, Ed is sane. His words evince that he understands the wrongfulness of his act. But under irresistible impulse, he is insane because he couldn't control his reaction to what he witnessed.

The Model Penal Code Test

The MPC contains a definition of insanity similar to, but broader than, the M'Naghten and irresistible impulse tests. This Model Penal Code test is also referred to as the *substantial capacity test*. The MPC reads:[8]

> A person is not responsible for criminal conduct if at the time of such conduct as a result of mental disease or defect he lacks substantial capacity either to appreciate the criminality [wrongfulness] of his conduct or to conform his conduct to the requirements of law.

The MPC approach is a combination of the M'Naghten and irresistible impulse tests. Borrowing from M'Naghten, this test requires that mental disease or defect cause a defendant to not appreciate the wrongfulness of their conduct. And the language "conform his conduct to the requirements of law" incorporates the irresistible impulse test.

But the MPC's approach differs; it isn't just a combination of M'Naghten and the irresistible impulse test. For example, the MPC requires substantial mental impairment. M'Naghten, on the other hand, requires impairment that is so severe that it prevents a person from knowing the wrongfulness of the act—that is, total impairment. The MPC test has been adopted by several jurisdictions, including Illinois, Kentucky, Vermont, and Washington.

Durham

Since 1871, New Hampshire has used the easiest insanity test to apply. Known as the Durham test, a defendant is not culpable if the crime would not have been committed but for the presence of a mental disease or mental defect. Today, only New Hampshire uses this test.

Guilty but Mentally Ill (GBMI)

In 1981, John Hinckley came close to assassinating President Ronald Reagan. The president, his press secretary James Brady, a Secret Service agent, and a police officer were wounded during Hinckley's attack with a handgun. All survived. But Brady's wound left him with a permanent brain injury. Hinckley committed the crime to impress actress Jodie Foster. At trial,

---

Model Penal Code test: Also known as the substantial capacity test.

Durham test: A test to determine legal insanity. A person is insane if the act is a product of disease or defective mental condition.

Hinckley was found not guilty by reason of insanity under the MPC test. As was true in the M'Naghten verdict 139 years earlier, there was both a public and legislative backlash to the decision. Legislatures throughout the nation reconsidered their insanity defenses.

Consequently, a few states abolished the defense altogether; others limited it. The federal system, for example, returned to the M'Naghten test after having switched from M'Naghten to the MPC test. Another change in a few states was the establishment of the **guilty but mentally ill** (GBMI) verdict. Pennsylvania's GBMI statute reads, in part, that a

> "person who timely offers a defense of insanity in accordance with the Rules of Criminal Procedure may be found 'guilty but mentally ill' at trial if the trier of facts finds, beyond a reasonable doubt, that the person is guilty of an offense, was mentally ill at the time of the commission of the offense, and was not legally insane at the time of the commission of the offense.[9]

A GBMI verdict is a finding of mental illness at the time of the crime, but not insanity as defined by the applicable legal test. Unlike a defendant who is found not guilty by reason of insanity, a defendant who is GBMI is punished. But psychological treatment is provided during incarceration.

GBMI is a supplement to, not a substitute for, the insanity defense. Most states that have GBMI also recognize M'Naghten. GBMI applies when a jury concludes that the defendant suffered from a mental illness, even though it didn't rise to the level of legal insanity. Even though the verdict is guilty, a judge may treat the illness as a mitigating factor at sentencing.

The Constitution and the Insanity Defense

Debate over whether the insane should be criminally absolved continues. Today, the defense is available in the federal system and in all but five states (Alaska, Idaho, Kansas, Montana, and Utah). In your next Digging Deeper, SCOTUS reviewed a defendant's claim that he had a due process right to present insanity as a defense to his jury.

DIGGING DEEPER 6.1

Does a defendant have a right to plead moral insanity to a jury?

Case: *Kahler v. Kansas*
Court: Supreme Court of the United States.   Citation: 589 U.S. ___
Year: 2020
Justice Kagan delivered the opinion of the court.

Guilty but mentally ill (GBMI): A determination that a defendant suffered from a mental illness at the time of the crime, but the illness doesn't satisfy the elements of the applicable insanity defense. A GBMI convictee is punished but provided mental health care during incarceration.

This case is about Kansas's treatment of a criminal defendant's insanity claim. In Kansas, a defendant can invoke mental illness to show that he lacked the requisite *mens rea* (intent) for a crime. He can also raise mental illness after conviction to justify either a reduced term of imprisonment or commitment to a mental health facility. But Kansas, unlike many States, will not wholly exonerate a defendant on the ground that his illness prevented him from recognizing his criminal act as morally wrong. The issue here is whether the Constitution's Due Process Clause forces Kansas to do so—otherwise said, whether that Clause compels the acquittal of any defendant who, because of mental illness, could not tell right from wrong when committing his crime. We hold that the Clause imposes no such requirement....

Kansas law provides that "[i]t shall be a defense to a prosecution under any statute that the defendant, as a result of mental disease or defect, lacked the culpable mental state required as an element of the offense charged." Under that statute, a defendant may introduce any evidence of any mental illness to show that he did not have the intent needed to commit the charged crime. Suppose, for example, that the defendant shot someone dead and goes on trial for murder. He may then offer psychiatric testimony that he did not understand the function of a gun or the consequences of its use—more generally stated, "the nature and quality" of his actions. *M'Naghten*, 10 Cl. & Fin., at 210, 8 Eng. Rep., at 722. And a jury crediting that testimony must acquit him. As everyone here agrees, Kansas law thus uses *M'Naghten*'s "cognitive capacity" prong—the inquiry into whether a mentally ill defendant could comprehend what he was doing when he committed a crime. If the defendant had no such capacity, he could not form the requisite intent—and thus is not criminally responsible.

At the same time, the Kansas statute provides that "[m]ental disease or defect is not otherwise a defense." In other words, Kansas does not recognize any additional way that mental illness can produce an acquittal.

This case arises from a terrible crime. In early 2009, Karen Kahler filed for divorce from James Kahler and moved out of their home with their two teenage daughters and 9-year-old son. Over the following months, James Kahler became more and more distraught. On Thanksgiving weekend, he drove to the home of Karen's grandmother, where he knew his family was staying. Kahler entered through the back door and saw Karen and his son. He shot Karen twice, while allowing his son to flee the house. He then moved through the residence, shooting Karen's grandmother and each of his daughters in turn. All four of his victims died. Kahler surrendered to the police the next day and was charged with capital murder. [He was tried, convicted, and sentenced to die.]

Before trial, Kahler filed a motion arguing that Kansas's treatment of insanity claims violates the Fourteenth Amendment's Due Process Clause. Kansas, he asserted, had "unconstitutionally abolished the insanity defense" by allowing the conviction of a mentally ill person "who cannot tell the difference between right and wrong."...

A challenge like Kahler's must surmount a high bar. Under well-settled precedent, a state rule about criminal liability—laying out either the elements of or the defenses to a crime—violates due process only if it "offends some principle of justice so rooted in the traditions and conscience of our people as to be ranked as fundamental."...

In *Powell* v. *Texas*, 392 U.S. 514 (1968), this Court explained why. There, Texas declined to recognize "chronic alcoholism" as a defense to the crime of public drunkenness. The Court upheld that decision, emphasizing the paramount role of the States in setting "standards of criminal responsibility." In refusing to impose "a constitutional doctrine" defining those standards, the Court invoked the many "interlocking and overlapping concepts" that the law uses to assess when a person should be held criminally accountable for "his antisocial deeds." "The doctrines of *actus reus*, *mens rea*, insanity, mistake, justification, and duress"—the Court counted them off—reflect both the "evolving aims of the criminal law" and the "changing religious, moral, philosophical, and medical views of the nature of man." Or said a bit differently, crafting those doctrines involves balancing and rebalancing over time complex and oft-competing ideas about "social policy" and "moral culpability"—about the criminal law's "practical effectiveness" and its "ethical foundations.".…

Nowhere has the Court hewed more closely to that view than in addressing the contours of the insanity defense. Here, uncertainties about the human mind loom large. ("Psychiatrists disagree widely and frequently on what constitutes mental illness, on [proper] diagnos[es, and] on cure and treatment.") Even as some puzzles get resolved, others emerge. And those perennial gaps in knowledge intersect with differing opinions about how far, and in what ways, mental illness should excuse criminal conduct.…

And twice before we have declined [to use the Constitution to create specific rules about the insanity defense]. In *Leland* v. *Oregon*, a criminal defendant challenged as a violation of due process the State's use of the moral-incapacity test of insanity—the very test Kahler now asks us to require. According to the defendant, Oregon instead had to adopt the volitional-incapacity (or irresistible-impulse) test to comply with the Constitution. We rejected that argument.

"[P]sychiatry," we first noted, "has made tremendous strides since [the moral-incapacity] test was laid down in *M'Naghten's Case*," implying that the test seemed a tad outdated. But still, we reasoned, "the progress of science has not reached a point where its learning" would demand "eliminat[ing] the right and wrong test from [the] criminal law." And anyway, we continued, the "choice of a test of legal sanity involves not only scientific knowledge but questions of basic policy" about when mental illness should absolve someone of "criminal responsibility." The matter was thus best left to each State to decide on its own. The dissent agreed (while parting from the majority on another ground): "[I]t would be indefensible to impose upon the States one test rather than another for determining criminal culpability" for the mentally ill, "and thereby to displace a State's own choice."

A half-century later, we reasoned similarly in *Clark*. There, the defendant objected to Arizona's decision to discard the cognitive-incapacity prong of *M'Naghten* and leave in place only the moral-incapacity one—essentially the flipside of what Kansas has done. Again, we saw no due process problem. Many States, we acknowledged, allowed a defendant to show insanity through either prong of *M'Naghten*. …

Kansas, he then contends, has altogether "abolished the insanity defense," in disregard of hundreds of years of historical practice. His central claim, though, is more confined. It is that Kansas has impermissibly jettisoned the moral-incapacity test for insanity. As earlier noted, both *Clark* and *Leland* described that test as coming from *M'Naghten*. But according to Kahler (and the dissent), the moral-incapacity inquiry emerged centuries before that decision, thus forming part of the English common-law heritage this country inherited. And the test, he claims, served for all that time—and continuing into the present—as the touchstone of legal insanity: If a defendant could not understand that his act was morally wrong, then he could not be found criminally liable. So Kahler concludes that the moral-incapacity standard is a "principle of justice so rooted in the traditions and conscience of our people as to be ranked as fundamental.".…

One point, first, of agreement: Kahler is right that for hundreds of years jurists and judges have recognized insanity (however defined) as relieving responsibility for a crime. …

But neither do we think Kansas departs from that broad principle. First, Kansas has an insanity defense negating criminal liability—even though not the type Kahler demands. As noted earlier, Kansas law provides that it is "a defense to a prosecution" that "the defendant, as a result of mental disease or defect, lacked the culpable mental state required" for a crime. That provision enables a defendant to present psychiatric and other evidence of mental illness to defend himself against a criminal charge. More specifically, the defendant can use that evidence to show that his illness left him without the cognitive capacity to form the requisite intent. ...

Second, and significantly, Kansas permits a defendant to offer whatever mental health evidence he deems relevant at sentencing. A mentally ill defendant may argue there that he is not blameworthy because he could not tell the difference between right and wrong. Or, because he did not know his conduct broke the law. Or, because he could not control his behavior. Or, because of anything else. In other words, any manifestation of mental illness that Kansas's guilt-phase insanity defense disregards—including the moral incapacity Kahler highlights—can come in later to mitigate culpability and lessen punishment. And that same kind of evidence can persuade a judge to replace any prison term with commitment to a mental health facility....

So Kahler can prevail here only if he can show (again, contra *Clark*) that due process demands a specific test of legal insanity—namely, whether mental illness prevented a defendant from understanding his act as immoral. Kansas, as we have explained, does not use that type of insanity rule. If a mentally ill defendant had enough cognitive function to form the intent to kill, Kansas law directs a conviction even if he believed the murder morally justified. In Kansas's judgment, that delusion does not make an intentional killer entirely blameless. Rather than eliminate, it only lessens the defendant's moral culpability. And sentencing is the appropriate place to consider mitigation: The decisionmaker there can make a nuanced evaluation of blame, rather than choose, as a trial jury must, between all and nothing. In any event, so Kansas thinks. Those views are contested and contestable; other States—many others—have made a different choice. But Kahler must show more than that. He must show that adopting the moral-incapacity version of the insanity rule is not a choice at all—because, again, that version is "so rooted in the traditions and conscience of our people as to be ranked as fundamental." And he cannot....

Early commentators on the common law proposed various formulations of the insanity defense, with some favoring a morality inquiry and others a *mens rea* approach....

Only with *M'Naghten*, in 1843, did a court articulate, and momentum grow toward accepting, an insanity defense based independently on moral incapacity. Still, *Clark* unhesitatingly declared: "History shows no deference to *M'Naghten* that could elevate its formula to the level of fundamental principle." As *Clark* elaborated, even *M'Naghten* failed to unify state insanity defenses. States continued to experiment with insanity rules, reflecting what one court called "the infinite variety of forms [of] insanity" and the "difficult and perplexing" nature of the defense.

And it is not for the courts to insist on any single criterion going forward. We have made the point before, in *Leland*, *Powell*, and *Clark*. Just a brief reminder: "[F]ormulating a constitutional rule would reduce, if not eliminate, [the States'] fruitful experimentation, and freeze the developing productive dialog between law and psychiatry into a rigid constitutional mold."...

We therefore decline to require that Kansas adopt an insanity test turning on a defendant's ability to recognize that his crime was morally wrong. Contrary to Kahler's view, Kansas takes account of mental health at both trial and sentencing. It has just not adopted the particular insanity defense Kahler would like. That choice is for Kansas to make—and, if it wishes, to remake and remake again as the future unfolds. No insanity rule in this country's heritage or history was ever so settled as to tie a State's hands centuries later. For that reason, we affirm the judgment below.

Justice Breyer, with whom Justice Ginsburg and Justice Sotomayor join, dissenting:

Like the Court, I believe that the Constitution gives the States broad leeway to define state crimes and criminal procedures, including leeway to provide different definitions and standards related to the defense of insanity. But here, Kansas has not simply redefined the insanity defense. Rather, it has eliminated the core of a defense that has existed for centuries: that the defendant, *due to mental illness*, lacked the mental capacity necessary for his conduct to be considered morally blameworthy. Seven hundred years of Anglo-American legal history, together with basic principles long inherent in the nature of the criminal law itself, convince me that Kansas' law " offends. . . principle[s] of justice so rooted in the traditions and conscience of our people as to be ranked as fundamental."...

A much-simplified example will help the reader understand the conceptual distinction that is central to this case. Consider two similar prosecutions for murder. In Prosecution One, the accused person has shot and killed another person. The evidence at trial proves that, as a result of severe mental illness, he thought the victim was a dog. Prosecution Two is similar but for one thing: The evidence at trial proves that, as a result of severe mental illness, the defendant thought that a dog ordered him to kill the victim. Under the insanity defense as traditionally understood, the government cannot convict either defendant. Under Kansas' rule, it can convict the second but not the first.

To put the matter in more explicitly legal terms, consider the most famous statement of the traditional insanity defense, that contained in *M'Naghten's Case*, 10 Cl. & Fin. 200, 8 Eng. Rep. 718 (H. L. 1843). Lord Chief Justice Tindal, speaking for a majority of the judges of the common-law courts, described the insanity defense as follows:

> "[T]o establish a defence on the ground of insanity, it must be clearly proved that, at the time of the committing of the act, the party accused was aboring under such a defect of reason, from disease of the mind, [1] as not to know the nature and quality of the act he was doing; or, [2] if he did know it, that he did not know he was doing what was wrong."

The first prong (sometimes referred to as "cognitive incapacity") asks whether the defendant knew what he was doing. This prong corresponds roughly to the modern concept of *mens rea* for many offenses. The second (sometimes referred to as "moral incapacity") goes further. It asks, even if the defendant knew what he was doing, did he have the capacity to know that it was wrong? Applying this test to my example, a court would find that both defendants successfully established an insanity defense. Prosecution One (he thought the victim was a dog) falls within *M'Naghten*'s first prong, while Prosecution Two (he thought the dog ordered him to do it) falls within its second prong....

I do not mean to suggest that *M'Naghten*'s particular approach to insanity is constitutionally required. As we have said, "[h]istory shows no deference to *M'Naghten*." *Clark* v. *Arizona*, 548 U.S. 735, 749 (2006). *M'Naghten*'s second prong is merely one way of describing something more fundamental. Its basic insight is that mental illness may so impair a person's mental capacities as to render him no more responsible for his actions than a young child or a wild animal. Such a person is not properly the subject of the criminal law. As I shall explain in the following section, throughout history, the law has attempted to embody this principle in a variety of ways. As a historical matter, *M'Naghten* is by far its most prominent expression, but not its exclusive one. Other ways of capturing it may well emerge in the future. The problem with Kansas' law is that it excises this fundamental principle from its law entirely.

The Due Process Clause protects those " principle[s] of justice so rooted in the traditions and conscience of our people as to be ranked as fundamental." Our "primary guide" in determining whether a principle of justice ranks as fundamental is "historical practice."...

Few doctrines are as deeply rooted in our common-law heritage as the insanity defense. Although English and early American sources differ in their linguistic formulations of the legal test for insanity, with striking consistency, they all express the same underlying idea: A defendant who, due to mental illness, lacks sufficient mental capacity to be held morally responsible for his actions cannot be found guilty of a crime. This principle remained embedded in the law even as social mores shifted and medical understandings of mental illness evolved. Early American courts incorporated it into their jurisprudence. The States eventually codified it in their criminal laws. And to this day, the overwhelming majority of U. S. jurisdictions recognize insanity as an affirmative defense that excuses a defendant from criminal liability even where he was capable of forming the *mens rea* required for the offense. ...

To see why Kansas' departure is so serious, go back to our two simplified prosecutions: the first of the defendant who, because of serious mental illness, believes the victim is a dog; the second of a defendant who, because of serious mental illness, believes the dog commanded him to kill the victim. Now ask, what moral difference exists between the defendants in the two examples? Assuming equivalently convincing evidence of mental illness, I can find none at all. In both cases, the defendants differ from ordinary persons in ways that would lead most of us to say that they should not be held morally responsible for their acts. I cannot find one defendant more responsible than the other. And for centuries, neither has the law.

More than that, scholars who have studied this subject tell us that examples of the first kind are rare....

Kansas' abolition of the second part of the *M'Naghten* test requires conviction of a broad swath of defendants who are obviously insane and would be adjudged not guilty under any traditional form of the defense. This result offends deeply entrenched and widely recognized moral principles underpinning our criminal laws....

For these reasons, with respect, I dissent.

In this decision, the court distinguished between cognitive incapacity and moral incapacity. Mr. Kahler insisted that M'Naghten's moral prong, the right–wrong element, has a long history in the United States, and it is, therefore, required by due process. But the majority of the court disagreed, for three primary reasons. First, while they agreed that the moral element of insanity has been around for a long time, it wasn't a part of criminal law for hundreds of years before the M'Naghten decision. Second, even after M'Naghten, state laws varied. Some incorporated moral elements; others didn't. As such, the moral element can't be deemed as a "fundamental" right under the due process clauses. And third, Kansas continues to allow a defendant to argue that their mental illness prevented them from forming specific intent. The court noted that this cognitive element existed hundreds of years before M'Naghten's moral element was added to the definition of insanity. If a state were to prevent a defendant from arguing both the absence of mens rea and insanity, the outcome would likely be different. In Table 6.1, you will find the relative popularity of the various insanity defenses in the United States.

PHOTO 6.1 James Kahler was convicted of capital murder in the shooting deaths of his estranged wife, their two teenage daughters, and his wife's grandmother, crimes his attorneys said he committed after his spouse took a lesbian lover and filed for divorce.

Newspaper Member / ASSOCIATED PRESS

TABLE 6.1 ■ State of the Insanity Defenses in the United States						
Test	M'Naghten	MPC	*Irresistible Impulse*	Durham	GBMI	Abolished
Number of jurisdictions using it	25	21	6	2	5	4

Note: The total exceeds 50 because it includes the 50 U.S. states, Washington, DC, and two of America's five inhabited territories.

Insanity Defense Procedure

As an affirmative defense, a defendant must plead, or provide notice, to the state and court that it is being asserted. This notice, which typically must occur within a specified number of days before trial, gives the prosecution time to evidence gather, including having its own mental health professionals assess the defendant.

Lay testimony may be used to prove insanity, but typically, expert testimony must be presented. Most states authorize the trial judge to appoint a psychiatrist or psychologist to assess the defendant. Because insanity is an affirmative defense, the burden falls to the defendant to establish a prima facie case of insanity before an assessment will be ordered. A defendant is permitted to commission his own assessment. In the case of an indigent defendant, the trial judge can arrange, at the court's expense, for an examination.

At trial, the defendant bears the burden of production. Generally, the defendant must present enough evidence to create a doubt of sanity. The states are split on the issue of persuasion. Some require that the prosecution disprove the insanity claim, usually beyond a reasonable doubt. In other jurisdictions, the defendant bears the burden of persuasion, usually by preponderance of the evidence. Federal law is the most favorable to the government. It requires the defendant to prove insanity by clear and convincing evidence.[10] This was another consequence of the Hinckley verdict.

In some places, one trial occurs, and the jury, or judge, determines both guilt and sanity. But a variant exists where bifurcated (two) hearings are conducted, with guilt and sanity tried separately.

What Happens to the Criminally Insane

A defendant found "not guilty by reason of insanity" is typically confined in a mental hospital until they are determined to be no longer dangerous. Some jurisdictions require the trial court to make a finding of dangerousness at the time of the verdict before confinement is ordered. A few jurisdictions have followed the Model Penal Code approach,[11] which requires automatic commitment following a finding of not guilty by reason of insanity. This is the rule in the federal system.[12]

The ideal is that the individual should receive mental care during commitment. But inadequate funding, security concerns, and overcrowding problems often stand in the way of effective treatment.

A person who has been committed is to be released when it is determined that they are no longer dangerous. The determination of dangerousness is left to the judge, not hospital administrators or mental health professionals—an often criticized practice. Patients, doctors, government officials, and even the judge can begin the process of release. Some states provide for periodic reviews of the patient's status in order to determine the propriety of release. The relevant federal statute reads like this, in part:[13]

> When the director of the facility in which an acquitted person is hospitalized... determines that the person has recovered from his mental disease or defect to such an extent that his release, or his conditional release under a prescribed regimen of medical, psychiatric, or psychological care or treatment, would no longer create a substantial risk of bodily injury to another person or serious damage to property of another, he shall promptly file a certificate to that effect with the clerk of the court that ordered the commitment.... The court shall order a discharge of the acquitted person or, on the motion of the attorney for the government or on its own motion, shall hold a hearing [to determine if the patient is dangerous].

The defendant has the burden of proving by clear and convincing evidence that he is no longer dangerous. As you have learned, convictees who were found "guilty but mentally ill" are entitled to treatment during their punishment, in prison or in the community.

Insanity at the Time of Trial

SCOTUS has held that it violates due process to try a defendant who is insane.[14] Specifically, the court is concerned that insanity can impede a defendant's ability to assist in mounting a defense. The test for determining insanity at the time of trial is different from what was discussed earlier. Insanity is found whenever a defendant lacks the capacity to understand the proceedings or to assist in the development of the defense. A defendant who is rational, able to testify coherently, and able to discuss the facts and defense strategy with their attorney is sane.

The burden of establishing incompetence is placed on the defendant in many jurisdictions. While this procedure comports with due process, requiring the defendant to establish incompetence by clear and convincing evidence does not. In *Cooper v. Oklahoma* (1996),[15] the Supreme Court held that the burden of proof can rest with defendant, but the standard of proof shall not exceed preponderance of evidence.

A defendant who is unable to stand trial because of mental incompetence is committed in a mental health facility until they regain sanity. But indefinite confinement is unconstitutional. Detention of 18 months or longer while awaiting competence to stand trial amounts to punishment that violates due process.[16] To hold the defendant longer, there must be an independent finding of dangerousness. In a similar case, SCOTUS determined that a person who has become insane after being sentenced to death may not be executed until the individual's sanity has returned.[17] Justice Marshall has stated, "It is no less abhorrent today than it has been for centuries to exact in penance the life of one whose mental illness prevents him from comprehending the reasons for the penalty or its implications."[18] Similarly, the court has held that mentally retarded individuals may not be executed.[19]

TABLE 6.2 ■ Insanity at the Time of the Crime and Trial	
Finding	*Disposition*
Insane at the time of the crime under M'Naghten, MPC, Durham, irresistible impulse	Not guilty. Institutionalized for treatment until it is determined the individual is no longer a threat to life.
Guilty but mentally ill	Punished for the crime. Treatment is provided during punishment.
Sane at the time of the crime but insane at the time of trial	Trial is postponed until the defendant is capable of assisting in their own defense and understands the nature of the proceedings.

Diminished Capacity

There are a few defenses that are commonly classified and taught in the mental state segment of criminal law. These fall under the heading *diminished capacity*. These defenses are incomplete; hence, if successful, they reduce a crime or its punishment, but they don't result in acquittal. In reality, these are mens rea defenses. Typically, the claim is that the defendant lacked the ability to form specific intent, leaving open the possibility of a conviction of a lesser, included, general intent crime—for example, manslaughter instead of murder or trespass instead of burglary.

Diminished capacity is sometimes raised by defendants who can't prove insanity but who believe that they didn't act with full volition. This defense was birthed in California in the 1950s. But California killed it in 1982, in response to a highly publicized murder case. Dan White, who was angry about an appointment he was denied, snuck into San Francisco's City Hall, sought out Mayor George Mascone and Supervisor (commonly referred to as a city council member in other states) Harvey Milk and killed them both with a handgun. In a highly publicized trial, White asserted that he suffered from a diminished capacity during the trial. One of many factors contributing to his mental state was hyperglycemia, or high blood sugar, according to the experts called by the defense. The jury concurred, finding him guilty of voluntary manslaughter. The verdict caused a stir, particularly in San Francisco's gay population because Milk was the first openly gay person elected to the Board of Supervisors. White was sentenced to a little more than 7 years in prison, served 5 years, spent 1 year in Los Angeles, returned to San Francisco, and committed suicide in 1985.[20]

White's trial took place in 1979. You may recall that Hinckley's attempted assassination of President Reagan occurred in 1981. The two events coalesced into an anti-insanity defense and law-and-order approach to criminal justice. California abolished the diminished capacity defense in favor of a harder to prove diminished actuality defense, and as you learned previously, several states rejected the MPC approach to insanity in favor of M'Naghten or another test. When the defense was debated in the California State Legislature, White's defense was referred to as the "Twinkie defense," a name that stuck, even though the defense never mentioned the snack cakes specifically when they referred to White's overconsumption of processed sugar.

Many states and the federal government continue to formally recognize the defense. The federal government's sentencing guidelines permit sentencing judges to "depart" from a recommended sentence if

A sentence below the applicable guideline range may be warranted if the defendant committed the offense while suffering from a significantly reduced mental capacity. However, the court may not depart below the applicable guideline range if

1. the significantly reduced mental capacity was caused by the voluntary use of drugs or other intoxicants;
2. the facts and circumstances of the defendant's offense indicate a need to protect the public because the offense involved actual violence or a serious threat of violence; or
3. the defendant's criminal history indicates a need to incarcerate the defendant to protect the public. If a departure is warranted, the extent of the departure should reflect the extent to which the reduced mental capacity contributed to the commission of the offense.[21]

If you are unsure of the difference between a "diminished capacity because of mental illness" defense and a "straight mens rea" defense, you are not alone. The differences vary by jurisdiction. Most are procedural. Diminished capacity, for example, is an affirmative defense; mens rea is not. A defendant must give notice that diminished capacity is an issue, and the defense must show the court that there is a factual basis (prima facie) for the defense before it may be presented to a jury.

If a defendant is not successful, the defense may not be presented to the jury. The defendant can still argue the mens rea point, but the court will not permit the defendant to call expert or other witnesses to prove that mental illness was a factor. Another difference concerns timing of the defense. Typically, mens rea is only an issue at the guilt phase—the trial. But diminished capacity may be raised, depending on the jurisdiction, at the guilt phase in an effort to persuade the jury to convict of a lesser offense, or at the sentencing phase to convince the judge to reduce the punishment.

Intoxication

A specific form of diminished capacity is intoxication, typically by drugs or alcohol. Some jurisdictions allow evidence of intoxication to be presented to prove that a defendant didn't form specific intent. Again, as an imperfect defense, conviction of a lesser included offense is possible.

Still, other states don't permit intoxication as a defense. These jurisdictions hold that a person's decision to get drunk or high as adequate mens rea to hold the person accountable for all resulting harm. Florida, for example, has done away with the defense altogether:

> Voluntary intoxication resulting from the consumption, injection, or other use of alcohol or other controlled substance as described in chapter 893 is not a defense to any offense proscribed by law.[22]

Some jurisdictions have taken a middle-of-the-road approach by either requiring extreme intoxication or forbidding its use in specific cases, such as driving when under the influence and vehicular battery and homicide. When a defendant convicted of murder challenged a decision to not permit him to argue involuntary intoxication to the jury, SCOTUS found no due process right to the defense.[23] In the unusual case of involuntary intoxication, the intoxication defense is perfect. Typically, a person is forced or tricked into an involuntary state of intoxication. But it is possible that it can occur accidentally, as long as it was genuinely unintended and not negligent.

Consider the following scenarios.

James lives in a state that permits evidence of voluntary intoxication as an imperfect defense. James gets very drunk in a bar and kills a man in a fight. James is charged with intentional murder. James is entitled to argue to the jury that his voluntary intoxication prevented him from forming the intent to kill and that he should be convicted of manslaughter.

James lives in a state that doesn't permit evidence of voluntary intoxication as an imperfect defense. James gets very drunk in a bar and kills a man in a fight. James is charged with intentional murder. James is not entitled to argue to the jury that his voluntary intoxication prevented him from forming the intent to kill.

James loses his job and discovers that his husband, Frank, is having a sexual affair. He seeks emotional help, is diagnosed as depressed, and begins taking a prescribed antidepressant. In a rare side effect of the drug, James unexpectedly and suddenly becomes violent while grocery shopping. He hits several people in the store before he is subdued. He is charged with three counts of battery. James is entitled to plead involuntary intoxication to the jury.

Intoxication: A defense that asserts a defendant was unable to form the required mens rea because of mental impairment resulting from alcohol or drugs.

QUESTIONS AND PROBLEMS

1. Define and distinguish the McNaghten, irresistible impulse, MPC, Durham, and GBMI tests.
2. Does a defendant have a due process right to present insanity as a defense to a jury? Explain your answer.
3. Explain the law of a defendant's insanity at the time of trial, including a comparison of the tests for insanity at the time a crime is committed to insanity at the time of trial.
4. Explain how the diminished capacity defense and the insanity defense differ.
5. Explain the intoxication defense.

For each of the following scenarios, apply the M'Naghten, irresistible impulse, and the MPC tests for insanity.

6. Shelby idolizes a social media influencer, Justin Jaffey. Like Justin, Shelby suffers from schizophrenia and depression. Shelby reads in an online blog that Justin has become very depressed, separating himself from friends and family. Shelby seeks him out and stabs him to death. When the police arrive at the scene, Shelby is sitting calmly next to Justin's body. The first officer on the scene, shocked by the scene, asks, "What happened?" Shelby replies, "I killed him so he can restart his life. When he awakes, he will be happy and no longer be ill. It won't be long now. You will see how happy he is and how pleased with me he will be."

7. Shelby idolizes a social media influencer, Justin Jaffey. Like Justin, Shelby suffers from schizophrenia and depression. Shelby reads in an online blog that Justin has decided to end his social media presence. Shelby finds Justin at home and knocks on the door; Justin answers, and Shelby pleads with him to change his mind. Justin becomes irritated by the conversation and begins to close the door. Shelby pushes the door back open, pulls out a knife, and stabs Justin to death. Shelby then cleans up the blood from the floor, puts Justin's body in the trunk of his car, and dumps him into a river. After he disposes of Justin's body, he calls a friend and says, "I can't tell you much, but I have done something horrible. I hope God forgives me."

8. Janice is in a meeting with her 10-year-old daughter's school principal to discuss disciplinary issues. When asked why she has been disobeying one of her teachers, the daughter begins to cry and said, "I am scared of him." When asked why she feared the teacher, the daughter said, "Because he touches me in my private areas." Janice feels her face become warm, then cold and clammy, and for a moment she feels lightheaded. She hugs her daughter and then becomes overwhelmed with anger and grief. She charges to the teacher's classroom, finds him in front of the class, and hits him repeatedly with a fire hydrant that she found along the way. The principal and another teacher stop Janice, who looks down at the teacher, bloody on the floor, and states, "You sick f**k, you got what you deserved. You will go to jail for what you have done."

I WAS YOUNG AND INNOCENT

Learning Objective: Explain infancy as a defense. Identify at least two differences between criminal and juvenile adjudications.

In recent years, schools referred close to 300,000 elementary and high school students to police, and between 2013 and 2018, almost 30,000 people under the age of 10 were arrested annually.[24]

Because children are presumed to lack the intellectual and moral capacity to form an evil intent and because they may prove to be more law-abiding, empathetic adults, the law sometimes excuses juvenile crime.

Youth, or *infancy*, is sometimes a perfect defense. Under the old Common Law, it wasn't possible, as a matter of law, for a person under the age of 7 to develop the mens rea to commit any crime. Between 7 and 14, a child was rebuttably presumed incapable of forming mens rea. The state could overcome the presumption by establishing that the child knew right from wrong.

In contemporary United States, two systems deal with juvenile offenders: the juvenile justice system and the criminal justice system. There is wide variance in the treatment of juvenile offenders across the United States, and the relationship of the two systems is complex. Often, both criminal and juvenile courts have concurrent jurisdiction. The process to decide whether a juvenile shall be tried as an adult or a juvenile varies between jurisdictions.

You may recall that the primary purposes of the juvenile justice system are to rehabilitate and reintegrate the child into society and to protect the public. Juveniles who are diverted into the juvenile justice system are not "punished," at least not the in the same way as in the criminal justice system. If guilty, a juvenile offender is found to be *delinquent* and ordered into education, counseling, and other rehabilitative programs. Commitment to a juvenile justice facility is also possible.

In most jurisdictions, violating any criminal law can be the basis of a delinquency case. In addition, certain status offenses, such as truancy or persistent disobedience of parents can also lead to a finding of delinquency.

Because the purpose of the juvenile justice system is different than the criminal justice system, the full array of constitutional rights that are enjoyed by criminal defendants is not available to juveniles—the right to a jury trial, for example. A few rights are so fundamental to ensuring a fair process, however, they extend to the juvenile justice system. The right to counsel is one.[25] See Table 6.3 for a comparison of the juvenile and criminal justice systems.

TABLE 6.3 ■ Juvenile and Criminal Justice Systems Comparison		
	Criminal Justice System	**Juvenile Justice System**
Objectives(s)	Punishment: deterrence, retribution, rehabilitation, restitution, restoration	Rehabilitation
Culpability	Criminal guilt	Delinquency
Types of offenses	Statutorily defined crimes	Statutorily defined crimes and status offenses
Fact finding hearing	Trial	Adjudication
Adjudication style	Adversarial, formal	Nonadversarial, less formal
Outcome	Sentence	Disposition
Due process	Full array of rights	Limited rights (e.g., no jury trial)

Infancy: A defense that asserts a defendant is not liable because of juvenile age.

The law is considerably different today than at the Common Law. Over 30 states have no statutory minimum age of criminal responsibility, and offenders as young as 12 have been prosecuted and punished for felonies. Courts in some of the states without statutory minimums have developed their own standards for determining whether a juvenile should be held accountable. In those states that have statutory minimums, the range is 7 to 10 years old.

Regardless of adult jurisdiction, juveniles are often referred by prosecutors into the juvenile justice system. This is more likely of drug, property damage, theft, threat, and simple battery cases than it is of violent felonies.

There is no minimum age for juvenile court jurisdiction. But states do define the point at which a person is an adult and no longer eligible to be adjudicated by juvenile court. By 2020, 44 states had a maximum age of 17 for juvenile court jurisdiction. Vermont permitted referrals into the juvenile system for offenders as old as 18, making it the only state allowing referrals for people older than 17. The other states cap juvenile court jurisdiction at 16.[26]

QUESTIONS AND PROBLEMS

1. Explain infancy as a defense.
2. Identify at least two differences between criminal and juvenile adjudications.

TO ERR IS HUMAN

Learning Objectives: Define and distinguish mistake of law, ignorance of law, legal impossibility, and mistake of fact from factual impossibility.

Benjamin Franklin wrote "but in this world nothing can be said to be certain, except death and taxes." But there is at least one other certainty of all people: They all make mistakes. Most mistakes are small, no harm is done, and the law is not involved. But a small number of mistakes are criminal. Two forms of mistakes are recognized in criminal law: legal and factual. For purposes of this area of law, a mistake refers to a person's knowledge about the law or the facts of the case. Although it is common to refer to a bad decision as a mistake, that is not the kind of mistake that can be used to excuse a crime. Generally, mistakes of fact are more successful defenses than mistakes of law.

Mistake of Law

A **mistake of law** occurs when a person commits an act believing it to be legal when it is not. Mistakes of law can be distinguished from ignorance of the law. The statement "Ignorance of the law is no excuse" is largely true. People have an obligation to be knowledgeable of the law, and the claim "I didn't know it was against the law" is not a defense. One exception is when ignorance of

---

Mistake of law: A defense that asserts a defendant's misunderstanding of the law mitigates culpability.

the law causes a defendant not to form specific intent. For example, SCOTUS decided that it isn't possible to "willfully" violate the tax laws when the taxpayer sincerely believes the tax is not owed.[27] Of course, this wouldn't apply if the mens rea requirement was only general intent or strict liability.

A mistake of law, as opposed to *ignorance of the law*, occurs when a person is aware of the law and believes they are complying with it when in fact, they are violating it. Again, if the mistake negates mens rea, the crime may be lowered to a lesser included offense. In rare circumstances, the mistake may excuse the crime for reasons beyond mens rea. To understand this, the ignorance of the law principle needs to be put into historical context. It came into being hundreds of years ago when crimes were fewer, they were malum in se, and community values and the law were closely aligned. In a modern, pluralistic society with complex and detailed laws aplenty, it is much easier to be wrong about, or unaware of, the law. While the law doesn't excuse unawareness, it has evolved to excuse, in rare instances, mistakes. The Model Penal Code identifies two instances when mistake of law is a valid excuse. Most of the states also recognize these:

1. When the law wasn't published or made reasonably available to the public or

2. When the defendant relied on a statute, judicial decision, or official interpretation of the law by an appropriate public official, even though that law or interpretation is later found to be wrong.[28]

Returning to taxes, imagine a taxpayer who wins $10,000 in an online gambling game. She doesn't know if she has to pay taxes on online income, so she makes a formal request for "guidance" of the Internal Revenue Service (IRS), the agency that enforces federal tax laws. She receives a letter from the IRS indicating that she isn't required to pay federal taxes on the winnings. But the IRS later informs her that it was wrong. She can't be prosecuted for the mistake, but she can be expected to pay the back taxes.

Bad legal advice from a friend, a government official who is not responsible for the giving the advice sought, or from an attorney are not legitimate excuses. The advice must be offered by an official who is responsible for enforcing the specific law that was violated.

The reverse is also possible—that is, a defendant believes the law is being broken when it is not. Norman, for example, believes he is required to pay taxes on his income from online gambling when he is not. In this case, it is a *legal impossibility* for Norman to commit the crime. Therefore, he is not guilty, even though he believes he has committed a legal wrong.

Mistake of Fact

A **mistake of fact** occurs when a defendant has committed the actus reus of a crime but hasn't formed the required mens rea because of misunderstanding of the facts. Consider Trudy, a shopper at an organic market. She fills a cart with fruit and nuts. At the register, the checker asks how many pomegranates she has in her basket, and she tells him she has 15. But Trudy miscounted; there were 17 of the fruit. Trudy has made a mistake of fact that excuses the crime of theft.

Mistake of fact: A defense that asserts a defendant's misunderstanding of the facts of the case mitigate culpability.

Factual impossibility is a related doctrine. It refers to situations where the mens rea to commit a specific intent crime is present, but the completion of the crime is factually impossible. However, a defendant may be guilty of attempting the specific intent offense, or of committing a lesser, included, general intent offense. In a case from the U.S. military, *United States v. Thomas*,[29] two men raped a dead woman they believed to unconscious. They were charged with attempted rape. The law the men were prosecuted under provided that only a living person can be raped. The defendants argued that the requirement of a living victim for the crime of rape should extend to the crime of attempted rape. Relying on the doctrine of factual impossibility, they argued that it is not possible to attempt to rape a person who can't be raped. Their argument was rejected by the court, and the men were court-martialed and sentenced to prison. While the court agreed that only a living person can be raped, attempted rape is different. The intent to commit a rape combined with the acts the men took in furtherance of this objective are adequate to establish the crime of attempt. This is the prevailing view. The following cases illustrate the law.

Pearl Pickpocket reaches into an empty pocket. She is not guilty of theft, but she is guilty of attempted theft.

With the intent to kill her, Patrick stabs Sandy in the heart while she is sleeping. But Sandy wasn't sleeping; she had died of a heart attack an hour earlier. Patrick is not guilty of murder, but he is guilty of attempted murder.

Bob buys a bag of powdered cocaine from Gary. As it turns out, Gary scammed Bob. The bag was full of baby powder. Bob is not guilty of purchasing a controlled substance, but he is guilty of attempting to purchase a controlled substance.

QUESTIONS AND PROBLEMS

1. Define and distinguish ignorance of law, mistake of law, and legal impossibility.
2. Define and distinguish mistake of fact from factual impossibility.

What mistake doctrine most applies to each of the following scenarios? Explain your answer, including what you determine the most likely legal outcome.

3. Tyler offers to sell Quint a large container of new iPhones that were stolen from a big-box technology retail store. Quint buys a container of them for $1,000. When Quint gets home and opens the container, he discovers that the individual boxes are filled with small pieces of wood. Unknown to the men, the police were monitoring their activities. Prosecutors are considering charging Quint with receiving stolen property, a specific intent crime.
4. Tyler lives in a state that doesn't permit right turns on red traffic lights, unless there is a sign indicating that right turn on red is permitted. Tyler previously lived in Ohio, which had the opposite rule—a right turn is permitted at a red light unless there is a sign forbidding it. On the second day after he moved to the state, he stopped at a red light, checked for oncoming cars, and turned right. He was ticketed for the offense and is defending against the citation by alleging that he was unaware of the law because he was from Ohio, where the turn is permitted.

I DID IT BECAUSE OF THE COPS

Learning Objective: Define, compare, and contrast subjective and objective entrapment.

Justin Laboy, an honor student at Park Vista High School in Florida with no criminal record, became immediately smitten with a new transfer student. As a boy from the Bronx and of Puerto Rican descent, Justin found Naomi Rodriguez, a Puerto Rican–Dominican girl from Queens, not only beautiful, but someone with whom he had much in common. The two began texting and seeing one another. He sang, danced, and wrote music for her. She let him kiss her on the cheek.

Before their school prom, Naomi asked Justin if he could get her marijuana. He said no, that he didn't do drugs. Naomi asked again. Eager to please her, he said he would try. Subsequently, she texted him several times inquiring if he had any luck. Eventually, he obtained a bag from a friend and gave it to her. She refused it as a gift, insisting that he take $25. He agreed. Not long thereafter, Justin was arrested, along with many others, for drug offenses. He would learn that his crush wasn't a high school student. She was a 25-year-old undercover police officer. Because he sold her the marijuana on school grounds, Justin's crime was a felony. He pled guilty and was sentenced to 3 years of probation. The felony conviction made him ineligible to join the United States military, his career objective.[30] Justin's case raises the question about how far the government can go in inducing a person into criminality. When a government goes too far, its conduct is known as *entrapment*.

Entrapment is an affirmative, perfect defense. The policy underlying entrapment is that it is morally wrong for a government to lure a person into committing a crime that they would not have committed without the government's inducement. The defense is recognized in all the states and the federal government. The line between offering the opportunity to commit a crime and unfairly drawing a person into crime is not easy to draw. Two tests have been created to determine if the government entrapped a person. They are known as the subjective and objective tests. A majority of the states and the federal government have adopted the subjective test. In addition to a minority of states, the MPC adopts the objective test. The test that is applied can make the difference between conviction and acquittal.

Subjective entrapment asks whether a defendant was mentally predisposed to commit the crime. A person is predisposed if they are ready and willing to commit a crime and only awaiting the opportunity. As expressed by SCOTUS, the subjective test is intended to distinguish between the "unwary innocent and the unwary criminal."[31]

Proof of subjective entrapment includes anything that demonstrates that the defendant was ready, willing, and able to commit the crime. A defendant's criminal history may be relevant. A history of drug convictions is relevant, for example, when a defendant claims entrapment in a drug offense prosecution. But a decades-old drug conviction isn't evidence of predisposition to steal from an employer. How hard the police had to work to get the defendant involved is also relevant. The defendant who becomes involved at the first opportunity or who requires little incentive is predisposed.

Subjective entrapment: A test used to determine if the state has gone too far in encouraging a defendant to commit a crime. This test focuses on the defendant's predisposition to commit the crime.

Creating an opportunity for a person to engage in crime is not entrapment per se, so police stings (undercover operations that often use deceit to catch offenders) are legitimate. A police officer posing as a teenager in an online chat room for purposes of catching child predators is an example.

Objective entrapment focuses on the conduct of the state, not on the defendant. For this reason, a defendant's criminal history is immaterial in the objective entrapment determination. Instead, the efforts that were made by the government to induce a person into the crime are considered. If excessive, a defendant has been entrapped. Under this model, it is possible for a defendant who is predisposed to commit a crime to be acquitted if the police go too far in drawing the defendant into the crime. This is a contrast with the subjective entrapment test, where the government may aggressively entice a predisposed defendant into a crime and still obtain a conviction.

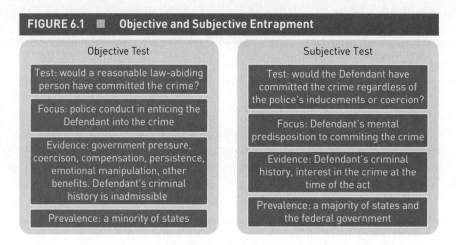

FIGURE 6.1 ■ Objective and Subjective Entrapment

Objective Test

Test: would a reasonable law-abiding person have committed the crime?

Focus: police conduct in enticing the Defendant into the crime

Evidence: government pressure, coercison, compensation, persistence, emotional manipulation, other benefits. Defendant's criminal history is inadmissible

Prevalence: a minority of states

Subjective Test

Test: would the Defendant have committed the crime regardless of the police's inducements or coercion?

Focus: Defendant's mental predisposition to commiting the crime

Evidence: Defendant's criminal history, interest in the crime at the time of the act

Prevalence: a majority of states and the federal government

Regardless of which test is applied, police are permitted to use lies and deceit to catch criminals. This is inherent in sting operations, such as when police pose as drug users to catch traffickers or as minors to catch sexual predators. Although these practices are permitted, they are relevant to the entrapment analysis, particularly in jurisdictions that employ the objective test.

One common limitation to the entrapment defense, both subjective and objective, is that it may not be used to defend against crimes of violence. The MPC takes this approach, as do most states. Procedurally, entrapment is an affirmative defense that puts the burden of production and persuasion on the defendant.

QUESTIONS AND PROBLEMS

1. Define and compare the subjective and objective entrapment tests.
2. Messalina is 35 years old. She was kicked out of her home by her parents at 15. To survive, she turned to selling drugs and prostitution. She was in and out of jail and

---

Objective entrapment: A test used to determine if the state has gone too far in encouraging a defendant to commit a crime. This test focuses on the conduct of the state's agents.

prison for sex and drug crimes until she was 30 years old. In total, she was convicted of prostitution on six occasions and possession of controlled substances on three occasions. At 30, she met James on the streets. He was homeless and a drug addicted but was determined to improve his life. The two became close and committed themselves to one another and to improving their lives. Messalina found a job as a cashier in a used furniture store, and James found day labor. Over 4 years, they were able to save enough to rent a nice apartment, and they were both free of drugs and other crime. Then tragedy struck. James died of a heart attack. Messalina was emotionally distraught, and without James's income, she was in financial distress. An undercover officer who knew her history of prostitution approached her a few weeks after James's death and offered her $50 a day to work for him as a prostitute. She turned down the request. A week later, she received a notice of eviction from the apartment. Aware of the notice, the officer approached Messalina again. He said, "You need to make money. Do you want to lose your home? The home you and James built? I can pay you $75 a day." She again refused the offer. Determined to keep the apartment, she took a second job. Even with it, however, she didn't earn enough to pay the rent and her other bills. Two days before the eviction was scheduled to occur, the officer approached Messalina again and offered to pay the $325 she owed in rent and $100 per day thereafter. She agreed. Was she entrapped? Apply the subjective and entrapment tests.

I DID IT A LONG TIME AGO

Learning Objective: Define statute of limitations and tolling.

Statute of limitations are laws that limit the maximum time within which the state must file a criminal action. The date of the crime is the starting point; the date the charges are filed is the end date. Typically, the more serious the crime, the longer the statute of limitation. Not all crimes have a statute of limitations. Serious crimes, such as murder, treason, and rape, often do not. Arkansas, for example, has no limitation on murder and some sex offenses, 6 years on serious felonies, 3 years on lesser felonies, and 1 year on most misdemeanors.[32]

In some circumstances, the clock on the statute of limitation is stopped. Known as tolling, this extends the time period for filing charges. The most common reason to toll a criminal statute of limitation is a defendant's fugitive status. A recent unusual example of tolling occurred during the COVID-19 pandemic. Several federal and state courts issued orders tolling all criminal and civil actions during court closures resulting from the COVID-19 pandemic.

There are at least two reasons for time-limiting prosecutions. First, due process requires reliable evidence to sustain a conviction. Like food, older physical and testimonial evidence

---

Statute of limitation: A period of time within which an actor must be charged with committing a crime or the opportunity to prosecute the actor is lost.

Tolling: A pause in a statute of limitations clock, resulting in a longer period of time within which a criminal charge may be filed.

can sour. Witnesses are less likely to accurately remember an event, witnesses die or otherwise become unavailable, and physical evidence can become tainted, change, dissipate, or break down. Therefore, the closer in time a defendant's trial is to the alleged crime, the more likely the evidence will be reliable. A second rationale for limiting the time within which a criminal action must be filed concerns personal responsibility and reformation. Some people believe that an individual shouldn't have to live their entire life in a state of fear of being apprehended and punished for crimes committed years or decades in the past.

PHOTO 6.2 A statute of limitations, known in civil law systems as a prescriptive period, is a law passed by a legislative body to set the maximum time after an event within which legal proceedings may be initiated.

serggn / iStock

QUESTIONS AND PROBLEMS

1. What is a statute of limitations?
2. Dr. Kimble has been charged with embezzlement. He is arrested, appears in court, and bail is set. He pays the bail, is released, and flees to Argentina. He is gone for 8 years before he returns to the United States. What impact does his time in Argentina have on the 7-year statute of limitations for embezzlement?

I HAD A RIGHT TO DO IT

A final reminder about a very important form of defense that you studied in Chapter 2: constitutional defense. If a defendant is prosecuted under a statute, or lower law, that violates the Constitution, the charges will be dismissed and, possibly, the law will be struck down.

IN A NUTSHELL

Like justification, society "excuses" some harmful acts for policy or humanistic reasons. The lack of moral culpability is an example. You saw this with mens rea earlier in the book, and in this chapter, it was discussed in the context of the insanity defense. One of the most controversial defenses, insanity acts as a complete defense, although the person found not guilty by reason of insanity may be institutionalized and treated until they are no longer a danger to others. Through the years, the insanity defense has been criticized and modified, and in recent years, a few states have abolished it altogether. For those jurisdictions that recognize it, there are four tests used to determine legal insanity: M'Naghten, irresistible impulse, MPC, and Durham. A few states supplement these with the guilty but mentally ill verdict, which results in both punishment and treatment of the convictee. Similarly, the acts of children are excused under the theory that a person must reach a certain level of maturity—cognitive, emotionally, and morally—to be criminally blameworthy.

There are other excuses that are driven by different policy objectives. The entrapment defense, for example, is intended to prevent the government from engaging in overzealous prosecutions that ensnare the innocent. Statute of limitations serve a due process purpose by demanding that a person be tried when the evidence is the freshest.

LEGAL TERMS

Durham test (p. 176)

guilty but mentally ill (p. 177)

infancy (p. 189)

intoxication (p. 187)

irresistible impulse test (p. 175)

mistake of fact (p. 191)

mistake of law (p. 190)

Model Penal Code test (p. 176)

M'Naghten test (p. 174)

Objective entrapment (p. 194)

Statute of limitations (p. 195)

Subjective entrapment (p. 193)

tolling (p. 195)

NOTES

1. Marisa M. Kashino, "The Definitive Oral History of the Bobbitt Case, 25 Years Later," *Washingtonian*, accessed July 1, 2020, Washingtonian.com.

2. Angela Paulsen, "Limiting the Scope of State Power to Confine Insanity Acquittees: *Foucha v. Louisiana*," *Tulsa L.J* 28 (1993): 537.

3. M'Naghten's Case, 8 Eng. Rep. 718 (H. L. 1843).

4. LaFave & Scott, Criminal Law § 4.2A(a)(Hornbook Series, St. Paul: West, 1986).

5. *State v. Johnson*, 290 N.W. 159 (Wis. 1940).

6. Model Penal Code, Tent. Draft 4, at 156.

7. LaFave & Scott at § 4.2(d).

8. Model Penal Code § 4.01(1).

9. 18 Pa. C.S.A. § 314.

10. 18 U.S.C. § 17.

11. Model Penal Code § 4.08.

12. 18 U.S.C. § 4243(a).

13. 18 U.S.C. § 4243(f).

14. *Dusky v. United States*, 362 U.S. 402 (1960).

15. 517 U.S. 348.

16. *Jackson v. Indiana*, 406 U.S. 715 (1972).

17. *Ford v. Wainwright*, 477 U.S. 399 (1986).

18. Id. at 417.

19. *Atkins v. Virginia*, 122 S. Ct. 2242 (2002).

20. Jay Mathews, "Dan White Commits Suicide," *Washington Post*. October 22, 1985, accessed July 18, 2020, Washingtonpost.com.

21. Federal Sentencing Guidelines Manual §5K2.13.

22. § 775.051, Fla. Stat.

23. *Montana v. Engelhoff*, 518 U.S. 37 (1996).

24. *Uniform Crime Reports*, Federal Bureau of Investigation (2019), accessed July 19, 2020, ucr. fbi.gov.

25. *In Re Gault*, 387 U.S. 1 (1967).

26. *Juvenile Age of Jurisdiction and Transfer to Adult Court Laws*, National Conference of State Legislatures (2020), accessed July 19, 2020, ncsl.org.

27. *Cheek v. United States,* 498 U.S. 192, 111 S. Ct. 604 (1991).

28. MPC§2.04.

29. 13 U.S.C.M.A. 278 (1962).

30. Ira Glass, "457: What I Did For Love," *This American Life*, February 10, 2012.

31. *Sherman v. United States*, 356 U.S. 369 (1958).

32. Ark. Code §5-1-109.

7 CRIMES AGAINST THE PERSON

On November 21, 1985, a 19-year-old woman was hitchhiking in Florida. John Brennan Crutchley, who was on his way to work, picked her up and agreed to take her to her destination after they made a brief stop at his home. When they arrived at his home, he tied a ligature around her neck, choked her into unconsciousness, and dragged her into the house. The woman woke to discover that she was nude and tied to Crutchley's kitchen island. In addition to repeatedly raping her, Crutchley drained and drank her blood, leading the media to dub him the Vampire Rapist. Although weakened by the loss of nearly half of her blood, the woman successfully escaped the next day while Crutchley was at work. All of this happened while Crutchley's wife and child were away visiting family for Thanksgiving. Subsequently, Crutchley was convicted of kidnapping and rape and sentenced to 25 years in prison. He was released 10 years later. However, Crutchley never fully returned to public life because he was found to have violated the terms of his parole only 1 day after his release. Still in a transition facility at the time, a judge ordered his parole revoked, and he was returned to prison. In 2002, he was found dead in his prison cell of autoerotic asphyxiation.

In searches of Crutchley's home and office after his arrest in 1985, police found evidence that linked him to several missing women. In prison, Crutchley bragged to other inmates that he murdered several women, including an ex-girlfriend. Years of investigation, extending well beyond Crutchley's death, were not successful in gathering enough evidence to link him to the deaths of anyone.[1] Adding to the oddity that was John Brennan Crutchley, the searches also discovered a cache of classified military documents that he apparently collected while working for National Aeronautics and Space Administration (NASA) contractors. Navy investigators considered charging him with espionage, and they also suspected that he was involved in the murders of two Navy women.[2]

Crutchley's case illustrates several crimes against the person, including kidnapping, rape, battery, and possibly murder. This chapter examines these and other crimes against the person. Homicide, the most serious crime against the person, is the subject of the next chapter. Subsequent chapters examine other crimes. Not all crimes can be covered. There are thousands of crimes in the codes of the federal government, the states, territories, and municipalities. The most common crimes will be reviewed in the upcoming chapters.

Each crime will be broken down into its elements. As you have already learned, most crimes require an act and mens rea. In some instances, these two elements are not singular. A crime may have two or three acts and multiple mens rea requirements. Also, many crimes include lesser offenses, and as you learned, these merge into the most serious offense. For example, a defendant who bludgeons a victim to death with a golf club has committed a murder and battery. If convicted of murder, the battery "merges" into the murder, and only the murder is punished; however, if the defendant is acquitted of the murder charge, conviction of battery is still possible.

STICKS AND STONES MAY BREAK MY BONES

Learning Objective: Define, compare, and contrast assault, battery, and mayhem at the Common Law and under the Model Penal Code (MPC).

Most children are familiar with the idiom "Sticks and stones may break my bones, but words won't ever harm me." This chapter addresses harm by sticks, stones, and—in spite of the idiom—words.

Assault, Battery, and Mayhem

At the Common Law, and in many jurisdictions today, assault and battery were two different crimes. A battery is an (1) unwanted, (2) intentional (3) touching of a person that is (4) harmful or offensive. The mens rea is general intent. It is enough that the actor intended the touching; an intent to cause harm or offense isn't required.

The actus reus of battery is a touching. Of course, touching a person with one's body satisfies this requirement. A touching by an inanimate object does as well—such as striking a person with a golf club. Nor is it necessary for the offender to be in physical possession of the object that touches the victim, so long as the defendant was the cause of the touching. A thrown baseball is an extension of the person who threw it. The touching element is also satisfied through the use of biological agents. Intentionally spreading a communicable disease, such as COVID-19, anthrax, or HIV, to another person is also battery.

An assault, on the other hand, doesn't require a touching. Historically, there were two forms of assault. The first is when a person is put into reasonable fear of an imminent battery. Returning to our golf club example, imagine that the defendant swings a golf club at the head of the victim, who successfully avoids being hit by jumping out of the way. Because the victim feared being hit and the threatened battery was imminent, the defendant committed an assault. Words do not satisfy the threat element; there must be an act that causes the victim to have a reasonable fear. Recall that reasonability is tested objectively. Not only must a defendant subjectively fear imminent harm, but society must recognize the fear to be rational and ordinary.

Now, imagine that an intended victim is looking the other way when the defendant swings the club and misses. Because the victim didn't experience apprehension, there is no assault. The second definition of assault fills in this gap. It defines an assault as an attempted battery; no

---

Assault: An intentional act that causes another person to have a reasonable fear of an imminent battery; or it is an attempted battery.

Battery: The intentional harmful or offensive touching of a person without consent.

apprehension by the intended victim is required. So the Common Law elements of battery say it is an (1) intentional (2) act (3) that causes another person to have a reasonable fear (4) of an imminent (5) battery; or it is an attempted battery.

Today, the MPC's approach is common. It combines assault and battery into one offense, graded by seriousness of harm, whether a deadly weapon was used, or the status of the victim. It also varies the mens rea requirement by factual context and actus reus:

§ 211.1. Assault

1. *Simple Assault.* A person is guilty of assault if he:
    a. attempts to cause or purposely, knowingly or recklessly causes bodily injury to another; or
    b. negligently causes bodily injury to another with a deadly weapon; or
    c. attempts by physical menace to put another in fear of imminent serious bodily injury.

Simple assault is a misdemeanor unless committed in a fight or scuffle entered into by mutual consent, in which case it is a petty misdemeanor.

2. *Aggravated Assault.* A person is guilty of aggravated assault if he:
    a. attempts to cause serious bodily injury to another, or causes such injury purposely, knowingly or recklessly under circumstances manifesting extreme indifference to the value of human life; or
    b. attempts to cause or purposely or knowingly causes bodily injury to another with a deadly weapon.

Aggravated assault under paragraph (a) is a felony of the second degree; aggravated assault under paragraph (b) is a felony of the third degree.

There are three forms of simple assault: purposeful, knowing, or reckless attempted battery; negligent bodily injury from a deadly weapon; and menacing. Menacing is an independent crime in many jurisdictions. Oddly, the MPC doesn't specify the mens rea, but presumably it would be purposeful or knowing. More than words are required to commit menacing assault. There must be a physical threat. Any act, beyond words, that would put a reasonable person in fear of imminent serious bodily harm qualifies. Backing a person into a corner, closing a door to trap a person, or raising one's fists are examples. Assault is increased to aggravated assault if either the (1) attempted or resulting bodily injury is serious or (2) a deadly weapon is used.

Francine is building and exploding pipe bombs in her backyard. She erects metal walls to guard against shrapnel hitting herself or others. Regardless, shrapnel of one bomb ricochets off one of the walls she constructed, flies into the neighbor's yard, and embeds itself in the skin of the neighbor. Francine has committed a misdemeanor simple assault under §211.1(1)(b).

Francine is building and exploding pipe bombs in her backyard. She takes no measures to protect herself or anyone else. The location of her activity is 30 feet from her neighbor's property line. The shrapnel of one bomb flies into the neighbor's yard and strikes the neighbor in the eye, causing permanent blindness in the eye. Francine has committed a second-degree felony aggravated assault under §211.1(2)(a).

Francine builds a pipe bomb with the intent of injuring her neighbor. She places the bomb 30 feet from where the neighbor is gardening. It explodes, but the neighbor is not hurt. Francine committed a third-degree felony aggravated assault under §211.1(2)(b).

Many states also have provisions that aggravate assaults that are committed against special classes of persons. New Jersey, for example, adopted the MPC provision mentioned earlier with amendments elevating assaults of police officers, firefighters, emergency medical technicians, teachers and other employees of public and private schools, judges, health care workers, child protective service workers, mass transit employees, and others to aggravated assaults, provided the victim's employment status is clearly identifiable, such as by a uniform.[3] Other variations in state law aggravate simple assault when committed in special locations, such as schools, or when they are committed using dangerous devices, such as guns and vehicles. See Table 7.1 for a summary of assault under the MPC and contemporary statutes.

TABLE 7.1 ■ Summary of Assault Under the MPC			
Crime	**Actus Reus**	**Mens Rea**	**Law**
Simple assault	Attempt to cause bodily injury	Purposeful, knowing, reckless	MPC
Simple assault	Bodily injury by deadly weapon	Negligence	MPC
Simple assault	Attempt using physical menace to create fear of imminent serious bodily injury	Purposeful	MPC
Aggravated assault	Attempt to cause serious bodily injury to another; causing serious bodily injury	Purposeful for attempt; purposeful, knowing, or reckless with extreme indifference to human life for actual injuries	MPC
Aggravated assault	Attempting to cause or causing bodily injury to another with a deadly weapon	Purposeful for attempt; purposeful or knowing for bodily injury	MPC
Aggravated assault	Simple assaults committed on victim of special status during the performance of their duties	Mens rea for simple assault plus scienter of victim's special status	State laws

Another special form of assault is mayhem. Mayhem has interesting historical roots. Hundreds of years ago in England, all men were expected to fight for the monarchy when called to service. In the interest of maintaining a population of able-bodied fighting men, injuring a

---

Mayhem: The intentional dismembering or disfiguring of another person without consent.

man in a manner that made him unable to fight was a felony punished by death. Severing a limb is an example. A punch in the face or the severing of a nose was not mayhem.

Today, many states include mayhem in their aggravated assault statutes. Others, such as California, continue to recognize mayhem as an independent crime. Its law defines the crime as this:

> Every person who unlawfully and maliciously deprives a human being of a member of his body, or disables, disfigures, or renders it useless, or cuts or disables the tongue, or puts out an eye, or slits the nose, ear, or lip, is guilty of mayhem. Mayhem is punishable by imprisonment in the state prison for two, four, or eight years.

And

> [a] person is guilty of aggravated mayhem when he or she unlawfully, under circumstances manifesting extreme indifference to the physical or psychological well-being of another person, intentionally causes permanent disability or disfigurement of another human being or deprives a human being of a limb, organ, or member of his or her body. For purposes of this section, it is not necessary to prove an intent to kill. Aggravated mayhem is a felony punishable by imprisonment in the state prison for life with the possibility of parole.[4]

California's approach is typical of those jurisdictions that continue to distinguish it from assault. The crime is graded by harm, and it expands the Common Law definition to include disfigurement.

Domestic Violence

As you read earlier, modern criminal codes commonly single out specific assaults for special attention. The identity of the victim is typically what distinguishes these assaults from others (e.g., battery on a police officer). *Domestic violence* is another example. It is estimated that one in four women and one in nine men have been victims of domestic violence. About 20 people are assaulted by an intimate partner every minute—or 10 million per year.[5] The prevalence of violence between intimate partners and family members led most states and the federal government to address the problem with specific assault laws and various forms of victim support.

Ohio's domestic violence law is typical. It reads, in part, as such:

A. No person shall knowingly cause or attempt to cause physical harm to a family or household member.

B. No person shall recklessly cause serious physical harm to a family or household member.

C. No person, by threat of force, shall knowingly cause a family or household member to believe that the offender will cause imminent physical harm to the family or household member.[6]

What most distinguishes domestic violence assault from other assaults are the victims. To satisfy the domestic violence statute, the victim must be a family or household member. Statutes vary in their definition of family or household members, but they commonly include spouses, children, parents, and other dependents.

The higher mens rea crime requires less harm; knowingly causing or attempting to cause physical harm is criminalized. The lower mens rea crime requires only recklessness, while requiring serious physical harm. Both attempted and the completed crimes are forbidden. Long before trial, the law involves itself in domestic violence cases in other ways. Some states mandate that police make arrests when probable cause of domestic violence exists, and courts routinely issue protected orders requiring alleged offenders and victims to remain apart from one another.

QUESTIONS AND PROBLEMS

1. What were the elements of battery at the Common Law?
2. What were the elements of assault at the Common Law?
3. Under the MPC, assault is graded by three factors. Name them.

Applying the Model Penal Code, determine if no assault, assault, or aggravated assault is committed in Questions 4 and 5. Cite the applicable section of section of MPC 211.1.

4. Kyle is standing on a subway platform, waiting for the 5:30 p.m. train home. He accidentally drops his cell phone next to the tracks. The tracks sit about 3 feet below the platform. Kyle checks the time, determines there are 3 minutes before the train will arrive, looks both ways, jumps down into the space next to the track, and retrieves his phone. When he begins to climb back up onto the platform, Jade stands in his way. Kyle can hear the train coming and begins to panic. Jade continues to obstruct him, laughs, and states, "What are you going to do now?"
5. Angry over not being hired by Ken, Jade buys a handgun, drives to Ken's home, waits for him to exit the house, takes aim, and shoots at him. The bullet misses and she exclaims, "Damn!" and drives away.

WORDS MAY HURT ME: THREAT

Learning Objective: Distinguish constitutionally protected speech from true threat.

In the last section, you were reminded of the childhood idiom "Sticks and stones may break my bones, but words won't ever harm me." In the context intended—a parent advising a child to shrug off the slights of other kids—the statement has value. It is developmental; it promotes antifragility. It can also reduce violence by offering the child a nonviolent way to deal with insults: to ignore them. But the statement isn't always true; sometimes, words can hurt, and sometimes, they can cause fear and apprehension. Often, the most hurtful words come from friends and family; sometimes, their words are well intended and true, but in other instances, they are malicious and untrue. Historically, true but hurtful words were not punished. In the

United States today, most hurtful, offensive, repugnant, and insulting words can't be criminalized because they are protected by the First Amendment. But there is a limit; there a few narrow exceptions to the First Amendment's protection.

In 1966, a group of protestors gathered at the Washington Monument in Washington, DC. The crowd broke into smaller groups. Robert Watts, 18 years old, chose to join a group that discussed police brutality. During the discussion, he stated that "[t]hey always holler at us to get an education. And now I have already received my draft classification as 1-A, and I have got to report for my physical this Monday coming. I am not going. If they ever make me carry a rifle, the first man I want to get in my sights is L. B. J. ... They are not going to make me kill my black brothers." Many of the listeners laughed. An undercover officer who heard the statement didn't find it funny, and Mr. Watts was later arrested, charged, and convicted of a federal statute that made it a crime to "knowingly and willfully... [make] any threat to take the life of or to inflict bodily harm upon the President of the United States." He appealed, eventually reaching SCOTUS. The high court set aside his conviction on free speech grounds. While the court affirmed the nation's interest in protecting its president, it didn't find Mr. Watts's words to be genuinely threatening:

> For we must interpret the language Congress chose "against the background of a profound national commitment to the principle that debate on public issues should be uninhibited, robust, and wide-open, and that it may well include vehement, caustic, and sometimes unpleasantly sharp attacks on government and public officials."

> The language of the political arena, like the language used in labor disputes, is often vituperative, abusive, and inexact. We agree with the petitioner that his only offense here was "a kind of very crude offensive method of stating a political opposition to the President." Taken in context, and regarding the expressly conditional nature of the statement and the reaction of the listeners, we do not see how it could be interpreted otherwise.[7]

The decision was short and didn't fully distinguish what speech may be punished from what may not. A few nuggets of precedent can be drawn from *Watts v. United States*. Hyperbole, particularly in the realm of political speech, is protected; threats that are conditioned upon unlikely events are protected; and the reaction of listeners is important as an indication of the speaker's intentions and apparent ability to follow through on the threat.

A threat that falls outside the protection of the First Amendment is known as a **true threat**. Social media enables threats to be amplified, communicated in new ways, and to be spread to millions of people instantaneously, thereby creating new issues. For example, does a social media posting need to be communicated directly to the target (e.g., through tagging)? What about passive communication, such as when the speaker and target are friends on Facebook, but the target wasn't tagged in the posting? Or is it enough to communicate a threat, even though it never reaches the target? The answer to the last question appears to be no; a threat must reach

---

True threat: The communication of a threat to cause serious harm or death to another person with the intent to cause, and a reasonable person would experience, fear.

its target, who must be objectively fearful—that is, the subjective reaction of the target isn't important. The question is whether a reasonable person would fear serious bodily harm from the speaker. But a confounding issue for courts has been whether the speaker must subjectively intend to cause fear. In the next Digging Deeper feature, SCOTUS addressed this question.

DIGGING DEEPER 7.1

Does a defendant have to intend to cause fear to commit a true threat?

Case: *Elonis v. United States*
Court: Supreme Court of the United States.   Citation: 575 U.S. 723
Year: 2015
Chief Justice Roberts delivered the opinion of the court.

Federal law makes it a crime to transmit in interstate commerce "any communication containing any threat. . . to injure the person of another." Petitioner was convicted of violating this provision under instructions that required the jury to find that he communicated what a reasonable person would regard as a threat. The question is whether the statute also requires that the defendant be aware of the threatening nature of the communication, and—if not—whether the First Amendment requires such a showing.

Anthony Douglas Elonis was an active user of the social networking website Facebook. Users of that website may post items on their Facebook page that are accessible to other users, including Facebook "friends" who are notified when new content is posted. In May 2010, Elonis's wife of nearly seven years, left him, taking with her their two young children. Elonis began "listening to more violent music" and posting self-styled "rap" lyrics inspired by the music. Eventually, Elonis changed the user name on his Facebook page from his actual name to a rap-style nom de plume, "Tone Dougie," to distinguish himself from his "on-line persona." The lyrics Elonis posted as "Tone Dougie" included graphically violent language and imagery. This material was often interspersed with disclaimers that the lyrics were "fictitious," with no intentional "resemblance to real persons." Elonis posted an explanation to another Facebook user that "I'm doing this for me. My writing is therapeutic."...

Elonis's co-workers and friends viewed the posts in a different light. Around Halloween of 2010, Elonis posted a photograph of himself and a co-worker at a "Halloween Haunt" event at the amusement park where they worked. In the photograph, Elonis was holding a toy knife against his co-worker's neck, and in the caption Elonis wrote, "I wish." Elonis was not Facebook friends with the co-worker and did not "tag" her, a Facebook feature that would have alerted her to the posting. But the chief of park security was a Facebook "friend" of Elonis, saw the photograph, and fired him....

"Moles! Didn't I tell y'all I had several? Y'all sayin' I had access to keys for all the f***in' gates. That I have sinister plans for all my friends and must have taken home a couple. Y'all think it's too dark and foggy to secure your facility from a man as mad as me? You see, even without a paycheck, I'm still the main attraction. Whoever thought the Halloween Haunt could be so f***in' scary?"...

Elonis's posts frequently included crude, degrading, and violent material about his soon-to-be ex-wife. Shortly after he was fired, Elonis posted an adaptation of a satirical sketch that he and his wife had watched together. In the actual sketch, called "It's Illegal to Say. . .," a comedian explains that it is illegal for a person to say he wishes to kill the President, but not illegal to explain that it is illegal for him to say that. When Elonis posted the script of the sketch, however, he substituted his wife for the President. The posting was part of the basis for Count Two of the indictment, threatening his wife:

"Hi, I'm Tone Elonis.

Did you know that it's illegal for me to say I want to kill my wife? . . .

It's one of the only sentences that I'm not allowed to say. . . .

Now it was okay for me to say it right then because I was just telling you that it's illegal for me to say I want to kill my wife. . . .

Um, but what's interesting is that it's very illegal to say I really, really think someone out there should kill my wife. . . .

But not illegal to say with a mortar launcher.

Because that's its own sentence. . . .

I also found out that it's incredibly illegal, extremely illegal to go on Facebook and say something like the best place to fire a mortar launcher at her house would be from the cornfield behind it because of easy access to a getaway road and you'd have a clear line of sight through the sun room. . . .

Yet even more illegal to show an illustrated diagram.

[diagram of the house]. . . ."

The details about the home were accurate. At the bottom of the post, Elonis included a link to the video of the original skit, and wrote, "Art is about pushing limits. I'm willing to go to jail for my Constitutional rights. Are you?"

After viewing some of Elonis's posts, his wife felt "extremely afraid for [her] life.". . .

A state court granted her a three-year protection-from-abuse order against Elonis (essentially, a restraining order). Elonis referred to the order in another post on his "Tone Dougie" page, also included in Count Two of the indictment:

"Fold up your [protection-from-abuse order] and put it in your pocket

Is it thick enough to stop a bullet?

Try to enforce an Order

that was improperly granted in the first place

Me thinks the Judge needs an education

on true threat jurisprudence

And prison time'll add zeros to my settlement . . .

And if worse comes to worse

I've got enough explosives

to take care of the State Police and the Sheriff's Department."

At the bottom of this post was a link to the Wikipedia article on "Freedom of speech. . . .

[Elonis also posted:]

"That's it, I've had about enough

I'm checking out and making a name for myself

Enough elementary schools in a ten mile radius

to initiate the most heinous school shooting ever imagined

And hell hath no fury like a crazy man in a Kindergarten class

The only question is . . . which one?"

[The FBI was contacted, and two agents visited Elonis.]

Following their visit, during which Elonis was polite but uncooperative, Elonis posted another entry on his Facebook page, called "Little Agent Lady," which led to Count Five:

"You know your s***'s ridiculous
　　when you have the FBI knockin' at yo' door
　　Little Agent lady stood so close
　　Took all the strength I had not to turn the b**** ghost
　　Pull my knife, flick my wrist, and slit her throat
　　Leave her bleedin' from her jugular in the arms of her partner
　　[laughter]
　　So the next time you knock, you best be serving a warrant
　　And bring yo' SWAT and an explosives expert while you're at it
　　Cause little did y'all know, I was strapped wit' a bomb
　　Why do you think it took me so long to get dressed with no shoes on?
　　I was jus' waitin' for y'all to handcuff me and pat me down
　　Touch the detonator in my pocket and we're all goin'
　　[BOOM!]
　　Are all the pieces comin' together?
　　S***, I'm just a crazy sociopath
　　that gets off playin' you stupid f***s like a fiddle
　　And if y'all didn't hear, I'm gonna be famous
　　Cause I'm just an aspiring rapper who likes the attention
　　who happens to be under investigation for terrorism
　　cause y'all think I'm ready to turn the Valley into Fallujah
　　But I ain't gonna tell you which bridge is gonna fall
　　into which river or road
　　And if you really believe this s***
　　I'll have some bridge rubble to sell you tomorrow
　　[BOOM!][BOOM!][BOOM!]"

[At trial, the jury was not instructed to find that Elonis intended to cause fear, and the prosecutor argued that his mental state was immaterial. He was convicted.]

The fact that the statute does not specify any required mental state, however, does not mean that none exists. We have repeatedly held that "mere omission from a criminal enactment of any mention of criminal intent" should not be read "as dispensing with it." This rule of construction reflects the basic principle that "wrongdoing must be conscious to be criminal." As Justice Jackson explained, this principle is "as universal and persistent in mature systems of law as belief in freedom of the human will and a consequent ability and duty of the normal individual to choose between good and evil." The "central thought" is that a defendant must be "blameworthy in mind" before he can be found guilty, a concept courts have expressed over time through various terms such as *mens rea*, scienter, malice aforethought, guilty knowledge, and the like. Although there are exceptions, the "general rule" is that a guilty mind is "a necessary element in the indictment and proof of every crime." We therefore generally "interpret[ ] criminal statutes to include broadly applicable scienter requirements, even where the statute by its terms does not contain them." ...

Elonis's conviction cannot stand. The jury was instructed that the Government need prove only that a reasonable person would regard Elonis's communications as threats, and that was error. Federal criminal liability generally does not turn solely on the results of an act without considering the defendant's mental state. That understanding "took deep and early root in American soil" and Congress left it intact here: Under Section 875(c), "wrongdoing must be conscious to be criminal."

There is no dispute that the mental state requirement in [the statute] is satisfied if the defendant transmits a communication for the purpose of issuing a threat, or with knowledge that the communication will be viewed as a threat. In response to a question at oral argument, Elonis stated that a finding of recklessness would not be sufficient. Neither Elonis nor the Government has briefed or argued that point, and we accordingly decline to address it. Given our disposition, it is not necessary to consider any First Amendment issues....

The judgment of the United States Court of Appeals for the Third Circuit is reversed, and the case is remanded for further proceedings consistent with this opinion.

[On remand, the appellate court affirmed Elonis's conviction because it found that the evidence supported a finding that Elonis had a knowing, and therefore also reckless, state of mind.]

The court avoided the First Amendment question by basing its *Elonis* decision on general criminal law principles, so it is unknown whether the First Amendment requires subjective intent by a speaker. If the court ever answers the constitutional question, it is reasonable to conclude that it will require subjective intent because it has done so in related cases. *Brandenburg v. Ohio*, for example, requires the speaker's words to be "directed" at causing imminent lawlessness. See Table 7.2 for a summary of several important true threat cases.

TABLE 7.2 ■ Important True Threat Cases	
Case	**Facts and Holding**
Elonis v. United States, 575 U.S. 723 (2015)	Defendant posted violent language and graphics about ex-wife, was charged, and was convicted of violating federal threat statute. Question before court was whether a defendant must intend to cause fear. Avoiding the First Amendment question, the court determined that basic criminal law principles require mens rea, so some form of intent is required. The court didn't specify what level of intent, although it held that negligence isn't adequate. On remand, his conviction was affirmed because the appellate court found the evidence supported a find that he acted either knowingly and recklessly, whichever applied.
Virginia v. Black, 535 U.S. 1094 (2002)	Statute made cross burning illegal and declared it to be prima facie evidence of intent to intimidate. Two different cases were heard. One was a cross burning at a KKK rally, and the second was on the property of an African American. The court held that cross burning may not itself be criminalized. But cross burning with intent to intimidate is not protected. Specifically, a true threat is a statement "where the speaker means to communicate a serious expression of an intent to commit an act of unlawful violence to a particular individual or group of individuals." In the KKK rally case, the defendants were exonerated because the court found no evidence of intent to intimidate; rather, the burning was a "statement of group identify and ideology." The opposite conclusion was reached about the burning on the property of the African American victims. Further, the court struck the statute's prima facie provision; intent may not be presumed from protected speech.

(Continued)

TABLE 7.1 ■ Important True Threat Cases *(Continued)*	
Case	**Facts and Holding**
RAV v. City of St. Paul, 505 U.S. 377 (1992)	Defendant and others erected and burned cross in yard of African American family. He was charged and convicted of statute forbidding speech about race, color, creed, religion, or gender that aroused anger or alarm. The statute was stricken because it was content based—it singled out messages about subjects. A more general statute forbidding any content that is likely to cause imminent lawlessness would be valid.
Planned Parenthood v. American Coalition of Life Activists, 290 F.3d 1058 (9th Cir., 2002)	Pro-life defendant published the names, photographs, and addresses of abortion doctors, three of whom were killed by activists. Also published names of 200 people associated with abortions online.
NCAA v. Claiborne Hardware Co., 458 U.S. 886 (1982)	During African American boycott of white merchants, defendant's statements that "Blacks who break the boycott are 'Uncle Toms' who will have their necks broken" was protected speech. "Mere advocacy" of violence doesn't alone remove speech from the protection of the First Amendment.
Brandenburg v. Ohio, 395 U.S. 444 (1969)	KKK rally on private land with cross burning; defendant's speech referred to "revengeance [sic]" on *iggers, Jews, Congress, president, and Supreme Court. Court announced what is known as the *Brandenburg test*: Speech is not protected if it is directed at and likely to incite imminent lawlessness. The defendant's speech was protected.

The cases found in Table 7.2 address threatening speech in different contexts. For example, the Brandenburg test sets forth a clear standard for speech that can cause people to erupt into violence. But it doesn't directly address threats to individuals that won't lead to violence but are likely to cause distress, disrupt lives, or that represent the last step before the speaker harms the target. Although SCOTUS has not precisely defined true threat, the following reflects a common understanding of the elements of the crime:

1. The speaker intends, purposely, knowingly, or recklessly, to

2. communicate a

3. serious expression of an intent to

4. commit an act of unlawful violence to a particular individual or group of individuals that would cause a

5. reasonable person to fear serious bodily harm or death;

6. the threat is communicated to, and received by, the target.

As is true of stalking and other related crimes, the defendant must have the apparent ability to carry it out, any conditions on the threat must be likely to occur, it must be imminent, and it must appear to a reasonable person that the speaker is likely to follow through on the threat. In some circumstances, such as a rally where emotions are inflamed, imminent refers to "in the moment." In others, the period may be longer. But a threat to harm someone in a year would not satisfy this expectation in most cases. Hypothetical expressions, jokes, satire, and fleeting statements made in the heat of the moment may not be punished. Consider, for example, the following statement by a litigant in a criminal case:

> There is not a day that goes by since I was sentenced at that courthouse that I have not dreamed about revenge and the utter hate I feel for the judge, and the utter hate I feel for the prosecuting attorney, and the utter hate I feel for the corporation that bound me in chains. There's not a day that goes by that I don't pray for the death and destruction upon the judge and upon every single person who sentenced me, and in front of witnesses, in front of everyone, and my utter hatred of you and of every other attorney there. You make me sick to my motherfucking stomach. And I hate you. And I hate the prosecuting attorney. And I hate Judge Calabrese. And I hate you all so very, very much. For the evil you did is unfreaking speakable and the lack of remorse I feel is because of the injustice done to me. You all can suck it because I hate you all with the bottomless, deepest hate of my heart.

The Illinois Court of Appeals overturned the defendant's expression because it didn't see an intent to commit imminent harm. The judges penned that a "person expressing a dream for revenge is not the same as an expression that the person intends to undertake physical retaliation or commit violence."[8]

Justice Sonia Sotomayer expressed concern over the lack of development of true threat law in a concurring opinion she wrote in the court's denial of certiorari in *Perez v. United States*.[9] The facts of the case reveal the seriousness of the matter. While partying on a beach with friends, Perez got drunk on a combination of grapefruit juice and vodka. He referred to the drink as a molly cocktail. When the group neared a liquor store, Perez was overheard by an employee talking about the drink. But the employee interpreted Perez's statement about the drink as a reference to to a homemade bomb that is known as a Molotov cocktail. The employee asked Perez about the bomb, and he replied that he didn't have a Molotov cocktail. But Perez continued his drunken banter by stating to a different employee that he did have a Molotov cocktail and that he could blow up the whole place. Perez and his friends left and returned; during this visit, Perez said he could blow up the world. Subsequently, the state of Florida prosecuted him for the statements under a statute that made it a felony to "threaten to throw, project, place, or discharge any destructive device with intent to do bodily harm to any person or with intent to do damage to any property of any person."

Perez was convicted and sentenced to 15 years in prison. SCOTUS denied certiorari because the First Amendment issue was not properly framed in the courts below. Justice Sotomayer concurred in the decision, but she was troubled by the outcome of the case. As she penned, "Robert Perez is serving more than 15 years in a Florida prison for what may have been nothing more than a drunken joke." She pointed out that the prosecutor who argued for the 15-year sentence acknowledged that Perez may have been nothing more than a "harmless drunk."

There are many threat statutes on the books today, at all levels of government. These laws focus on different acts and intended victims (e.g., direct, personal threats; computer and online threats; terroristic threats such as bombings; and singling out classes of people for protection, such as government officials). Various names are given to the same crimes. Threat, for example, is known as harassment is some criminal codes. The basic First Amendment rules already described apply to all statutes that criminalize speech.

QUESTIONS AND PROBLEMS

1. What are the basic elements of a true threat?

Are the following true threats? Explain your answer.

2. Victor I. Ninel is a member of the Communist Organization of Southern Truckers. The organization adheres to the philosophy that the government and capitalism must be overthrown by violent revolution. He publishes a pamphlet with the statement, "Someday, the economy will falter and the people will be displeased. On that day, Mr. President, Mr. Governor, police officers, and military personnel, we are coming for you. And if you stand in the way, your life will be sacrificed for the greater good."
3. Burt believes Ernie has eaten his candy. Burt sends Ernie a text, "You will pay for eating my gummies, and soon." Ernie, replies, "I didn't do it. Not me. I think it was Elmo." In a social media posting the next day tagging Ernie, Burt wrote, "Candy thieves and liars are wrong; with a knife, I can make them sing a song." Two days later, while at work, Burt waves to get Ernie's attention. When Ernie looks, Burt pulls a knife with a 4-in. blade out of his belt and slowly pretends to run the blade across his neck. As he reaches the end of his neck, he points the knife at Ernie.

UNFOLLOW ME: STALKING

Learning Objective: Identify and explain the typical elements of stalking statutes.

Before the 1990s, a person who was harassed and threatened by another, but not assaulted, found little help in the law. The target of the threat could obtain a civil protective, or restraining, order from a court. A civil protective order commands a person to keep their distance from the victim. A violation of a protective order is punished as contempt of court. For many reasons, civil protective orders aren't adequate to address domestic violence. One reason is that they are reactive. It is commonly said that a protective order is "just a piece of paper." It doesn't protect anyone on its own, and police are handcuffed from acting until the order is violated. In many cases, this means that nothing is done until after the victim has been battered or murdered. Another reason is that there are limits to how long a person may be incarcerated for contempt of court that don't apply to the crime of stalking. There are also important procedural differences. The victim, not the state, bears the burden of applying for, and satisfying the evidentiary standard for, issuance of the order. In an effort to proactively prevent harm, all states have **stalking** laws today. The first was California in 1990.[10]

Stalking: A pattern of intentional acts that cause another person to reasonably fear serious bodily harm or death.

The typical stalking statute requires (1) two or more intentional acts, commonly referred to as a pattern; (2) that would cause a reasonable person to fear; (3) imminent; (4) serious bodily injury. The mens rea is often akin to the MPC's knowing; purposely causing the fear isn't required. New Mexico's stalking law is a good example:

30-3A-3. Stalking; penalties

A. Stalking consists of knowingly pursuing a pattern of conduct, without lawful authority, directed at a specific individual when the person intends that the pattern of conduct would place the individual in reasonable apprehension of death, bodily harm, sexual assault, confinement or restraint of the individual or another individual.

B. As used in this section:
1. "lawful authority" means within the scope of lawful employment or constitutionally protected activity; and
2. "pattern of conduct" means two or more acts, on more than one occasion, in which the alleged stalker by any action, method, device or means, directly, indirectly or through third parties, follows, monitors, surveils, threatens or communicates to or about a person.

C. Whoever commits stalking is guilty of a misdemeanor. Upon a second or subsequent conviction, the offender is guilty of a fourth degree felony.

D. In addition to any punishment provided pursuant to the provisions of this section, the court shall order a person convicted of stalking to participate in and complete a program of professional counseling at the person's own expense or a domestic violence offender treatment or intervention program.

Repeated visits of a Girl Scout to sell cookies or annoying calls to a neighbor to complain about a barking dog, even if unwanted, are not examples of stalking.

In most jurisdictions, the defendant must intend the acts. In MPC terms, the defendant must act knowingly, recklessly, or in some states, negligently. Jurisdictions differ in whether the defendant must also intend to cause the victim to be fearful. Arkansas is an example of a state that requires both intentionality in the act and the outcome. Its law declares that "[a] person commits stalking in the second degree if he or she knowingly engages in a course of conduct that harasses another person and makes a terroristic threat with the *purpose* of placing that person in imminent fear of death or serious bodily injury [emphasis added]."[11]

The actus reus standards are high. Some jurisdictions require the alleged victim to have both subjective and objective fear of serious bodily harm; others require only objective fear. To be objectively reasonable, the subjective feelings of the victim are not determinative; a jury would have to conclude that a person of ordinary reason, intelligence, and judgment would have experienced fear of serious bodily injury. Additionally, the alleged stalker must possess the apparent ability to cause serious bodily harm. The statute also specifically exempts conduct that occurs under the authority of law and that which is constitutionally protected. For example, a police detective's surveillance of a criminal suspect isn't stalking. The most likely example of constitutionally protected acts are free assembly, free speech, and the free press. For example, an investigative reporter who follows a public official who is believed to be corrupt is protected by the First Amendment. The inclusion of this provision in any criminal law is unnecessary because the Constitution trumps the statute regardless.

Stalking is graded in all jurisdictions. Violating a restraining order, the level of intent, history of stalking and threat, and age of the victim are common factors in the grading and enhancement of stalking offenses.

Naturally, stalking and threat laws intersect. One distinguishing characteristic is the requirement of a pattern of conduct for stalking. Most stalking laws require acts; words aren't adequate. A true threat, on the other hand, doesn't require an act beyond speaking or writing. State laws vary in how they name, define, and grade these crimes. Later in the book, you will learn more about terrorism and terrorist threat as illustrations of state and federal stalking and threat laws.

Some victims feel abandoned by the law because the definitions of true threat and stalking are so narrow that some threatening speech and conduct goes unpunished. Remember, however, that just because a threatening communication or act isn't a crime doesn't mean that the law is entirely toothless. The legal standard for issuing restraining orders is lower than what is required to prove stalking or true threat, and violations of these orders can lead to jail time. Other criminal laws, such as trespass, often also come into play in harassment and stalking cases.

PHOTO 7.1 Following a person is an example of the type of conduct that can form the basis of the crime of stalking.

MachineHeadz / iStock

QUESTIONS AND PROBLEMS

1. What are the elements of the typical stalking statute?
2. Ellie is interested in Dylan. They see one another a couple times a week at a coffee shop. She asks him to have coffee. He declines, telling her that he is engaged to a woman he loves. Ellie asks him again the next time they meet. Dylan declines again and asks her to stay away from him. She calls 2 days later and says, "I know you have someone else. But I think we would be wonderful together. All I want is to have a cup of coffee." He hangs up and calls the police. Applying the typical elements of stalking, has Ellie committed stalking? Explain your answer.

SEX OFFENSES

Learning Objective: Identify and explain the elements of Common Law rape; compare those to modern sexual assault statutes.

This section examines sex offenses. There are many sex offenses found in criminal codes. They can be grouped into two categories. In the first are sex acts or sexually motivated acts that are prohibited because they violate the autonomy of, and harm, people; rape, sexual assault, and child molestation fall into this category. The second category contains sex acts or sexually motivated acts that are prohibited for moral reasons; incest, sodomy, bestiality, prostitution, and obscenity are among them. In this chapter, you will learn about the former. The others will be covered in a later chapter. By their nature, sex offenses often have lesser included crimes. All rapes, for example, are batteries.

Rape and Sexual Assault

The crime of rape dates to antiquity, and in most societies, it was punished harshly. Perspectives on the harm of rape have varied considerably between cultures and over time within some societies. For example, at the old Common Law, wives and daughters were considered the property of the husbands and fathers. The chastity of a daughter was important to a family, socially and materially. Consequently, rape was treated as a legal trespass for a period of time. Eventually, the physical and emotional harm resulting from assault and the invasion of a woman's bodily autonomy were recognized as reasons to punish rape. Eventually, rape was punished by death at the early Common Law. This approach was adopted in the colonies and was dominant until SCOTUS found capital punishment for rape to be unconstitutional.

This historical context also framed early definitions of rape. At one time, it was defined as sexual intercourse with a woman by an adult man, not her husband, using force. This old definition is anachronistic; only men could commit rape, minors were incapable of committing the offense, only women could be raped, husbands could not rape their wives, and physical force had to be used, often with a requirement of resistance by the victim.

Advances in women's rights, data on the frequency of the crime, a greater appreciation for the psychological and physical harm caused by rape, and an awareness that men and boys are also raped led legislatures throughout the nation to change rape laws in the 20th century. Today, minors and women can be punished for, and men can be the victims of, rape.

Physical force continues to be required in a few states. In others, the question is entirely one of consent. Threat of harm, duress, and incapacitation (e.g., sleeping, being intoxicated) of the victim all satisfy this element in jurisdictions that don't require force.

The "marital rape exception" was part of the law for centuries. It rested on the ideas that women consented to sex with their husbands and that prosecutions of husbands would undermine family harmony and threaten the stability of communities. In 1975, South Dakota became the first state to criminalize marital rape. Today, all jurisdictions have spousal rape

---

Rape: Sexual intercourse or another sex act with another person without consent.

laws, although a few states treat the crime differently than rape between unmarried persons. Two common differences are to impose the old Common Law requirement of physical force and to grade spousal rape as lower than other rape. Another common exception applies in spousal *statutory* rape cases. This is explained later in this section.

The early Common Law also forbade sodomy, which has been defined variously to include anal sex, fellatio, cunnilingus, and bestiality. Sodomy laws were often aimed at gay men, although they were sometimes used to punish heterosexual conduct too. Today, the Fourteenth Amendment protects the sexual freedom of competent, consenting adults. Two significant SCOTUS cases in this regard are *Lawrence v. Texas* (2003)[12] and *Obergefele v. Hodges* (2015).[13] *Lawrence* involved the prosecution of Mr. Lawrence for violating a state statute that forbade sexual contact between men. Police discovered Mr. Lawrence having sex with Tyron Garner during a raid that was conducted in response to a false report by a jealous lover of Mr. Garner. In its invalidation of the Texas law criminalizing homosexual conduct, the court said that "[t]he petitioners are entitled to respect for their private lives. The state cannot demean their existence or control their identity by making their private sexual conduct a crime. Their right to liberty under the Due Process Clause gives them the full right to engage in their conduct without intervention from the government." Then in 2015, SCOTUS extended its reasoning to include the right of same-sex couples to legally marry in *Obergefell v. Hodges*. One remnant of old sodomy laws, bestiality, continues to be recognized in every state.

The Model Penal Code, when first issued, contained several of the Common Law's elements that are now out of date, so many states that adopted the MPC's rape provisions have since amended them. In the late 2010s and into 2020, the American Law Institution, the publishers of the MPC, engaged in an intensive examination of the provision with the intent of modernizing it. Although all states have updated their rape laws, they have not done so in a uniform manner. Both the mens rea and actus reus elements of the crime vary. The elements of a typical modern statute in codes that continue to distinguish rape from other forms of sexual assault are seen in Kansas's law:

Kan. Stat. 21-5503. Rape

a. Rape is:
1. Knowingly engaging in sexual intercourse with a victim who does not consent to the sexual intercourse under any of the following circumstances:
   A. when the victim is overcome by force or fear; or
   B. when the victim is unconscious or physically powerless;
2. knowingly engaging in sexual intercourse with a victim when the victim is incapable of giving consent because of mental deficiency or disease, or when the victim is incapable of giving consent because of the effect of any alcoholic liquor, narcotic, drug or other substance, which condition was known by the offender or was reasonably apparent to the offender;
3. sexual intercourse with a child who is under 14 years of age;
4. sexual intercourse with a victim when the victim's consent was obtained through a knowing misrepresentation made by the offender that the sexual intercourse was a medically or therapeutically necessary procedure; or

5. sexual intercourse with a victim when the victim's consent was obtained through a knowing misrepresentation made by the offender that the sexual intercourse was a legally required procedure within the scope of the offender's authority.

The statute continues by grading each of these offenses by their seriousness, with (a)(1)-(3) as higher than (a)(4)-(5). Note that the mens rea is knowingly engaging in sexual intercourse with the victim. As is true of most law today, the requirement of the use of force to overcome the victim has been broadened to include unconsciousness, physical powerlessness, incapacity due to intoxication or mental disease, and deceiving the victim into believing the act is needed for medical reasons or required by law. Take note of another element of the law; it requires "sexual intercourse." At the old Common Law, rape was limited to the penetration of the vagina by a man's penis. Kansas, like other states, redefined sexual intercourse as "any penetration of the female sex organ by a finger, the male sex organ or any object. Any penetration, however slight, is sufficient to constitute sexual intercourse."

The same Kansas statute criminalizes sex offenses that don't involve penis–vagina penetration, such as hand and digital contact with sex organs, fellatio, and cunnilingus under separate provisions. Many states do this; they have independent provisions for rape, sodomy, and statutory rape. Not every state organizes its penal code in this way. A few states have consolidated sex crimes against the person under a single label—commonly, sexual assault. In these jurisdictions, the various forms of sexual assault (e.g., touching of genitals, intercourse, sodomy) are graded differently and often have differing mens rea, even though they carry the same name. Effectively, sexual assault consolidation has little impact on the elements or punishment of these crimes. An example of a consolidated approach is found in Connecticut, which classifies the crimes in this way:[14]

First-Degree Sexual Assault includes sexual intercourse through the use of force, with a person under 13 years of age (provided there is at least two years difference in age), and intercourse with a person who is mentally incapacitated. The use of a deadly weapon, an intent to disfigure and otherwise physically harm the victim, the circumstances evince a reckless disregard for life and the victim suffers serious physical harm, and when there are multiple abusers are all factors that aggravate the crime. This is a Felony A or B crime, with A being the most serious.

Spousal Sexual Assault refers to vaginal intercourse, fellatio, or cunnilingus between spouses that occurs through force or threat of force. A Felony B crime.

Aggravated Sexual Assault of Minor refers to engaging in any sex act with a person under 13 years of age who has been kidnapped, stalked, when violence was used to commit the act, the victim was disfigured or suffered serious physical injury, the victim and assailant were strangers, there was more than one victim, and when the defendant had prior conviction of violent sexual assault. Felony A.

Second-Degree Sexual Assault includes sexual intercourse with a person aged 13 to 16 and there is at least three years difference in age, the victim is in the custody of the law or a hospital, and many other categories of victims. Felony B or C.

Third-Degree Sexual Assault includes sexual contact (not just intercourse) through the use of force, the threat of force, and sexual contact with a relative. Felony D, but Felony C if the victim is less than 16 years of age. The crime is also aggravated if committed with a firearm.

Fourth-Degree Sexual Assault refers to many other instances of sexual contact, including sex with animals or human corpses, school students abused by adult volunteers and coaches, and any person over the age of 20 who is in a position of power over the victim. Class A misdemeanor, but Class D felony if the victim is under the age of 16.

Under Connecticut law, Class A felonies are punished by 10 to 50 years in prison or 25 years to life imprisonment; Class B felonies, 1 to 40 years; Class C felonies, 1 to 10 years; class D, 1 to 5 years; Class A misdemeanor, no time to 1 year; Class B misdemeanor, no time to 6 months. There is also a graduated scale of fines for each class.

Most rape statutes are drafted with the assumption that the defendant is the person who commits the act. In the next Digging Deeper, we consider the question of whether a man who didn't commit the act of penetrating a woman can be convicted of rape.

DIGGING DEEPER 7.2

Does a man commit rape when he uses another man's penis to penetrate a woman?

Case: *Dusenbery v. Commonwealth of Virginia*
Court: Supreme Court of Virginia.   Citation: 263 S.E.2d 392 (Va. 1980)
Year: 1980
Before l'Anson, C. J., and Carrico, Harrison, Cochran, Poff, and Compton, J. J.

Per curiam.
Indicted for rape of "T. M. against her will and by force, in violation of Section 18.2-61" of the Code, William Donald Dusenbery was convicted in a bench trial and sentenced to confinement in the penitentiary for five years. Upon consideration of a presentence report, the trial court suspended the sentence and placed defendant on indefinite probation.

At approximately 10:30 p. m. on September 16, 1978, T. M. and J. G., both 16 years of age, parked their car in a secluded area and partially undressed in preparation for sexual intercourse. Defendant, a part-time security guard wearing a uniform, badge, handcuffs, and a holstered pistol, appeared at the window with a flashlight, ordered the couple to get out, and demanded identification. Defendant told them that he would take them to the authorities or report their conduct to their parents unless they finished what they had started and allowed him to watch. The couple entered the back seat of the car, discussed the options, and agreed to attempt to perform the act in defendant's presence. Defendant watched as the couple undressed and the boy assumed the superior position. Complaining that the boy had not penetrated the girl, defendant thrust his head and shoulders through the open window, seized the boy's penis, and forced it "partially in" the girl's vagina.

Defendant contends that the evidence is insufficient to support his conviction under Code § 18.2-61 because "the evidence is clear that [he] did not 'carnally know' the alleged victim" within the meaning of that statute.

In felony cases, principals in the second degree and accessories before the fact are accountable "in all respects as if a principal in the first degree." Code § 18.2-18. But, by definition, there can be no accessory without a principal. Although *conviction* of a principal in the first degree is not a condition precedent to conviction of an accessory, Code § 18.2-21, "before the accessory to a crime can be convicted as such, it must be shown that the crime has been committed by the principal." Since the evidence fails to show that J. G. committed rape, defendant cannot be convicted as a principal in the second degree. The question remains whether the evidence is sufficient to prove that defendant committed that crime as a principal in the first degree.

With respect to certain crimes, the law regards a person who acts through an innocent agent as a principal in the first degree. *See* W. La Fave and A. Scott, Criminal Law 496-97 (1972); R. Perkins, Criminal Law 644-45 (2d ed. 1969); ALI Model Penal Code § 2.06(2) (a) (Proposed Official Draft 1962). In some jurisdictions, this rule has been applied in rape cases where the accused forced an innocent third party to have carnal knowledge of an unwilling victim. But the "innocent agent" rule cannot be applied here, for it is antithetical to the construction this Court has placed upon Virginia's rape statute.

Our prior decisions establish that one element of rape is the penetration of the female sexual organ by the sexual organ of the principal in the first degree. Whether Dusenbery's conduct constituted an offense other than rape is not a question before us on appeal. We hold only that the evidence is insufficient to prove that defendant carnally knew the prosecutrix within the intendment of Code § 18.2-61 as construed by this Court, and the judgment must be reversed. The case will be remanded for further proceedings if the Commonwealth be so advised, provided that defendant may not be retried for rape.

Reversed and remanded.

The outcome of this case may be different in other jurisdictions. For example, if the law were worded to prohibit all forms of forcible or incapacitated sex, the defendant would be guilty. Even more, many modern statutes would include the boyfriend as a victim. In such a case, the security guard would be guilty of two acts of sexual assault.

QUESTIONS AND PROBLEMS

What follows is an old definition of rape. What is different in most rape statutes today?

The carnal knowledge of a woman by a man, who is not her husband, using physical force that overcomes her resistance.

STATUTORY RAPE

Learning Objectives: Identify the elements of statutory rape. Identify and contrast the mens rea that is required in most jurisdictions with the mens rea required in a minority of jurisdictions for statutory rape.

An oddly named crime, statutory rape occurs when an adult has sexual relations with a consenting minor. Because the law assumes that a minor is unable to fully appreciate the nature and consequences of sex, consent is irrelevant.

The basic elements of statutory rape are (1) sexual intercourse with a (2) person under a specific age. The purpose of the law was to protect girls from sexual exploitation by older men—particularly from pregnancy and damage to the victim's reputation. Just as the law of rape has evolved, so, too, has the law of statutory rape. Today, the prohibition applies to men and women, girls and boys. And the policy undergirding the law has broadened. Today, protecting victims from psychological and physical harm is emphasized.

The actus reus of modern statutory rape is sexual intercourse, or other sex acts, with a person below a specified age. Often, statutes require that the defendant be of a minimum age or grade the offense by the relative ages of the victim and defendant. Alabama does this:[15]

First-degree rape: For someone age 16 or older to have sexual intercourse with someone under age 12; life in prison or 10 to 99 years.

Second-degree rape: For someone age 16 or older to have sexual intercourse with someone between age 12 and 16, when the actor is at least two years older; 2 to 20 years in prison.

Because the law is intended to protect people that society deems too young to make informed, mature decisions about sex, victim consent is immaterial.

In most jurisdictions, statutory rape has no mens rea element. It is a strict liability crime. In these jurisdictions, it doesn't matter if the defendant has a good-faith belief that the victim is old enough to consent. This is true, even in cases of age fraud. A defendant who has sex with a victim who told the person that they are older, or who even shared a fake identification that confirms the lie, is guilty of statutory rape. A minority of states excuse the conduct when there has been a reasonable mistake of age. Minnesota's statutory rape statute is strict liability, except when a defendant who is less than 10 years older than the victim has a reasonable belief the victim is 16 years or older.[16]

State statute declares it to be a Felony B Sexual Assault, punishable by 2 to 6 years in prison, for a *"person who is 18 years of age or older to have sex with a person who is under the age of 16."* Juliet, 18 years old, is a first-year student at Shakespeare College. She meets Romeo in her literature class. Romeo is 6' tall with a mustache. The two regularly meet for coffee and study together for weeks. During that time, Romeo tells Juliet that he graduated from Montague High School, where he played varsity tennis. They had intercourse for the first time 2 months after they met. As it turns out, Romeo graduated from high school early. He turned 16 years

---

Statutory rape: Sexual intercourse or another sex act with a minor; consent is immaterial.

old 2 months after their sexual relationship began. Juliet has committed felony sexual assault because the statute has no mens rea requirement. She is on her way to prison.

Or consider the same facts, but change the law to state that it is a Felony B Sexual Assault, punishable by 2 to 6 years in prison, for a *"person who is 18 years of age or older to have sex with a person who is under the age of 16, provided that the older person doesn't reasonably believe the younger person is 16 years of age or older."* In this scenario, it is reasonable for Juliet to assume Romeo is older than 16 because he told her that he is a high school graduate, participated in high school athletics, is a college student, and because of his physical appearance. Therefore, she could be acquitted under this statute.

QUESTIONS AND PROBLEMS

1. What are the elements of statutory rape in most jurisdictions?
2. Set aside the law. Do you believe it is just to hold a person criminally liable for statutory rape when a reasonable person has also believed the victim to be an adult?

STATUTES OF LIMITATIONS AND SEX CRIMES

Learning Objective: Describe the rationale and statutory outcomes of the movement to eliminate or extend the statute of limitations for sex crimes.

Another issue in contemporary sexual assault law is whether prosecution of the crime should be bound in time. Most crimes, and civil actions as well, must be filed within a certain period of time, or they are lost. These limiting laws are known as statutes of limitation. There are a few common exceptions; homicide, treason, and crimes against humanity are not limited. They can be pursued until the defendant's last breath is drawn.

Several reasons have been advanced for time-limiting prosecutions. The most compelling concern is reliable fact-finding, which is made difficult by the passage of time. There are several ways fact-finding is negatively impacted by time:

- The deterioration or total loss of physical evidence

- The unavailability of witnesses who have died, become incompetent, or left the jurisdiction

- The fallibility and unreliability of memory generally; specifically, how time distorts memory

Other reasons for limiting the time within which prosecutions must be started include these:

- The prevention of fraud, which is easier to commit as time passes.

- Holding defendants accountable for acts that occurred when social and legal standards were different is unfair.

- At some point, a person should be given peace of mind and the opportunity to move forward without fear of the past.

- Encouraging victims to pursue their claims as soon as possible improves fact-finding and may serve the public good by identifying and punishing an offender who is a threat to others.

Rape and sexual assault have historically been bound by time limitations. In recent decades, there has been a movement to extend or eliminate the statute of limitations for sex offenses. In cases of child sexual assault, the time for victims to report their crimes is extended into adulthood because children are often unaware of the law or afraid to report abuse. States vary considerably in this area of the law. There are three approaches: a fixed limit, a conditional limit, and no limit. A fixed limit refers to a set period of time after an offense within which a prosecution must be filed or the case is lost. The same offense may have very different statutes of limitation between states. Florida, for example, has a limit of 10 years and Indiana, 21 years. Some states create conditions that extend the time. Extending the period until a certain amount of time after a victim reaches adulthood is one example. Proof of a crime by DNA evidence, as is one condition in Texas, is another. And finally, some states have no limit, such as North Carolina.

QUESTIONS AND PROBLEMS

1. What is a statute of limitation?
2. What are the three approaches to statute of limitations in rape cases?

PUNISHING SEX OFFENDERS

Learning Objective: Identify and explain two or more special aspects of punishing sex offenders.

How crimes are punished won't be discussed for every crime you learn in this book. Today, imprisonment and fines are the default punishment for most crimes. But of course, there are other forms of punishment. Convictees are sentenced to death, community service, drug and psychological treatment, house arrest, restitution, and the rare act of shaming, such as when a defendant who drove on a sidewalk to pass a school bus that had stopped to pick up children was ordered to stand in an intersection holding a sign that read "Only an idiot would drive on the sidewalk to avoid a school bus."[17] There are two special aspects of punishing sex offenders that warrant discussion: the death penalty and sex offender registration.

Recall that death was the punishment for rape for hundreds of years. In the United states, this ended with *Coker v. Georgia*, 433 U.S. 584 (1977). In *Coker*, SCOTUS held that the death penalty is grossly disproportionate and violative of the Eighth Amendment's prohibition of cruel and unusual punishments for the crime of rape of an adult woman. Thirty-one years later, the court extended its reasoning to the rape of children in *Kennedy v. Louisiana*, 554 U.S. 407 (2008). Consequently, imprisonment, fines, occasionally psychological treatment, and registration are the common punishments.

In 1947, California became the first state that required sex offenders who had served their time and were back in the community to register with law enforcement and for that information to be made available to the public. The intent of sex offender registration is to enable police to monitor offenders and to empower the public to protect itself. In 1994, the federal government enacted the Jacob Wetterling Crimes Against Children and Sexually Violent Offender Registration Act, requiring states to enact sex offender registration systems. Two years later, the act was amended to also require community notification of registered sex offenders in the Adam Walsh Child Protection and Safety Act of 2006, more commonly known as the Sex Offender Registration and Notification Act (SORNA). States that didn't comply were threatened with loss of federal funding for law enforcement. A few states chose not to comply, largely due to the expenses associated, and in a few states that complied, courts invalidated their systems. Today, the vast majority of states have mandatory registration and notification that complies with SORNA.

It is both a state and federal crime to fail to register. SORNA has a grading system. The most serious offenses require registration and check-ins with police every 3 months, for life; a middle tier requires check-ins every 6 months for 25 years; and the lowest-level offenders are required to check in annually for 15 years. In most jurisdictions, local law enforcement agencies have databases where anyone can enter an address and determine if sex offenders live in their neighborhood. A new twist on these laws is emerging in the states: mandatory digital tracking of offenders. Many states now require sex offenders to wear GPS monitoring devices that are attached to the individual to detect if they enter forbidden areas, such as school zones or day cares. For the same purpose, some jurisdictions require computer monitoring.

A limitation on computer monitoring was announced in 2017, when SCOTUS invalidated a North Carolina law that forbade a released sex offender from using social media.[18] The law restricted the individual's access to social media sites, such as Twitter and Facebook, because teens frequent the platforms. But the court found the restriction to be too broad. By blanket-banning access, the individual's right to access acceptable, nonteen contact is prevented, not allowing him to exercise core First Amendment free speech. Citing an earlier case, the majority wrote that [w]hile in the past there may have been difficulty in identifying the most important places (in a spatial sense) for the exchange of views, today the answer is clear. It is cyberspace—the "vast democratic forums of the Internet." It is implicit in the court's reasoning, as suggested by a concurring opinion by three of the justices, that a state has the authority to restrict access to teen-specific sites and to teens themselves.

A minority of jurisdictions also provide for "chemical castration" and postrelease civil commitment of dangerous offenders. Chemical castration refers to the administration of a drug that lowers testosterone in males and thereby reduces the likelihood that they will commit sex offenses. The federal government[19] and a large number of states also have statutory law enabling authorities to seek civil commitment of dangerous sex offenders both preconviction and after they have been convicted, served their sentences, and been released from prison.

Generally, commitment continues indefinitely, until the individual is deemed to no longer be a threat. Consequently, people have been "civilly" imprisoned for decades. The process of civil commitment is different from both the typical criminal and civil case. Because it involves a significant restraint of liberty, certain constitutional protections apply. Conversely, because civil commitment isn't intended to punish (and therefore, isn't criminal), not all constitutional protections apply. The right to counsel is an example of a right that applies. The protection against double jeopardy does not apply here, even if the respondent was previously convicted of the offense that is used to prove that the respondent should be committed.

SCOTUS has affirmed these laws, provided certain standards are met. In *Kansas v. Hendricks*, 521 U.S. 346 (1997), the Kansas Sexually Violent Predator Act was upheld against double jeopardy and due process challenges. Key to the law's affirmation was its expectation that the respondent be found to be dangerous to others as a consequence of "mental abnormality" or "personality disorder." Further, the condition must be so serious that the respondent is likely to engage in sexually violent behavior in the future.

QUESTIONS AND PROBLEMS

1. Set aside the law. Do you agree with SCOTUS that the death penalty is disproportionate and violative of the Eighth Amendment's cruel and unusual punishments clause? Explain your answer.
2. What are the advantages and disadvantages of having sex offenders register after they have served their time in prison and otherwise satisfied their criminal sentences?

RAPE SHIELD LAWS

By the nature of the adversarial system, crime victims are expected to tell, and retell, their stories. In the case of a sexual assault, the accuser recounts their story to the first-on-the-scene police officer, possibly to other officers and sexual assault counselors, nurses and physicians who conduct sexual assault exams, and prosecutors; eventually, they testify at trial. Rape victim advocates allege that this retelling is a form of revictimization.[20] Adding to the trauma of the experience and resulting process was a long-standing defense practice of challenging the character of the complainant. This often took the form of immaterial and harassing questioning at trial. For example, defense attorneys would inquire into the complainant's sexual history in an effort to prove consent through prior sexual conduct or simply to discredit the witness in the eyes of the jury. Another line of questioning would delve into the complainant's sexual history with the defendant, again with the purpose of establishing consent to the specific alleged rape through prior consent to have sex with the defendant.

All of this retelling and the stress of testifying at trial is believed to dissuade many sexual assault victims from reporting their assaults. Beginning in the 1970s, there was a social movement aimed at changing the evidence rules in sexual assault cases to reduce the emotional trauma of sexual assault accusers. These changes also reflected a change in social values. At one time, female promiscuity was believed to be relevant to the determination of consent. But today, society sees little connection between sexual promiscuity and consent. The movement was successful in achieving the enactment of rape shield laws throughout the state and the federal government. Each jurisdiction's law makes evidence of an accuser's sexual history inadmissible, with a few exceptions. Common exceptions include the following:

- Evidence of a history sexual conduct between the accuser and defendant

- Evidence that is offered to prove another man was the source of found semen or other physical evidence

- When the Constitution requires admission of the evidence

- Evidence that is offered to prove that a defendant had a reasonable, but mistaken, belief of consent

- Evidence that a pattern of conduct or behavior on the part of the accuser is so similar to the conduct or behavior in the case that it is relevant to the issue of consent

A majority of states include the first three in their laws; the last two are less common.

A few states have gone further than limiting the evidence of an accuser's sexual history to opening the door to evidence about a defendant's criminal history. Evidence of prior crimes for the purpose of proving guilt is prohibited for all crimes. A crime must be proved, beyond a reasonable doubt, by facts specific to the alleged crime. Regardless, a few states permit evidence of prior sexual assaults to be admitted for the purpose of proving guilt.

Rape shield laws are controversial. The adversarial system is premised on truth being found through oral testimony that is subject to cross-examination. This principle is so important that it is protected by the Sixth Amendment's rights to both confront and cross-examine one's accusers and the state's witnesses. Rape shield laws squarely face off with these Sixth Amendment principles, as well as the Fifth and Fourteenth Amendment's due process and equal protection protections. The philosopher Jeremy Bentham penned, "Evidence is the basis of justice: to exclude evidence, is to exclude justice."[21] To date, calls by defense attorneys and many scholars to invalidate or limit rape shield laws have met with little success in state courts.

QUESTIONS AND PROBLEMS

1. What is a rape shield law?
2. What are the common exceptions to rape shield?

Rape shield laws: Statutory law intended to limit evidence about an alleged victim's sexual history or to permit evidence of a defendant's criminal history at trial.

KIDNAPPING AND FALSE IMPRISONMENT

Learning Objective: Identify the elements of, and compare and contrast, kidnapping and false imprisonment.

Kidnapping was a crime at the Common Law, and today, it is a crime in all 50 states and under federal law. The MPC's definition, which is common in state laws, reads as such:

> A person is guilty of kidnapping if he unlawfully removes another from his place of residence or business, or a substantial distance from the vicinity where he is found, or if he unlawfully confines another for a substantial period in a place of isolation, with any of the following purposes:
>
> **a.** to hold for ransom or reward, or as a shield or hostage; or
>
> **b.** to facilitate commission of any felony or flight thereafter; or
>
> **c.** to inflict bodily injury on or to terrorize the victim or another; or
>
> **d.** to interfere with the performance of any governmental or political function.
>
> Kidnapping is a felony of the first degree unless the actor releases the victim alive and in a safe place, in which case the crime is lowered to a felony of the second degree.

For a kidnapping to occur, the initial grab must be unlawful. A police officer who makes an lawful arrest or a guardian who takes control of a ward doesn't commit kidnapping. But a parent who has been legally declared to be an unfit parent commits kidnapping if they take their child.

Most states, and the MPC, require that a victim be removed from a safe place, moved, or confined. States vary considerably in the definition of these terms. Under the MPC, unlawfully removing a person from their home or business satisfies this element, as does movement, known as *asportation*, of the victim a "substantial distance." So pointing a gun at a person, ordering them into a car, and driving miles away satisfies this element. Some jurisdictions only require slight movement, although movement that is incidental to the crime doesn't create a kidnapping. For example, a robber who orders a store cashier to walk from one end of a counter to the other to access the cash register has not committed kidnapping. However, almost all jurisdictions treat a change of location that increases the risk to the victim as satisfying the asportation element. A jogger in a park who is stopped, threatened at gunpoint, and moved 50 feet away into a heavily wooded area to hide a sexual assault has been kidnapped. In addition to removal from a safe place and asportation, this element is satisfied by confinement in a place of isolation. The MPC requires that the confinement be for a substantial period of time. Codes do not specify how much time is "substantial." As is true of the movement requirement, many jurisdictions connect the confinement to the defendant's intention. If a bank teller is confined for 15 minutes during a bank robbery to prevent the teller from alerting the police, the defendant is less likely

---

Kidnapping: To unlawfully remove another from his place of residence or business, or a substantial distance from the vicinity where he is found, or to unlawfully confine another for a substantial period in a place of isolation, to commit a felony upon the person, to hold for ransom, or for another evil purpose.

to have committed a kidnapping than if the teller is ordered into an office for the same period of time so the defendant can commit a sexual assault. The last element of the MPC and many state laws concerns the defendant's *intention* in taking the victim hostage. The MPC requires that the defendant intends to seek ransom or reward, to use the victim as a hostage or shield, to use the hostage to commit a felony or flee from a crime, to harm or terrorize the hostage, or to interfere with governmental or political functions.

The MPC definition of kidnapping leaves gaps. Consider these scenarios:

- An offender who closes and locks a closet door on a person who is inside picking their day's clothes and refuses to open it for an hour because they think it is funny doesn't commit kidnapping because there isn't asportation.

- An offender who takes a hostage with the intention of committing a nonviolent misdemeanor hasn't committed kidnapping because nonviolent misdemeanors don't quality as predicate offenses.

But these crimes don't go unpunished under the MPC. They are examples of kidnapping's first cousin **false imprisonment**, also known as false restraint.

The MPC defines felony restraint as restraining a person unlawfully in circumstances exposing the victim to risk of serious bodily harm and when a person is held in involuntary servitude; misdemeanor false imprisonment is the act of voluntarily and unlawfully restraining a person in a way that substantially interferes with that person's liberty.[22]

On March 1, 1932, Charles A. Lindbergh, the 20-month-old baby of Charles and Ann Lindbergh, was kidnapped from their home. Part of the ladder that was used to reach the second-floor window and footprints leading to and from the window of entry were discovered. Charles Lindberg was an aviator, military officer, inventor, and, to most of America, a national treasure. His popularity drew national attention to the kidnapping. As happens more than once in any century, the crime became known as the "crime of the century." Tragically, the baby was eventually found dead, and Bruno Richard Hauptmann was arrested, tried, convicted, and executed for the murder. During the investigation, the Federal Bureau of Investigation, which didn't have direct investigative authority, provided invaluable assistance to state authorities.[23]

The absence of federal authority led to the quick adoption the Federal Kidnapping Act, also known as the Lindbergh Law. The law empowers federal authorities to pursue kidnappings that cross state lines with their victims. Ironically, the timing of the enactment of the law caused it to be named the Lindbergh Law, and today, it is commonly assumed that the Lindbergh kidnapping was the reason Congress acted. But that is only partially true. The federal kidnapping statute had already been proposed, and the first congressional hearing on the bill occurred just days before the Lindbergh toddler was taken. In fact, kidnappings were common throughout the United States during the Great Depression. The original motivation for the law was a large number of kidnappings, labeled the "snatch racket," orchestrated by crime

---

False Imprisonment: To restrain a person's liberty of movement without consent.

syndicates. The victims of these kidnappings were often transported between states, making it difficult for the police of any one state to effectively bring the body snatchers to justice. The snatch racket included among its victims several high-profile targets, including an heir to the Anheuser-Busch beer empire.[24] But the Lindbergh kidnapping put the legislative process on steroids. The federal law was enacted quickly, even before Hauptmann was captured. Ironically, the law wouldn't even have applied to the Lindbergh crime even if it had been in existence when Hauptmann took little Charles because Hauptmann never crossed state lines with the baby.

The Federal Kidnapping Statute of 1932 is still good law. Recall that the states possess the general police power, which includes punishing kidnappers. So the law doesn't make all kidnappings federal crimes. It applies to kidnappings where the victims are transported across state lines; an act of moving a victim between states creates federal jurisdiction under the interstate commerce clause. The law defines federal kidnapping as (1) the unlawful (2) taking and confinement and (3) asportation of (4) another person (5) by use of force, threat, fraud, or deception.[25] Regardless of whether federal criminal jurisdiction exists, federal authorities often assist local police in kidnapping cases.

QUESTIONS AND PROBLEMS

1. Identify the elements of kidnapping under the MPC.
2. Identify the elements of felony restraint and misdemeanor false imprisonment under the MPC.
3. What is required for the federal government to have jurisdiction over a kidnapping?
4. Joy waives down a taxi, gets into the vehicle, and instructs the driver to take her to an address that is about a 40-minute drive away. The two have a nice talk during the drive, piquing a romantic interest in Joy by the driver. After 20 minutes, the driver asks Joy if she would like to "go out one night for drinks." Joy declines. The driver asks her out a second time. Joy becomes uncomfortable asks him to stop the car. The driver immediately stops the car on a busy street, but he locks the doors and refuses to let her out. For 5 minutes, he tries to convince her that they would have fun and might be a wonderful couple. She begins to scream, the driver unlocks the door, and she exits the taxi. Under the MPC, what crime is committed in that scenario? Explain your answer.

ABUSE AND NEGLECT

Learning Objective: Distinguish the crime of abuse from the crime of neglect.

Abuse is a crime of commission; neglect is a crime of omission. Both crimes apply to intimate relationships—to people who have a legal duty to care for another person. Abuse and neglect

---

Abuse: The intentional act of causing harm to a person who is, by law, under an actor's care.

Neglect: The failure to care for a person who is, by law, under an actor's care, such failure resulting in harm to the ward.

statutes are intended to protect people who can't protect themselves, such as children, mental health patients, and other incapacitated people.

All jurisdictions in the United States recognize both the crimes of abuse and neglect. Many states have separate code provisions for each protected group (e.g., children, wards of institutions). Virginia's law concerning the abuse of neglect of children reads:

§ 18.2-371.1. Abuse and neglect of children; penalty; abandoned infant

   A. Any parent, guardian, or other person responsible for the care of a child under the age of 18 who by willful act or willful omission or refusal to provide any necessary care for the child's health causes or permits serious injury to the life or health of such child is guilty of a Class 4 felony. For purposes of this subsection, "serious injury" includes but is not limited to (i) disfigurement, (ii) a fracture, (iii) a severe burn or laceration, (iv) mutilation, (v) maiming, (vi) forced ingestion of dangerous substances, and (vii) life-threatening internal injuries....

   1. Any parent, guardian, or other person responsible for the care of a child under the age of 18 whose willful act or omission in the care of such child was so gross, wanton, and culpable as to show a reckless disregard for human life is guilty of a Class 6 felony.

   2. If a prosecution under this subsection is based solely on the accused parent having left the child at a hospital or emergency medical services agency, it shall be an affirmative defense to prosecution of a parent under this subsection that such parent safely delivered the child to a hospital that provides 24-hour emergency services or to an attended emergency medical services agency that employs emergency medical services personnel, within the first 14 days of the child's life. In order for the affirmative defense to apply, the child shall be delivered in a manner reasonably calculated to ensure the child's safety.

   B. Any parent, guardian, or other person having care, custody, or control of a minor child who in good faith is under treatment solely by spiritual means through prayer in accordance with the tenets and practices of a recognized church or religious denomination shall not, for that reason alone, be considered in violation of this section.[26]

In addition, there are other provisions in the Virginia law that criminalize specific abuses of children, including using a tongue while kissing a child, exposing a minor to pornography, and tattooing a minor except in the presence of a parent or medical professional.

A difficult question to answer in the area of child abuse is where to draw the line between acceptable corporal punishment and abuse. Historically, the law shied away from family matters, leaving child-rearing, including discipline, to parents. But this has changed in recent decades. Neighbors, friends, and strangers are more likely than in the past to involve themselves when abuse or neglect is suspected, typically invoking the law and pressuring child protective and law enforcement authorities to intervene. Statutes, such as the Virginia law, that require "serious injury" or "excessive corporal punishment" implicitly recognize the authority of parents to use corporal punishment, even if it results in minor injury. Hawaii goes a step further and legislatively endorses corporal punishment that is not intended to cause harm and is administered with "due regard for the age and size of the minor and is reasonably related to the purpose of safeguarding or promoting the welfare of the minor, including the prevention or punishment of the minor's misconduct."[27] In states that only require an "injury" and don't explicitly recognize the authority of parents or school officials to use corporal punishment, whether a whipping that causes minor injury constitutes child abuse or not is unclear. The line between legitimate parental discipline and child abuse, and how those ideas are processed, is the subject of the next Digging Deeper.

DIGGING DEEPER 7.3

Is a spanking that leaves a handprint on the skin child abuse?

Case: *Bountiful City v. Baize*
Court: Supreme Court of the State of Utah
Year: 2021
JUSTICE PEARCE, opinion of the Court

After hours of unsuccessful attempts to calm his four-year-old who was throwing a series of temper tantrums, Nathan Baize spanked his son three times. During the tantrums, Baize's son kicked Baize and hit him in the face. The child also kicked and punched his grandmother. Baize later told a police detective that he spanked his son as a "last resort." Evidence at trial showed that Baize struck his son with enough force to leave bruises in the shape of a handprint on the child's bottom that were visible two days later.

Bountiful City charged Baize with child abuse under [state statute]. That provision makes it a Class C misdemeanor to "inflict upon a child physical injury" with "criminal negligence." The district court convicted Baize after a bench trial....

Baize had his four-year-old son (Son) for weekend parent-time. Son acted up and threw multiple temper tantrums. Son's mother (Mother) testified that Baize had emailed her and that the emails indicated Son had been "yelling and screaming." Son "was saying terrible things, he was going to hurt people. He was mad. He wanted to go home. He was upset. Completely distraught." A Bountiful City Police Department detective (Detective) similarly testified that, based on his interview with Baize, Son was "out of control," "throwing temper tantrums, using foul language, [and] saying that he wanted [Baize] dead."...

One of Son's tantrums occurred in a grocery store parking lot. According to Detective, when Baize came out of the store, Baize found Son "kicking and punching his grandmother," who was with Son in a parked car. Son also repeatedly "jump[ed] up and down, 'slamming his rear end on the bottom of the car seat.'" Id. (quoting Detective). The tantrum continued for approximately an hour until Son calmed down enough that Baize could strap the child into his car seat.

But the reprieve from Son's tantrums proved temporary. Once they returned home, Son resumed fighting with Baize. Baize told Detective that he tried various disciplinary interventions. This included talking to Son, putting him in a corner, and "everything but physical force." Finally, "the only thing... [Baize] thought would help would [be to] spank [Son]."

Baize then put Son "over his knee and warned him that he was going to be spanked unless he calmed down." Son "continued to swear and tell Baize that he hated him." Id. Baize then spanked Son on his bottom. Son continued his tantrum. Baize warned Son again. And then he spanked Son a second and third time. Baize told Detective the spanking was a "last resort."

The morning after the incident, Baize called Mother and asked that she pick up Son hours earlier than planned. That evening, Mother noticed bruising on Son's bottom. Id. Son told Mother what had happened. Id. Mother then called the Division of Child and Family Services (DCFS).

[Subsequently] Bountiful City charged Baize with a Class C criminal misdemeanor of child abuse... for "inflict[ing] upon a child physical injury" with "criminal negligence."...

> The [abuse] statute defines "physical injury" as: an injury to or condition of a child which impairs the physical condition of the child, including: (i) a bruise or other contusion of the skin; (ii) a minor laceration or abrasion; (iii) failure to thrive or malnutrition; or (iv) any other condition which imperils the child's health or welfare and which is not a serious physical injury."...

> [Another statute] "provides that the defense of justification may be claimed... when the actor's conduct is reasonable discipline of minors by parents, guardians, teachers, or other persons in loco parentis...." This defense is "not available if the offense charged involves causing... serious physical injury."...

Mother testified that she saw "bruising, fingerprints... lines on [Son's] bottom, bruising... [and] little spots on his bottom that are bruised." Mother's photograph of the bruising was introduced into evidence without objection. Mother testified that the images accurately portrayed Son's bruising. Id.

Detective similarly testified that the photograph depicted bruising in the shape of "a finger or a handprint," as well as other bruising and redness consistent with diaper rash. Detective presumed that Son "slamming his butt up and down into the car seat" was the cause of the additional bruising. Detective testified that he was unaware of any reports that Son required medical attention for the redness and bruising. Mother confirmed that Son required no medical attention.

Baize's trial counsel argued that spanking Son "was not a gross deviation from the standard of care based on [the] facts [and] specific evidence that [was introduced]." He also argued that Baize "did not take an unjustifiable risk to cause bruising." Id. Baize's counsel emphasized the circumstances leading up to the incident, including that Son "kicked and punched" his grandmother, caused bruising to himself by jumping up and down in his car seat, and engaged in "[t]hreatening behavior, hitting, yelling." The spanking, counsel explained, was the only tool Baize had left "as a parent" after exhausting other options. Moreover, it was done in a "controlled manner," was "not done out of anger"...

The City acknowledged that it is not "illegal or wrong" for parents to discipline their children, including by spanking. Nevertheless, the City repeatedly pushed for a rule that "when you spank a child to the point where there is physical injury... you come to a Class C misdemeanor child abuse." The law "clearly states," the City asserted, that it "is a violation when you leave physical injury [and] that's always going to be a gross deviation. Parents aren't supposed to leave physical injury on their children."...

The court then found that "the level of contusion, the bruising on the buttocks of the child" indicated that the spanking "was just too hard," and therefore the "discipline was a gross deviation from the standard of care that an ordinary person would exercise." [The trial court convicted the defendant and the appellate court affirmed the conviction.]

The court of appeals similarly concluded it was "clear" the district court analyzed whether Baize's discipline was the "reasonable discipline" a parent can apply without criminal penalty. The court of appeals pointed to the district court's conclusion that Baize's "discipline was a gross deviation from the standard of care," which came after the district court recognized that "[a] parent should be allowed to discipline his children in an appropriate way." The court of appeals reasoned that "gross deviation from the standard of care" is "simply a variation in nomenclature describing the concept of reasonableness," and therefore it was unnecessary for the district court to "explicitly invoke the numbers" of the relevant statutory subsections or explicitly use the words "reasonable" or "unreasonable."...

We disagree with the court of appeals' conclusion that it is "clear from the record" that the district court actually and correctly conducted a "reasonable discipline" analysis....

The court of appeals based its conclusion on this portion of the district court's analysis:

> [A] parent should be allowed to discipline his children in an appropriate way. But the level of contusion, the bruising on the buttocks of the child causes me to come to the conclusion that [the] discipline was a gross deviation from the standard of care that an ordinary person would exercise. It was just too hard.

The court of appeals reasoned that "gross deviation from the standard of care" is "simply a variation in nomenclature describing the concept of reasonableness."...

[The court explained that the gross deviation from the standard of care and reasonable discipline standards are different, the former being the mens rea element of the crime and the latter an affirmative defense.] When the defendant has presented sufficient evidence to put the affirmative defense of "reasonable discipline" at issue, then the prosecution must also disprove that defense beyond a reasonable doubt.

Because of the district court's comments appearing to approve of the City's incorrect interpretation of the Statute's requirements, we are unsure whether the court correctly analyzed the reasonable discipline defense. In other words, to the extent the district court considered whether Baize's discipline was reasonable, we have no visibility into what facts the district court might have considered to make that determination. Without that detail, we cannot meaningfully review the district court's decision. Thus, we order remand to permit the district court to clarify its ruling.

Although we hold that the court of appeals was largely correct in its construction of the Child Abuse Statute, we nevertheless hold that the court erred when it concluded that it was "clear" the district court correctly applied the Statute's "reasonable discipline" defense. On the findings in front of us, we are unable to ascertain whether the district court addressed the defense and, if it did, what was the basis for a determination that Baize's discipline was not reasonable. We therefore vacate Baize's conviction and remand to the district court to squarely address Baize's reasonable discipline defense. The district court may, if it deems helpful, permit further evidence and argument on that question, and conduct any other proceedings necessary to address the "reasonable discipline" defense.... But the court must enter findings and conclusions on the question of "reasonable discipline" sufficient to permit meaningful appellate review.

The mens rea of abuse and neglect is typically on the high end. The previous Virginia example establishes a willful standard, something close to knowing or purposeful under the MPC. If lower, the risk that bad parenting will be criminalized would be possible. A religious exemption is provided for in the Virginia law and the laws of the majority of other states.

As you learned in an earlier chapter, most jurisdictions also have laws that require certain classes of people to report child abuse or neglect to a law enforcement authority. Teachers, health care and social workers, and police officers are examples.

QUESTIONS AND PROBLEMS

1. Are the crimes of abuse and neglect crimes of commission or omission? Explain your answer.
2. After reflecting on the competing values of family autonomy and the protection of children, draft a child neglect law. What is the mens rea and actus reus?

HUMAN TRAFFICKING AND ENSLAVEMENT

Learning Objective: Identify the typical elements of the crime of human trafficking.

Human enslavement isn't just a phenomenon of the past. It is estimated that there are more enslaved people in the 21st century than at any time in history. Victims are found in every nation of the world and in every state in the United States. Victims may be transported between states or nations, or not. The most common reasons people are trafficked and enslaved are for labor, sex, forced marriage, and the harvesting of organs and tissue. It is estimated that tens of millions of people are trafficked around the world, with hundreds of thousands in the United States.[28] Many victims in the United States can be found working in brothels, adult entertainment clubs, restaurants, and in the agricultural industry.

Human trafficking is the recruitment, transportation, harbor, or confinement of persons through force, threat, coercion, or deceit for purposes of labor, sexual acts, or other exploitation. Traffickers use similar methods to recruit and traffic their victims. One method, for example, is to offer an adult victim a job abroad and to pay the victim's travel expenses. Then when in the new home, the victim is stripped of their passport, cash, and other identifying documents and told that they must repay the debt to the trafficker through labor or sex, lest they will be deported or arrested. Sadly, many children are sold by their parents into forced labor or sexual servitude. In some regions of the world, kidnapping trafficking victims is common.

The Trafficking Victims Protection Act of 2000[29] (TVPA) was groundbreaking federal legislation that has been actively used to address international and interstate trafficking cases. Although the TVPA is the primary piece of federal legislation, there are other federal statutes that criminalize trafficking and exploitation. The Mann Act, which predates the TVPA, is such a law. It makes the interstate transportation of people for the purpose of prostitution or other

---

Human trafficking: The knowing recruitment, transportation, harbor, isolation, solicitation, or enticement of an individual into labor, sexual services, or servitude through force, threat, or deceit.

PHOTO 7.2 Modern human trafficking involves the sale and control of people for labor and sex.

filadendron / iStock

illegal sex crimes a federal offense.[30] In an effort to address intrastate trafficking, all 50 states, Washington, DC, and the U.S. territories have enacted counterpart laws. The typical trafficking law has the following elements:

1. Knowing

2. recruitment, transportation, harbor, isolation, solicitation, or enticement of an individual into

3. labor, sexual services, or servitude

4. through force, threat, or deceit

It is common for codes to either aggravate the crime, or to have a separate prohibition, if the victim is a minor or suffers serious injury. Of course, traffickers are also liable for the other crimes that attend trafficking, including kidnapping, rape, and false imprisonment.

QUESTIONS AND PROBLEMS

What are the typical elements of the crime of human trafficking?

CIVIL RIGHTS CRIMES

Learning Objective: Identify and define Section 1983 actions and at least one federal criminal civil rights law.

Nearly all states and the federal government have civil rights laws. These laws can be divided into two categories:

1. Civil and criminal remedies for harmful acts that are motivated by race, sex, religion, and other bias; and

2. Civil and criminal remedies for violations of constitutionally protected rights.

Let's begin with the first. You may recall from Chapter 2 that the First Amendment's free speech clause protects a broad range of expression, including offensive and hateful speech. The purpose behind the First Amendment's protection of speech is to create a free market of ideas that will advance society through scientific discovery, innovation, medical advances, and creative thought and expression. Free expression also advances the constitutional republic by ensuring uninhibited, open, and robust debate about the most controversial matters. Naturally, this includes criticism of law, government, and public officials. As Justice Robert Jackson wrote, "If there is any fixed star in our constitutional constellation, it is that no official... can prescribe what shall be orthodox in politics, nationalism, religion, or other matters of opinion or force citizens to confess by word or act their faith therein."[31]

Illustrative is *Brandenburg v. Ohio* (1969),[32] a case where a Ku Klux Klan leader in Ohio was charged with advocating violence for statements he made at a rally on private property where he and other men, donned in Klan robes, burned a cross. The men were on the property with the consent of the owner. Brandenburg said there would be "revengeance" against n***ers and Jews, and he claimed that Congress, the Supreme Court, and the president were oppressing the Caucasian race. He further called for African Americans to return to Africa and Jewish Americans to Israel. Brandenburg was charged under Ohio's criminal syndicalism statute, which forbade "advocat[ing]... sabotage, violence, or unlawful methods of terrorism as a means of accomplishing industrial or political reform" and for "voluntarily assembl[ing] with any society, group, or assemblage of persons formed to teach or advocate the doctrines of criminal syndicalism." SCOTUS held that threatening speech may only be regulated if (1) it is likely to result in (2) imminent lawlessness and (3) the speaker intends to cause that lawlessness. Applying this standard, the court struck down Ohio's law as too broad. The Brandenburg test, which overruled an earlier test, remains the law today.

In the 1992 decision *R.A.V. v. St. Paul*,[33] several teenagers burned a cross on the lawn of a Black family that lived in their neighborhood. They were charged and convicted of violating the following ordinance:

Whoever places on public or private property a symbol, object, appellation, character-ization or graffiti, including, but not limited to a burning cross or Nazi swastika, which

---

Civil rights laws: Statutory laws that offer civil and criminal remedies for violations of constitutionally protected rights and for harmful acts that are motivated by race, sex, religion, and other bias.

one knows or has reasonable ground to know arouses anger, alarm, resentment in others on the basis of race, color, creed, religion, or gender, commits disorderly conduct and shall be guilty of a misdemeanor.

SCOTUS reversed the convictions because the ordinance was viewpoint discriminatory—it singled out a specific belief, or viewpoint, for punishment. It didn't, for example, make it unlawful to arouse anger, alarm, or resentment on the basis of political beliefs, sexual orientation, or hairstyle. The government is not permitted to decide what ideas, or the expression of them, are acceptable, and not.

One year later, the court issued a decision in *Wisconsin v. Mitchell*. The bias law at issue in this case was different than in *Brandenburg* and *R. A.V.* It didn't regulate speech; it enhanced the punishment of harmful conduct that was racially motivated. The defendant, Mitchel, was one of a group of young Black men who beat a white teen to the point of unconsciousness, leaving him in a coma state for 4 days. Mitchell was charged and convicted of aggravated battery. At sentencing, his punishment was increased from a maximum of 2 years in prison to an actual sentence of 4 years because his crime was racially motivated. Wisconsin statute permitted the enhancement if a crime was motivated by "race, religion, color, disability, sexual orientation, national origin, or ancestry." The court found the law to be focused on conduct, not speech, and historically, motives of all kinds were considered in punishment. Accordingly, the court upheld the penalty enhancement.

A decade later, SCOTUS reviewed another cross-burning case, *Virginia v. Black*. In this case, defendants from three independent cases were heard together. The three defendants had all burned crosses on private property. Two defendants burned crosses on the property of African Americans, and the third defendant, Mr. Black, burned his cross on private property with the consent of the owner as part of a KKK rally. All three defendants were charged under a law that forbade burning a cross with an intent to intimidate others. The law also created a presumption that the burning of a cross was intended to intimidate other people. Although similar in facts, the legal issue in this case was different than in *Brandenburg*. Brandenburg was prosecuted for his speech. In this case, Black and the other defendants were prosecuted for the act of cross burning. But those acts were intended to send a message. This combination of speech and act is known as *expressive conduct*. Expressive conduct is protected by the First Amendment, but not the extent of pure speech. SCOTUS concluded that the state may criminalize conduct that is intended to intimidate, provided it does so in a viewpoint-neutral manner. This statute was viewpoint neutral; any cross burning intended to intimidate, regardless of the motive or the identities of the persons involved, fell within the grasp of the prohibition. However, the court found the statute's presumption of intent invalid because there could be many messages intended by cross burning. Even the KKK used cross burning to convey multiple messages. The group burns crosses to intimidate others, to express solidarity, as a symbol of ideology, and ritualistically. The first of these four may be criminalized; the last three are protected expression. The law was "overbroad," meaning that its net caught both protected and unprotected speech. The court noted that there have been cases where crosses were burned for reasons that have nothing to do with race whatsoever. As such, Black's conviction was overturned.

To summarize, laws that punish hateful thought or expression are unconstitutional. But conduct that is otherwise illegal may be punished more severely when it is motivated by specific forms of hatred.

With an understanding of how the First Amendment limits the criminalization of bias, let's return to the two types of offenses that may be regulated. This is a criminal law text, so our focus will be on criminal laws, with one exception—a federal civil lawsuit that is commonly used to sue police officers, corrections officers, and other criminal justice officials. We will start there.

In criminal law, police, corrections, and other government officials can be sued under state and federal laws for violating constitutionally and statutorily created rights. 18 U.S.C. §1983 provides that every person who (1) "under color of state law" (2) deprives another person of a legally protected right is liable in damages, and possibly, subject to injunctive relief. This type of lawsuit is commonly known as a "1983 action." The federal government and state governments can't be sued under §1983, although other laws may allow a plaintiff to sue them. To be liable under §1983, an individual must act under color of state law. States create and empower local governments, so anyone acting under city, township, county, or state authority is subject to §1983. Territories and Washington, DC, are included within the law's grasp. The following are examples of when §1983 applies:

An overzealous city police officer breaks down the door of a home without first obtaining a warrant.

A state corrections officer brutally beats an inmate who has made her mad.

A city police officer shoots a shoplifter who is fleeing the scene of the crime.

However, an FBI agent who beats a confession out of a suspected terrorist is acting under color of federal law and, therefore, is not subject to liability under §1983.

Prevailing plaintiffs can be awarded money damages, attorneys fees, and court costs. In some circumstances, a court can enjoin, or order, a defendant to stop or change the conduct that led to the deprivation. Although states can't be enjoined or held liable, injunctions against local governments (e.g., police departments) are allowed.

Civil rights plaintiffs have to jump several hurdles to be successful. The first is *sovereign immunity*. This doctrine dates back to old England; it stood for the principle that the monarch could do no wrong. Sovereign immunity was brought to the United States by British colonists and still survives today, so a person can only sue the government if it consents. Federal and state governments have enacted waivers of sovereign immunity. But they are limited. To succeed in suing a government itself, a plaintiff must establish that a waiver of immunity exists.

There are other barriers for plaintiffs to navigate. Individual defendants under §1983 can raise their own personal immunity defenses. Two are common: *absolute immunity* and *qualified immunity*. In rare cases, officials are absolutely immune from not only liability but from the process of defending lawsuits. In practice, this means that a case is quickly reviewed, and if it

---

§1983 Action: A federal law that allows a person to sue people acting under color of state law for federal civil rights violations.

alleges liability for a judicial act, it is immediately dismissed. Judicial immunity extends to anyone acting under a judge's order, including police officers who are executing warrants and other court orders. The rationale for absolute immunity is that the nature of the judicial function is to make difficult decisions, and to hold judges accountable for their mistakes would make judges tentative to judging, if not wholly deter them from it.

The second personal defense is qualified immunity. This immunity isn't absolute; an official is liable if a clearly established right is violated. Even if a defendant is shielded by qualified immunity, the case will proceed longer than in cases of absolute immunity because more facts have to be found. The qualified immunity standard has been criticized in recent years, particularly in the context of police shootings of Black men and women because many lower courts have held that the facts of a precedential case must be identical, or nearly, to the facts of the case under review. If the facts are not nearly identical, then there isn't a clearly established right to apply. Under this approach, it is rare for plaintiffs to overcome qualified immunity.

Civil rights violations can also be crimes. Many criminal civil rights laws were enacted to combat the Ku Klux Klan's terrorization of African Americans, Catholics, Jews, homosexuals, and other minority groups. These laws target both individuals and government officials who violate civil rights. Table 7.3 has a summary of federal civil rights laws.

TABLE 7.3 ■ Federal Civil Rights Laws Important to Criminal Justice

Law	Civil or Criminal	Prohibited Acts and Mens Rea
Civil Actions for Violations of Rights, 42 U.S.C. §1983	Civil	Violations of civil rights by people (not the federal or state governments) acting under color of state law can result in damages award or injunctive relief. Although civil, this law is included because it is commonly enforced against police and other criminal justice officials.
Conspiracy Against Civil Rights, 18 U.S.C. §241	Criminal	Two or more people conspire to injure, oppress, threaten, or intimidate a person from enjoying constitutional rights.
Deprivation of Rights under Color of Law, 18 U.S.C. §242	Criminal	A person acting under color of *any* law willfully deprives another person of a constitutional right while the individual is purporting or pretending to be acting under the authority of law.
Violent Interference With Federal Rights, 18 U.S.C. §245	Criminal	To use or threaten to use force to willfully interfere with any person because of race, color, religion, or national origin and because the person is participating in a federally protected activity, such as voting, public education, employment, jury service, travel, or the enjoyment of public accommodations, or helping another person to do so.

Law	Civil or Criminal	Prohibited Acts and Mens Rea
The Matthew Shepard and James Byrd Jr. Hate Crimes Prevention Act of 2009, 18 U.S.C. § 249	Criminal	Willfully causing bodily injury (or attempting to do so with fire, firearm, or other dangerous weapon) when (1) the crime was committed because of the actual or perceived race, color, religion, national origin of any person, or (2) the crime was committed because of the actual or perceived religion, national origin, gender, sexual orientation, gender identity, or disability of any person.
Church Arson Prevention Act of 1996, 18 U.S.C. § 247	Criminal	Intentionally defacing, damaging, or destroying religious property because of the religious nature of the property, so long as the crime is committed in or affects interstate commerce; intentionally obstructing or attempting to obstruct, by force or threat of force, an individual's enjoyment of his or her religious beliefs; intentionally defacing, damaging, or destroying any religious real property because of the race, color, or ethnic characteristics of any individual associated with the property.
Intimidation of Voters, 18 U.S.C. § 594 National Voter Registration Act, 42 U.S.C. § 1973gg-10(1)	Criminal	Section 594 makes it illegal to use intimidation, threats, or coercion, or attempt to use any of these means, to interfere with the right of another to vote or vote as the individual chooses, or to cause the individual to vote or not vote for any particular candidate for federal office. Section 1973gg-10(1) of Title 42 criminalizes, in a federal election, to intimidate, threaten, or coerce a prospective registrant or voter from registering to vote, voting, or attempting to register or vote, or for urging another to register or vote.
Freedom of Access to Clinic Entrances Act of 1994, 18 U.S.C. § 248	Criminal	To use force, threat of force, or physical obstruction to intentionally injure or intimidate a person (1) because he or she has been obtaining or providing reproductive health services, or (2) because he or she is lawfully exercising the right of religious freedom at a place of worship. The statute also makes it unlawful for a person to intentionally damage or destroy the property of a facility because it provides reproductive health services, or because it is a place of worship.

QUESTIONS AND PROBLEMS

1. What are the elements of a §1983 action?
2. What is the difference between absolute and qualified immunity?

The City of Amity, California, is considering the ordinances found in Questions 3 and 4. Is each constitutional under the First Amendment? Explain your answer, citing the controlling SCOTUS precedent.

3. Resolved, hatred is widespread and systemic in our community. A socially and personally destructive force, hatred must be eradicated. Therefore, it shall be a misdemeanor for any person to express themselves in public in a manner that intimidates, harasses, demeans, or disparages a person, or group of people, on the account of race, gender, sexual orientation, physical ability, or religious belief.
4. Resolved, hatred is widespread and systemic in our community. Acts of hatred that harm others are a scourge that must be addressed. Therefore, the crimes of battery, assault, and stalking shall be charged as aggravated and the penalty increased for conviction if the defendant targeted the victim on the account of race, gender, sexual orientation, physical ability, or religious belief.

IN A NUTSHELL

Along with treason and terrorism, crimes involving physical harm to another person are the most serious. The most serious of them, homicide, is the subject of your next chapter. Battery, or the unwanted harmful or offensive touching of another person, has existed since the old Common Law. The touching doesn't have to be direct. Touching someone with an extension of the body, such as a baseball bat, or with a thrown object, such as a baseball, both satisfy that actus reus element. Batteries are graded by nature and severity, with serious harm, sexual battery, and battery against special classes of people punished more severely. Police officers, teachers, and other public officials are examples of aggravation classes, at least when they are battered because of, or during, their jobs. Assault is the sibling of battery. There are two forms of assault: attempted battery and putting another person in fear of an imminent battery.

In the digital era, the crimes of true threat and stalking are on steroids. The ability to monitor and overwhelm a person with threatening expression and conduct, and the inability of victims to escape it, are problems. Generally, expression is protected by the First Amendment, and therefore, it may not be criminalized. This includes offensive and personal comments. But several exceptions exist, such as when a person intends and is likely to incite imminent lawlessness and when a true threat is uttered. Not yet precisely defined, a true threat is a communication that is intended to lead the victim to belief that the speaker will commit violence against the victim, and a reasonable person would feel so threatened. The related crime of stalking is focused on conduct, not expression. Because it is not a regulation of pure speech, the state has greater authority to regulate it than it does speech. Stalking is a pattern of conduct that is intended, and likely, to cause fear of serious bodily injury or death in another person.

Rape is also an old Common Law crime. The elements of rape have changed considerably since the 1970s. It was once defined as vaginal intercourse between a man and a woman, not his wife, without her consent, by use of force. Today, men and women may both commit rape, the requirement of resistance by the victim is not required, and spouses may be raped. In some jurisdictions, rape continues to be defined as penis–vagina intercourse. In others, this act and all other sex acts are consolidated into one crime, or set of crimes, with gradations of punishment. Vaginal sex continues to be graded highly because of the fear of pregnancy. Even in those jurisdictions with an independent rape statute, other forced sex acts are criminalized under sexual assault statutes.

Kidnapping is the crime of taking and moving a person with the intent to commit another evil act, such as rape and murder, to collect a ransom, to hold hostage, or to interfere with a political or governmental function. In those instances when an offender restrains the freedom of a victim but doesn't have a motive enumerated for kidnapping, the lesser crime of false imprisonment is committed.

Finally, there is a portfolio of civil rights and "bias" crimes. Again, limited by the First Amendment, governments may not regulate hate speech. But they may punish criminal acts more harshly if they are motivated by the victim's race, religion, or other factors, and they may punish a person who intentionally violates or interferes with a person's civil rights. The civil version of these laws, 42 U.S.C. §1983, offers individuals whose rights have been violated by state and local police officers the opportunity to sue the officers in federal court, where they can receive money damages. In some cases, the civil version may order local governments to stop illegal practices or to change their policies.

LEGAL TERMS

1983 action (p. 237)

Abuse (p. 228)

assault (p. 200)

battery (p. 200)

civil rights laws (p. 235)

false imprisonment (p. 227)

Human trafficking (p. 233)

Kidnapping (p. 226)

mayhem (p. 202)

neglect (p. 228)

rape (p. 215)

rape shield laws (p. 225)

stalking (p. 212)

statutory rape (p. 220)

true threat (p. 205)

NOTES

1. Cat McAuliffe, "The Life and Death of John Brennan Crutchley, AKA the Vampire Rapist," *Ranker*, September 15, 2017, accessed Ranker.Com on August 22, 2020.

2. *John Brennan Crutchley: The Vampire Rapist*. TruecrimeLabpod, Episode 1 Notes, November 27, 2019, accessed Truecrimelabpod.com on August 22, 2020.

3. NJ Rev Stat § 2C:12-1 (2013).

4. CA Penal Code § 203, et seq. (2019).

5. National Coalition Against Domestic Violence. Data retrieved from NCADV.org on September 13, 2020.

6. O.R.C. §2919.25.

7. *Watts v. United States*, 394 U.S. 705 (1969).

8. *People v. Wood*, 2017IL App (1st)143135.

9. *Perez v. United States*, 580 U.S. ___ (2017).

10. Brian L. McMahon, *Constitutional Law—Unreasonable Ambiguity: Minnesota's Amended Stalking Statute is Unconstitutionally Vague*. 24,(1998).

11. AR Code § 5-71-229 (2017).

12. *Lawrence v. Texas*, 539 U.S. 558 (2003).

13. *Obergefell v Hodges*, 576 U.S. 644 (2015).

14. Conn. Gen. Stat. §§53a-70, et. Seq.

15. Ala. Code §§ 13A-6-61 – 62.

16. Minn. Stat. 609.345.

17. David M. Reutter, *For Shame! Public Shaming Sentences on the Rise*, Human Rights Defense Center, February 4, 2015, accessed Prisonlegalnews.org on October 10, 2020.

18. *Packingham v. North Carolina*, 582 U.S. ___ (2017).

19. SCOTUS affirmed the constitutionality of federal civil commitment of sex offenders against a federalism challenge in *United States v. Comstock*, 560 U.S. 126 (2010).

20. For a discussion of how the process employed by inquisitorial systems lessens the impact of process on rape victims, see L. E. Ellison, "A Comparative Study of Rape Trials in Adversarial and Inquisitorial Criminal Justice Systems" (PhD. diss., University of Leeds, 1997).

21. J. Bentham, *The Rationale of Evidence*, 1843, found at oll.libertyfund.org on October 15, 2020.

22. MPC §212.

23. Lindbergh Kidnapping, U.S. Federal Bureau of Investigation, accessed FBI.gov on October 16, 2020.

24. Barry Cushman, *Headline Kidnappings and the Origins of the Lindbergh Law*, 55 St. Louis U. L.J. 1293 (2010-2011).

25. 18 U.S.C. §1201.

26. Va. Code § 18.2-371.1.

27. Haw. Rev. Stat. §703-309.

28. Polaris Project. *Myths, Facts, and Statistics*. Found at polarisproject.org on October 25, 2020.

29. 22 U.S.C. §7101, et seq.

30. 18 U.S.C. §§ 2421-2424.

31. *West Virginia State Board of Education v. Barnette*, 319 U.S. 624 (1943).

32. *Brandenburg v. Ohio*, 395 U.S. 444 (1969).

33. *R.A.V. v. City of St. Paul*, 505 U.S. 377

8 HOMICIDE

On March 9, 2003, Ryan Holle, 20 years old, enjoyed a night of partying with friends. At the party, three of his friends discussed going to the house of a known drug dealer to get something to eat. They also mentioned robbing her of cash and drugs. Because one of the men was the on-again, off-again boyfriend of the woman's daughter, Jessica Snyder, Ryan didn't believe they intended to rob her. In the morning, one of the men asked to borrow Ryan's car to go to the home. A hungover Ryan handed over his car keys. As it turned out, the men were serious; they planned to steal a safe that was believed to be full of drugs. They encountered Jessica during their burglary, the situation turned violent, and one of the men beat Jessica in the head until she was dead. The three burglars were convicted of murder. So was Ryan. Even though he was not present at the scene of the crime and he had no intention to rob or hurt the victim, Ryan received the same sentence as the other three men: a lifetime in prison without the possibility of parole.

Did the act of loaning his car, with the belief that they intended to commit a nonviolent robbery, make Ryan, who had no criminal record, as blameworthy as the man who bludgeoned the victim to death? The prosecutor thought so. He commented, "No car, no crime." Ryan's attorney saw it differently. She said that "the worst thing he was guilty of was partying too much and not being discriminating enough in who he was partying with." Subsequently, Florida Governor Rick Scott reduced Ryan's sentence to 25 years of imprisonment. The victim's mother, who found her daughter with her head crushed and teeth knocked out, had insult added to emotional injury when she was convicted and sentenced to 3 years in prison for possession of a pound of marijuana that was found in the safe.[1]

The only crimes for which a person may be executed in the United States are murder, treason, and, possibly, a few other crimes against the state. SCOTUS has found capital punishment disproportionate under the Eighth Amendment's cruel and unusual punishments clause for other serious crimes, including the rape of adults and children. Statutory law continues to punish espionage and drug kingpin activity with death. Whether death is proportional to these crimes under the Eighth Amendment is unknown. The former is more likely than the latter.

Historically, treason and murder are considered to be the most serious of crimes because *both* were considered murder. Treason is the murder, or at least attempted murder, of the state. The reason murder has, and is, subjected to the most severe punishment is obvious, even instinctive. All peoples of the world place a high value on human life. For a long period of Western history, it was the Christian belief that life was God's creation, and to wrongfully take it was a mortal sin.

Later, this belief was supplemented by philosophical humanism—the belief that human life and autonomy are inherently valuable.

Homicide is the taking of another person's life, but not all homicides are crimes. Soldiers kill, as do state executioners. Neither act of homicide is criminalized. This is not without its critics. The French Enlightenment philosopher Voltaire wrote, "It is forbidden to kill; therefore all murderers are punished unless they kill in large numbers and to the sound of trumpets." Voltaire was questioning whether killing in the name of the state was heroic, or even just. Regardless, most societies not only excuse, but require soldiers to kill. Other examples of lawful homicides are the justified and excused killings you learned about in an earlier chapter, such as self-defense and acts of insanity.

If you have already read the chapter on the two essential elements, it won't surprise you to learn there are different forms of unlawful homicides that are distinguished by their respective mens rea. The first criminalized homicide at the old Common Law was murder.

OLD SCHOOL MURDER

Learning Objective: Identify, compare, and contrast express murder and the three implied forms of murder at the Common Law.

In the early Common Law, murder was defined as the (1) killing of a (2) human being with (3) malice aforethought. The mens rea, malice aforethought, is a high mental state. A killer had to possess, in advance of the act of killing, the specific intent to cause the victim's death. Over time, the courts expanded the definition of murder. By the 15th century, the following forms of murder were recognized. The first is sometimes referred to as express murder and the other three as implied murder, or implied malice:

- Malice aforethought murder

- Intent to commit serious (grievous) bodily harm murder

- Depraved heart murder

- Felony murder

Malice Aforethought Murder

The actus reus of murder is the unlawful killing of a human being. The modifier "unlawful" is used to distinguish murder from the excused and justified homicides that you learned about in Chapter 3. You also learned about causation in that chapter. A person is blameworthy for another person's death only when he is the legal cause of death. You may recall that in order to be

---

Express murder: The taking of human life with malice aforethought.

Implied murder: The taking of human life during an act that is intended to inflict serious bodily harm, with the wanton and reckless disregard for life, or during the commission of a felony.

the legal cause of death, an act must be both the but-for cause and the proximate cause, the latter being satisfied when a victim's death is a reasonably foreseeable consequence of an act. Any means of causing another person's death satisfies the actus reus element. In most cases, victims are directly killed by the perpetrator, such as through the use of a knife, gun, blunt object, or poison. But it is also possible to be liable for the death of a person who causes their own death. For example, a husband who repeatedly struck his wife and ordered her to jump into a river was convicted of murder because she complied and drowned.[2]

For there to be a killing, there must be a death. At one time, death was defined as the cessation of blood flow and breathing. This created a problem when medical science developed to the point where a person's blood circulation and respiration could be mechanically maintained but the person had no hope of recovering brain function. Today, either brain death or a combination of the cessation of brain, circulation, and respiration functions are used to determine death.

The mens rea of malice aforethought murder has two parts, malice and aforethought. An ordinary definition of malice is to be possessed of hatred, to act out of an evil or ill will. Indeed, the early mens rea was focused on moral guilt. Over time, mens rea developed from moral to cognitive guilt. The question of culpability shifted from one's heart to state of mind. Malice evolved into the desire to cause the death of the victim. It is an example of an early specific intent crime.

PHOTO 8.1 Dr. Jack Kevorkian, a physician who was prosecuted on several occasions and convicted once for assisting terminally ill patients in ending their lives. In this photo, he is advocating for an enlarged role for the Ninth Amendment.

Proximate cause: A test used to determine if an act is the legal cause of a result. A result must be foreseeable to be the proximate cause of an act.

Brain death: Irreversible cessation of all functions of the entire brain. The legal standard to determine if death has occurred.

Malice aforethought murder: An act of homicide that was committed with the specific intent of causing the victim's death. The first murder under the Common Law that continues to the standard for the most culpable form of murder.

For there to be a murder, a perpetrator's malicious intent must be formed before—aforethought—the murderous act happens. "Premeditated" and "deliberate" are commonly used synonyms for aforethought. Clearly, a defendant who devotes hours to studying the efficacy of various poisons to kill and who waits weeks until the right moment presents itself to lace a victim's drink has acted with premeditation. Whether a defendant who suddenly becomes enraged and shoots a victim all in a few seconds has acted with aforethought is a harder case. Case law varies. Most courts have deemphasized the measurement of time in favor of examining whether there was adequate time for the defendant to form a malicious state of mind before completing the killing. Other doctrines, such as provocation, must also be factored into these decisions. You will learn more about these considerations later in this chapter. The following scenarios illustrate classical malice aforethought murder:

Pearl is fired from her job by Jolene. Pearl is determined to make Jolene pay with her life. She sits outside of Jolene's home for several days, looking for patterns in her movement and planning the best time to kill her. She follows through one day, killing Jolene with a knife to the throat when she returns home from the gym.

Dustin Corleone wants to make a name for himself as a gangster. He uses his car to run down and kill Julie Rudyani, a federal prosecutor who has earned a reputation as a gang-busting prosecutor.

Intent to Do Serious Bodily Harm Murder

The second form of murder that has been recognized for hundreds of years is when a person acts with the intent to seriously injure another person, but death results. For example, Jamar strikes Nolan in the leg with a metal bar, intending to break his leg. Nolan's tibia breaks in a compound fracture. The wound becomes infected, causing Nolan's death. Jamar is liable for murder, even though he didn't intend to cause Nolan's death. The following are the elements of this form of implied murder, **intent to cause serious bodily injury murder**:

1. An act

2. taken with the specific intent

3. to cause the victim serious bodily harm

4. that results in the death of the victim.

Recall the role of inferences in proving mens rea. A jury may infer from a dangerous act that death was intended. No reasonable jury could conclude that the blow to Nolan's leg was

---

Intent to cause serious bodily injury murder: An act of homicide that results from a defendant's specific intent to cause serious, or grievous, bodily injury. Treated as murder under the Common Law and commonly classified as second-degree murder today.

intended to kill him. But a blow to the head with a metal bar is different. These facts illustrate the deadly weapon doctrine, or the inference of specific intent to kill that a jury may draw from the use of a deadly weapon. The Model Penal Code (MPC), which continues to recognize the deadly weapon doctrine, defines deadly weapon as "any firearm, or other weapon, device, instrument, material or substance, whether animate or inanimate, which in the manner it is used or is intended to be used is known to be capable of producing death or serious bodily injury."[3] As the rule makes clear, the intrinsic nature or the manufacturer's intended purpose of an item is not dispositive. It is about how an object is used. The definition is so broad that a jury can infer deadly intent from almost any item. A tennis racquet, for example, is a deadly weapon when used by Aryana to beat someone about the head. Deadly chemical agents and communicable diseases are also deadly weapons. The best example of the emphasis on use, not inherent status, is the human body. The hand that offers comfort, that renders aid to the needy, that creates great works of art can also be a deadly weapon in a few states, including Colorado. And it isn't only the hand; legs, feet, teeth—actually, the entire body—if employed harmfully, convert into a deadly weapon.[4]

If a jury decides that a defendant intended to cause less than serious bodily injury and death resulted, the lesser crime of manslaughter has been committed. A more thorough discussion about manslaughter follows shortly. Consider the following examples:

> Jubilant that her candidate for president won the election, Parker runs out of her house into her suburban neighborhood, cheering and randomly firing her rifle. One her gunshots kills a neighbor. Parker has not committed murder because there was no intent to cause serious bodily harm.

> Ruby, who knows she is infected with COVID-19, spits in the mouth of a police officer during her arrest. She proclaims, "I hope you get f*cking sick, you thug. I have the 'rona, and you will soon have it too." The officer dies from respiratory failure caused by COVID-19. Ruby has committed murder.

Depraved Heart Murder

Depraved heart murder refers to circumstances where a defendant lacks specific intent but acts with reckless and wanton disregard for life. To rise to the level of depraved heart murder, an act must be more than negligent, or even grossly negligent. The act must pose a high, wanton risk of death. Further, the risk must be disregarded. The actor's subjective awareness of the risk doesn't have to be proved. The objective test is applied; the defendant is liable if a reasonable person would have been aware of the risk. The risk of death itself must be

---

Deadly weapon doctrine: An inference of deadly intent when a person kills another with an object that is designed to kill or has been used in a manner that can kill.

Depraved heart murder: A homicide that results from the reckless and wanton disregard of life. Treated as murder at the Common Law, it is commonly classified as second-degree murder or first-degree manslaughter today.

very high—in fact, probable. So the following must be proved by a prosecutor in depraved heart murder:

1. An act that

2. poses a high, wanton risk to life;

3. a reasonable person would have been aware of the risk;

4. the defendant disregarded the risk;

5. killed a human being.

Consider these scenarios:

A police officer tases a fleeing shoplifting suspect who is running along the roofline of a building, causing the suspect to fall to his death. The officer has committted depraved heart murder.

A hunter shoots and kills a schoolchild while attempting to kill a deer that is standing in the playground of the schoolyard where the child is enjoying recess. The hunter has committed depraved heart murder.

Return to Parker, our jubilant citizen in the earlier scenario. This is a more difficult case. Her actions are clearly negligent, but whether they pose a high, wanton risk to life is unclear. Most likely, she would be convicted of a lesser form of homicide, such as negligent manslaughter. Manslaughter will be explained later in this chapter.

A famous case of depraved heart murder occurred in San Francisco in 2001 when Diane Whipple was killed by her neighbors' dogs as she was reaching for the key to open the door to her apartment. You will read about this sensational and tragic case, where the very fine distinctions between murder and manslaughter standards are examined, in the next Digging Deeper.

DIGGING DEEPER 8.1

Is not controlling dangerous dogs that kill a person depraved heart murder?

Case: *People v. Knoller*
Court: Supreme Court of California. Citation: 41 Cal.4th 139 (Cal. 2007)
Year: 2007
Justice Kennard delivered the opinion of the court.

In 1998, Pelican Bay State Prison inmates Paul Schneider and Dale Bretches, both members of the Aryan Brotherhood prison gang, sought to engage in a business of buying, raising, and breeding Presa Canario dogs. This breed of dog tends to be very large, weighing over 100 pounds, and reaching over five feet tall when standing on its hind legs. A document found in defendants' apartment describes the Presa Canario as "a gripping dog... always used and bred for combat and guard... [and] used extensively for fighting...."

Prisoners Schneider and Bretches relied on outside contacts, including Brenda Storey and Janet Coumbs, to carry out their Presa Canario business. Schneider told Coumbs that she should raise the dogs.

As of May 1990, Coumbs possessed four such dogs, named Bane, Isis, Hera, and Fury. Hera and Fury broke out of their fenced yard and attacked Coumbs's sheep. Hera killed at least one of the sheep and also a cat belonging to Coumbs's daughter. Coumbs acknowledged that Bane ate his doghouse and may have joined Fury in killing a sheep.

[The defendant and her husband, Noel, met Schneider while representing a corrections officer in his prison. Eventually, the defendants agreed to take the dogs, but only after they were told about the sheep and cat attacks.]

Defendant Knoller thereafter contacted Dr. Donald Martin, a veterinarian for 49 years, and on March 26, 2000, he examined and vaccinated the dogs. With his bill to Knoller, Dr. Martin included a letter, which said in part: "I would be professionally amiss [sic] if I did not mention the following, so that you can be prepared. These dogs are huge, approximately weighing in the neighborhood of 100 pounds each. They have had no training or discipline of any sort. They were a problem to even get to, let alone to vaccinate. You mentioned having a professional hauler gather them up and taking them.... Usually this would be done in crates, but I doubt one could get them into anything short of a livestock trailer, and if let loose they would have a battle.

To add to this, these animals would be a liability in any household, reminding me of the recent attack in Tehama County to a boy by large dogs. He lost his arm and disfigured his face. The historic romance of the warrior dog, the personal guard dog, the gaming dog, etc., may sound good but hardly fits into life today."...

On April 1, 2000, both defendants and a professional dog handler took custody of the dogs from Coumbs. Bane then weighed 150 pounds and Hera 130 pounds. Coumbs told both defendants that she was worried about the dogs, that Hera and Fury should be shot, and that she was also concerned about Bane and Isis....

Between the time defendants Noel and Knoller brought the dogs to their sixth-floor apartment in San Francisco and the date of the fatal mauling of Diane Whipple on January 26, 2001, there were about 30 incidents of the two dogs being out of control or threatening humans and other dogs. Neighbors mentioned seeing the two dogs unattended on the sixth floor and running down the hall. Codefendant Noel's letters to prisoner Schneider confirmed this, mentioning one incident when defendant Knoller had to let go of the two dogs as they broke from her grasp and ran to the end of the hall. Noel described how the dogs even pushed past him and "took off side by side down the hall toward the elevator in a celebratory stampede!! 240 lbs. of Presa wall to wall moving at top speed!!!" In a letter to inmate Schneider, defendant Knoller admitted not having the upper body strength to handle Bane and having trouble controlling Hera.

When neighbors complained to defendants Noel and Knoller about the two dogs, defendants responded callously, if at all. In one incident, neighbors Stephen and Aimee West were walking their dog in a nearby park when Hera attacked their dog and "latched on" to the dog's snout. Noel was unable to separate the dogs, but Aimee threw her keys at Hera, startling Hera and causing Hera to release her grip on the Wests' dog. On another day, Stephen West was walking his dog when he encountered Noel with Bane. Bane lunged toward West's dog, but Noel managed to pull Bane back. When Stephen West next saw Noel, West suggested that Noel muzzle the dogs and talk to dog trainer Mario Montepeque about training them; Noel replied there was no need to do so. Defendants Knoller and Noel later encountered Montepeque, who advised defendants to have their dogs trained and to use a choke collar. Defendants disregarded this advice. On still another occasion, when dog walker Lynn Gaines was walking a dog, Gaines told Noel that he should put a muzzle on Bane; Noel called her a "bitch" and said the dog Gaines was walking was the problem.

There were also instances when defendants' two dogs attacked or threatened people. David Moser, a fellow resident in the apartment building, slipped by defendants Knoller and Noel in the hallway only to have their dog Hera bite him on the "rear end." When he exclaimed, "Your dog just bit me," Noel replied, "Um, interesting." Neither defendant apologized to Moser or reprimanded the dog. Another resident, Jill Cowen Davis, was eight months pregnant when one of the dogs, in the presence of both Knoller and Noel, suddenly growled and lunged toward her stomach with its mouth open and teeth bared. Noel jerked the dog by the leash, but he did not apologize to Davis. Postal carrier John Watanabe testified that both dogs, unleashed, had charged him. He said the dogs were in a "snarling frenzy" and he was "terrified for [his] life." When he stepped behind his mail cart, the dogs went back to Knoller and Noel. On still another occasion, the two dogs lunged at a six-year-old boy walking to school; they were stopped less than a foot from him.

One time, codefendant Noel himself suffered a severe injury to his finger when Bane bit him during a fight with another dog. The wound required surgery, and Noel had to wear a splint on his arm and have two steel pins placed in his hand for eight to 10 weeks.

Mauling victim Diane Whipple and her partner Sharon Smith lived in a sixth-floor apartment across a lobby from defendants. Smith encountered defendants' two dogs as often as once a week. In early December 2000, Whipple called Smith at work to say, with some panic in her voice, that one of the dogs had bitten her. Whipple had come upon codefendant Noel in the lobby with one of the dogs, which lunged at her and bit her in the hand. Whipple did not seek medical treatment for three deep, red indentations on one hand. Whipple made every effort to avoid defendants' dogs, checking the hallway before she went out and becoming anxious while waiting for the elevator for fear the dogs would be inside. She and Smith did not complain to apartment management because they wanted nothing to do with defendants Knoller and Noel.

On January 26, 2001, Whipple telephoned Smith to say she was going home early. At 4:00 p.m., Esther Birkmaier, a neighbor who lived across the hall from Whipple, heard dogs barking and a woman's "panic-stricken" voice calling, "Help me, help me." Looking through the peephole in her front door, Birkmaier saw Whipple lying facedown on the floor just over the threshold of her apartment with what appeared to be a dog on top of her. Birkmaier saw no one else in the hallway. Afraid to open the door, Birkmaier called 911, the emergency telephone number, and at the same time heard a voice yelling, "No, no, no" and "Get off." When Birkmaier again approached her door, she could hear barking and growling directly outside and a banging against a door. She heard a voice yell, "Get off, get off, no, no, stop, stop." She chained her door and again looked through the peephole. Whipple's body was gone and groceries were strewn about the hallway. Birkmaier called 911 a second time.

At 4:12 p.m., San Francisco Police Officers Sidney Laws and Leslie Forrestal arrived in response to Birkmaier's telephone calls. They saw Whipple's body in the hallway; her clothing had been completely ripped off, her entire body was covered with wounds, and she was bleeding profusely. Defendant Knoller and the two dogs were not in sight.

The officers called for an ambulance. Shortly thereafter, defendant Knoller emerged from her apartment. She did not ask about Whipple's condition but merely told the officers she was looking for her keys, which she found just inside the door to Whipple's apartment.

An emergency medical technician administered first aid to Whipple, who had a large, profusely bleeding wound to her neck. The wound was too large to halt the bleeding, and Whipple's pulse and breathing stopped as paramedics arrived. She was revived but died shortly after reaching the hospital.

An autopsy revealed over 77 discrete injuries covering Whipple's body "from head to toe." The most significant were lacerations damaging her jugular vein and her carotid artery and crushing her larynx, injuries typically inflicted by predatory animals to kill their prey. The medical examiner stated that although earlier medical attention would have increased Whipple's chances of survival, she might ultimately have died anyway because she had lost one-third or more of her blood at the scene. Plaster molds of the two dogs' teeth showed that the bite injuries to Whipple's neck were consistent with Bane's teeth....

The jury found Knoller guilty of second degree murder; it also found both Knoller and Noel guilty of involuntary manslaughter and owning a mischievous animal that caused the death of a human being.... [The trial court ordered a new trial on the second-degree murder conviction, finding that the jury was given a bad definition of the mens rea required. The court concluded that the mens rea should be a defendant *subjectively knows, based on everything, that the conduct that he or she is about to engage in has a high probability of death to another human being.* Both the prosecution and defense appealed the decision. On appeal, the trial court was told that its high probability standard was wrong. The court of appeals instructed it to use something closer to the MPC standard: "appreciation and conscious disregard of a likely risk of... serious bodily injury." The court of appeals decision was appealed to the California Supreme Court. What follows is that court's decision on the mens rea requirement.]

Murder is the unlawful killing of a human being, or a fetus, with malice aforethought. At issue here is the definition of "implied malice. Second degree murder is the unlawful killing of a human being with malice aforethought but without the additional elements, such as willfulness, premeditation, and deliberation, that would support a conviction of first degree murder. [M]alice may be either express or implied. It is express when there is manifested a deliberate intention to take away the life of a fellow creature. It is implied, when no considerable provocation appears, or when the circumstances attending the killing show an abandoned and malignant heart." Defendant Knoller was convicted of second degree murder... "abandoned and malignant heart" is far from clear... implied malice requires a defendant's awareness of the risk of death to another....

We conclude that a conviction for second degree murder, based on a theory of implied malice, requires proof that a defendant acted with conscious disregard of the danger to human life. In holding that a defendant's conscious disregard of the risk of serious bodily injury suffices to sustain such a conviction, the Court of Appeal erred....

[Now, turning to the trial's court mens rea definition:] In granting Knoller a new trial, the trial court properly viewed implied malice as requiring a defendant's awareness of the danger that his or her conduct will result in another's *death* and not merely in serious bodily injury. But the court's ruling was legally flawed in other respects....

The court stated that a killer acts with implied malice when the killer "*subjectively knows, based on everything, that the conduct that he or she is about to engage in has a high probability of death* to another human being."...

> Nor does [our precedent] require a defendant's awareness that his or her conduct has a *high probability* of causing death. Rather, it requires only that a defendant acted with a "conscious disregard for human life."
>
> *[Therefore, the Supreme Court found that both the trial court and court of appeals were applying wrong tests. It remanded the case back to the trial court, where the defendant was retried using the standard it announced above: that Ms. Knoller was aware of the danger that her conduct would result in Ms. Whipple's death and consciously disregarded that risk. Knoller was retried, found guilty of second-degree murder again, and sentenced to 15 years to life in prison. She was denied parole in 2019. One final note: The full story of the defendants and their relationship to Mr. Schneider is bizarre. Conduct your own research to learn more.]*

Felony Murder

Ryan Holle, the man who loaned his car keys to the wrong men in our opening scenario, committed **felony murder**, the fourth and final form of murder at the Common Law. Felony murder holds that a person is liable in murder for any death that occurs during, or as a result of, the commission of a felony. Sometimes wrongly characterized as transferred intent, felony murder is a combination of constructive intent and agency/vicarious liability between co-conspirators. An actor need not have the intent to kill, or even harm, the victim. In fact, there isn't a requirement that anyone intends harm. The death can be accidental.

As is true of all murders, the act (specifically, the felony) and the death must be causally connected. The death must be a consequence of the crime, not a coincidence. Historically, the death and the predicate felony had to be proximately related (i.e., the death had to be foreseeable). While the proximate cause test requires a greater connection than the "but-for" test, it isn't highly rigorous. Under the proximate cause test, the defendant need not commit the act that directly causes the victim's death. The actor only needs to be a principal or accessory before the fact to the felony. Holle's act of loaning his car to the men who committed the murder made him an accomplice to the burglary and, therefore, to the murder. As another illustration, consider the case of Cole Allen Wilkins. He stole several kitchen appliances from a home under construction. He loaded them into the bed of a truck, and in a rush to leave the site, he didn't tie them down. On the freeway, a boxed stove fell from the truck. It caused three accidents, the third killing a driver. Wilkins was charged and convicted of felony murder. Thirteen years later, his conviction was reduced to manslaughter by an appellate court, a crime for which he was sentenced to serve 4 years in prison, one-third the length of time he had already served.[5]

The prosecutions of Holle, Wilkins, and many other people raise questions about the purpose and justice of felony murder. The rationale for the rule is obvious—to deter and punish potentially dangerous conduct. Whether these objectives are achieved, and if so, whether the punishment is in proportion to the deed, is sometimes questionable. Also, dispensing with the

---

Felony murder: A homicide that is a consequence of the commission of a felony. Co-conspirators are guilty of felony murder, regardless of which conspirator committed the homicidal act. Treated as murder at the Common Law and commonly classified as first- or second-degree murder today.

traditional requirement of mens rea is concerning, especially for a crime that can be punished with death.

Another reason felony murder didn't seem as harsh hundreds of years ago as it does today is that all felons were executed. So people convicted of felony murder were sentenced to death twice: once for the underlying felony and the second for felony murder. Eventually, however, felonies began to be graded and punished differently, but felony murder hung on. This created situations where the underlying felony was punished with imprisonment and the felony murder with death. In an effort to address these concerns, many states limit felony murder to the commission of felonies that inherently threaten life, such as arson, burglary, rape, robbery, aggravated battery, kidnapping, and drug trafficking. Another way several state legislatures have limited the scope of felony murder has been to change the proximate cause test to **agency theory**. Under agency theory, a defendant is liable only for the actions of co-conspirators.

Putting all of this together, felony murder is defined as such:

1. The killing of a human being by any person (not just the defendant or a co-felon)

2. during the commission of a named felony and

3. the felony is the proximate cause of the homicide, or alternatively, co-felons are operating in agency with one another.

Let's apply felony murder to a conspiracy to bank robbery. The two robbers, Daniel and Aryana, agree that no one should be hurt during the robbery. Defendant Daniel suggests that they put blanks in their guns to reduce the chances of an accidental shooting. Regardless, Aryana loads her gun with live ammunition. During the robbery, a bank guard draws his weapon. Reflexively, Aryana shoots the security guard, inflicting a fatal wound. Obviously, Aryana is guilty of malice aforethought murder. Daniel is also guilty of murder, even though he didn't intend to kill anyone and he didn't pull the trigger. His status as a co-felon in the robbery is all that is required to establish his liability for felony murder. Effectively, the felony murder rule establishes vicarious liability between Aryana and Daniel. This is true, regardless of whether the proximate cause or agency test is applied.

Let's take the bank robbery scenario to another level. During the robbery, a frightened bank patron runs out the front door into the street and is struck and killed by an ambulance that is rushing to the hospital. Applying the proximate cause test, both Daniel and Aryana have committed felony murder, even though neither of them intended to harm the patron, and a third party, the driver of the ambulance, was the direct cause of death. Neither would be guilty of felony murder if agency theory is applied.

In our third robbery scenario, the security guard shoots and kills Daniel. Under agency theory, Aryana has not committed felony murder; however, the law is not uniform between states that employ the proximate cause test. For most states, co-felons are not responsible for

---

Agency theory (felony murder): Co-conspirators are equally responsible in murder for foreseeable deaths resulting from the commission of a named felony that is caused by a co-conspirator.

the justified homicides of their colleagues in crime. But in a minority of states, they are just as responsible for the justified killings of their co-felons as they are for anyone else.

Other examples of felony murder include the following:

Miley and Cyrus break into what they believe is an abandoned home with the intention of burning it down. Much to their surprise, the owner appears and threatens them with a candlestick. Cyrus wrestles the candlestick from the owner and beats him about the head with it until he is dead. Cyrus has committed malice aforethought murder, and Miley has committed felony murder because the owner's death is a foreseeable consequence of the burglary.

Miley and Cyrus break into what they believe is an abandoned home with the intention of burning it down. Much to their surprise, the owner appears and fires a weapon at them; the bullet misses the robbers, passes through a window, and kills a neighbor. The owner's use of deadly force was justified. Miley and Cyrus, however, are guilty of felony murder because the death is a consequence of the burglary.

Miley and Cyrus break into what they believe is an abandoned home with the intention of burning it down. Much to their surprise, the owner appears and fires a weapon into the air, and they run to their car and speed away. One block away, they hit and kill a child in the road. Both Miley and Cyrus have committed felony murder because the death is a foreseeable consequence of the burglary.

Felony murder is a very serious crime. In many jurisdictions, it is punished in the same way as malice aforethought murder, with decades to life in prison, and in Pennsylvania and a few other states, life without the possibility of parole. SCOTUS has also set a few boundaries, such as in the 1982 case *Enmund v. Florida*,[6] where it was decided that capital punishment is disproportionate for someone who aided and abetted but did not themselves kill, attempt to kill, or intend to kill. The court 5 years later tweaked this decision in *Tison v. Arizona* by holding that a conspirator who is a major participant in a felony and who acted with at least a reckless disregard for life may be punished as a murderer.[7] The court subsequently limited that decision to adults. Juveniles may not be executed for felony murder.[8]

Whether it is just to treat offenders who don't intend to cause death or who don't commit the act that causes death as equal to premeditated killers is under scrutiny. Also, punishing juveniles with long terms of imprisonment for felony murder is a matter of contemporary discussion. There are also concerns that African Americans are disproportionately impacted by felony murder. These concerns are likely to receive legislative and judicial attention in the years to come.

Corpus Delicti

In 1661, three English men were executed for murder in what is known as Perry's Case. The body of the victim was never found, but one of three men confessed to murdering the victim. He also implicated the other two. Much to the surprise of the community, the victim reappeared after the men were executed. This and other similar cases led to the development of the corpus delicti rule.[9] Because it was developed in response to a murder case and because it translates to "body of the crime," corpus delicti is often misunderstood to require that a victim's remains be found as a condition of a murder prosecution. While having the body is helpful to a prosecutor's case, it is not required. The corpus delicti rule demands that a prosecutor have proof of the crime beyond a defendant's confession. The rule was an early recognition of what modern social science research has confirmed: Innocent people falsely confess.

Although important, corpus delicti isn't a difficult hurdle for prosecutors in most cases. It doesn't require proof that the defendant committed the crime, only that the crime was committed. In Perry's Case, there were only two pieces of evidence: the confession of one of the three defendants and the disappearance of the alleged victim. But the absence of a person isn't evidence of murder. There are many reasons people go missing. Many forms of evidence, both direct and circumstantial, can be used to establish corpus delicti. An eyewitness to the crime, a text from the victim expressing the expectation that she is about to be killed, or a room with the furniture knocked over and the alleged victim's blood on the floor may all be used to establish that the crime occurred. Once corpus delicti has been established, a prosecutor is free to introduce a defendant's confession. Corpus delicti has been expanded to nearly all crimes. Today, a prosecutor must show a jury that a house was burned in an illegal manner or that property was indeed taken unlawfully before introducing confessions for arson or larceny.

QUESTIONS AND PROBLEMS

1. What are the elements of express murder at the Common Law?
2. What are the elements of intent to inflict serious bodily harm murder at the Common Law?
3. What are the elements of depraved heart murder at the Common Law?
4. What are the elements of felony murder at the Common Law?

For Questions 5 through 8, identify whether express murder or a form of implied murder is committed. If implied, identify which form of murder. Explain your answers thoroughly, addressing the elements of the crime you choose.

5. Emmy learns that Thea has stolen a valuable tennis racquet from her. Angry, Emmy drives to the local tennis club where Thea is playing, muttering to herself, "After I am finished with her, she won't play tennis for a long time." Emmy locates her, runs onto the court, screams, "You are a crime committer," pulls out a knife, and jabs it into Thea's leg. The knife opens Thea's femoral artery, killing her. What form of murder, if any, has Emmy committed?
6. Shante and Megan decide to rob a liquor store. During the robbery, Shante pushes a customer out of the way to get to the cash register. The customer falls back, hits his head on a freezer containing ice cream, and dies from his head wound. What form of murder, if any, has Megan committed?
7. Jealous of his roommate's academic achievements, Albert I. Stine put arsenic in her drink, killing her. What form of murder, if any, has Albert committed?
8. Roger Shags is a local K-9 police officer. His dog, Scooby, is highly effective in catching and restraining fleeing suspects. But in recent months, Shags has noticed a change in the dog. He has become more aggressive and less obedient. In three separate

instances in 2 months, Scooby bit the necks and faces of suspects rather than focusing on the arms and legs as he was trained. On four occasions, Scooby disobeyed Shag's commands to release suspects. An emergency room physician that treated one of the suspects commented that the wounds were serious and that the dog was dangerous. Later, Shags released and ordered Scooby to catch Fred, whom Shags suspected of possessing cocaine. Scooby brought Fred down, began biting his neck, and ignored Shag's commands to stop the attack. Eventually, Shags was able to pull the dog off, but not until after he had opened Fred's jugular vein, killing him. What murder, if any, has Shags committed?

LIFE, NOT DEATH: MANSLAUGHTER

Learning Objective: Identify, compare, and contrast provocation, combat, and the imperfect defense forms of manslaughter.

The harshness of the single penalty for murder (death) caused courts to be creative in avoiding murder verdicts in cases where defendants didn't act with malice. But avoiding sentences of death created its own problem; blameworthy homicides went unpunished. While capital punishment was extreme, so was freeing the person who committed the homicide with no punishment whatsoever. By the 1300s, a formal alternative was established: a lesser form of wrongful homicide—manslaughter.[10] All forms of manslaughter were punished with life in prison rather than death. There are two reasons a homicide may be treated as manslaughter rather than murder. First, because the defendant possessed a lesser mens rea than required for murder. Recall that to be convicted of murder, a defendant has to possess malice aforethought, intend to cause seriously bodily harm, act with reckless and wanton disregard of life, or be a part of a felony that results in death. Yet people sometimes people kill with a lesser mental state. The second reason, as you learned in earlier chapters, is that an imperfect defense can reduce a crime from murder to manslaughter.

Losing My Cool: Provocation

The classic manslaughter is the heat of passion, or provoked, homicide. Heat of passion manslaughter occurs when a defendant, in response to that person's provocation, kills the victim impulsively, without thinking. The response is so sudden that it is not possible for the defendant to form malice aforethought. The elements of this defense are as follows:

1. The defendant intentionally killed a human being.

2. The killing was committed in the heat of passion.

3. The victim provoked the defendant in a manner that a reasonable person could have lost self-control.

Heat of passion: The provoked, impulsive killing of a person.

4. The provocation was the immediate cause of the homicide.

5. The defendant did not have time to cool off.

The crime has a subjective mens rea element—general, rather than specific intent. Specifically, the provocation must push a defendant into a diminished mental state that forecloses the possibility of developing malice aforethought.

In addition to the subjective, there is an objective element. The provocation must be so severe that a reasonable person might have also lost self-control. The state of mind of the defendant is immaterial. After all, some people take offense to everything, and other people take offense to nothing. The test is objective: Would a reasonable person have been provoked to kill? If this question is answered yes, a defendant's homicide is reduced from murder to manslaughter. However, words alone, no matter how offensive, are rarely enough to establish the provocation defense. A specific elf (OK—Buddy, if you must know) may kill in response to being referred to as a "cotton-headed ninny muggins," but a reasonable elf wouldn't.

The reasonable person test, used throughout the law, was once easier to apply. But America's increased cultural, religious, and racial diversity are confounding to the test. It is argued, for example, that the definition of a reasonable person should be particularized to the defendant's identity. For example, a white man is killed by an African American man in response to a push and a racial slur. Should the reasonableness of the homicide be assessed from the perspective of a reasonable African American, or should it be evaluated from a reasonable person of no identity (raceless, genderless, etc.)? What about the reverse? Consider the homicide by a person of the Jewish faith of a vandal that is caught painting a swastika and destroying headstones in a Jewish cemetery. Should the reasonable person be defined as a reasonable Jewish person? Now, consider a third case. An interracial couple, white and Black, approach a known white supremacist and begin to kiss and fondle each other in front of him. If he reacts by killing one of them, should his homicide be viewed through the lens of a reasonable white supremacist? These are difficult questions that are answered differently by the courts.

The classic provocation is to find one's spouse sexually engaged with a third person. As the Latin phrase *in flagrante delicto* expresses, the spouse must be caught in the sexual act for this defense to be legitimate. A spouse who learns about a spouse's infidelity by text, email, from a nosey neighbor, or even by admission of the unfaithful spouse over dinner is not entitled to the protection of the provocation defense. For example, in a Louisiana case, a man was not entitled to a reduction in his murder conviction for shooting his estranged wife and lover in a bar after the wife told the husband that the boyfriend was good in bed.[11] A different outcome was reached, however, in a Massachusetts case where a wife confirmed her husband's suspicions of her infidelity by stating, while pointing to her crotch, "You will never touch this again because I have got something bigger and better for it." The appellate court ordered a retrial of the defendant with instructions that the jury be given the option of finding heat of passion manslaughter, in addition to murder; he was found not guilty of both charges.[12] Essentially, the court equated the shocking verbal admission of adultery to discovering a spouse physically engaged with a lover.

Because the defense is rooted in the moment—in reflex—the homicide must occur immediately in response to the provocation. If the defendant has had time to cool off, the defense isn't valid. A few seconds, maybe a few minutes, between the provocation and the homicide can be immediate. But not hours. Consider the following scenarios:

Breonna, who is cooking dinner, hears her 10-year-old son screaming for help from outside the house. Knife in hand, she runs outside and discovers a 30-year-old man slapping and pushing her son. She becomes enraged and stabs the man with the knife, inflicting a mortal wound. She is charged with murder. Breonna may argue heat of passion manslaughter to the jury.

Breonna returns from work to discover her 10-year-old son with bruises on his face. He tells her that their 30-year-old neighbor, Randall, hit him for running through his yard. Breonna stews for an hour, becoming more enraged as time passes. She loads a gun, walks over to Randall's home, knocks on the door, and shoots and kills Randall when he answers the door. Breonna has had time to form malice aforethought and is guilty of murder.

Mutual Combat

A second form of manslaughter occurs when two or more people agree to fight and one unintentionally kills the other. Mutual combat, as it is known, was once common in the United States. Boys fought on school playgrounds, and men brawled in bars. Until the early 1800s, even dueling was permitted in some states. The United States lost one of its prominent early citizens, Alexander Hamilton, to a duel in 1804. Hamilton was killed by Aaron Burr, who was vice president of the United States at the time, over political and personal disagreements. Early state laws commonly permitted fighting, as long as no one was seriously injured or killed. The elements of the defense of mutual combat are

1. Two or more adults
2. voluntarily consent
3. to assault one another,
4. and the assaults are proportional.

The cultural setting is different today. Fighting is discouraged in favor of discussion or the involvement of authorities, and only a handful of criminal codes continue to explicitly permit consensual fighting. Where permitted, mutual combat is a complete defense to assault and battery. But death is never justified. If a defendant unintentionally kills a fellow combatant, the defense of mutual combat is incomplete; the homicide is reduced from murder to manslaughter. The rationale for the reduction is that both parties were, at least partially, at fault. An alternative rationale is they both assumed some measure of risk. Of course, if a defendant can be shown to have intentionally killed an opponent, then heat of passion or malice aforethought murder has been committed. Similarly, mutuality assumes proportional violence. DeShawn and Andrew, for example, are not liable for punches to the stomach and nose if they agree to a fist fight. But mutual combat doesn't apply if one picks up a plank of wood and hits the other in the head. In this case, a battery has been committed.

Even though mutual combat is generally prohibited, there are exceptions, such as for-sport fighting. A losing boxer may not, for example, claim that the winner committed battery. Texas recognizes the defense of consent to assault and battery in three instances.

Texas Penal Code §22.06

a. The victim's effective consent or the actor's reasonable belief that the victim consented to the actor's conduct is a defense to prosecution under Section 22.01 (Assault), 22.02 (Aggravated Assault), or 22.05 (Deadly Conduct) if:

    1. the conduct did not threaten or inflict serious bodily injury; or

    2. the victim knew the conduct was a risk of:

        A. his occupation;

        B. recognized medical treatment; or

        C. a scientific experiment conducted by recognized methods.

b. The defense to prosecution provided by Subsection (a) is not available to a defendant who commits an offense described by Subsection (a) as a condition of the defendant's or the victim's initiation or continued membership in a criminal street gang.

See Figure 8.1, The Criminal Homicide Equation, for a summary of the various forms of homicide.

FIGURE 8.1 ■ The Criminal Homicide Equation
THE CRIMINAL HOMCIDE EQUATION
Express Murder = Malice Aforethought + Concurring Act + Death Caused by Defendant
Implied Murder = High Degree of Intent But Less Than Malice + Concurring Act + Death Caused by Defendant
Manslaughter = Reckless or Negligence + Concurring Act + Death Caused by Defendant
Felony Murder = No Intent or Negligence + No Act + Death Caused by Someone Other Than the Defendant

Imperfect Defenses

In Chapter 5, you learned that self-defense can be perfect or imperfect. If all of its elements are satisfied, a defendant goes free. As a reminder, the elements of self-defense are (1) an unprovoked (2) imminent threat (3) of bodily harm (4) requiring force to avoid the harm, and (5) the amount of force used was reasonable. There are circumstances when self-defense only partially absolves a defendant of liability. Take, for example, a case where a person unreasonably, but genuinely, believes that force is necessary. A second example is when a defendant is privileged to use nondeadly force to repel an attacker, but they use deadly force. In most states, these cases are punished as manslaughter. A third example applies in states that require retreat. If a defendant chooses to kill an intruder in the home rather than retreat, the crime may be reduced to manslaughter, provided the defendant's belief that the attacker presented a threat of serious bodily injury or death is reasonable. In a state that doesn't require retreat, however, the outcome would be different. The defendant would be guilty of no crime. These incomplete defenses, as you may have already surmised, are mens rea defenses with fancy names.

> Reese is having an extramarital affair. Although her husband has never been violent with her, he has told her on many occasions that women who cheat are the lowest form of humanity and that no one would blame a man for killing an unfaithful wife. One afternoon, she is with her lover when her husband comes home unexpectedly. Hearing his truck, she runs to the window and sees him jump out of his truck and run for the house. Fearing that he knows she is in the house with her lover, Reese grabs a handgun and shoots her husband the moment he enters the home. As it turns out, he was rushing home to get a tool that he needed for work. Reese didn't possess malice aforethought, and her belief that she needed to use deadly force was genuine, but it proved unnecessary and unreasonable. She has committed manslaughter.

> Jose is landscaping his yard. Suddenly, a man appears with a broom handle and hits him in the head, causing a laceration on Jose's forehead that begins to bleed. The attacker raises the broom handle above Jose's head a second time, with the apparent intent to hit Jose again. Jose grabs a hatchet he was using in the yard and strikes two blows to the attacker's chest, killing him. Jose's use of deadly force was excessive. He is guilty of manslaughter.

> Jose is landscaping his yard. Suddenly, a man appears with an ax. He wrongly claims that Jose has caused him to lose his job. He threatens to hit him with the axe. Jose is standing 15 feet from the man and can easily retreat into his house. Instead, he waits for the man to attack and shoots him with a handgun. Jose lives in a retreat state. He is guilty of manslaughter.

Misdemeanor Manslaughter

Felony murder is limited to felonies. The lower-crime counterpart is misdemeanor manslaughter. As is apparent from its name, this crime occurs when a death is a consequence of the commission of a misdemeanor. Similar to felony murder, many states limit misdemeanor manslaughter to specific, dangerous misdemeanor offenses. These statutes differ in how they list the possible predicate offenses. Some list specific crimes; others refer to inherently dangerous crimes, or they distinguish between crimes malum prohibitum and malum in se. The elements are identical to those of felony murder, except, of course, the level of the predicate offense.

1. The killing of
2. a human being

3. during the commission or attempted commission of a named misdemeanor, and

4. the misdemeanor is the proximate cause of the homicide.

State law permits the open carry of firearms, but it prohibits, as a misdemeanor, openly brandishing firearms in a menacing manner. State law also declares that any death resulting from the commission of a misdemeanor that involves a threat of life to another person to be misdemeanor manslaughter. Two days after an election, Tim unholsters his weapon in a public park and waves it around while screaming, "The election was stolen. I am killing someone who voted the wrong way today." Tyrell, who is standing nearby, witnesses the act, has a heart attack, and dies. Tim has committed misdemeanor manslaughter.

The state has the same misdemeanor manslaughter law just described. Tyrell grabs a handful of candy valued at $4 from the shelf of a store and runs away. The store clerk is frightened by the incident and dies from heart failure. Tyrell has not committed misdemeanor manslaughter.

State law requires dental hygienists to earn 10 continuing education credits per year to remain licensed. State law defines misdemeanor manslaughter as death resulting from malum in se misdemeanors. Anong has been a licensed hygienist for 10 years. During her 11th year, the birth of her second child and the death of her husband prevented her from finishing the last two hours of continuing education credit. As such, her license was suspended. Under state law, it is a misdemeanor to practice without a license. She accidentally cuts a patient's gum during a cleaning. The laceration leads to an infection that kills the patient. Anong has not committed misdemeanor manslaughter because the crime of failing to complete her continuing education is malum prohibitum.

QUESTIONS AND PROBLEMS

1. What are the elements of manslaughter caused by provocation?
2. What are the elements of mutual combat manslaughter?
3. What are the elements of misdemeanor manslaughter?
4. Referring to the earlier white supremacist scenario, it can be argued that racism is unreasonable, and as such, the reasonableness test should not be used in this manner. Do you agree? If so, do you believe that a racial epithet that is uttered toward a person of color should be evaluated through the lens of how a reasonable person of color would respond? Should the government favor one set of beliefs over others? What are the dangers and advantages of doing this? Discuss fully.

Identify what form of manslaughter, if any, is committed in each of the following scenarios. Explain your answers thoroughly, addressing the elements of the crime you choose.

5. Brooke suffers from arachnophobia, the fear of spiders. Her fear is so extreme that she has received counseling for it—without success—for years. One of her coworkers, Scut, is a known bully. He learns of her fear, brings a large spider to work, and threatens to throw it on her. Faced with the creature, she reaches for her purse, takes out a gun, and fatally shoots Scut. She also puts a round into the spider as it attempted to escape.

> **6.** State law defines misdemeanor manslaughter as a homicide resulting from the commission of a malum in se misdemeanor. State law also declares the purposeful serving of tainted or spoiled food a misdemeanor. Keenan owns a restaurant. His most popular meal is roasted pork. One morning, he discovers that he has 5 pounds of spoiled pork in his freezer. He sets it aside, intending to discard it. He forgets to throw it out and later cooks and serves it, killing a diner.

MURDER ISN'T WHAT IT USED TO BE: MODERN LAW

Learning Objective: Identify, compare, and contrast the various forms of criminal homicide under the MPC with their counterparts, if any, under the Common Law.

The distinction between murder and manslaughter continues today, but with even finer distinctions. In most jurisdictions, there are two grades of murder, commonly referred to as first and second degree, and two or more grades of manslaughter, commonly known as voluntary, involuntary, reckless, and negligent. With the understanding that state approaches to the grading and punishment of homicides vary, we will use the MPC as our model of modern homicide law.

The MPC, Section 210, begins by stating that all four mens rea—purposeful, knowledgeable, reckless, and negligent—form the basis of criminal homicide. There are three forms of criminal homicide: murder, manslaughter, and negligent homicide.

Homicide is murder, a felony of the first degree, when committed with

- purpose or

- knowingly or

- recklessly, under circumstances manifesting extreme indifference to the value of human life, and

- during the commission of, or flight from, robbery, rape, deviate sexual intercourse by force or threat, arson, burglary, kidnapping, or felonious escape, reckless is rebuttably presumed.

This is similar to the Common Law. Purposeful and knowing murders are the counterpart to malice aforethought murder; the reckless with extreme indifference murder is the counterpart to depraved heart murder; and the final form is the MPC's version of the felony murder. It adds a twist to the Common Law felony murder rule: It presumes recklessness and extreme indifference if one of the specified crimes is being committed. If the presumption is overcome by a defendant, the lesser crime of manslaughter will be found.

Manslaughter is graded as a felony of the second degree and is defined as a homicide committed by reckless behavior (without extreme indifference to life) or while under the "influence of extreme mental or emotional disturbance for which there is reasonable explanation or excuse." The determination of the reasonableness of this type of homicide is assessed through the eyes (or, more aptly, the mind) of the defendant at the time of the crime. Finally, homicides that are caused by negligence are labeled negligent homicides, punished as felonies of the third degree. The chart in Table 8.1 compares the Common Law and MPC approaches to homicide.

TABLE 8.1 ■ Homicide Under the MPC and Common Law	
Common Law	**MPC**
Malice aforethought murder	Purposeful; murder; felony of the first degree
Depraved heart murder	Knowing; reckless with extreme indifference; murder; felony of the first degree
Intent to do serious bodily harm murder	Knowing; reckless; murder; felony of the first degree
Felony murder	Presumption of reckless or indifference to life if homicide occurs during or flight from sex crimes, robbery, arson, burglary, kidnapping, or felonious escape; murder; felony of the first degree
Provocation	Yes, if extreme mental or emotional disturbance; manslaughter; felony of the second degree
Manslaughter	Reckless; murder; felony of the first degree
Wasn't criminalized	Negligence

In many states, there are more forms of murder than under the MPC. Murder in the first degree often includes purposeful and knowing homicides, and murder in the second degree includes provoked and other homicides where malice aforethought is absent. Similarly, states divide manslaughters by blameworthiness—commonly into voluntary and involuntary categories.

Typically, voluntary, or first-degree, manslaughters are committed recklessly, while involuntary manslaughters, also known as negligent or second-degree manslaughters, are homicides that are caused by negligence. Two examples of involuntary manslaughter are *Commonwealth of Massachusetts v. Michelle Carter* and *Roberson v. Texas*. In the first case, Michelle Carter was convicted by a juvenile court of involuntary manslaughter for encouraging her long-distance boyfriend to commit suicide. Because they lived far from one another, their communications were by text and phone. Before his death, the victim had shared his suicidal feelings with Ms. Carter on many occasions. She had dissuaded him from committing suicide on many previous occasions before not only encouraging him, but assisting him in planning his death.[13] In *Roberson*, a woman was convicted of manslaughter for falsely alleging that her lover was raping her, causing her husband, who had discovered the two romantically engaged, to shoot and kill the man.[14]

Many states have added vehicular homicide or manslaughter to their criminal codes. In most cases, vehicular homicide is treated similarly to involuntary manslaughter. However, cases of gross negligence, such as driving 70 miles per hour through a school zone, may be charged higher. The next Digging Deeper addresses whether a drug dealer is liable for manslaughter in the death of a customer who overdoses.

DIGGING DEEPER 8.2

Is a drug dealer criminally liable for the death of a customer who overdoses?

Case: *Maryland v. Thomas*
Court: Court of Appeals of Maryland.   Citation: 464 Md. 133, 153, 211 A.3d 274, 285
(2019)
Year: 2019
S. Adkins delivered the opinion of the court.

The past twenty years have seen a dramatic increase in heroin use, abuse, and accessibility. Unsurprisingly, Maryland has experienced a correlating spike in heroin and opioid-related deaths. Our State, and Marylanders alike, seek tools to combat this epidemic. We are asked to consider under what circumstances the dangers of heroin would justify holding a dealer liable for involuntary manslaughter for supplying the means by which his customer fatally overdoses....

[We hold that] there was sufficient evidence to convict Thomas of gross negligence involuntary manslaughter.

[The facts were not in dispute. The victim was discovered sitting on a toilet, dead from a heroin overdose. Phone records showed that the victim called the defendant 28 times in 22 minutes. Also, there were several text messages from the victim to the defendant.

Some read, "I got $30, man, call me, please." June 25, 2015, at [23:48] hours, "Call me." June 25, 2015, [23:48], "I'll come to you." June 26, 2015, at two minutes past midnight,... "I'm here, I need 4."... June 26, 2015, at [00:05] hours, "Yo, I'm here."

A subsequent search of the defendant's home discovered large quantities of heroin, much of it packed in the same manner as was found near the victim's body. Evidence was also submitted about the public's general knowledge of the dangerousness of heroin. The defendant confessed to selling the victim the heroin, knew he was young, found the time he received the calls and texts from the victim unusual, and while he acknowledged knowing that heroin can cause death, he was surprised that the amount he sold the victim killed him.]

The State presented two possible theories for an involuntary manslaughter conviction: unlawful act manslaughter and gross negligence manslaughter. The court determined that Thomas could be convicted under either theory. Specifically, the judge concluded that Thomas was grossly negligent because the testimony would have shown that "it is well known that, in fact, the use of heroin can cause death," and Thomas' statement to police demonstrated that he was so aware....

In Maryland, involuntary manslaughter is a common law felony.... Involuntary manslaughter is the unintentional killing of a human being, irrespective of malice. There are generally thought to be three varieties of involuntary manslaughter: (1) unlawful act manslaughter—"doing some unlawful act endangering life but which does not amount to a felony"; (2) gross negligence manslaughter—"negligently doing some act lawful in itself"; and (3) "the negligent omission to perform a legal duty." For the latter two categories of involuntary manslaughter, "the negligence [must] be criminally culpable"—i.e., grossly negligent. The present case involves only the second variety: gross negligence involuntary manslaughter.

The State must also demonstrate a "causal connection between such gross negligence and death... to support a conviction, although it is not essential that the ultimate harm which resulted was foreseen or intended." This includes actual, but-for causation and legal causation. The legal cause analysis "turns largely upon the foreseeability of the consequence" of the defendant's acts or omissions and whether "the ultimate harm is one which a reasonable man would foresee as being reasonably related to the acts of the defendant."...

Maryland case law describing the 'gross negligence' necessary to support a conviction for involuntary manslaughter equated 'gross negligence' with a 'wanton or reckless disregard for human life.'... The act must "manifest[] such a gross departure from what would be the conduct of an ordinarily careful and prudent person under the same circumstances so as to furnish evidence of indifference to the consequences." Moreover, the defendant, or an ordinarily prudent person under similar circumstances, should be conscious of this risk. See id. Still, these definitions, while somewhat descriptive, are of limited practical use.

It is difficult to draw an exact line dividing gross negligence from the lower ordinary negligence standard, or from the higher depraved-heart standard. Although, as recognized by Judge Moylan, these mentes reae exist one-after-the-other on a continuum of culpability....

Our courts have discussed gross negligence involuntary manslaughter in four main contexts: automobiles, police officers, failure to perform a duty, and weapons. None of these provide a perfect analog for heroin distribution, but, together, they create a helpful tableau depicting how we assess a defendant's level of negligence....

It is undisputed that Thomas was knowingly engaged in the unregulated selling of a CDS with no known medical benefit—an addictive and useless poison—to customers in a region suffering from an epidemic of heroin and opioid abuse and deaths. The agreed facts provide that Thomas was surprised that Colton fatally overdosed from four bags of Banshee heroin. Assuredly, he may have felt pangs of conscience. But these facts do not overcome the risk and inherent dangerousness of the underlying activity. Indeed, according to the agreed statement of facts, "anyone in Thomas' situation would understand the dangers of heroin, and its propensity to harm physically, if not kill, individuals who are ingesting it." The agreed facts also include a description of what Detective Johns, testifying as an expert in CDS investigations, would say at a trial—that Worcester County "has been consumed with heroin overdoses, some resulting in deaths, and that these overdoses have resulted in an acute awareness of the dangers of heroin." In his words, "heroin kills, and everyone knows it." His proffered testimony is consistent with data collected by the State of Maryland's Department of Health and Mental Hygiene regarding fatal overdoses from heroin and other opioids. In 2015, the year Colton died, there were 1,259 deaths from alcohol and drugs in Maryland—86% of these were opioid-related. In this State, fatal overdoses from heroin rose dramatically between 2011 and 2015, from 247 to 748 overdoses, vastly exceeding the number of deaths caused by any other drug, including fentanyl.

It is also fair to infer that Thomas subjectively knew an overdose was possible based on his statement that Colton "couldn't have overdosed off [the amount] I sold him." It is enough that Thomas knew about the overdose risks of heroin. That he knew about the risk but wrongly estimated the amount of heroin sufficient to kill his customer does not remove his conduct from the reckless and wanton category. Again, involuntary manslaughter does not involve an intent to kill, but only a reckless disregard of another person's life....

A reasonable person in Thomas' place would have understood that Colton was desperate for heroin and would have realized that increased the risk of the transaction. The facts state that Colton had been abusing heroin for approximately four-and-a-half years, and Thomas knew he was a "young boy" who had been in prison in Pennsylvania sometime in the past. On the night of his fatal overdose, Colton called Thomas 27 or 28 times between 11:45 p.m. and 12:07 a.m.—more than one call per minute—until Thomas finally answered. Colton also sent multiple text messages to Thomas in that same timeframe, imploring him to "call me, please" and stating that he would "come to [Thomas]" to get the heroin. Moreover, Thomas recognized that it was "unusual" for him to meet Colton at midnight and that he "usually met him earlier." All of these facts support the inference that Colton was desperately in need of heroin and might well ingest the entire four bags of heroin immediately. It is also relevant to distinguish the systematic and sustained heroin distributor from the infrequent or inexperienced provider. The agreed statement of facts reveals a substantial amount about Thomas' heroin distribution practices. Thomas resupplies his heroin stock "every two to three days," when he travels to Delaware to purchase five bundles (50–65 total bags of heroin) for $300. Thomas is a heroin abuser, himself; presumably consumes between 24 to 36 bags of each resupply; and sells the remainder for $10–$15 per bag, an amount which consistently nets him a profit. At the time of his arrest, Thomas possessed 13.10 grams (60 bags) of heroin. From all this, it is evident that Colton was not Thomas' only client and that Thomas consistently distributed heroin to a substantial network of associates. Thus, we can infer that Thomas was aware of the risk to life posed by consistent heroin abuse, cognizant of its ill-effects, and, yet, continued to sell the drug notwithstanding its danger....

Based on his own admissions, Thomas should have reasonably concluded that Colton was also likely to use all four bags in one shot—as Thomas himself does—a fact he implicitly recognized when he stated that "he couldn't have overdosed off what I sold him" because it was only four bags. Thomas sold Colton four bags of heroin, likely to be used at once, without knowing anything about the composition of the heroin he sold, about what other substances Colton was taking or might have used that day, or about Colton's tolerance given his age and recent incarceration. To knowingly distribute a dangerous, and sometimes lethal, substance without such information qualifies as "a gross departure from what would be the conduct of an ordinarily careful and prudent person under the same circumstances." Failure to obtain this information represents an "indifference to [the] consequences" that may result.

[The conviction for gross negligence involuntary manslaughter is affirmed.]

Often, lower forms of murder and manslaughter are lesser included offenses of higher forms of the crimes. A prosecutor who isn't confident that purpose or extreme indifference to life can be proved is likely to stack the higher form of murder with a reckless or negligent manslaughter charge. In addition to increasing the probability of a single conviction, it can produce two guilty verdicts. Although the convictions will merge for purposes of punishment, it guards against a defendant walking free should one of the convictions be overturned on appeal. Derek Chauvin, the Minneapolis police officer who murdered George Floyd in 2020, is an example. Chauvin was convicted of three forms of homicide. The first, second-degree murder, required the state to prove that Chauvin killed Floyd during the commission of an assault. The second, third-degree murder, is Minnesota's depraved heart murder. And the third, second-degree manslaughter, is Minnesota's negligent homicide law. Chauvin was sentenced to 22.5 years in prison for second-degree murder. But if that conviction were to be reversed, he would remain in prison for his other convictions.

Because of the gravity of taking life, murder continues to be punished severely. Twenty-eight states statutorily authorize capital punishment for murder. Regardless, few executions are performed in the United States. Twenty-two people were executed in 2019 and 15 in 2020.[15] Instead, most murderers are sentenced to long terms of prison, often life or life without the possibility of parole. Because of the variance in the wrongfulness among the different forms of manslaughter, a common punishment doesn't exist. Sentences vary from very short, sometimes suspended terms of imprisonment for negligent homicide to decades of time for voluntary manslaughter.

QUESTIONS AND PROBLEMS

1. What is the MPC mens rea counterpart to the Common Law malice aforethought?
2. What is the MPC mens rea counterpart to the Common Law depraved heart murder?
3. What is the MPC mens rea counterpart to the Common Law intent to inflict serious bodily harm murder?
4. What is the Common Law mens rea counterpart to the MPC negligent homicide?

DEATH BEFORE BIRTH: FETICIDE

Learning Objective: Explain why a mother may choose to abort a fetus without committing feticide.

Feticide is the destruction or homicide of a fetus. Feticide was not a crime at the Common Law. Murder was defined as the killing of a human being, and life didn't begin until a person was born alive. Today, about 40 states criminalize the act of killing a fetus. These states vary in how they determine when the fetus is protected by homicide laws. Some states, such as Alabama, protect fetuses from the moment of conception.[16] A few states require that a fetus be more developed. One method is to protect the child when it quickens, or when it first moves, which can be as early as 10 weeks. This is the Michigan approach.[17] Still other states wait until a fetus is viable—capable of living on its own, outside the womb.[18] Viability varies but can be as early as 24 weeks. Where murdering a fetus is criminalized, it is typically found in the criminal code as a form of murder, or it increases the punishment for the murder or battery of the mother.

No discussion of feticide is complete without addressing abortion rights. In what is one of the best-known, and most controversial, SCOTUS decisions, *Roe v. Wade* (1973),[19] a pregnant woman possesses a right to decide to end her pregnancy, subject to minimal regulations. The *Roe* court decided that the liberty right extends from conception until fetal viability. Specifically, the court held that a woman's right to abort was absolute during the first trimester of pregnancy, subject to reasonable regulations during the second trimester, and could be forbidden when viability was reached in the third trimester, except when the life or health of the mother is threatened by the pregnancy.

In the 1992 decision *Casey v. Planned Parenthood*,[20] the court affirmed the right to abortion, as it had done several times before, until viability. But it set aside the trimester analysis in favor of a standard that forbids regulations that "unduly burden" the pre-viability right. A regulation is unduly burdensome if it places a "substantial obstacle in the path of a woman seeking an abortion of a nonviable fetus." The court applied this test to the restrictions imposed by Pennsylvania and held that the state's requirement that a woman notify her spouse about the pregnancy to be unduly burdensome. But it upheld a 24-hour waiting period, informed consent (disclosure of the details and risks of the procedure), and parental consent for minors, subject to the option of a court giving approval in special circumstances, such as when a girl doesn't have a parent available or the pregnancy is the result of parental rape. Since *Casey*, several other cases have applied the unduly burdensome standard.

Why can a person who attacks a mother causing a miscarriage be prosecuted for feticide, but a mother can terminate the same fetus without liability? Because the fetus, and the liberty right to her body, are held by the mother. The law balances the liberty and health interests of the mother against the state's interests in protecting the fetus. Indeed, the mother's health interest is taken very seriously by the court. It has affirmed time and again since *Roe* that the government can't force a woman to complete a pregnancy if it threatens her health or life. A third party, on the other hand, has no health or liberty interests to balance against the state's interests; feticide by any person except the mother and the medical professionals who provide protected abortive services may be punished.

QUESTIONS AND PROBLEMS

1. What is feticide?
2. What was the holding in *Roe v. Wade*?
3. How did *Casey v. Planned Parenthood* both affirm and change the *Roe v. Wade* decision?
4. A state enacts the following statute. Discuss the constitutionality of the various requirements of the law.

Protecting Fathers, Parents, and Viable Fetuses Act

Any mother who elects to abort a fetus, under any circumstance, shall be required to do the following:

1. She must show proof to the physician, clinic, hospital, or other medical professional that she has informed the father of the fetus of the pregnancy and of her decision to abort.
2. If the mother is less than 16 years of age, she shall also be required to show proof that she has informed her parents of the pregnancy and that she has obtained their consent to the abortion.
3. No abortion shall be performed after a fetus is independently viable.

KILLED WITH KINDNESS: ASSISTED SUICIDE

Learning Objective: Define assisted suicide and explain what crimes are committed by the act, if not protected by law.

At one time, suicide was a crime—a serious crime. The offender was punished with a dishonorable burial in a public highway with a stake driven through the body, and all property was forfeited to the crown. Blackstone explained it this way:

> [T]he law of England wisely and religiously considers that no man hath a power to destroy life but by commission from God, the author of it; and as the suicide is guilty of a double offense, one spiritual, in evading the prerogative of the Almighty, and rushing into his immediate presence uncalled for; the other temporal, against the king, who hath an interest in the preservation of all his subjects, the law has, therefor e, ranked this among the highest crimes, making it a peculiar species of felony, a felony committed on one's self.[21]

Attempted suicides were misdemeanors and, accordingly, subject to lesser punishment. The British treatment of suicide was transported to the American colonies, although a few decriminalized the act early in their histories. Six of the 13 states had decriminalized suicide by 1798.[22] Today, suicide is criminalized throughout the United States. This isn't universally true, although many nations continue to treat suicide and attempted suicide as crimes.

But this doesn't close the book on criminal law and suicide. Assisted suicide remains a legal and controversial problem. Assisted suicide refers to a second party helping an individual, at their request, to die. It comes up most often in the context of a physician providing a patient who is terminally ill and suffering with the means to die. In many states, assisting death is criminal homicide.

A famous case of physician assisted suicide is that of Dr. Jack Kevorkian. Popularly known as "Dr. Death," Kevorkian helped nearly 2 dozen terminally ill patients die in the 1990s. After several unsuccessful prosecutions, he was convicted of second-degree murder and sentenced to prison. What was different in his final prosecution was his role. In the earlier cases, he provided the mechanism of death but didn't "push the button." In the case where he was convicted, Kevorkian administered the injection that caused his patient to die.

During and after his release, Kevorkian advocated for the right to die and for the right of physicians to assist terminally ill patients to die. He was also a proponent of the Ninth Amendment, believing that it secured many rights not protected by the other amendments. Unsurprisingly, he contended that the right to die was one of the rights guaranteed by the Ninth Amendment.[23]

Attempts to protect the individual's right to die, and by extension the right to have the help of another person, have failed. SCOTUS held in 1997 that the Fourteenth Amendment's protection of liberty doesn't include the right to die.[24]

PHOTO 8.2 Dr. Jack Kevorkian, a physician who was prosecuted on several occasions and convicted once for assisting terminally ill patients in ending their lives. In this photo, he is advocating for an enlarged role for the Ninth Amendment.

Bill Pugliano / Stringer / Getty Images

But there are a handful of states that explicitly permit physician-assisted suicide for terminally ill patients. In 2019, Hawaii's Death With Dignity Act became effective. For the Hawaii law to apply, the patient

- shall be at least 18 years old;

- shall have a terminal, incurable, and irreversible disease that will result in death within 6 months, confirmed by two physicians;

- shall make two oral requests to die, at least 20 days apart;

- shall make a signed, written request that is witnessed by two people (one unrelated to the patient);

- shall be not suffering from depression or another condition that might interfere with the patient's ability to make an informed decision.

QUESTIONS AND PROBLEMS

1. Does a person have a constitutional right to die?
2. What does Hawaii's Death With Dignity Act require before a physician may assist a patient to die?

IN A NUTSHELL

The ancient definition of murder, a killing with malice aforethought, has stood the test of time. Some states continue to use the precise language of the Common Law to describe murder. Even in those that don't, they only use different words to express the same idea. Over hundreds of years, so-called implied murders were developed to address situations where offenders didn't act maliciously, but who were nonetheless highly blameworthy. All three—intent to commit serious bodily injury, depraved heart, and felony murder—continue to be recognized in most jurisdictions. Also, manslaughter was developed to address situations where defendants were even less blameworthy, such as when provoked or when they acted recklessly or negligently.

The variety of mentes raea that were slowly recognized in the Common Law and formed the basis of the murder/manslaughter distinction were organized by the drafters of the MPC into four levels: purpose, knowing, reckless, and negligent. This approach has been adopted by most jurisdictions, with variations.

The level of intent is most often what decides what grade of homicide is to be charged, with purposeful murder at the top and negligent homicide at the bottom. The gradation of crimes is tricky. Many factors are considered, including the offender's criminal and mental health history, motive, whether the offense was committed with a weapon, whether the victim suffered, and the impact of the crime on the victim. Overlap exists in some jurisdictions between the bottom end of the punishment for a higher crime and the top end of the next-lower crime. For example, the prison range for first-degree murder may be 30 years to life, and the range for second-degree murder may be 20 years to 40 years. So it is possible for a person convicted of second-degree murder to be sentenced to less time than another person convicted of first-degree murder.

Another change to the Common Law is the crime of feticide. Killing a fetus was not a crime for hundreds of years, although a person could be punished for battery or murder of the mother. Feticide is a crime today nearly everywhere, subject to the exception of the constitutionally protected right of a mother to end a pregnancy.

LEGAL TERMS

agency theory (p. 253)

brain death (p. 245)

deadly weapon doctrine (p. 247)

Depraved heart murder (p. 247)

express murder (p. 244)

felony murder (p. 252)

heat of passion (p. 256)

implied murder (p. 244)

intent to cause serious bodily injury murder (p. 246)

malice aforethought murder (p. 245)

proximate cause (p. 245)

NOTES

1. A. Liptak, "Serving Life for Providing Car to Killers," *New York Times*, December 4, 2007, and J. Wallace, "Governor and Cabinet Cut Two Prison Sentences in Rare Clemency Action," *Tampa Bay Times*, June 24, 2015, accessed November 23, 2020, Tampabay.com.

2. *State v. Myers*, 7 N.J. 465, 81 A.2d 710 (1951).

3. MPC §210.04.

4. *People v. Ross*, 831 P.2d 1310 (1992).

5. The case had a long and torturous history. Wilkins's conviction was overturned because of police misconduct. He was retried, convicted, and sentenced to 16 years to life. In 2020, his conviction was reduced to manslaughter, and he was resentenced to 4 years in prison, about a third of the time he already spent in prison. See Alma Fausto and Tony Saavedra, "Man Driving Truck That Dropped Stove on California Freeway, Killing a Deputy, Is Set Free," *East Bay Times*, March 11, 2020, accessed November 25, 2020, eastbaytimes.com.

6. *Enmund v. Florida*, 458 U.S. 782 (1982).

7. *Tison v. Arizona*, 481 U.S. 137, 158 (1987).

8. *Roper v. Simmons*, 543 U.S. 551 (2005).

9. Tom Barber, "The Anatomy of Florida's Corpus Delicti Doctrine," *The Florida Bar Journal* 74 (2000): 80.

10. Thomas A. Green, "The Jury and English Law of Homicide 1200–1600," *Michigan Law Review* 74 (1975–1976): 413, 473.

11. *State v. Thorne*, 633 So. 2d 773 (La. App. 5 Cir. 1994).

12. *Commonwealth v. Schnopps*, 383 Mass. 178, 417 N.E.2d 1213 (1981). On retrial where the jury was instructed that they could find murder or heat of passion manslaughter, Schnopps was again convicted of murder. 390 Mass. 722 (1984).

13. "*Commonwealth v. Carter*: Trial Court Convicts Defendant of Involuntary Manslaughter Based on Encouragement of Suicide," *Harvard Law Review* 131 (2018): 918.

14. *Roberson v. Texas*, Court of Appeals, Ft. Worth (2010).

15. Death Penalty Information Center. Accessed December 3, 2020, deathpenaltyinfo.org.

16. Ala. Code 13A-6-1.

17. Mich. Comp. Laws Ann. § 750.322.

18. Md. Criminal Law Code Ann. § 2-103.

19. *Roe v. Wade*, 410 U.S. 113 (1973).

20. *Casey v. Planned Parenthood*, 505 U.S. 833.

21. Lawrence T. Hammond, Jr., "Attempted Suicide," *North Carolina Law Review* 40 (1962): 323.

22. Helen Y. Chang, "A Brief History of Anglo-Western Suicide: From Legal Wrong to Civil Right," *Southern University Law Review* 46 (2018): 150, 174.

23. Fred Charatan, "Dr. Kevorkian Found Guilty of Second-Degree Murder," *U.S. National Library of Medicine*, April 10, 1999. Accessed on October 7, 2021, https://www.ncbi.nlm.nih.gov.

24. *Washington v. Glucksberg*, 521 U.S. 702 (1997).

9 CRIMES AGAINST PROPERTY

In 2019, the tabloid newspaper *National Enquirer* reported that Jeff Bezos, the founder of Amazon and, at the time, the wealthiest person on Earth, had an extramarital affair. The story included text messages sent between Mr. Bezos and his paramour. In response, Bezos hired an investigator to determine how the *National Enquirer* acquired his private texts. He also alleged that the story was politically motivated. The parent company of the *National Enquirer*, American Media, Inc. (AMI), responded to the inquiry and to Bezos's allegation that it had political motives by sending Bezos a message threatening to release intimate photos of him and his lover if he didn't agree to several terms, including a "public, mutually-agreed upon acknowledgement from the Bezos Parties, released through a mutually agreeable news outlet, affirming that they have no knowledge of basis for suggesting that AM's coverage was politically motivated or influenced by political forces." Bezos made the entire matter, including AMI's messages, public. He alleged that AMI was attempting to blackmail him.[1]

This chapter is titled "Crimes Against Property." Of course, property doesn't feel pain, hunger, or emotion, nor does it have an interest in financial security. But people do. So the subject of the crimes in this chapter is property, but it is people who are harmed.

The Common Law has long protected property rights. The Framers believed property and economic rights were fundamental liberties that were important features of human autonomy and necessary to the nation's economic vitality. Alexander Hamilton commented at the Constitutional Convention that "[one duty of government] is the personal protection and security of property." James Madison, the lead author of the Constitution, wrote that "government is instituted to protect property of every sort." The Fifth Amendment, and later the Fourteenth Amendment, protected property from the government by requiring due process of law before it is taken, just compensation by the government when taken, and limiting takings for purpose of "public use." As did their model, the Framers left it to the states to protect people and their property from one another.

Property crime is common and expensive. In 2019, there were an estimated 6,925,677 larcenies, burglaries, and arsons in the United States. Larceny accounted for more than 70% of these crimes. While property crimes may not be as heinous as battery, murder, and rape, the repercussions on victims' emotional, physical, and financial health are often serious. Although property crime is frequent, its rate declined significantly in the late 2010s, as shown in Table 9.1.

These data don't include one of the most frequently violated property crimes: trespass.

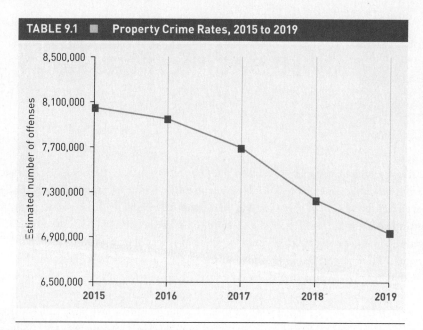

TABLE 9.1 ■ Property Crime Rates, 2015 to 2019

Source: FBI. 2019. "Crime in the United States." Accessed December 2020. ucr.fbi.gov..

FORGIVE ME MY TRESPASSES

Learning Objective: Identify, describe, and apply the elements of trespass.

To unlawfully enter—or remain on property—is criminal **trespass**. This crime is closely connected to property and tort law. Criminal trespass, for example, borrows property law's framing of the right to property (e.g., who has a right to use property, when, and how). If a defendant charged with criminal trespass claims that he had a right to be on the property, the criminal court will turn to property law to decide if the claim is legitimate.

In this context, property refers to real property and land and things permanently attached to it, such as homes, garages, barns, and fences. Personal property is everything else. Interfering with a person's possession or use of personal property is typically treated not as a trespass, but as larceny or mischief. These crimes are discussed later in this chapter.

The MPC, §221, identifies two forms of trespass. The first occurs when a person enters or surreptitiously remains in a building with knowledge that he has no legal right (no "privilege" or "license") to be there. This offense is graded higher if the act occurs at night, for the same reason burglaries at night are considered more serious than during the day. You will read more about this in a short time. The second form of trespass occurs when the actor is put on notice of his trespass by actual communication, fencing, or signage—the classic "No Trespassing" sign, as seen in Photo 9.1. The MPC refers to this type of offender as a defiant trespasser. Exceptions to criminal trespass are recognized, such as for abandoned property.

Trespass: For an actor to enter or remain on property with knowledge that they have no legal right to be on the property.

PHOTO 9.1 To unlawfully enter—or remain on property—is criminal trespass.

traviswolfe/iStock

Many states follow the MPC, requiring actual knowledge that the person had no right to be on the property. Therefore, the backpacker who inadvertently hikes onto private property that adjoins a public wilderness area has not committed trespass. But the outcome would be different if the backpacker jumped a fence or ignored a private-property sign.

Sometimes, it isn't clear if a person has a right to be on, or to use, property. This is where property law fills in some blanks. Ownership of property doesn't always end the analysis. The question is whether the actor has a right to use the property in the way they did, at the time they did. Consider the landlord–tenant relationship. A landlord's ownership of an apartment building doesn't give the landlord license to enter a tenant's apartment at any time. Instead, the lease agreement and statutory law define the rights of the landlord. Typically, landlords have contractual and statutory rights to inspect their property periodically, with notice to the tenant, and to enter to make repairs and address emergencies. Other entries by the property owner are criminal trespass.

Another example is privately owned businesses that are open to the public. With a few exceptions, such as when public accommodations laws require a business to provide service to a person (i.e., no matter their race, sex, sexual orientation, etc.) or an individual has another legal right to be on the grounds (e.g., police or code inspectors in the performance of their duties), business owners are free to decline service and exclude people from their businesses. People who refuse to leave—or return when they have been told they are not welcome—are trespassers.

So far, we have only examined private lands. But it is possible to trespass on public lands as well. Some public lands are highly restricted, such as military bases and critical infrastructure facilities. Scaling a fence at an army base, water treatment plant, chemical storage facility, pipeline, communication facility, or nuclear power plant is often subject to prosecution under special trespass laws that are graded higher than other trespasses, sometimes elevating the crime from a misdemeanor to a felony.

Trespass of areas normally open to the public also occurs when an actor crosses the line between lawful use of the property and unlawful use:

> A person has a right to stand in front of a courthouse and hand out literature about the unfairness of the criminal justice system. The same person who blocks the door to the courthouse and prevents people from entering commits criminal trespass (and possibly other crimes).

> Protestors have a First Amendment right to gather and to express their opinions in a public space, but they commit criminal trespass (and possibly other crimes) if they block traffic during their protest.

The siege of the United States Capitol on January 6, 2021, saw hundreds of trespassers. One of the defendants is alleged to have said he wouldn't be charged for his acts because "the Capitol building is owned by the people, so again, nothing will happen."[2] This is, of course, wrong. Every person doesn't have the right to access or use any publicly owned space anytime they want. Entering or remaining on public space in violation of posted rules or after being ordered to leave is trespass, and using force to enter or remain is either aggravated trespass or a separate crime. The trespasses and other crimes committed at the Capitol will be discussed in greater detail in Chapter 12.

As you read earlier, trespass to personal property is most often categorized as something other than trespass. A few exceptions can be found in state laws—trespass to automobiles, for example. The following Illinois statute does this:

Criminal trespass to vehicles

    a. A person commits criminal trespass to vehicles when he or she knowingly and without authority enters any part of or operates any vehicle, aircraft, watercraft, or snowmobile.

    b. Sentence. Criminal trespass to vehicles is a Class A misdemeanor.[3]

As a lesser included offense, trespass merges into the next crime, burglary.

QUESTIONS AND PROBLEMS

1. What are the elements of trespass?

Has trespass been committed in the following two scenarios? Explain your answer.

2. Lorne Cartwright owns thousands of acres of land in Nevada. He hired a surveyor who mapped his land, and he and his sons fenced most of it. The surveyor made an error

that included 100 acres of a neighbor's land. Lorne rode his horse on this area of land. His neighbor wants him arrested for trespass.

3. Ping owns an electronics store. In response to an outbreak of a deadly virus, she requires everyone in the store, employees and customers, to wear masks and to socially distance. Ira enters the store without a mask. Ping asks Ira to either put on a mask or to leave. Ira refuses to don a mask or to leave, stating, "This is a free country, and you are a public business. I don't have to wear what you say."

HOME SWEET HOME

Learning Objective: Identify and compare and contrast the elements of burglary and breaking and entering.

Closely related to trespass is burglary. At the Common Law, burglary was defined as this:

1. The breaking and entering

2. of another's dwelling

3. at night

4. for the purpose of committing a felony once inside.

The first element required a breaking and entering into the home. Passing through an unlocked door or window didn't satisfy this element. Over time, the breaking requirement was softened to include any act that changed the conditions under which the actor entered the home. So opening a closed door or window constituted a breaking in most jurisdictions, even though the act of passing through either if opened remained outside of the definition. Additionally, "constructive breakings," or when an actor uses fraud or force to gain entry, eventually satisfied the breaking element of burglary. So if a burglar poses as a telephone repair worker to gain entry, then the breaking element has been satisfied. The same is true if the owner consents to the burglar's entry under threat or the use of force.

After the breaking, an entry of the home had to occur. The burglar's body doesn't have to fully enter the home; an arm stretched in through a window to grab a diamond earring is satisfactory.

The second element is that the structure broken into had to be another person's dwelling. Breaking into a building that was not commonly inhabited was not burglary at the Common Law. The home didn't have to be inhabited at the time of the breaking. It was enough that the structure was commonly used for sleeping. The occupant doesn't have to be the owner; the presence of a tenant or guest made the structure a dwelling. Applying these rules, apartments and hotels were considered dwellings, as were buildings that multipurposed as a person's business

---

Burglary: The breaking and entering of a structure with the intent to commit a felony.

and home. Reflecting an archaic legal perspective, in 1888 a New York court concluded that churches were dwellings, regardless of whether anyone lived inside, because they were the "mansion house of God."[4] Also, the dwelling had to belong to another person; it was not possible to burglarize one's own home.

Many modern statutes have broadened the property element of burglary to include more than homes. Among the states that do this, many continue to punish burglaries of dwellings more severely than other structures. Virginia's law is an example of the old school approach:

§ 18.2-89. Burglary; how punished

If any person breaks and enters the dwelling house of another in the nighttime with intent to commit a felony or any larceny therein, he shall be guilty of burglary, punishable as a Class 3 felony; provided, however, that if such person was armed with a deadly weapon at the time of such entry, he shall be guilty of a Class 2 felony.

Idaho has expanded burglary to include other properties:

18-1401. BURGLARY DEFINED. Every person who enters any house, room, apartment, tenement, shop, warehouse, mill, barn, stable, outhouse, or a building other than one defined in section 18-1401A, Idaho Code, tent, vessel, vehicle, trailer, airplane, or railroad car with intent to commit any theft or any felony is guilty of burglary.

The third element required that the offense happen at night. The distinction between daytime and nighttime crimes involving habitation is very old. You saw this distinction earlier with trespass. The rationale for the special nighttime protection is intuitive. The home is a safe sanctuary where most people let their guards down. For both animals and people, sleep is a vulnerable time. When suddenly awakened, people don't always think clearly. The likelihood of instinctive and possibly, unnecessary, violence in response to an intruder is greatest while asleep. Blackstone put it this way:

[T]he malignity of the offense does not so properly arise from its being done in the dark, as in the dead of night, when all the creation, except beasts of prey, are at rest; when sleep has disarmed the owner and rendered his castle defenceless.[5]

For these reasons, the law seeks to deter nighttime intrusions into homes. Historically, dawn and dusk were used to define nighttime. Moonlight, eclipses, and other phenomena were not considered. Today, a few jurisdictions continue to require that the crime occurs at night. Most have abandoned this element, although they continue to grade nighttime burglaries as more serious than daytime intrusions. Similarly, as is seen in the Virginia law presented earlier, some states aggravate the crime if the burglar possesses a weapon, explosives, or other dangerous tools. For those who continue to distinguish night from day, sunset and sunrise are often used to draw the line between night and day. In some jurisdictions, to ensure that an actor has committed the crime during the night, not during twilight, the breaking must occur no less than 30 minutes after dusk and before dawn.

The final element concerns the intent of the breaking and entering: The actor must intend to commit a felony when inside. The states are split on the predicate crime element. In some states, all felonies qualify. In others, the predicate felonies are limited, commonly to theft, murder, felonious assault, rape, and arson. This element distinguishes burglary from breaking and entering and trespass. To enter a person's land without legal right and without a breaking is trespass; to break in and enter without legal right and without the intention of committing a felony is a breaking and entering; and to break in and enter without legal right and possibly at night, with the intention to commit a felony, is burglary. See Figure 9.1 for a comparison of trespass, breaking and entering, and burglary.

FIGURE 9.1 ■ Trespass, Breaking and Entering, and Burglary

From Trespass to Burglary

Unlawful Entry or Remaining = Trespass

Unlawful Entry + Breaking + Entry = Breaking + Entering

Unlawful Entry + Breaking + Entering + Intent to Commit Felony + Possibly Night + Possibly Dwelling = Burglary

---

Mable Wood owns a home that sits across a public street from a golf course. Tired of golfers crossing the street and walking onto her property to retrieve their bad drives, she posts "No Trespassing" signs in her yard. Ima Rude hits a ball into Mable's yard, steps over the "No Trespassing" sign, and retrieves the ball. Ima committed criminal trespass.

Marv and Harry are homeless. On a cold night, they break into Kevin's house to get warm. They committed breaking and entering and the lesser included offense of trespass.

Marv and Harry are broke. For several days, they surveilled a neighborhood of valuable homes and identified a home they believed was vacant. They broke a window, crawled in, and stole $5,000 in jewelry, electronics, and cash. They committed burglary as well as the lesser included offenses of trespass and breaking and entering.

In summary, the elements of contemporary burglary are as follows:

1. The unlawful
   the actor's knowledge that no right or license to be there existed

2. breaking and entering

3. into a building
   variously defined as a dwelling, any building, specific buildings, automobiles, or some combination of these

4. at night
   in some states, at any time

5. with the intention to commit a felony.
   variously defined as any felony or one of several enumerated felonies

QUESTIONS AND PROBLEMS

1. What were the elements of burglary at the Common Law?
2. How is contemporary burglary different from the Common Law?
3. Distinguish burglary from breaking and entering.

WHERE THERE'S SMOKE, THERE'S FIRE

Learning Objective: Identify, describe, and apply the elements of arson.

2020 became a punchline as the year everyone wants to forget. In addition to COVID-19, the year saw raging wildfires in the U.S. West and buildings set ablaze during riots. Many of the wildfires were intentionally started, as were the burnings of public buildings. These acts illustrate our next crime, **arson**. The elements of arson at the Common Law were the

1. malicious

2. burning of a

3. dwelling house of

4. another.

Both the mens rea and actus reus were narrow. The act had to be malicious, only a dwelling could be burned (not other property), and a person wasn't guilty of arson for torching their own home, even if the intent was to file a fraudulent insurance claim.[6] This definition included outhouses and the area directly around the home ("curtilage"), as long as the area was commonly occupied by people. The burning of businesses and other structures was not arson.

To have been a burning, the dwelling must have been damaged, although evidence of a small burn, leaving only a charring, was enough to prove arson. However, the damage had to be made by the fire itself. Smoke discoloration from a fire that didn't touch the house was not arson. Oddly, causing a dwelling to explode was not arson, unless the house burned as a consequence of the explosion.

Modern law has broadened arson in several respects. To illustrate, read West Virginia's arson statute:

§61-3-1. Burning, etc., of a dwelling or outbuilding; first degree arson; penalty; definitions

    a. Any person who willfully and maliciously sets fire to or burns, or who causes to be burned, or who aids, counsels, procures, persuades, incites, entices or solicits

---

Arson: The purposeful, intentional burning of a structure.

any person to burn, any dwelling, whether occupied, unoccupied or vacant, or any outbuilding, whether the property of or herself or of another, shall be guilty of arson in the first degree and, upon conviction thereof, be sentenced to the penitentiary for a definite term of imprisonment which is not less than two nor more than twenty years....

b. As used in subsection (a) of this section:

1. "Dwelling" means any building or structure intended for habitation or lodging, in whole or in part, regularly or occasionally, and shall include, but not be limited to, any house, apartment, hotel, dormitory, hospital, nursing home, jail, prison, mobile home, house trailer, modular home, factory-built home or self-propelled motor home;

2. "Outbuilding" means any building or structure which adjoins, is part of, belongs to, or is used in connection with a dwelling, and shall include, but not be limited to, any garage, shop, shed, barn or stable.

West Virginia retains the high mens rea standard, willful and malicious, and the dwelling requirement. Varying from the Common Law, it criminalizes the burning of one's own dwelling. As was true at the Common Law, it includes outbuildings. The West Virginia code continues by creating second-degree arson, which applies to properties that are not homes:

§61-3-2. Burning, etc., of other buildings or structures; second degree arson; penalty

Any person who willfully and maliciously sets fire to or burns, or who causes to be burned, or who aids, counsels, procures, persuades, incites, entices or solicits any person to burn, any building or structure of any class or character, whether the property of himself or herself or of another, not included or prescribed in the preceding section, shall be guilty of arson in the second degree and, upon conviction thereof, be sentenced to the penitentiary for a definite term of imprisonment which is not less than one nor more than ten years.

Finally, the code makes the burning of personal property an arson of the third degree:

§61-3-3. Burning personal property of another of the value of five hundred dollars or more; third degree arson; penalty

Any person who willfully and maliciously sets fire to or burns, or who causes to be burned, or who aids, counsels, procures, persuades, incites, entices or solicits any person to burn, any personal property of any class or character, of the value of not less than $500, and the property of another person, shall be guilty of arson in the third degree and, upon conviction thereof, be sentenced to the penitentiary for a definite term of imprisonment which is not less than one nor more than three years. ...

This grading scheme is common. Because of a greater threat to life, the burning of a home continues to be the highest form of arson. But today, all states criminalize burning other structures as well. Many states specifically include forests, farming lands, and vehicles (cars, boats, recreational vehicles) in the list of properties protected by their arson laws.

PHOTO 9.2 Arson occurred during protesting and rioting over the death of George Floyd, who was killed by a police officer in May 2020.

Sipa USA via AP

The mens rea varies across the states. Some, like West Virginia, continue to expect the highest form of intent—purposeful, knowing, or malicious. Others have reduced the mens rea element to recklessness.

The federal government also has arson laws. Obviously, they apply to federal properties. But the United States has extended its reach beyond its property to state and local properties that were purchased with, or supported by, federal monies. On May 30, 2020, two New York attorneys—Urooj Rahman, 31, and Colinford Mattis, 32—are alleged to have thrown a homemade bomb, a Molotov cocktail, into an unoccupied New York City police van during a Black Lives Matter protest. It exploded, but no one was hurt.[7]

Because the New York City police department receives federal funding, the United States asserted jurisdiction, charging the two with several federal crimes, including arson. The relevant federal statute, 18 U.S.C. §844(i) reads,

Whoever maliciously damages or destroys, or attempts to damage or destroy, by means of fire or an explosive, any building, vehicle, or other real or personal property used in interstate or foreign commerce or in any activity affecting interstate or foreign commerce shall be imprisoned for not less than 5 years and not more than 20 years, fined under this title, or both; and if personal injury results to any person, including any public safety officer performing duties as a direct or proximate result of conduct prohibited by this subsection, shall be imprisoned for not less than 7 years and not more than 40 years, fined under this title, or both; and if death results to any person, including any public safety officer performing duties as a direct or proximate result of conduct prohibited by this subsection, shall also be subject to imprisonment for any term of years, or to the death penalty or to life imprisonment.

These cases, and others with similar facts, were pending when this book went to press. Whether the federal government's claim of jurisdiction is legitimate—as well as the guilt of the accused attorneys—remains to be seen.

QUESTIONS AND PROBLEMS

1. What were the elements of arson at the Common Law?
2. How is contemporary arson different from the Common Law?
3. For the following scenario, explain whether arson at the Common Law and in contemporary law is committed: Bradford burns down a local grocery. The owner of the grocery lives 10 miles from his store.

YOU BREAK IT, YOU PAY FOR IT

Learning Objective: Identify, describe, and apply the elements of criminal mischief.

Arson is one way to damage or destroy property. All other acts of intentional damaging property are known as **criminal mischief**. Texas's statute is typical:

Sec. 28.03. CRIMINAL MISCHIEF. (a) A person commits an offense if, without the effective consent of the owner:

1. he intentionally or knowingly damages or destroys the tangible property of the owner;

2. he intentionally or knowingly tampers with the tangible property of the owner and causes pecuniary loss or substantial inconvenience to the owner or a third person; or

3. he intentionally or knowingly makes markings, including inscriptions, slogans, drawings, or paintings, on the tangible property of the owner.

The statute continues by grading the offense by the nature of the property and the amount of actual or possible harm. Most cases of mischief are misdemeanors. But more serious cases are felonies. Tampering with a critical system, such as water supply and fire alarm and suppression, is an example of an offense that is graded highly because of the threat to life. Financial harm, even when there is no threat to life, is also a factor. The amount of damage, in dollar terms, can make the difference between misdemeanor and felonious mischief.

Criminal mischief: Intentionally damaging, destroying, defacing, or tampering with the personal property of another person.

The absence of the owner's consent is an element in every jurisdiction, and most require a high mens rea—purposeful, knowing, and, occasionally, reckless. The actus reus can be causing damage, destroying, or simply tampering with the property. Like Texas, most criminal mischief statutes refer to tangible property. This includes all forms of physical property, both real and personal. Intangible property includes things like patents, copyrights, licenses, and software. The following are examples of what does and doesn't qualify as criminal mischief.

In the nighttime hours and without permission, Bang Sih painted a mural of a famous chef on the side of Horizon's headquarters, a telecommunications company. He committed criminal mischief.

Duke Davidson, the founder of an anti-Semitic organization, got drunk and without permission went into a Jewish graveyard and painted swastikas on four headstones. He committed criminal mischief.

Randall is with a group of kids. He is challenged by one of the boys to hit a streetlamp with a rock. After three attempts, he hits and breaks the light. He committed criminal mischief.

Jada lives next door to Will. A fence separates their properties. She was told by the previous owner of her house that the fence falls on her property. She paints both sides of the fence. Will objects and hires a surveyor, who determines that the fence is just inside of Will's property line. Jada is not guilty of criminal mischief because she acted negligently.

QUESTIONS AND PROBLEMS

1. What are the elements of criminal mischief?

Has criminal mischief been committed in the following scenarios?

2. Tony is mowing his lawn. The lawnmower picks up and propels a rock through a stained glass window of his neighbor's historic home.
3. Tony disagrees with his neighbor's support of a candidate for governor. To demonstrate his disagreement, he throws a rock through a stained-glass window of the neighbor's historic home.

STOLEN TREATS ARE THE SWEETEST

Learning Objective: Identify, describe, and compare the elements of larceny, larceny by trick, and identity theft.

In 2019, there was almost $6 billion in automobile theft, $1.4 billion in currency theft, $323 million in stolen electronics, and billions more lost to other forms of personal property theft.[8] The legal term for theft is "larceny." There are specific forms of larceny, such as embezzlement and robbery, which will be discussed after this section on traditional larceny.

Larceny

Larceny was defined at the Common Law as

1. The trespassory taking

2. and carrying away (*asportation*)

3. personal property

4. of another person

5. with an intent to permanently deprive the owner of possession.

As was true of trespass, criminal law turns to property law to determine if the first element is satisfied—whether a taking is lawful or trespassory. Ironically, if a person acquired property lawfully and then stole it, which is known as conversion, no crime was committed at the old Common Law. For example, Bailey loans Kiley her horse. It wasn't larceny for Kiley to not return it because her initial acquisition was lawful. Eventually, courts filled this hole in two ways. The first won't be a surprise to you because you have seen it before. They created a legal construct, or fiction—*constructive possession*. This doctrine held that employers retained possession of their property when it was in the actual physical possession of their employees. Therefore, if an employee converted the property, they were taking it from the employer's possession and, hence, committing a trespass. But this didn't fully remedy the problem because constructive possession was limited to the workplace. To protect others from property conversion, the crime of embezzlement was created.

The second element is asportation, or the carrying away of the property. The slightest movement satisfies the asportation requirement. The third element limits larceny to personal property. Land and fixtures to land were not protected by larceny. This is because land is immovable. Other laws protect an owner's, or rightful possessor's, interest in land, such as trespass. The fourth element is obvious: The property must belong to another person. That can be an owner or a person who has the right to possess the property.

Finally, the mens rea element. An actor must intend to permanently deprive the owner of the object. If a person who steals cash from another's pocket when they aren't looking spends all of the money, it is a safe bet that the actor intended to permanently deprive the owner of the money. The classic teenage automobile joyride is a more difficult case, particularly if the teen is caught quickly after the car snatching. If the teen isn't caught until 2 days later, the mens rea element is more easily proven.

In addition to the inference of time, creating a substantial risk that the owner will be permanently deprived of the use or value of the property satisfied the mens rea element. Imagine, for example, taking a valuable collectible baseball. If the baseball is taken, used in a game, and returned with marks that greatly reduce its value and make it unusable for display or trade,

---

Larceny: The trespassory taking and carrying away (asportation) personal property of another person with an intent to permanently deprive the owner of possession.

larceny is committed. If the mens rea element can't be proven, the actor may still be prosecuted for trespass, and if the property is damaged, for criminal mischief.

Larceny by Trick

Initially, a person didn't commit larceny if they deceived a property owner into handing over their property. This wasn't considered a "trespass." Eventually, a permutation of larceny was developed to cover acquisition through deceit, larceny by trick. The elements of this crime were the same, except the use of deceit or false statement was substituted for the trespassory-taking element. To satisfy the mens rea, the defendant had to intend to deceive the owner at the time the untrue statement was made.

Alfred opens the gate to Fred's farm, finds a cow, leads it away, has it butchered, and sells the meat. Alfred has committed larceny.

Alfred asks Fred if he can borrow his cow for 2 weeks, for milking. Fred agrees, and Alfred leads the cow away. A week later, unexpectedly desperate for cash, Alfred decides to have the cow butchered and to sell the meat. Alfred didn't commit larceny because he acquired the cow lawfully. Nor did he commit larceny by trick because he didn't intend to deceive the owner at the time he acquired the cow.

Milly Drysdale works at a bank as a teller. She pockets $2,000 of the bank's money and later spends it on alcohol and clothes. She has committed larceny under the doctrine of constructive possession.

Milly Drysdale is a bank manager. Her mother desperately needs $50,000 to close on a purchase of a new home. Her mom expected to return the $50,000 to Milly the following day when she closed on the sale of her current home. Milly took $50,000 out of the bank's vault and gave it to her mom, intending to return it to the vault after her mom closed on the sale of her house. Unfortunately, the sale fell through after her mom closed on the new home purchase, and Milly wasn't able to return the money to the safe. Milly has not committed larceny because she didn't intend to permanently deprive the bank of the money.

Milly Drysdale tells a neighbor that she has an opportunity to invest in a start-up company that will earn lots of money, fast. The neighbor gives Drysdale $5,000 to invest in the company. There is no start-up. Drysdale intended to keep the money all along. Drysdale has committed larceny by trick.

Identity Theft

The use of another person's identifying information to commit a predicate offense, such as fraud, is big business today. But identity theft isn't new. In the 16th century, Martin Guerre, a Frenchman, left his family. Several years later, a man appeared in town, claiming to be Guerre.

Larceny by trick: The use of deceit to acquire the personal property of another with the intent to permanently deprive the owner of possession.

His wife, and others, believed he looked like her husband, and she welcomed him home. Although they lived together for years and had two children, people in the village became suspicious. When the man made claim to a deceased relative's estate, he was tried for impersonation and arson. He was acquitted. He was tried a second time in another city and convicted. He appealed and appeared to be persuading the appellate judges that he was indeed Martin Guerre when, much to his chagrin, the real Martin Guerre appeared before the court. The imposter, whose real name was Arnaud du Tilh, was executed.

People assume the identity of others for a variety of unsavory reasons, including *inter alia* to commit fraud, to obstruct justice, to harass the victim of the theft or other people in the victim's name, to obtain access to secret information or places, and to vote illegally. Identity theft and impersonation crimes are located throughout criminal codes, including larceny, fraud, and computer crime provisions. The federal government and most, if not all, of the states have identity theft statutes. "Identity" is commonly defined as personal data, such as social security and tax identification numbers, driver's license number, date of birth, and personal name.

The common elements of identify theft in state statutes are

1. The unlawful and

2. intentional use of another person's identity

3. to commit fraud or another crime.

These elements are easily seen in the primary federal identify theft law, Federal Identity Theft and Assumption Deterrence Act of 1998, which declares it a crime whenever "[a]ny person who knowingly transfers or uses, without lawful authority, a means of identification of another person with the intent to commit, or to aid or abet, any unlawful activity that constitutes a violation of Federal law, or that constitutes a felony under any applicable State or local law."

QUESTIONS AND PROBLEMS

1. What are the elements of larceny?
2. How does larceny by trick vary from larceny?
3. What are the elements of identity theft?

Is larceny or larceny by trick committed in the following scenarios?

4. Rhonda asks Roberta if she can borrow $500, promising to repay it in a week. Roberta gives Rhonda the cash. Three days later, Rhonda's son is unexpectedly arrested. She uses the $500 to post his bail. She can't repay Roberta as agreed.
5. Rhonda is visiting with Roberta. She sees $500 in cash hidden in a cookie jar. She takes the money when Roberta isn't looking. She later spends the money on a flat-screen television.

YOUR FIRST MISTAKE WAS TRUSTING ME

Learning Objective: Identify and describe the elements of embezzlement, false pretenses, and mail fraud.

As discussed earlier in this chapter, the trespassory-taking requirement of larceny left a gap in the law. Entrusting nonowners with the care of property is common in life, particularly in fiduciary relationships—legal relationships involving trust. Bank officers, lawyers, accountants, and financial advisors are fiduciaries. It also happens when property is left with service people for repair or improvement and when hotels hold luggage for guests; it is very common between family and friends. So why wasn't conversion a crime hundreds of years ago? One author suggests that it was because people of the time conceived of the public and private law distinction differently. Early in the Common Law, a traditional theft was perceived as a threat to the public order. Therefore, it was treated as a crime. Taking property that was given in trust, on the other hand, was seen as a private affair. Courts didn't turn a blind eye to conversions. Victims could seek compensation in civil court.[9] Another factor you have seen before also inhibited the expansion of larceny by early courts; it was a felony punished with death. As you learned, the doctrine of constructive possession partially filled in the gap. But it didn't address nontrespassory takings outside of the employment setting. For this, courts eventually created the crime of embezzlement.

Embezzlement

Embezzlement is defined as such:

1. The lawful acquisition of possession

2. of personal property of another

3. and then converting it

4. with an intent to permanently deprive the owner of it.

An important distinction between larceny and embezzlement is the timing of the mens rea. For larceny, the actor must intend to steal property at the time the property is taken. An embezzler, on the other hand, may develop the intent to steal after lawfully acquiring the property. The act of taking the property for one's own use after lawfully receiving it is referred to as conversion. The majority view is that the embezzler must intend to permanently deprive the owner of the property. However, a minority view is that the embezzler only needs to intend to convert the property, even if temporarily. For example, an accountant who converts a client's money (intending to return it) to cover a short-term deficit is guilty of embezzlement under the latter approach but not under the former approach.

Embezzlement: The conversion of lawfully acquired property with the intent to permanently deprive the owner of the property.

Conversion: The act of a trustee in using or interfering with property that has been entrusted to them.

Even with the addition of larceny by trick and embezzlement, a gap in the law of theft remained when a person used fraud to steal title, as opposed to taking possession, of property. Recall that because other criminal and civil laws, such as trespass, could be used to eject trespassers to land, there was no need for a crime of larceny of real property. But it was possible to steal a "title," or proof of ownership, to land. The title to real property is found in a written document called a deed. You may have heard of a title to a car. Title is proof of ownership of the car in the same way that a deed is proof of ownership of land. To steal ownership of real or personal property is the crime of **false pretenses**. The elements of this crime include the following:

1. A false representation

2. of a material fact

3. known to be false

4. made for the purpose of causing

5. and causes

6. the victim to pass title to property.

The actus reus of false pretenses is the use of a false representation—an untruth—of material fact to acquire the property. Opinions and feelings are not facts. To qualify, the factual representation must be of past or present fact. A statement about a future fact isn't sufficient. The fact must be about a past or present fact. The line between a statement known to be true today about a future event and a statement about a future event that turns out to not happen is different. For example, it is a false pretense statement to ask someone to loan money, with the understanding that they will be repaid tomorrow with money that is in a bank account today. It is a statement of future fact to ask someone to loan money, with the understanding that they will be repaid with money that will be deposited into their banking account tomorrow. The former can be the basis of false pretense, if untrue. The latter can't.

The misrepresentation can't be of any fact. Only important, or material, facts form the foundation of false pretense. An objective test is used to determine materiality—that is, a fact is material if it would influence a reasonable person's decision to transfer title. Also required for the actus reus is the victim actually transferring title to the defendant. Transfer can occur in any way (e.g., physically, electronically).

False pretense has a double mens rea requirement. First, the defendant must know that the statement of material fact is false. Mistake of fact is a legitimate defense to this crime. However, many modern statutes have widened this element to include reckless misrepresentations. Second, the defendant must intend for the representation to cause the victim to transfer title.

Gill Bates takes his iPad to a big-box technology store, which has a dedicated group of technicians who provide service and support—the TechnoTeam. Gill discusses his interest in adding gaming software to the device with Jobe Steves. Jobe falls in love with Gill's iPad and decides to steal it. He promises Gill that he will add the software at no cost. Gill leaves the iPad with him, and Jobe takes it home, intending to keep it. Jobe has committed larceny by trick because he used deceit to acquire and permanently deprive Gill of the device.

Gill Bates takes his iPad to a big-box technology store, which has a dedicated group of technicians who provide service and support—the TechnoTeam. Gill leaves his iPad with Jobe Steves, a member of the TechnoTeam, to add new gaming software. Jobe gives him a quote on the price, checks it in, and the next day decides to steal it. Jobe has committed embezzlement because he converted the device after lawfully acquiring it.

Jobe Steves offers to buy HardMacro, a small computer hardware company, and the land and buildings where the company does its work. Gill Bates, the owner, agrees to sell for $10 million, provided he will be paid immediately. Jobe assures Gill that he has the money in his bank account and writes a check. Gill signs over the deed and other documents transferring ownership, only to discover later that Jobe doesn't have any money in his account. Jobe has committed false pretenses.

Other Fraud Crimes

State and federal criminal codes contain many specialized fraud crimes. Among them are laws addressing tax fraud, investment and securities fraud, bank fraud, charitable giving fraud, election fraud, campaign finance fraud, political fraud, and telemarketing fraud. There are fraud laws that criminalize kickbacks to physicians for prescribing or referring patients to medical products, for cheating Medicare and other federal assistance programs, and for dialing back the mileage on an automobile to increase its value.

Typically, for mens rea, these laws require knowledge of the deception with an intent to financially or otherwise benefit in some manner. While the actus reus of these crimes varies by subject matter, an act of deception for financial or other benefit is the common denominator. The "benefit" element is sometimes a high hurdle for prosecutors to jump. Two cases illustrate the problem.

Former Governor of New Jersey Chris Christie sought the support of city mayors and other officials for his 2013 reelection bid. The mayor of Fort Lee, New Jersey, declined to support Christie's campaign. To punish the mayor, Christie supporters who were Port Authority officials decided to create problems for the mayor by reducing the number of lanes long reserved at the George Washington Bridge's toll plaza for Fort Lee's morning commuters. To disguise their political retribution, the officials claimed the lane realignment was part of a traffic study. As part the plan, they asked Port Authority traffic engineers to collect traffic data, and they arranged to pay an extra toll collector overtime. The lane closures caused 4 days of traffic gridlock, resulting in a public outcry. The lanes were reopened when the Port Authority's executive director discovered what was happening and countermanded the orders of his subordinates.

The two Port Authority officials who were responsible for the scheme were charged and convicted of federal wire and program fraud and conspiracy to commit those crimes. In 2020, SCOTUS overturned the convictions because the fraud laws forbid "any scheme or artifice to defraud, or for obtaining money or property by means of false or fraudulent pretenses, representations, or promises," and the defendants didn't commit their fraud to obtain money or property. In the words of Justice Kagan, writing for the court,

> The evidence the jury heard no doubt shows wrongdoing—deception, corruption, abuse of power. But the federal fraud statutes at issue do not criminalize all such conduct. Under settled precedent, the officials could violate those laws only if an object of their dishonesty was to obtain the Port Authority's money or property.[10]

A second case illustrates the same point, with a First Amendment twist. It is the subject of your next Digging Deeper.

DIGGING DEEPER 9.1

Is it fraud to lie about being a decorated military veteran?

Case: *United States v. Alvarez*
Court: Supreme Court of the United States.   Citation: 567 U.S. 709
Year: 2012
Justice Kennedy delivered the opinion of the court.

Lying was his habit. Xavier Alvarez, the respondent here, lied when he said that he played hockey for the Detroit Red Wings and that he once married a starlet from Mexico. But when he lied in announcing he held the Congressional Medal of Honor, respondent ventured onto new ground; for that lie violates a federal criminal statute, the Stolen Valor Act of 2005. 18 U. S. C. §704.

In 2007, respondent attended his first public meeting as a board member of the Three Valley Water District Board. The board is a governmental entity with headquarters in Claremont, California. He introduced himself as follows: "I'm a retired marine of 25 years. I retired in the year 2001. Back in 1987, I was awarded the Congressional Medal of Honor. I got wounded many times by the same guy." None of this was true. For all the record shows, respondent's statements were but a pathetic attempt to gain respect that eluded him. The statements do not seem

PHOTO 9.3 Xavier Alvarez lied about being a veteran and about receiving the medal of honor.

State Bar of California

to have been made to secure employment or financial benefits or admission to privileges reserved for those who had earned the Medal.

Respondent was indicted under the Stolen Valor Act for lying about the Congressional Medal of Honor at the meeting....

"[A]s a general matter, the First Amendment means that government has no power to restrict expression because of its message, its ideas, its subject matter, or its content." As a result, the Constitution "demands that content-based restrictions on speech be presumed invalid ... and that the Government bear the burden of showing their constitutionality."

In light of the substantial and expansive threats to free expression posed by content-based restrictions, this Court has rejected as "startling and dangerous" a "free-floating test for First Amendment coverage. . . [based on] an ad hoc balancing of relative social costs and benefits." Instead, content-based restrictions on speech have been permitted, as a general matter, only when confined to the few "'historic and traditional categories [of expression] long familiar to the bar.'" Among these categories are advocacy intended, and likely, to incite imminent lawless action, see *Brandenburg v. Ohio*; obscenity (e.g., *Miller v. California*); defamation, *New York Times Co. v. Sullivan*; speech integral to criminal conduct, *Giboney v. Empire Storage & Ice Co*; so-called "fighting words," *Chaplinsky v. New Hampshire*; child pornography, *New York v. Ferber*; fraud, *Virginia Bd. Of Pharmacy v. Virginia Citizens Consumer Council, Inc*; true threats, *Watts v. United States*; and speech presenting some grave and imminent threat the government has the power to prevent, *Near v. Minnesota ex rel. Olson*, although a restriction under the last category is most difficult to sustain.

Absent from those few categories where the law allows content-based regulation of speech is any general exception to the First Amendment for false statements. This comports with the common understanding that some false statements are inevitable if there is to be an open and vigorous expression of views in public and private con-versation, expression the First Amendment seeks to guarantee....

The Court has never endorsed the categorical rule the Government advances: that false statements receive no First Amendment protection. Our prior decisions have not confronted a measure, like the Stolen Valor Act, that targets falsity and nothing more....

[The Court distinguished the Stolen Valor Act from lying to government officials and perjury, which cause serious harm.]

The Act by its plain terms applies to a false statement made at any time, in any place, to any person....

Permitting the government to decree this speech to be a criminal offense, whether shouted from the rooftops or made in a barely audible whisper, would endorse government authority to compile a list of subjects about which false statements are punishable. That governmental power has no clear limiting principle. Our constitutional tradition stands against the idea that we need Oceania's Ministry of Truth. See G. Orwell, *Nineteen Eighty-Four* (1949) (Centennial ed. 2003). Were this law to be sustained, there could be an endless list of subjects the National Government or the States could single out....

The Government is correct when it states military medals "serve the important public function of recognizing and expressing gratitude for acts of heroism and sacrifice in military service," and also "'foste[r] morale, mission accomplishment and esprit de corps' among service members."...

But to recite the Government's compelling interests is not to end the matter. The First Amendment requires that the Government's chosen restriction on the speech at issue be "actually necessary" to achieve its interest....

The Government points to no evidence to support its claim that the public's general perception of military awards is diluted by false claims such as those made by Alvarez.... As one of the Government's amici notes "there is nothing that charlatans such as Xavier Alvarez can do to stain [the Medal winners'] honor....

The Government has not shown, and cannot show, why counterspeech would not suffice to achieve its interest. The facts of this case indicate that the dynamics of free speech, of counterspeech, of refutation, can overcome the lie. Respondent lied at a public meeting. Even before the FBI began investigating him for his false statements "Alvarez was perceived as a phony," Once the lie was made public, he was ridiculed online, see Brief for Respondent 3, his actions were reported in the press, and a fellow board member called for his resignation....

The remedy for speech that is false is speech that is true. This is the ordinary course in a free society. The response to the unreasoned is the rational; to the uninformed, the enlightened; to the straight-out lie, the simple truth. ...

In addition, when the Government seeks to regulate protected speech, the restriction must be the "least restrictive means among available, effective alternatives." There is, however, at least one less speech-restrictive means by which the Government could likely protect the integrity of the military awards system. A Government-created database could list Congressional Medal of Honor winners. Were a database accessible through the Internet, it would be easy to verify and expose false claims....

The Nation well knows that one of the costs of the First Amendment is that it protects the speech we detest as well as the speech we embrace. Though few might find respondent's statements anything but contemptible, his right to make those statements is protected by the Constitution's guarantee of freedom of speech and expression. The Stolen Valor Act infringes upon speech protected by the First Amendment.

[Justices Alito, Thomas, and Scalia dissented. The reversal of Alvarez's conviction by the Court of Appeals was affirmed.]

In addition to the plethora of substantive fraud laws, there are also laws that target the means of committing fraud. The federal government, for example, criminalizes the use of the U.S. mail and wire services to commit fraud. Wire services is defined to include wire (including telephone), radio, and television. Although found in two separate statutes, mail and wire fraud mirror one another. To prove one or both, the United States must prove the following:

1. The use of either mail or wire communications in the foreseeable furtherance

2. of a scheme and intent to defraud another of either property or honest services

3. involving a material deception of fact.

The wire and mail fraud laws are quite broad, and when paired with RICO (Racketeer Influenced and Corrupt Organizations Act), which you learned about in Chapter 4, they are powerful prosecutorial tools—quite possibly, too broad and powerful. The use of computers to commit fraud and other crimes is discussed in the next chapter.

QUESTIONS AND PROBLEMS

1. What are the elements of embezzlement?
2. What distinguishes larceny, larceny by trick, embezzlement, and false pretenses?

THE SHAKEDOWN

Learning Objective: Identify, describe, and apply the elements of extortion.

Commonly known as blackmail, **extortion** is the use of a threat to extract money, property, or something of value from another person. Extortion and robbery, which is your next crime, both rely on threats. However, the threat in a robbery must be of immediate harm, while extortion involves a threat of future harm. At the old Common Law, only public officials could be blackmailed. Contemporary extortion is much broader in its definition:

1. The act of taking or acquiring property or something of value

2. of another

3. using a threat

4. with an intent to permanently deprive the owner of the property.

The actus reus is the acquisition of another person's property and the communication of a threat. In some jurisdictions, actual receipt of the property must occur. In others, the threat is enough to establish attempted extortion.

A threat of future physical harm satisfies the threat element, as do threats to injure another's reputation, business, financial status, or family relationship. As in the case of robbery, the threat may be directed at one person and the demand for property made on another. For example, if Victor states to Bjorn, "If you don't give me $5,000 by 5 p.m., I will kill your child," Victor has committed extortion, even though he has not threatened Bjorn.

The threatened conduct or condition itself need not be illegal to be extortion. Threats to disclose that a member of the Daughters of the American Revolution isn't actually descended from a person who was involved in America's struggle for independence or to make public that a church pastor had a child from an extramarital affair are both extortions, provided they are made with the intent to squeeze money from their subjects.

This brings us back to Jeff Bezos, the founder of Amazon. Threatening to disclose an extramarital affair unless money is paid is extortion, even though infidelity is no longer a crime. But AMI's case is more complicated. The case illustrates the fine line between negotiations and

---

Extortion: The acquisition of the property of another by threat with the intent to permanently deprive the owner of the property.

blackmail. Every day in business and law, people negotiate agreements where the terms can be interpreted as threats, often involving information that one of the parties may want to keep private. Several key factors in drawing the line can be identified—the truth of the allegations, whether the money or relief sought is reasonable, and whether relief sought is designed to remedy the harm alleged.

Consider the case of famed *Riverdance* dancer Michael Flatley. He was accused by Tyna Marie Robertson of rape. Her lawyer, Attorney D. Dean Mauro, sent Flatley a letter demanding a large monetary settlement, or he would "go public" with a client's accusation that Flatley raped her. Flatley denied the allegation and sued Robertson and Mauro. The California Supreme Court held that Mauro had committed extortion, Flatley was cleared of the allegation, and he subsequently won a multimillion dollar judgment against his accuser for extortion and defamation.[11] That the threat to publicize the alleged rape didn't appear to remedy the alleged wrongdoing was an important factor in the case. Applying these factors to the Bezos case, there is an apparent disconnect between AMI's alleged defamation—that it was motivated by politics—and the action it threatened—to publish embarrassing photos of Bezos and his lover. Yet there are factors weighing in AMI's favor, including that the demand is for a statement by Bezos, not for money or property, and it can be reasonably argued that a Bezos statement better addresses the alleged wrong (defamation) than a huge amount of cash. Also, AMI's threat lacks details. Unlike Mauro's letter, which created a deadline for response, AMI's letter invited negotiation. Bottom line, whether AMI was negotiating a settlement or blackmailing Bezos is unclear.

While extortion is largely a state offense, there are also federal blackmail laws. It is a crime, for example, for federal officers to extort members of the public, to be involved in an extortion that interferes with or occurs in interstate or international commerce, and to extort individuals by threatening to expose violations of federal law.

QUESTIONS AND PROBLEMS

1. What are the elements of extortion?

Explain whether embezzlement has been committed in the scenarios found in Questions 2 through 4.

2. Terri is the accountant for The Great Ming, a Pan-Asian restaurant. The owners discovered that Terri had transferred $8,000 of their money into her bank account. They told Terri that if she didn't return the money in 3 days, they would report her conduct to the police.

3. Alexa intends to text a nude picture of herself to her boyfriend, Robert. She accidentally sends it to Roberta, an acquaintance in her contacts. Roberta replies to her with this message: "Thanks for the pic. If you don't give me $250 by midnight tonight, I am snapping and tweeting it to everyone I know."

4. Carlos declines Rhonda's request to borrow his car for 3 hours. Rhonda tells Carlos that if he doesn't allow her to use it, she will tell his parents that he has been using methamphetamine.

STICK 'EM UP

Learning Objective: Identify, describe, and apply the elements of robbery.

Robbery and larceny are siblings. The elements of robbery include the following:

1. A trespassory taking

2. and carrying away

3. the personal property of another

4. from that person or in their presence

5. using either force or threat of force

6. with an intent to permanently deprive them of it.

Many of the elements of robbery are the same as for larceny. There must be a trespassory taking, asportation, and an intent to steal. What distinguishes robbery from larceny is the use of force.

To satisfy this element, the property must either be directly taken from the victim or taken in their presence. Holding a gun on a victim while stripping a watch from his wrist is a robbery. Taking property directly from a victim is easy enough. The alternative "in the presence of" the victim can be more difficult to determine. The prevailing rule is that the property must be within the control of the victim at the time of the act.

The force itself has to be more than what is required to take the property. For example, it is larceny, not robbery, to snatch a phone from an unexpecting person's hands and run away. It would be robbery if the victim sees the thief coming, pockets the phone, and the thief hits the victim in the face and removes the phone while the victim is disoriented from the blow.

Actual force doesn't have to be used. Threatening force is sufficient to prove the crime. The person who points a gun at a person walking a dog and states, "Give me your dog or I'll fill you with bullets," has committed a robbery, even though there was no physical contact. Most states require the threatened harm to be contemporaneous with the act; threats of future harm do not prove robbery. Threats to third parties, such as family members, are the same as to the victim.

Rob Rotten breaks into Stephanie's home, holds a gun on her, and orders her to stand in a doorway while he opens her safe and steals her jewelry and other valuables. Rob has committed robbery (and burglary).

Rob Rotten breaks into Stephanie's home, opens her safe, and steals her jewelry and valuables. She is out of town on work but can see Rob on her phone's video security app. The security app has a two-way communication system. Stephanie tells Rob to stop, that the police are on the way. He points a gun at the camera and threatens to shoot her if he is caught. Rob has not committed robbery because his threat was of future harm, he didn't take the property in Stephanie's physical presence, and she didn't have control over the property at the time he took it.

Robbery: The taking of personal property from another using force with the intent to permanently deprive the owner of the property.

The states vary in how the threat is evaluated. In some, the victim must subjectively experience fear. In others, the test is whether a reasonable person would have feared for life or limb. This is the subject of the next Digging Deeper.

DIGGING DEEPER 9.2

Is it robbery for two people to "ask" for money while surrounding a person?

Case: In Re T. J. H.
Court: Court of Special Appeals of Maryland. 2019 Md. App. LEXIS 99
Year: 2019
Judge Leahy delivered the opinion of the court.

On May 19, 2017, eighteen-year-old Yolanda Lopez had just picked up her baby from the babysitter after school. While walking home through a Baltimore City alley, two girls approached Ms. Lopez from behind and asked her where she was going. Ms. Lopez explained that "[she] didn't pay attention to them because, at first, [she] thought they weren't even talking to [her]. And then they kept following [her], asking [her] many times where [she] was going." After telling the two girls that she was going home, they continued to follow her, and Ms. Lopez testified that

> they started walking next to me, one on one side of me and the other one on the other side. And they asked me for money. And then I said, "No, I don't have any money." And then she said, "Let me see." And one of them grabbed the diaper bag I had for my baby and started to look through it to see if I had any money, and she only found $40. And then they just stayed there, I don't know, and gave back the diaper bag. But I never touched it. She's the one who did everything. I never touched it.

The diaper bag was hanging on the stroller at the time one of the girls grabbed it. After obtaining the $40 from the diaper bag, the confrontation continued and "one [of the girls] started to say, 'I want more money.'" Ms. Lopez replied that she did not have any more money. According to Ms. Lopez, the following interaction took place:

> [T]hey started to touch me a lot and I honestly got very nervous and I was afraid. And I called—no, [*5] I wanted to call other people, but there was no one there. And I just wanted to go quickly to see if there was someone who could help me.

> And then one of them went in front of me and I had my baby in the carrier, and said, "Okay. I want more money." "I don't have any more money." I didn't know how to tell her in English "just take everything," but I didn't know. I just was showing with gestures. And one of them took my baby and said, "If you don't give me my money, I'm not going to give you your baby." And at that moment, my body got very weak, watery. I don't know how to explain it, but it's a very bad sensation.

At that moment, Ms. Lopez saw her brother-in-law, Bardales Ayala, leaving his home nearby and called out his name for help. Mr. Ayala testified that he turned when he heard his name and saw that "two young people... were... just [walking] away from [Ms. Lopez]."...

Before this Court, T. J. H. argues that the State's evidence was insufficient to support the juvenile court's finding of her involvement in robbery. Pointing out that there are two "modalities" of robbery—commonly referred to as the force modality and the intimidation modality—T. J. H. contends that the evidence "does not support the intimidation modality of robbery because a reasonable person in Ms. Lopez's position would not have been 'in fear of bodily harm.'" Specifically, T. J. H. avers, that both before and during the taking of Ms. Lopez's $40, "there was no *demand* for money; there was no implication of a weapon; and there were no threats of any kind." T. J. H. notes that Ms. Lopez testified that she was intimidated only *after* the taking of the $40, making that testimony irrelevant to the robbery analysis. T. J. H. also argues that the State's evidence was insufficient to support the force modality of robbery because "Ms. Lopez did not resist; was not injured; and the force used was that, and only that, necessary to remove the money from Ms. Lopez's possession."

In response, the State concedes that there was no evidence to support the force modality of robbery. The State maintains, however, that the threats and demand for money were implicit in T. J. H.'s conduct. The State argues, further, that the juvenile court was "not limited to Lopez's precise words... [and] could consider the way in which she relayed the events [in her testimony]." The State argues, therefore, that Ms. Lopez's testimony supported a reasonable inference that "Lopez felt intimidated because a reasonable person under the same circumstances would have felt intimidated."

In determining whether there has been a threat of force or intimidation, an objective test "focusing on the accused's actions" must be applied. This test considers "whether an ordinary, reasonable person under the circumstances would have been in fear of bodily harm." As such, proof of actual fear and the actual display of a weapon are not necessary "if the means employed are calculated to instill fear in the heart or mind of a reasonable man[,]" and, if the circumstances "reasonably... cause the owner to surrender his property."

Here, Ms. Lopez testified that while walking home in an alley with only her infant son, T. J. H. and the other girl approached her from behind and asked multiple times where she was going. After telling the girls that she was going home, they continued to follow Ms. Lopez and surrounded her, one girl standing on each side as they asked her for money. Ms. Lopez testified that after telling the girls that she did not have any money, one of the girls stated "let me see" and grabbed Ms. Lopez's diaper bag from the stroller and searched it until she found the $40. She testified, further, that she "never touched" the diaper bag when it was taken from her possession.

These facts and circumstances, and the reasonable inferences deducible therefrom, were found by the juvenile court as showing the intimidation element of robbery. We cannot say that the magistrate's conclusion was clearly erroneous. Although Ms. Lopez testified that the girls "asked" for money, the girls did so while physically surrounding Ms. Lopez and her infant child in an alley with no one else around. A reasonable person in Ms. Lopez's position could have interpreted the actions of T. J. H. and her accomplice as both an intimidating demand for money *and* a threat of bodily harm to her and her infant.

[The lower court's finding that the juvenile was delinquent for committing robbery and other charges was affirmed.]

Robbery is a crime in every state. The federal government criminalizes robberies when federal monies or interstate commerce is involved. Robbery of a bank that is federally insured by the United States is an example. Because of the threat to life, robbery is graded higher than larceny, and robberies that result in injury are punished more severely than those that don't. Some jurisdictions also aggravate the crime if committed with a weapon or against people who are particularly vulnerable.

Florida's robbery statute illustrates many of the principles just discussed:

§812.13, Fla. Stat.

1. "Robbery" means the taking of money or other property which may be the subject of larceny from the person or custody of another, with intent to either permanently or temporarily deprive the person or the owner of the money or other property, when in the course of the taking there is the use of force, violence, assault, or putting in fear.

2. a. If in the course of committing the robbery the offender carried a firearm or other deadly weapon, then the robbery is a felony of the first degree, punishable by imprisonment for a term of years not exceeding life imprisonment or as provided in...

   b. If in the course of committing the robbery the offender carried a weapon, then the robbery is a felony of the first degree, punishable as provided in...

   c. If in the course of committing the robbery the offender carried no firearm, deadly weapon, or other weapon, then the robbery is a felony of the second degree.

QUESTIONS AND PROBLEMS

1. What are the elements of robbery?

Has Perry committed robbery in the following scenarios? Explain your answers.

2. Perry Pursesnatcher sees Margaret window shopping with her purse draped over her arm. He runs up to her from behind, slips the purse off her arm, and runs away with it.
3. Perry Pursesnatcher sees Margaret window shopping with her purse draped over her arm. He runs up to from behind and grabs her purse. Margaret feels the purse move and grabs it with the other hand. The two struggle for 30 seconds before Perry is able to free the purse from her and run away.

TOO HOT TO HANDLE

Learning Objective: Identify, describe, and apply the elements of receiving and selling stolen property.

In an effort to deter larceny, criminal laws target not only the theft but the business of theft. One such law that is found in all the states is receiving, possessing, and selling stolen property, which is defined as a person who

---

Receiving, possessing, and selling stolen property: The act of receiving, possessing, or selling property that is known to be stolen with the intent of permanently depriving the owner of the property.

1. receives property

2. that has been stolen

3. with knowledge of its stolen character

4. with an intent to deprive the owner of the property.

The mens rea of this offense is knowing the property's stolen or "hot" character. The jurisdictions are split on their use of subjective or objective mens rea tests. In a jurisdiction that requires subjective knowledge, a prosecutor has a large hurdle to jump. It must be proven that the defendant actually knew the property was stolen. If the objective test is employed, a prosecutor must only show that a reasonable person would have known that the property was stolen.

Jafari posts an advertisement in MyLocalMarket, a buying and selling app that geo-targets buyers and sellers. He posts, "Electronics. Need to sell fast. Very Cheap. Northwood High School Parking Lot, 8 p.m. to 10 p.m. tonight." Sammi is 18, had a sheltered childhood, and her friends and family commonly make fun of her for being innocent and naïve. Sammi arrives at 8:00. Jafari has new, boxed laptops and printers. Sammi buys a laptop for about half of retail. Sammi lives in a state that requires subjective knowledge. She is not guilty of receiving stolen property because she didn't know of its stolen character.

Consider the same facts, except Sammi lives in a state that employs the objective test. Sammi is guilty of receiving stolen property because a reasonable person would have known the laptop was stolen.

Most jurisdictions criminalize the possession of stolen property, as well as the receipt, as long as the other elements are met (e.g., intent to deprive the owner). Consequently, an individual who becomes aware of an item's stolen character after innocently receiving it isn't privileged to sell it.

The actus reus of receiving the property may occur by actual or constructive possession. Constructive possession occurs when the receiver has control over the property, regardless of physical possession. A defendant who directs a fence to leave stolen computer tablets in a warehouse owned by the defendant has received the property when they are placed in the warehouse. A quid pro quo transaction is not required. Stolen property that is acquired as a gift is no different than if it had been purchased.

The received property must be stolen. Property from larcenies, robberies, embezzlement, extortion, false pretenses, and other theft crimes are all stolen for the purposes of selling and receiving stolen property laws. As is true of other property crimes, the intent to deprive the owner element refers to not only taking possession and using an item, but to any use that greatly reduces the property's value, even if it is returned.

Sellers, also known as fences, of stolen property are also liable. In Florida, for example, "any person who traffics in, or endeavors to traffic in, property that he or she knows or should know was stolen" commits a felony.[12] It is also a federal felony to sell or receive stolen items in interstate or international commerce or on federal lands.[13]

QUESTIONS AND PROBLEMS

1. What are the elements of receiving and selling stolen property?

Did Joanne commit the crime receiving stolen property in the following scenarios? Explain your answer.

2. Joanne is with her girlfriend Tammi. Joanne and Tammi see a pair of expensive sunglasses, and Joanne states, "Those are awesome. I would love to have them. But we don't have the money right now. Someday, they are mine." The two split up and continue shopping. Thirty minutes later in the car, Tammi hands Joanne the sunglasses. They still have the price tag on them. Tammi says to her, "Why wait? We got the five-finger discount today." Joanne tears off the tag, puts them on, and thanks Tammi.

3. Joanne is with her girlfriend Tammi. Joanne and Tammi see a pair of expensive sunglasses, and Joanne states, "Those are awesome. I would love to have them. But we don't have the money right now. Someday, they are mine." The two split up and continue shopping. Thirty minutes later in the store parking lot, Tammi hands Joanne the sunglasses. They still have the price tag on them. Tammi says to her, "Why wait? We got the five-finger discount today." Joanne replies, "That's not right. We are taking them back. But first, I want to try them out. We will come back with them after we eat." She puts them on, price tag and all, and wears them during their lunch.

CONSOLIDATING THEFT CRIMES

Learning Objective: Describe the MPC's theft consolidation provisions.

Although all of the theft crimes you just learned about were independent at the Common Law, and continue to be—in part or whole, in some places—most states have followed the MPC's approach and enacted consolidated theft statutes. The purpose in consolidating theft crimes is to eliminate the archaic differences between the crimes that developed over hundreds of years and to reduce disparities in punishments between the various forms of theft. The primary mens rea and actus reus elements of each crime that you learned about continue to exist. For example, embezzlement continues to require lawful acquisition followed by a conversion. And all of the crimes continue to require an intent to permanently deprive the owner of the property. What is different is that in a consolidated theft law, they are all labeled "theft" and the punishment for each of them is the same, as determined by the value of the property stolen. Section 223.7 of the MPC brings together the following forms of theft:

1. Theft by taking (includes Common Law larceny and embezzlement)

2. Theft by deception (includes Common Law false pretenses)

3. Theft by extortion

4. Theft of property known to be mislaid, misdelivered, or lost, and no reasonable attempt to find the rightful owner is made

5. Receiving stolen property

6. Theft of professional services by deception or threat

7. Conversion of entrusted funds

8. Unauthorized use of another's automobile

The MPC states that thefts are felonies of the third degree if the amount stolen exceeds $500 or if the property stolen is a firearm, automobile, airplane, motorcycle, motorboat, or other vehicle; and, in cases of receiving stolen property, if the receiver of the property is a fence, then it is a felony of the third degree regardless of the property's value. Thefts of property valued $50 to $499 are misdemeanors, and if the value is less than $50, the crime is a petty misdemeanor. The MPC classifies all unauthorized uses of automobiles as misdemeanors. See Figure 9.2 for a summary of the MPC approach to theft.

FIGURE 9.2 ■ The Model Penal Code Approach to Theft

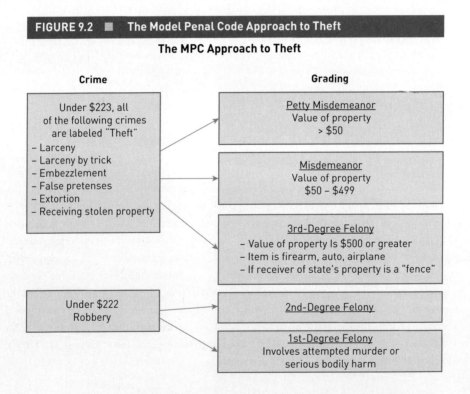

The MPC Approach to Theft

Of course, the states haven't adopted the MPC's consolidation verbatim. The MPC was published in 1962. At that time, $500 meant more than it does today, so modern codes often require the loss to be greater than $500 to be classified as a felony. Another variation from the MPC is that many states have more grade levels than the MPC, with grades determined by both the value of the property and many other factors, such as whether the item stolen was a firearm or explosive, or the theft occurred during a riot, fire, war, or natural disaster. In a few farming states, theft of livestock is laddered up in punishment.

A couple of the theft crimes continue to be treated independently by the MPC—robbery, for example, because it involves a threat to life. If during the commission of a theft the defendant inflicts serious bodily injury upon another, threatens serious bodily injury, or threatens to commit a felony of the first or second degree, there is a robbery. It is a felony of the second degree unless the defendant attempts to kill or cause serious bodily injury, in which case it is a felony of the first degree.[14]

Like robbery, forgery is also treated as a separate offense. Forgery is discussed in greater detail in the next chapter.

QUESTIONS AND PROBLEMS

1. Describe the MPC's consolidation of theft offenses.

IN A NUTSHELL

Early property crimes were developed at a time when society held different values about property, the role of civil and criminal law, and business relationships. Burglary is no longer limited to homes, nor at night. Arson has been broadened from homes to include all structures, in most jurisdictions.

Similarly, the independent and idiosyncratic nature of the individual Common Law theft crimes, which were out of date by the 20th century, were standardized in most states following the issuance of the MPC. Today, most nonviolent forms of stealing are labeled as theft by the states. This includes larceny, larceny by trick, embezzlement, false pretenses, and extortion. The grading of these crimes recognizes both modern and historic priorities, such as the idea that nighttime burglaries are more serious than daytime. Robbery continues to be treated differently than theft—not because of the value of the property involved, but because it is more threatening to life than the other forms of theft.

LEGAL TERMS

arson (p. 280)

burglary (p. 277)

conversion (p. 288)

criminal mischief (p. 283)

embezzlement (p. 288)

extortion (p. 294)

Larceny (p. 285)

larceny by trick (p. 286)

receiving, possessing, and selling stolen
    property (p. 299)

Robbery (p. 296)

trespass (p. 274)

NOTES

1. A. Au-Yeung and J. Bezos, "Details Blackmail Attempt by Publisher of 'National Enquirer.'" *Forbes*, February 7, 2019, accessed December 21, 2020, from Forbes.com.

2. *Wilmington Man Charged with Online Threats, Witness Tampering Regarding his Participation in Protests at U.S. Capitol*, Press Release, U.S. Department of Justice, January 15, 2021, accessed March 18, 2021, from Justice.Gov. Press Release.

3. 720 ILCS 5/21-2

4. *People v. Richards*, 108 N.Y. 137, 15 N.E. 371 (1888).

5. Blackstone Commentaries, p. 224. (1769)

6. 5 Am. Jur. 2d Arson 2 (1962).

7. Two Brooklyn Residents and a Greene County Resident Charged in Connection with Molotov Cocktail Attacks on the NYPD. Press Release, United States Attorney for the Eastern District of New York, May 31, 2020.

8. Property stolen and recovered in the United States in 2019, by type and value, accessed December 18, 2020, from Statistica.com.

9. G. P. Fletcher, "The Metamorphosis of Larceny," *Harvard Law Review* 89 (1976): 469.

10. *Kelly v. United States*, 590 U.S. ___ (2020).

11. *Flatley v. Mauro*, 39 Cal.4th 299 (Cal. 2006).

12. §812.019 Fla.Stat.

13. 18 U.S.C.§2315.

14. MPC §221.

10 COMMERCIAL AND CYBERCRIME

In early 2018, Patrick Reames received a 1099 from Amazon's self-publishing arm, CreateSpace. A 1099 is an Internal Revenue Service (IRS) form that is used to report self-employment income. CreateSpace had reported to the IRS that Mr. Reames had earned tens of thousands of dollars on CreateSpace selling his book, *Lower Days Ahead*. Normally, an author would be excited to learn that he is earning royalties. But there was a problem: Mr. Reames didn't have a book listed with CreateSpace. Nor did he write *Lower Days Ahead*. In his words,

> I did the "sneak peek" on the inside and the book appeared to be some computer gener-ated story, with no paragraph or chapter structure. Each sentence was in quotes and each was ended with a carriage return... not the way any human would write. At that moment, it seemed to me that this "author" that shared my name was hoping some poor soul would be stupid enough to buy this fraud of a book and boom, they would get a healthy payday. No, at this point, I hadn't really connected this book to my problem.... I know I'm not the only Patrick Reames in the world, not even the only one in the U.S. I was also sure that this ridiculous book wouldn't ever sell enough copies to generate $10 in royalties, much less almost $25K—especially since it was only on Amazon's site for 11 weeks total in 2017.... Using Amazon's own calculator, a book that sells for $440 would yield the author about $270, plus or minus. This means that the fraudulent book *Lower Days Ahead* sold about 90 copies in 11 weeks. Simply stated, there is no way in hell that 90 people in 11 weeks fell for this Amazon-hosted scam. After an additional few minutes of thought, it occurred to me that the only purpose that could be served by this "book" and the account set-up with my credentials was to launder money.

Indeed, the book was a computer-generated work, the creators used stolen credit cards to buy many copies of it, and they subsequently pocketed the author's royalties.[1] True to the title of the book, Mr. Reames had lower days ahead of him. His fight to correct the record was pro-tracted and difficult.

This story illustrates a common phenomenon: cybercrime. In Mr. Reames's case, there are several crimes rolled into one, including credit card theft, improper access and use of privileged data, and theft by computer.

You studied larceny, false pretenses, and basic fraud in the last chapter. This chapter takes a deeper dive into specific commercial crimes and cybercrimes. Although independent of one another, the combination of commercial and cybercrime is common today. In the first half of this chapter, you will study other forms of theft that are commonly found in the business and commercial world. These are commonly known as "white-collar" crimes—a term referring to the white, button-down shirts that were once the common dress of men in business.

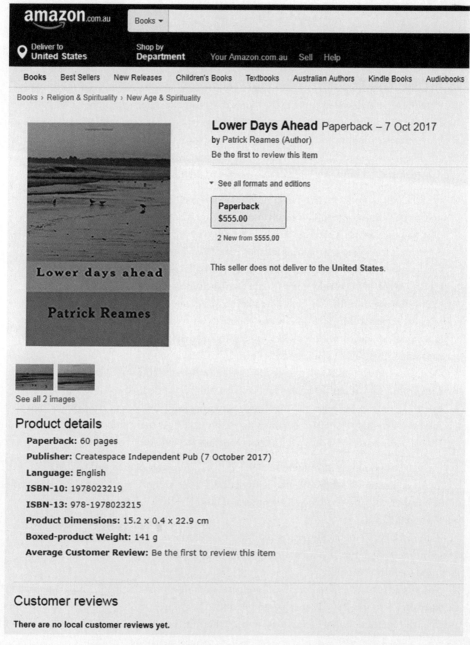

PHOTO 10.1 This fake book sold more than 60 times on Amazon using Patrick Reames's name and social security number.

FAKING IT: FORGERY

Learning Objectives: Identify, describe, and apply the elements of forgery, cyberforgery, and uttering.

Forgery is a specific type of fraud. Forgery is the

1. making, using, or altering of a

2. false document (or the alteration of existing documents making them false) or item of value

3. that is passed (uttered)

4. to another person

5. with an intent to defraud.

The author Oscar Wilde said, "Imitation is the sincerest form of flattery." But the victims of forgery and counterfeiting may not feel complimented when they calculate their losses. There are several acts that fulfill the actus reus of forgery. The creation of a false document, or the alteration of a genuine document, is the most obvious. But the act of using a false or altered document—"uttering"—is also considered forgery. Including the word "use" enables the prosecution of actors who don't alter or create false documents to be prosecuted, provided they possess the requisite mens rea. Additionally, the document must be passed to another person or business. This can occur in person, through the mail, or by other methods.

An attendant circumstance of forgery is that the document must be passed to a person. For purposes of theft laws, persons include people *and* businesses. The latter includes sole proprietorships, corporations, nonprofit corporations, and other legally recognized business organizations.

Finally, the mens rea is intent to defraud. The MPC requires purpose to defraud or knowledge that a fraud is being perpetuated.[2]

Forgery may be prosecuted under general fraud or forgery-specific statutes. Many jurisdictions also have computer forgery laws. Georgia's criminal code, for example, includes the following prohibition:

O.C.G.A §16-9-93(d)

Computer Forgery. Any person who creates, alters, or deletes any data contained in any computer or computer network, who, if such person had created, altered, or deleted a tangible document or instrument would have committed forgery under Article 1 of this chapter, shall be guilty of the crime of computer forgery. The absence of a tangible writing directly created or altered by the offender shall not be a defense to the crime of

---

Forgery: To make and utter a false document with the intent to defraud another person.

computer forgery if a creation, alteration, or deletion of data was involved in lieu of a tangible document or instrument.

What is significant about this Georgia provision, and others like it, is that it brings digital (intangible) documents within the grasp of the law, and it recognizes "cyberuttering." Email transmissions and uploading and posting digital documents are forms of cyberuttering.

A few states distinguish forgery and uttering. Forgery is the crime of creating or altering a document. Uttering is the use of the document. Both require an intent to defraud. As mentioned previously, other jurisdictions combine the two into a single crime, or include them both in a broader fraud statute.

Kayla creates a fake check using a digital publishing program and remotely deposits it into her savings account at the Fourth National Bank. Kayla has committed (cyber)forgery.

Kayla creates a fake check to be used in a bank fraud training program. She distributes the check to the students at the training. She hasn't committed forgery because she lacked an intent to defraud.

QUESTIONS AND PROBLEMS

1. What are the elements of forgery?
2. How do modern cyberforgery statutes amend "traditional" forgery laws?

FUNNY MONEY: COUNTERFEITING

Learning Objective: Identify, describe, and apply the elements of counterfeiting.

Counterfeiting is a crime under federal and state laws. A "counterfeit" is a replication or faux version of a document or item. There are many different laws that forbid the creation or transfer of counterfeit items for the purposes of defrauding another person. These include, inter alia:

- United States money

- Documents (forgeries)

- Art and antiquities

- Securities

- Postage stamps

- Intellectual property

Counterfeiting: To make a duplication of an original document with such similitude that a reasonable person would be defrauded.

- Legal documents, such as certificate of birth or death, driver's license, official employment identification, certificates of authenticity or ownership

- Products (e.g., "knockoffs," including pharmaceuticals and other medical supplies)

Counterfeiting often overlaps with other crimes, such as forgery and fraud. Criminal and civil counterfeiting laws can be found through federal and state laws. They are found in the securities, commercial, intellectual property, governmental operations, and criminal sections of codes. The common elements of counterfeiting are these:

1. Creation of a

2. copy of an original item of value

3. with sufficient similitude to convince a person of ordinary caution that it is real

4. uttered or used

5. with intent

6. to defraud.

The foundational federal counterfeiting law is as follows:

18 U.S. Code § 471

Whoever, with intent to defraud, falsely makes, forges, counterfeits, or alters any obligation or other security of the United States, shall be fined under this title or imprisoned not more than 20 years, or both.

"Obligation or other security" includes U.S. currency. So this is the statute that applies to the classic money counterfeiter. The same section of the U.S. code criminalizes the uttering of counterfeited securities, the possession of counterfeiting tools, and extends these counterfeiting laws to foreign securities, such as counterfeiting and using the Chinese Yuan to defraud someone in the United States.

The "intent to defraud" element of counterfeiting has been interpreted in two ways. First, an actor can defraud the person to whom the funny money is given as a form of payment. Second, any use of the counterfeit has the effect of defrauding the United States itself by injuring the integrity of the dollar. If counterfeit currency was widespread, trust in the U.S. dollar would dissipate, injuring the U.S. economy and the American people. Money counterfeiting is a federal crime because the authority to create a national currency is delegated exclusively to the federal government in Article I, Section 8 of the U.S. Constitution.

A counterfeit doesn't have to be identical to the original. But it must have "sufficient similitude," or similarity, to deceive a person of ordinary caution into believing it is genuine. Simply producing the likeness of paper or coined money, or the instruments to create them, is not counterfeiting. There must be an accompanying intent to defraud. There is no requirement, however, of an utterance.

PHOTO 10.2 There are many different laws that forbid the creation or transfer of counterfeit items for the purposes of defrauding another person.

megaflop/iStock

Frank B. Rassa, an adept computer graphics artist, creates images of the U.S. dollar, prints them, and intends to use them to buy a new computer graphics program. Frank is committing counterfeiting, as well as other crimes.

Frank B. Rassa, an adept computer graphics artist and thespian, creates images of the U.S. dollar, prints them, and intends to use them in a community play, Catch Me If You Can. *Frank is not committing counterfeiting because he lacks an intent to defraud.*

QUESTIONS AND PROBLEMS

1. What are the basic elements of counterfeiting?
2. Brock William, broke and drunk, draws a picture of Alexander Hamilton and adds other text that appears on the $10 bill on a cocktail napkin. He attempts to pay for beer at the liquor store with the napkin. Has he committed counterfeiting?

YOU'VE GOT MAIL: POSTAL CRIMES

Learning Objective: Identify and describe mail fraud and two other postal crimes, specifying the elements of mail fraud.

Just as it does with the authority to coin money, the Constitution delegates postal authority to the federal government. Congress created the United States Post Office Department, now the United States Post Office, in 1792 through the Postal Service Act. This enabling law also declared it a crime to steal the mail, making theft of it one of the oldest federal crimes. The Postal Service Act also created a postal police, the U.S. Postal Inspection Service. Today, the agents of this office investigate tens of thousands of cases per year, arresting more than 10,000 people annually for mail fraud, robbery and burglary of post offices, theft, illegal mailing of explosives and other dangerous materials, drug offenses, money laundering, threat, sexual predation, human trafficking, and many other crimes.[3] In 1792, the maximum punishment for mail theft was death. Mail thieves aren't executed today, but crimes involving the mail continue to be punished severely. See Table 10.1 for a listing of postal crimes.

TABLE 10.1 ■ Postal Crimes

Crime	Statute	Punishment
Mail fraud	18 USC §§1341 & 1342; USC § 1345; 39 USC §§3005 & 3007	Varied, up to 20 in prison and fines
Theft/receipt of stolen mail	18 USC §§1708 & 1709	Up to 5 years in prison and fines
Destruction of mailbox	18 USC §§1705	Up to 3 years in prison and fines
Mailing bombs, poisons, weapons, and other dangerous articles	18 U.S.C. §1716	1 year; up to 20 years in prison if the intent is to injure; capital punishment if death results
Burglary of postal facility	18 USC §2115	Up to 20 years in prison and fines
Child exploitation: mailing obscene materials to children and mailing child pornography	18 USC §1470; 2251 et seq.	Varied; up to 50 years in prison and fines
Mailing controlled substances	21 USC 841§§841–843	Varied
Using the mail for extortion	18 USC §876	Up to 10 years in prison and fines
Identity theft	18 USC §§1028–1029	Varied
Money laundering	18 USC §§1956 & 1957	Varied
Mailbox restriction: placing items in mailbox, except U.S. mail by official mail carrier	Title 18, Section 1725	Fines up to $5K for individuals & $10K for organizations

Mail fraud: To commit (or attempt) an illegal scheme using the mail.

Money laundering: To conduct a financial transaction with money known to have been obtained illegally with the intent to conceal it, carry on a crime, avoid a reporting requirement, or to commit a tax crime.

Let's look specifically at the mail fraud statute, 18 USC §§1341. Originally enacted "to prevent the frauds which are mostly gotten up in the large cities... by thieves, forgers, and rapscallions generally, for the purpose of deceiving and fleecing the innocent people in the country,"[4] mail fraud has become a darling of federal prosecutors because nearly all crimes involve either mail or wire communication and because violations are severely punished.

The elements of mail fraud are for a person to

1. devise or intend to devise a scheme to defraud (or to perform specified fraudulent acts) and

2. the use of the mail for the purpose of executing, or attempting to execute, the scheme (or specified fraudulent acts).

The mens rea is high: the intent to defraud. Other federal fraud laws require that the actor's misrepresentation—the lie—be "material." To be material, the fact lied about must be so important that it influenced the victim's decision to buy, sell, or act. The mail fraud statute is silent on this matter. SCOTUS explained why materiality is part of the "scheme to defraud" element in the Digging Deeper case, *Neder v. United States.*

DIGGING DEEPER 10.1

Must a scheme to defraud involve a material lie to commit mail fraud?

Case: *Neder v. United States*
Court: United States Supreme Court
Year: 1999
C. J. Rehnquist delivered the opinion of the court.

In the mid-1980s, petitioner Ellis E. Neder, Jr., an attorney and real estate developer in Jacksonville, Florida, engaged in a number of real estate transactions financed by fraudulently obtained bank loans. Between 1984 and 1986, Neder purchased 12 parcels of land using shell corporations set up by his attorneys and then immediately resold the land at much higher prices to limited partnerships that he controlled. Using inflated appraisals, Neder secured bank loans that typically amounted to 70% to 75% of the inflated resale price of the land. In so doing, he concealed from lenders that he controlled the shell corporations, that he had purchased the land at prices substantially lower than the inflated resale prices, and that the limited partnerships had not made substantial down payments as represented. In several cases, Neder agreed to sign affidavits falsely stating that he had no relationship to the shell corporations and that he was not sharing in the profits from the inflated land sales. By keeping for himself the amount by which the loan proceeds exceeded the original purchase price of the land, Neder was able to obtain more than $7 million. He failed to report nearly all of this money on his personal income tax returns. He eventually defaulted on the loans.

Neder also engaged in a number of schemes involving land development fraud. In 1985, he obtained a $4,150,000 construction loan to build condominiums on a project known as Cedar Creek. To obtain the loan, he falsely represented to the lender that he had satisfied a condition of the loan by making advance sales of 20 condominium units. In fact, he had been unable to meet the condition, so he secured additional buyers by making their down payments himself. He then had the down payments transferred back to him from the escrow accounts into which they had been placed. Neder later defaulted on the loan without repaying any of the principal. He employed a similar scheme to obtain a second construction loan of $5,400,000, and unsuccessfully attempted to obtain an additional loan in the same manner.

Neder also obtained a consolidated $14 million land acquisition and development loan for a project known as Reddie Point. Pursuant to the loan, Neder could request funds for work actually performed on the project. Between September 1987 and March 1988, he submitted numerous requests based on false invoices, the lender approved the requests, and he obtained almost $3 million unrelated to any work actually performed.

Neder was indicted on, among other things, 9 counts of mail fraud, in violation of 18 U. S. C. § 1341; 9 counts of wire fraud, in violation of § 1343; 12 counts of bank fraud, in violation of § 1344; and 2 counts of filing a false income tax return....

We also granted certiorari in this case to decide whether materiality is an element of a "scheme or artifice to defraud" under the federal mail fraud (18 U. S. C. § 1341), wire fraud (§ 1343), and bank fraud (§ 1344) statutes. The Court of Appeals concluded that the failure to submit materiality to the jury was not error because the fraud statutes do not require that a "scheme to defraud" employ *material* falsehoods. We disagree....

We first look to the text of the statutes at issue to discern whether they require a showing of materiality. In this case, we need not dwell long on the text because, as the parties agree, none of the fraud statutes defines the phrase "scheme or artifice to defraud," or even mentions materiality....

That does not end our inquiry, however, because in interpreting statutory language there is a necessary second step. It is a well-established rule of construction that "where Congress uses terms that have accumulated settled meaning under... the common law, a court must infer, unless the statute otherwise dictates, that Congress means to incorporate the established meaning of these terms....

The Government does not dispute that both at the time of the mail fraud statute's original enactment in 1872, and later when Congress enacted the wire fraud and bank fraud statutes, actionable "fraud" had a well-settled meaning at common law. Nor does it dispute that the well-settled meaning of "fraud" required a misrepresentation or concealment of *material* fact. Indeed, as the sources we are aware of demonstrate, the common law could not have conceived of "fraud" without proof of materiality....

Thus, under the rule that Congress intends to incorporate the well-settled meaning of the common-law terms it uses, we cannot infer from the absence of an express reference to materiality that Congress intended to drop that element from the fraud statutes. On the contrary, we must *presume* that Congress intended to incorporate materiality unless the statute otherwise dictates....

Accordingly, we hold that materiality of falsehood is an element of the federal mail fraud, wire fraud, and bank fraud statutes.

[The court remanded the case to the U.S. Court of Appeals for further action.]

The actus reus of mail fraud is straightforward. Any use of the mail in a fraudulent scheme, no matter how small, satisfies this element. So sending a letter between conspirators about their crime, mailings to victims, or receiving payments through the mail all add a federal crime to a predicate state or federal offense. Section 1341 extends the reach of the law beyond the U.S. mail to "private or commercial interstate carriers." FedEx and UPS are examples of private interstate carriers.

Mail fraud is a commonly charged crime because most conspiracies and fraud crimes require communication between conspirators and between conspirators and victims. Commending about the popularity of mail fraud as a prosecutorial tool, one former federal prosecutor wrote that

> To federal prosecutors of white collar crime, the mail fraud statute is our Stradivarius, our Colt .45, our Louisville Slugger, our Cuisinart—and our true love. We may flirt with RICO, show off with 10b-5, and call the conspiracy law "darling," but we always come home to the virtues of 18 U.S.C. 1341, with its simplicity, adaptability, and comfortable familiarity.[5]

Mail fraud is also popular with prosecutors because of its hefty punishment; a convictee can be fined and spend as many as 20 years in prison. This makes mail fraud an effective prosecutorial bargaining chip. Mail fraud's sibling, wire fraud, extends the reach of these laws to radio, telephone, television, and cyber communications.[6]

In 2020, a huge mail and wire fraud case was announced in Minnesota. The U.S. Attorney for the District of Minnesota charged 60 defendants with a telemarketing scheme that bilked $300 million from over 150,000 mostly elderly victims. The prosecutors alleged that the defendants, over a period of 20 years, used the mail and telephone service to defraud the victims. In the prosecutor's press release, the crime was described this way:

> The telemarketers often claimed—falsely—to be calling with an offer to reduce the monthly cost of an existing subscription. In reality, the company had no existing relationship with the victim-consumers and was actually fraudulently signing the victim-consumers up for expensive and entirely new magazine subscriptions.

> The effect was that a single consumer went from having one magazine subscription to, at times, more than a dozen, all with different fraudulent magazine companies, each "sold" under the auspices of "reducing" the consumer's monthly rate.[7]

QUESTIONS AND PROBLEMS

1. What are the elements of mail fraud?
2. Identify three or more postal crimes.

FEELING INSECURE: SECURITIES FRAUD

Learning Objective: Identify, describe, and apply the elements of securities fraud.

Securities refers to both stocks and commodities. Stock represents ownership of a fraction of a "publicly held" company. Ownership of a private company is held by a single or small group of people, often the founders of the company. Their ownership interest is not publicly traded. These individuals are wholly responsible for the management of the corporation, they suffer its losses, and they benefit from its profits.

When a company goes public, the individual owners sell their ownership interest in the company in small pieces. Each piece of ownership is known as a stock share. Companies typically issue millions of shares that are bought and sold in stock exchanges around the world, such as the New York, Nasdaq, Tokyo, London, Shanghai, and Indonesia exchanges.

Commodities are tangible goods that are traded. Private owners make this choice to go public for a variety of reasons, including to raise money to pay business debts or to expand the company. Agricultural items, such as corn and wheat, and precious metals, such as silver, are commodities. In addition to stocks and commodities, there are other forms of securities, such as bonds. There is a body of laws, state and federal, that regulates the buying, selling, and trading of securities. These laws forbid various forms of securities fraud, which is knowingly using a scheme or artifice to defraud a person in connection to a securities transaction.

Corporate securities fraud occurs when corporate officials use a corporation to commit fraud or they intentionally withhold or lie about the corporation with the intention of causing the value of the corporation's stock to change. This occurred with Luckin Coffee. Founded in 2017, Chinese-based Luckin was intended to be a competitor to Starbucks, which is very popular in China. Luckin grew rapidly, opening over 4,000 stores in less than 20 years. Its stock soared in value, and it was a popular stock to investors in the United States. Then in late 2019, it was discovered that the company's chief operating officer and other corporate executives had been overreporting the company's sales by over $300 million. Luckin was immediately delisted from the stock exchanges, its stock plummeted in value, an investigation took place, and executives were fired. After a few months, Luckin reached an agreement with the U.S. Securities and Exchange Commission to pay $180 million in fines, and its stock was relisted;[8] by early 2021, the value of its stock began to rise.

Individual securities fraud occurs when a person defrauds others for personal gain through securities trading and through insider trading.[9] These crimes are commonly committed by corporate officials, stockbrokers and traders, and bankers. If the executives in the Luckin Coffee

---

Securities fraud: To knowingly use a scheme or artifice to defraud a person in connection to a securities transaction.

Insider trading: When a fiduciary uses information not available to the public to make a securities transaction.

scandal benefited from their fraud, they are guilty of securities fraud in the same way as the company itself. Securities fraud occurs when a person

1. knowingly uses or attempts to use a scheme or artifice

2. with an intent to defraud any person
   a. in connection with a security or
   b. obtains, by means of false or fraudulent pretenses, representations, or promises, any money or property in connection with the purchase or sale of any commodity for future delivery, or any option on a commodity for future delivery, or any security.[10]

There are a multitude of ways that securities fraud happens. It can be as simple as lying about the value of a company's assets or the number of customers it has been serving with the intent of persuading people to buy the company's stock. Or it can be done through complex schemes that involve continual and hard-to-track transfers of monies that have the effect of making a company's finances appear different than reality. These forms of "cooking the books" come in many varieties, such as Ponzi and pyramid schemes. The mens rea is intent. Mistaken statements that induce another person to buy or sell stock isn't fraud. Finally, the third element requires a connection, a nexus, between the lie or scheme and the purchase or sale of the security. Said another way, the lie (or scheme) must be the cause of the victim's decision to buy or sell.

Insider trading refers to the buying and selling of stocks by executives and others who are closely tied to the corporation. Most of the time, insiders are allowed to trade in their company's stocks. It is a common practice, for example, for companies to use their own stock as a form of salary or as performance bonuses. Illegal insider trading, on the other hand, refers to situations where individuals trade on the stock market with the benefit of information that is not available to the general public. Interestingly, insider trading isn't specifically found in federal code. The crime has been created out of the prohibition of securities fraud. For this reason, the crime is often challenged as violating the basic principle of legality—that crimes must be created, with specificity, by the legislature. Regardless, the crime has withstood these challenges and continues to be developed by the courts. Calls for legislative action to create and better define insider trading had not been successful by early 2021. The elements of criminal insider trading are the

1. trade

2. of a security

3. on the basis of material information about the security

4. with knowledge that the information is not public

5. with knowledge that the material information was obtained through a fiduciary relationship.

As you can see, insider trading has a double mens rea requirement: the actor must have knowledge the information isn't public and knowledge that the information was initially disclosed by someone who had a fiduciary relationship with the company. Knowledge has been interpreted to mean both subjective and objective knowledge. So if an actor should have known, but ignored the facts, that the information was fraudulently disclosed by a person "in the know," the crime has been committed. This can apply down the line of a series of tippers, although the further down the line it goes, the less likely a trader would have the facts to conclude that the original tip occurred in violation of a fiduciary duty.

Material information is any data that would influence a reasonable investor's decision to trade. The fifth element requires that the information be obtained in breach of fiduciary relationship. As an example, let's return to Luckin Coffee. Hypothetically, if an executive of the company who wasn't involved in the fraud learned at a meeting that the fraud had been discovered and that it was to be publicly announced the next day, it would be illegal insider trading for that individual to sell their shares before the public announcement. This element has been interpreted to include tips to people who don't have a fiduciary duty to the company, as long as the source of the information was in a fiduciary relationship with the company.

Returning to Luckin Coffee, if the corporate executive who didn't commit the fraud but learned about it at the meeting were to tip off a friend who immediately sold their shares of Luckin Stock, the friend would be guilty of criminal insider trading. However, the mens rea requirement of third-party liability is twofold. First, the third party must know, or have reason to know, that the information was not public (scienter), and second, they must intend to defraud the buyers of the stock. Simply having knowledge of the secret that will cause the stock to fall in value establishes the intent to defraud.

> Martha is friends with Sam, the chief executive officer of GetThereFast, a delivery company. Sam tells Martha that his company has reached an agreement to provide delivery for Amazon. The deal is expected to cause GetThereFast's stock to skyrocket overnight. Martha buys $100,000 of the stock immediately after their discussion. Martha is guilty of illegal insider trading.

> Berman is deputy attorney general of the state. He learns through his job that VirusDefense, Inc., a corporation that has been developing a pharmaceutical to treat COVID-19 is being investigated, in secret, for falsifying the success of the drug in its trials. Berman sells his VirusDefense, Inc., stock that evening. He is guilty of illegal insider trading.

Individual violators can be imprisoned for 20 years and fined as much as $5 million. Corporative fines can be as great as 5 times that amount.

QUESTIONS AND PROBLEMS

1. What are the elements of individual securities fraud?
2. What are the elements of insider trading?

Apply the elements of insider trading to the following scenarios.

1. Haris Canda is vice president of research for CardioElectro, Inc., a publicly traded company. Researchers in Haris's labs have invented a revolutionary heart valve. The company plans to announce its work and apply for a patent in the upcoming weeks. Haris tells a friend, Opa C. Hamilton, about the valve and the company's intention to go public soon. Opa purchases 1,000 shares of CardioElectro, Inc., stock 2 hours later. Has Opa committed insider trading? Apply all of the elements of the crime and fully explain your conclusion.

2. Haris Canda is vice president of research for CardioElectro, Inc., a publicly traded company. Researchers in Haris's labs have invented a revolutionary heart valve. The company plans to announce its work and apply for a patent in the upcoming weeks. Haris tells a friend, Opa C. Hamilton, about the valve and the company's intention to go public soon. The next day Opa goes to the RiversEdge Racquet and Fitness Club to play in a regular mixed-doubles league. He is assigned a partner, Oma Java. During a break in their match, Opa says to Oma, "I hear that CardioElectro, Inc., is an up-and-coming company; the stock shows promise." That night, Oma buys 100 shares of the company. Has Oma committed insider trading? Apply all of the elements of the crime and fully explain your conclusion.

HIDING IN PLAIN SIGHT: MONEY LAUNDERING

Learning Objective: Identify, describe, and apply the elements of money laundering.

One of the challenges to large-scale criminal enterprises is what to do with the money they earn. Federal and states laws require banks to report large deposits, withdrawals, and transfers of money at banks and other financial institutions. This type of activity, in turn, can be a red flag to law enforcement authorities, so criminals create methods to conceal, known as cleaning or laundering, the illegal origins of their dirty money. Two common ways to launder dirty money are to channel it through a legitimate business and to hide its origin through multiple and complex banking transactions. Walter White, in the television drama *Breaking Bad*, concealed the earnings from his drug enterprise by laundering them through a car wash. Specifically, he inflated car wash sales to account for the illegal cash he was channeling through the business.

The federal Money Laundering Control Act, found at 18 U.S.C. §§ 1956 and 1957, criminalizes more than traditional laundering. It is a violation of the Act for any person to:

1. conduct, or attempt to conduct, a financial transaction

2. knowing the money involved in the transaction is the product of illegal activity

3. with the intent to one of the following:
    a. carry on a "specified unlawful activity"
    b. commit tax evasion or tax fraud
    c. conceal or disguise the nature, location, source, ownership, or control of proceeds of the specified unlawful activity
    d. avoid a financial transaction reporting requirement.

"Financial transaction" includes obvious bank transactions, such as a deposit, withdrawal, or transfer of funds, loan, and the creation of a trust. But the definition extends well beyond banking matters. All purchases, gifts, and pledges count as financial transactions. So the only act that is *not* a transaction appears to be maintaining personal possession of the property. The list of "specified unlawful activities" is long. About 250 violations of federal, state, and local law fall into this box. Therefore, nearly all crimes qualify. A handful of examples are murder, rape and other sex crimes, theft and fraud, tax crimes, extortion, immigration violations, espionage, firearms violations, gambling, kidnapping, mischief, obscenity, and obstruction of justice.

There are two mens rea elements for laundering money. The first is knowledge that the money is a product of unlawful activity, and the second is the specific intent to commit one of the four acts previously listed in element number 3 of the Money Laundering Control Act: to carry on, evade taxes, conceal, or avoid reporting.

A conviction of the federal Money Laundering Control Act is punished with confiscation of the monies, huge fines, and long prison sentences. Most states have money laundering laws that are similar to the federal statute.

QUESTIONS AND PROBLEMS

1. What are the elements of money laundering?

TAKE A BYTE OUT OF CRIME: CYBERCRIME

Learning Objective: Identify and describe the three types of computer crimes.

Per the cliche, there isn't anything new under the sun. At their core, cybercrimes are traditional crimes that are committed using (or they are aimed at) modern technology. The objectives of cybercrimes are not new; cybercriminals steal, injure people and property, and invade privacy.

Generally, there are three types of computer crimes. The first is when a computer is the target of a traditional crime. Stealing a computer, destroying a computer, and installing malware to damage a computer are examples. The second form of computer crime is when a computer is itself the instrument of a crime, such as using a computer to spread damaging malware or to disrupt computing services. The third category of computer crime occurs when a computer is used as a tool, or it is an accessory, to crime. Using a computer to plan a riot on the U.S. Capitol, as occurred in 2021 during Congress's counting of the electoral votes for president and vice president, is an example. Law enforcement officers scoured social media sites, email, and websites in search of evidence of intent and planning by the rioters. This framework can be seen in Figure 10.1, Types of Computer Crime.

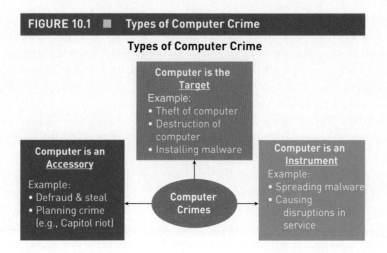

FIGURE 10.1 ■ Types of Computer Crime

Types of Computer Crime

Computer is the Target
Example:
- Theft of computer
- Destruction of computer
- Installing malware

Computer is an Accessory
Example:
- Defraud & steal
- Planning crime (e.g., Capitol riot)

Computer is an Instrument
Example:
- Spreading malware
- Causing disruptions in service

Computer Crimes

While computer crimes may not be different in type from traditional crimes, cybercrimes do present a difference in degree. Computers make it possible to defraud millions, rather than hundreds, of people; to overwhelmingly harass people from great distances; and to access accounts and records in stunning numbers, at breathtaking speed, and from any location. Many of the crimes that you have already read about, and will in future chapters, can be committed using computers. Every jurisdiction approaches prosecution of crimes involving computers differently. In some instances, computer crimes are prosecuted under traditional laws. In others, there may be specific cybercrime laws. The remainder of this chapter is devoted to examining cybercrimes not discussed elsewhere in this book.

Cyberstalking

As you learned in Chapter 7, stalking and true threats are prohibited by criminal laws in all of the states. Add a computer to these crimes, and you have specific criminal statutes that apply.

The federal and nearly all state governments criminalize **cyberstalking**. At the federal level, the Communications Decency Act is an important player. It makes it a crime when any person

> by means of a telecommunications device knowingly makes, creates, or solicits, and initiates the transmission of any comment, request, suggestion, proposal, image, or other communication which is obscene, lascivious, filthy, or indecent, with the intent to annoy, abuse, threaten or harass another person.[11]

Two other federal statutes punish actors who use mail, any interactive computer service, or any facility of interstate or foreign commerce "to kill, injure, harass, or place under surveillance with intent to kill, injure, harass, or intimidate, or cause substantial emotional distress to a person,"[12] and who "transmit in interstate or foreign commerce any communication containing

---

Cyberstalking: The crime of using internet communications to send obscene, abusive, or harassing language with the intent to harass or threaten another person.

any threat to kidnap any person or any threat to injure the person of another."[13]And there are other federal laws that criminalize harassment by telephone.

As an example of a state law, Washington defines the crime in this way:

RCW 9.61.260: Cyberstalking

1. A person is guilty of cyberstalking if he or she, with intent to harass, intimidate, torment, or embarrass any other person, and under circumstances not constituting telephone harassment, makes an electronic communication to such other person or a third party:
    a. Using any lewd, lascivious, indecent, or obscene words, images, or language, or suggesting the commission of any lewd or lascivious act;
    b. Anonymously or repeatedly whether or not conversation occurs; or
    c. Threatening to inflict injury on the person or property of the person called or any member of his or her family or household.

"Electronic communication" includes electronic mail, internet-based communications, pager service, and electronic text messaging. A violation is a misdemeanor unless the actor is a family member and has been convicted of harassing the victim before or death is threatened, in which case it is a felony.

You learned in Chapter 7 that a threat must rise to the level of being a "true threat" to be punished. Lesser harassment or offenses are protected by the First Amendment. Although this area of First Amendment law is very much in development, you may recall that the elements of a true threat, in the doctrine's current form, are as follows:

1. The speaker intends, purposely, knowingly, or recklessly, to

2. communicate a

3. serious expression of an intent to

4. commit an act of unlawful violence to a particular individual or group of individuals that would cause a

5. reasonable person to fear serious bodily harm or death;

6. the threat is communicated to, and received by, the target.

In-person stalking typically involves conduct, which takes it beyond the protections of the First Amendment. Cyberstalking is different. It typically only involves speech that is communicated over the internet. Therefore, cyberstalking statutes raise free speech concerns, particularly when they criminalize words that are "annoying" or "harassing" or "offensive." Remember, offensive and annoying speech is protected. It may be regulated only when it causes a reasonable concern of serious bodily harm. In 2019, a federal district judge invalidated a cyberstalking law that criminalized nonthreatening speech. You can read an excerpt of that decision in your next Digging Deeper.

PHOTO 10.3 Cybercriminal at work.

Daniel E. Hall

DIGGING DEEPER 10.2

Is a person guilty of cyberstalking for being persistently annoying?

Case: *Rynearson v. Ferguson*
Court: United States District Court for the Western District of Washington
Year: 2019
Opinion by Judge Leighton

Rynearson is an online author and activist who regularly writes online posts and comments to the public related to civil liberties, including about police abuse and the expansion of executive power in the wake of September 11. Rynearson's writings are often critical—and sometimes harshly so—of local public figures and government officials. These writings are well within the traditions of independent American political discourse, and are intended both to raise the awareness of other citizens regarding the civil-liberties issues that Rynearson writes about, and to hold civic and political leaders accountable to the community through pointed criticism.

This sort of expression is at the very heart of political speech which the First Amendment most strongly protects. Many of Rynearson's online posts and comments relate to a detention provision in the National Defense Authorization Act ("NDAA") of 2012. Specifically, Section 1021, which was found for authorizing the (unconstitutional) detention of American citizens without trial under the laws of war. Given his interest in indefinite-detention issues, Rynearson became interested years ago in public and civic organizations in the Seattle area that memorialize and seek to present the lessons of the Japanese American internment in World War II....

In the past, Rynearson has regularly posted on public Facebook pages criticizing the leadership of public and civic organizations, either because their leaders failed to condemn the NDAA or because they vocally and strongly support politicians who voted for or signed the NDAA, such as Governor Jay Inslee and former President Barack Obama. For example, in February 2017, Rynearson wrote a series of public posts on Facebook criticizing Clarence Moriwaki, the founder of the Bainbridge Island Japanese American Exclusion Memorial ("Memorial"), for failing to criticize Governor Inslee and President Obama for voting for/signing the NDAA.

The thrust of Rynearson's posts was that Moriwaki should be removed from his role as board member and de facto spokesperson for the Memorial because Moriwaki used thelessons of the internment, and his role with the Memorial, to criticize Republican politicians (chiefly, President Trump) in many media articles or appearances related to the Memorial, but failed to criticize Democratic politicians. Rynearson's posts often include invective, ridicule, and harsh language (but no profanity, obscenity, or threats) intended to criticize or call into question the actions and motives of these civic leaders and other public figures. He reasonably fears prosecution under the cyberstalking statute for such posts. In fact, the Bainbridge Island Police Department referred a police report to the Kitsap County Prosecutor finding probable cause for cyberstalking based on such critical posts to and about Moriwaki.

For a period of time, from March 2017 to January 2018, Rynearson was also subject to a civil protection order imposed by the Bainbridge Island Municipal Court based on posts critical of Moriwaki. The cyberstalking statute was one of the statutes invoked by the Municipal Court in imposing the protection order. The order imposed sharp limits on Rynearson's speech, such as barring the use of Moriwaki's name in the titles or domain names of webpages. The order has now been vacated on the ground that it was impermissibly based on Rynearson's constitutionally protected speech....

In 2004, Washington enacted one of the first state statutes directly criminalizing cyberstalking. The statute provides:

A person is guilty of cyberstalking if he or she, with intent to harass, intimidate, torment, or embarrass any other person, and under circumstances not constituting telephone harassment, makes an electronic communication to such other person or a third party:

a. Using any lewd, lascivious, indecent, or obscene words, images, or language, or suggesting the commission of any lewd or lascivious act;

b. Anonymously or repeatedly whether or not conversation occurs; or

c. Threatening to inflict injury on the person or property of the person called or any member of his or her family or household.

Over the years, the Supreme Court has enumerated certain "well-defined and narrowly limited" classes of speech that remain unprotected by the First Amendment. The unprotected speech is limited to (a) obscenity, (b) defamation, (c) fraud, (d) incitement, (e) true threats, and (f) speech integral to criminal conduct. Speech that does not fall into these exceptions remains protected.

Section 9.61.260(1)(b)'s breadth—by the plain meaning of its words—includes protected speech that is not exempted from protection by any of the recognized areas just described. [The law under review] criminalizes a large range of non-obscene, non-threatening speech, based only on (1) purportedly bad intent and (2) repetition or anonymity. The terms "harass, intimidate, torment, or embarrass" are not defined by the statute. When statutory terms are undefined, Washington courts generally give them their ordinary meaning, including the dictionary definition. The dictionary definition of "harass" includes "to vex, trouble, or annoy continually or chronically," and the meaning of "torment" incudes "to cause worry or vexation to." "Embarrass" means "to cause to experience a state of self-conscious distress." As a result, even public criticisms of public figures and public officials could be subject to criminal prosecution and punishment if they are seen as intended to persistently "vex" or "annoy" those public figures, or to embarrass them....

Moreover, the Supreme Court has consistently classified emotionally distressing or outrageous speech as protected, especially where that speech touches on matters of political, religious or public concern. This is because "in public debate our own citizens must tolerate insulting, and even outrageous, speech in order to provide 'adequate breathing space' to the freedoms protected by the First Amendment."...

For the reasons given here, this Court concludes that [the provision of the cyberstalking law applied to Rynearson] is facially unconstitutional.

Sexting and Revenge Porn

Two new trends are **sexting** and so-called **revenge porn**. Phones with cameras along with social media, texting, and email capabilities have made it possible to instantly snap and transmit pictures and video to others. Sexting refers to the voluntary self-taking and sending of nude and sexually explicit photos and video. Sexting is increasingly common, among both adults and juveniles. Between consenting adults, sexting is First Amendment protected. But sexually provocative images of children are not constitutionally protected, even if self-produced by a juvenile. Sexting is a risky activity. Embarrassment, loss of employment, and emotional distress sometimes result from sexting. Fear of public disclosure of sexted images makes individuals who have sent compromising photos or videos vulnerable to harassment and extortion.

To prevent sexting, a minority of states have enacted prohibitions. These laws vary. Some states punish juveniles who sext, others only punish adults who sext with juveniles, and a third approach is to require that the sender and recipient be distant from one another in age (e.g., 2 years or greater), punishing the elder of the two. An intent to sext is required by most of these laws. The person who has a photo open on a cell phone and accidentally sends it to another person isn't guilty of sexting.

Florida's law targets minors. "A minor commits the offense of sexting if he or she knowingly uses a computer... to transmit or distribute to another minor any photograph or video of any person which depicts nudity... and is harmful to minors." To be harmful to minors, a depiction

---

Sexting: The voluntary self-taking and electronic communication of nude or sexually explicit photos and videos.

Revenge porn: The use of voluntarily sent nude or sexually explicit photos or videos to harm the sender.

must be "obscene." Obscene is a term of art in First Amendment law that demands that the image appeal to "prurient," morbid sexual interests; be patently offensive; and not have serious literary, artistic, political, or scientific value. You will learn more about obscenity in an upcoming chapter. The first conviction under Florida's law is treated as a noncriminal offense. Subsequent convictions are misdemeanors. In states without sexting laws, child pornography and sexual exploitation laws may be used to prosecute sextors.

Beyond consensual sexting is "revenge porn" and sextortion. Revenge porn occurs when a recipient of voluntarily sent nude images makes those images public without the consent of the person in the images. Although referred to a "revenge" porn, the laws forbidding this conduct are not limited to cases with a revenge motive, as can be seen in Arizona's law:

Arizona Revised Statutes § 13-1425

PHOTO 10.4 An anti-sexting campaign poster

Callum Moffat/Mirrorpix/Newscom

It is unlawful for a person to intentionally disclose an image of another person who is identifiable from the image itself or from information displayed in connection with the image if all of the following apply:

1. The person in the image is depicted in a state of nudity or is engaged in specific sexual activities.

2. The depicted person has a reasonable expectation of privacy. Evidence that a person has sent an image to another person using an electronic device does not, on its own, remove the person's reasonable expectation of privacy for that image.

3. The image is disclosed with the intent to harm, harass, intimidate, threaten or coerce the depicted person.

As you have seen before, prosecutors must prove two mens rea, which attach to the two actus reus elements: an intent to disclose and an intent to harm, harass, intimidate, threaten, or coerce. The final verb in that list, to "coerce," is colloquially known as "sextortion." Sextortion

---

Sextortion: The use of voluntarily sent nude or sexually explicit photos or videos to extort the sender.

mirrors the elements of extortion, except that it limits the coercive means to threatening to make nude and sexually explicit images public.

In the *In Re S. K.* case, found in your next Digging Deeper, a counterintuitive prosecution took place—a teenage victim of revenge porn was prosecuted for sexting.

DIGGING DEEPER 10.3

Is a victim of revenge porn guilty of sexting?

Case: *In Re S. K.*
Court: Maryland Court of Appeals
Year: 2019
Opinion by J. Getty.

During the 2016–17 school year, two sixteen-year-old females, A. T. and S. K., and a seventeen-year-old male, K. S., were best friends attending Maurice J. McDonough High School in Charles County, Maryland. S. K. and A. T. had been friends since elementary school. The trio had a group chat on their cell phones in which they would communicate with one another by text message. A. T. stated the group chat was used, among other things, to send silly photos and videos to "one-up" each other. The trio frequently hung out together and trusted one another to keep their group text messages private.

In October, A. T. and K. S. received a text message containing a video recording from S.K.'s cell phone number. The video was approximately one minute in length and showed S. K. performing fellatio on a male. The male's identity and age were not established in the testimony at the adjudication hearing although A. T. testified that she knew him. In the video, S. K. is nude and her upper torso, including an exposed breast, is visible throughout most of the video. The nude male's mid-torso and erect penis are shown during the majority of the video, although an unfocused view of his face is visible momentarily at the video's conclusion. The male appears to be the one filming the video through an extended reach of his arm, similar to taking a selfie.

In December, S. K. and K. S. had a falling out. Commenting on the falling out, A. T. testified: We all used to be friends. And at the time [K. S.] just really dislikes her. And you can ask anybody in his sixth period class. Cause we used to eat lunch together. And he would always write on the board like, saying she's a slut or saying any type of thing.

K. S. began urging A. T. to go with him to the school resource officer to report the video of S. K. Eventually, A. T. relented. K. S. testified he was worried about S. K. and wanted her to receive help. However, A. T. testified that the motives of K. S. were not so pure. A. T. testified that K. S. was bragging around school about S. K. going to jail if he were to report the text message to the school resource officer. She stated, "He has a strong hate towards her. And he kinda [sic] just pulled me along with him because he knew I would be on his side."

A. T. and K. S. went to the school resource officer, Officer Eugene Caballero of the Charles County Sheriff's Office. At the meeting, A. T. and K. S. told Officer Caballero about the video. At that point, K. S. possessed the video as an email attachment. He displayed the email and video on Officer Caballero's computer. Officer Caballero then instructed K. S. to delete the video from his email account.

After receiving a copy of the video from K. S., Officer Caballero met with S. K. at the Robert D. Stethem Educational Center in Charles County. S. K. was read her Miranda rights and agreed to speak with Officer Caballero. In his police report, Officer Caballero stated S. K. cried during their meeting and was upset that the video was going around the school. S. K. was under the impression that Officer Caballero met with her to stop the video from further distribution to other students. At no point during this meeting did Officer Caballero inform S. K. that she was considered a suspect for criminal activity. S. K. provided Officer Caballero with a written statement admitting that she was in the video and had only sent it to her two friends.

The police report was referred to the State's Attorney for Charles County who had discretion as to whether to file the criminal charges. After review, the State charged S. K., as a juvenile, with three counts as follows: Count 1: filming a minor engaging in sexual conduct... Count 2: distributing child pornography... and Count 3: displaying an obscene item to a minor....

The adjudicatory hearing was held on April 27, 2017, before the Circuit Court of Charles County sitting as a juvenile court. S. K. was represented by the Office of the Public Defender. A. T., K. S., and Officer Caballero testified during the hearing. At the conclusion of the hearing, Count 1, filming a minor engaging in sexual conduct, was dismissed because there was no evidence presented that S. K. was filming the video. At the end of closing argument, the juvenile court found S. K. involved as to Counts 2 and 3.

At a subsequent disposition hearing on May 18, 2017, S. K. was placed on electronic monitoring until June 9, 2017, and supervised probation administered by the Department of Juvenile Services....

For the first time, this Court is confronted with the complexities of the sociocultural phenomenon of sexting by minors in the context of Maryland's criminal statutes as applied in a juvenile proceeding. We are asked to determine whether it is a violation of the child pornography statute for a sixteen-year-old minor female to distribute a one-minute video via text message to her best friends in which she is engaging in sexual conduct that is not criminal. Further, we are asked whether the distribution of the text message video qualifies as an "item" codified in the obscenity statute criminalizing the display of obscene matter to a minor.

Central to this issue is the dominant role cell phones play in our society. In *Riley v. California*, Chief Justice John Roberts observed that "modern cellphones... are now such a pervasive and insistent part of daily life that the proverbial visitor from Mars might conclude they were an important feature of human anatomy." Undoubtedly, smartphone use has become ubiquitous across all generations. However, Generation Z, loosely comprising of those born after 1997, has a distinctive relationship with this technology. Unlike the Silent Generation, Baby Boomers, Generation X, or Millennials, Generation Z has never known life without access to a smartphone....

Consistent with the rise in smartphone usage, at least 18.5% of middle and high schoolers report having received sexually explicit images or videos on their phones or computers....

Although the majority of states have passed legislation to amend their child pornography statute relative to sexting, Maryland is one of twenty-one states that have not passed any such legislation and thus permit teenagers to be charged under the child pornography statute....

Occasionally, other state courts have considered the breadth of their child pornography statute vis-à-vis sexting. In *State v. Gray*, the Washington Supreme Court addressed whether a seventeen-year-old boy's act of "electronically sending an unsolicited picture of his erect penis to an adult woman" violated the language of [a Washington statute] that "[a] person commits the crime of dealing in depictions of a minor engaging in sexually explicit conduct in the second degree when he or she... [k]nowingly... disseminates... any visual or printed matter that depicts a minor engaged in an act of sexually explicit conduct." 189 Wash.2d 334, 337 (2017). The majority upheld the conviction, holding that the statute was unambiguous, thus the minor's conduct violated the statute....

The court determined there was nothing under the statute which indicated a natural person and a minor cannot be the same person. Further, if the Washington State Legislature had intended to exclude minors, it would have explicitly done so. As to the policy arguments, the court commented:

> We understand the concern over teenagers being prosecuted for consensually send-ing sexually explicit pictures to each other. We also understand the worry caused by a well-meaning law failing to adapt to changing technology. But our duty is to interpret the law as written and, if unambiguous, apply its plain meaning to the facts before us.

In a recent Colorado case, a male teenager was romantically involved with two female teenagers during the 2012–2013 school year. *People in Interest of T. B.*, 2019 WL 2495514 (June 17, 2019 Co.). He exchanged nude selfies by text message with the females. The male kept the photos on his cell phone, and when he was arrested in 2013 on an unrelated sexual assault charge, police discovered the photographs of the nude females on his cell phone. He was charged and adjudicated delinquent for sexual exploitation of a child....

As to the dangers of child pornography, the Supreme Court stated:

> The distribution of photographs and films depicting sexual activity by juveniles is intrinsically related to the sexual abuse of children in at least two ways. First, the materials produced are a permanent record of the children's participation and the harm to the child is exacerbated by their circulation. Second, the distribution network for child pornography must be closed if the production of material which requires the sexual exploitation of children is to be effectively controlled. Indeed, there is no seri-ous contention that the legislature was unjustified in believing that it is difficult, if not impossible, to halt the exploitation of children by pursuing only those who produce the photographs and movies. While the production of pornographic materials is a low-profile, clandestine industry, the need to market the resulting products requires a visible apparatus of distribution. The most expeditious if not the only practical method of law enforcement may be to dry up the market for this material by imposing severe criminal penalties on persons selling, advertising, or otherwise promoting the product.

With this historical backdrop, we now turn to an analysis of the statute [under which S. K. was prosecuted].

The 1978 child pornography statute [under which S. K. was prosecuted] prohibits a "per-son" from knowingly distributing "any matter, visual representation, or performance... that depicts a minor engaged as a subject in... sexual conduct." Sexual conduct is defined in CR § 11-101(d) as (1) human masturbation; (2) sexual intercourse; or (3) whether alone or with another individual or animal, any touching of or contact with: (i) the genitals, buttocks, or pubic areas of any individual; or (ii) breasts of a female individual."...

S. K. contends this case is about whether [the statute] permits the prosecution of a minor for transmitting a visual representation of herself engaged in consensual, legal sexual conduct. S. K. argues the answer is no, stating the statute was intended to protect, not prosecute, minors victimized and exploited in the production of sexually explicit videos....

S. K. is certainly "a person" to which this statute would apply. We refuse to read into the statute an exception for minors who distribute their own matter, and thus we believe S. K.'s adjudication as delinquent under [the statute] must be upheld.

We do not find any ambiguity in this text and, therefore it is our duty to interpret the law as written and apply its plain meaning to the facts before us....

This case presents a unique challenge. On the one hand, there is no question that the State has an overwhelming interest in preventing the spread of child pornography and has been given broad authority to eradicate the production and distribution of child pornography. On the other hand, S. K., albeit unwisely, engaged in the same behavior as many of her peers. Here, S. K. is prosecuted as a "child pornographer" for sexting and, because she is a minor, her actions fell directly within the scope of the statute. The General Assembly has consistently expanded the scope of the statute to assist in the eradication of any form of child pornography. As written, the statute in its plain meaning is all encompassing, making no distinction whether a minor or an adult is distributing the matter. Therefore, based on this intent and the unambiguous language, we believe S. K.'s conduct falls within the purview of the statute. In affirming this adjudication, however, we recognize that there may be compelling policy reasons for treating teenage sexting different from child pornography. In response to this case, legislation was introduced in the 2019 Legislative Session that was not passed but in light of these policy concerns, such legislation ought to be considered by the General Assembly in the future.

[Conviction affirmed.

In dissent, Justice Hotten argued that "person" and "minor" should be interpreted to mean two different people and that minors, the group the law was intended to protect, can't be guilty of the crime.]

Stay Out of My (Cyber)space

Hundreds of years ago, people who would skulk around homes, under windows and eaves—"eavesdroppers"—were punished for their privacy invasions. Today, the greatest threat to privacy is electronic. Accessing a person's cell phone, laptop, or online accounts opens a doorway to a depth and breadth of information about a person that has never been possible before. In moments, a hacker can obtain financial information, friends and family contact data, work information, private thoughts, photos, and a treasure trove of location and tracking data that may date back for years. Because of this, computer privacy law is an important and growing area.

All jurisdictions have laws that regulate access to, and the use of, computers and digital data. Much of this law is civil and regulatory. But a growing body of criminal law is developing. You read about some of these laws in prior chapters, such as identity theft statutes.

There are many federal criminal statutes that protect computer access and data privacy.

The Computer Fraud and Abuse Act (CFAA) criminalizes "unauthorized access" to computers for the purpose of committing fraud or extortion, harming hardware or software, stealing and selling data, and for other nefarious reasons. This is the federal government's go-to law to prosecute computer hacking.

Also significant is the Federal Wiretap Act, as amended by the Electronics Communications Privacy Act (ECPA).[14] The former only applied to telephone calls. The ECPA broadened the Wiretap Act to include digital communication. These laws protect wire, oral, and electronic communications as they are occurring and when stored. The following prohibitions are among the many protections of the ECPA:

- Intruding into, intercepting, or attempting to intercept any wire, oral, or electronic communications

- Disclosing or attempting to disclose the contents of any wire, oral, or electronic communication knowing that the information was obtained through the interception of communications

- Using or attempting to use the contents of any wire, oral, or electronic communication knowing that the information was obtained through the interception of communications

- Intentionally disclosing or attempting to disclose the contents of communications intercepted legally knowing that the information was intercepted in connection with a criminal investigation

- Preventing electronic communication service providers from divulging the contents of a communication being transmitted.

The Wiretap Act has several exceptions. For example, companies that provide communications services, such as telecommunications companies and internet service providers (ISPs), may access data as needed to maintain their service. Most significantly is the exception that applies in criminal procedure. The Wiretap Act establishes the requirements for law enforcement to obtain wiretap orders, which are the equivalent of a traditional search warrant under the Fourth Amendment of the Constitution, only with additional hurdles the government must jump.

The mens rea for Wiretap Act and ECPA violations is intent. Negligent interceptions or disclosures are not criminal acts. Violations of these two laws are felonies that carry up to 5 years in prison.

The ECPA applies to intercepted or tapped communications. The Stored Communications Act (SCA)[15] protects records stored by service providers. Unauthorized access to these files is criminalized. Specifically, the law declares it a felony if a person "intentionally accesses without authorization a facility through which an electronic communication service is provided or... intentionally exceeds an authorization to access that facility; and thereby obtains, alters, or prevents authorized access to a wire or electronic communication while it is in electronic storage."

The SCA contains exceptions. Again, service providers can access the data when needed for maintenance. An important exception applies to government access. If a communication has been in storage for 180 days or less, the government must obtain a warrant to obtain it. If the communications have been in storage for over 180 days, or the user has accessed the data, the government can provide notice to the customer and then issue a subpoena to obtain the records. The distinction in time harks back to a time when users downloaded their data to their personal computers, and any data left with the ISPs was either abandoned or intended to be backup storage. At the time, Congress decided that abandoned and backup data wasn't entitled to the same privacy protections as original, real-time data. This rationale is out of date in a world where forever cloud storage is commonly used for the most sensitive of data. Changes to these provisions of the SCA are likely in the years to come. Like the ECPA, an actor must intentionally commit the act of accessing the data. Violations are punished with as many as 10 years in prison.

There are other federal laws that protect the privacy of intellectual property, medical data, and national security. And as mentioned earlier in this chapter and in prior chapters, there are federal laws that protect children from sexual exploitation and violence, and the states all protect privacy in internet communications and data storage.

Malware

The crimes discussed so far represent a specific breed of computer crime—where the computer is the instrument of wrongdoing. But a computer can also be the target of a crime. A laptop, desktop, server, and other hardware can be physically destroyed. These acts can be punished under traditional property crime laws.

Computers are also harmed by malicious software—malware—that has been introduced into a computer. Malware comes in many forms, including viruses, worms, ransomware, spyware, and phishing. They are similar in that they enter a computer or system and modify, damage, destroy, record, or transmit information. A virus is a form of malware that spreads through infected files. A virus is triggered when the file is opened. Worms are similar, except they are self-executing. They spread without attaching to files. They can rapidly "worm" their way through entire systems. Ransomware refers to malware that takes control or "hijacks" a computer, rendering it unusable by the user until payment is made to reopen the computer for use. Spyware collects information on users and uses it to target marketing to the user or to commit fraud. Finally, phishing refers to use of spam, fake text or email messages, or fraudulent websites to defraud people. In addition to the harm caused to computers and systems and the economic losses that individuals, corporations, and countries experience, malware threatens life. Medical implants, hospital equipment, and critical infrastructure all rely on healthy hardware and software.

The introduction of malware into computers with the intent to cause damage or commit fraud is covered by the federal CFAA, as discussed earlier in this chapter. State laws also criminalize this conduct. An example is Nebraska's law:

Neb. Rev. Stat. §28-1345.

Unlawful acts; harming or disrupting operations; penalties.

(1) Any person who accesses or causes to be accessed any computer, computer system, computer software, or computer network without authorization or who, having accessed any computer, computer system, computer software, or computer network

---

Malware: Software that is designed to damage, gain access, or disrupt computers and computer systems.

with authorization, knowingly and intentionally exceeds the limits of such authorization shall be guilty of an offense if he or she intentionally: (a) Alters, damages, deletes, or destroys any computer, computer system, computer software, computer network, computer program, data, or other property; (b) disrupts the operation of any computer, computer system, computer software, or computer network; or (c) distributes a destructive computer program with intent to damage or destroy any computer, computer system, computer network, or computer software. [The statute continues by grading the offense by the amount of loss caused.]

The actor must knowingly and intentionally exceed her authorization and must intentionally cause one of the listed outcomes (e.g., alter, damage). This high mens rea standard frees the innocent party who spreads malware from guilt.

QUESTIONS AND PROBLEMS

1. Identify the three types of computer crime.
2. In the *In Re S. K.* case, which was featured in the Digging Deeper feature (Reading Activity 10.3), a juvenile who had been the victim of revenge porn was prosecuted for having sent the video that was used to harass her. Make your best policy arguments in favor of holding her criminally liable for sexting *and* for not holding her liable.
3. Are the following cyberstalking statutes consistent with the First Amendment's protection of free speech? Explain your answers.
   It shall be a misdemeanor of the first degree for any person, with an intent to harass or annoy another person, to make two or more electronic communications that do, in fact, harass or annoy the person.
   It shall be a misdemeanor in the first degree for any person, with an intent to cause another person to fear serious bodily harm or death, to make two or more electronic communications that do, in fact, and reasonably, cause the recipient of the communications to fear seriously bodily harm or death.

IN A NUTSHELL

The network of commercial criminal law, along with its counterpart civil commercial law, is intended to protect the U.S. economic system. Individual investors rely on the law to protect their savings, investments, and retirement.

Independently, white-collar crime and cybercrime are costly and harmful. When computers are used to commit white-collar crime, the frequency of these crimes, and the resulting harm, explodes. Historic crimes, such as forgery and counterfeiting, continue to be important in deterring and punishing these crimes. But they don't fully address the problems of modernity. Accordingly, all of the states and the federal government have enacted laws that are aimed specifically at both cybercrime and white-collar crime.

The federal government, through its interstate and international commerce powers, actively prosecutes white-collar crime and cybercrime. The mail and wire fraud statutes, securities fraud laws, ECPA, and RICO are among the most powerful tools federal prosecutors have in their belts. Likewise, the states, with varied approaches, prosecute the same crimes.

LEGAL TERMS

Counterfeiting (p. 308)

cyberstalking (p. 320)

Forgery (p. 307)

insider trading (p. 315)

mail fraud (p. 311)

malware (p. 331)

money laundering (p. 311)

revenge porn (p. 324)

securities fraud (p. 315)

sexting (p. 324)

sextortion (p. 325)

NOTES

1. Krebs on Security "Money Laundering Via Author Impersonation on Amazon?", accessed January 8, 2021, https://krebsonsecurity.com/2018/02/money-laundering-via-author-impersonation-on-amazon/.

2. MPC §224.1

3. *United States Postal Inspection Service: Because the Mail Matters*. Publication 162. U.S. Postal Service. Accessed January 9, 2020. USPS.com.

4. *McNally v. United States*, 483 U.S. 350, 356 (1987).

5. Jed S. Rakoff, *The Federal Mail Fraud Statute (Part 1)*, 18 Duquesne L. Rev. 771 (1980).

6. 18 U.S.C. §1343.

7. U.S. Attorney's Office for the District of Minnesota, "Sixty Defendants Charged In $300 Million Nationwide Telemarketing Fraud Scheme," press release; October 28, 2020,anuary 10, 2021. j ustice.gov.

8. Nick Brown, "Luckin Coffee Agrees to Pay $180 Million to Settle SEC Fraud Charges," *Daily Coffee News*, December 22, 2020, dailycoffeenews.com.

9. The primary laws of insider trading are found at 15 U.S.C. §78j and Securities and Exchange Commission Rule 10b-5, 17 C.F.R. § 240.10b-5, promulgated thereunder.

10. 18 U.S.C. §1348.

11. 47 U.S.C. § 223(a)(1)(A).

12. 18 U.S.C. §2261(A).

13. 18 U.S.C. §875(c).

14. 18 U.S.C. §§2510 et seq.

15. 18 U.S.C. §§2701 et seq.

11 CRIMES THAT INVOLVE THE PUBLIC GOOD

In 1990, the United States was briefly in the prostitution business. As you might suspect, the path the federal government traveled to find itself in control of a brothel was not straight. (Congress didn't decide one day that the public good demanded a federal brothel.) The story begins in the early 1960s when a private party opened an illegal brothel named the Mustang Bridge Ranch in Storey County, Nevada, about 20 miles from the gambling town of Reno. Several years after it opened, the ranch was purchased by Joe and Sally Conforte. They renamed the brothel the Mustang Ranch. Politically connected, the Confortes successfully lobbied the Nevada legislature to legalize prostitution. They were successful, and since the early 1970s, with subsequent amendments to the original law, counties have been empowered to permit regulated prostitution, except in the state's largest cities. Ironically, that means one area where prostitution isn't legal is in Sin City itself, Las Vegas.

PHOTO 11.1 The Mustang Ranch brothel in the early 2020s

Debra Reid/Associated Press

After the law was changed, the Confortes persuaded Storey County to permit prostitution, and the Mustang Ranch became the first licensed brothel in Nevada in 1971. Joe was a high roller with a big personality. He kept tough bodyguards near and survived assassination attempts, but eventually, one of his associates killed a professional boxer who had been having an affair with Sally and who had bragged that he was going to take over the brothel. Joe's associate was prosecuted by a friend of Joe, tried by a judge who was a friend of Joe, and acquitted by a jury which included several people to whom Joe was a landlord. In the late 1980s, Joe found himself in legal trouble—maybe the worst kind of legal trouble: tax fraud. After being convicted of tax fraud, Conforte fled the nation, and the ranch was seized by the government. Bankruptcy was filed, and the U.S. Trustee in Bankruptcy briefly operated the business before it was sold. Its new owners were subsequently convicted of fraud and conspiracy, and the business was closed again. For years, it was on-again, off-again. In 2020, however, the Mustang Ranch was in full operation, qualifying for small-business coronavirus relief funds.[1]

Prostitution is one of the many crimes against the public and against the government that will be examined in the next two chapters. The crimes in this chapter are characterized in a variety of ways. It is common, for example, to refer to prostitution, obscenity, and gambling as victimless or **morality crimes**. Vagrancy, panhandling, public urination, and disorderly conduct are examples of **quality-of-life crimes**. And other crimes in this chapter involve harm to the public at large. Pollution and animal welfare crimes are examples. The first crime to be discussed is prostitution. See Table 11.1 for a listing of crimes against the public good.

TABLE 11.1 ■ Types of Crimes Against the Public Good		
Quality-of-Life Crimes	*Morality Crimes*	*Larger Public Good*
Drugs use and distribution	Prostitution	Animal cruelty and neglect
Public exposure/nudity	Lewdness	Environmental degradation
Gambling	Obscenity	
Noise	Adultery	
Vagrancy, loitering, sleeping in public	Gambling	

THE OLDEST PROFESSION

Learning Objective: Identify, describe, and apply the elements of prostitution.

In *On the City Wall* (1888), the author Rudyard Kipling described the character Lalun as "a member of the most ancient profession in the world." Whether prostitution is the oldest profession is unknown, but there is no doubt that trading in sex is ancient. It is also known in the animal world, where the females of some species appear to trade sex for food and security.

Society views about prostitution vary by time, both within and between communities. There are societies where it was widely accepted during one period of time only to be treated as shameful, even criminal, during other periods. In contemporary United States, prostitution is illegal in every state except Nevada, where, as you learned, counties may permit it in rural areas.

Morality crimes: Acts that are prohibited because they offend the values of society.

Quality-of-life crimes: Acts that are believed to reduce the public's enjoyment of public spaces, lower the value of property, or otherwise reduce the quality of public life.

The elements of **prostitution** are

1. providing or agreeing to provide

2. sexual services

3. in exchange for compensation.

In most jurisdictions, the actor doesn't have to provide sexual services. Agreeing to provide them is satisfactory. Providing or agreeing to provide sex implies a high level of mens rea—some form of specific intent.

The second element, sexual services, includes all forms of sex, fellatio, intercourse, cunnilingus, and the touching of the sex organs. Today, the genders of the parties are immaterial.

The third element is the quid pro quo of prostitution. Sexual promiscuity is not only lawful; it is a constitutionally protected right. Receiving pay for the same conduct changes matters. Although money is a common form of compensation, any item of value (e.g., drugs or legal services) can be used as compensation.

Buying sex is also a crime. In some states, the elements of prostitution are broadened to include people, commonly known as "johns," who buy, or offer to buy, sex. In others, the crime of **solicitation** is used to punish johns. Solicitation occurs when a person with "the purpose of promoting or facilitating its commission he commands, encourages or requests another person to engage in specific conduct which would constitute such crime."[2] While often associated with prostitution—though specific solicitation of prostitution laws can be found in some states—most jurisdictions criminalize the inducement or encouragement of any crime (e.g., solicitation of murder or theft).

Whether prostitution should be criminalized is a perennial policy debate. In favor of forbidding it are the arguments that many people, particularly women, are victimized by the crime and often these victims are trafficked and enslaved; that it is degrading to everyone involved; and that it is immoral. On the other side, proponents of decriminalizing prostitution argue that women are victimized by criminalization itself; that it doesn't prevent trafficking, but instead emboldens it; that sexually transmitted diseases could be better controlled if it was legalized and regulated; that it is an outlet for sexually aggressive men; that it can be taxed (organized crime would be removed from the equation); and that society should respect the autonomy of consenting adults to make commercial and intimate decisions for themselves.

QUESTIONS AND PROBLEMS

1. What are the elements of prostitution?
2. Identify reasons prostitution should be criminalized and why it should be permitted.

Prostitution: Agreeing to provide, or providing, sexual services in exchange for compensation.

Solicitation: Encouraging, enticing, or encouraging another to commit a crime.

ALL IN THE FAMILY

Learning Objective: Identify, describe, and apply the elements of incest.

In 2015, *New York Magazine* published an interview with a 17-year-old girl who had reunited with her father after 12 years apart. Shortly after they reunited, they began to engage in physical play. The play led to intercourse—the girl's first sexual experience. In the interview, the girl said, "We plan to move to New Jersey where we can be safe under the law since adult incest isn't illegal there, and once I'm there, I'll tell everyone. I'll call my mom and let her know that we are in love and we are having children." She continued by saying that they intend to marry. But the marriage won't be formally registered with the state. Although New Jersey permits incestuous sex, it doesn't permit incestuous marriages.[3]

Incest, or sex between consenting adults of the same family, is a crime in most states. Two policy reasons are advanced for making these relationships a crime. First, it is morally wrong. Most people react to incestuous relationships with disgust. It is a cultural taboo known throughout much of the world. Second, in response to the suggestion that incest is a victimless crime, opponents point out that the children of these relationships are at a higher-than-average risk of congenital defects and disease. Medical research supports this concern, particularly between first-degree relatives (e.g., parents and children, full siblings), where the likelihood is much greater than between second-degree relatives (e.g., grandparents and grandchildren, aunts and uncles, nieces and nephews, and half siblings) and third-degree relatives (e.g., first cousins). Possibly, the health of the children of incestuous relationships was the cause of the historical taboo.

A few states also forbid sex and marriage between a parent and a stepchild. Nebraska is such a state. Its incest law declares that "any person who shall knowingly intermarry or engage in sexual penetration with any person who falls within the degrees of consanguinity set forth in [another statute] or any person who engages in sexual penetration with his or her stepchild who is under nineteen years of age commits incest," a felony.[4] As you read earlier, New Jersey and a few other states don't prohibit incestuous liaisons, even though marriage isn't permitted.

The elements of incest are as follows:

1. To engage in sexual intercourse

2. with another person within a specified degree of consanguinity (family relationship)

3. with knowledge of the relationship.

The mens rea is typically high—actual knowledge of the family relationship. If two people meet for the first time as adults, begin a sexual relationship, and subsequently learn they are siblings who were separated when they were infants, no crime is committed.

Because one of the purposes of criminalizing incest is to prevent the birth of unhealthy children, sexual intercourse is the prohibited conduct in most states. Other forms of sex are not punished. Jurisdictions that prohibit incestuous sex typically also criminalize marriage. An attendant circumstance is the relationship. Both biological and adoptive relationships satisfy the element, as long as they fall within the degree of consanguinity. This prevents a father and daughter from terminating parental rights to open the door to a relationship. Their biological connection remains. The same is true of relationships between parents and adoptive children, or between adoptive siblings, even though the health of the children born from these relationships is not at risk of congenital disease or abnormalities.

For financial reasons, spouses adopting one another has been on the rise in recent years. For example, a person may create a trust and name their children as beneficiaries with the intent of shielding the money from being taken to satisfy a civil judgment. To do this, one spouse may adopt the other. Even if this process is successful in warding off a creditor, it creates an incest problem.

State law forbids incest by persons within one degree of consanguinity. Peter and Rachel, first cousins, fall in love and begin a sexual relationship. They have not committed incest because they have a third-degree relationship.

QUESTIONS AND PROBLEMS

1. What are the elements of incest?
2. Rachel and Tim are biological siblings who were separated when they were ages 4 and 5. They meet at a bar when they are 21 and 22, fall in love, and decide to marry. A week before the wedding, they discover through DNA tests that they are siblings. They decide their love for one another is too important to give up. They decide to continue with the marriage but to not have children. Have they committed incest in a state that forbids relationships within one degree of consanguinity?

COVETING THY NEIGHBOR'S SPOUSE

Learning Objective: Identify, describe, and apply the elements of adultery.

For a long period of time, sex outside of marriage was a crime. Today, most states have repealed their adultery crimes. But the crime continues to be recognized, at least in the books, in a minority of states. New York, for example, has this statute:

Section 255.17

A person is guilty of adultery when he engages in sexual intercourse with another person at a time when he has a living spouse, or the other person has a living spouse.

Adultery is a class B misdemeanor. (90 days in jail and/or fine)

The elements of criminal adultery are::

1. Sexual intercourse with

2. someone other than one's spouse, or with a married person with

3. knowledge of the marital status.

An actor's knowledge that they are married, or that their lover is married, is the required mens rea. So a person who is deceived into believing their lover is single is not guilty of the crime. The actus reus is commonly sexual intercourse. Other forms of sex don't give rise to liability. In Illinois, "a person commits adultery when he or she has sexual intercourse with another not his or her spouse, if the behavior is open and notorious."[5] Presumably, the statute identifies two separate actus reus—sexual intercourse in private as well as an open and notorious relationship—not the single actus reus that a couple's physical liaisons shall be open and notorious. Another jurisdictional variation in the crime is the requirement that the spouse of the married party be the complainant. Reports of infidelity by others or discovery by police are not adequate to sustain a prosecution in these jurisdictions.

Even where forbidden, adultery is rarely enforced. This is largely due to the lack of interest in prosecuting the crime by the general public. This is illustrated by the high-profile case of the 45th president of the United States, Donald Trump. He admitted to adultery while living in New York, where adultery remains a crime. Yet his admission garnered little legal attention. Many years ago, a legal scholar suggested an explanation for why the crime remains on the books, even though it is unenforced. He wrote that "most unenforced criminal laws survive in order to satisfy moral objections to our established modes of conduct. They are unenforced because we want to continue our conduct, and unrepealed because we want to preserve our morals."[6]

An unanswered question is whether having an adulterous relationship is a protected liberty interest under the Fourteenth Amendment in the same way that other sexual and procreative conduct—such as same-sex marriage and interracial marriage, both once forbidden—have been found to be.

PROBLEMS AND QUESTIONS

1. What are the elements of adultery?
2. Abebi was born in Niger, where arranged marriages are common. Young girls are often married to older men who bring money and status to the relationship. Against her wishes, Abebi was married to 30-year-old man when she was 14. He forced her to quit school to stay home to care for him. Still unhappy at 18, she fled Niger for the United States. She met other Nigerian immigrants who told her that her marriage wasn't valid in the United States. Three months after her arrival in the United States, she met a man and began a sexual relationship. Her husband from Niger found her, notified authorities, and asked that she be prosecuted for adultery. Has she committed adultery? Explain your answer.

I KNOW IT WHEN I SEE IT

Learning Objective: Identify, describe, and apply the elements of the Miller obscenity test.

In 1972, Herbert Streicher, a young man and former U.S. Marine, was hired as lighting director for a low-budget pornographic film. When the film's male lead didn't show, Streicher, who would be given the screen name Harry Reems, was paid $100 to assume the lead. The movie, *Deep Throat*, became a sensation, catapulting sexual pornography into the mainstream. But social conservatives weren't excited about the movie. Contributing to the film's success was the media attention that followed multiple police raids of a New York movie theater where it was being shown. The raids followed a decision by a New York judge that the film was legally obscene; in the judge's words, the film was "a Sodom and Gomorrah gone wild before the fire."

In 1974, Mr. Reems was arrested in New York and extradited to Tennessee, where he and several others were tried for federal conspiracy to transport obscene materials across state lines. He was convicted by the jury, even though he had waived all interests in the film in his acting contract and had nothing to do with the film's sales or distribution. The convictions of all of the defendants were subsequently reversed on appeal.[7]

The cultural impact of the movie was enduring. It began a more permissive trend toward sexually explicit expression, setting the stage for an explosion in pornography when the internet came of age, and the film's title would subsequently be used by the journalists Carl Bernstein and Bob Woodward to describe one of their most important information sources in President Nixon's Watergate scandal.[8]

Governments have long regulated to protect morality. These laws criminalize immoral conduct, speech, and the middle area between the two, known as expressive conduct or symbolic speech.

Of the three, governmental authority over conduct is the greatest. In a constitutional sense, regulations of conduct are valid if the government has a rational basis for them. Usually, simply having a history of disapproval of conduct and a law that is reasonably designed to address that conduct is constitutional. Regulating indecent speech is different.

Restrictions of words, art, paper publications, internet postings, broadcasts, and film that are deemed morally wrong, disgusting, vulgar, or lewd are subject to First Amendment free speech review. Once actively enforced, few prosecutions for indecency occur today. One reason is the relaxation of social norms. As is true of adultery, the public interest in punishing immoral conduct has declined considerably in recent decades. Additionally, indecency laws often regulate First Amendment protected speech.

You may recall that even though the First Amendment refers to "speech," SCOTUS has interpreted the clause to protect many forms of expression, including this list:

- Verbal communication

- Nonverbal communication, such as body gestures

- Written communication, such letters, newspapers, pamphlets

- Digital communication, such as email, websites, and social media

- Artistic expression, such as paintings and sculpture

- Video and film

- Expressive conduct, such as wearing clothes with a message or burning a flag

- Donating to political candidates and causes

Not all speech is equal. Political speech, for example, receives greater protection than commercial speech. This is a reflection of the values that underpin protecting expression. Creating an environment that is open and rich in political discourse is more important to a free state than getting the word out about half-priced pumpkin spice lattes. Advertising isn't unprotected; it is less protected. Similarly, expressive conduct is less protected because it is a mix of speech and conduct, the latter not being protected by the First Amendment when in its pure form. In the context of lewd or nude expressive conduct, SCOTUS, in a complex 5–4 plurality decision in *Barnes v. Glen theater, Inc.*, held that nude dancing is protected by the First Amendment but only within its "outer perimeters."[9] That is another way of saying that classic nude dancing in a bar is only marginally protected. The court acknowledged that nudity can be expressive but also found that the state had a neutral and legitimate interest in regulating nudity. But the state's authority is limited to requiring the most private area of the body to be covered. In the court's words:

> Likewise, the requirement that the dancers don pasties and a G-string does not deprive the dance of whatever erotic message it conveys; it simply makes the message slightly less graphic. The perceived evil that Indiana seeks to address is not erotic dancing, but public nudity. The appearance of people of all shapes, sizes and ages in the nude at a beach, for example, would convey little if any erotic message, yet the state still seeks to prevent it. Public nudity is the evil the state seeks to prevent, whether or not it is combined with expressive activity.

Subsequently, the court reviewed nude dancing again in *Pap's A.M. v. City of Erie*.[10] In this case, the court affirmed Barnes while also making clear that courts should apply the **O'Brien test** to public nudity cases. The elements of the O'Brien test are as follows:

1. The regulation must be within the constitutional power of the government.

2. The regulation furthers an important or substantial governmental interest.

3. The interest must be unrelated to the suppression of free expression.

4. Any incidental restriction on speech must be no greater than is essential to the furtherance of the governmental interest.

Applying O'Brien, the court concluded that the government didn't intend to suppress expression, that the restrictions on expression were minimal, and that the government had a substantial interest in protecting public order and morality. One justice agreed in the outcome but disagreed in the reasoning. Justice Souter didn't find the state's interest in morality or order to be substantial. But he was persuaded that the secondary effects of nude-dancing establishments on the property values of neighbors and other interests were substantial. Other justices also concurred but would have required less of the government (a simple rational basis, not substantial interest) to uphold the law.

O'Brien test: A test used to determine if expressive conduct is entitled to First Amendment free speech protection.

Morally objectionable expression is found in many mediums: writing, audio recordings, photographs, and video. And as Harry Reems learned the hard way, speech that offends morality is sometimes criminalized under the theory that it is degrading to both actors and consumers and because it threatens social stability. Speech that is so lewd, morally objectionable, or lascivious that it loses First Amendment protection is known as obscenity. Everything less than obscenity, including what is commonly known as pornography, is protected.

Drawing the line between acceptable and unacceptable speech is difficult. As Justice Potter Stewart wrote about defining **obscenity**, "I shall not today attempt further to define the kinds of material I understand to be embraced within that shorthand description; and perhaps I could never succeed in intelligibly doing so. *But I know it when I see it*, and the motion picture involved in this case is not that."[11]

Today, the **Miller test,** announced in the 1973 SCOTUS case *Miller v. California*, is used to define obscenity.[12] Under the Miller test, expression is obscene if these conditions apply:

- The average person applying contemporary community standards would find that the work, taken as a whole, appeals to a prurient interest and

- the work depicts or describes, in a patently offensive way, sexual conduct specifically defined by the applicable state law, and

- the work, taken as a whole, lacks serious literary, artistic, political, or scientific value.

There is a lot packed into the Miller test. First, the work must appeal to a prurient interest. A shameful or morbid sexual interest is prurient. The prurient decision is based on community standards. The Miller case was decided in 1973, before the internet. Today, with porn widely available and consumed by a broad audience and greater sexuality in advertising and popular media than in the past, the idea that community values differ from national values is questionable.

The second prong of the test requires that the speech depict sexual conduct that is prohibited by law and that the depiction be patently offensive. The third prong creates a zone of protection for works that may satisfy the first two elements of the Miller test but are nonetheless protected because they serve a larger societal need.

Images of a child's genitalia in a medical textbook that is intended to teach future physicians how to identify sexual abuse are protected.

Publication of the same photos on the internet with the intent of appealing to a pedophile's sexual appetites, on the other hand, are not protected and could be punished.

Obscenity: A category of speech that is not protected by the First Amendment. The Miller test is used to determine if speech is obscene.

Miller test: A test used to determine if speech is so morally objectionable—obscene—that it loses the protection of the First Amendment.

As the internet's booming pornography industry proves, what is socially and legally accept-able today is much broader than in the past. Nearly all forms of common consensual adult sex may be displayed. This includes, among other acts, intercourse, felatio, and cunnilingus. The sex of the participants is immaterial today. Yet there are forms of sexual conduct that clearly fall outside of the protection of the First Amendment. Sex with children and bestiality are examples.

SCOTUS has held that depictions of sex with children is unprotected because of the physi-cal and emotional harm that it causes.[13] On the other hand, the court struck down a federal law that criminalized the creation and distribution of digital images of sex involving children because no children were harmed in the making of the imagery.[14] Because of the heightened privacy interests people have in their homes, SCOTUS has also decided that a homeowner (or renter) can't be punished for possession of obscenity in the home.[15] However, returning to the harm rationale, possession of child pornography in the home is unprotected.[16]

In another line of cases, the authority of governments to protect minors from viewing sexual content has been affirmed. For example, a state may prohibit the distribution and sale of erotic materials to minors, even if the materials are not obscene. On the other hand, attempts to con-trol what appears on the internet to prevent children from viewing age-inappropriate content have failed because they have been overbroad; they limited adult access to the content too.

Although far less enforced than in the past, all of the states and the federal government have obscenity laws. For the federal government, laws that prohibit sending obscene materials in the mail are the most commonly enforced. Virginia's obscenity laws are similar to what are found in other states. A writing, painting, video, or other form of expression is obscene when it, taken as "a whole, has as its dominant theme or purpose an appeal to the prurient interest in sex—that is, a shameful or morbid interest in nudity, sexual conduct, sexual excitement, excretory functions or products thereof or sadomasochistic abuse, and which goes substantially beyond customary limits of candor in description or representation of such matters and which, taken as a whole, does not have serious literary, artistic, political or scientific value."

Unsurprisingly, the statute tracks the language of the Miller test. The law continues by criminalizing the production, publication, sale, possession, and financing of obscenity. Schools, universities, and museums are generally exempted from prosecution under the law. Another feature of the law that is found in other state statutes is a presumption-of-age provision. A jury may infer that a person is a minor if a pornographic work depicts, by text, title, or appearance, that the person is under the age of 18.[17]

QUESTIONS AND PROBLEMS

1. What are the elements of the Miller test?
2. Andrea was the victim of sexual abuse as a child. Now an adult, she writes about her experiences in an internet blog. In the first blog, she explained that the purpose of the blog is to educate the public about the harms caused by sexual abuse of children, to use her story to activate for legal change, and to facilitate her own healing. In her blogs, she details her sexual abuse, including drawings that depict what happened to her. The

blog becomes popular with other victims of rape and abuse. But it is also a source of enjoyment for pedophiles. She was made aware of this by police, who asked her to stop blogging about her abuse. She refuses and is prosecuted for obscenity. Apply the Miller test to her case.

I DON'T WANT TO SEE IT

Learning Objectives: Identify, describe, and apply the elements of public indecency and describe the contemporary equal protection issue with these laws.

The last section discussed indecent expression. There are also laws that address public indecency, or the public display of the sexual areas of the body as well as having sex in public. Recall from the earlier discussion that regulations of conduct easily pass constitutional analysis. As long as they don't violate a specific constitutional right, such as equal protection of the laws, they only need to be rational to be valid.

Public decency laws vary considerably. Every state prohibits public nudity, and most states prohibit sex in public, even when the private areas of the lovers are not visible to others.

How "public" is defined also varies. Obviously, public spaces, such as parks and government buildings, fall within the reach of these laws. Private spaces, including inside a home, may also be subject to public decency legislation. Undressing in front of a first-floor window of a home that sits close to a public street and sidewalk in a crowded neighborhood is public indecency. The outcome would be different if the home is located in a rural area, many acres away from the nearest home and hundreds of feet from the lightly traveled road that leads to the home. The analysis is objective; would a reasonable person have known that they were visible to other people?

The required mens rea is another area of difference between the states. Some jurisdictions require the actor to have a sexual intent; others do not. Consider the case of Jeffrey Toobin, lawyer, author, and media personality. In 2020, during the COVID-19 shut-in, Mr. Toobin was on a Zoom call with colleagues. During a time when he mistakenly thought his video was muted, Mr. Toobin could be seen masturbating. Apparently, he was on two Zoom calls simultaneously—the work call and a sex call with another party. Mr. Toobin was ultimately fired from his post at the *New Yorker* magazine after 27 years of employment as a staff writer.[18] Did he commit the crime of indecency? To answer this question, the elements of New York's indecency laws must be examined. The relevant code provisions are as follows:

N.Y. Penal Law §245.00. Public Lewdness

A person is guilty of public lewdness when he or she intentionally exposes the private or intimate parts of his or her body in a lewd manner or commits any other lewd act: (a) in a public place, or (b) (i) in private premises under circumstances in which he or she may readily be observed from either a public place or from other private premises, and with intent that he or she be so observed, or (ii) while trespassing, as defined in section

140.05 of this part, in a dwelling as defined in subdivision three of section 140.00 of this part, under circumstances in which he or she is observed by a lawful occupant. Public lewdness is a class B misdemeanor.

§245.01. Exposure of a person

A person is guilty of exposure if he appears in a public place in such a manner that the private or intimate parts of his body are unclothed or exposed. For purposes of this section, the private or intimate parts of a female person shall include that portion of the breast which is below the top of the areola. This section shall not apply to the breastfeeding of infants or to any person entertaining or performing in a play, exhibition, show or entertainment. Exposure of a person is a violation.

Assuming the reported facts are true, Mr. Toobin wasn't guilty of public lewdness because his exposure was accidental—he lacked the mens rea of intentionally exposing himself. Additionally, it appears that he didn't intend to be seen, at least not by his coworkers. The exposure statute is a more difficult question. As written, it appears to be a strict liability crime; no mens rea is mentioned. Even if construed as a strict liability crime, there is another question: Was he in a public place? Most likely, a virtual work meeting would be treated as the equivalent to being in the office. But it is plausible that a court could find otherwise.

Let's look at another example. Maine's indecent conduct law is as follows:

Maine, 17A-§854. Indecent Conduct

1. A person is guilty of indecent conduct if:
   A. In a public place:
      1. The actor engages in a sexual act...
      2. The actor knowingly exposes the actor's genitals under circumstances that, in fact, are likely to cause affront or alarm;
   B. In a private place, the actor exposes the actor's genitals with the intention that the actor be seen from a public place or from another private place; or
   C. In a private place, the actor exposes the actor's genitals with the intention that the actor be seen by another person in that private place under circumstances that the actor knows are likely to cause affront or alarm.

The areas of the body that may not be exposed in public typically include the anus, vagina, penis, pubic areas, and, on women, anything below the top of the areola of the breast. Many states expressly exempt breastfeeding from their public indecency laws.

A contemporary issue in public indecency law is whether the Fourteenth Amendment's equal protection clause commands that men and women be treated the same under public decency laws. Specifically, women are prohibited from exposing their breasts in public or to children in private; men aren't. The case of Tilli Buchanan is an example. In 2019, she and her husband were hanging drywall in their home. Drywall can be messy, so the two removed their shirts to keep their clothes clean. Ms. Buchanan also removed her bra. Three children of the husband's, varying in age from 9 to 13, discovered the two. The children asked why she was topless, and as it was later explained, "Tilli... considers herself a feminist and she wanted to make a point that everybody should be fine with walking around their house or elsewhere with skin showing."

Subsequently, the children told their mother what they witnessed, Mom reported the incident to state welfare officials, and Mrs. Buchanan was charged with three counts of lewdness in front of a child—a Class A misdemeanor, punishable with jail time, fines, and mandatory sex registration. With the assistance of the American Civil Liberties Union (ACLU), Ms. Buchanan challenged the law as violative of the equal protection clause because it treated men and women differently. The argument failed, and Ms. Buchanan pled guilty to a lesser crime, lewdness in front of an adult, and was ordered to pay a $600 fine. The reduction in the crime avoided Ms. Buchanan being listed on the sex offender registry. Ironically, to operationalize the plea agreement, she had to confess to exposing her breasts to an adult—her husband—in order to be guilty of the lesser offense.[19] In many states, this wouldn't be possible because their indecency laws expressly exempt nudity in front of spouses.

Ms. Buchanan wasn't the first legal challenge of its type. An international group, Free the Nipple, campaigns to decriminalize female toplessness and supports women who are criminally charged for exposing their breasts. While most courts have rejected both First Amendment expression and Fourteenth Amendment equal protection claims to be topless in public, a contrary decision was made by the 10th Circuit Court of Appeals in *Free the Nipple—Ft. Collins v. City of Ft. Collins* (2019), which is the subject of your next Digging Deeper.

DIGGING DEEPER 11.1

Does it violate equal protection for a state to allow a man to be topless but not a woman?

Case: *Free the Nipple—Ft. Collins v. City of Ft. Collins, CO*
Court: 10th Circuit Court of Appeals
Year: 2019
Circuit Judge Phillips

In 2015, after substantial public debate, the Fort Collins city council enacted this public-nudity ordinance:

No female who is ten (10) years of age or older shall knowingly appear in any public place with her breast exposed below the top of the areola and nipple while located: (1) In a public right-of-way, in a natural area, recreation area or trail, or recreation center, in a public building, in a public square, or while located in any other public place; or (2) On private property if the person is in a place that can be viewed from the ground level by another who is located on public property and who does not take extraordinary steps, such as climbing a ladder or peering over a screening fence, in order to achieve a point of vantage.... The prohibition [on female toplessness] does not extend to women breastfeeding in places they are legally entitled to be.

Fort Collins, Colo., Mun. Code § 17-142(b), (d). Any person who violates this ordinance "shall be guilty of a misdemeanor" and "shall be punished" by a fine of up to $2,650, or up to 180 days in jail, or both.

The Plaintiffs immediately sued the City in federal district court, alleging that the public-nudity ordinance violates the Free Speech Clause of the First Amendment and the Equal Protection Clause of the Fourteenth Amendment to the U.S. Constitution, as well as the Equal Rights Amendment to the Colorado Constitution....

[T]he Plaintiffs moved for a preliminary injunction blocking enforcement of the ordinance and "prohibit[ing] [the City] from discriminatorily arresting [the] Plaintiffs, and all others similarly situated, when they engage in the protected activity of standing topless in public places in Fort Collins, Colorado. The City countered with a motion to dismiss....

The district court first addressed the City's motion to dismiss. It granted the motion on the Plaintiffs' free-speech claim, agreeing with the City that "topless protests" aren't protected speech, but allowed the Plaintiffs' (federal) Equal Protection Clause and (state) Equal Rights Amendment claims to proceed. Next, the court turned to the Plaintiffs' preliminary-injunction motion. After holding a hearing on the matter, it granted the motion, ruling that the ordinance likely violated the Equal Protection Clause, and issued the requested injunction....

The Equal Protection Clause and Gender-Based Classifications

"No State shall... deny to any person within its jurisdiction the equal protection of the laws." U.S. Const. amend. XIV, § 1. The Equal Protection Clause, as the U.S. Supreme Court has interpreted it, directs "that all persons similarly situated should be treated alike." "At a minimum," it requires that any statutory classification be "rationally related to a legitimate governmental purpose." But more stringent judicial scrutiny attaches to classifications based on certain "suspect" characteristics.

Gender, for instance, "frequently bears no relation to ability to perform or contribute to society," and statutes that differentiate between men and women "very likely reflect outmoded notions" about their "relative capabilities." As a result, gender based classifications "call for a heightened standard of review," a standard dubbed "intermediate scrutiny" because it lies "[b]etween the extremes of rational basis review and strict scrutiny." To survive intermediate scrutiny, a gender-based classification needs "an exceedingly persuasive justification." The classification must serve "important governmental objectives" through means "substantially related to" achieving those objectives....

The district court characterized as "little more than speculation" the City's claim that banning only female toplessness furthered important governmental objectives. Instead, the court found: The ordinance discriminates against women based on the generalized notion that, regardless of a woman's intent, the exposure of her breasts in public (or even in her private home if viewable by the public) is necessarily a sexualized act. Thus, it perpetuates a stereotype engrained in our society that female breasts are primarily objects of sexual desire whereas male breasts are not. As a result, the court concluded, the Plaintiffs demonstrated "a strong likelihood that they will succeed at the permanent injunction trial in establishing that [the city's public-nudity ordinance] violates the Equal Protection Clause....

The City challenges this conclusion on appeal. It argues that, "in light of the differences between male and female breasts," prohibiting only female toplessness is substantially related to an important governmental objective, as a sizeable majority of other courts have found. We address the City's argument in two parts. First, we discuss the focus of the City's defense—the physical differences between male and female breasts—and explain how such differences affect the constitutional analysis. Second, we determine whether the City's female only toplessness ban survives constitutional scrutiny.

a. Physical Differences

In defending the constitutionality of its public-nudity ordinance, the City emphasizes the physical, social, and sexual characteristics particular to the female breast. Citing a Wikipedia article (which is titled "Breast" but discusses only the female version) the City argues that women's breasts "have social and sexual characteristics," although their "primary function" is breastfeeding infants. The article, as quoted by the City, describes female breasts ("and especially the nipples") as "among the various human erogenous zones" and claims that "it is common to press or massage them with hands or orally before or during sexual activity." Breasts, the City claims, "can figure prominently in a woman's perception of her body image and sexual attractiveness" and "have a hallowed sexual status" in Western culture, "arguably more fetishized than either sex's genitalia." But "the sexualization of women's breasts," according to the City, "is not solely a product of societal norms, but of biology." Research suggests that women's breasts have greater "tactile sensitivity" than men's....

[A]s we inquire into a gender-based classification's objectives, we must beware of stereotypes and their potential to perpetuate inequality. "Even if 16 stereotypes frozen into legislation have 'statistical support,'" we must "reject measures that classify unnecessarily and overbroadly by gender when more accurate and impartial lines can be drawn."

The City argues that the inherently sexual nature of the female breast, as opposed to the male breast, raises "myriad concerns" with "permitting adult females to go topless in public without restriction." The City refers us to the preliminary-injunction hearing, where three city officials—the deputy city manager, the assistant chief of police, and the city aquatics supervisor—described some of these concerns. The officials testified that female toplessness could disrupt public order, lead to distracted driving, and endanger children. Citing these concerns, the City claims that prohibiting only female toplessness serves to protect children from public nudity, to maintain public order, and to promote traffic safety. We address each rationale in turn.

Protecting Children From Public Nudity

The capacity to breastfeed is the first attribute that, the City claims, sets the female breast apart. Yet the City's public-nudity ordinance expressly exempts breastfeeding women from the female-toplessness ban, so even children who weren't exposed to their mothers' breasts as breastfeeding infants may still see a naked female breast if they pass a woman breastfeeding in public—her right under state law.

The need to protect children arises, instead, from the City's fear of topless women "parading in front of elementary schools, or swimming topless in the public pool"—scenarios that it described to the court at the preliminary-injunction hearing. But laws in the neighboring cities of Boulder and Denver, and in many other jurisdictions, allow female toplessness, and the City presented no evidence of any harmful fallout.

And absent contrary proof we, like the district court, doubt that without a female-toplessness ban on the books, topless women would "regularly walk[] through downtown Fort Collins," "parad[e]" past elementary schools, or swim in public pools.

We're left, as the district court was, to suspect that the City's professed interest in protecting children derives not from any morphological differences between men's and women's breasts but from negative stereotypes depicting women's breasts, but not men's breasts, as sex objects....

In support of this view, the district court relied on the testimony of Dr. TomiAnn Roberts, a psychology professor and witness for the Plaintiffs. At the preliminary-injunction hearing, Dr. Roberts testified that our society's sexualization of women's breasts—rather than any unique physical characteristic—has engrained in us the stereotype that the primary purpose of women's breasts is sex, not feeding babies. The district court found Dr. Roberts credible and concluded, based on her testimony, that "the naked female breast is seen as disorderly or dangerous because society, from Renaissance paintings to Victoria's Secret commercials, has conflated female breasts with genitalia and stereotyped them as such."

But laws grounded in stereotypes about the way women are serve no important governmental interest. To the contrary, legislatively reinforced stereotypes tend to "create a self-fulfilling cycle of discrimination."...

Maintaining Public Order and Promoting Traffic Safety

In the abstract, we agree that public order and traffic safety are important governmental objectives. The absence of either could be fatal. But the justification for a gender-based classification "must be genuine, not hypothesized," and "it must not rely on overbroad generalizations."...

A female-only toplessness ban strikes us as an unnecessary and overbroad means to maintain public order and promote traffic safety "when more accurate and impartial lines can be drawn."...

For instance, the City could abate sidewalk confrontations by increasing the penalties for engaging in offensive conduct. And to reduce distracted driving, the City could target billboards designed to draw drivers' eyes from the road. But the City can't impede women's (and not men's) ability to go topless unless it establishes the tight means–ends fit that intermediate scrutiny demands. We recognize that ours is the minority viewpoint. Most other courts, including a recent (split) Seventh Circuit panel, have rejected equal-protection challenges to female-only toplessness bans....

For these reasons, we affirm the district court's order granting the Plaintiffs' motion for a preliminary injunction, and we remand the case to the district court for further proceedings consistent with this opinion.

As the judges acknowledged, their decision was contrary to the decisions of other appellate courts. Furthermore, the decision is limited by the procedural posture of the case. The court didn't render a final decision on the matter; it affirmed a preliminary injunction by the trial court. A preliminary injunction is a legal tool that is used early in a case to temporarily stop the enforcement of a law. It is possible for the trial or circuit court judges to change their minds at the end of the full case and hold that the equal protection clause is not violated. That won't happen in the *Ft. Collins* case because the city repealed the law and decided to not appeal the decision you just read. Finally, the court didn't hold that a person has a constitutional right to "free the nipple" in public. In fact, it rejected the First Amendment free speech claim. Instead, it held that it violates due process to treat men and women differently. If a government were to enforce such a law against both men and women, equal protection wouldn't be an issue. Anyone challenging such a law would have to take another run at the First Amendment speech theory or attempt to create a new liberty right to nudity under the Fourteenth Amendment.

Finally, there are nonsexual but indecent or unsanitary acts that are punished under indecency laws. Public urination and defecation, for example, are universally prohibited. Some states prohibit these acts through their health codes, some use public indecency laws (because a sex organ has been exposed), and a few states have specific criminal laws.

As you have learned, there are many laws that criminalize speech, conduct, and expressive conduct with the intent to protect public morality. Because morality isn't the strongest argument in favor of government authority and because these laws often encroach on liberties, they are often subjected to constitutional testing. Figure 11.1 illustrates the application of the Constitution to morality laws.

FIGURE 11.1 ■ Lewd Conduct and Speech: Constitutional Analysis

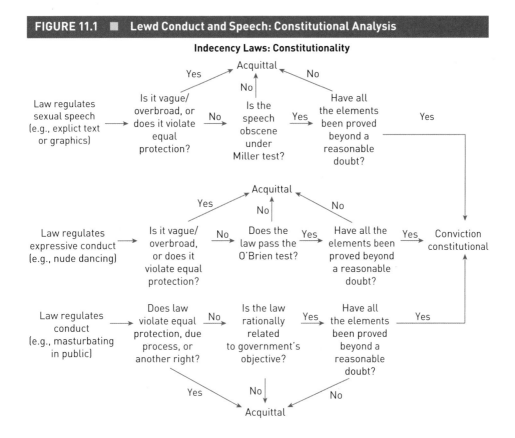

Indecency Laws: Constitutionality

QUESTIONS AND PROBLEMS

1. What are the elements of public indecency?

Use the following state public indecent exposure law to answer Questions 2 and 3:

A person is guilty of indecent exposure if he or she (A) appears (1) in a public place or (2) in private premises under circumstances in which he or she may readily be observed from either a public place or from other private premises (B) in such a manner that he or she disregards the likelihood that their (C) intimate body parts will be exposed to another person who is not a spouse.

For purposes of this section, the anus, genitals, and pubic area of a person are intimate parts of any person. The breast of a woman below the top of the areola is also an intimate part.

2. Nick Jackelson is golfing at a public golf course that is located in the middle of a residential area. After an hour of play, Nick decides that he needs to urinate. The clubhouse is a distance away and he doesn't want to delay his play, so he finds a tree and urinates behind it. He is seen unzipping and urinating, however, from 400 feet away by a resident of the neighborhood. He is charged under the state statute above. Analyze whether he is guilty of public exposure under this law.

3. Aryana lives in a large home that sits in the center of an acre of land. There are homes on three sides of the house, each also sitting in the center of an acre of land. After playing tennis and returning home on a hot day, she removes her shirt and bra in the kitchen to be put into the laundry. A neighbor, using a pair of binoculars, sees her through an open window that faces the neighbor's home. Analyze whether she is guilty of public exposure under the state statute above. Also discuss any constitutional defenses that are available to her that were discussed in this chapter.

LUCK OF THE DEVIL

Learning Objective: Identify, describe, and apply the elements of gambling and the tests that are used to distinguish games of chance from skill.

Gambling is the activity of risking something of value in a game or contest with the hope of increasing one's assets. Betting on horse races and card games, playing bingo for money, and pulling a roulette wheel in a casino are all forms of gambling. Historically, gambling has been deemed immoral, a vice, and harmful. The involvement of organized-crime syndicates in gambling has contributed to its reputation as a vice and to what is sometimes intense regulation and criminalization.

Gambling is a crime under state laws and federal law. However, most states have legalized certain forms of gambling. State lotteries are an example, as are state-approved casinos. The legal gambling industry is known as *gaming*. Gaming is a highly regulated business. There are strict rules governing ownership and operation of casinos. It is also heavily taxed. Some jurisdictions collect as much as half of large winnings, in addition to taxing operators. Online gambling is the subject of many federal and state laws.

The elements of a typical gambling prohibition are

1. The wager or bet
2. of something of value, known as consideration
3. in a game or contest of chance
4. with knowledge of the risk of loss and possible gain.

The actus reus of gambling is the making of a wager. The mens rea is knowledge that there is both risk of loss and the possibility of winning. The consideration and possible rewards are

Gambling: A wager or bet of something of value in a game of chance with knowledge of the risk of loss and gain.

usually cash, but they don't have to be. Anything of value may be wagered or won, and the two may be different in the same gambling transaction. A home may be wagered against the possibility of winning cash, or vice versa.

An important element of gambling is that the bet or wager must be on a game of chance, not skill. The line between the two can be difficult to draw. In some instances, legislatures have expressly defined specific games or contests as either chance or skill. In the absence of statutory clarity, the decision is left to the courts.

There are three tests used to make this determination in the United States. Most jurisdictions use the **dominant factor test**. This test asks which factor, skill or luck, was more than 50% of the cause of the outcome. If skill prevails, the game is lawful. If it is more chance than skill, the game is unlawful. The second test, the **material element test**, doesn't assess dominance. Instead, it asks whether chance was significant to the outcome. It is possible for skill to be dominant but still considered gambling under this test. Finally, a small number of states adheres to the **any chance test**. As the name implies, if chance is a factor at all, a contest is labeled gambling. New York is a statutorily explicit material element jurisdiction, as can be seen in Section 1 of its gambling law:

N.Y. Penal Law §225

1. "Contest of chance" means any contest, game, gaming scheme or gaming device in which the outcome *depends in a material degree* upon an element of chance, notwithstanding that skill of the contestants may also be a factor therein.

2. "Gambling." A person engages in gambling when he stakes or risks something of value upon the outcome of a contest of chance or a future contingent event not under his control or influence, upon an agreement or understanding that he will receive something of value in the event of a certain outcome.

Let's apply these tests to a few fact patterns.

Annie Oh registers to compete in a national competitive gun and rifle contest. Only individuals who have won several local competitions qualify to participate. Registration is $250. The first-prize winner receives a trophy and $25,000. The contest involves shooting targets at a varieties of distances and using two different weapons. Annie is not gambling under any of the tests because the contest is one of skill.

Standford W. Ong, a billionaire, enjoys flouting his money and showing off. He and a group of other wealthy men and women gather to "cut cards for cash." The game is simple

---

Dominant factor test: One of three tests used to determine if a game or contest is one of chance or skill. Whichever most contributes to the outcome of a game or contest is determinative.

Material element test: One of three tests used to determine if a game or contest is one of chance or skill. If chance is a material element, even if not dominant, in the outcome of a game or contest, the game is one of chance.

Any chance test: One of three tests used to determine if a game or contest is one of chance or skill. If chance is a factor, no matter how small, in the outcome of a game or contest, the game is one of chance.

and high-stakes. They each cut the cards (remove a random stack) from a deck of standard playing cards, and whomever has the largest card on the bottom of their stacks wins $50,000. Stanford has committed gambling under all three tests because the outcome of the game is 100% chance.

Rose Peter bets on the outcome of a professional baseball game. Armed with a PhD in statistics, he relies on player and team data to place his bets. Regardless of the probabilities he calculates, he is committing gambling under the any chance test because chance remains a factor. A player, for example, may become injured during the game. Most likely, he satisfies both the material factor and dominant factor tests, provided state law doesn't expressly characterize sports betting as gambling.

Gambling does not include bona fide business transactions valid under the law of contracts, including but not limited to contracts for the purchase or sale at a future date of securities or commodities, and agreements to compensate for loss caused by the happening of chance, including but not limited to contracts of indemnity or guaranty and life, health, or accident insurance. Life insurance contracts are defined as not being gambling under the law, although they share the risk and payoff elements of gambling.

Many states exempt small-money charitable events, or "social gambling" (e.g., church bingo night), from gambling prohibitions. Laws exempting social gambling typically require that each player be on equal terms. Said another way, skill can't be a factor. The game only involves luck. Hawaii's social gambling provision is an example:

Hawaii Rev. Stat. §712-1231 Social gambling; definition and specific conditions, affirmative defense

a. Definition. "Social gambling" means gambling in which all of the following conditions are present:

1. Players compete on equal terms with each other; and
2. No player receives, or becomes entitled to receive, anything of value or any profit, directly or indirectly, other than the player's personal gambling winnings; and
3. No other person, corporation, unincorporated association, or entity receives or becomes entitled to receive, anything of value or any profit, directly or indirectly, from any source, including but not limited to permitting the use of premises, supplying refreshments, food, drinks, service, lodging or entertainment; and
4. It is not conducted or played in or at a hotel, motel, bar, nightclub, cocktail lounge, restaurant, massage parlor, billiard parlor, or any business establishment of any kind, public parks, public buildings, public beaches, school grounds, churches or any other public area; and
5. None of the players is below the age of majority; and
6. The gambling activity is not bookmaking [a gambling business].

Gambling is typically a misdemeanor. In addition to fines and jail time, some jurisdictions forfeit a convicted gambler's winnings to the government.

QUESTIONS AND PROBLEMS

1. What are the elements of gambling?
2. Harmony Beth is a rising star in the chess world. Having won local, state, and national titles, she is competing in her first international match. Bobby Fish is a chess enthusiast and online gambler. He has monitored her career, learns who her first opponent is to be, calculates the probabilities based on their prior records, and decides to wager $25,000 that she will win her first match. Has Bobby committed the crime of gambling under any of the chance tests?
3. Research the game of backgammon and discuss whether it is a game of chance or skill under each of the three chance tests.

CHILLIN' OUT

Learning Objective: Describe the due process and free speech limitations on loitering and vagrancy laws.

Vagrancy and loitering are crimes in many places. Vagrancy can encompass a lot of conduct. Loitering, or hanging out in a public space for extended periods of time without purpose, homelessness, having no apparent livelihood, and street begging are different forms of vagrancy that have been criminalized in United States. Once commonly enforced, both contemporary values and constitutional law have limited this form of quality-of-life crime. As to the former concern, vagrancy laws tend to criminalize poverty and homelessness, a form of social control that is out of step with modern America. As to the latter, these laws give rise to due process and free speech concerns.

At the Common Law, a *vagrant* was one who wandered from place to place with no means of support, except the charity of others. At one time, in early English law, vagrancy applied to disorderly persons, rogues (dishonest wanderers), and vagabonds (homeless people with no means of support). Vagrants were jailed, whipped, and conscripted into military service. Beginning in the 1880s, it was common in the United States for statutes to prohibit a wide range of behavior as vagrancy. These statutes were drafted so broadly that police officers had considerable discretion in their enforcement. This discretion was used to control the "undesirables" of society.

Many vagrancy statutes had the effect of making the status of being homeless, a gambler, or addicted to drugs a crime. This situation ended in 1972 when SCOTUS handed down *Papachristou v. City of Jacksonville*, 405 U.S. 156 (1972), where it held that a vagrancy statute that prohibited "persons wandering or strolling around from place to place without any lawful purpose or object" and for men who are able to work to be "habitually living upon the earnings of their wives or minor children" to be "too precarious for a rule of law." The court noted that police had so much discretion under the law that they could arbitrarily pick and choose who to enforce the law against, particularly disadvantaging the "the poor and the unpopular." For these reasons, the law was deemed to be violative of the due process and cruel and unusual clauses of the Constitution.

Subsequently, states amended their laws to add specific forbidden acts to loitering. An example of a "loitering plus" law was New York's ban on vagrancy or loitering when accompanied with begging for money. However, because begging was determined to be free speech, the law was stricken down in a federal appeals court.[20] Other loitering plus laws forbid sleeping on sidewalks and public benches, aggressive panhandling, and loitering when paired with gang membership. Many of these laws have also been invalidated because they violated due process or the First Amendment. In the next Digging Deeper case, a Boise law that forbade the use "any of the streets, sidewalks, parks, or public places as a camping place at any time" was challenged by several homeless plaintiffs under the theory that to criminalize sleeping in public spaces is on par with criminalizing their homeless status.

DIGGING DEEPER 11.2

Does it violate the Eighth Amendment to punish a homeless person for sleeping in a public area?

Case: *Martin v. City of Boise*
Court: Ninth Circuit Court of Appeals.   Citation: 920 F. 3d 584
Year: 2019
Circuit Judge Berzon

"The law, in its majestic equality, forbids rich and poor alike to sleep under bridges, to beg in the streets, and to steal their bread." —Anatole France, *The Red Lily*

We consider whether the Eighth Amendment's prohibition on cruel and unusual punishment bars a city from prosecuting people criminally for sleeping outside on public property when those people have no home or other shelter to go to. We conclude that it does.

The plaintiffs-appellants are six current or former residents of the City of Boise ("the City"), who are homeless or have recently been homeless. Each plaintiff alleges that, between 2007 and 2009, he or she was cited by Boise police for violating one or both of two city ordinances. The first, Boise City Code § 9-10-02 (the "Camping Ordinance"), makes it a misdemeanor to use "any of the streets, sidewalks, parks, or public places as a camping place at any time." The Camping Ordinance defines "camping" as "the use of public property as a temporary or permanent place of dwelling, lodging, or residence." Id. The second, Boise City Code § 6-01-05 (the "Disorderly Conduct Ordinance"), bans "[o]ccupying, lodging, or sleeping in any building, structure, or public place, whether public or private... without the permission of the owner or person entitled to possession or in control thereof."...

Boise has a significant and increasing homeless population....

There are currently three homeless shelters in the City of Boise offering emergency shelter services, all run by private, nonprofit organizations. [And they are not large enough to accommodate all of the homeless who seek shelter.]...

The Eighth Amendment states: "Excessive bail shall not be required, nor excessive fines imposed, nor cruel and unusual punishments inflicted." U.S. Const., Amend. VIII. The Cruel and Unusual Punishments Clause "circumscribes the criminal process in three ways." First, it limits the type of punishment the government may impose; second, it proscribes punishment "grossly disproportionate" to the severity of the crime; and third, it places substantive limits on what the government may criminalize. It is the third limitation that is pertinent here.

"Even one day in prison would be a cruel and unusual punishment for the 'crime' of having a common cold." *Robinson v. California*, 370 U.S. 660, 667 (1962)....

Robinson, the seminal case in this branch of Eighth Amendment jurisprudence, held a California statute that "ma[de] the 'status' of narcotic addiction a criminal offense" invalid under the Cruel and Unusual Punishments Clause. The California law at issue in *Robinson* was "not one which punishe[d] a person for the use of narcotics, for their purchase, sale or possession, or for antisocial or disorderly behavior resulting from their administration"; it punished addiction itself. Recognizing narcotics addiction as an illness or disease—"apparently an illness which may be contracted innocently or involuntarily"—and observing that a "law which made a criminal offense of... a disease would doubtless be universally thought to be an infliction of cruel and unusual punishment," *Robinson* held the challenged statute a violation of the Eighth Amendment.

In *Powell v. Texas*, 392 U.S. 514 (1968), however, the Court elaborated on the principle first articulated in *Robinson*. Powell concerned the constitutionality of a Texas law making public drunkenness a criminal offense. Justice Marshall, writing for a plurality of the Court, distinguished the Texas statute from the law at issue in *Robinson* on the ground that the Texas statute made criminal not alcoholism but conduct—appearing in public while intoxicated. "[A]ppellant was convicted, not for being a chronic alcoholic, but for being in public while drunk on a particular occasion. The State of Texas thus has not sought to punish a mere status, as California did in *Robinson*; nor has it attempted to regulate appellant's behavior in the privacy of his own home."...

The *Powell* plurality opinion went on to interpret *Robinson* as precluding only the criminalization of "status," not of "involuntary" conduct. "The entire thrust of *Robinson*'s interpretation of the Cruel and Unusual Punishment Clause is that criminal penalties may be inflicted only if the accused has committed some act, has engaged in some behavior, which society has an interest in preventing, or perhaps in historical common law terms, has committed some actus reus. It thus does not deal with the question of whether certain conduct cannot constitutionally be punished because it is, in some sense, 'involuntary.'"...

Thus, five Justices gleaned from *Robinson* the principle "that the Eighth Amendment prohibits the state from punishing an involuntary act or condition if it is the unavoidable consequence of one's status or being." This principle compels the conclusion that the Eighth Amendment prohibits the imposition of criminal penalties for sitting, sleeping, or lying outside on public property for homeless individuals who cannot obtain shelter. As Jones reasoned, "Whether sitting, lying, and sleeping are defined as acts or conditions, they are universal and unavoidable consequences of being human." Moreover, any "conduct at issue here is involuntary and inseparable from status—they are one and the same, given that human beings are biologically compelled to rest, whether by sitting, lying, or sleeping." As a result, just as the state may not criminalize the state of being "homeless in public places," the state may not "criminalize conduct that is an unavoidable consequence of being homeless—namely, sitting, lying, or sleeping on the streets."

Our holding is a narrow one. Like the Jones panel, "we in no way dictate to the City that it must provide sufficient shelter for the homeless, or allow anyone who wishes to sit, lie, or sleep on the streets... at any time and at any place." We hold only that "so long as there is a greater number of homeless individuals in [a jurisdiction] than the number of available beds [in shelters]," the jurisdiction cannot prosecute homeless individuals for "involuntarily sitting, lying, and sleeping in public." That is, as long as there is no option of sleeping indoors, the government cannot criminalize indigent, homeless people for sleeping outdoors, on public property, on the false premise they had a choice in the matter.

Here, the two ordinances criminalize the simple act of sleeping outside on public property, whether bare or with a blanket or other basic bedding. The Disorderly Conduct Ordinance, on its face, criminalizes "occupying, lodging, or sleeping in any building, structure or place, whether public or private" without permission. Boise City Code § 6-01-05. Its scope is just as sweeping as the Los Angeles ordinance at issue in *Jones*, which mandated that "no person shall sit, lie or sleep in or upon any street, sidewalk or other public way." The Camping Ordinance criminalizes using "any of the streets, sidewalks, parks or public places as a camping place at any time."

We conclude that a municipality cannot criminalize such behavior consistently with the Eighth Amendment when no sleeping space is practically available in any shelter.

Although a government may not prohibit conduct that is inherent to a person's status, it may limit conduct that interferes with the function of property, interferes with the rights of others, or threatens harm or property destruction. For example, a homeless person may not block a sidewalk when sleeping or physically obstruct people from using public spaces while panhandling.

QUESTIONS AND PROBLEMS

Read the following vagrancy statutes and assess whether they violate the Eighth Amendment. Explain your answers.

1. No person shall sleep or eat in or upon any sidewalk, public park, or other outdoor public space.
2. No person shall block or obstruct any sidewalk, or, upon a public space, block access to any building, while sleeping or eating.

JUST SAY NO

Learning Objective: Describe the federal Controlled Substances Act (CSA), including the factors that are used to determine a drug's classification and the acts that are criminalized.

All jurisdictions make it a crime to possess, manufacture, cultivate, and sell specific drugs. They also regulate the manufacturing, distribution, and sale of alcohol. The policy reasons for controlling mind-altering and addictive substances are many. Through overdoses and intoxicated driving, they cause death. Drug use and sales also cause losses in work productivity, users commit thefts and other crimes to pay for their drugs, rape and human trafficking is facilitated, and families are destroyed by drug addiction. On the other hand, the overcriminalization of drugs has its downsides. Potentially helpful medical treatments are foreclosed, as in the case of medical marijuana. Drug criminalization is also very expensive, in both law enforcement and punishment. The United States has the largest prison population, per capita, in the world. A large number of state inmates and nearly 50% of all federal prisoners are serving sentences for drug crimes. Federal initiatives such as "Just Say No" and "Zero Tolerance" reflect the federal government's interest in deterring and punishing drug use.

The disproportionate impact that drug laws, particularly at the federal level, have had on African Americans also raises racial inequity questions. For these and other reasons, many states have begun to decriminalize marijuana, reduce punishments for other drug crimes, shift from a retributive to rehabilitative approach in punishment, and level out disparities in punishment between drugs. Many states have created drug courts, which are intended to focus on treatment and rehabilitation of offenders.

Regardless of modern changes, drug crimes and their enforcement continue to be robust. All of the states and the federal government have comprehensive drug laws. The federal government's law is referred to as the Comprehensive Drug Abuse and Prevention Act of 1970, or, in short, the Controlled Substances Act (CSA).[21] Not all substances that can impact a person's mental or physical state are regulated. Coffee and tea, for example, contain caffeine, a stimulant. But caffeine isn't regulated. Nor is hemlock, the poisonous plant that was used to create the drink that killed the Greek philosopher Socrates. Nor are all drugs and chemicals that are regulated by the CSA. There are, for example, over-the-counter and prescription drugs not subject to the CSA's provisions and many chemicals and substances that are consumed, applied to the body, or used in other ways that are regulated under other food and drug laws, but not the CSA.

But hundreds of "dangerous" drugs do fall under the grasp of the CSA, which places drugs into "schedules," or categories, based upon (1) their potential for abuse, (2) their medicinal value, and (3) whether they can be used safely. Schedule I contains the most harmful, least valuable, and least safe drugs and Schedule 5, the opposite.

Clever drug dealers and users find ways to circumvent the CSA. Identifying narcotic or hallucinogenic natural substances that aren't on the schedules is one way. Congress addressed this problem by authorizing federal law enforcement officials to temporarily and permanently list new chemicals in the schedules. A second work-around is the creation of synthetic or analog drugs, also known as designer drugs. A designer drug is a scientifically created fake that replicates the effects of a naturally occurring drug. Because the chemical makeup of a designer drug differs from the scheduled drug, it was lawful to possess, use, and distribute under the original CSA. Through a 1986 amendment to the CSA, synthetic or analog drugs began to be regulated in the same manner as the substances they mimic. See Table 11.2 for a summary of the five schedules.

Schedule I drugs are strictly forbidden. Not only may they not be possessed or distributed generally, but they can't be prescribed by doctors. Drugs in the other four schedules may be prescribed, subject to regulations that become increasingly stringent as a drug moves up the schedule ladder.

TABLE 11.2 ■ Federal CSA Schedules		
Schedule	**Description**	**Examples**
I	Substances that have a high potential for abuse and no currently accepted medical use; no accepted safe way to use the drug, even under medical supervision	Heroin, marijuana, LSD, peyote
II	Substances that have a high potential for abuse and can lead to physical or psychological dependence; may be prescribed in limited circumstances	Morphine, methamphetamine, oxycodone, and methadone
III	Substances that can lead to moderate or low physical dependence or high psychological dependence; may be prescribed	Some steroids, drugs with high levels of codeine, pain relievers with hydrocodone, some barbiturates
IV	Substances that can lead to limited physical dependence or psychological dependence; may be prescribed	Valium®, Xanax®
V	Substances that can lead to limited physical or psychological dependence; may be prescribed	Drugs with low levels of codeine, including cough medicines

There are several different acts that the CSA criminalizes, including, inter alia, for a person to do the following:

- Possess a controlled substance

- Manufacture, distribute, or dispense, or possess with intent to manufacture, distribute, or dispense, a controlled substance

- Create, distribute, or dispense, or possess with intent to distribute or dispense, a counterfeit substance

- Distribute controlled substances near highway rest stops and truck stops

- Distribute controlled substances near schools and colleges

- Distribute controlled substances to, or employ in a distribution operation, a minor

- Commit drug offenses as part of a continuing criminal enterprise (a large-scale drug operation)

- Endanger life during the manufacturing of controlled substances

There are many other crimes defined in the CSA, such as altering the labeling or packaging of scheduled substances that are sold and prescribed.

For possession and distribution offenses, the mens rea is expressly identified as knowing or intentional. What exactly a defendant must "know" has been the subject of considerable litigation for many years, and there is disagreement among the federal courts. Is it enough for a defendant to knowingly possess, cultivate, or distribute a drug, but not know it is a controlled substance; or must a defendant have actual knowledge that the drug appears in the schedules; or must a defendant know a substance is a narcotic or has mind-altering effects? SCOTUS answered the CSA mens rea question in the 2015 case *McFadden v. United States*,[22] where it held that there are two ways the government can prove a defendant acted knowingly:

That knowledge requirement may be met by showing that the defendant knew he possessed a substance listed on the schedules, even if he did not know which substance it was. Take, for example, a defendant whose role in a larger drug organization is to distribute a white powder to customers. The defendant may know that the white powder is listed on the schedules even if he does not know precisely what substance it is. And if so, he would be guilty of knowingly distributing "a controlled substance."

The knowledge requirement may also be met by showing that the defendant knew the identity of the substance he possessed. Take, for example, a defendant who knows he is distributing heroin but does not know that heroin is listed on the schedules. Because ignorance of the law is typically no defense to criminal prosecution, *Bryan v.United States*, 524 U.S. 184, 196 (1998), this defendant would also be guilty of knowingly distributing "a controlled substance."

A violation of the CSA is graded by the drug's classification in the schedules, the quantity of the substance, criminal history, and the type of drug crime. Sale and distribution, for example, are punished more severely than possession. Selling to a minor—or on or near school grounds—also elevates an offense. Drug offenses range from misdemeanors with little jail time and fines for possession of lower-level drugs to life imprisonment for large-scale operations that manufacture and distribute Schedule I or II drugs.

All of the states have enacted controlled substances acts that are similar to the federal CSA. There is little variation in what acts are criminalized between the states. Possession, cultivation, manufacturing, and distribution are illegal everywhere. Occasionally, states schedule drugs differently than the federal government. In recent years, this has been true of marijuana. While it continues to be a Schedule I drug under the federal CSA, many states now permit its medical and recreational use. The disconnect between state and federal law creates a dilemma. Legal use under state law can still be punished under federal law. In recent years, the United States has been largely hands-off, respecting the decisions of the states. But it could, at any time, begin to enforce the federal CSA on people who are using drugs lawfully under state law. The greatest difference in drug laws in the United States is in punishment. For example, the same crime may result in a fine in one state and years in prison in another.

There is a drug that causes many deaths and injuries, contributes to family discord and financial distress, and causes many people to do very stupid things—alcohol. But it is widely popular, and the experiment to prohibit it throughout the nation, which required a constitutional amendment (Eighteenth), failed. Not only did it lead to greater crime, but it was a leading cause in the rise of organized crime. Reversing prohibition required another amendment, the Twenty-First, making it possible for alcohol to be widely available today. It is also regulated, but not to the extent of the drugs found in the CSA.

There are many alcohol-related crimes. Public drunkenness laws prohibit being intoxicated in a public place. Minimum drinking-age laws establish the youngest a person may be to buy, possess, serve, or consume alcohol. These laws also forbid adults from providing alcohol to minors. Merchants holding liquor licenses may be subject to criminal penalties for not complying with liquor laws, such as selling alcohol on holidays, Sundays, or Election Day, as well as for selling alcohol to minors. A merchant who violates these laws may also be subject to the civil penalty of revocation of liquor license.

Alcohol and automobiles are a deadly combination. All states have laws that criminalize driving while under the influence of alcohol or drugs, often known by the shorthand DUI, DWI, or OVI. These statutes are of two types. The first prohibits the operation of a motor vehicle while under the influence of any drug, including alcohol. To prove this charge, the quantity of the drug or alcohol in the defendant's system is not the focus. Instead, whether the substance has impaired a driver's ability to safely operate their vehicle is examined. In these cases, field sobriety tests are helpful. These are tests performed at the location where police have stopped the driver. The tests are used to assess coordination, spatial relations, and other driving-related skills.

The second type of DUI law prohibits driving a motor vehicle any time a person's blood-alcohol level (BAL) is above a stated amount. The states vary in their BAL limits, although 8 hundredths of a percent (0.08) and 10 hundredths of a percent (0.10) are common, although some states have reduced their BAL to .05. The effect of these laws is that an irrebuttable presumption that a vehicle can't be operated safely is created. Under such statutes, evidence that a person can safely operate a motor vehicle with a blood-alcohol level greater than the maximum allowed is not permitted.

All states also prohibit the possession of open containers of alcohol in the passenger areas of automobiles that are be driven on public roads. Alabama's open container law, in part, reads:

> It is unlawful for a person to have in his or her possession alcoholic beverages in an open container in the passenger area of a motor vehicle of any kind on a public highway or right-of-way of a public highway of this state.[23]

The code exempts buses and other vehicles for hire when the driver holds a commercial driver's license, has containers in the trunk or other closed compartments of a car or behind the seat of a truck that doesn't have a trunk or a separate enclosed storage area, and when a driver doesn't have knowledge of the presence of the container. A container is considered "open" if its state "is other than in the manufacturer's sealed condition."

Today, drunk drivers who kill others are prosecuted under special vehicular homicide statutes, as discussed in Chapter 8. Similarly, most states have statutes that punish DUI drivers who cause serious bodily injury to others.

Finally, as you learned earlier in this chapter, the acts of manufacturing, possessing, and distributing drugs may be criminalized. But the status of being drug addicted may not. The same is true of alcoholism. It may not be punished, but public intoxication, selling alcohol to minors, and driving a vehicle under the influence of alcohol are conduct that may be punished.

QUESTIONS AND PROBLEMS

1. What are the three variables that are used to determine the appropriate schedule level for a drug under the federal CSA?
2. Randy "Red" is addicted to cocaine. He is also penniless. He begs his dealer, Brandy, to give him a fix, with a promise to pay her in the future. She declines but offers an alternative. She hands him a transparent baggie of white powder and instructs him to deliver it to a man in a public park. He is told to collect $500 from the man. For this, she will give him a small amount of cocaine. He asks, "What is in the bag?" Brandy, replies, "Do you want your stuff or not? Just deliver it." He does as instructed, is arrested at the scene by federal agents, and is subsequently charged with distributing cocaine. Did Red possess the mens rea of possession and distribution under the CSA?
3. Sydnee and Haley recently met at a college Helping the Homeless meeting. They had coffee after the meeting, where they discussed their shared passion to help the homeless. After their coffee, Sydnee told Haley that she had to miss the next meeting of the group and asked her to deliver a box to the group's president. Haley agreed. Much to her surprise, federal agents intervened when she handed the box to the group president and arrested them both; subsequent testing of the box's contents revealed that it contained methamphetamine. Haley was charged with possession and distribution of a controlled substance. Did Haley possess the mens rea of possession and distribution under the federal CSA?

JUDGE THE HEART OF A MAN BY HIS TREATMENT OF ANIMALS

Learning Objectives: Describe how animal rights have evolved from the Common Law to modernity.

The human–animal relationship has a long and complicated history. For thousands of years, many people have viewed animals as resources to be used as needed. Others, particularly adherents of some Eastern religions, such as Jainism, Hinduism, and Buddhism, believe animals have souls and are sentient (or, at the least, respect their welfare). Historically, the Western world fell more into the former philosophy. Animal cruelty was not a crime at the Common Law. Animals were treated as inanimate property. They could be used and treated in any manner. This has changed. The earliest roots of animal rights in the United States trace back to the 1800s, but the animal rights movement has accelerated in recent decades.

Simultaneous to recent changing societal values about animal rights, a second, related concern about animal cruelty has surfaced. It appears than when unchecked, animal abuse is a precursor to violence against people. Although this idea has been the subject of academic research and law enforcement attention in recent years, the idea isn't new. St. Francis of Assisi, who lived in the 13th century, is thought to have remarked that "*if you have men who will exclude any of God's creatures from the shelter of compassion and pity, you will have men who will deal likewise with their fellow men.*"[24] The philosopher Immanuel Kant expressed the same belief; the opening quote of this section is Kant's.[25]

The combination of the change in society's values about animal welfare and an interest in preventing future violence against people have coalesced to drive new animal rights laws. Animal cruelty and welfare laws vary considerably between the states. They differ in language, acts criminalized, and punishment. The following offenses are commonly recognized:

- Cruelty

- Abandonment

- Neglect

- Bestiality

Many exceptions to these laws exist for farming, meat, and the entertainment industries. Three of the listed acts are crimes of commission. The fourth, neglect, is a crime of omission. Statutory law imposes a duty of care that didn't exist at the Common Law. Ohio's cruelty laws are typical. In addition to criminalizing animal fighting, abandonment, injuring, poising, and other specific inhumane acts, Ohio forbids cruelty generally:

O.R.C. §959.13: No person shall:

1. Torture an animal, deprive one of necessary sustenance, unnecessarily or cruelly beat, needlessly mutilate or kill, or impound or confine an animal without supplying it during such confinement with a sufficient quantity of good wholesome food and water;

2. Impound or confine an animal without affording it, during such confinement, access to shelter from wind, rain, snow, or excessive direct sunlight if it can reasonably be expected that the animals would otherwise become sick or in some other way suffer. Division (A)(2) of this section does not apply to animals impounded or confined prior to slaughter. For the purpose of this section, shelter means a man-made enclosure, windbreak, sunshade, or natural windbreak or sunshade that is developed from the earth's contour, tree development, or vegetation;

3. Carry or convey an animal in a cruel or inhuman[e] manner;

4. Keep animals other than cattle, poultry or fowl, swine, sheep, or goats in an enclosure without wholesome exercise and change of air, nor feed cows on food that produces impure or unwholesome milk;

5. Detain livestock in railroad cars or compartments longer than twenty-eight hours after they are so placed without supplying them with necessary food, water, and attention, nor permit such stock to be so crowded as to overlie, crush, wound, or kill each other.

The United States has several laws that regulate the treatment of animals. The Animal Welfare Act of 1966 is America's most significant animal rights regulation. The AWA establishes the minimal acceptable care for certain animals that are used in entertainment and exhibition, traded and sold, transported, and used in research. The statute covers many warm-blooded animals, including dogs, cats, rabbits, and primates. Farm animals, fish, horses, birds, and other animals are excluded from the statute's mandates. The AWA requires dealers, researchers, and people who exhibit protected animals to provide adequate housing, nutrition, veterinary care, and protection from the natural elements.

A famous AWA case involved the author Ernest Hemingway. Hemingway's home in the Florida Keys has been made into a museum, and it has inhabitants that are popular to both locals and tourists: polydactyly, or six- or seven-toed, cats. They live in the museum, but freely roam the museum and the acre of land that is part of the museum. In 2003, a volunteer at the museum expressed concern for the welfare of the animals to the United States Department of Agriculture (USDA) after a cat had wandered off museum grounds. The USDA is the agency charged with enforcing the AWA. The USDA asserted jurisdiction over the situation because the cats were used in advertising, cat memorabilia was sold, and the use of the cats met the definition of being an exhibit under the law.

The USDA inspectors concluded that the museum had to obtain an exhibition license and that the cats needed protection, even though the evidence showed that the cats enjoyed a pampered life. The best evidence came from an investigator from the People for the Ethical Treatment of Animals (PETA), which was hired by the USDA to assess the situation. The investigator wrote that "what I found was a bunch of fat, happy and relaxed cats. God save the cats."[26]

Regardless, the USDA required the museum to obtain an exhibition license, erect a higher fence, install electric wire, or, in the alternative, hire a night watchperson to ensure that the cats didn't leave the property. The agency also demanded that the museum provide the cats with separate sleeping cages and elevated resting surfaces. The museum litigated the orders, arguing that the federal government's authority under the commerce clause didn't extend to the museum or the cats. It lost at both the trial and appellate levels.[27]

The United States acted to protect animals again in a 1999 law that was intended to criminalize "crush videos." In these videos, people torture, mutilate, and kill small animals to satisfy the sexual fetishes of viewers. They are referred to as crush videos because the earliest videos featured women using high heels to crush mice and other small animals. These acts are criminal in all 50 states. But internet-distributed videos present jurisdictional problems for the states. Often, the location of their creation and broadcast is unknown and difficult to ascertain. This is where federal law steps in to fill the gaps.

The original federal law, which criminalized "depictions" of animal cruelty, was invalidated by SCOTUS on First Amendment grounds.[28] The court determined it too overbroad because it forbade the distribution of videos of depictions of animal cruelty, not actual cruelty. Congress quickly amended the law to make it a crime to distribute videos that (1) depict actual conduct in which one or more non-human animals are intentionally crushed, burned, drowned, suffocated, impaled, or otherwise subjected to serious bodily injury and (2) are obscene. By narrowing the law to videos of genuine cruelty, not just depictions, and by requiring that a video meet the test for obscenity, the amended law was upheld by a federal appellate court.[29]

To animal rights activists, however, the new law didn't go far enough. It only criminalized videos of cruelty, not the acts of cruelty themselves. In 2020, the Preventing Animal Cruelty and Torture Act (PACT) changed this situation. The law makes it a crime for a person to engage in crushing or creating a crush video. Crushing is defined as "actual conduct in which one or more living non-human mammals, birds, reptiles, or amphibians is purposely crushed, burned, drowned, suffocated, impaled, or otherwise subjected to serious bodily injury."

There are two open issues with these laws. First, given that all 50 states forbid animal cruelty, the need for federal intervention in what is a traditional state matter is questionable. Second, the extent to which Congress's authority over interstate commerce gives it the jurisdiction to criminalize crushing is unclear.

QUESTIONS AND PROBLEMS

1. Describe how animal rights have evolved from the Common Law to modernity.

THIS LAND WAS MADE FOR YOU AND ME

Learning Objective: Identify three or more federal environmental protection laws and identify the most common mens rea of environmental crimes.

In 2013, Walmart pled guilty to six counts of negligently violating the federal Clean Water Act. And, yes, if you are wondering, corporations can commit and be punished for crimes. As reported by the United States Justice Department,

> Walmart did not have a program in place and failed to train its employees on proper hazardous waste management and disposal practices at the store level. As a result, hazardous wastes were either discarded improperly at the store level—including being put into municipal trash bins or, if a liquid, poured into the local sewer system—or they were improperly transported without proper safety documentation to one of six product return centers located throughout the United States.... Federal laws that address the proper handling, storage, and disposal of hazardous wastes exist to safeguard our environment and protect the public from harm.

Through a plea agreement, Walmart was ordered to pay more than $81 million in fines.[30] In an even larger case, colloquially known as "Dieselgate," Volkswagen, the automobile manufacturer, was discovered to have installed a "defeat device" that falsified the pollution emissions data in over 500,000 cars, making them in violation of the Clean Air Act. Specifically, the device underreported nitrogen-oxide emissions (NOx)—a pollutant that is believed to cause lung cancer. The amount of cheating varied, but some cars that reported as under the limit were actually emitting 40 times the limit.

PHOTO 11.2 Volkswagen, the automobile manufacturer, was discovered to have installed an "defeat device" that falsified the pollution emissions data in over 500,000 cars, making them in violation of the Clean Air Act.

Ilari Nackel/iStock

The company, whose headquarters in Wolfsburg, Germany, is seen in Photo 11.2, attempted to cover up its offenses during the investigation. Ultimately, the corporation pled guilty to three felonies stemming from the cover-up: conspiracy, making false statements to authorities, and obstruction of justice. It was fined $2.8 billion and agreed to pay an additional $1.5 billion in civil damages. In addition, several executives and employees of Volkswagen were personally charged with obstructing the investigation. The scandal wreaked havoc on Volkswagen stock, causing it to plummet. A couple of years after the initial criminal charges were filed, a handful of executives were charged with new securities crimes. The government's theory in this set of accusations is that the executives' failure to timely disclose the scandal to stockholders was fraudulent.[31]

As the world has become more densely populated, the use of chemicals in industry has risen; the amounts of pollutants that have been introduced into the ground, water, and air have skyrocketed; and the human impact on animals continues to reach new levels. A body of environmental laws have been enacted to protect people from harm, animals from extinction and cruelty, and to protect the natural beauty and integrity of the environment for its own sake.

All of the states regulate the environment. But the interstate, often international, nature of many acts of pollution and environmental degradation and the expenses of enforcing complex, highly technical, time-intensive environmental laws have left the federal government in the lead. The U.S. Environmental Protection Agency (EPA) is the federal government's chief enforcer, and it has a cadre of inspectors, investigators, and scientists to bring to the task. The list of federal environmental laws is long. It includes, inter alia:

- Clean Air Act (CAA) is a comprehensive federal law that regulates air quality. Among other things, this law authorizes EPA to establish National Ambient Air Quality Standards to protect public health and welfare and to regulate emissions of hazardous air pollutants.[32]

- Clean Water Act (CWA) regulates the discharge of pollutants into the waters of the United States.[33]

- Comprehensive Environmental Response, Compensation, and Liability Act (CERCLA or Superfund) provides federal monies to clean up uncontrolled or abandoned hazardous waste sites as well as accidents, spills, and other emergency releases of pollutants and contaminants into the environment. Through CERCLA, EPA was delegated the authority to enforce its mandates against the parties responsible for any release and to compel their cooperation in the cleanup.[34]

- Endangered Species Act (ESA) provides a program for the conservation of threatened and endangered plants and animals and the habitats in which they are found. This law is enforced by the U.S. Fish and Wildlife Service and U.S. National Oceanic and Atmospheric Administration.[35]

- Federal Insecticide, Fungicide, and Rodenticide Act (FIFRA) provides for federal regulation of pesticide distribution, sale, and use.[36]

- Marine Protection, Research, and Sanctuaries Act (MPRSA), also referred to as the Ocean Dumping Act, generally prohibits (1) transportation of material from the United States for the purpose of ocean dumping; (2) transportation of material from anywhere for the purpose of ocean dumping by U.S. agencies or U.S.-flagged vessels; (3) dumping of material transported from outside the United States into the U.S. territorial sea.[37]

- Nuclear Waste Policy Act (NWPA) supports the use of deep geologic repositories for the safe storage and/or disposal of radioactive waste.[38]

- Resource Conservation and Recovery Act (RCRA) gives EPA the authority to control hazardous waste from cradle to grave. This includes the generation, transportation, treatment, storage, and disposal of hazardous waste.[39]

- Toxic Substances Control Act (TSCA) of 1976 provides EPA with authority to require reporting, recordkeeping and testing requirements, and restrictions relating to chemical substances and/or mixtures. Certain substances are generally excluded from TSCA, including, among others, food, drugs, cosmetics, and pesticides.[40]

Few environmental laws existed before 1900. And those that were in existence before the 20th century were largely regulatory. When Congress declared crimes, they were low-level misdemeanor public welfare offenses that required no mens rea. Beginning in the 1960s, there has been a proliferation of environmental laws, with regulatory, civil, and criminal provisions. Today, many environmental crimes are felonies that are severely punished. With this evolution from a few regulatory offenses to a large set of serious crimes came a shift away from strict liability.

The mens rea for most environmental crimes is knowing. As is common in other crimes with this mens rea, knowledge that the acts were taken is all that is required. A prosecutor doesn't have to prove that a defendant knew the law was violated, nor is there a scienter requirement (e.g., proof that the defendant knew a discarded substance is toxic). Many of these offenses are felonies punished with large fines and years in prison. Offending corporations can be banned from contracting with the government in the future.

For some environmental crimes, there are are both felony offenses, requiring knowledge, and misdemeanor counterparts (or civil liability) that only require proof of negligence. The knowing standard has been criticized as being potentially unfair because environmental regulations are so complex that it is possible for innocent people to be convicted. Other complex criminal laws, such as tax, require more.

QUESTIONS AND PROBLEMS

1. Identify and briefly describe three federal environmental criminal laws that we discussed in this chapter.
2. PlastiCO, a plastics company, had a team of scientists evaluate its chemical use and disposal policies. The team concluded that it was permitted under the Clean Air Act to "scrub" and release a certain amount of a chemical into the atmosphere. The team's calculations were wrong. PlastiCO discharged twice the allowed amount of the poison into the air. It has been charged with violating the CAA. It has defended itself by alleging that it acted in good faith, and, therefore, it lacked the mens rea to commit the crime. Is it correct? Analyze the defense.
3. ColorCO, a company that manufactures house paint, has a process to dispose of its chemical waste. The process involves pumping the waste through a pipe into a holding tank, where it is eventually drained into trucks and transported to disposal facilities. Unknown to anyone working at ColorCO, an environmental vandal opened a small area of the pipe, allowing for some of the waste to leach into the groundwater. The Environmental Protection Agency discovers the situation, and ColorCO is charged with violating the Clean Water Act. ColorCO has defended itself by alleging that it acted in good faith, and therefore, it lacked the mens rea to commit the crime. Is it correct? Analyze the defense.

IN A NUTSHELL

Morality and quality-of-life crimes are found in the statutes of all of the states, territories, and the federal government. Many of these crimes are less frequently enforced than in the past, such as adultery and obscenity. Crimes involving children, the environment, and animals are more common and more aggressively enforced than in the past. The difference between the two groups lies in their objectives. Those in the former group are often "victimless" morals crimes, while the latter offenses have potential victims to protect or harms to prevent.

Immoral conduct may be controlled simply because a community objects to it, provided the laws don't discriminate by religion, race, ethnicity, sex, and sexual orientation. If a law does, or if it restricts speech, the law must overcome the strict Miller test to be legitimate. Laws that regulate the betwixt area—expressive conduct—must jump a hurdle that is higher than pure conduct but lower than speech.

LEGAL TERMS

any chance test (p. 353)

dominant factor test (p. 353)

Gambling (p. 352)

material element test (p. 353)

Miller test (p. 343)

morality crimes (p. 336)

obscenity (p. 343)

O'Brien test (p. 342)

prostitution (p. 337)

quality-of-life crimes (p. 336)

solicitation (p. 337)

NOTES

1. J. Coates, "Nevada Brothel Thanks IRS for Its New Bottom Line," *Chicago Tribune*, October 23, 1990, Chicagotribune.com; and "Joe Conforte Talks About Bonavena Shooting," *KTVN Channel 2 News*, accessed February 4, 2021, Ktvn.com.

2. MPC § 5.02(1).

3. A. Tsoulis-Reay, "What It's Like to Date Your Dad: The Cut," *New York Magazine*, January 15, 2015, thecut.com.

4. Neb. Rev. Stat. §28-703.

5. 720 ILCS 5/11-35.

6. D. L. Rhode, "Op-Ed: Why Is Adultery Still a Crime?" *Los Angeles Times*, May 2, 2016, accessed February 11, 2021, latimes.com.

7. *United States v. Battista*, 646 F.2d 237 (6th Cir. 1981). See also *United States v. Peraino*, 645 F.2d 548 (6th Cir. 1981).

8. Shortly before his death, Mark Felt, who had been associate director of the Federal Bureau of Investigation, disclosed that he was Deep Throat, the source for Woodward and Bernstein. The authors confirmed the claim. D. von Drahle, "FBI's No. 2 Was 'Deep Throat': Mark Felt Ends 30-Year Mystery of the *Post*'s Watergate Source," *Washington Post*, June 1, 2005, washingtonpost.com.

9. *Barnes v. Glen theater, Inc.*, 501 U.S. 560 (1991).

10. *Pap's v. City of Erie*, 529 U.S. 277 (2000).

11. *Jacobellis v. Ohio*, 378 U.S. 184 (1964).

12. *Miller v. California*, 413 U.S. 15 (1973).

13. *New York v. Ferber,* 458 U.S. 757 (1982).

14. *Ashcroft v. Free Speech Coalition,* 535 U.S. 234 (2002).

15. *Stanley v. Georgia,* 394 U.S. 557 (1969).

16. *Osborne v. Ohio,* 495 U.S. 103 (1990).

17. Va. Code Ann. §18.2-325, et seq.

18. O. Darcy, "Jeffrey Toobin Fired From *The New Yorker* After Exposing Himself on a Zoom Call," *CNN Business,* November 11, 2020, CNN.com.

19. Utah woman suffers setback in fighting criminal charges for being topless in own home. *USA Today,* January 22, 2020, USAToday.com.

20. *Loper v. New York City Police Department,* 999 F.2d 699 (2nd Circuit 1993).

21. 21 U.S.C. §801 et. seq.

22. *McFadden v. United States,* 576 U.S. 186 (2015).

23. Ala. Code § 32-5A-330.

24. See D. P. Gushee, "Can a Sanctity-of-Human-Life Ethic Ground Christian Ecological Responsibility?" *Notre Dame Journal of Law, Ethics & Public Policy* 23, no. 67 (2009): 471, 490.

25. Animals and Ethics, "Internet Encyclopedia of Philosophy," accessed February 23, 2021, https://iep.utm.edu/anim-eth/.

26. L. Alvarez, "Cats at Hemingway Museum Draw Tourists, and Legal a Battle," *New York Times,* December 22, 2012, http://www.nytimes.com.

27. 907 Whitehead Street, Inc., d.b.a. *Ernest Hemingway Home and Museum, v. Gipson,* 701 F.3d 1345 (11th Cir. 2012).

28. *United States v. Stevens,* 559 U.S. 460 (2010).

29. *United States of America v. Richards,* 755 F.3d 269, 271, 273 (5th Cir. 2014).

30. *Walmart Pleads Guilty to Federal Environmental Crimes, Admits Civil Violations, and Will Pay More Than $81 Million.* Press Release, U.S. Department of Justice. May 28, 2013, accessed February 24, 2021, archives.fbi.gov.

31. Alexander Pappas, "Revisiting Criminal Culpability Under the Clean Air Act Under Dieselgate," *Georetown Law Blog,* October 9, 2018, law.Georgetown.edu; and "Volkswagen Top Executives Charged With Market Manipulation," *BBC News,* September 24, 2019, bbc.com.

32. 42 U.S.C. §7401 et seq. (1970).

33. 33 U.S.C. §1251 et seq. (1972).

34. 42 U.S.C. §9601 et seq. (1980).

35. 16 U.S.C. §1531 et seq. (1973).

36. 7 U.S.C. §136 et seq. (1996).

37. 16 USC § 1431 et seq. and 33 USC §1401 et seq. (1988).

38. 42 U.S.C. §10101 et seq. (1982).

39. 42 U.S.C. §6901 et seq. (1976).

40. 15 U.S.C. §2601 et seq. (1976).

12 CRIMES AGAINST THE PEOPLE

On January 6, 2021, Congress convened to count the votes of electors for vice president and president, as required by the Twelfth Amendment to the United States Constitution. The counting of the votes of the members of the Electoral College by Congress is the final step in certifying the president-elect and vice-president-elect. Prior to January 6, President Donald J. Trump, who lost his reelection bid to Joseph Biden, engaged in a campaign to reverse the outcome through dozens of failed court challenges, calls for the electors to change their votes, pressure on state officials to change their states' vote counts, pressure on Vice President Mike Pence and members of Congress to reject several electoral votes for former Vice President Joseph Biden and to declare President Trump the victor, and an intense appeal to supporters in what became known as "Stop the Steal." Consequently, thousands of people attended a "Save America" rally in front of the White House during the January 6 meeting of Congress. At that gathering, President Trump and other speakers addressed the crowd, reiterating the claim that the election was stolen and encouraging them to march to the Capitol. Subsequently, thousands of people walked down Pennsylvania Avenue to the Capitol.

Within a short time after arriving at the Capitol, a mob overcame the police who were protecting the building and its residents. Some of attendees forced their way into the building on the first floor; others scaled the walls and the scaffolding that had been erected for the upcoming presidential inauguration. To gain entry, the mob assaulted officers, killing one. Inside, they made their way through the building into members' offices and onto the floors of both the House of Representatives and the Senate.

Videos, photos, and social media postings surfaced in the days following the insurrection that evinced a wide range of crimes. Some of the actors intended to disrupt Congress; others had expressed interest in murdering Vice President Mike Pence, Speaker of the House Nancy Pelosi, and other members of Congress. Several insurrectionists proudly posted or permitted photos to be taken of themselves during the events, including a man who was seated in the Speaker of the House's office with his feet on her desk, another who waved to a camera as he was stealing the Speaker's lectern, and yet another who was seated in the vice president's chair at the dais of the Senate Chamber. One insurrectionist was killed, and three other people died as a result of the riot, bringing the total dead to five.

The attack on the Capitol was the first since the British invaded and burned the building during the War of 1812. The behavior of the mob, of President Trump and other elected officials, and the apparent unpreparedness of Capitol police all shocked the nation—and the world. Immediately, there were calls for the suspects to be tried for treason and other crimes. Indeed, the crimes of January 6, 2021, will leave an indelible mark on America. The social, economic, and political causes of that dark day will be studied and discussed for decades.

In criminal law terms, a plethora of crimes that are the subject of this chapter—crimes against the "state" or against the "people"—occurred that day. Trespass, theft, assault, and sedition are the most obvious examples of crimes against the people. But as you will read in this chapter, there are many others.

Your study of this category of crimes begins with the most serious, treason.

ET TU, BRUTE

Learning Objective: Identify, describe, and apply the elements of treason.

Treason and murder have long been the most serious crimes in the Common Law—murder because it takes life, treason because it is an attempt to murder a nation. In Dante's *Inferno*, there is a special place reserved for traitors. Although most historians believe it apocryphal, William Shakespeare, in his play *Julius Caesar*, portrays dictator Julius Caesar uttering the words "Et tu, Brute," or *You, too, Brutus*, as Brutus joins the mob in its assassination of the dictator.

Traitors to the Crown were punished harshly throughout England's early history. King Henry VIII had two of his wives executed on the theory that their alleged marital infidelities were acts of treason. Treason was often punished more severely than murder. Murderers were typically executed quickly, while traitors were disemboweled, quartered, and subjected to torture before death. The family of a traitor was punished as well. Through corruption of blood, a traitor's property was forfeited to the Crown, and no titles or other family rights could be inherited from the traitor. This scarred a family for generations.

The British perspective on treason was transmitted to America. The Framers wrote and spoke about the dishonor and harm of treason. At the same time, they were leery of it. The British had used treason as a weapon to oppress political opponents and to suppress dissent in the American colonies. For example, speaking ill of the King or of the Crown's policies was sometimes punished as treason. Many Framers were treated as traitors to the British Crown even before the American Revolution began. So they included treason in the Constitution—the only crime to appear there—not to emphasize its importance, but to prevent its abuse. Article III, Section 3 reads:

> Clause 1: Treason against the United States shall consist only in levying War against them, or in adhering to their Enemies, giving them Aid and Comfort. No Person shall be convicted of Treason unless on the Testimony of two Witnesses to the same overt Act, or on Confession in open Court.

> Clause 2: The Congress shall have Power to declare the Punishment of Treason, but no Attainder of Treason shall work Corruption of Blood, or Forfeiture except during the Life of the Person attainted.

Treason: Levying war on, or adhering to the enemies of, a nation.

Congress implemented Clause 1, and the resulting elements of the offense are as follows:

18 U.S.C. §2381. Treason

1. A person who owes an allegiance to the United States,
2. *Levies* war or *Adheres* to an enemy of the United States and
3. commits an overt act and
4. possesses treasonable intent.

The first element applies treason law to "a person who owes an allegiance to the United States." Citizens of the United States clearly fall into this category, as may classes of noncitizens, such as members of the military and permanent residents, who both swear allegiance to the United States.

There are two forms of treason: (1) levying war against the United States and (2) adhering to an enemy of the United States, giving them aid and comfort. The second requires adhering to an enemy nation, or a foreign power. The first doesn't. An enemy is a nation that Congress has declared war upon or at least has authorized the president to use military force against.

Regardless of which form of treason is charged, the government must prove that an "overt act" in furtherance of the treason was taken. Requiring an overt act was the Framers' way to protect against one of the abuses they witnessed under British rule: the use of treason to punish dissenting speech. The First Amendment also protects the right to criticize governmental policies and officers. The treason clause requires the overt act be proved by a confession in open court or by the testimony of two witnesses.

The mens rea of treason isn't specifically identified in the Constitution, but specific intent to betray the nation is most likely required. It is possible, therefore, to provide aid and comfort to an enemy and not be guilty of treason.

A United States soldier offers medical care to a suffering enemy soldier. Although aid and comfort have been provided, there was no intent to betray the United States.

A United States soldier, who is fighting in a war declared by Congress, gives her unit's movement plans and other strategic information to a soldier of an enemy. At the time she hands them over, she states, "America doesn't belong here. The more setbacks we see, the more likely we will leave your country for good." The soldier has provided aid and comfort to the enemy.

The definition of "levying war" was considered for the first time only a few years after the Constitution was ratified. The case involved Aaron Burr, vice president under President Thomas Jefferson and the man who killed Alexander Hamilton in a duel. But his murder of Hamilton wasn't treason. He was tried for treason in 1807 for allegedly planning to seize part of the United States and Mexico with the intention of creating a new nation. Burr, a rendering of whom can be seen in Photo 12.1, and his codefendants were acquitted at a trial that was presided over by the Chief Justice of the United States John Marshall. Their case resulted in the Supreme Court decision *Ex Parte Bollman and Ex Parte Swartwout* (1807).[1]

In *Ex Parte Bollman*, SCOTUS held that planning an insurrection—conspiracy alone—against the United States isn't an overt act. Further, the fact that the men traveled to the place where the co-conspirators were to gather didn't satisfy the overt act element. Chief Justice John Marshall wrote, on behalf of the court, that an "actual assemblage of men for the purpose of executing a treasonable design" must occur. Because the alleged conspirators hadn't reached this point in the plot, if real, they were acquitted.

In a WWII-era case, *Cramer v. United States*,[2] the Supreme Court issued another narrow interpretation of treason. Mr. Cramer was born in Germany, served in the German military during WWI, and subse-

PHOTO 12.1 Aaron Burr, circa 1810. Was he a traitor?

Science History Images / Alamy Stock Photo

quently moved to the United States, where he earned U.S. citizenship, was gainfully employed, and crime free. He remained close to his family and friends in Germany, and he sympathized with Germany in its conflicts with other European nations before and during WWII.

Before the United States entered WWII, Cramer developed a friendship with two German men who returned to Germany to support the Nazis. Subsequently, but during the war, the men returned to the United States. They contacted Cramer, and the men met casually on a couple of occasions. Even though he was suspicious of their intentions, Cramer denied having ever been told why or how they returned to the United States. It would later be revealed that they were in the United States to commit sabotage. There was no evidence that Cramer assisted them in their sabotage efforts. Cramer was charged and convicted of treason. He was sentenced to 45 years in prison and a fine of $10,000. On appeal, SCOTUS reversed his conviction, writing that

> [t]he crime of treason consists of two elements: adherence to the enemy; and rendering him aid and comfort. A citizen intellectually or emotionally may favor the enemy and harbor sympathies or convictions disloyal to this country's policy or interest, but so long as he commits no act of aid and comfort to the enemy, there is no treason. On the other hand, a citizen may take actions which do aid and comfort the enemy—making a speech critical of the government or opposing its measures, profiteering, striking in defense plants or essential work, and the hundred other things which impair our cohesion and diminish our strength—but if there is no adherence to the enemy in this, if there is no intent to betray, there is no treason....

In addition to a narrow interpretation of what constitutes levying war or offering aid and comfort to the enemy, the court held that subjective intent must be proven, even if by inference.

The court found insufficient evidence that Cramer committed an overt act or that he harbored a specific intent to betray the United States.

The treason clause also addresses the punishment for treason. Congress may punish it with death, imprisonment, fines, and a prohibition of holding federal office in the future, but it may not issue an attainder or impose corruption of blood or forfeiture beyond the life of the traitor. The attainder language forbids Congress from declaring a person guilty of treason, a power that Parliament exercised. Instead, treason defendants are entitled to be tried before courts of law. Corruption of blood was an old Common Law punishment that deprived family members from inheriting property or titles of nobility. The prohibition of corruption of blood means that a traitor's family may inherit money and property that is not taken from the offender as punishment, such as fines.

The overt act and double witness requirements are high bars. Consequently, there have been fewer than 50 treason convictions in United States history and none whatsoever in last several decades. Alternatively, federal prosecutors turn to related felonies that don't require two witnesses, such as seditious conspiracy, espionage, or unlawful disclosure of national security secrets. Most of the states have treason laws that parallel federal law. See Table 12.1 for a list of prominent treason cases.

TABLE 12.1 ■ Prominent Treason Cases

Year	Defendant(s)	Facts	Outcome
1794	Philip Vigol and John Mitchell	Two of many tax protestors in what is known as Whiskey Rebellion. Several charged with treason.	Convicted and sentenced to death. President George Washington pardoned both.
1807	Aaron Burr	Alleged to have planned an insurrection to make part of the United States and Mexico an independent nation.	Acquitted
1859	John Brown	One of several men charged by Virginia with treason for inciting a rebellion of slaves in the Harpers Ferry Raid.	Convicted. The first person executed for treason in the United States.
1862	William Mumford	Mumford tore down a U.S. flag from a public building during the Civil War.	Convicted and executed in front of the building where the act occurred.
1865	Mary Surratt	Surratt was a co-conspirator in the assassination of President Abraham Lincoln.	Convicted. The first woman executed by the United States.
1942+	Several defendants	Several people were charged with joining the Axis powers during WWII.	Various outcomes, including convictions with years to life imprisonment. Some later received commutations.

(Continued)

TABLE 12.1 ■ Prominent Treason Cases (Continued)			
Year	Defendant(s)	Facts	Outcome
1949	Iva Toguri D'Aquino, aka Tokyo Rose	Toguri D'Aquino was alleged to have assisted the Japanese Empire through radio transmissions of propaganda to U.S. soldiers. Her conviction was controversial because the evidence was little and of questionable credibility.	President Gerald Ford issued a full pardon in 1977.
1952	Tomoya Kawakita	Kawakita was born in the U.S. but was living in Japan when it attacked Pearl Harbor in 1941. He remained in Japan, where he was also a citizen. During the war, he worked as an interpreter in a factory that used American POW labor. He returned to the U.S. after the war, and after being identified by a former POW, he was charged with treason. He defended himself by claiming he acted under duress and that he didn't owe the U.S. allegiance during the war. His appeals to SCOTUS failed.	Convicted and sentenced to death. President Dwight D. Eisenhower commuted the sentence to life imprisonment, and President John F. Kennedy ordered his release on the condition that he return to Japan. Kawakita is the last person convicted of treason against the United States.

Misprision of treason, or the failure to report known treason, is also a crime. The elements under federal law are that

1. Whoever, owing allegiance to the United States and

2. having knowledge of the commission of any treason against them

3. conceals and does not, as soon as may be, disclose and make known the same to the President or to some judge of the United States, or to the governor or to some judge or justice of a particular State.

Misprision of treason is punished with as many as 7 years in prison.

At the time of the writing of this book, the attack on the U.S. Capitol had just occurred, and much is to be learned about the intentions and acts of the people involved. For the defendants who entered the building and assaulted officers, the overt act element has been satisfied, even applying Justice Marshall's requirement that there be an "assemblage" of people. But establishing an intent to betray the United States will prove to be more difficult. If history is an accurate predictor, federal prosecutors will charge other crimes, not treason.

Misprision of treason: The crime of failing to report known treason to authorities.

Closely related to treason is the crime of inciting violence against the government. Under 18 U.S.C. §2383,

1. Whoever incites, sets on foot, assists, or engages in

2. any rebellion or insurrection

3. against the authority of the United States or the laws thereof,

4. or gives aid or comfort thereto

is guilty of rebellion or insurrection. Unlike treason, a defendant doesn't have to owe allegiance to the United States to be guilty of insurrection. Punishment for violations carry as many as 10 years in prison, a fine, and disqualification from holding federal office.

A more controversial law, the Smith Act,[3] reaches beyond violent conduct. It criminalizes advocating the overthrow of government. In the language of the law,

whoever knowingly or willfully advocates, abets, advises, or teaches the

duty, necessity, desirability, or propriety of overthrowing or destroying the government of the United States or the government of any State, Territory, District or Possession thereof, or the government of any political subdivision therein,

by force or violence, or by the assassination of any officer of any such government; or

whoever, with intent to cause the overthrow or destruction of any such government, prints, publishes, edits, issues, circulates, sells, distributes, or publicly displays any written or printed matter advocating, advising, or teaching the duty, necessity, desirability, or propriety of overthrowing or destroying any government in the United States by force or violence, or attempts to do so; or

whoever organizes or helps or attempts to organize any society, group, or assembly of persons who teach, advocate, or encourage the overthrow or destruction of any such government by force or violence; or becomes or is a member of, or affiliates with, any such society, group, or assembly of persons, knowing the purposes thereof

is guilty of advocating the overthrow of government. If convicted, a defendant can be fined, imprisoned up to 20 years, and shall be ineligible for employment by the United States for 5 years. The constitutionality of the law is in question because it criminalizes speech, not conduct. The law was upheld by SCOTUS in the 1951 decision *Dennis v. United States*, subject to the limitation that the words that are the subject of the prosecution present a clear and present danger to the United States, as outlined in the *Schenck* decision discussed in the following paragraphs.[4] Six years later, SCOTUS reversed the convictions of 14 communists who were charged under the Smith Act in *Yates v. United States*. The defendants were convicted of joining and organizing a communist organization and teaching communism, a political ideology that included the need for a violent revolution to overthrow capitalism and bring about social and political change. Applying *Dennis*, the court concluded that the

First Amendment's clear and present danger test draws a line between belief and advocacy and that the defendants didn't cross that line. In the words of Justice John Marshall Harlan, writing for the court,

> In failing to distinguish between advocacy of forcible overthrow as an abstract doctrine and advocacy of action to that end, the District Court appears to have been led astray by the holding in *Dennis* that advocacy of violent action to be taken at some future time was enough. It seems to have considered that, since "inciting" speech is usually thought of as something calculated to induce immediate action, and since *Dennis* held advocacy of action for future overthrow sufficient, this meant that advocacy, irrespective of its tendency to generate action, is punishable, provided only that it is uttered with a specific intent to accomplish overthrow. In other words, the District Court apparently thought that *Dennis* obliterated the traditional dividing line between advocacy of abstract doctrine and advocacy of action.

The effect of *Dennis, Yates,* and other cases is the minimization of the Smith Act. Furthermore, as you will read in just a few minutes, the clear and present danger test has been replaced, at least during peacetime, with the Brandenburg test. This test further restricted the authority of government to regulate speech that suggests violence or advocates hate. Specifically, Brandenburg requires speech to be directed at, and likely to produce, imminent lawlessness before it may be punished.

Professor Vostrom teaches political theory at NorthSouth State University. The readings in his political theory course include books and pamphlets by the communists Karl Marx and V. I. Lenin. During his lectures, he mentions on several occasions that he believes a violent revolution is both likely to occur and is needed to bring Americans into a state of equality. His speech is protected because he is teaching a theory in an academic context that is unlikely to incite anyone to violence.

Professor Vostrom teaches political theory at NorthSouth State University; specifically, he teaches communist theory. At the request of a local union, he has been delivering lectures on communist theory and workers' rights at the union's monthly meetings for the past year. Two weeks ago, the employees of a steel plant who are represented by the union went on strike. On the evening of June 2, city police officers attempted to move the striking workers away from the plant. Violence erupted, and a worker was shot and killed. Thirty minutes later, Vostrom stood in front of the workers, who were angry and grieving the loss of their "comrade," and yelled, "The time is now. You must rise and fulfill the promise of this nation and of Marx. Take control of this plant, as the great communist and worker revolutionaries

---

Clear and present danger test: Developed by SCOTUS in Schenck v. United States, this First Amendment doctrine limited the authority of government to regulate speech advocating violence to words that present a clear and present danger to government. Likely replaced by the Brandenburg test.

Brandenburg test: Developed by SCOTUS in *Brandenburg v. Ohio*, this First Amendment doctrine limits the authority of government to regulate speech advocating violence to words that are directed at, and are likely to produce, imminent lawlessness.

of Russia, China, and Cuba took control of their nations—and their industries. You have the power. There are more of us than there are supervisors or police. Arm yourself and act now!" Vostrom's speech is unprotected because it is directed at, and likely to produce, imminent lawlessness.

Finally, it is also unlawful to willfully interfere with, impair, or cause disloyalty, insubordination, or mutiny in the United States military.[5] The conduct is punished with fines and up to 10 years in prison during peacetime. During war, the maximum prison time increases to 20 years.[6]

QUESTIONS AND PROBLEMS

1. What are the elements of treason?
2. Michail Gorba Chef is a citizen of the Russian Federation. As a spy in his country's Foreign Intelligence Service, he is sent to the United States to collect military intelligence. He is caught by the U.S. Federal Bureau of Investigation and charged with treason. Is he guilty of treason? Explain your answer.
3. Robert Brown, born and reared in New Hampshire, uses social media to define a plan to kill the president of the United States, Toby Bartlet, and to take control of the federal government. Over a period of a year, he recruits 200 people from across the United States to join him in an invasion of the White House on the day of Bartlet's second inauguration. The plan calls for assassinating the president during the inaugural address at the Capitol building while others storm the White House. Members of the group armed themselves, and Brown acquired handheld missile launches and two armored vehicles. Under the leadership of Brown, a former colonel in the U.S. Marines, the group created a detailed plan. The day before the inauguration, all 200 are arrested in hotels located in Washington, DC, and Maryland. The weapons and vehicles were seized. Is Brown guilty of treason? Explain your answer.

SLEEPING WITH THE ENEMY

Learning Objective: Identify, describe, and apply the elements of seditious conspiracy.

After the Electoral College declared former Vice President Joe Biden the victor of the 2020 presidential election—but before the riot at the Capitol—President Donald Trump held a meeting in the White House. In addition to the president, former National Security Advisor and advisor to the president Michael Flynn, attorney Sidney Powell, Chief of Staff Mark Meadows, White House counsel Pat Cipollone, and advisor to the president Rudy Giuliani were in attendance. The group is reported to have discussed declaring martial law and using the military, at gunpoint, to seize voting machines and to rerun the elections in Georgia, Pennsylvania, Michigan, and Wisconsin. At least two in the meeting, Cipollone and Meadows, objected. When the meeting became public, journalists and scholars raised concerns about the antidemocratic and seditious nature of the discussion.[7]

Sedition has been a crime since America's earliest days. Unfortunately, these laws had been used to stifle and punish dissent during British rule, and by the Framers themselves, for the same purpose. Enacted only 8 years after the ratification of the Bill of Rights, the Alien and Seditions Acts of 1798 made it a crime to write false, scandalous, or malicious stories about the government; increased the residency period required to become a citizen; and increased the president's authority to deport dangerous aliens. Targeted at the opponents of President John Adams and the Federalists, several publishers and other supporters of Thomas Jefferson were convicted of sedition.

The provisions of the sedition laws suppressing the press and punishing political speech were controversial. Thomas Jefferson, James Madison, and other prominent Americans openly opposed them. After the law expired by its own sunset provision, Congress reimbursed the paid fines for all those who had been convicted under its authority.[8]

Sedition became an issue again as the nation entered WWI in 1917. There was opposition to the decision to enter the conflict at home, much of it coming from unpopular voices—émigré's from Russia and Europe, communists, anarchists, and pacifists. The dissenters opposed both the U.S. entry into the war and the military draft, which had never been used in America before. Opponents engaged in an antiwar campaign that involved fiery lectures, pamphleting, and, in some cases, encouraging men to evade the draft. There were genuine fears in the general public and in Congress that antiwar advocacy threatened the security of the United States. The recent fall of the Russian Empire to communism intensified these concerns. In response, Congress enacted the Espionage Act of 1917. It prohibited interference with the draft or military operations, insubordination by military personnel, and support of the enemy during wartime.

The Espionage Act was followed by the Sedition Act of 1918. Although referred to by that name, the law wasn't named the Sedition Act. It was, in reality, an amendment to the Espionage Act. It expanded the reach of the Sedition Act to include, during wartime, "disloyal, profane, scurrilous, or abusive language" about the United States, its flag, or the military. Causing others to have contempt for the United States was also made a crime. The postmaster general was given the authority to investigate the use of the mail to deliver items that contained prohibited language.

Many people were prosecuted under the two laws, including labor leaders, communist sympathizers, and peace activists. The broad reach of the laws, particularly the Sedition Act's criminalization of speech, was constitutionally challenged on many occasions. SCOTUS affirmed the laws in three cases in 1919. In the most famous of the cases, *Schenck v. United States*,[9] Charles Schenck, a socialist, was convicted of conspiracy to violate the Espionage Act for distributing pamphlets that encouraged men to refuse the draft. Justice Oliver Wendel Holmes, writing for the court, penned that the "question in every case is whether the words used are used in such circumstances and are of such a nature as to create a clear and present danger that they will bring about the substantive evils that Congress has a right to prevent." This announced a new

---

Sedition: Speech or acts that inspire a person to rebel against government. The First Amendment limits the authority of government to punish sedition.

free speech test that would be used to draw the line between protected and unprotected speech: Does the speech create a clear and present danger?

Holmes offered what has become a famous example of a clear and present danger: "The most stringent protection of free speech would not protect a man in falsely shouting fire in a theater and causing a panic." The court determined that Schenck's efforts to undermine the draft created a clear and present danger. His conviction was affirmed. In two more cases, *Debs v. United States*[10] and *Frohwerk v. United States*,[11] the court upheld convictions for speech deemed a clear and present danger.

In one of SCOTUS's most interesting stories, Justice Holmes, a conservative man from a privileged background who had served the Union bravely in the Civil War, decided less than a year later that he, and the court, were wrong. Influenced by young progressives whom he was mentoring, he disavowed his own clear and present danger test because he concluded that, as it was being applied, speech was underprotected. Unable to persuade his colleagues to apply the clear and present danger test differently or to abandon it, Holmes wrote one of the most famous dissents in SCOTUS history. The case was *Abrams v. United States*.

In *Abrams,* the Court reviewed the convictions of two Russian immigrants who distributed pamphlets (by throwing them out the windows of a building onto the streets of New York City) that expressed opposition to U.S. involvement in the communist revolution in Russia. Specifically, the defendants called for a general strike by workers, going so far as to suggest that violence may be necessary if the strike wasn't successful in changing America's policy.

As it had done in the *Schenck, Debs*, and *Frohwerk* cases, the court affirmed the convictions, finding the content of the pamphlets to be a clear and present danger to the security of the nation. In his dissent, joined by Justice Louis Brandeis, Holmes penned that ideas, good and bad, need to be heard. "The ultimate good desired is better reached by free trade in ideas... that the best test of truth is the power of the thought to get itself accepted in the competition of the market, and that truth is the only ground upon which their wishes safely can be carried out." This idea became commonly known as the *marketplace of ideas*.

Holmes and Brandeis didn't believe the leaflets were a serious threat to national security, referring to them as silly. Furthermore, their subject was Russia, with whom the United States was not at war. In important language, Holmes and Brandeis advanced a new First Amendment test, advocating that only speech that so "imminently threaten[s] immediate interference with the lawful and pressing purpose of the law that an immediate check is required to save the country" may be regulated. This is now familiar to you. Nearly 60 years later, SCOTUS adopted Holmes's imminent lawlessness standard in *Brandenburg v. Ohio*, as discussed earlier in this chapter and in Chapter 7. That test protects speech until it is directed at causing imminent lawlessness and is likely to produce such lawlessness. More protective of speech than the clear and present danger test, *Brandenberg* remains the law today, at least during peacetime. Because the clear and present danger test hasn't been explicitly overruled, it is possible that it could be resurrected during wartime.

Through *Brandenberg* and other cases, the First Amendment's protections of free speech and press limit the reach of the crime of sedition. As you learned in earlier discussions, political speech is the highest form of expression. Disagreement with government, political hyperbole, and satire are protected. See Table 12.2 for a summary of significant SCOTUS treason, sedition, and riot cases.

TABLE 12.2 ■ Significant SCOTUS Treason, Sedition, and Riot Cases		
Crime	Case	Holding
Treason	Ex Parte Bollman & Ex Parte Swartwout (1807)	Conspiring, planning, and even traveling to the venue of the intended crime are not adequate to prove treason.
Treason	Cramer v. United States (1945)	Subjective intent to levy war or adhere to the enemy must be proved, and simply associating with traitors, without rendering aid and comfort, is not treason.
Sedition, riot, disorderly conduct	Schenck v. United States, Debs v. United States, and Frohwerk v. United States (1919)	Speech may be regulated if it presents a clear and present danger.
Sedition, riot, disorderly conduct	Brandenburg v. Ohio (1969)	Speech may be regulated if it is directed at, and likely to produce, imminent lawlessness. The test was first suggested by Justice Holmes in Abrams v. United States (1919).

Today, the federal government doesn't have a general sedition law. Instead, it criminalizes conspiracies to commit sedition. One of the distinguishing characteristics between seditious conspiracy and overthrow of government, espionage, and treason is the lack of an overt act. As is true of all conspiracies, the agreement between the conspirators is the full actus reus of the crime, subject to the First Amendment's limitations that were just outlined. The elements of federal seditious conspiracy are as follows:

1. Two or more persons

2. in any State or Territory, or in any place subject to the jurisdiction of the United States

3. conspire to

4. overthrow or put down or
   destroy by force the Government of the United States or
   to levy war against them or
   to oppose by force the authority thereof or
   by force to prevent, hinder, or delay the execution of any law of the United States
   or by force to seize, take, or possess any property of the United States.[12]

Violators can be fined under this title or imprisoned not more than 20 years, or both.

QUESTIONS AND PROBLEMS

1. What are the elements of federal seditious conspiracy?
2. Describe the history of sedition and SCOTUS's First Amendment approaches to it.

I SPY WITH MY EYE

Learning Objective: Identify, describe, and apply the elements of espionage.

The last section discussed sedition and made references to the related crime of espionage. Spying for the enemy, a form of espionage, can injure a nation's security and finances and cause loss of life.

Federal espionage law is broad, overlapping, and confusing. As one scholar put it,

> [The Espionage Act] comprises some of the most confusing and ambiguous federal criminal law on the books. Despite its title, courts agree that the various provisions of the Espionage Act punish much more than traditional espionage. Not only do some provisions apply to government insiders who disclose national security information to the press, but some also appear to leave open the possibility of prosecutions against the press itself, as well as any other downstream publishers (including ordinary citizens).[13]

18 U.S.C. §§ 793 and 794 are the general espionage prohibitions. Section 793 criminalizes the gathering, transmitting to an unauthorized person, or losing of national defense information, and Section 794 makes it a crime for a person to deliver, or attempt to deliver, national defense information to foreign agents or subjects of foreign countries with intent or reason to believe that it is to be used to the injury of the United States or to the advantage of a foreign nation. The required mental state of these crimes varies. Section 793 requires gross negligence. Section 794, on the other hand, requires intent or at least reason to believe that the information will be used to injure the United States or will give advantage to a foreign nation.

Other federal espionage laws include these:

- Computer Espionage. 18 U.S.C. § 1030(a)(1) makes it unlawful to knowingly access a computer without authorization, or beyond the scope of one's authorization, and thereby obtain information that has been classified for national defense or foreign relations reasons, with intent or reason to believe that such information is to be used to the injury of the United States or to the advantage of a foreign nation.

- Communication or Receipt of Classified Information. 50 U.S.C. § 783 makes it unlawful for any officer or employee of the United States, or of any federal department or agency, to communicate to any person whom he or she knows or has reason to believe to be an agent of a foreign government, any information classified by the president or by the head of such department or agency as affecting the security of the United States, knowing or having reason to know that such information has been so classified. Conversely, it is unlawful for a foreign agent to knowingly receive classified information from a U.S. government employee, unless special authorization has been obtained.

- Disclosing Intelligence Identities. 50 U.S.C. § 421 prohibits the unauthorized disclosure of information identifying certain U.S. intelligence officers, agents, informants, or sources.

Espionage: A synonym for spying.

- Foreign Agent Registration. 18 U.S.C. § 951 makes it unlawful for foreign agents to act as such without notifying the attorney general, unless the agent is entitled to a statutory exemption from the registration requirement.

In addition to foreign spies, there have been many disloyal Americans who have been prosecuted under espionage laws for selling state secrets to foreign governments. Ethel and Julius Rosenberg, Robert Hanssen, and Aldrich Ames are four people who became household names after they were discovered to have spied for the Soviet Union. In recent years, the focus has been on economic and national security spying by the Chinese.

Sometimes, the line between patriot and traitor is unclear. Free speech, particularly of a political nature, is fundamental to a constitutional republic. Government is held accountable and self-governance is advanced when the people are informed. Conversely, secrecy is sometimes warranted. Revealing future battle plans or the names of U.S. spies abroad can threaten national security, and kill people. Several whistleblowers have tested the national security/openness dilemma. For these individuals, disclosing national secrets can be an act of patriotism. Daniel Ellsberg, an analyst in the Department of Defense, with the assistance of Anthony Russo, leaked the Pentagon Papers in 1969. The documents revealed lies by successive presidential administrations about the Vietnam War. Hailed by many—and demonized by others—Ellsberg was charged with espionage, and *The New York Times* and *The Washington Post* were ordered to stop printing the papers. Ellsberg was not convicted, and *The Washington Post* won the right under the First Amendment to publish them in *New York Times Co. v. United States* (1971).[14]

Equally controversial were the releases of classified information by Chelsea Manning to Wikileaks and Edward Snowden to several newspapers. Both were charged under the Espionage Act. Manning pled guilty, was sentenced to 35 years in prison, and was freed through a commutation by President Barack Obama. Snowden fled the United States, and as of 2021, he was living n Russia and was still wanted by the United States. Like Ellsberg, Manning and Snowden are whistleblowers to some people, villains to others.

QUESTIONS AND PROBLEMS

1. Distinguish espionage from sedition.
2. Research the Snowden and Manning cases. Are either liable for espionage? Are the two equally culpable? Explain your answers.

THE CONSTITUTION ISN'T A SUICIDE PACT

Learning Objective: Identify, describe, and apply the elements of domestic and international terrorism.

In 1949, Justice Robert Jackson wrote a dissent in a case where the court set aside a man's conviction for breaching the peace. Jackson believed the court had gone so far in protecting the defendant's individual rights that the justice put the public at risk. He wrote that "if the Court does not temper its doctrinaire logic with a little practical wisdom, it will convert the constitutional Bill of Rights into a suicide pact."[15] The pithy comment, commonly reduced to *The Constitution isn't a suicide pact*, caught on, and it is commonly found in media and legal writings.

Acts of terrorism typically involve traditional crimes, such as murder, battery, and property destruction. What makes terrorism different from these crimes is the intent of the actors. Terrorism involves more than the specific intent to destroy property or to murder; rather, it uses those outcomes to cause fear in the people generally or to influence a government's conduct or policy. The law recognizes both domestic and international terrorism. 18 U.S.C. § 2331 defines *domestic terrorism* as follows:

1. Violent acts or acts that are dangerous to human life

2. that are a violation of the criminal laws of the United States or of any State, or that would be a criminal violation if committed within the jurisdiction of the United States or of any
    State and

3. appear to be intended
     i. to intimidate or coerce a civilian population; or
     ii. to influence the policy of a government by intimidation or coercion; or
     iii. to affect the conduct of a government by mass destruction, assassination, or
         kidnapping; and

4. occur primarily within the territorial jurisdiction of the United States.

The definition of *international terrorism* is the same, except that the acts must occur "primarily outside the territorial jurisdiction of the United States." If the methods used, the people that are coerced or intimidated, or the location the actors flee to after the crime are beyond the United States, the crime is an act of international terrorism. Capital punishment or life imprisonment is imposed if the terroristic act causes death. Otherwise, long prison sentences, including life, are possible.

Zack failed to pay his U.S. taxes for several years. Angry that the United States won a lawsuit against him to collect the past-due taxes, he plants a deadly virus in the local federal building, killing 50 people. Zack has not committed terrorism because he lacks the intent to intimidate or coerce the people or to influence federal policy.

Zack is unhappy with the U.S. human rights policy for China. He sends the U.S. Department of State an anonymous message, threatening to kill Americans if the policy is not changed. There is no change in policy, so Zack plants a deadly virus in the local federal building, killing 50 people. He follows the act with an audio message to a local radio station, stating, "The virus that started in the federal building is a warning. If the United

States doesn't change its human rights policy regarding China within 30 days, more people will die." Zack is committing terrorism because he intends to intimate and coerce the population by committing deadly acts.

QUESTIONS AND PROBLEMS

1. What are the elements of domestic terrorism? How does it differ from international terrorism?
2. How does terrorism differ from traditional murder and other crimes of violence?
3. Angry over losing his job at the U.S. Social Security Administration, Andrew plants a bomb in the federal building where he worked. He detonates it, destroying the building, killing 100 people, and wounding another 120 people. He moves to another city to avoid detection and remains low-key. Regardless, he is caught a year later. Has he committed domestic terrorism? Explain your answer.

TO UNPEACEABLY ASSEMBLE

Learning Objective: Identify, describe, and apply the elements of riot under federal law.

The First Amendment protects the right to peaceably assemble. By definition, this right involves acts by more than one person. Throughout U.S. history, the free speech, press, grievance petition, and assembly rights have been critical to social change. Abolitionists, suffragettes, civil rights advocates, LGBTQ advocates, and religious groups have all relied upon these rights to spread their messages and to advocate for social and legal change.

As you have read before in this book, no right is absolute. Rights, while expansive, are bound by narrowly and strictly construed exceptions. The First Amendment itself establishes a significant boundary to the right to gather with other people—only peaceable assemblies are protected. Accordingly, it is legitimate for governments to criminalize breaches of the peace. Even when peaceful, reasonable time, place, and manner (TPM) rules may further limit free speech and assemblies. Examples of reasonable TPM restrictions are to require demonstrators in public streets and sidewalks to not impede foot or automobile traffic and to set maximum decibel-level limits in neighborhoods at night. Another limitation exists: when individuals' rights come into conflict with one another. The rights of one person end where the rights of others begin. In no case, however, may government engage in viewpoint discrimination. Consider the following examples:

A statute that criminalizes interfering with the free flow of traffic may be enforced against demonstrators who choose to block a street because it is a viewpoint-neutral, TPM restriction.

A city's decision to deny a permit to a group of people who want to gather in a public park to protest a recent court verdict because city officials believe the group's message is incendiary violates the viewpoint neutrality rule and is invalid.

A group of demonstrators received a permit to meet in a public park. They follow the city's TPM rules. But during their event, violence erupts. Chairs and fists are thrown, a small child who was playing nearby is injured, and park benches are overturned. To restore order, and pursuant to state law that authorizes police and other officials to make arrests and clear public spaces during riots, police officers order everyone to leave the area. One of the demonstrators refuses, citing the permit as her authorization to be in the area. She has committed trespass.

There are many laws that regulate unlawful and destructive conduct in public spaces. Four are discussed in this section: riot, disorderly conduct, trespass, and destruction of public property.

PHOTO 12.2 The Capitol riot of January 6, 2021.

Anadolu Agency / Contributor

Riot and disorderly conduct are cousins. All states forbid both, as does the federal government. Riot laws vary in the conduct that is prohibited and the number of people required. Texas, for example, requires at least seven people in the group. An individual charged must knowingly engage in conduct that

1. creates an immediate danger of damage to property or injury to persons;

2. substantially obstructs law enforcement or other governmental functions or services; or

3. by force, threat of force, or physical action deprives any person of a legal right or disturbs any person in the enjoyment of a legal right.[16]

Three people can make a riot under federal law:

1. an act or acts of violence by one or more persons part of an assemblage of three or more persons, which act or acts shall constitute a clear and present danger of, or shall result in, damage or injury to the property of any other person or to the person of any other individual or

2. a threat or threats of the commission of an act or acts of violence by one or more persons part of an assemblage of three or more persons having, individually or collectively, the ability of immediate execution of such threat or threats, where the performance of the threatened act or acts of violence would constitute a clear and present danger of, or would result in, damage or injury to the property of any other person or to the person of any other individual.[17]

Using these definitions, a person violates the antiriot law for any of these acts:

1. Inciting a riot

2. Organizing, promoting, encouraging, or participating in, or carrying on a riot

3. Commiting any act of violence in furtherance of a riot

4. Aiding or abetting others in riot[18]

Of course, the United States must have jurisdiction over the acts, which means that an alleged rioter must travel in, or use a facility of, interstate or foreign commerce to be guilty of federal riot. The use of the mail, internet, telephone, and wire and cellular communication all satisfy the interstate commerce requirement. Riot is punished with a fine and as much as 5 years in prison.

Returning to the Capitol siege, seen in Photo 12.2, one of the most frequently charged crimes was trespass, which appears in a few different forms in the United States Code. One is the offense of entering or remaining on restricted buildings or grounds,[19] defined as

1. knowingly entering or remaining

2. in any restricted building or grounds

3. without lawful authority to do so.

Offenders are punished with as much as 1 year of imprisonment and a fine, unless the actor is carrying a firearm or dangerous weapon or significant bodily injury occurs, in which case the fine can be larger and the possible prison term increases to 10 years.

Another crime that many of the Capitol siege defendants were charged with applies specifically to the Capitol building. The violent entry and disorderly conduct statute makes it a crime, among other acts, to willfully and knowingly

A. enter or remain on the floor of either House of Congress or in any cloakroom or lobby adjacent to that floor, in the Rayburn Room of the House of Representatives, or in the Marble Room of the Senate, unless authorized to do so pursuant to rules adopted, or an authorization given, by that House;

B. enter or remain in the gallery of either House of Congress in violation of rules governing admission to the gallery adopted by that House or pursuant to an authorization given by that House.[20]

This crime is punished with as much as 6 months imprisonment and a fine.[21]

You learned about criminal mischief, or damaging property, in Chapter 9. Governments across the country have special mischief laws that punish the destruction of public property. In the case of the Capitol riot, many defendants were charged with destruction of federal property. 18 U.S.C. § 1361. Destruction of Federal Property

Whoever willfully injures or commits any depredation against any property of the United States, or of any department or agency thereof, or any property which has been or is being manufactured or constructed for the United States, or any department or agency thereof, or attempts to commit any of the foregoing offenses, shall be punished as follows:

If the damage or attempted damage to such property exceeds the sum of $1,000, by a fine under this title or imprisonment for not more than 10 years, or both; if the damage or attempted damage to such property does not exceed the sum of $1,000, by a fine under this title or by imprisonment for not more than 1 year, or both.

QUESTIONS AND PROBLEMS

1. What are the elements of federal riot?
2. Rasheed, Jazmine, and Peter object to a federal law that authorizes the president of the United States to use military force to help the government of another country that is involved in a civil war. They decide to protest outside of the White House. During their protest, they recite the slogan, "No guns, no force, no later remorse!" Their message catches on with people in the streets. After 15 minutes, over 100 people are yelling the slogan at the top of their lungs. Have Rasheed, Jazmine, and Peter committed federal riot? Explain your answer.
3. Rasheed, Jazmine, and Peter object to a federal law that authorizes the president of the United States to use military force to help the government of another country that is involved in a civil war. They decide to protest outside of the White House. During their protest they recite the slogan, "No guns, no force, no later remorse!" Their message catches on with people in the streets. After 15 minutes, over 100 people are yelling the slogan at the top of their lungs. As the group chants, the three pull metal bars and Molotov cocktails from a box and distribute them. Using a bullhorn, Rasheed yells, "Make change happen! Stop this injustice!" At that moment, Jazmine and Peter begin climbing the fence to the White House. Several members of the crowd help them over the fence, while others grab the metal bars and begin swinging them around. Have Rasheed, Jazmine, and Peter committed federal riot? Explain your answer.

DISORDER IN THE COURT

Learning Objective: Compare and contrast civil, criminal, direct, and indirect contempt.

People have many reasons, social and legal, to not obey court orders. Exhibiting disrespect toward and failing to comply with an order of a court is contempt of court. The contempt power is an inherent judicial authority and often, a statutorily recognized authority.

There are four forms of contempt. *Direct contempt* refers to acts that occur in the presence of a judge. Although direct contempt usually occurs in the courtroom, judges' chambers and office area are included. *Indirect contempt* refers to a violation of a court order that occurs outside of the presence of the court.

Criminal contempt is imposed to punish a person for violating a court order. Civil contempt, by contrast, it a punishment. It is intended to coerce a person into complying with a court order. For example, if Mary refuses to testify at a trial despite an order to testify, the judge may order her confined until she complies. Once she testifies, Mary is free. Consequently, civil contemnors "hold the keys to their jail cells"; criminal contemnors do not. In theory, one who has been held in civil contempt can be punished for criminal contempt after complying with the court order. In practice, this seldom occurs, presumably because judges and prosecutors feel that the acts taken to coerce compliance also adequately serve as punishment. Regardless of the form of contempt, intentional conduct is required. This is obvious in cases of disruptive outbursts that occur in the presence of a judge. It can be more difficult in indirect contempt cases.

The contempt power is significant. Indirect criminal contemnors are entitled to the protections of other criminal defendants, such as a right to a trial, assistance of counsel, and proof beyond a reasonable doubt. Direct criminal contemnors have no such rights because the act took place in the presence of a judge. However, a person held in direct contempt is to be given the opportunity to speak before sentence is imposed, and both the contempt citation and its sentence may be appealed and reviewed for fairness.

Civil contemnors have greater rights than criminal contemnors, but less than criminal defendants. A contemnor does not possess all of the rights of a criminal defendant because civil contempt is not considered a criminal action. Of course, if an appellate court determines that the underlying order is unlawful, the civil contemnor is released. However, the individual may be charged with criminal contempt for failure to comply with the order before it was held unlawful by an appellate court. The fact that a court order may be nullified at some future date does not justify noncompliance. Court orders must be obeyed to ensure the orderly administration of justice. See Table 12.3 for a comparison of the four types of contempt.

The contempt power is broad, but limited. Yelling and cursing at or questioning the integrity of the court all fall on the wrong side of the law. But the line between civil disagreement and contempt is sometimes thin. In your next Digging Deeper case, *In Re Dearman v. State*, the line between an attorney's advocacy for a client and contempt is discussed.

Contempt: Willfully disobeying a judge's command or official court order, or causing a disruption in court. Contempt can be direct (within the judge's notice) or indirect (outside the court and punishable only after proved to the judge). It can also be civil contempt (disobeying a court order in favor of an opponent) or criminal contempt.

25

TABLE 12.3 ■ The Four Types of Contempt		
	Criminal	*Civil*
Direct	Shouting to a judge during a hearing, "F*ck you, I don't care what you say. You are an idiot, and if I weren't handcuffed, I would kick your ass." The judge fines the actor $200.	An attorney disobeys a judge's order to stop talking. The judge tells the attorney that they will be fined $10 for every word uttered from that point forward.
Indirect	A judge issues an order to a witness to produce documents to the police within 48 hours. The witness refuses. The judge sentences the witness to 2 days in jail.	A judge issues an order to a witness to produce documents to the court within 48 hours. The witness doesn't produce the documents. The judge orders the witness jailed until the documents are produced.

DIGGING DEEPER 12.1

Is it contemptuous for an attorney to repeatedly object over a judge's order to stop?

Case: *In Re Dearman v. State*
Court: Supreme Court of Alabama
Year: 2020

Justice Mendheim

H. Chase Dearman petitioned this Court for a writ of certiorari to review the Court of Criminal Appeals' decision affirming, without an opinion, the Mobile Circuit Court's order finding Dearman in direct contempt....

On August 30, 2018, Dearman, an attorney, was representing James Markese Wright at Wright's probation-revocation hearing before the circuit court; Judge James T. Patterson was the circuit-court judge presiding over the hearing. During the course of the probation-revocation hearing, the following exchange occurred between Dearman and Judge Patterson:

> [Wright's probation officer]: During the search [of Wright's house], I ended up locating in the kitchen drawer, what was later determined to be a controlled substance.
> [The State]: Specifically, what was it?
> [Wright's probation officer]: AK-47 Herbal Incense.
> [The State]: Would that be on the streets known as—
> Mr. Dearman: I object. This officer has no training in narcotics whatsoever. This is not a regular drug and regularly identifiable. And in addition to that, the district court found no probable cause on this case, the facts of which the court is now hearing.
> The Court: All right.
> Mr. Dearman: We've had a preliminary hearing.

The Court: Alabama Rules of Evidence, Article 11, Miscellaneous Rules, Rule 1101, rules inapplicable. These rules, other than those with respect to privileges, do not apply in the following situations: preliminary questions of fact, grand jury, miscellaneous proceedings including proceedings for extradition or rendition, preliminary hearing in criminal cases, sentencings, granting and revoking probation.

Mr. Dearman: Judge, in district court—

The Court: No. They don't apply.

Mr. Dearman: May I finish my objection?

The Court: No, you may not. There's no objection here. They don't apply. The Rules of Evidence don't apply here.

Mr. Dearman: I have an objection for the record.

The Court: No, sir. The rules don't apply. The rules don't apply, Mr. Dearman.

Mr. Dearman: The Judge is talking over me.

The Court: The rules don't apply.

Mr. Dearman: My objection—

The Court: The rules don't apply.

Mr. Dearman: My objection is—

The Court: The rules don't apply.

Mr. Dearman: My objection is—

The Court: The rules don't apply.

Mr. Dearman: Okay. Let me know when I can speak.

The Court: You're not going to speak. If you're going to make an objection, you're not going to speak.

Mr. Dearman: May the record reflect that I'm not allowed to make—

The Court: Get him out of here. Take the lawyer out. Get out.

Mr. Dearman: May the record reflect—

The Court: Get out.

Mr. Dearman: —that I am being ordered out of the courtroom—

The Court: Get out.

Mr. Dearman: —and the Judge has lost his temper—

The Court: Get out.

Mr. Dearman: —again.

The Court: Get out. Take him back.

(Proceedings concluded.)

On the same day of the hearing, the circuit court entered the following order:

"Based on his conduct before this court this date at hearing on the probation revocation of his client, James Markese Wright, and specifically his conduct after this court advised Mr. Dearman that per Ala. R. Evid. 1101(b)(3), the rules of evidence do not apply to granting or revoking probation, and because of his contemptuous conduct cted [sic] toward this court immediately after this Rule of Evidence was pointed out to him, this court finds attorney Chase Dearman in direct contempt of court....

"This matter was immediately disposed of by undersigned ordering Mr. Dearman to leave [the] courtroom..., and this court will take no further action in this regard—this time. However, please be advised that further outbursts of this nature may lead to other sanctions...."

Dearman argues that his conduct at the August 30, 2018, hearing did not "constitute an act of direct contempt." Dearman's brief, p. 14: Dearman argues that he was not challenging the circuit court's authority at the August 30, 2018, hearing, but was attempting "to put a timely and complete objection on the record" in defending his client. In so arguing, Dearman argues that the Court of Criminal Appeals' decision is in conflict with Hawthorne, supra....

In *Hawthorne*, an attorney used the phrase "sons of bitches" during closing argument. There was no objection made by opposing counsel at the time the phrase was used, and the trial court took no immediate action to stop or to reprimand the attorney for using the phrase. It was not until the opposing side was giving its closing argument that the attorney's use of the phrase "sons of bitches" was objected to as inappropriate. The trial court agreed, stating that "'it was highly improper to use that language in the courtroom.'" Ten days later, the trial court gave the attorney "an opportunity to be heard as to whether he should be held in contempt of court for using the phrase 'sons of bitches.'" Following the hearing, the trial court "issued an order finding the [attorney] guilty of direct criminal contempt of court." The attorney appealed to the Court of Criminal Appeals.

On appeal, the Court of Criminal Appeals stated that "the question is whether the conduct amounts to direct criminal contempt of court" as defined by [statutory law]. The Court of Criminal Appeals stated that, "while the language used was unprofessional, indecorous, unnecessary, and unbecoming of a member of the bar, the record is devoid of any evidence that 'immediate action [was] essential to prevent diminution of the court's dignity and authority before the public.'" The Court of Criminal Appeals further stated that "the record is devoid of sufficient evidence that the [attorney's] use of the phrase 'sons of bitches' 'obstruct[ed] the administration of justice'" or interrupted, disturbed, or hindered the court's proceedings.

In the present case, the circuit court held Dearman in contempt because he repeatedly attempted to make a specific objection after the circuit court determined that the Alabama Rules of Evidence did not apply at the August 30, 2018, probation-revocation hearing. It appears that the circuit court believed that the objection Dearman was attempting to make was related to that particular ruling. However, it is unclear from the record the exact objection that Dearman sought to assert. It is certainly true that the circuit court made its position clear that the Alabama Rules of Evidence do not apply in a probation-revocation proceeding, but it is unclear if Dearman was attempting to object to that particular ruling. The only objections on the record that Dearman made during the probation-revocation hearing are as follows:

> Mr. Dearman: I object. This officer has no training in narcotics whatsoever. This is not a regular drug and regularly identifiable. And in addition to that, the district court found no probable cause on this case, the facts of which the Court is now hearing.

Dearman then noted that "we've had a preliminary hearing," at which point the circuit court read from Rule 1101, Ala. R. Evid., which states that the Alabama Rules of Evidence do not apply in probation-revocation hearings. Immediately thereafter, Dearman stated: "Judge, in district court—." It is at this point that the circuit court would not permit Dearman to continue to speak. Therefore, based on the facts before us, there is nothing indicating that Dearman was attempting to continually object to the circuit court's ruling that the Alabama Rules of Evidence do not apply in a probation-revocation hearing. Dearman stated that he had "an objection for the record," but the circuit court responded, "No sir." Dearman then attempted to state his objection, three times, beginning his objection with "My objection..." or "My objection is..." Each time, however, the circuit court spoke over Dearman and then told Dearman that "you're not going to speak. If you're going to make an objection, you're not going to speak." This statement of the circuit court indicates that not only was the circuit court not allowing Dearman to object to its determination that the Alabama Rules of Evidence did not apply to the hearing (if that was even Dearman's objection), but that Dearman could make no objection whatsoever.

As did the Court of Criminal Appeals in *Hawthorne*, we conclude in the present case that the record is devoid of any evidence that Dearman's conduct "disturb[ed] the court's business" and that "immediate action [was] essential to prevent diminution of the court's dignity and authority before the public." The evidence before us indicates that Dearman, by trying to make an objection on the record to preserve the issue for appellate review, was simply trying to engage the court in the business before it, not detract from it. The immediate action taken by the circuit court in silencing Dearman was not to prevent Dearman from diminishing the court's dignity or authority, but to prevent Dearman from asserting a necessary objection on behalf of his client.... Dearman specifically stated that his intent was "only to fulfill my duty as the advocate for my client." Dearman further explained that he believed that "if you do not put [a specific objection] on the record, you've lost it forever, and that was all I was simply trying to do. There was no intent on my behalf." Dearman's understanding of the law is correct.

[Dearman's conviction for contempt is] REVERSED and REMANDED.

QUESTIONS AND PROBLEMS

1. Distinguish direct from indirect contempt.
2. Distinguish civil from criminal contempt.
3. Judge Erik Kneehouse orders Katy to turn over an automobile and its title to Megan by June 1. Katy refuses. Judge Kneehouse orders that Katy be jailed until she complies. What form of contempt is represented in this hypothetical?
4. Judge Erik Kneehouse is conducting a juvenile justice proceeding. An attorney becomes enraged at a decision of the court. She knocks over a chair and screams, "You are an idiot. How can you be so heartless and stupid?!" Judge Kneehouse holds the attorney in contempt and fines her $500. What form of contempt is represented in this hypothetical?

LIAR, LIAR PANTS ON FIRE

Learning Objective: Identify, describe, and apply the elements of perjury.

Perjury was a crime at the Common Law and continues to be prohibited by statute in all states. The elements of perjury are these:

1. The making of a

2. false statement

3. with knowledge that it is false

4. while under oath or affirmation.

Perjury: Lying while under oath or affirmation.

To convict a person of perjury, the prosecution must prove a high level of mens rea: knowledge of the falsity of a statement. As with other crimes, juries are permitted to infer a defendant's knowledge from the surrounding facts.

A statement must be made while under oath to be subject to perjury. Taking an oath to God is ancient; it relied on a witness's fear of eternal damnation to elicit the truth. For those individuals who have a religious objection to "swearing," the law permits an "affirmation." This is simply an affirmation by the witness that they understand truthful testimony is required by law. The purpose of oaths and affirmations are the same. They appeal to the conscience of the witness to be truthful, they formally message the significance of the proceeding, and they remind witnesses that there are legal consequences for lying. The law treats an affirmation in the same manner as it does an oath. Here are examples of both:

Oath: "Do you solemnly state that the evidence you shall give in this matter shall be the truth, the whole truth, and nothing but the truth, so help you God?"

Affirmation: "Do you solemnly state, under penalty of perjury, that the evidence that you shall give in this matter shall be the truth, the whole truth, and nothing but the truth?

Perjury laws apply to more than testifying in court. It is perjurious to lie in affidavits, to knowingly present falsities in any document signed before a notary public, for a police officer to submit a complaint and affidavit for a warrant that contains facts known to be untrue, to lie in a deposition before a court reporter (e.g., for deposition), to lie to a grand jury, to falsely testify before Congress, and in many other circumstances.

Some jurisdictions require that the false statement be "material," or important to the matter. This requirement prevents prosecutions for trivial lies. Some jurisdictions have defined *materiality* as any fact that may affect the outcome of a case. If a statement is not material, even if untrue, perjury hasn't been committed.

Reggie committed a murder. At trial, he decides to testify. When asked where he was at the time of the murder, he tells the court that he was with his girlfriend, 20 miles away from the scene of the murder. Reggie has committed perjury.

Reggie is called as a witness in a murder trial. A few months before, he saw the defendant thrust a knife into the victim. When asked his name by the prosecutor, he answers, "Reggie Hawkins." His legal name is Robert Reginald Hawkins, but he prefers Reggie. Although he knows his answer is untrue, the statement isn't material to the case and, therefore, not perjurious.

A related crime is subornation of perjury. This crime occurs when one convinces or procures another to commit perjury. One who commits subornation is treated as a perjurer for the purpose of sentencing.

Subornation of perjury: The crime of asking or forcing another person to lie under oath.

In addition to being a crime in every state, perjury has been made criminal by statute in the United States. 18 U.S.C. § 1621 reads:

Whoever (1) having taken an oath before a competent tribunal, officer, or person, in any case in which a law of the United States authorizes an oath to be administered, that he will testify, declare, depose, or certify truly . . . is true, willfully and contrary to such oath states or subscribes any material matter which he does not believe to be true. . . .

Of course, truth is a complete defense to a charge of perjury. Truth is not always easy to determine, and in most close cases, prosecutors don't prosecute. This is largely due to the stringent mens rea element.

In some instances, unsworn lies are punished. Lying to police, for example, can be punished. In most jurisdictions, filing false police reports, even though the reports are unsworn, are misdemeanors. Typically, actual knowledge that the statement is false is required. Although this crime is commonly a misdemeanor, Michigan has a particularly strict law. To threaten a terroristic act falsely can be punished with as many as 20 years in prison and a fine of up to $20,000.[22] Lying to police can also lead to an obstruction of justice charge.

QUESTIONS AND PROBLEMS

1. What are the elements of perjury?
2. Preeda, a deputy state auditor, is called to testify before a grand jury in an investigation of government corruption. In preparation, she reviews notes from the meetings and other documents. When testifying, she confuses the dates of two meetings and testifies falsely. The error puts the grand jury on the wrong investigative track, and they spend weeks pursuing a theory that proves untrue. Frustrated, the grand jury charges Preeda with perjury. Has she committed the crime? Explain your answer.

GETTING IN THE WAY

Learning Objective: Identify, describe, and apply the elements of obstruction of justice.

In the last section, you learned that lying to the police is a crime in some jurisdictions. Even in the absence of a specific statute, lying to the police may be prosecuted as obstruction of justice. Any act that interferes with the investigation or administration of a criminal case is obstruction.

Obstruction statutes come in many different forms. One variety focuses on who is obstructed (e.g., police, child welfare officers), and another variety is aimed at specific conduct (e.g., lying, hiding from authorities). Obstruction of justice is a commonly charged crime, sometimes being used when other more serious offenses can't be proven. Typically, obstruction of justice occurs when

---

Obstruction of justice: Intentionally interfering with the investigation or prosecution of a criminal case.

1. a person intentionally

2. destroys, alters, conceals or disguises physical evidence, plants false evidence, furnishes false information; or induces a witness having knowledge material to the subject at issue to leave the state or conceal himself or herself; or possessing knowledge material to the subject at issue, he or she leaves the jurisdiction or conceals himself

3. with the intent to prevent the apprehension or obstruct the prosecution or defense of any person.

Destroying evidence of a crime, hiding a suspect, lying to investigators, or planting fake evidence of a crime to throw police off the trail of an investigation are examples of criminal obstruction of justice. But any form of obstruction can be prosecuted. In 2020, Shanynn Kemp was sentenced to 3 years imprisonment for obstructing justice. Her husband, Daniel Kemp Sr., was an active duty solider in the U.S. Army. During an investigation of him for the rape of a minor, Ms. Kemp harassed the minor to the point of dissuading her from providing law enforcement with all the information she had about the alleged rape.[23]

The mental state of obstructing justice is demanding. The act of concealing, destroying, and such must be intentional. Moreover, the actor must intend to impede a prosecution or defense. A mother who launders a child's bloody shirt, believing her child hurt herself, is not guilty of obstruction when she later learns that the blood belonged to a victim of the child's rage.

Many high-profile defendants have been charged, investigated, or convicted of obstruction. President Richard M. Nixon was investigated for obstructing the investigation of the Watergate affair, but he was pardoned by President Gerald Ford before prosecutors could act. In 2015, Robel Phillipos, Dias Kadyrbayev, and Azamat Tazhayakov, friends of Boston Marathon bombing defendant Dzhokhar Tsarnaev, were all convicted of obstructing justice and conspiracy to obstruct justice. After the bombings, Kadyrbayev and Tazhayakov, who had been texting with Tsarnaev, went into his dorm room and collected several items, including a laptop, thumb drive, Vaseline, and a backpack. They later destroyed several of the items. The third friend, Phillipos, lied to federal investigators. They were sentenced to 6, 3.5, and 3 years in prison respectively.[24]

PHOTO 12.3 Jake Angeli Chansley, the "QAnon Shamon," was convicted of obstructing Congress for his role in the Captiol riot of January 6, 2021.

JT/STAR MAX/IPx

A separate crime from obstructing justice, obstructing governmental operations is forbidden by the federal and many state governments. Returning to the Capitol riot, several defendants were charged with obstructing an official governmental proceeding. One of the most notorious of the rioters, Jake Angeli Chansley, or the "QAnon Shamon," seen in Photo 12.3, pled guilty to obstructing an official proceeding for his role in causing Congress to stop its presidential certification session.[25]

QUESTIONS AND PROBLEMS

1. What are the elements of obstruction of justice?
2. Michael is a college athletic director. He learns that the State Bureau of Investigation (SBI) has begun an investigation into college admissions fraud involving his college and an independent college admissions advisor, Rick Sang. He has done business with Sang for years. After receiving a call from the SBI, where he scheduled a time to discuss the case with the special agent in charge of the investigation, Michael packed up his most prized possessions, emptied his bank account, and without telling anyone where he was going, moved to another state. Has Rick committed obstruction of justice? Explain your answer.

GIVE ME YOUR TIRED, YOUR POOR, YOUR HUDDLED MASSES YEARNING TO BREATHE FREE

Learning Objective: Identify, describe, and apply the elements of illegal entry into the United States.

It is theorized that the first peoples arrived in the Americas from Asia via the Bering Land Bridge as long as 20,000 years ago. Over thousands of years, the entire continent was settled. In the 1600s, English, Spanish, and Dutch immigrants first appeared in the eastern lands of what is now known as the United States. Subsequently, immigrants from all over the world, including France, Ireland, Germany, Italy, Africa, Russia, China, Japan, and Mexico, bringing with them a diversity of religious beliefs and customs, continue to join our country until this day.

This history earned the United States the reputation as the place for new beginnings—a beacon on the hill offering opportunity and freedom. These sentiments are reflected in the sonnet "The New Colossus" by Emma Lazarus, which appears on the Statue of Liberty. It reads, in part,

"Give me your tired, your poor,

Your huddled masses yearning to breathe free,

The wretched refuse of your teeming shore.

Send these, the homeless, tempest-tost to me,

I lift my lamp beside the golden door!

Unfortunately, while true, this history is also tarnished. First and most obviously, the ancestors of many African Americans were brought to the United States in enslavement. Second, not every group of free aliens has been welcomed with open arms. Third, some of America's immigration policies have been ethnically or racially discriminatory. For example, the Nationality Act of 1790 limited naturalization to white people of good character who had lived in the United States longer than 2 years; German and Irish immigrants were disfavored in the mid-19th century; and in 1882, Chinese became the first and only group of people to be expressly excluded because of their nationality.

Regardless of this history, the United States continues to be the most popular destination for migrants. Today, the United States has the largest number of immigrants, in both raw numbers and as a percentage of the population, of any nation. Of the U.S. population of 340 million people, more than 40 million were born in another nation. About 77% of those individuals entered the United States legally, and 45% have become naturalized citizens. One quarter of America's immigrants come from Mexico, with China and India being tied at 6% each for the second-most common countries of origin. Asian immigration is rising at a faster pace than other ethnicities.[26]

To administer the modern immigration enterprise, a substantial amount of law and bureaucracy have been created. Most of the law is regulatory, but a minority of it is criminal. One of the most prominent criminal provisions is illegal entry, which is defined as any alien who

1. enters or attempts to enter the United States at any time or place other than as designated by immigration officers, or

2. eludes examination or inspection by immigration officers, or

3. attempts to enter or obtains entry to the United States by a willfully false or misleading representation or the willful concealment of a material fact.

A first conviction for illegal entry can be punished with a fine and as much as 6 months in prison, and subsequent offenses are punished with a fine and as much as 2 years incarceration.[27] Under other laws, these offenders are also subject to deportation. Reentry by aliens who were excluded for criminal convictions is a separate offense that can be punished with as many as 10 years imprisonment. If the prior conviction is for an aggravated felony, the prison time increases to a maximum of 20 years. If a crime is an aggravated felony, it is a matter of federal law, irrespective of how an act is defined by state law. So some misdemeanors under state law are classified as aggravated felonies for purposes of federal immigration law. Murder, rape, sexual crimes against minors, drug trafficking, obstruction of justice, theft and burglary convictions that are sentenced to more than year in prison, and many other crimes qualify.

Other immigration and naturalization crimes exist, such as lying or omitting information on immigration and naturalization forms. Although this policy area is strongly federal, many states have laws that address immigrant involvement in state-funded education and social services, licensing of professions and trades, voting, and public office eligibility.

QUESTIONS AND PROBLEMS

1. What are the elements of illegal entry into the United States?
2. Rudolph entered the United States legally. Four years later, he earned permanent resident alien status. Three years later, he was charged, convicted, and sentenced to 2 years in prison for burglary. After his release, he was deported and ordered not to return to the United States. Regardless, he is found in the United States 2 years later. What is the maximum amount of time he can be sentenced to serve in prison if convicted of illegal reentry?

THE BEST GOVERNMENT MONEY CAN BUY

Learning Objective: Identify and describe at least one campaign finance crime and one electoral integrity crime.

Money in politics has long been a concern. The concern that donors can influence the policy decisions of the officials they support is held by people across the political spectrum. If the amount of money spent is any gauge, there is a reason to worry. The 2020 elections were the costliest in history. Over $14 billion was spent, doubling the amount spent in the 2016 election. Over $6 billion of the spending in 2020 was on the presidential campaign alone. Large individual donations account for 42% of the money raised; individual donations, 22%; self-funding, 13%; and political action committees, 5%.[28]

Beyond regulating the money of campaigns, there is a body of election law aimed at protecting the integrity of the electoral process, defining voter eligibility, and protecting voting rights. A few of the laws concerning voting rights were covered in Chapter 7. This discussion begins with the criminal aspects of campaign finance and ends with electoral integrity.

The leading federal campaign finance law is the Federal Election Campaign Act (FECA)[29] and the regulations issued by the agency responsible for enforcing it, the Federal Election Commission (FEC). Much of the law is regulatory and is enforced by the FEC through administrative processes. But there are criminal provisions that are enforced with regularity by the Department of Justice. Finance laws regulate who can donate, how much can be donated, and how the money may be used.

As to who may donate in federal elections, citizens and permanent residents may donate. Foreign nationals who are not permanent residents of the United States, foreign governments, and foreign corporations are forbidden from donating to federal elections. Also, individuals and corporations who are doing business with the federal government are forbidden from giving to congressional and presidential elections.

Attempts to bypass donor eligibility and donation limitation restriction by so-called conduit contributions, or when one person makes a contribution in their own name with someone else's money, are also prohibited. In a controversial decision, SCOTUS decided that domestic corporations, unions, and other organizations have a First Amendment right to contribute to federal electoral candidates.[30]

Federal law details how much money may be donated and to whom. For example, in 2022 individuals are limited to donating $2,900 to each specific candidate, $5,000 to political action committees ($10,000 to specific forms of political action committees), and $36,500 to national party committees. The Democratic and Republican parties have three national party committees each: for the party generally, for House of Representatives races, and for Senate races. The laws detail many other aspects of campaign donations, including how gifts of property, food, and other items of value ("in-kind" donations) are handled, gifts to third-party candidates, and distinguishing between primary and general elections. It is a crime for a donor to give, or a candidate or party to receive, donations that exceed the legal limitations.

FECA, House, and Senate rules also limit how candidates and parties may use campaign donations. The rule is liberal, allowing political spending as well as campaign spending. Television, social network, billboard, radio, and all other forms of advertising; campaign travel; food for social events involving campaign or political staff; renting spaces for rallies and meetings; for legal expenses resulting from the election; and, if victorious, the expenses of moving to Washington, DC, are a few of the many examples of campaign spending. The money may also be used on future campaigns.

Political spending includes donations to other campaigns, donations to charities, and legal expenses resulting from the position itself. The most significant limitation on the use of donations is the ban on personal use. A candidate may not, for example, buy a home or other items for personal use, pay for a wedding or a funeral (unless a campaign employee dies on the job), or pay off a student loan debt.

State and federal laws also protect the electoral process. Voter fraud and voter intimidation are examples of laws that fall into this category. Voter fraud describes many acts. Voting more than once in an election, voting or registering to vote in another person's name, using a fraudulent ballot, voting when ineligible (underage, not a resident, or not a citizen), and buying votes are examples. In most jurisdictions, the mens rea of these crimes is at least a knowing violation. A mistaken belief by new state residents that they are eligible to vote after 4 months of residency when the minimum is 6 months, for example, is not a crime. Fraud by election officials is also prohibited. So an election officer who knowingly counts fraudulent ballots, counts votes from ineligible voters, or who tampers with votes has committed a crime.

Interfering with another's person vote is also a crime under both federal and state laws. Specifically, intimidating voters is illegal everywhere. Under federal law, it is a crime for any person, including election officials, to intimidate, threaten, or coerce a person, or attempt to do so, "for the purpose of interfering with" that person's right to vote or to vote as he may choose.[31] It is also a crime to knowingly and willfully intimidate, threaten, or coerce any person, or attempt to do so, for "registering to vote, or voting," or for "urging or aiding" anyone to vote or register to vote.[32] And it is a crime to, "by force or threat of force," willfully injure, intimidate, or interfere with any person because they are voting or have voted or "in order to intimidate" anyone from voting.[33] These laws also forbid election fraud, such as delivering fraudulent ballots and reporting fraudulent results. The punishment for violating these laws is a fine or up to 5 years in prison, or both.

QUESTIONS AND PROBLEMS

1. Randy has already reached the limit on how much he can donate to Sam's campaign to be elected to the U.S. Senate. He asks Michelle if she would contribute to Sam's campaign in her own name if he gave her the cash. She agreed. What crime, if any, has been committed?

2. Sam is elected to the U.S. Senate. She has $350,000 of leftover campaign donations. She uses several thousand dollars to move to Washington, DC, $100,000 to pay attorneys who represented her in election disputes, and she bought land in the Virgin Islands for her retirement. Were her uses of the money lawful?

TO IGNORE EVIL IS TO BECOME AN ACCOMPLICE TO IT

Learning Objective: Identify, describe, and apply the elements of genocide.

In 1865, Captain Henry Wirz of the Confederate Army was tried for what are now known as "war crimes." In the last year of the Civil War, Wirz served as the commandant of Andersonville Prison, located in Camp Sumter in Georgia. Andersonville, which housed Union prisoners of war, was vastly overcrowded. While under Wirz's control, prisoners were physically abused and malnourished, and the poor sanitary conditions made it a cesspool of disease. Consequently, 29% of the inmates of the prison died. News accounts accompanied by photos of survivors whose emaciated conditions put the inhumanity of their treatment into full form spread across the nation after the war. Wirz was arrested, convicted after a long trial, and hanged.

Contemporary historians question the fairness of the trial. It is pointed out many of the conditions in the prison were outside of his control. Wirz complained that as an alien (he was Swiss), he was an easy scapegoat for the crimes of the Confederacy and the mistakes of the Union Army, which had not taken advantage of opportunities to free the prisoners during the war. At his trial, Wirz was denied the right to call all of his witnesses to testify, and he was alleged to have committed murder but the government never identified a victim. Ironically, historians agree, guilty or not, Wirz was denied due process—a fundamental human right. Wirz maintained his innocence until he was hanged. At his execution, Wirz said to his executioner, "I know what orders are... and I am being hanged for obeying them."[34] This defense—following orders—will be heard again by the world after WWII. It was uttered by many of the German and Japanese defendants who were tried for crimes against humanity at the Nuremberg and Tokyo trials.

Up to this point, this book has examined offenses that occur in the United States during peacetime. In certain circumstances, citizens and resident aliens of the United States are accountable in the United States for offenses committed abroad. Military personnel, for example, can be punished under the Uniform Code of Military Justice for acts committed anywhere in the world. Additionally, the United States has treaty obligations that require it to adhere to, and to enforce, international criminal prohibitions. Beyond treaties, basic humanity impresses upon the individual an obligation to act when cruelty is witnessed. As Martin Luther King Jr. wrote, "To ignore evil is to become an accomplice to it."[35]

The first international trials for **crimes against humanity** took place in the aftermath of WWII. The magnitude of both world wars can't be understated. WWII, specifically, resulted in an estimated 70 to 80 million deaths, or 3% of the world's population. Over half of the dead were civilians. Six million Jewish people were killed in the Holocaust. As a nation, the Soviet Union was hardest hit, with an estimated 20 to 27 million dead. China lost as many as 20 million; Germany, 6 to 9 million; Japan, 2.5 to 3.1 million; Italy, the United Kingdom, and the United States, over 400,000 each. Nearly all of the military dead were men. But millions of women were murdered and raped around the world.

An example of the depth of inhumanity that occurred in WWII comes from a horrific event that is unknown to most Americans. In 1942, 16 U.S. bombers with a total of 80 airmen, under the command of Lt. Colonel Jimmy Doolittle, flew over Tokyo and other cities in Japan, bombing industrial and military targets. While ordered to not bomb the Japanese emperor's palace, bombers flew over it. The objective of the Doolittle Raid, as it would later be labeled, was more psychological warfare than military strategy. By demonstrating that the U.S. could reach the Japanese islands, specifically the emperor, the U.S. intended to demoralize the Japanese and to uplift the Americans, who had been stunned by the Japanese attacks on Pearl Harbor. This half of the story is well known. It is what happened after the mission that is less known.

Because the aircraft carrier, the *USS Hornet*, that transported the airmen to Japan was sighted by the Japanese while at sea, the airmen had to lift off earlier than planned. The early departure meant that they didn't have enough fuel to return to the aircraft carrier. Regardless, the men, all volunteers, continued with the mission. Three were killed in action, and one crew landed in the Soviet Union. All of the other planes crashed in China, a U.S. ally. The Chinese people and foreign missionaries hid and assisted the airmen in evading capture by the Japanese. In their search for the Americans, and to punish the Chinese, Japanese soldiers tore through villages, raping women, intentionally spreading deadly pathogens, razing entire villages and cities, and murdering. In addition to executing three American fliers, the Japanese are estimated to have killed 250,000 Chinese. One bombing raid led to a quarter million civilian deaths.[36]

In 1945 and 1946, the Allied powers—the Soviet Union, United Kingdom, United States, and France—tried 199 German soldiers, political leaders, and professionals for war crimes, crimes against humanity, and crimes against peace. Formally known as the International Military Tribunal—informally as the Nuremberg trials—161 men were convicted and 37 were sentenced to death.[37] A second set of trials of Japanese war criminals began in 1946. The International Military Tribunal of the Far East, the Tokyo Trial, was conducted by 11 nations. Twenty-eight leaders of the Japanese government and military were charged with crimes against humanity, war crimes, and crimes against peace. All were convicted at trials that lasted longer than 2 years. Seven of the defendants were sentenced to death, 16 to life imprisonment, two to lesser prison terms, two died before the trials ended, and one was found insane.[38] In the decades after the Nuremberg and Tokyo trials, several other ad hoc tribunals were created around the world to try alleged international criminals.

Crimes against humanity: Genocide, maltreatment of civilians, and torture and maltreatment of combatants are forms of crimes against humanity.

The United Nations (UN) was another product of WWII, having been created to promote peace and security around the world. Under the leadership of Eleanor Roosevelt, the newly founded UN developed the Universal Declaration of Human Rights (UDHR). The UDHR recognizes 30 rights, including life, liberty, and security of the person; to be free of enslavement; to equal protection; to privacy; to freedom of conscience, religion, and speech; and to be free of arbitrary arrest, exile, and detention. While all the members of the UN, which is nearly every country today, have agreed to the UDHR, it is not legally binding. Regardless, most nations have agreed to hold their citizens accountable for international crimes through treaties. The world's first standing court, the International Criminal Court (ICC), was created in 1998 and became operational in 2002 through an agreement known as the Rome Statute. Considered a court of "last resort," the ICC can try individuals only if their home nations don't. It has the authority to investigate and prosecute genocide, war crimes, crimes against humanity, and the crime of aggression (violations of peace). Over 120 nations have agreed to the jurisdiction of the ICC. The United States is not among them.

As part of its obligations under several treaties, however, the U.S. Congress has enacted several statutes that enable the nation to prosecute its citizens for crimes against humanity. Genocide, war crimes, torture, and the recruitment of child soldiers are among the crimes against humanity that the federal government punishes.

One of the most horrendous of crimes is genocide. Genocide involves the attempted elimination of an entire group of people who belong to the same race, ethnicity, religion, or nationality. The list of human atrocities is stunningly long. About 6 million Jewish people were murdered in the Holocaust of WWII, as many as 3 million people were killed by the Khmer Rouge in Cambodia in the 1970s, nearly 800,000 in the Rwandan Genocide of 1994, and as many as 1.8 million Armenians were murdered in the early 20th century by the Ottoman Empire.

Genocide is defined by federal law as

1. whoever, whether in time of peace or in time of war and

2. with the specific intent to destroy, in whole or in substantial part,

3. a national, ethnic, racial, or religious group
   a. kills members of that group or
   b. causes serious bodily injury to members of that group or
   c. causes the permanent impairment of the mental faculties of members of the group through drugs, torture, or similar techniques or
   d. subjects the group to conditions of life that are intended to cause the physical destruction of the group in whole or in part or
   e. imposes measures intended to prevent births within the group; or
   f. transfers by force children of the group to another group.

All acts of genocide in the United States are covered by the statute, and any person present in the United States who has committed genocide in another nation may be punished under this statute. The law also applies to acts of genocide abroad if committed by a citizen, permanent resident, or other person owing allegiance to the United States. Punishment for genocide is death, life imprisonment or less, and a fine as much as $1,000,000.[39]

War crimes are also criminalized. The definition of a war crime comes from treaty law, including the Geneva and Hague Conventions. The law applies to acts within the United States and abroad, committed by or against members of the U.S. military or any U.S. national (citizen, permanent resident, or person owing allegiance to the U.S.) during times of armed conflict. Examples of war crimes are rape and sexual assault, murder, medical experimentation, and torture. If death results, the actor may be sentenced to capital punishment. Otherwise, the crime is punished with as much as life in prison.[40] The recruitment of child soldiers is also forbidden. Any person under the age of 15 is deemed a child. This crime is punished with as many as 20 years in prison or life imprisonment if the child dies while serving as a soldier.[41]

Independent from the war crimes law just discussed, another federal law specifically forbids torture by individuals acting under the authority of the United States when outside of the nation. Specifically, the infliction of severe physical or mental pain or suffering (other than pain or suffering incidental to lawful sanctions) upon a person within the actor's custody or physical control is punished with death (if death results), as much as life imprisonment.[42]

QUESTIONS AND PROBLEMS

1. What are the elements of genocide?
2. Two defenses raised at the Nuremberg trials were duress and due process. In the first, the defendants asserted that they were following orders—orders issued by a ruthless government that was intolerant of dissent. The second defense was that it was wrong to punish the defendants for their crimes because there was no international law to break. Indeed, there was no United Nations and no international law forbidding crimes against humanity. And they were tried by an international tribunal, not by a German or other court. Discuss each defense, making your best argument in support of *and* against the defendants.

IN A NUTSHELL

Crimes against the state involve acts that threaten the integrity of governmental institutions, such as contempt and perjury; threaten government itself, such as treason or sedition; or threaten the people collectively and individually, such as terrorism and crimes against humanity. The Framers' history with England and with themselves in the early years made them wary of treason and sedition. They, therefore, included in the Constitution the elements of, and evidence needed to prove, treason. The requirement of two witnesses, treasonous intent, and an overt act make the crime so hard to prove that it has only been charged a few times—and not at all in the past 50 years. Alternatively, prosecutors turn to espionage and other laws to prosecute treasonous acts.

The misuse of the crime of sedition by the British, and by the Framers themselves, has left it with a stain. Today, the First Amendment's protection of speech guards against the use of sedition to punish dissent. At the federal level, sedition isn't a crime, but seditious conspiracy is.

The political and social turmoil of recent years is a reminder of the importance of legal guardrails in terms of security and liberty. Criminal law is needed to protect public property, people, and to ensure the orderly and equitable use of public goods. At the same time, the Constitution's limits on governmental authority are essential to protect the rights of dissent, including being able to speak and demonstrate in public spaces.

Perhaps the most significant offense isn't treason, but a crime against humanity. The idea of trying persons for violating international, or universal, human rights is relatively new. As codified in U.S. law, genocide, torture, using children in war, and other war offenses can be tried and punished in the United States if committed against or by a citizen or national. Although new, this is an area of criminal law that is likely to expand in the future.

LEGAL TERMS

Brandenburg test (p. 380)

clear and present danger test (p. 380)

contempt (p. 392)

crimes against humanity (p. 405)

espionage (p. 385)

Misprision of treason (p. 378)

obstruction of justice (p. 398)

Perjury (p. 396)

Sedition (p. 382)

subornation of perjury (p. 397)

Treason (p. 374)

NOTES

1. Ex Parte Bollman and Ex Parte Swartwout, 8 U.S. 75 (1807).

2. *Cramer v. United States*, 325 U.S. 1 (1945).

3. 18 U.S.C. §2385.

4. See, for example, *Dennis v. United States*, 341 U.S. 494 (1951) and *Yates v. United States*, 354 U.S. 298 (1957).

5. 18 U.S. Code § 2387.

6. 18 U.S. Code § 2388.

7. Kimberly Wehle, "No, Flynn's Martial Law Plot Isn't Sedition. But It's Not Necessarily Legal Either," *Politico*, December 24, 2020, Politico.com.

8. See 70 Am. Jur. 2d 70.

9. *Schenck v. United States*, 249 U.S. 47 (1919).

10. *Debs v. United States*, 249 U.S. 211 (1919).

11. *Frohwerk v. United States*, 249 U.S. 204 (1919).

12. 18 U.S.C. §2384.

13. M. R. Papandrea, "National Security Information Disclosures and the Role of Intent," *William & Mary Law Review* 56 (2015): 1381.

14. *New York Times Co. v. United States*, 403 U.S. 713 (1971).

15. *Terminiello v. Chicago*, 337 U.S. 1 (1949).

16. Tex. Penal Code § 42.02.

17. 18 U.S. Code § 2102.

18. 18 U.S. Code § 2101.

19. 18 U.S. Code § 1752(a)(1).

20. 40 U.S. Code § 5104(e).

21. 40 U.S. Code § 5109.

22. Michigan Penal Code § 750.543.

23. "Wife of U.S. Army Soldier Sentenced to Prison for Obstruction of Justice." Press Release. U.S. Department of Justice, July 22, 2020, justice.gov.

24. R. Sanchez, "Boston Bomber's Friends Sentenced to Prison," *CNN*, June 5, 2015, CNN.com.

25. Chansley was convicted under 18 U.S.C. 1512(c). Section 1503 criminalizes obstructions of federal court proceedings, and Section 1505 criminalizes obstructions of Congress and regulatory proceedings. It is likely that Chansley was charged under Section 1512 because the penalties are higher than in Section 1505.

26. A. Budiman, "Key Findings About U.S. Immigrants," *Pew Research Center*, August 20, 2020, Pewresearch.org.

27. 8 U.S. Code § 1325.

28. "2020 Election to Cost $14 Billion, Blowing Away Spending Records," *Center for Responsible Politics*, October 28, 2020, Opensecrets.org.

29. 52 U.S.C. §30101, et seq.

30. *Citizens United v. Federal Election Commission*, 558 U.S. 310 (2010).

31. 18 U.S.C. § 594.

32. 52 U.S.C. § 20511(1).

33. 18 U.S.C. § 245(b)(1)(A).

34. K. D. Stringer, "The Andersonville Trial, 1865," *History.Net*, accessed April 2, 2021, history.net.

35. Hearings Before the Subcommittee on Executive Reorganization of the Committee on Government Operations, United States Senate, Eighty-Ninth Congress, Second Session, December 14 and 15, 1966, Part 14. Washington DC: United States Government Printing Office, 1967.

36. J. M. Scott, "The Untold Story of the Vengeful Japanese Attack After the Doolittle Raid," *Smithsonian Magazine*, April 15, 2015, smithsonianmag.com.

37. Nuremberg Trials, "Holocaust Encyclopedia," *The Holocaust Memorial Museum*, accessed March 31, 2021, https://encyclopedia.ushmm.org.

38. The Tokyo War Crimes Trials, "The American Experience," *PBS*, accessed March 31, 2021, PBS.org.

39. 18 U.S. Code § 1091.

40. 18 U.S. Code § 2441.

41. 18 U.S. Code § 2442.

42. 18 U.S. Code § 2340 et seq.

GLOSSARY

§1983 Action: A federal law that allows a person to sue people acting under color of state law for federal civil rights violations.

Abuse: The intentional act of causing harm to a person who is, by law, under an actor's care.

Accessory after the fact: A person who assists a principal or accessory in avoiding arrest or prosecution after a crime is committed.

Accessory before the fact: A person who is involved in the planning or preparation of a crime but isn't present during its commission.

Accomplice: Depending on the jurisdiction, a synonym for a person involved in a crime that is not a principal in the first degree.

Accusatorial: An element of the adversarial system that places the burden of proof on the state and otherwise gives the benefit of doubt to the defendant.

Actus reus: A voluntary physical movement—a muscle contraction—that is part of a crime. Some crimes do not require a physical act; the voluntary decision to not act satisfies the actus reus of a crime.

Adjudication: The process of a case in court, from start to finish. It is also used to refer to the final outcome, or judgment, of a case. In criminal law, this refers to a finding of guilty or not guilty.

Adversarial system: A system of adjudication where the state and defendant are competitors with independent investigations and theories of the case. The two parties are active in the development of the case, with the court in a more passive role, overseeing the process and ensuring due process. Common Law nations, such as the United States, use the adversarial system.

Affirmative defenses: Special defenses that must be raised and proved by a defendant. Affirmative defenses involve facts that reduce or fully extinguish a defendant's culpability, even if the forbidden acts are committed.

Agency theory (felony murder): Co-conspirators are equally responsible in murder for foreseeable deaths resulting from the commission of a named felony that is caused by a co-conspirator.

Alibi: A affirmative, factual defense where the defendant alleges that they were in another location at the time of a crime.

Any chance test: One of three tests used to determine if a game or contest is one of chance or skill. If chance is a factor, no matter how small, in the outcome of a game or contest, the game is one of chance.

Arson: The purposeful, intentional burning of a structure.

As-applied challenge: An assertion that a statute is invalid as it is applied in a specific case, even though it is valid generally.

Assault: An intentional act that causes another person to have a reasonable fear of an imminent battery; or it is an attempted battery.

Attempt: When a person intends to cause prohibited harm, takes steps in furtherance of the intent, but the harm doesn't occur.

Attendant circumstances: Facts or conditions that must be proved, along with the mens rea and actus reus, for a defendant to be convicted.

Attending circumstance: A fact required to prove a crime that attends a mens rea or actus reus element.

Battered person syndrome defense: Where a person who inflicts lethal or nonlethal force on an intimate partner asserts either self-defense or insanity due to psychological and physical abuse so intense that they fear for their life and, sometimes, the lives of children or other family members.

Battery: The intentional harmful or offensive touching of a person without consent.

Beyond a reasonable doubt: Standard of proof required to convict a defendant in a criminal case. While the standard has not been precisely quantified, it is less than beyond all doubt and considerably more than preponderance of evidence.

Bills of attainder: A legislative decision to punish a person or legal entity (e.g., companies) without a judicial trial. The Constitution forbids bills of attainder.

Brain death: Irreversible cessation of all functions of the entire brain. The legal standard to determine if death has occurred.

Brandenburg test: Developed by SCOTUS in *Brandenburg v. Ohio*, this First Amendment doctrine limits the authority of government to regulate speech advocating violence to words that are directed at, and are likely to produce, imminent lawlessness.

Burglary: The breaking and entering of a structure with the intent to commit a felony.

Castle doctrine: A rule that a person is not required to retreat from an attack in a home. Today, statutory law in some states includes automobiles and other spaces in the zone where retreat is unnecessary.

Checks and balances: A structural feature of government that keeps the three branches of government accountable through the sharing of powers with one another.

Civil law: A branch of law concerned with the private rights of individuals. It is intended to provide individuals with a legal mechanism to be compensated for their injuries by the people who harm them.

Civil Law: A comprehensive approach to law that has written codes issued by legislative bodies as a primary source of law. Civil Law was founded in 7th-century Italy and subsequently spread throughout Europe and to the colonies and territories of European nations. The majority of the nations of the world fall into this family of law today.

Civil rights laws: Statutory laws that offer civil and criminal remedies for violations of constitutionally protected rights and for harmful acts that are motivated by race, sex, religion, and other bias.

Clear and convincing evidence: Standard of proof that is applied in civil and administrative cases in which substantial personal interests are at stake (e.g., deportation and retraining orders). It is also applied to specific criminal law matters, such as the determination of whether a defendant's right to bail should be limited. The standard is defined as evidence that is substantially more likely to be true than not.

Clear and present danger test: Developed by SCOTUS in *Schenck v. United States*, this First Amendment doctrine limited the authority of government to regulate speech advocating violence to words that present a clear and present danger to government. Likely replaced by the Brandenburg test.

Co-conspiratory hearsay rule: An exception to the hearsay rule for statements by conspirators made during the planning and commission of a target crime.

Common Law: A comprehensive approach to law that relied, in its early development, on courts—not legislatures—to create law. They did this by deciding the law of individual cases. That law then became precedent for future like cases. Founded in 11th-century England, it spread to England's colonies and territories and was brought to the United States by colonists. The Common Law is a lower form of law than constitutional and statutory law.

Complete attempt: When a person completes all the acts required to commit a specific intent crime, but the prohibited harm doesn't occur.

Concurrence: The requirement that an act be the product of mens rea.

Constitutional law: The most fundamental law of the United States. As the highest form of law, all other forms of law are invalid if contrary to the U.S. Constitution.

Constitutionalism: Having fundamental law that limits the authority of government. In this text, it is a reference to the increasingly important role of the U.S. Constitution to criminal law.

Constructive intent: A legal fiction; an inference. Proof of intent from the act itself, context, or other facts.

Contempt: Willfully disobeying a judge's command or official court order, or causing a disruption in court. Contempt can be *direct* (within the judge's notice) or *indirect* (outside the court and punishable only after proved to the judge). It can also be *civil contempt* (disobeying a court order in favor of an opponent) or *criminal contempt*.

Contract law: A form of civil law where two or more persons create an agreement that may be enforced in court.

Conversion: The act of a trustee in using or interfering with property that has been entrusted to them.

Counterfeiting: To make a duplication of an original document with such similitude that a reasonable person would be defrauded.

Crime of omission: A crime that involves a failure to act. The actus reus is omitted from the standard requirement of actus reus, mens rea, and concurrence for there to be a crime.

Crime: An act that society finds so harmful, threatening, or offensive that it is forbidden and punished.

Crimes against humanity: Genocide, maltreatment of civilians, and torture and maltreatment of combatants are forms of crimes against humanity.

Criminal law: A branch of law, and legal study, that defines criminal offenses and defenses to criminal accusations.

Criminal mischief: Intentionally damaging, destroying, defacing, or tampering with the personal property of another person.

Criminal procedure law: (1) The steps and processes that are used to adjudicate a criminal case. (2) The constitutional limitations on the state's criminal law authority.

Cyberstalking: The crime of using internet communications to send obscene, abusive, or harassing language with the intent to harass or threaten another person.

Dangerous proximity test: A test to determine if an actor crossed the line from preparation to attempt. A person is dangerously proximate to the completion of a crime when it is possible to complete it immediately, or when the final step has been started.

Deadly force: An amount of force that a reasonable person believes is likely to result in death or serious bodily injury.

Deadly weapon doctrine: An inference of deadly intent when a person kills another with an object that is designed to kill or has been used in a manner that can kill.

Defendant: A litigant who is sued is referred to as the defendant.

Defense: Law or fact that is used to reduce or fully eliminate criminal liability.

Depraved heart murder: A homicide that results from the reckless and wanton disregard of life. Treated as murder at the Common Law, it is commonly classified as second-degree murder or first-degree manslaughter today.

Dominant factor test: One of three tests used to determine if a game or contest is one of chance or skill. Whichever most contributes to the outcome of a game or contest is determinative.

Dual sovereignty: A doctrine that empowers multiple sovereigns to prosecute and punish an individual for the same crime without violating the prohibition of double jeopardy.

Due process: Found in the Fifth and Fourteenth Amendments, a requirement that government provide a fair process when taking life, liberty, or property. In addition to procedural requirements, due process also includes substantive rights, such as the right to privacy.

Duress: A doctrine that excuses illegal conduct because it was caused by a threat of serious bodily harm or death.

Durham test: A test to determine legal insanity. A person is insane if the act is a product of disease or defective mental condition.

Element analysis: The assignment of a separate mens rea to each element of an offense.

Element: A part of a crime. For conviction, each element must be proved beyond a reasonable doubt.

Embezzlement: The conversion of lawfully acquired property with the intent to permanently deprive the owner of the property.

Equal protection: Found expressly in the Fourteenth Amendment and implicitly in the Fifth Amendment, a guarantee that government won't, without a compelling reason, treat people differently because of race, national origin, religion, or alienage.

Espionage: A synonym for spying.

Ex post facto law: A law that declares an act to be criminal after it has occurred. The Constitution forbids ex post facto laws.

Excessive force exception: An exception to the rule that a person who provokes an attack is not entitled to the protection of self-defense. It applies when the person attacked responds with unreasonable force.

Exclusionary rule: A judicially created rule that requires evidence that is illegally obtained by the state to be excluded from the trial of the defendant.

Excuse: Conduct that is illegal but forgiven, or at least, the punishment is reduced because of the circumstances faced by the defendant.

Executive orders: Law and declarations created by the president of the United States and the governors of states that are issued to implement their responsibilities. The status of an executive order, relative to other forms of law, varies.

Express murder: The taking of human life with malice aforethought.

Extortion: The acquisition of the property of another by threat with the intent to permanently deprive the owner of the property.

Facial challenge: An assertion that a statute is invalid on its face and, therefore, should be stricken in its entirety.

Fact finder: The person or body responsible for weighing the evidence and deciding what evidence is true. Both judges and juries are fact finders. In criminal law, a defendant has a right to have a jury of peers find the facts in the ultimate determination of guilt. Judges find facts when issues arise before, during, and after trial. Judges only find the facts in regard to the ultimate question of guilt when a defendant has waived the right to a jury trial.

Factual cause: For an act to be a substantial factor in an outcome. Most jurisdictions use the "but-for" test to determine if an act is the factual cause of a harm.

Factual guilt: To commit the elements of a crime.

False Imprisonment: To restrain a person's liberty of movement without consent.

Federalism: The division of governmental power between the federal and state governments.

Felonies: Serious crimes that may be punished with imprisonment of 1 year or longer.

Felony murder: A homicide that is a consequence of the commission of a felony. Co-conspirators are guilty of felony murder, regardless of which conspirator committed the homicidal act. Treated as murder at the Common Law and commonly classified as first- or second-degree murder today.

Folkways: Expected rules of behavior that have evolved to give order to life.

Foreseeable: An outcome of an act that a reasonable person anticipates as possible.

Forgery: To make and utter a false document with the intent to defraud another person.

Gambling: A wager or bet of something of value in a game of chance with knowledge of the risk of loss and gain.

General intent: Purposefully causing an act, but not the outcome (harm) of the act.

Grading: A system of classifying crimes by seriousness and corresponding punishment.

Grand jury: A group of citizens who decide if probable cause to believe a suspect has committed a crime exists.

Guilty but mentally ill (GBMI): A determination that a defendant suffered from a mental illness at the time of the crime, but the illness doesn't satisfy the elements of the applicable insanity defense. A GBMI convictee is punished but provided mental health care during incarceration.

Habeas corpus: A Latin phrase that translates to "you have the body." In law, it is a command to bring a detained person to a court to determine if the detention is lawful.

Hearsay: A statement about what someone else said (or wrote or otherwise communicated). Generally, hearsay evidence is inadmissible at trial to prove the hearsay's truth. There are many exceptions to the hearsay rule.

Heat of passion: The provoked, impulsive killing of a person.

Human trafficking: The knowing recruitment, transportation, harbor, isolation, solicitation, or enticement of an individual into labor, sexual services, or servitude through force, threat, or deceit.

Imperfect defense: A defense that partially relieves a defendant of criminal liability or mitigates punishment.

Implied murder: The taking of human life during an act that is intended to inflict serious bodily harm, with the wanton and reckless disregard for life, or during the commission of a felony.

Inchoate crime: A started but unfinished crime.

Incomplete attempt: When a person starts but doesn't complete all of the acts required to commit a specific intent crime.

Indictment: Also known as a true bill, a formal criminal charge issued by a grand jury.

Infancy: A defense that asserts a defendant is not liable because of juvenile age.

Infractions: Minor offenses that may be treated as civil or administrative offenses or as minor crimes. These are typically punished with administrative sanctions, fines, and rarely with very short terms of imprisonment.

Inquisitorial system: A method of investigation and adjudication found in Civil Law nations, such as France and Italy. Characterized as a continuous investigation, courts play an active role in the entire process, including the evidence gathering and theory development of a case.

Insider trading: When a fiduciary uses information not available to the public to make a securities transaction.

Intent to cause serious bodily injury murder: An act of homicide that results from a defendant's specific intent to cause serious, or grievous, bodily injury. Treated as murder under the Common Law and commonly classified as second-degree murder today.

Intentional tort: Injury to person or property damage that was intended by the defendant.

Intervening and superseding cause: An independent act (or external force) that is unforeseeable and breaks the causal chain between the defendant's act and the result.

Intoxication: A defense that asserts a defendant was unable to form the required mens rea because of mental impairment resulting from alcohol or drugs.

Irresistible impulse test: A test to determine legal insanity; the loss of control due to mental disease that is so great that a person cannot stop from committing a crime.

Judicial review: The authority of courts to review the acts of the legislative and executive branches for constitutionality.

Justification: Conduct that is legal, even though it causes harm.

Kidnapping: To unlawfully remove another from his place of residence or business, or a substantial distance from the vicinity where he is found, or to unlawfully confine another for a substantial period in a place of isolation, to commit a felony upon the person, to hold for ransom, or for another evil purpose.

Knowing: The second-highest form of mens rea under the Model Penal Code. A defendant knowingly acts when the result of an act is "practically certain."

Larceny by trick: The use of deceit to acquire the personal property of another with the intent to permanently deprive the owner of possession.

Larceny: The trespassory taking and carrying away (*asportation*) personal property of another person with an intent to permanently deprive the owner of possession.

Last act test: A test to determine if an actor crossed the line from preparation to attempt. An actor commits an attempt if the final step toward completion of a crime occurs.

Legal cause: Similarity between the intended and actual result of an act, and the similarity between the intended manner used to bring about a result and the actual manner that caused the result.

Legal construct: A fiction that is used to connect reality with legal doctrine; an adjustment to the law through a logical presumption, inference, or imputation.

Legal guilt: The idea of investigating and adjudicating criminal suspects using a just process. Factually guilty people may be punished less harshly or not at all when treated unfairly in the process.

M'Naghten test: A test to determine legal insanity. It is also known as the right–wrong test.

Magna Carta: Also known as the Great Charter of Liberty. Forced upon King John in 1215, it represents the first appearance of rule of law.

Mail fraud: To commit (or attempt) an illegal scheme using the mail.

Malice aforethought murder: An act of homicide that was committed with the specific intent of causing the victim's death. The first murder under the Common Law that continues to the standard for the most culpable form of murder.

Malum in se: An act that is prohibited because it is inherently wrong.

Malum prohibitum: An act that is prohibited by law but isn't inherently wrong.

Malware: Software that is designed to damage, gain access, or disrupt computers and computer systems.

Material element test: One of three tests used to determine if a game or contest is one of chance or skill. If chance is a material element, even if not dominant, in the outcome of a game or contest, the game is one of chance.

Mayhem: The intentional dismembering or disfiguring of another person without consent.

Mens rea: The mental aspect of criminality. The intention or knowledge part of a crime.

Miller test: A test used to determine if speech is so morally objectionable—obscene—that it loses the protection of the First Amendment.

Misdemeanors: Crimes that are punished with imprisonment of less than 1 year.

Misprision of treason: The crime of failing to report known treason to authorities.

Mistake of fact: A defense that asserts a defendant's misunderstanding of the facts of the case mitigate culpability.

Mistake of law: A defense that asserts a defendant's misunderstanding of the law mitigates culpability.

Model Penal Code (MPC): A recommended criminal code created by a group of scholars and practicing attorneys. Most states have enacted portions of the MPC.

Model Penal Code test: Also known as the substantial capacity test.

Money laundering: To conduct a financial transaction with money known to have been obtained illegally with the intent to conceal it, carry on a crime, avoid a reporting requirement, or to commit a tax crime.

Morality crimes: Acts that are prohibited because they offend the values of society.

Mores: Expected rules of behavior that are grounded in morality. The word is pronounced "more-ray."

Motive: A person's reason for acting or for desiring the outcome of an act. Motive leads to mens rea and actus reus. Prosecutors are not required to prove motive but often do.

Mutual combat: A rule that participants who agree to fight are not liable for minor injuries resulting from the fight.

Natural and probable consequences doctrine: A rule that holds that accomplices are criminally liable for the unplanned but foreseeable crimes of the principal in the first degree that are committed during the planned crime.

Necessity: A doctrine that excuses illegal conduct because it was necessary in order to avoid greater harm. Also known as "choice of evils" defense.

Neglect: The failure to care for a person who is, by law, under an actor's care, such failure resulting in harm to the ward.

Negligence: A defendant acts negligently when the resulting harm or material element of a crime occurs because the defendant has taken a substantial and unjustifiable risk, even if the risk is not perceived, so long as the risk involves a gross deviation from the standard of conduct that a law-abiding person would observe.

Negligent tort: Injury to a person or property damage resulting from another person's failure to act reasonably.

New judicial federalism: The interpretation of state constitutions independent from the U.S. Constitution. State constitutions may enlarge, but not reduce, the rights found in the U.S. Constitution.

Norms: Expected behaviors.

O'Brien test: A test used to determine if expressive conduct is entitled to First Amendment free speech protection.

Objective entrapment: A test used to determine if the state has gone too far in encouraging a defendant to commit a crime. This test focuses on the conduct of the state's agents.

Obscenity: A category of speech that is not protected by the First Amendment. The Miller test is used to determine if speech is obscene.

Obstruction of justice: Intentionally interfering with the investigation or prosecution of a criminal case.

Offense analysis: The assignment of a single mens rea to an offense.

Ordinance: Law made by local legislative bodies, such as city councils. A lower form of law to constitutional and statutory law.

Overbreadth doctrine: A criminal prohibition that includes acts that may be criminalized and constitutionally protected acts. Overbroad statutes are invalid.

Overt act: An act taken in furtherance of a crime. Proof of an overt act in furtherance of the target crime is required to prove conspiracy in some jurisdictions.

Parties: The persons involved in a dispute. If the dispute is in court, the parties are also known as litigants.

Perfect defense: A defense that completely relieves a defendant of criminal liability.

Perjury: Lying while under oath or affirmation.

Pinkerton rule: A conspirator is liable for the foreseeable acts of co-conspirators that occurred during the planning and commission of the target crime.

Plaintiff: A litigant who files a civil suit is referred to as a plaintiff.

Precedent: A prior case that is similar in facts.

Preponderance of the evidence: Standard of proof used to decide who wins in a civil case. It is also used in criminal law for specific questions, but never in the determination of guilt. A plaintiff must persuade the fact finder that its claim is more likely true (greater than 50%) than not to satisfy the preponderance standard.

Presumption of innocence doctrine: In the United States and many other nations, the state has the obligation to prove a defendant's guilt. In the United States, the state must prove every element of the crime beyond a reasonable doubt. A defendant begins the process innocent and is not obliged to put on a defense.

Principal in the first degree: A person who commits a prohibited act.

Principal in the second degree: A person who is present and provides assistance in the commission of a crime but who doesn't commit the prohibited act.

Private law: Also known as civil law; any law that concerns the relationship of one person to another.

Privilege and immunities: Found in both Article IV and the Fourteenth Amendment, these clauses guarantee a limited number of rights against the federal government and fair treatment of states between their citizens and citizens of other states.

Probable cause: The standard of proof required by the Fourth Amendment to the Constitution of the United States for a search or seizure to be conducted. An officer has probable cause when the facts available to the officer warrant a person of reasonable caution in the belief that contraband or evidence of a crime is present.

Probable desistence test: A test to determine if an actor crossed the line from preparation to attempt. It asks whether in the ordinary and natural course of events, without interruption from an outside source, would the defendant have completed the crime?

Prostitution: Agreeing to provide, or providing, sexual services in exchange for compensation.

Proximate cause (felony murder): Co-conspirators are equally responsible in murder for any foreseeable death resulting from the commission of a named felony, regardless of who committed the act (including third parties) that causes the death.

Proximate cause: A test used to determine if an act is the legal cause of a result. A result must be foreseeable to be the proximate cause of an act.

Public law: Any law that concerns the relationship of an individual and government.

Punitive damages: Money damages in a civil suit that exceed compensation and are intended to punish and deter future misconduct.

Purpose: The Model Penal Code's highest level of mens rea; similar to the Common Law's strict liability. A defendant acts with purpose when there is a desire to cause the result.

Quality-of-life crimes: Acts that are believed to reduce the public's enjoyment of public spaces, lower the value of property, or otherwise reduce the quality of public life.

Rape shield laws: Statutory law intended to limit evidence about an alleged victim's sexual history or to permit evidence of a defendant's criminal history at trial.

Rape: Sexual intercourse or another sex act with another person without consent.

Rational basis test: The default test under the equal protection clause and due process clauses. It is applied whenever a law doesn't involve a suspect classification or a fundamental right. The least demanding test under the Fourteenth Amendment, a law will survive review if it is supported by a legitimate governmental interest and the law is rationally related to that interest.

Reasonable suspicion: Less than probable cause, and therefore an exception to the Fourth Amendment's probable cause requirement; police officers are sometimes permitted to conduct brief detentions and limited searches when a reasonable suspicion of criminality, supported by specific and articulable facts, is present. Reasonable suspicion is but more than a mere scintilla or a hunch, although an officer's experience may inform the decision.

Receiving, possessing, and selling stolen property: The act of receiving, possessing, or selling property that is known to be stolen with the intent of permanently depriving the owner of the property.

Recidivism: To commit a new crime after being punished for a different crime.

Reckless: A defendant acts with indifference to consequences and indifference to the safety and rights of others. Recklessness involves less care than ordinary negligence.

Referendum: Law created directly by the people through a process of gathering a minimum number of voter signatures to place a constitutional amendment or a statutory equivalent on an election ballot for consideration by the general voting public.

Regulation: Law that is created by administrative agencies. A lower form of law to constitutional and statutory law.

Res ipsa loquitor test: A test to determine if an actor crossed the line from preparation to attempt; translates to "the thing speaks for itself." An attempt has taken place if at the moment the actor stopped moving toward the completion of the crime, it was clear that the actor's purpose was to commit the crime. Evidence of the actor's purpose must "manifest," or be self-evident, from the acts themselves.

Restorative justice: A philosophy of justice that focuses on repairing the harm caused by a crime and restoring the victim, offender, and community to their pre-offense state. The restorative justice model is less formal and more focused on the needs of the parties and community than the adversarial model.

Retreat to the wall doctrine: A rule that a person must avail themselves of all safe opportunities to retreat from an attack before using deadly force to repel the attack.

Revenge porn: The use of voluntarily sent nude or sexually explicit photos or videos to harm the sender.

RICO: An acronym for Racketeer Influenced and Corrupt Organizations Act, a federal conspiracy statute.

Robbery: The taking of personal property from another using force with the intent to permanently deprive the owner of the property.

Rule of consistency: A person may not be convicted of conspiracy if all of the alleged co-conspirators have been acquitted.

Rule of law: The idea that all people, including government leaders, are subject to the law.

Rule of lenity: If there are two or more reasonable interpretations of a statute, the interpretation that most favors the defendant is to be adopted.

Scienter: A form of specific intent; having specific knowledge.

SCOTUS: Supreme Court of the United States.

Securities fraud: To knowingly use a scheme or artifice to defraud a person in connection to a securities transaction.

Sedition: Speech or acts that inspire a person to rebel against government. The First Amendment limits the authority of government to punish sedition.

Selective incorporation doctrine: The determination that a right found in the Bill of Rights is fundamental and necessary to an ordered liberty, and therefore, applies to the states.

Separation of powers: The division of governmental authority between the legislative, executive, and judicial branches.

Severability: A doctrine that enables a court to remove unconstitutional provisions of a law, leaving the remainder of the law intact.

Sexting: The voluntary self-taking and electronic communication of nude or sexually explicit photos and videos.

Sextortion: The use of voluntarily sent nude or sexually explicit photos or videos to extort the sender.

Solicitation: Encouraging, enticing, or encouraging another to commit a crime.

Specific intent: Purposely acting with the intention of causing a specific outcome (harm).

Stalking: A pattern of intentional acts that cause another person to reasonably fear serious bodily harm or death.

Stand-your-ground doctrine: A rule that a person is not required to retreat from an attack, in any space, before defending with lethal force.

Stare decisis: Latin for "stand by a thing decided." The doctrine holds that prior legal decisions shall be binding on future cases when the facts of the prior and current case are similar.

State action: A command, decision, or act that can be attributed to a government.

Statute of limitation: A period of time within which an actor must be charged with committing a crime or the opportunity to prosecute the actor is lost.

Statutory law: Law made by the U.S. Congress and state legislatures. Statutory law is the primary form of law that defines crimes, defenses to crimes, and the processes used in criminal cases. A lower form of law than constitutional law.

Statutory rape: Sexual intercourse or another sex act with a minor; consent is immaterial.

Strict liability crime: A crime that has no mens rea element; proof of actus reus is all that is required for guilt.

Strict liability tort: A form of liability that is not concerned with state of mind, or fault. If a person is responsible for the act that results in injury or damages, even though unintentional and the person was acting reasonably, liability exists.

Strict scrutiny test: Laws that discriminate using a suspect classification or that encroach upon a fundamental right are reviewed by courts under the strict scrutiny test. To satisfy equal protection or due process, such laws must be supported by a legitimate compelling governmental interest, be narrowly tailored, and use the least restrictive means possible to accomplish the government's purpose.

Subjective entrapment: A test used to determine if the state has gone too far in encouraging a defendant to commit a crime. This test focuses on the defendant's predisposition to commit the crime.

Subornation of perjury: The crime of asking or forcing another person to lie under oath.

Substantial relationship test: Laws that discriminate between people by sex are reviewed by courts under the substantial relationship test. To satisfy equal protection, such laws must be supported by an important and legitimate governmental interest, and the law is substantially related to that interest.

Substantial steps test: A test to determine if an actor crossed the line from preparation to attempt. An act(s) that strongly corroborates an actor's purpose to commit a specific harm is a substantial step. It is the MPC approach, followed by many states.

Substantive criminal law: The law that identifies and defines crimes and the defenses to criminal accusations.

Supremacy clause: Article IV, Clause 2 of the Constitution of the United States makes clear that when the federal government and states have concurrent jurisdiction, federal law is superior when the two are in conflict.

Suspect classification: Laws that discriminate between people by race, alienage, national origin, and religion are suspect.

Target crime: The crime that conspirators plan to commit. Also referred to as the substantive offense.

Tolling: A pause in a statute of limitations clock, resulting in a longer period of time within which a criminal charge may be filed.

Tort: A civil wrong not arising out of a contract. There are three forms of tort: negligence, intentional, and strict liability.

Transferred intent: A legal fiction. If the harm that a defendant specifically intends to inflict on a person or object falls to another, the defendant's specific intent applies to the unintended victim.

Treason: Levying war on, or adhering to the enemies of, a nation.

Trespass: For an actor to enter or remain on property with knowledge that they have no legal right to be on the property.

True threat: The communication of a threat to cause serious harm or death to another person with the intent to cause, and a reasonable person would experience, fear.

Vicarious liability: Criminal culpability for the acts of another person.

Victim compensation fund: Public monies that reimburse crime victims for their medical, psychological, property, and other expenses.

Victim impact evidence: Oral or written testimony by a victim of the physical, psychological, financial, and other harm caused by a crime. This evidence may not be considered in the guilt determination but may be considered at sentencing or in parole, probation, clemency, and pardon decisions.

Victim-in-fact: A person or legal entity that is harmed by another. In civil cases, the victim-in-fact may sue to be compensated for injuries. In criminal law, a victim-in-fact does not have the legal authority to prosecute the offender.

Victim-in-law: The government when acting as a public prosecutor.

Void for vagueness: A criminal prohibition that is so imprecise that a person doesn't know if a specific act is prohibited. Vague statutes violate due process and are invalid.

Warrant: A judicially issued authorization for police to conduct a search or seizure.

Wharton's Rule: A prohibition of punishment for conspiracy when the target offense requires two or more people.

Withdrawal exception: An exception to the rule that a person who provokes an attack is not entitled to the protection of self-defense. It applies when the person who provoked the attack retreats from the encounter but is pursued by the person initially attacked.

Writ: A court order.

Year-and-a-day rule: An old Common Law rule that relieves a defendant of murder if the victim lives longer than a year and day. Many jurisdictions have abolished the rule, extended it to 3 years and a day, or modified it in other ways.

INDEX